COMMERCE
OF
THE PRAIRIES

By Josiah Gregg

EDITED BY
MAX L. MOORHEAD
FOREWORD BY
MARC SIMMONS

UNIVERSITY OF OKLAHOMA PRESS

NORMAN AND LONDON

To Amy

Library of Congress Catalog Card Number: 54–10055.
ISBN: 0–8061–1059–7

Copyright © 1954 by the University of Oklahoma Press, Publishing Division of the University. All rights reserved. Manufactured in the U.S.A. First printing, 1954; second printing, 1958; third printing, 1974; fourth printing, 1990.

Commerce of the Prairies is Volume 17 in the *American Exploration and Travel Series*.

COMMERCE OF THE PRAIRIES

AMERICAN EXPLORATION AND TRAVEL

Josiah Gregg

Redrawn from a photograph of an old daguerrotype for
reproduction in William E. Connelley's
Doniphan's Expedition (1907)

CONTENTS

ILLUSTRATIONS

ARRIVAL OF THE CARAVAN AT SANTA FÉ

FOREWORD

BY MARC SIMMONS

IN THE VAST sea of books dealing with the historic, old Santa Fe Trail, one title shines brightly above all others—Josiah Gregg's *Commerce of the Prairies*. It is at once the classic account of the overland trade between the United States and Mexico, and a recital of the author's personal experiences and observations as a participant in that stirring phase of frontier history. Today, the book remains as useful and readable as the year it was first published, 1844.

Although *Commerce of the Prairies* has passed through many editions, the one edited by the late Max L. Moorhead in 1954 and reprinted here must be considered by any standard of measurement as the best. His meticulous combing of primary and secondary sources allowed him to add a series of highly authoritative footnotes to Gregg's text, illuminating obscure points and identifying certain people and place-names not sufficiently covered in the original. It is difficult to imagine that anyone else could have done a better job.

Professor Moorhead, an intelligent, dedicated, and gracious scholar, contends in his Preface that it would be dangerous to speak of his new edition of Gregg as definitive. By that, we can take him to mean that he did not wish to appear presumptuous. Paul Horgan, a leading Gregg biographer, however, was under no such constraints when he pronounced Moorhead's *Commerce of the Prairies* to be "the definitive modern edition."

One other supportive comment is perhaps worth quoting here. In his landmark compilation, *The Santa Fe Trail, A Historical Bibliography* (1971), author Jack D. Rittenhouse argued that Gregg's volume "stands as a cornerstone of all studies on the Santa Fe Trail in the early period," and he urged newcomers to the field to read it first. He also concurred with Horgan as to the superiority of the Moorhead edition.

The biographical introduction written by Professor Moorhead provides readers the necessary background concerning Gregg's life before he entered the Santa Fe trade and after he left it and presents the circumstances surrounding the writing of *Commerce of the Prairies*. Nothing, therefore, needs to be added in that direction. But a word or two can be included here about the recent resurgence of interest in Santa Fe Trail history, a phenomenon that can only produce an expanded readership for the Gregg book.

In May, 1987, President Ronald Reagan signed a congressional bill establishing the Santa Fe National Historic Trail, thereby bringing the old pioneer route under the jurisdiction of the National Park Service, for purposes of preservation and interpretation. The new law, an amendment to the National Trails System Act, provided for the marking of the trail along 950 miles from a point near Old Franklin, Missouri, through Kansas, Oklahoma, and Colorado, to the terminus on the central plaza of Santa Fe, New Mexico.

Coinciding with passage of the law, history-minded citizens banded together to form the nonprofit, educational Santa Fe Trail Association, committed to publicizing the trail's story and commemorating the major events associated with it. Both the legislation and the organization represented a latter-day expression of the same spirit that had animated, at least in part, Josiah Gregg when he determined to record and memorialize the Santa Fe Trail in the pages of his book. He sensed that he was participating in a grand and unrepeatable adventure, and he wished to document what he could before recollection of the details slipped away and was lost to future generations.

At one point Gregg wrote that he had developed a "passion

for prairie life," and after he abandoned the overland trade, he observed wistfully that: "Scarcely a day passes without my experiencing a pang of regret that I am not now roving at large upon those western plains." He had become captivated by life on the open trail, and there can be no doubt that his travels to Santa Fe and back proved to be the central event in his varied career. Without those journeys, there would have been no *Commerce of the Prairies*, and his name would have sunk, unremembered, into the bottomless gulf of the past.

As it is, memory of Josiah Gregg remains fresh. As Professor Moorhead aptly remarked, he wrote fully and reliably and he knew whereof he spoke. Those qualifications guarantee that Gregg will continue to find an audience among the reading public as well as among scholars who see in his book a faithful source of information. Under the circumstances, it seems fitting to classify Josiah Gregg as an enduring writer within the ranks of those who chronicled the development of the American West.

EDITOR'S PREFACE

Commerce of the Prairies has been recognized for more than a hundred years as the classic description of the early southern plains and as the epic of the Santa Fé Trail. What has set it above other personal narratives of early western travel more than all else is its genuineness. Josiah Gregg, though an amateur as a writer and a naturalist, was a professional trader, an experienced frontiersman, and a keen observer. To this day historians, botanists, ethnologists, and other scholars still find his descriptions inspiring and reliable, and their popular appeal seems only to have increased with the passage of time. J. Frank Dobie, the foremost exponent of Southwestern lore, names Gregg's narrative as his personal favorite.

My own research on early American trade with Mexico during the last seven years has convinced me of what I had suspected at the outset, that Gregg's information is at once the fullest and the most reliable of all firsthand accounts. While my investigations in the local and national collections of the United States and Mexico have allowed me to clarify and correct a number of Gregg's statements, they most often merely have substantiated them. The panorama of his interests has sent me to specialized references in many fields, but the results of my checking have almost always been the same: *Gregg knew what he was talking about.*

The present edition is justified not only by the scarcity of the original volumes, but also by the accumulation in recent years of much important new evidence. It is always dangerous to speak of the definitive, but this new evidence has made it possible, at least, to approach that much desired goal. This is the first edition of Gregg's complete text, notes, and maps which also contains a biographical introduction, critical notes, and a list of the author's sources. The introduction and several of the notes would have been impossible but for the indefatigable scholarship of Maurice G. Fulton, whose *Dairy & Letters of Josiah Gregg* has opened new horizons for the setting in which Gregg's narrative was written. The *Diary & Letters* together with Paul Horgan's masterful introduction have at long last given the public a full biography of the author. My own sketch of Gregg's life is based in large part on this work.

Other acknowledgments, particularly for materials made available to me, are due the following: Barbara Kell, reference librarian of the Missouri Historical Society at St. Louis; Floyd C. Shoemaker, secretary of the State Historical Society of Missouri at Columbia; Don Rickey, Jr., librarian of the Frank Phillips Collection of the University of Oklahoma at Norman; C. Boone McClure, director of the Panhandle-Plains Historical Museum at Canyon, Texas; E. R. Rochambeau, of Amarillo, who is at present establishing Gregg's route across the Texas panhandle; Aldon B. Bell, of Perryton, Texas; Arthur J. O. Anderson, of the Historical Society of New Mexico at Santa Fé; and George P. Hammond, director of the Bancroft Library of the University of California at Berkeley. Visits to the latter two collections were made financially possible by faculty research grants from the University of Oklahoma for another but related study. The few materials from the official archives at Washington and Mexico City, likewise obtained for another project, were supplied through funds from the American Philosophical Society at Philadelphia.

For special advice on the wide variety of subjects encompassed by Gregg, I am indebted to many of my colleagues on the University of Oklahoma faculty and most particularly to Professors J. Kester Svendsen, Department of English; George J. Goodman, Plant Sciences; Ralph E. Olson, Geography; Robert E. Bell, Anthropology; and John O. Beach, Oklahoma Geological Survey. I wish also to thank my wife, Amy, for her patient assistance in reading copy and proof. Errors of all kinds are my very own.

The text of *Commerce of the Prairies* which I have used is that of the first edition (1844). In editing it, I have preserved the origi-

nal spelling, punctuation, and phrasing, but I have indicated in footnotes the revisions made by Gregg in his second edition (1845).
Gregg's footnotes were marked by asterisks in the original, but I
have herein numbered them along with my own, distinguishing
them from mine by attaching his signature. The glossary of Spanish
words is from the second edition, there being none in the first, and
Gregg's bibliography, absent in all previous editions, is of my own
reconstruction from his informal references to his sources. With the
exception of the portrait of Gregg, all illustrations and the maps are
from the original edition of *Commerce of the Prairies*.

Norman, Oklahoma   Max L. Moorhead

INDIAN ALARM ON THE CIMARRON RIVER

INTRODUCTION

I. THE AUTHOR

JOSIAH GREGG best served posterity by capturing the fleeting time and changing space of the West when it was young. Long before the onward march of civilization could alter the natural landscape and primitive life of the Great Plains, and before trained scientists and historians arrived on the changing scene, Gregg was there taking notes. The product of his efforts, the only book he ever finished, has placed subsequent generations forever in his debt.

Who was this pioneer historian of the Santa Fé Trail, this amateur naturalist of the prairies? Until the last fifty years little more was known of him than what his own book revealed, and that much never satisfied the curious. It was all there was until the twentieth century. Then the value of his work was rediscovered by students of Western history and literature, and gradually skilled research unearthed the details of his life. Today only a few important facts still elude his biographers.[1]

[1] In the order of their publication the important biographies of Gregg are: [Charles S. Sargent ?], "Josiah Gregg," *Garden and Forest*, Vol. VII, No. 2 (January 10, 1894), 12; William E. Connelley, editorial note in John T. Hughes, *Doniphan's Expedition and the Conquest of New Mexico and California* (1907), 162–77; William E. Connelley, "Dr. Josiah Gregg, Historian of the Old Santa Fe Trail," *Proceedings of the Mississippi Valley Historical Association*, Vol. X, Part 2 1919–20), 334–48; Ralph Emerson Twitchell, *Dr. Josiah Gregg, Historian of the Santa Fe Trail* (1924); John Thomas Lee, "The Authorship of Gregg's *Commerce of the Prairies*," *Mississippi Valley Historical Review*, Vol. XVI, No. 4 (March, 1930), 451–66; John Thomas Lee, "New Found Letters of Josiah Gregg," *Proceedings of the American Antiquarian Society*, Vol. XL, No. 2 (April, 1930), 47–68; John Thomas Lee, "Josiah Gregg and Dr. George Engelmann," *ibid.*, Vol. XLI, No. 4 (October, 1931), 355–404; Paul Horgan, "Josiah Gregg Himself" in Maurice G. Fulton (ed.), *Diary & Letters of Josiah Gregg* (1941–44), I, 3–40; II, 3–30.

Josiah Gregg's ancestors were Scotsmen who came to America in the seventeenth century as refugees from the tyranny of England's Charles the First. His father, Harmon Gregg, a Kentucky wheelwright turned farmer, married one Suzannah Smelser of Pennsylvania and sired a brood of seven: four sons and three daughters. Josiah was the youngest son, born on July 19, 1806, in Overton County, Tennessee. His home, however, was ever on the move—westward. He was taken to Illinois when he was three and to Missouri when he was six, and for a period of four years the Greggs were on the very rim of civilization. Under repeated attack by pro-British Indians during the War of 1812, Cooper's Fort in Howard County, Missouri, offered scant facility for schooling; but when peace came, the Greggs took up a farm some distance from the palisade. For several years thereafter young Josiah was in regular attendance at a log-cabin school in the woods.

A frail child with an intellectual bent, Josiah was something of a misfit on the family farm, but he was in his natural element at the schoolhouse. So well did he master his studies that soon he was tutoring others in the rudiments of mathematics. He became keenly observant of the world about him and eager to master every technique of understanding it. By the time he was twelve he had fashioned from wood a serviceable quadrant, and one of his favorite hobbies was ascertaining the heights of trees with it, checking his calculations afterward with actual measurements. At sixteen he was studying to be a surveyor. By this time he had developed the habit of keeping notebooks, of jotting down mathematical rules, formulae, and personal observations. And it was during these same early years that he met and fell in love with good books. The Greggs soon realized that one son, at least, would be a man of science and letters.

Other boys on the Missouri frontier married early and reared large families, but Josiah shied away from the fairer sex. He never married. Knowledge was his only love; the prairies his only real home. Several professions beckoned, but no one long held his full attention. When he was eighteen he opened a school near Liberty, Missouri, and tried his hand at teaching. One year was enough of that. When the family moved farther west in the fall of 1825, to the vicinity where Independence was soon established, he decided to study medicine. He applied for an apprenticeship under Dr. John Sappington (later famous for his research on fevers), but when this application was rejected, he turned to law. Young Gregg soon found that legal principles were too much for him and was disturbed over his failure, but his difficulty was more physical than mental. His health had never been good, and now, at the age of twenty-four, he suffered the first of his several serious illnesses. Chronic dyspepsia and consumption confined Gregg to his room and prevented exertion of both mind and body for almost a year. He gave up law.

Curiously enough, the very infirmity which denied him one career opened the road to his true destiny. When their packaged curatives failed to restore his health, Gregg's doctors prescribed a trip to the high prairies, to the great out-of-doors, and in May of 1831 he joined a merchant caravan at Independence that was bound for Santa Fé. New Mexico was eight hundred miles away—beyond rolling prairies and arid plains that were inhabited only by nomadic Indians and wild animals—but there was family precedent for this adventure. Two of Gregg's brothers, first Jacob and then John, had followed the Santa Fé Trail during the previous decade. Neither, however, became so thoroughly identified with it as Josiah.

The cure worked with surprising speed. After two weeks on the road the invalid was out of his dearborn and on a pony, and during the six weeks consumed by the trip he mastered a book on Spanish grammar and was able to use the new tongue on arrival in New Mexico. Gregg had a facility for languages. He also had a head for figures, and on his first trip he earned his way as a bookkeeper, hired by Jesse Sutton, one of the merchants. Almost unwittingly Gregg had become a businessman, a Santa Fé trader.

For the next nine years, from 1831 to 1840, Gregg crossed and recrossed the Great Plains four times with merchant caravans, trading American dry goods and hardware for Mexican silver and mules. In the fall of 1833 he returned from his apprentice journey but embarked again the following spring, this time as Sutton's partner and also as captain of the wagon train. This trip took him beyond Santa Fé to the interior cities of Mexico, and he did not return to the States until the fall of 1836. The next spring he was off again for another year and a half, returning in the fall of 1838. On his fourth and last expedition to Santa Fé, Gregg blazed a completely new trail, a route which was a favorite in the next decade with California-bound gold seekers. That spring, in 1839, Gregg organized a caravan at Van Buren, Arkansas, struck out through the settlements in Indian Territory, and then followed the Canadian River into New Mexico. This new and more southerly trail provided his animals with earlier spring pasturage than the regular trail afforded, and this earlier pasturage in turn enabled his wagons to enter the market at Santa Fé a month ahead of his competitors.

Gregg reaped the rewards of his boyhood hobbies on this pioneering venture. With quadrant and pocket compass he was able to mark his position and keep his bearings on the oceans of grass with a minimum of error. His longitudes, latitudes, and other observations were duly recorded in his ever-present notebooks, and from these records he published in 1845 the most complete and reliable map of the prairies then in existence. Notes on his charts and in his book show that he knew, or at least suspected, the true location of the Red River's source by 1846,[2] thus anticipating Captain Randolph B. Marcy, who corrected the errors of Lieutenant Pike and Major Long in this matter.

It may be presumed that Gregg, having remained in the Santa Fé trade for nine years, was at least moderately successful as a merchant. According to his business associates, he used good judgment in estimating the Mexican markets, purchased wisely from the wholesalers, and conducted his operations with decorum and honesty. During his overland trips and the long winters of storekeeping in Santa Fé and Chihuahua he became well acquainted with the most successful men in the trade and highly esteemed by them. Yet he was never one to seek new friends.

The complicated and formal life of cities, even of rustic frontier towns, never set well with Gregg. He detested meeting people and was unduly modest in the presence of his intellectual superiors. His few close associates valued his friendship highly, but he was hardly

2 "Map of the Prairies," *Diary & Letters*, I, opposite p. 94. Gregg's map appearing in his own book, engraved in 1844, was also published in Sidney E. Morse and S. Breese, *North American Atlas* (New York, Harper & Bros., 1842–45), Plate 33.

an amiable person. Chronic illness and characteristic impatience with the shortcomings of his inferiors made him something of a crank. Above all he was an escapist, forever fleeing to his beloved prairies. There and only there he breathed as a free, happy, and well man.

In the spring of 1840, Gregg returned from New Mexico for the last time, but his travels were by no means over. The very next summer he returned to the prairies, making a brief tour from Fort Smith, Arkansas, across the Choctaw and Chickasaw nations of Indian Territory to Cache Creek and Chouteau's Fort on the border of Comanche country, and back again to Fort Smith by way of the Seminole nation. In the following year, 1841, he escorted a drove of mules to the Republic of Texas and sold them for enough to purchase some land. But these trips were never solely for business, nor even for health. Along the entire route Gregg incessantly made notes: on the lay of the land, the composition of the soil, the quality of the water, the species of trees, the attitudes of the people, and even the vagaries of Texas politics.

On his return from Texas, Gregg settled for a time at Van Buren. There he aided in making a new survey of the town and then, in partnership with his brother John and a George Pickett, established a general store. Although he occasionally transacted business for the firm while he was in the East, Gregg never became an active partner. A new profession had beckoned.

Sometime in 1842 Gregg began mulling over his travel notes. During his nine years in the Santa Fé trade he had learned a great deal about its origin and development, about the intricacies of caravan travel and camp life on the plains. He had also learned much about the Indians, the plants and animals, and the mineral resources of the Far West. His field notes, recorded as they were with characteristic precision, constituted a veritable encyclopedia of Western Americana, and much of the information had widespread public appeal. Gregg was about to become an author.

In July of 1843 he went east to prepare his manuscript and find a publisher. His trying experiences as an author and the success of his literary endeavors merit special attention elsewhere, but it may be said here that they were attended with much less reward in his time than in later years. The *Commerce of the Prairies* was off the press in July of 1844, and although Gregg was shortly at work on a second edition, other affairs engaged most of his time.

Having now tried his hand at schoolteaching, study of law, overland trading, storekeeping, surveying, and authoring, Gregg now turned back to an unfulfilled youthful aspiration. His own delicate health together with the scientific turn of his mind had once induced him to study medicine; and although denied the opportunity, he had never abandoned interest. Over the years he had collected a number of medical books and, in ministering to the ailments of caravan comrades, he had established something of a reputation as a successful practitioner. Now, in the autumn of 1845, he enrolled in the medical school at the University of Louisville. For two semesters he attended six lectures a day and pored over his books each night; but instead of pursuing the prescribed curriculum, he accepted an honorary degree at the following spring commencement and left for home. A mystery surrounds the circumstance of this award. More than a year passed before Gregg would consent to bear the title "Doctor," and then it was only when he established a medical practice in Mexico.

Meanwhile, in the spring of 1846, Gregg felt himself in need of another "tour of health" and joined a caravan of Santa Fé traders being organized at Independence by an old friend, Samuel C. Owens. It was with some uneasiness that he planned to visit New Mexico again, for copies of his book had undoubtedly reached that province; and its uncomplimentary remarks about the governor, Manuel Armijo, might well have antagonized the old tyrant. To be on the safe side, therefore, Gregg wrote a friend at Santa Fé inquiring into the delicate situation. This letter, having long been buried among the recipient's papers, may now be added to the growing collection of "Greggiana."[3] Scarlet fever in his sister's family delayed Gregg's departure for Santa Fé, but he sent his books, in-

[3] "My dear Sir:
    "You will doubtless be surprised to learn that I am again 'on the wing' for Santa Fé—a mere tour for health. I hope to get off sometime during the present month—as I expect to go in company with S. C. Owens. However, if Owens delays too late, and I meet with a convenient opportunity and an agreeable party, I will go sooner.
    "It is unnecessary for me to write you a long letter now, as there is no particular news, and what there is, you will hear by the *avant-courriers:* in fact, I hope to have the pleasure of saluting you in *propia persona*, in a few days after the receipt of this.

struments, and other baggage ahead in Owens's wagons and overtook them on horseback a few days later. He never completed the journey.

That spring the United States and Mexico went to war, and Gregg yielded to the importunities of patriotism. At the instigation of Congressman Archibald Yell and Senator Ambrose Sevier, both of Arkansas, he joined the volunteers of that state who were on their way to join General John Wool's army in a march on Chihuahua. By the time Gregg decided to enlist, the wagons with all his baggage were too far along to turn back, and Gregg, returning on horseback, was able to retrieve only a few portable items.

Just what part Gregg played in the Mexican War has never been fully ascertained. Unofficially he was a war correspondent. He submitted several articles from the front to western newspapers, including his own eyewitness report on the celebrated battle of Buena Vista. His official duties, he said, were not entirely either civilian or military, although he was supposed to receive the pay and honors of a major. From his diary it would appear that he served largely as guide and interpreter for the army, but official records show that

"The principal object of this little *carta* is to solicit you to 'feel the pulse' of your friend the Gov. and others, perhaps, and see if you can get from them, how I will be received. This can be done by mentioning among them that I am on the way there: their remarks will indicate their temperment to some degree at least.

"Should you fancy that I would be particularly ill-treated, I should be glad [if] you would inform me by some one who may come out to meet me: in fact, I hope you will write me, at all events, if you have an opportunity. Though should you by chance think that circumstances & my safety required it, I would be glad (and would pay all charges) if you would send a *correo*, if no prompt conveyance should present itself.

"Now, as to myself, my own opinion is that I will be in no sort of danger, & therefore feel no *recelos*: still I might be mistaken; and the foregoing precautions have been suggested by a friend arrived from there, who seems more timorous than myself.

"It is hardly necessary for me to solicit you that the foregoing remains strictly confidential.

"Truly your Friend,

"*Josiah Gregg*

"P. S. I will get Dr. Waldo to superscribe and send this letter to prevent suspicion. I write in English, that the Mexicans, who bear it, would not undertsand it very well, even if the seal were broken."

Josiah Gregg to Manuel Alvarez, Independence, Mo., May 7, 1846, MS, Historical Society of New Mexico at Santa Fé, B. M. Read Collection, Folder G, No. 158.

much of the cartographical data which he collected for his own note-book was incorporated into reports for the War Department.[4]

As far as General Wool was concerned, Gregg was a nuisance and a malicious gossip whose stories for the press were far too criti-cal. And to the men in the ranks, Gregg was anything but a comrade. His scientific and hypochondriac preoccupations became the butt of their jokes, and their pranks were merely encouraged by his indig-nation. Gregg thought the enlisted men crude and the officers stupid. At Saltillo he was impatient for the army to march on Chihuahua and for a time even entertained delusions of his own military grandeur. He wrote his brother John that if influence were brought to bear in the right places, a regular commission might be forthcoming, but that he would accept nothing short of a lieutenant-colonelcy. Most of all he wanted to be quit of General Wool, and that occasion soon arrived.

A regiment of Missouri volunteers under Colonel Alexander Doniphan had moved toward Chihuahua from the north with orders to support Wool's operations, but the regiment, finding that Wool had not yet marched, took the city of Chihuahua alone and sent an express to Saltillo for further orders. At the head of the dispatch riders was James Collins, a trader, who brought word to Gregg that the merchant caravan from Independence with all his precious books and instruments aboard had arrived at Chihuahua with Doniphan's troops. There was also bad news. Samuel Owens was dead. He had been elected colonel of a special battalion of merchants and wagoners and was killed in action less than twenty miles from Chihuahua.

Gregg had little difficulty in getting General Wool's permission to accompany Collins and the express on its return. The general probably considered it good riddance. At any rate, Gregg made the dangerous ride through enemy-held territory to Chihuahua. Colonel Doniphan was ready and waiting for marching orders when they arrived, and the orders were to repair at once to Saltillo. There was barely time for Gregg to recover his lost baggage and visit old mer-chant friends, but the weary march back to Saltillo had its compen-sations. With the Missouri volunteers was a university-trained na-

4 *Report of the Secretary of War, March 1st, 1849* (31 Cong., 1 sess., *Senate Executive Document No. 32*), 8, 51–57.

turalist from Germany, Dr. Frederick Adolph Wislizenus, whose companionship and conversations provided a much-needed intellectual stimulus. The two were soon comparing notes and exchanging scientific information.[5] There were also a number of traders with the column, among them Samuel Magoffin and his bride, Susan, whose diary has added such charm to Santa Fé literature.[6] Shortly before reaching Saltillo, Gregg and Magoffin entered into a business partnership. The arrangements called for Gregg to return to the States and buy goods in the East while Magoffin prepared to market them in northern Mexico. The war was not yet over, but Gregg's enlistment was.

Leaving his instruments and books in Saltillo, Gregg proceeded to Philadelphia and New York. In the latter city he was in the very act of buying about forty thousand dollars worth of goods when a telegram from Magoffin cut him short. Unforeseen difficulties had arisen, and the deal was off. Gregg was bitterly disappointed, but as long as he was in the East, he visited his publisher and then went to Washington. There he met President Polk and several congressmen whom he sounded out on prospects for employment with the government. Nothing came of these meetings, however; so he returned to Missouri.

Since his valuables were still in Mexico, Gregg decided to go back to Saltillo, but this time in a different role—as Dr. Gregg, physician. He reached Saltillo in the autumn of 1847 and entered practice with another American, Dr. G. M. Prevost. Gregg had all the patients he wanted and time to spare for other pursuits. The army of occupation was still there, and between patients Gregg gave Spanish lessons to American officers and their families. He was almost as much at home in Mexico as on the prairies, and if only he could make himself as much at ease in American society, he wrote John, he would be willing to live in the United States. As it was, new interests lured him even farther to the south.

[5] In the preface of his next book the naturalist acknowledged Gregg's aid in fixing points on his map, especially in northeastern Mexico. Frederick Adolph Wislizenus, *Memoir of a Tour to Northern Mexico* (30 Cong., 1 sess., *Senate Miscellaneous Document No. 26*), 4, 138.

[6] Stella M. Drumm (ed.), *Down the Santa Fe Trail and into Mexico; the Diary of Susan Shelby Magoffin, 1846–1847.*

In the spring of 1848, Dr. Gregg deserted his practice in favor of a far-flung field trip. A botanical expedition would take him to Mexico City, to the Mexican west coast, and finally to California. Gregg had long been interested in the flora of the prairies and of the Mexican desert, and to judge from the numerous identifications in his *Commerce of the Prairies*, he knew something of botanical taxonomy as early as 1844. Such interest had doubtlessly been stimulated by his brief medical training at Louisville and his association with Dr. Wislizenus, but his main inspiration stemmed from Dr. George Engelmann, an eminent botanist in St. Louis.[7] The progress of a novice in natural science is eloquently revealed by Gregg's correspondence with Engelmann.[8]

While with the army in 1846, Gregg had collected about two hundred varieties of Mexican plants, about half of them in bloom. These he sent to Engelmann with profuse apologies for his lack of method in handling, preserving, enumerating, and classifying the specimens and with due appreciation for the professor's alternate words of scolding and praise. By the following year, Gregg's apologies had become rarer, and it may be assumed that his own techniques had improved. Entering the country late in 1847, by April of 1849 he had collected some seven hundred specimens and, in response to a request, was preparing a copy of his field notes for Engelmann. This task led him to envision a new book, one based on the memoranda of his current trip and entitled "Roving Abroad." But fate ruled that it should never be published in his time. Gregg's last known letter to Engelmann was mailed from Mazatlán, on the Pacific coast of Mexico, June 30, 1849. He was sending the botanist two herbariums, one of 650 specimens and another, duplicating most of the first, of 600.

If Gregg sought recognition for his contributions to science, he was ultimately well rewarded. Twice the American Botanical Society proposed his name for a genus of plants, and it was only because an

[7] George Engelmann (1809–84) was born at Frankfort on the Main, Germany, and came to St. Louis in 1833 as a physician and botanist. There he built up a large medical practice and in 1856 organized the St. Louis Academy of Science.

[8] Twelve of Gregg's letters to Engelmann, dating from April of 1846 to June of 1849, have been found and published by Lee in his "Josiah Gregg and Dr. George Engelmann," *Proc. of the Amer. Antiq. Soc.*, Vol. XLI, No. 4 (October, 1931), 355–404.

older *Greggia* existed that he was deprived of the high honor.[9] Several members of the Society did give his name to new species, however, and a total of twenty-three different plants came to bear the designation *greggi*.[10]

As a would be naturalist Gregg dabbled in other sciences besides botany. One of his letters to a former medical school professor reveals that he had been collecting Mexican birds, and their skins were ultimately given to Engelmann for presentation to museums.[11] His geological interests were confined to collecting and sending Engelmann a number of rocks with suitable comments, but his interest in geography ran deeper. His field instruments now included a sextant, a prismatic compass, binoculars, and a barometer; and while in Mexico City he combed the national archives for manuscript maps of the republic in preparation for what he thought would be the most accurate map of Mexico yet published. There is no indication from his diary or letters that he made any study of the native races of the country, though his anthropological contributions had already won future acclaim. His data on the plains and pueblo Indians appearing in *Commerce of the Prairies*, while admittedly not entirely from his own observations, anticipated by many years the first systematic classification of these tribes by professional ethnologists.

From Mazatlán, Gregg sailed to San Francisco. There, fortunately for posterity, he left his Mexican field notes with Jesse Sutton, his former partner, who was now a California resident. As he prepared to strike out for the gold diggings of the interior, Gregg may have had a premonition, for he instructed Sutton to forward the notebooks to John Gregg should anything happen to himself.

There was no further news from Josiah Gregg until October of 1849, when he wrote from a roaring mining camp on Trinity River called Rich Bar. His reputation must have preceded him, for the

[9] [Sargent ?], "Josiah Gregg," *Garden and Forest*, Vol. VII, No. 2 (January 10, 1894), 12.

[10] A list of these species has been prepared by T. J. Fitzpatrick, curator of the University of Nebraska herbarium. Engelmann, who honored Gregg with some of these names, acknowledged the "very fine herbarium" which Gregg sent him from Mexico. Engelmann, "Botanical Appendix," in Wislizenus, *Memoir of a Tour to Northern Mexico*, 87.

[11] Letter to Dr. George W. Bayless, Mazatlán, June 30, 1849, in *Diary & Letters*, II, 335; John Gregg to George Engelmann, Shreveport, La., December 24, 1850, postscript, *ibid.*, I, 389.

settlers there commissioned him to lead an expedition across the mountains to the coast in search of a long-lost bay. What was needed was a direct road to the sea and a harbor that would obviate the long and devious supply road from San Francisco. A harbor of sorts was known to exist somewhere on the northern coast, for a Trinidad Bay had been discovered by a Spanish navigator, Bruno Heceta, in 1776. It was now mistakenly supposed to lie at the mouth of Trinity River.

In the late autumn of 1849, Captain Gregg and a party of seven started across the Coast Ranges. Had the weather been good, the trip should have taken them eight days. It took a full month. Their progress was impeded not only by early snows, steep ascents, and thick forests, but also by the leader's interminable stopping to observe the flora and fauna en route. Passing through the redwoods, they could make but two miles a day, for Gregg felt obliged to measure each new arboreal giant. Their supplies ran out, and they had to forage, but finally they reached the sea.

They came out of the wilderness at the mouth of Little River (near present Trinidad, in Humboldt County), not far below the real Trinidad Bay. Not recognizing it, they pursued the coastline northward for about eleven miles until they encountered Big Lagoon. Then, retracing their route, they reached Trinidad Head (which they named "Gregg's Point"), but again failed to recognize the adjacent water as the object of their search. Atop this bold promontory, overlooking the present town of Trinidad, Gregg ascertained his position and inscribed on a large tree the latitude, barometrical reading and temperature at high noon, the date, and his own name. Proceeding southward, short of supplies and short of temper, the men quarreled, especially with Captain Gregg, and one of their tiffs gave name to Mad River. Shortly after crossing this stream, one of the party discovered a very large bay which was hidden from the sea by its protective bar and the omnipresent fog; and presuming this to be the one discovered by the Spaniards, they named it "Trinity Bay." Shortly afterwards, when a maritime expedition "discovered" it again, its present name, Humboldt Bay, was applied in honor of the celebrated German naturalist. On its shore towns were soon laid out —Arcata and Eureka—and the interior mining camps had their seaport, but Gregg was never to profit from the discovery.

For several weeks his party rested, and then it pressed on southward, hoping to reach San Francisco. South of the bay it discovered and named other landmarks, the Van Duzen and Eel rivers. But travel on the coast became so difficult that the party split into two groups, each seeking its own way back. Gregg's division eventually turned back into the hinterland, and when they reached Clear Lake, the errant naturalist met with his last adventure. Exhausted from travel, exposure, and starvation, Gregg suffered a bad fall from his horse which ended his pain completely. He died on February 25, 1850, and was buried on the spot. The only chronicle of Gregg's California adventure, written by one of the survivors,[12] refers to him as the "old gentleman," but he was not yet forty-four.

Gregg's gravesite is lost and, more tragically, so also are the notes he so painstakingly made in the wilderness of northern California. Dr. G. W. Bayless, who knew Gregg at Louisville, learned of his death tardily and from garbled reports, but his tribute was particularly apt:

> It seems a curious coincidence that he should have sacrificed his life to the interests of science on the waters of the bay that bears the name of the great philosopher whose example he was following in the study of nature, 'Twere a fit place for him to die.[13]

Actually, of course, death did not overtake Gregg on Humboldt Bay, but discovering it had been the paramount achievement of his fatiguing last journey.

II. THE BOOK

THE GREATEST MONUMENT in memory of Josiah Gregg is his own book, *Commerce of the Prairies*. It was a labor of love. The copious memoranda of his Santa Fé travels had been gathering dust

[12] Lewis K. Wood, "The Discovery of Humboldt Bay." This narrative was published as an article in the Eureka, California, *Humboldt Times* in 1856 and 1863; printed as a separate pamphlet in 1873; paraphrased in Anthony Jennings Bledsoe's *Indian Wars in the Northwest* (1885), chap. 1; and included as a facsimile reprint in the *Quarterly of the Society of California Pioneers*, Vol. IX, No. 1 (March, 1892).

[13] Dr. George W. Bayless to Prof. Charles W. Short, Hazelwood [Missouri], March 16, 1851, in *Diary & Letters*, I, 399.

for three years before the idea of writing a book took root. Another year passed before he went East to complete the manuscript, and still another before it was published in 1844. Since doubt arose in later years that Gregg was really the author, the history of its preparation and publication is of more than passing interest.

From Gregg's own diary and letters it would appear that the first draft of the manuscript was prepared in Philadelphia during the latter half of 1843 and under the most distressing circumstances. Shortly after his arrival in that city, an illness (diagnosed as influenza) cost Gregg over a month of writing time and so much of his hair that he had to shave off the remainder and wear a toupee until it grew out anew. The noise of city streets also distressed him, and further delays attended his shuttling back and forth between Philadelphia and Camden—and from one boarding house to another—in a vain search for comfort. Eventually his health improved, and he became inured to urban distractions; but writing itself, he complained, was proving far more difficult than he had anticipated. However, encouragement came from former business associates—in particular from Thomas C. Rockhill, a Philadelphia wholesale merchant—and at long last the manuscript was presentable.

Armed with letters of recommendation from Rockhill, Gregg arrived in New York on November 25, 1843. He took his manuscript first to Harper and Brothers, but they turned it down. In December he came to terms with D. Appleton and Company, but after a few months the contract was cancelled by "mutual agreement." This falling out, in March of 1844, was apparently linked with Gregg's ghost-writer trouble. Doubtlessly the manuscript needed considerable grooming, especially if Gregg's letters are an indication of his literary style, but the man assigned to the task was insufferable.

Louis Fitzgerald Tasistro, an Irish actor, linguist, and self-styled "Count," had just written a book,[14] and it was probably on this recommendation that Gregg agreed to let him rework the manuscript. It was a mistake. Tasistro's facile pen was guided by artistic imagination and scant regard for the facts. Gregg, on the other hand, considered his own style adequate and the truth sacred. Before the end

---

[14] *Travels in the Southern States: Random Shots and Southern Breezes* (New York, Harper & Bros., 1842).

of December, 1843, he was trying to extricate himself from the agreement; but Tasistro threatened to sue, and a complete settlement was not reached until March, 1844, about the time the contract with Appleton was dissolved. Since Gregg and Tasistro were at serious odds as early as December, the latter's influence on the finished manuscript was probably slight. One of Tasistro's passages, however, did slip into print in the advance copies, but it seems to have been deleted before the first edition was complete. Gregg referred to it as "a page of fiction written by friend T. for which I had a peculiar repugnance."[15]

Gregg did need editorial help, and even before he retrieved his manuscript from Tasistro, he turned for assistance to another. John Bigelow proved to be a more fortunate choice. A young lawyer at the time, Bigelow had just finished dressing up another travelogue for publication,[16] and was recommended to Gregg by no less a personage than William Cullen Bryant. Later Bigelow made a name for himself on Bryant's New York *Evening Post* and after that as a diplomat and as an author of several historical works. At first he was merely Gregg's legal counsel in the difficult task of repossessing the manuscript. Tasistro finally agreed to release it, on March 21, 1844, for a financial consideration that was subsequently arranged by arbitration.

Events now took a better turn. Before the end of March new arrangements for publishing were made, this time with J. and Henry G. Langley. It was agreed that two thousand copies would be printed; Gregg would get a thousand at cost to sell on his own account; he would receive ten per cent of the profits on the second thousand, which the publishers would market; and he could obtain

---

[15] Gregg to John Bigelow, Independence, Mo., September 6, 1844, *Diary & Letters*, I, 147. Since no significant changes were made in the second edition's text, it must be presumed that the objectionable passage was eliminated during the first printing. Gregg complained later that he had been charged forty dollars "for altering stereotype plates, etc." when the account with his first publisher was finally drawn up. Gregg to Bigelow, Independence, May 8, 1846, *ibid.*, I, 190.

[16] This was Benjamin Moore Norman's *Rambles in Yucatan*, which went through seven editions by 1849. Margaret Clapp, *Forgotten First Citizen: John Bigelow*, 26; Lee, "The Authorship of Gregg's *Commerce of the Prairies*," *Miss. Valley Hist. Rev.*, Vol. XVI, No. 4 (March, 1930), 466.

copies of the latter at a discount of thirty-five per cent on the retail price.[17]

Bigelow found the task of polishing the manuscript comparatively easy—except for Gregg's refusal to brook literary "frills"—and at last the work went to press. Gregg left for the West on June 30, 1844, with a hundred advance copies, but the completed edition was not out until July 22, 1844. It appeared in two duodecimo volumes (of 320 and 318 pages) and bore the ponderous title: *Commerce of the Prairies: or the Journal of a Santa Fé Trader, during Eight Expeditions Across the Great Western Plains and a Residence of Nearly Nine Years in Northern Mexico. Illustrated with Maps and Engravings.* It was dedicated to Gregg's Philadelphia friend, Thomas C. Rockhill.

The success of the book sales-wise was not instantaneous, but the publishers were encouraged to begin preparations for a second edition within a few months after the first was issued. Only very minor changes were made in the text of the new edition, but Gregg added a second preface, an alphabetical index, and a glossary of Spanish words. Revision proved unnecessary, and it took only a few years for public demand to exhaust available copies and clamor for more. Altogether, *Commerce of the Prairies* went through fourteen printings (seven during Gregg's own short lifetime) and came from presses in England and Germany as well as the United States.[18]

[17] Gregg, entry for March [?], 1844, *Diary & Letters*, I, 141.

[18] A search of catalogues and check lists yields the following citations: *Commerce of the Prairies* (2 vols., New York, H. G. Langley, 1844); *ibid.* (2 vols., London, Wiley & Putnam, 1844); *ibid.*, 2nd and 3rd eds. (2 vols., New York, J. and H. G. Langley, 1845); *Karawanenzüge durch die westlichen Prairieen und Wanderungen in Nord-Mejico*, translated by Martin B. Lindau ([2 vols. ?], Leipzig and Dresden, Arnoldische Buchhandlung, 1845–); *Wanderungen durch die Prairieen und das nördlich Mexiko*, translated by Gottlob Fink (2 vols. in 1, Stuttgart, Franck, 1847); *Karawanenzüge durch die westlichen Prairieen und Wanderungen in Nord-Mejico*, translated by Lindau (2 vols. in 1, Leipzig and Dresden, Arnold, 1848); *Commerce of the Prairies* (2 vols., Philadelphia, J. W. Moore, 1850); *Wanderungen durch die Prairieen und das nördlich Mexiko*, translated by Fink (2 vols. in 1, Stuttgart, Franck, 1851); *Commerce of the Prairies* (2 vols., Philadelphia, Moore, 1851); *ibid.* (2 vols., Philadelphia, Moore, 1855); *Scenes and Incidents in the Western Prairies* (2 vols. in 1, Philadelphia, Moore, 1856); *Commerce of the Prairies*, edited by Reuben Gold Thwaites (2 vols., XIX and XX of *Early Western Travels*, Cleveland, Arthur H. Clark Co., 1905); *The Commerce of the Prairies*, edited and abridged by Milo Milton Quaife (2 vols. in 1, Chicago, R. R. Donnelley & Sons Co., 1926); *A Reprint of Commerce of the Prairies* (2 vols. in 1, Dallas, Southwest Press, 1933).

Fortune, however, did not accompany fame. In 1846 the Langley brothers went into bankruptcy, and the stereotype plates along with unpaid royalties went into the hands of the receivers. It is doubtful that Gregg ever recovered his original investment in the book, since he died four years afterward, but he was spared during his lifetime the challenge of his literary integrity.

No one questioned Gregg's authorship of *Commerce of the Prairies* until fifty years after its first publication. Then Bigelow wrote two letters which were made public. The first, addressed to a writer in *Garden and Forest*, a New York magazine, was printed in the issue of January 10, 1894.[19] The second, to L. Bradford Prince, president of the Historical Society of New Mexico, was written on September 12, 1907, but not published until 1924.[20] Taken out of context and broadly interpreted, some of Bigelow's statements were quite misleading. Witness, for example, this eye-opening annotation in Wagner's bibliography of Western travel literature:[21] "Bradford Prince says that this book was written by John Bigelow, a reporter on the N. Y. *Post*, 1844, from Gregg's notes." An equally bald assertion was made by Bigelow's son, in a letter to John Thomas Lee, on June 12, 1929: "John Bigelow took the 'log of the ship,' or field notes of a busy explorer and created therefrom a readable book."[22]

These disturbing remarks were made long after the fact. Bigelow was only twenty-six when he worked on Gregg's manuscript. He was seventy-six when he wrote to *Garden and Forest* and ninety when he addressed Prince. His son, an elderly man at the time he wrote Lee, knew the circumstances only from early family conversations. Unfortunately, the diaries which both Gregg and Bigelow kept were not explicit on the point at issue.

Bigelow's entry for December 29, 1843, offers the first hint. There came to his office that day "a gentleman by the name of Gregg,

[19] Quoted in Sargent [?], "Josiah Gregg," *Garden and Forest*, Vol. VII, No. 2 (January 10, 1894), 12.
[20] Quoted in Twitchell, *Dr. Josiah Gregg, Historian of the Santa Fé Trail*, 12–13.
[21] Henry Raup Wagner, *The Plains and the Rockies: A Bibliography of Original Narratives of Travel and Adventure, 1800–1865*, 59.
[22] Poultney Bigelow to John Thomas Lee, June 12, 1929, quoted in part in Lee, "The Authorship of Gregg's *Commerce of the Prairies*," *Miss. Valley Hist. Rev.*, Vol. XVI, No. 4 (March, 1930), 451–66.

formerly Santa Fe trader, who has some memoranda of his travels which he wishes me to revise and chastise in case the man who has them in hand should modify his terms into a respectable quantum. He left me promising to call tomorrow if occasion should arise."[23] It would appear from this that the manuscript was still in the form of rough notes, or memoranda, but such was not the case. As Tasistro still held it at this date, Bigelow had not yet seen it. According to Gregg's records, he had written out eighteen chapters in clean copy from his original notes more than nine weeks previously and had come to New York with an almost complete draft over a month before he met Bigelow.[24]

Gregg's diary mentions the young lawyer only once. In what appears to be a late entry for March (no day given), he summarized events occuring since February 26: "Owing to the rascality and ill-temper of Tasistro I withdrew my MS from him about this time (or a little before) and got the aid of one John Bigelow to assist me to finish revising or preparing my work for the press."[25] Both diaries specify that Bigelow's job was to revise the manuscript to make it publishable.

Bigelow's only entry dealing with his actual literary contribution was for June 9, 1844: "I have finished my work on Gregg's book. It will get out next week. I have *noticed* it in the *Dem. Review* and had Eames notice it in the New York *World*."[26] A later entry for the same month (day not indicated) indicates the value of his service. "I

[23] John Bigelow's entries dealing with Gregg were transcribed in 1930 from the original manuscript in the New York Public Library by his daughter and literary executor, Grace Bigelow, for Lee, who quotes them in the article just cited.

[24] Letters to John Gregg, Philadelphia, October 19, and New York, December 1, 1843, in *Diary & Letters*, I, 130, 135. At the latter date Gregg had still to do "two or three weeks writing—then maps, etc. all tedious work."

On January 3, 1844, Bigelow's diary notes that Gregg had called a second time about his book. "He said that he had engaged Tasistro but did not like the way he was working, and if he could only get the affair out of his hands he would place it in mine." And on March 2, Bigelow reveals how deeply Gregg was involved. "I have been for the past week endeavoring to help Gregg out of his difficulties with Tasistro. T. insists on $200 more at first for his work on Gregg's book. G's firmness afterwards brought him to put with $500 or an arbitration." The latter was resorted to on March 1 with Bigelow serving as Gregg's counsel, but on Tasistro's complaint that he was not equally represented, the arbiters adjourned. Nothing in the diary indicates the final result, but by the end of the month, the break with Tasistro seems to have been complete.

[25] *Diary & Letters*, I, 140–41.

have settled with Gregg for a draft on the Langleys for 2 per cent on the sales of the book until the same amounts to $100 in addition to the cash already received, $100, which will make $200 for my work." Bigelow's biographer asserts that this was the most the young lawyer had yet received for his literary efforts.[27] The extent of his assistance, however, is not specified in either diary.

Gregg's letters are equally noncommittal. While calling the attention of his brother to Bigelow's book notice in the *Democratic Review*, Gregg glosses over the reviewer's identity and further connection with the book.[28] Nowhere in his correspondence with John Gregg, in whom he usually confided, does he mention Bigelow by name or indicate having received literary assistance from any source. Was he ashamed? For the information they supplied others received acknowledgment in the preface of his book, but Bigelow was ignored completely. It is equally notable that neither Gregg nor his book is mentioned even once by Bigelow in his extensive autobiography.[29] Seemingly, young Bigelow, who was already planning to give up his law practice for a writing career when he worked on Gregg's book, would have insisted on recognition of some kind in the finished product, but there was none. Yet, from the subsequent correspondence between the two, it would appear that their mutual respect and esteem were none the worse for the slight. Was Bigelow ashamed of his work? Or did he feel, as he later admitted, that his own contribution was inconsequential? Certainly Gregg considered the book his own work, for he referred to it as such in his letters to Bigelow. Nowhere in this correspondence does he pluralize the possessive pronoun—except in reference to the preface of the second edition, which he specifically instructed Bigelow to rewrite.[30]

The reader of *Commerce of the Prairies* must occasionally raise an eyebrow at the apparent erudition of its frontier-bred author. The allusions to Cervantes's immortal *Don Quixote*—to the Knight er-

[26] Charles Eames was a personal friend of Bigelow and a college lecturer who, like Bigelow himself, contributed occasional book reviews to the newspapers.

[27] Clapp, *Forgotten First Citizen*, 28.

[28] Letter to John Gregg, New York, June 9, 1844, in *Diary & Letters*, I, 142–43.

[29] John Bigelow, *Retrospections of an Active Life*.

[30] Letters to Bigelow, Liberty, Mo., October 14, 1844; New York, December 25, 1844; Washington City, December 31, 1844, in *Diary & Letters*, I, 150–56.

rant himself, to his faithful liege Sancho, and to the damsel of his dreams, Dulcinea—are not so unlikely. Gregg's familiarity with this classic is borne out by an earlier entry in his diary.[31] But the fine touch of an educated man is suggested by the verbatim quotations from Bacon's essays and the casual allusions to the verse of Burns and Cowper and the attributes of Mercury, Minerva, and Aesculapius, of classical mythology.

Bigelow's college education could have supplied these fine touches, but it is also conceivable that Gregg drew from his own knowledge, for he, too, read well. According to John Gregg, Josiah's education beyond his log-cabin schooling was largely self-administered but hardly meager. He mastered the Spanish language, learned to read French and Italian, and at least worked at German, Latin, and Greek. "He never professed a knowledge of anything in literature, except what he understood critically correct." Books were his lifelong companions, but "he never professed to know or understand anything—even in literature—in which he was not well versed."[32] Obituary praise from a brother may hardly be accepted at face value, but these particular remarks were made long before the authorship of *Commerce of the Prairies* was ever called into question. While the personal letters of Gregg indicate that he was more addicted to clichés than to fine quotations, he did own good books. An inventory of the personal effects he sent to Santa Fé in 1846 lists about seventy volumes, among which were twenty-five dictionaries (English, Spanish, French, and Italian), five or six travel and history books, and some two dozen works of real literary merit by such authors as Pope, Voltaire, Racine, and Molière.[33] If these were indicative of his earlier reading, Gregg's aforementioned erudition becomes less unlikely.

The diaries of Gregg and Bigelow, as we have seen, are noncommittal on the delicate subject of authorship. Bigelow's entries boil down to the statement that Gregg wanted him to "revise and chastise" the manuscript; Gregg's mention is reduced to the admis-

[31] Entry for March 10, 1840, *ibid.*, I, 50.
[32] John Gregg to Dr. George Engelmann, Shreveport, La., December 25, 1850, *ibid.*, I, 377–89.
[33] "Memorandum of Sundries Packed in Box and Trunk," *ibid.*, I, 199–200, (n.).

sion that he hired Bigelow to help him to finish "revising or preparing" it for the press. Both indicate that the manuscript was in need of editorial work, but Bigelow's aforementioned letter to *Garden and Forest* fifty years later affirms rather than denies that Gregg was the true author. How others inferred the contrary is difficult to see.

"We were soon at work together," Bigelow recalled. "He had previously confided his notes to Count Louis Fitzgerald Tasistro, subsequently and for many years a translator in the State Department at Washington, but their views of the way in which the work they were engaged upon should be executed were so widely divergent that their partnership was speedily dissolved. As I became acquainted with Mr. Gregg I had no difficulty in discerning the cause of their incompatibility. He had no notions of literary art and he knew it, but he was morbidly conscientious, and nothing would induce him to state anything that he did not positively know as if he did know it, or to overstate anything. Tasistro had no such infirmity. Then Gregg had about as little imagination as any man I ever knew, while Tasistro had such an excess of it that he had no difficulty in believing and affirming things that never happened. It was not strange, therefore, that they soon parted with opinions of each other not in the least improved by their association.

"I soon found that all I had to do was to put his notes into as plain and correct English as I knew how, *without in the least modifying the proportions of his affirmations*. [Emphasis supplied.] He would not allow his version of a fact to be expanded or contracted a hair's-breadth, no matter what might be the artistic temptation, nor however unimportant the incident; he always had the critics of the plains before his eyes, and would sooner have broken up the plates and reprinted the whole book than have permitted the most trifling error to creep into his description of the loading of his mules or the marshaling of one of his caravans. . . .

"Whatever the value his book possesses—and as a history of the trans-Mississippi commerce before the invasion of the railway, it has, I think, great and enduring value—was due to him and him only. My laundry work added no more value to the washing of it than the washing and ironing adds to the value of a new garment."

In his subsequent letter to L. Bradford Prince, also cited above, Bigelow merely reinforces these opinions. Two of his statements in fact leave the ghost-writer thesis practically untenable. Even the literary style appears to be Gregg's own. "It is due to him to say that my task was a comparatively easy one; and his statements, though never picturesque, were so lurid, so realistic, and so unpretendingly honest, that they needed little illuminating or refining from his editor." Nor did Gregg draw on Bigelow's store of quotations or make use of material outside his own knowledge if the following is taken at face value: "In our debates over the manuscript I remember nothing so well as his intolerance of any literary 'frills' which his old companions on the Plains could make sport of as borrowed feathers. On the other hand he was extremely careful about the exactness of every statement that he made and I do not think he allowed a word to be printed in that book that he would not have been willing to make an oath to."

From all available evidence—direct and indirect—it would appear that Gregg was the author and that Bigelow's contribution was merely editorial. Nothing in the writings of either indicates the contrary. Had Gregg's travel notes been rewritten by the urbane lawyer, the book would never have enjoyed such lasting appeal. As it was, Bigelow's editorial pencil spared much of Gregg's faulty grammar and prosaic expression, and Tasistro (an authority on the subject) failed to improve the colloquial spelling and usage of his borderland Spanish. Lacking the literary excellence that these critics could have supplied, *Commerce of the Prairies* became a classic of Western Americana because of the authenticity of its information and the earthiness of its style.

Although fundamentally the story of the Santa Fé trade, Gregg's masterpiece is packed with prairie lore and human adventure. Other writers have drawn heavily from its vivid descriptions of Western phenomena: cloudbursts on the high plains, desert mirages, buffalo hunts, prairie-dog towns, horse stampedes, Indian alarms, and New Mexican revolutions. Historians, ethnologists, naturalists, and bibliophiles have cherished it for generations. Gregg's was not the first book on its subject nor the last, but few would deny that it was the finest.

COMMERCE OF THE PRAIRIES

VOLUME I

PREFACE

In adding another to the list of works which have already been published, appearing to bear more or less directly upon the subject matter of these volumes, I am aware that my labors make their appeal to the public under serious disadvantages. Topics which have occupied the pens of Irving and Murray and Hoffman, and more recently, of Kendall, the graphic historiographer of the "Texan Santa Fé Expedition,"[1] may fairly be supposed to have been so entirely exhausted, that the entrance of a new writer in the lists, whose name is wholly unknown to the republic of letters, and whose pretensions are so humble as mine, may be looked upon as an act of literary hardihood, for which there was neither occasion nor excuse. In view of this 'foregone conclusion,' I trust I may be pardoned for prefacing my literary offering with a few words in its justification,—which will afford me an occasion to explain the circumstances that first led to my acquaintance with life upon the Prairies and in Northern Mexico.

For some months preceding the year 1831, my health had been gradually declining under a complication of chronic diseases, which defied every plan of treatment that the sagacity and science of my medical friends could devise. This morbid condition of my system,

[1] The references are to Washington Irving's *Tour on the Prairies* (Philadelphia, Carey, Lea & Blanchard, 1835), Charles Augustus Murray's *Travels in North America* (2 vols. London, R. Bentley, 1839), Charles Fenno Hoffman's *A Winter in the West* (2 vols. New York, Harper, 1835) and *Wild Scenes in Forest and Prairie* (2 vols. London, R. Bentley, 1839), and George Wilkins Kendall's *Narrative of the Texan Santa Fé Expedition* (2 vols. New York, Harper, 1844).

which originated in the familiar miseries of dyspepsia and its kindred infirmities, had finally reduced me to such a state, that, for nearly a twelvemonth, I was not only disqualified for any systematic industry, but so debilitated as rarely to be able to extend my walks beyond the narrow precincts of my chamber. In this hopeless condition, my physicians advised me to take a trip across the Prairies, and, in the change of air and habits which such an adventure would involve, to seek that health which their science had failed to bestow. I accepted their suggestion, and, without hesitation, proceeded at once to make the necessary preparations for joining one of those spring Caravans which were annually starting from the United States, for Santa Fé.

The effects of this journey were in the first place to re-establish my health, and, in the second, to beget a passion for Prairie life which I never expect to survive. At the conclusion of the season which followed my first trip, I became interested as a proprietor in the Santa Fé Trade, and continued to be so, to a greater or less extent, for the eight succeeding years. During the whole of the above periods I crossed the Prairies eight different times; and, with the exception of the time thus spent in traveling to and fro, the greater part of the nine years of which I speak, were passed in Northern Mexico.

Having been actively engaged and largely interested in the commerce of that country and across the Prairies, for so long a period, I feel that I have at least had opportunities for observation, upon the subjects of which I have ventured to treat, superior to those enjoyed by any writers who have preceded me. But not even an attempt has before been made to present any full account of the origin of the Santa Fé Trade and modes of conducting it; nor of the early history and present condition of the people of New Mexico; nor of the Indian tribes by which the wild and unreclaimed regions of that department are inhabited. I think I may also assure my readers that most of the facts presented in my sketch of the natural history of the Prairies, and of the Indian tribes who inhabit them, are now published for the first time. As I have not sought to make a treatise upon these subjects, I have not felt compelled, for the purpose

4

of giving my papers symmetry and completeness, to enter to any extent upon grounds which have already been occupied by other travellers; but have contented myself with presenting such matters and observations as I thought least likely to have come before under the notice of my readers.

I am perfectly sensible, however, that, in the selection of matter, and in the execution of my work, it is very far from being what it should be, and what, in more capable hands, it might have been. I only trust, that, with all its imperfections, it may be found to contain some new and not unimportant facts, which may be thought, in some measure, to justify my appearance for once in the capacity of a book-maker; for which vocation, in all other respects, I am free to confess myself very poorly qualified.

This work has been prepared chiefly from a journal which I have been in the habit of keeping from my youth upward, and in which I was careful to preserve memoranda of my observations while engaged in the Santa Fé Trade,—though without the remotest intention of ever appropriating them to the present purpose. In addition, however, I have embraced every opportunity of procuring authentic information through others, upon such matters as were beyond my own sphere of observation. From materials thus collected I have received much assistance in the preparation of the chapters from the sixth to the fifteenth inclusive, of the first volume, which are chiefly devoted to the early history of New Mexico, and the manners, customs and institutions of its people. For favors thus conferred, I beg in particular to make my acknowledgments to Elisha Stanley, Esq., and Doctors Samuel B. Hobbs and David Waldo, whose names have been long and favorably associated with the Santa Fé Trade.[2]

[2] Elisha Stanley, originally of Connecticut, was engaged in the Missouri trade with Santa Fé at least as early as 1825. He was elected captain of the caravan of 1831.

Dr. Samuel B. Hobbs, of Clinton, Missouri, was Gregg's favorite physician. The records of the American consul list him among the merchants at Santa Fé in 1837 and again in 1839.

Dr. David Waldo (1802–78) was born in Virginia, came to Missouri in 1826, studied medicine at Transylvania University (at Lexington, Kentucky), and practiced for a short time before entering the Santa Fé trade about 1828. He became a Mexican citizen in 1831 and by 1846 had amassed a large fortune in the overland

Though myself cradled and educated upon the Indian border, and familiar with the Indian character from my infancy, I am yet greatly indebted, for information upon that subject, to many intelligent Indian traders, and others resident upon our border, with whose ample experience I have been frequently favored.

Yet, while I recognize my indebtedness to others, I feel bound, in self-defence, to reclaim in a single case, at least, the *waifs* of my own pen, which have been dignified with a place in the pages of a contemporary writer. During the years 1841 and 1842, I contributed a number of letters upon the history and condition of the Santa Fé Trade, etc., to the Galveston "Daily Advertiser" and the "Arkansas Intelligencer," under the signatures of "J.G." and "G.," portions of which I have occasion to insert in the present volumes. In Captain Marryat's recent work, entitled "Monsieur Violet," I was not a little annoyed (when I presume I ought to have been flattered) to find large portions of this correspondence copied, much of it *verbatim*, without the slightest intimation or acknowledgment whatever, of the source from whence they were procured. The public are already so familiar with the long series of literary larcenies of which that famous work was the product, that I should not have presumed to emphasize my own grievance at all here, but that the appearance of the same material, frequently in the same words, in these volumes, might, unless accompanied by some explanation, expose me to a charge of plagiarism myself, among those who may never have seen my original letters, or who are not yet aware that "Monsieur Violet" was an offering which had evidently been intended for the altar of Mercury rather than of Minerva.[3]

---

trade. During the Mexican War he served first as a translator for the American occupational forces in New Mexico and later as a captain with the Missouri volunteers in the march on Chihuahua. After the war he married, at Independence, Mo., but continued in the trading and freighting business. Connelley, n., in Hughes, *Doniphan's Expedition*, 133–34; Robert Glass Cleland, *This Reckless Breed of Men: The Trappers and Fur Traders of the Southwest*, 210–11.

[3] Frederick Marryat, *Travels and Adventures of Monsieur Violet among the Snake Indians and Wild Tribes of the Great Western Prairies* (3 vols. London, Longman, Brown & Green, 1843). The plagiarization from Gregg appears in Vol. I, chap. 13. Kendall complains in the preface to his *Narrative of the Texan Santa Fé Expedition* that Marryat pilfered whole chapters from his work.

6

In my historical sketches of New Mexico, it might have been naturally expected that some notice would be taken of the Texan Santa Fé Expedition of 1841, the events of which are so closely connected with the history of that country. I declined, however, to enter upon the topic; for I considered that none who had seen Mr. Kendall's account of that ill-fated enterprise, would have any inducement to consult these pages upon the subject; and for those who had not, I felt sure the best thing I could do, was to direct their attention at once to its attractive pages.[4]

The maps which accompany the present work will be found, I believe, substantially correct; or more so, at least, than any others, of those regions, which have been published. They have been prepared, for the most part, from personal observations. Those portions of the country which I have not been able to observe myself, have chiefly been laid down from manuscript maps kindly furnished me by experienced and reliable traders and trappers, and also from the maps prepared under the supervision of United States surveyors.

The arrangement I have adopted seems to require a word of explanation. That the reader may the better understand the frequent notices, in the course of my personal narrative, of the Santa Fé Trade, the first chapter has been devoted to the development of its early history. And, though the results of my observations in Northern Mexico and upon the Prairies, as well as on the border, are sometimes interspersed through the narrative, I have, to a great degree,

---

[4] The Texan–Santa Fé expedition was a semi-official attempt by the Lone Star republic to annex the New Mexican settlements east of the Río Grande as being within its territory as claimed in 1836. In the spring of 1841 about 270 volunteer soldiers under General Hugh McLeod and some 50 civilians (commissioners, merchants, and a few curious tourists like Kendall, editor of the New Orleans *Picayune*), set out on foot from Texas. On reaching the frontier settlements, they found the New Mexicans in arms against them. Most of the party were captured by a ruse, disarmed, and conducted on a harrowing "death march" from Santa Fé to Chihuahua (where they were imprisoned for a time) and ultimately to Mexico City. In New Mexico, where feeling against Texas was high, their treatment was particularly barbarous. Eventually the survivors were freed and allowed to return to their homes. Kendall's narrative became the classic account of the misadventure. Another eyewitness version was written by an Englishman, Thomas Falconer, as "Notes on a Journey Through Texas and New Mexico Made in the Years 1841 and 1842," in the *Journal of the Royal Geographical Society of London*, Vol. XIII (1843), 199–222. A modern study is H. Bailey Carroll's *The Texan Santa Fe Trail*.

digested and arranged them into distinct chapters, occupying from the sixth to the fifteenth, inclusive, of the first volume, and the seven last chapters, of the second. This plan was resorted to with a view of giving greater compactness to the work, and relieving the journal, as far as possible, from cumbrous details and needless repetitions.

J.G.

New York, June 12, 1844

CHAPTER I

Origin and progressive Development of the Santa Fé Trade—Captain Pike's Narrative—Pursley—La Lande—Expedition of McKnight and others—Glenn—Becknell—Cooper—Sufferings of Captain Becknell and his Companions—First Introduction of wheeled Vehicles—Colonel Marmaduke—Hostility of the Indians—Recriminations—Indian Ethics —Increase of Outrages—Major Riley's Escort—Annoyed by the Indians—Government Protection—Composition of a Caravan.

THE OVERLAND TRADE between the United States and the northern provinces of Mexico, seems to have had no very definite origin; having been rather the result of accident than of any organized plan of commercial establishment.[1] For a number of years its importance attracted no attention whatever. From Captain Pike's narrative[2] we learn, that one James Pursley, after much wandering over the wild and then unexplored regions west of the Mississippi, finally fell in with some Indians on the Platte river, near its source in the Rocky Mountains; and obtaining information from them respecting the settlements of New Mexico, he set out in company with a party of these savages, and descended, in 1805, to Santa Fé, where

[1] It is now known that Frenchmen crossed the plains to trade with Santa Fé in 1739, 1749, 1750, and 1751, but the Spaniards allowed few of these adventurers to return. When Spain acquired the Louisiana territory, she commissioned a naturalized citizen, Pedro (Pierre) de Vial, to blaze a trail between St. Louis and Santa Fé in 1792, but although Vial traversed almost exactly what was later called the Santa Fé Trail, Spanish caution and secrecy prevailed over bold enterprise, and no important commerce flowed over this road until it was rediscovered and tested by Americans thirty years later. Louis Houck, *The Spanish Regime in Missouri*, I, xxiv.

[2] Zebulon Montgomery Pike, *An Account of Expeditions to the Sources of the Mississippi and Through the Western Parts of Louisiana* (Philadelphia, C. & A. Conrad, 1810). Several editions followed, the most fully annotated of which is Elliott Coues (ed.), *The Expeditions of Zebulon Montgomery Pike* (3 vols., New York, F. P. Harper, 1895).

9

he remained for several years—perhaps till his death. It does not appear, however, that he took with him any considerable amount of merchandise.[3]

Although Captain Pike speaks of Pursley as the first *American* that ever crossed the desert plains into the Spanish provinces, it is nevertheless related by the same writer, that, in consequence of information obtained by the trappers, through the Indians, relative to this isolated province, a merchant of Kaskaskia, named Morrison,[4] had already dispatched, as early as 1804, a *French Creole*, by the name of La Lande, up Platte river, with directions to push his way into Santa Fé, if the passage was at all practicable. The ingenious emissary was perfectly successful in his enterprise; but the kind and generous treatment of the natives overcame at once his patriotism and his probity. He neither returned to his employer nor accounted for the proceeds of his adventure. His expansive intellect readily conceived the advantages of setting up in business for himself upon this 'borrowed' capital; which he accordingly did, and remained there, not only unmolested, but honored and esteemed till his death, which occurred some fifteen or twenty years afterward—leaving a large family, and sufficient property to entitle him to the fame of *rico* among his neighbors.[5]

The Santa Fé trade attracted very little notice, however, until the return of Captain Pike,[6] whose exciting descriptions of the new

[3] James Purcell came from Bardstown, Kentucky, to Missouri in 1799, left for Santa Fé in 1802, and arrived there in 1805, according to Pike, who met him there in 1807. Pike calls him Pursley, but an item in the *Missouri Intelligencer* of April 10, 1824, announced the recent arrival of a James Purcell, who had been a citizen of Santa Fé for nineteen years. Hiram Martin Chittenden, *The American Fur-Trade of the Far West*, II, 493.

[4] William Morrison (d. 1837), originally of Pennsylvania, was a merchant at Kaskaskia from 1790 to his death. He traded extensively throughout Illinois and Upper Louisiana and maintained a fleet of river boats plying between Pittsburgh and New Orleans.

[5] Jean Baptiste Lelande played the dual role of spy and debt-dodger in 1807. Pike, a friend of Morrison, had promised to collect the money due him from Lelande. Before his own capture by the Spaniards, Pike sent an emissary to Santa Fé ostensibly to collect from Lelande but actually to obtain a more intimate commercial and military knowledge of the country. On Pike's arrival at Santa Fé, Lelande pretended to be a prisoner himself and tried to pump incriminating information from the American officer, but to no avail.

[6] This celebrated officer, who was afterwards promoted to the rank of General, and died in the achievement of the glorious victory at York, Upper Canada, in 1813,

El Dorado spread like wildfire throughout the western country. In 1812, an expedition was fitted out under the auspices of Messrs. McKnight, Beard, Chambers, and several others (in all about a dozen), who, following the directions of Captain Pike across the dreary western wilds, finally succeeded in reaching Santa Fé in safety. But these new adventurers were destined to experience trials and disappointments of which they had formed no conception. Believing that the declaration of Independence by Hidalgo, in 1810, had completely removed those injurious restrictions which had hitherto rendered all foreign intercourse, except by special permission from the Spanish Government, illegal, they were wholly unprepared to encounter the embarrassments with which despotism and tyranny invariably obstruct the path of the stranger. They were doubtless ignorant that the patriotic chief Hidalgo had already been arrested and executed, that the royalists had once more regained the ascendency, and that all foreigners, but particularly Americans, were now viewed with unusual suspicion.[7] The result was that the luckless traders,

was sent, in 1806, on an exploring expedition up the Arkansas, with instructions to pass to the sources of the Red River, for which those of the Canadian were then mistaken. Captain Pike, however, even passed around the head of the latter; and, crossing the mountain with an almost incredible degree of peril and suffering, he descended upon the Río del Norte with his little party, then but fifteen in number. Believing himself now upon Red River, within the then assumed bounds of the United States, he erected a small fortification for his company, till the opening of the spring of 1807 should enable him to continue his descent to Natchitoches. As he was within the Mexican territory, however, and but sixty to eighty miles from the northern settlements, his position was soon discovered, and a force sent out to take him to Santa Fé, which, by a treacherous manoeuvre, was effected without opposition. The Spanish officer assured him that the Governor, learning he had missed his way, had sent animals and an escort to convey his men and baggage to a navigable point on *Red River* (Rio Colorado), and that his Excellency desired very much to see him at Santa Fé, which might be taken on their way. As soon, however, as the Governor had Captain Pike in his power, he sent him with his men to the Commandant General at Chihuahua, where most of his papers were seized, and he and his party were sent under an escort, via San Antonio de Bexar, to the United States.

The narrative of Captain Pike gives a full account of this expedition, both previous and subsequent to its interruption by the Spaniards; but as this work is now rarely met with, the foregoing note may not be deemed altogether supererogatory. Many will believe and assert to the present day, however, that this expedition had some connection with the famous project of Aaron Burr; yet the noble and patriotic character of the officer who conducted it, will not permit us to countenance such an aspersion.—GREGG. [Gregg's own notes, as distinguished from those of the editor, are hereinafter indicated in this manner.]

[7] Miguel Hidalgo y Costilla (1753–1811) was a parish priest whose revolt, inaugurated September 16, 1810, became more nearly a race war than an inde-

immediately upon their arrival, were seized as spies, their goods and chattels confiscated, and themselves thrown into the *calabozos* of Chihuahua, where most of them were kept in rigorous confinement for the space of nine years; when the republican forces under Iturbide getting again in the ascendant,[8] McKnight and his comrades were finally set at liberty. It is said that two of the party contrived, early in 1821, to return to the United States in a canoe, which they succeeded in forcing down the Canadian fork of the Arkansas.[9] The stories promulgated by these men soon induced others to launch into the same field of enterprise, among whom was a merchant of Ohio, named Glenn, who, at the time, had an Indian trading-house

---

pendence movement. His undisciplined Indian army destroyed the life and property of Spaniards and Mexicans alike. Defeated, Hidalgo fled to the north but was captured, unfrocked, condemned, and shot with several of his comrades. Although seeking independence from the Spaniards, Hidalgo's movement acknowledged the authority of the king, then a French prisoner. American sympathies were openly with his revolution.

[8] Agustín de Iturbide (1783–1824) was not a republican, but a royalist. He opposed the revolution from its inception to 1820, when Spain itself succumbed to liberalism. Then, unable to crush the republicans in Mexico, he effected a compromise with them in 1821 by which both sides proclaimed the independence of Mexico as a monarchy with an established church and guaranteed racial equality. Iturbide became the first emperor, in 1822, but was exiled in 1823 and shot the following year when he tried to return.

[9] The known members of the interned party were Robert McKnight, James Baird, Samuel Chambers, Benjamin Shrive, Alfred Allen, Michael McDonough, William Mines, Peter Baum, Thomas Cook, and Carlos Miers, an interpreter.

Robert McKnight (*ca.* 1789–1846), a Virginian by birth, joined his brother John and Thomas Brady at St. Louis in 1809 in a mercantile adventure. Attracted by Pike's published account, he and nine others left for Santa Fé in May of 1812. Arrested as spies, they were confined, some at Chihuahua and others at Durango, for nine years. John McKnight went to Durango in 1821 and returned to St. Louis with his brother the next year. In the fall of 1822 the McKnight brothers and eight others went out to trade in the Comanche country, where John was reportedly killed by the Indians. After returning from this adventure in 1824, Robert went to New Mexico, renounced his nationality, became a Mexican citizen, and married in Chihuahua. In 1828 he gained possession of the Santa Rita copper mine in what is now southern New Mexico, made a fortune, but abandoned operation of the mine because of frequent attacks by the Apache.

Of the others, James Baird (d. 1826), of Pennsylvania, returned to the Santa Fé trade after his release in Mexico. In 1825 he, Samuel Chambers, and two others established a distillery near Taos, New Mexico. Baird became a Mexican citizen and settled at El Paso del Norte, where in 1826 he protested to his government against the inroads being made by Americans on the Mexican beaver-trapping business. *American State Papers, Foreign Affairs*, IV, 207–13; Chittenden, *American Fur Trade*, II, 497–500; Cleland, *This Reckless Breed of Men*, 122–23; Kate L. Gregg (ed.), *The Road to Santa Fe*, 267.

near the mouth of the Verdigris river. Having taken the circuitous route up the Arkansas towards the mountains, this pioneer trader encountered a great deal of trouble and privation, but eventually reached Santa Fé with his little caravan, before the close of 1821, in perfect safety.[10]

During the same year, Captain Becknell, of Missouri, with four trusty companions, went out to Santa Fé by the far western prairie route. This intrepid little band started from the vicinity of Franklin, with the original purpose of trading with the Iatan or Comanche Indians; but having fallen in accidentally with a party of Mexican rangers, when near the Mountains, they were easily prevailed upon to accompany them to the new emporium, where, notwithstanding the trifling amount of merchandise they were possessed of, they realized a very handsome profit. The fact is, that up to this date New Mexico had derived all her supplies from the Internal Provinces by the way of Vera Cruz; but at such exorbitant rates that common calicoes, and even bleached and brown domestic goods, sold as high as two and three dollars per *vara* (or Spanish yard of thirty-three inches). Becknell returned to the United States alone the succeeding winter, leaving the rest of his company at Santa Fé.[11]

The favorable reports brought by the enterprising Captain, stimulated others to embark in the trade; and early in the following

[10] The expedition of Hugh Glenn and Jacob Fowler followed the Arkansas to the site of present Pueblo, Colorado. Glenn and three others went to Santa Fé, obtained a trapping license, and in company with Fowler worked the headwaters of the Río Grande in southern Colorado. Fowler, a prominent surveyor, was from Covington, Kentucky. Glenn was from Cincinnati. For their adventures, see Elliott Coues (ed.), *The Journal of Jacob Fowler.*

[11] William Becknell, Indian fighter and veteran of the War of 1812, left the Missouri River with his party on September 1, 1821, encountered the Spanish dragoons on November 13, accompanied them to San Miguel del Vado, and arrived at Santa Fé on November 16. The recent separation from Spain, they learned, had ended the restrictive trade policy, and so Becknell with one companion returned with the good tidings, leaving Santa Fé on December 13 and arriving in Missouri after forty-eight days. Becknell made several trapping and trading expeditions to the west after 1821, carried mail for the Santa Fé road-survey party in 1825, established a ferry across the Missouri about 1828, and in 1832 commanded a militia company in the Black Hawk War. He also served in the Missouri legislature as a representative from Saline County. F. F. Stephens, "Missouri and the Santa Fé Trade," in *Missouri Historical Review*, Vol. XI, No. 4 (July, 1917), 291–94. For a record of his first Santa Fé expedition, kept by his brother, see "The Journals of Capt. Thomas Becknell, from Boone's Lick to Santa Fé, and from Santa Cruz to Green River," *ibid.*, IV, No. 2 (January, 1910), 68–84.

May, Colonel Cooper and sons, from the same neighborhood, accompanied by several others (their whole number about fifteen), set out with four or five thousand dollars' worth of goods, which they transported upon packhorses. They steered directly for Taos, where they arrived without any remarkable occurrence.[12]

The next effort of Captain Becknell was attended with very different success. With a company amounting to near thirty men, and perhaps five thousand dollars' worth of goods of various descriptions, he started from Missouri, about a month after Colonel Cooper. Being an excellent woodsman, and anxious to avoid the circuitous route of the Upper Arkansas country, he resolved this time, after having reached that point on the Arkansas river since known as the 'Caches,' to steer more directly for Santa Fé, entertaining little or no suspicion of the terrible trials which awaited him across the pathless desert. With no other guide but the starry heavens, and, it may be, a pocket-compass, the party embarked upon the arid plains which extended far and wide before them to the Cimarron river.

The adventurous band pursued their forward course without being able to procure any water, except from the scanty supply they carried in their canteens. As this source of relief was completely exhausted after two days' march, the sufferings of both men and beasts had driven them almost to distraction. The forlorn band were at last reduced to the cruel necessity of killing their dogs, and cutting off the ears of their mules, in the vain hope of assuaging their burning thirst with the hot blood. This only served to irritate the parched palates, and madden the senses of the sufferers. Frantic with despair, in prospect of the horrible death which now stared them in the face, they scattered in every direction in search of that element which they had left behind them in such abundance, but without success.

Frequently led astray by the deceptive glimmer of the mirage, or false ponds, as those treacherous oases of the desert are called, and not suspecting (as was really the case) that they had already ar-

---

[12] Benjamin Cooper was accompanied by two nephews, Braxton and Stephen Cooper. They left Howard County, Missouri, and after meeting the Arkansas, continued up it to the Rockies and entered New Mexico from the northern or mountain branch of the trail. Stephen Cooper led another party in 1823 and in 1825 assisted in marking the road from Missouri to the New Mexico boundary. After leaving the Santa Fé trade, he went to California. K. Gregg (ed.), *Road to Santa Fe*, 21, 24, 69.

rived near the banks of the Cimarron, they resolved to retrace their steps to the Arkansas. But they were no longer equal to the task, and would undoubtedly have perished in those arid regions, had not a buffalo, fresh from the river's side, and with a stomach distended with water, been discovered by some of the party, just as the last rays of hope were receding from their vision. The hapless intruder was immediately dispatched, and an invigorating draught procured from its stomach. I have since heard one of the parties to that expedition declare, that nothing ever passed his lips which gave him such exquisite delight as his first draught of that filthy beverage.

This providential relief enabled some of the strongest men of the party to reach the river, where they filled their canteens, and then hurried back to the assistance of their comrades, many of whom they found prostrate on the ground, and incapable of further exertion. By degrees, however, they were all enabled to resume their journey; and following the course of the Arkansas for several days, thereby avoiding the arid regions which had occasioned them so much suffering, they succeeded in reaching Taos (sixty or seventy miles north of Santa Fé) without further difficulty. Although travellers have since suffered excessively with thirst upon the same desert, yet, having become better acquainted with the topography of the country, no other equally thrilling incidents have subsequently transpired.[13]

It is from this period—the year 1822—that the virtual commencement of the Santa Fé Trade may be dated. The next remarkable era in its history is the first attempt to introduce wagons in these expeditions. This was made in 1824[14] by a company of traders, about

[13] There are a number of inconsistencies in this account of Becknell's second expedition. According to the journal, the party consisted of twenty-one men instead of nearly thirty, their goods were worth $3,000 instead of "perhaps five thousand," and they did not turn back from the Cimarron crossing and go by way of Taos but pushed on to Santa Fé by way of San Miguel del Vado. The journal does not record the suffering from thirst on the Cimarron crossing but does indicate an important point which Gregg misses. There were three wagons on this expedition, the first to be used on the Santa Fé Trail. "The Journals of Capt. Thomas Becknell," *Mo. Hist. Rev.*, Vol. IV, No. 2 (January, 1910), 79–80.

[14] Wagons were first used in 1822. See above, n. 13. Becknell's journal on this point is substantiated by the diary of the Fowler party which, returning from New Mexico in 1822, followed for at least two days the wagon trace left by Becknell. See entry for July 1, 1822, in Coues (ed.), *Journal of Jacob Fowler*, 167.

eighty in number, among whom were several gentlemen of intelligence from Missouri, who contributed, by their superior skill and undaunted energy, to render the enterprise completely successful. A portion of this company employed pack-mules: among the rest were owned twenty-five wheeled vehicles, of which one or two were stout road-wagons, two were carts, and the rest dearborn carriages— the whole conveying some $25,000 or $30,000 worth of merchandise. Colonel Marmaduke, the present Governor of the State of Missouri, having formed one of the party, has been pleased to place his diary of that eventful journey at my disposal; but want of space necessarily compels me to pass over the many interesting and exciting incidents which it contains.[15] Suffice it to say that the caravan reached Santa Fé with much less difficulty than must have been anticipated from a first experiment with wheeled vehicles. The route, indeed, appears to have presented fewer obstacles than any ordinary road of equal length in the United States.

It was not until several years after this experiment, however, that adventurers with large capital began seriously to embark in the Santa Fé trade. The early traders having but seldom experienced any molestations from the Indians, generally crossed the plains in detached bands, each individual rarely carrying more than two or three hundred dollars' worth of stock. This peaceful season, however, did not last very long; and it is greatly to be feared that the traders were not always innocent of having instigated the savage hostilities that ensued in after years. Many seemed to forget the wholesome precept, that they should not be savages themselves because they dealt with savages. Instead of cultivating friendly feelings with those few who remained peaceful and honest, there was an occasional one always disposed to kill, even in cold blood, every Indian that fell into their power, merely because some of the tribe had committed some outrage either against themselves or their friends.

[15] For the diary, see F. A. Sampson (ed.), "Santa Fe Trail: M. M. Marmaduke Journal (1824)," in *Mo. Hist. Rev.*, Vol. VI, No. 1 (October, 1911), 1–10. Meredith Miles Marmaduke (1791–1864), originally of Virginia, was a colonel of militia in the War of 1812. He came to Missouri about 1824, settled at Old Franklin, and engaged in the Santa Fé trade from 1824 to about 1830. After that he held several offices in Missouri, including that of governor (1844), and was a strong Unionist during the Civil War.

Since the commencement of this trade, returning parties have performed the homeward journey across the plains with the proceeds of their enterprise, partly in specie, and partly in furs, buffalo rugs and animals. Occasionally, these straggling bands would be set upon by marauding Indians, but if well armed and of resolute spirit, they found very little difficulty in persuading the savages to let them pass unmolested; for, as Mr. Storrs very justly remarks, in his representation presented by Colonel Benton, in 1825, to the United States Senate,[16] the Indians are always willing to compromise when they find that they cannot rob "without losing the lives of their warriors, which they hardly ever risk, unless for revenge or in open warfare."

The case was very different with those who through carelessness or recklessness ventured upon the wild prairies without a sufficient supply of arms. A story is told of a small band of twelve men, who, while encamped on the Cimarron river, in 1828, with but four serviceable guns between them, were visited by a party of Indians (believed to be Arrapahoes), who made at first strong demonstrations of friendship and good will. Observing the defenceless condition of the traders, they went away, but soon returned about thirty strong, each provided with a *lazo*, and all on foot. The chief then began by informing the Americans that his men were tired of walking, and must have horses. Thinking it folly to offer any resistance, the terrified traders told them if one animal apiece would satisfy them, to go and catch them. This they soon did; but finding their requests so easily complied with, the Indians held a little parley together, which resulted in a new demand for more—they must now have two apiece. "Well, catch them!" was the acquiescent reply of the unfortunate

[16] Augustus Storrs, a native of New Hampshire, accompanied the caravan under Becknell and Marmaduke which left Missouri in May, 1824, and on his return gave Senator Thomas Hart Benton of Missouri a detailed report entitled *Answers of Augustus Storrs, of Missouri, to Certain Queries upon the Origin, present State, and future Prospects, of Trade and Intercourse between Missouri and the Internal Provinces of Mexico, propounded by the Hon. Mr. Benton, Jan. 5, 1825,* which was published in *Senate Document No. 7* (18 Cong., 1 sess., Washington, Government Printing Office, 1825). The often quoted report was submitted in support of Benton's bill for the authorization of a government-sponsored survey and marking of the Santa Fé road, which became law in March, 1825. Storrs was captain of the Santa Fé caravan of 1825 and the same year was appointed United States consul at Santa Fé, the first to hold the office.

band—upon which the savages mounted those they had already secured, and swinging their lazos over their heads, plunged among the stock with a furious yell, and drove off the entire *caballada* of near five hundred head of horses, mules and asses.[17]

The fall of 1828 proved still more fatal to the traders on their homeward trip; for by this time the Indians had learned to form a correct estimate of the stock with which the return companies were generally provided. Two young men named McNees and Monroe, having carelessly lain down to sleep on the banks of a stream, since known as McNees's creek,[18] were barbarously shot, with their own guns, as it was supposed, in very sight of the caravan. When their comrades came up, they found McNees lifeless, and the other almost expiring. In this state the latter was carried nearly forty miles to the Cimarron river, where he died, and was buried according to the custom of the Prairies.[19]

Just as the funeral ceremonies were about to be concluded, six or seven Indians appeared on the opposite side of the Cimarron. Some of the party proposed inviting them to a parley, while the rest, burning for revenge, evinced a desire to fire upon them at once. It is more than probable, however, that the Indians were not only innocent but ignorant of the outrage that had been committed, or they would hardly have ventured to approach the caravan. Being quick of perception, they very soon saw the belligerent attitude assumed by some of the company, and therefore wheeled round and attempted to escape. One shot was fired, which wounded a horse and brought the Indian to the ground, when he was instantly riddled with balls! Almost simultaneously another discharge of several guns followed, by which all the rest were either killed or mortally

[17] A similar incident, possibly the same, was reported by the road-survey party early in 1826, but the Indians were identified as Pawnees rather than Arapahoes. Benjamin H. Reeves to Secretary of War James Barbour, Fayette, Mo., April 15, 1826, in K. Gregg (ed.), *Road to Santa Fe*, 231.

[18] Known now as Corrumpa Creek. Daniel Monroe and young McNees, son of Samuel McNees, were both from Franklin, Missouri.

[19] These funerals are usually performed in a very summary manner. A grave is dug in a convenient spot, and the corpse, with no other shroud than its own clothes, and only a blanket for a coffin, is consigned to the earth. The grave is then usually filled up with stones or poles, as a safe-guard against the voracious wolves of the prairies.—GREGG.

wounded, except one, who escaped to bear to his tribe the news of their dreadful catastrophe!

These wanton cruelties had a most disastrous effect upon the prospects of the trade; for the exasperated children of the desert became more and more hostile to the 'pale faces,' against whom they continued to wage a cruel war for many successive years. In fact, this same party suffered very severely a few days afterwards. They were pursued by the enraged comrades of the slain savages to the Arkansas river, where they were robbed of nearly a thousand head of mules and horses. But the Indians were not yet satisfied. Having beset a company of about twenty men, who followed shortly after, they killed one of their number, and subsequently took from them all the animals they had in their possession. The unfortunate band were now not only compelled to advance on foot, but were even constrained to carry nearly a thousand dollars each upon their backs to the Arkansas river, where it was *cached* (concealed in the ground) till a conveyance was procured to transfer it to the United States.[20]

Such repeated and daring outrages induced the traders to petition the Federal Government for an escort of United States troops. The request having been granted, Major Riley,[21] with three companies of infantry and one of riflemen, was ordered to accompany the caravan which left in the spring of 1829. The escort stopped at Chouteau's Island, on the Arkansas river, and the traders thence pursued their journey through the sand-hills beyond.[22] They had hardly advanced

[20] This treasure was recovered by the military escort in 1829, according to the recollections of one of its members, although the official records say nothing of it. Otis E. Young, *The First Military Escort on the Santa Fe Trail, 1829,* 86–87, citing Milton E. Bryan, "The Flight of Time: Adventures on the Plains, Sixty Years Ago," Troy (Kansas) *Chief,* June 9, 1887, p. 8.

[21] Bennett Riley (1787–1853), of Virginia, served in the War of 1812, became a major in 1828, and in the same year was given command of an escort for the Santa Fé caravan. Major Riley appears to have been the first to use oxen on the Santa Fé Trail, there being four oxcarts in his supply train. Later he was with General Winfield Scott in Mexico, and in 1849, as brigadier-general, was sent to California, where he became the last territorial governor. The report of his escort service appears in Young, *The First Military Escort on the Santa Fe Trail* and in Fred S. Perrine, "Military Escorts on the Santa Fe Trail," *New Mexico Historical Review,* Vol. II, Nos. 2 and 3 (April, July, 1927), 175–93, 269–304; Vol. III, No. 3 (July, 1928), 265–300.

[22] Chouteau Island was in the upper ford of the Arkansas River, about midway between present-day Lakin and Hartland, Kansas, where the river flows northeastward. K. Gregg (ed.), *Road to Santa Fe,* 256–57. The name dates from the

six or seven miles, when a startling incident occurred which made them wish once more for the company of the gallant Major and his well-disciplined troops. A vanguard of three men, riding a few hundred yards ahead, had just dismounted for the purpose of satisfying their thirst, when a band of Kiawas, one of the most savage tribes that infest the western prairies, rushed upon them from the immense hillocks of sand which lay scattered in all directions. The three men sprang upon their animals, but two only who had horses were enabled to make their escape to the wagons; the third, a Mr. Lamme, who was unfortunately mounted upon a mule, was overtaken, slain, and scalped before any one could come to his assistance.[23] Somewhat alarmed at the boldness of the Indians, the traders dispatched an express to Major Riley, who immediately ordered his tents to be struck; and such was the rapidity of his movements, that when he appeared before the anxious caravan every one was lost in astonishment. The reinforcement having arrived in the night, the enemy could have obtained no knowledge of the fact, and would no doubt have renewed the attack in the morning, when they would have received a wholesome lesson from the troops, had not the *reveille* been sounded through mistake, at which they precipitately retreated. The escort now continued with the company as far as Sand creek,[24] when, perceiving no further signs of danger, they returned to the Arkansas, to await the return of the caravan in the ensuing fall.

The position of Major Riley on the Arkansas was one of serious and continual danger. Scarce a day passed without his being sub-

---

spring of 1816, when Auguste P. Chouteau, returning from an expedition to New Mexico with Julius De Munn and Joseph Philbert, was attacked by Pawnees. Retreating to this island, they survived the attack, but the following year were arrested in Mexican territory and sent back to the United States without their goods. Chittenden, *American Fur Trade*, II, 497–500; Edwin James, *Account of an Expedition from Pittsburg to the Rocky Mountains . . . from the Notes of Major S. H. Long* (Vols. XIV–XVII of Reuben Gold Thwaites [ed.], *Early Western Travels*) XV, n. 134.

[23] Samuel Craig Lamme, of Kentucky, had recently become a merchant at Franklin, Missouri, with stores also at Liberty and Independence. Ironically enough, he was one of those who petitioned President Jackson for military protection of the caravan. Lewis E. Atherton, "Business Techniques in the Santa Fe Trade," in *Mo. Hist. Rev.*, Vol. XXXIV, No. 3 (April, 1940), 335–41.

[24] Sand Creek, when joined by Bear Creek, becomes the northern fork of the Cimarron River. The Santa Fé Trail crossed it about fifty miles after leaving the Arkansas.

jected to some new annoyance from predatory Indians. The latter appeared, indeed, resolved to check all further concourse of the whites upon the Prairies; and fearful of the terrible extremes to which their excesses might be carried, the traders continued to unite in single caravans during many years afterwards, for the sake of mutual protection. This escort under Major Riley, and one composed of about sixty dragoons, commanded by Captain Wharton,[25] in 1834, constituted the only government protection ever afforded to the Santa Fé trade, until 1843, when large escorts under Captain Cook[26] accompanied two different caravans as far as the Arkansas river.

Of the composition and organization of these trading caravans, I shall take occasion to speak, from my own experience, in the following chapters.

[25] Clifton Wharton (d. 1848), a Pennsylvanian, entered the army in 1818 and became a captain in 1826. For his report on the escort service in 1834, see Perrine, "Military Escorts on the Santa Fe Trail," *N. Mex. Hist. Rev.*, Vol. II, No. 3 (July, 1927), 269–304. Gregg was captain of the caravan escorted by Wharton until Gregg resigned on June 27, at the Arkansas crossing. *Ibid.*, II, 301–304.

[26] Philip St. George Cooke (1809–95) was one of the great figures in the opening of the trans-Mississippi West. A Virginian, he graduated from West Point in 1827 and spent the next forty-six years in the army, serving in the Blackhawk, Mexican, and Civil wars. For the details of his escort command in 1843, see his *Scenes and Adventures in the Army*, 236–82. Cooke also wrote *The Conquest of New Mexico and California*.

CHAPTER II

Head Quarters of the Santa Fé Trade—Independence and its *Locale*—
A Prairie Trip an excellent Remedy for Chronic Diseases—Supplies for
the Journey—Wagons, Mules, and Oxen—Art of Loading Wagons—
Romancing Propensity of Travellers—The Departure—Storms and
Wagoncovers—Quagmires—Tricks of marauding Indians—Council
Grove—Fancy *versus* Reality—Electioneering on the Prairies—The Or-
ganization—Amateur Travellers and Loafers—Duties of the Watch—
Costumes and Equipment of the Party—Timbers for the Journey.

PEOPLE WHO RESIDE at a distance, and especially at the North,
have generally considered St. Louis as the emporium of the Santa
Fé Trade; but that city, in truth, has never been a place of rendezvous, nor even of outfit, except for a small portion of the traders who
have started from its immediate vicinity. The town of Franklin on
the Missouri river, over a hundred and fifty miles further to the
westward, seems truly to have been the cradle of our trade; and, in
conjunction with several neighboring towns, continued for many
years to furnish the greater number of these adventurous traders.[1]
Even subsequently to 1831, many wagons have been fitted out and
started from this interior section. But as the navigation of the Missouri river had considerably advanced towards the year 1831, and
the advantages of some point of debarkation nearer the western

---

[1] Old Franklin, across the Missouri River from Booneville, was founded in
1816 and made the seat of Howard County the following year. It was the most
important town west of St. Louis until 1828, when it was washed away by high
waters. Many of the houses were removed two miles back from the river, where
New Franklin was established, but the town never regained its former importance.
Jonas Viles, "Old Franklin: A Frontier Town of the Twenties," in *Miss. Valley
Hist. Rev.*, Vol. IX, No. 4 (March, 1923), 269–82.

frontier were very evident, whereby upwards of a hundred miles of troublesome land-carriage, over unimproved and often miry roads, might be avoided, the new town of Independence, but twelve miles from the Indian border and two or three south of the Missouri river, being the most eligible point, soon began to take the lead as a place of debarkation, outfit and departure, which, in spite of all opposition, it has ever since maintained.[2] It is to this beautiful spot, already grown up to be a thriving town, that the prairie adventurer, whether in search of wealth, health or amusement, is latterly in the habit of repairing, about the first of May, as the caravans usually set out some time during that month. Here they purchase their provisions for the road, and many of their mules, oxen, and even some of their wagons —in short, load all their vehicles, and make their final preparations for a long journey across the prairie wilderness.

As Independence is a point of convenient access (the Missouri river being navigable at all times from March till November), it has become the general 'port of embarkation' for every part of the great western and northern 'prairie ocean.' Besides the Santa Fé caravans, most of the Rocky Mountain traders and trappers, as well as emigrants to Oregon, take this town in their route. During the season of departure, therefore, it is a place of much bustle and active business.

Among the concourse of travellers at this 'starting point,' besides traders and tourists, a number of pale-faced invalids are generally to be met with. The Prairies have, in fact, become very celebrated for their sanative effects—more justly so, no doubt, than the most fashionable watering-places of the North. Most chronic diseases, particularly liver complaints, dyspepsias, and similar affections, are often radically cured; owing, no doubt, to the peculiarities of diet, and the regular exercise incident to prairie life, as well as to the purity of the atmosphere of those elevated unembarrassed regions. An invalid myself, I can answer for the efficacy of the remedy, at least in my own case. Though, like other valetudinarians, I was dis-

[2] Independence, about five miles east of present Kansas City, was laid out and made the seat of Jackson County in 1827. After the deluge at Franklin, Independence was the main fitting-out center for the caravans until 1844, when the steamboat landing there was destroyed by flood. It was then supplanted by Westport Landing in what is now Kansas City.

posed to provide an ample supply of such commodities as I deemed necessary for my comfort and health, I was not long upon the prairies before I discovered that most of such extra preparations were unnecessary, or at least quite dispensable. A few knickknacks, as a little tea, rice, fruits, crackers, etc., suffice very well for the first fortnight, after which the invalid is generally able to take the fare of the hunter and teamster. Though I set out myself in a carriage, before the close of the first week I saddled my pony; and when we reached the buffalo range, I was not only as eager for the chase as the sturdiest of my companions, but I enjoyed far more exquisitely my share of the buffalo, than all the delicacies which were ever devised to provoke the most fastidious appetite.

The ordinary supplies for each man's consumption during the journey, are about fifty pounds of flour, as many more of bacon, ten of coffee and twenty of sugar, and a little salt. Beans, crackers, and trifles of that description, are comfortable appendages, but being looked upon as *dispensable* luxuries, are seldom to be found in any of the stores on the road. The buffalo is chiefly depended upon for fresh meat, and great is the joy of the traveller when that noble animal first appears in sight.

The wagons now most in use upon the Prairies are manufactured in Pittsburg; and are usually drawn by eight mules or the same number of oxen. Of late years, however, I have seen much larger vehicles employed, with ten or twelve mules harnessed to each, and a cargo of goods of about five thousand pounds in weight.[3] At an early period the horse was more frequently in use, as mules were not found in great abundance; but as soon as the means for procuring these animals increased, the horse was gradually and finally discarded, except occasionally for riding and the chase.

Oxen having been employed by Major Riley for the baggage wagons of the escort which was furnished the caravan of 1829, they were found, to the surprise of the traders, to perform almost equal to mules. Since that time, upon an average about half of the wagons

[3] The so-called "Pittsburg wagon" was a modified version of the historic Conestoga and was often called by that name. For a full description of the Conestoga and its variations, see John Omwake, *The Conestoga Six-Horse Bell Teams of Eastern Pennsylvania.*

in these expeditions have been drawn by oxen. They possess many advantages, such as pulling heavier loads than the same number of mules, particularly through muddy or sandy places; but they generally fall off in strength as the prairie grass becomes drier and shorter, and often arrive at their destination in a most shocking plight. In this condition I have seen them sacrificed at Santa Fé for ten dollars the pair; though in more favorable seasons, they sometimes remain strong enough to be driven back to the United States the same fall. Therefore, although the original cost of a team of mules is much greater, the loss ultimately sustained by them is usually less,—to say nothing of the comfort of being able to travel faster and more at ease. The inferiority of oxen as regards endurance is partially owing to the tenderness of their feet; for there are very few among the thousands who have travelled on the Prairies that ever knew how to shoe them properly. Many have resorted to the curious expedient of shoeing their animals with 'moccasins' made of raw buffalo-skin, which does remarkably well as long as the weather remains dry; but when wet, they are soon worn through. Even mules, for the most part, perform the entire trip without being shod at all; though the hoofs often become very smooth, which frequently renders all their movements on the dry grassy surface nearly as laborious as if they were treading on ice.

The supplies being at length procured, and all necessary preliminaries systematically gone through, the trader begins the difficult task of loading his wagons. Those who understand their business, take every precaution so to stow away their packages that no jolting on the road can afterwards disturb the order in which they had been disposed. The ingenuity displayed on these occasions has frequently been such, that after a tedious journey of eight hundred miles, the goods have been found to have sustained much less injury, than they would have experienced on a turnpike-road, or from the ordinary handling of property upon our western steam-boats.

The next great difficulty the traders have to encounter is in training those animals that have never before been worked, which is frequently attended by an immensity of trouble. There is nothing, however, in the mode of harnessing and conducting teams in prairie travelling, which differs materially from that practised on the public highways throughout the States,—the representations of certain travellers to the contrary, notwithstanding.[4] From the amusing descriptions which are sometimes given by this class of writers, one would be apt to suppose that they had never seen a wagon or a team of mules before, or that they had just emerged for the first time from the purlieus of a large city. The propensity evinced by these writers for giving an air of romance to everything they have either seen or heard, would seem to imply a conviction on their part, that no statement of unvarnished facts can ever be stamped with the seal of the world's approbation—that a work, in order to prove permanently attractive, should teem with absurdities and abound in exaggerated details. How far such an assumption would be correct, I shall not pause to inquire.

At last all are fairly launched upon the broad prairie—the miseries of preparation are over—the thousand anxieties occasioned by wearisome consultations and delays are felt no more. The charioteer, as he smacks his whip, feels a bounding elasticity of soul within him, which he finds it impossible to restrain;—even the mules prick up their ears with a peculiarly conceited air, as if in anticipation of that change of scene which will presently follow. Harmony and good feeling prevail everywhere. The hilarious song, the *bon mot* and the witty repartee, go round in quick succession; and before people have had leisure to take cognizance of the fact, the lively village of Independence, with its multitude of associations, is already lost to the eye.

It was on the 15th of May, 1831, and one of the brightest and most lovely of all the days in the calendar, that our little party set out from Independence. The general rendezvous at Council Grove was our immediate destination. It is usual for the traders to travel thus far in detached parties, and to assemble there for the purpose of entering into some kind of organization, for mutual security and defence during the remainder of the journey. It was from thence that the formation of the *Caravan* was to be dated, and the chief interest of our journey to commence; therefore, to this point we all

[4] Among others, Gregg obviously had in mind Thomas Jefferson Farnham. See Farnham's *Travels in the Great Western Prairies, the Anahuac and Rocky Mountains, and in the Oregon Territory* (New York, Greeley & McElrath, 1843), 4⁻.5

looked forward with great anxiety. The intermediate travel was marked by very few events of any interest. As the wagons had gone before us, and we were riding in a light carriage, we were able to reach the Round Grove,[5] about thirty-five miles distant, on the first day, where we joined the rear division of the caravan, comprising about thirty wagons.

On the following day we had a foretaste of those protracted, drizzling spells of rain, which, at this season of the year, so much infest the frontier prairies. It began sprinkling about dark, and continued pouring without let or hindrance for forty-eight hours in succession; and as the rain was accompanied by a heavy north-wester, and our camp was pitched in the open prairie, without a stick of available timber within a mile of us, it must be allowed that the whole formed a prelude anything but flattering to valetudinarians. For my own part, finding the dearborn carriage in which I had a berth not exactly waterproof, I rolled myself in a blanket and lay snugly coiled upon a tier of boxes and bales, under cover of a wagon, and thus managed to escape a very severe drenching.

It may be proper to observe here, for the benefit of future travellers, that in order to make a secure shelter for the cargo, against the inclemencies of the weather, there should be spread upon each wagon a pair of stout Osnaburg sheets,[6] with one of sufficient width to reach the bottom of the body on each side, so as to protect the goods from driving rains. By omitting this important precaution many packages of merchandise have been seriously injured. Some have preferred lining the interior of the wagon-body by tacking a simple strip of sheeting all around it. On the outward trips especially, a pair of Mackinaw blankets can be advantageously spread betwixt the two sheets, which effectually secures the roof against the worst of storms. This contrivance has also the merit of turning the blankets into a profitable item of trade, by enabling the owners to evade the customhouse officers, who would otherwise seize them as contraband articles.

[5] Round Grove was on the headwaters of Cedar Creek, between present Olathe and Gardner in Johnson County, Kansas. By the road surveyed in 1825 it was 13 miles and 22 chains (of 66 ft.) from the ford of the Big Blue (Topeka) River. K. Gregg (ed.), *Road to Santa Fe*, 190.
[6] A coarse linen fabric manufactured in Osnabrück, Germany.

The mischief of the storm did not exhaust itself, however, upon our persons. The loose animals sought shelter in the groves at a considerable distance from the encampment, and the wagoners being loth to turn out in search of them during the rain, not a few of course, when applied for, were missing. This, however, is no uncommon occurrence. Travellers generally experience far more annoyance from the straying of cattle during the first hundred miles, than at any time afterwards; because, apprehending no danger from the wild Indians (who rarely approach within two hundred miles of the border), they seldom keep any watch, although that is the very time when a cattle-guard is most needed. It is only after some weeks' travel that the animals begin to feel attached to the caravan, which they then consider about as much their home as the stock-yard of a dairy farm.

After leaving this spot the troubles and vicissitudes of our journey began in good earnest; for on reaching the narrow ridge which separates the Osage and Kansas waters (known as 'the Narrows'),[7] we encountered a region of very troublesome quagmires. On such occasions it is quite common for a wagon to sink to the hubs in mud, while the surface of the soil all around would appear perfectly dry and smooth. To extricate each other's wagons we had frequently to employ double and triple teams, with 'all hands to the wheels' in addition—often led by the proprietors themselves up to the waist in mud and water.

Three or four days after this, and while crossing the head branches of the Osage river, we experienced a momentary alarm. Conspicuously elevated upon a rod by the roadside, we found a paper purporting to have been written by the Kansas agent, stating that a band of Pawnees were said to be lurking in the vicinity! The first excitement over, however, the majority of our party came to the conclusion that it was either a hoax of some of the company in advance, or else a stratagem of the Kaws (or Kansas Indians), who, as well as the Osages, prowl about those prairies, and steal from the caravans, during the passage, when they entertain the slightest hope that their maraudings will be laid to others. They seldom venture

[7] The Narrows separate the affluents of Wakarusa Creek, a tributary of the Kansas, and Ottawa Creek, which feeds the Osage, and are found just west of Baldwin, in Douglas County, Kansas. The distance from Round Grove was 30 miles, according to Gregg's own table. See below, Vol. I, chap. 16, n. 4.

28

further, however, than to seize upon an occasional stray animal, which they frequently do with the view alone of obtaining a reward for returning it to its owner. As to the Pawnees, the most experienced traders were well aware that they had not been known to frequent those latitudes since the commencement of the Santa Fé trade. But what contributed as much as anything else to lull the fears of the timid, was an accession to our forces of seventeen wagons which we overtook the same evening.

Early on the 26th of May we reached the long looked-for rendezvous of Council Grove,[8] where we joined the main body of the caravan. Lest this imposing title suggest to the reader a snug and thriving village, it should be observed, that, on the day of our departure from Independence, we passed the last human abode upon our route; therefore, from the borders of Missouri to those of New Mexico not even an Indian settlement greeted our eyes.

This point is nearly a hundred and fifty miles from Independence, and consists of a continuous stripe of timber nearly half a mile in width, comprising the richest varieties of trees; such as oak, walnut, ash, elm, hickory, etc., and extending all along the valleys of a small stream known as 'Council Grove creek,' the principal branch of the Neosho river. This stream is bordered by the most fertile bottoms and beautiful upland prairies, well adapted to cultivation: such indeed is the general character of the country from thence to Independence. All who have traversed these delightful regions, look forward with anxiety to the day when the Indian title to the land shall be extinguished, and flourishing 'white' settlements dispel the gloom which at present prevails over this uninhabited region. Much of this prolific country now belongs to the Shawnees and other Indians of the border, though some portion of it has never been allotted to any tribe.

Frequent attempts have been made by travellers to invest the Council Grove with a romantic sort of interest, of which the following fabulous vagary, which I find in a letter that went the rounds of

[8] Council Grove, now the seat of Morris County, Kansas, was a heavily timbered bottom of the Neosho about one hundred and sixty acres in extent which offered excellent pasturage. Since passing The Narrows, Gregg had crossed 110-Mile Creek (30 miles), Bridge Creek (8 miles), and Big John Spring (15 miles), from which Council Grove was 2 miles, according to his table.

our journals, is an amusing sample: "Here the Pawnee, Arapaho, Comanche, Loup and Eutaw Indians, all of whom were at war with each other, meet and smoke the pipe once a year." Now it is more than probable that not a soul of most of the tribes mentioned above ever saw the Council Grove. Whatever may be the interest attached to this place, however, on account of its historical or fanciful associations, one thing is very certain,—that the novice, even here, is sure to imagine himself in the midst of lurking savages. These visionary fears are always a source of no little merriment to the veteran of the field, who does not hesitate to travel, with a single wagon and a comrade or two, or even alone, from the Arkansas river to Independence.

The facts connected with the designation of this spot are simply these. Messrs. Reeves, Sibley and Mathers, having been commissioned by the United States, in the year 1825, to mark a road from the confines of Missouri to Santa Fé, met on this spot with some bands of Osages, with whom they concluded a treaty, whereby the Indians agreed to allow all citizens of the United States and Mexico to pass unmolested, and even to lend their aid to those engaged in the Santa Fé trade; for which they were to receive a gratification of eight hundred dollars in merchandise. The commissioners, on this occasion, gave to the place the name of 'Council Grove.'[9]

But, although the route examined by the Commissions named above, was partially marked out as far as the Arkansas, by raised mounds, it seems to have been of but little service to travellers, who continued to follow the trail previously made by the wagons, which is now the settled road to the region of the short 'buffalo grass.'

The designation of 'Council Grove,' after all, is perhaps the most appropriate that could be given to this place; for *we* there held

[9] For the treaty, journals, and correspondence of the survey party, see K. Gregg (ed.), *Road to Santa Fe*. Benjamin Reeves, of Howard County, Missouri, had been a legislator in Kentucky and became politically prominent in Missouri after his arrival there in 1819. He was elected lieutenant governor in 1824 but resigned to join the road commission. George Champlin Sibley (1782–1863) was born in Massachusetts, accompanied his family to North Carolina in 1788, and in 1805 entered the Indian service as assistant factor at Fort Bellefontaine. After twenty years as a factor, he was appointed to conduct the Santa Fé road survey. Thomas Mather (1795–1853), a native of Connecticut, removed to Illinois in 1818 and became a merchant at Kaskaskia in partnership with James L. Lambe. He was a member of the Illinois legislature prior to his appointment to the road commission.

a 'grand council,' at which the respective claims of the different 'aspirants to office' were considered, leaders selected, and a system of government agreed upon,—as is the standing custom of these promiscuous caravans. One would have supposed that electioneering and 'party spirit' would hardly have penetrated so far into the wilderness: but so it was. Even in our little community we had our 'office-seekers' and their 'political adherents,' as earnest and as devoted as any of the modern school of politicians in the midst of civilization. After a great deal of bickering and wordy warfare, however, all the 'candidates' found it expedient to decline, and a gentleman by the name of Stanley, without seeking, or even desiring the 'office,' was unanimously proclaimed 'Captain of the Caravan.'[10] The powers of this officer were undefined by any 'constitutional provision,' and consequently vague and uncertain: orders being only viewed as mere requests, they are often obeyed or neglected at the caprice of the subordinates. It is necessary to observe, however, that the captain is expected to direct the order of travel during the day, and to designate the camping-ground at night; with many other functions of a general character, in the exercise of which the company find it convenient to acquiesce. But the little attention that is paid to his commands in cases of emergency, I will leave the reader to become acquainted with, as I did, by observing their manifestations during the progress of the expedition.

But after this comes the principal task of organizing. The proprietors are first notified by 'proclamation' to furnish a list of their men and wagons. The latter are generally apportioned into four 'divisions,' particularly when the company is large—and ours consisted of nearly a hundred wagons,[11] besides a dozen of dearborns and other small vehicles, and two small cannons (a four and six pounder), each mounted upon a carriage. To each of these divisions, a 'lieutenant' was appointed, whose duty it was to inspect every ravine and creek on the route, select the best crossings, and superintend what is called in prairie parlance, the 'forming' of each encampment.

[10] Elisha Stanley. See above, Preface, n. 2.
[11] About half of these wagons were drawn by ox-teams, the rest by mules.—The capital in merchandise of the whole caravan was about $200,000.—GREGG.

Upon the calling of the roll, we were found to muster an efficient force of nearly two hundred men without counting invalids or other disabled bodies, who, as a matter of course, are exempt from duty. There is nothing so much dreaded by inexperienced travellers as the ordeal of guard duty. But no matter what the condition or employment of the individual may be, no one has the smallest chance of evading the 'common law of the prairies.' The amateur tourist and the listless loafer are precisely in the same wholesome predicament— they must all take their regular turn at the watch. There is usually a set of genteel idlers attached to every caravan, whose wits are forever at work in devising schemes for whiling away their irksome hours at the expense of others. By embarking in these 'trips of pleasure,' they are enabled to live without expense; for the hospitable traders seldom refuse to accommodate even a loafing companion with a berth at their mess without charge. But then these lounging *attachés* are expected at least to do good service by way of guard duty. None are even permitted to furnish a substitute, as is frequently done in military expeditions, for he that would undertake to stand the tour of another besides his own, would scarcely be watchful enough for the dangers of the Prairies. Even the invalid must be able to produce unequivocal proofs of his inability, or it is a chance if the plea is admitted. For my own part, although I started on the 'sick list,' and though the prairie sentinel must stand fast and brook the severest storm (for then it is that the strictest watch is necessary), I do not remember ever having missed my post but once during the whole journey.

The usual number of watches is eight, each standing a fourth of every alternate night. When the party is small the number is generally reduced; while in the case of very small bands, they are sometimes compelled for safety's sake to keep one watch on duty half the night. With large caravans the captain usually appoints eight 'sergeants of the guard,' each of whom takes an equal portion of men under his command.

The heterogeneous appearance of our company, consisting of men from every class and grade of society, with a little sprinkling of the softer sex, would have formed an excellent subject for an artist's pencil. It may appear, perhaps, a little extraordinary that females should have ventured across the Prairies under such forlorn auspices. Those who accompanied us, however, were members of a Spanish family who had been banished in 1829, in pursuance of a decree of the Mexican congress, and were now returning to their homes in consequence of a suspension of the decree.[12] Other females, however, have crossed the prairies to Santa Fé at different times, among whom I have known two respectable French ladies, who now reside in Chihuahua.

The wild and motley aspect of the caravan can be but imperfectly conceived without an idea of the costumes of its various members. The most 'fashionable' prairie dress is the fustian frock of the city-bred merchant furnished with a multitude of pockets capable of accommodating a variety of 'extra tackling.' Then there is the backwoodsman with his linsey or leather hunting-shirt—the farmer with his blue jean coat—the wagoner with his flannel-sleeve vest—besides an assortment of other costumes which go to fill up the picture.

In the article of fire-arms there is also an equally interesting medley. The frontier hunter sticks to his rifle, as nothing could induce him to carry what he terms in derision 'the scatter-gun.' The sportsman from the interior flourishes his double-barrelled fowling-piece with equal confidence in its superiority. The latter is certainly the most convenient description of gun that can be carried on this journey; as a charge of buck-shot in night attacks (which are the most common), will of course be more likely to do execution than a single rifle-ball fired at random. The 'repeating' arms have lately been brought into use upon the Prairies, and they are certainly very formidable weapons, particularly when used against an ignorant savage foe. A great many were furnished beside with a bountiful supply of pistols and knives of every description, so that the party made altogether a very brigand-like appearance.

During our delay at the Council Grove, the laborers were employed in procuring timber for axle-trees and other wagon repairs, of which a supply is always laid in before leaving this region of substantial growths; for henceforth there is no wood on the route for

[12] The decree of expulsion was issued at Mexico City, March 20, 1829, and ten Spanish men and six women accompanied the caravan from Santa Fé that was met on the Arkansas by Major Riley and escorted to Missouri. Young, *The First Military Escort*, 142, 201.

these purposes; not even in the mountains of Santa Fé do we meet with any serviceable timber. The supply procured here is generally lashed under the wagons, in which way a log is not unfrequently carried to Santa Fé, and even sometimes back again.

CHAPTER III

OWING TO THE DELAYS of organizing and other preparations, we did not leave the Council Grove camp till May 27th. Although the usual hour of starting with the prairie caravans is after an early breakfast, yet, on this occasion, we were hindered till in the afternoon. The familiar note of preparation, "Catch up! catch up!" was now sounded from the captain's camp, and re-echoed from every division and scattered group along the valley. On such occasions, a scene of confusion ensues, which must be seen to be appreciated. The woods and dales resound with the gleeful yells of the light-hearted wagoners, who, weary of inaction, and filled with joy at the prospect of getting under way, become clamorous in the extreme. Scarcely does the jockey on the race-course ply his whip more promptly at that magic word 'Go,' than do these emulous wagoners fly to harnessing their mules at the spirit-stirring sound of 'Catch up.' Each teamster vies with his fellows who shall be soonest ready; and it is a matter of boastful pride to be the first to cry out—"All's set!"

The uproarious bustle which follows—the hallooing of those in pursuit of animals—the exclamations which the unruly brutes call forth from their wrathful drivers; together with the clatter of bells—the rattle of yokes and harness—the jingle of chains—all conspire to produce a clamorous confusion, which would be altogether incomprehensible without the assistance of the eyes; while these alone would hardly suffice to unravel the labyrinthian manoeuvres and hurly-burly of this precipitate breaking up. It is sometimes amusing to observe the athletic wagoner hurrying an animal to its post—to see him 'heave upon' the halter of a stubborn mule, while the brute as obstinately 'sets back,' determined not to 'move a peg' till his own pleasure thinks it proper to do so—his whole manner seeming to say, "Wait till your hurry's over!" I have more than once seen a driver hitch a harnessed animal to the halter, and by that process haul 'his mulishness' forward, while each of his four projected feet would leave a furrow behind; until at last the perplexed master would wrathfully exclaim, "A mule will be a mule any way you can fix it!"

"All's set!" is finally heard from some teamster—"All's set," is directly responded from every quarter. "Stretch out!" immediately vociferates the captain. Then, the 'heps!' of drivers—the cracking of whips—the trampling of feet—the occasional creak of wheels—the rumbling of wagons—form a new scene of exquisite confusion, which I shall not attempt further to describe. "Fall in!" is heard from head-quarters, and the wagons are forthwith strung out upon the long inclined plain, which stretches to the heights beyond Council Grove.

After fifteen miles' progress, we arrived at the 'Diamond Spring'[1] (a crystal fountain discharging itself into a small brook), to which, in later years, caravans have sometimes advanced, before 'organizing.' Near twenty-five miles beyond we crossed the Cottonwood fork of the Neosho,[2] a creek still smaller than that of Council Grove, and our camp was pitched immediately in its further valley.

[1] Known also as Diamond of the Plains, Diamond of the Desert, and Jones Spring, Diamond Spring was a favorite with all travelers. It is located about 4 miles north of the railroad station of the latter name, in Morris County, Kansas. By the road surveyed in 1825 it was 16 miles and 32 chains beyond Council Grove. K. Gregg (ed.), *Road to Santa Fe*, 60, 254.

When caravans are able to cross in the evening, they seldom stop on the near side of a stream—first, because if it happens to rain during the night, it may become flooded, and cause both detention and trouble: again, though the stream be not impassable after rain, the banks become slippery and difficult to ascend. A third and still more important reason is, that, even supposing the contingency of rain does not occur, teams will rarely pull as well in 'cold collars,' as wagoners term it—that is, when fresh geared—as in the progress of a day's travel. When a heavy pull is just at hand in the morning, wagoners sometimes resort to the expedient of driving a circuit upon the prairie, before venturing to 'take the bank.'

We experienced a temporary alarm during the evening, while we lay encamped at Cottonwood, which was rather more boisterous than serious in its consequences. The wagons had been 'formed' across the neck of a bend in the creek, into which the cattle were turned, mostly in their yokes; for though, when thoroughly trained, teamsters usually unyoke their oxen every night, yet at first they often leave them coupled, to save the trouble of re-yoking them in their unruly state. A little after dark, these animals started simultaneously, with a thundering noise and rattle of the yokes, towards the outlet protected by the wagons, but for which obstacle they might have escaped far into the prairie, and have been irrecoverably lost, or, at least, have occasioned much trouble and delay to recover them. The cause of the fright was not discovered; but oxen are exceedingly whimsical creatures when surrounded by unfamiliar objects. One will sometimes take a fright at the jingle of his own yoke-irons, or the cough of his mate, and, by a sudden flounce, set the whole herd in a flurry. This was probably the case in the present instance; although some of our easily excited companions immediately surmised that the oxen had scented a lurking Pawnee.

Our route lay through uninterrupted prairie for about forty miles—in fact I may say, for five hundred miles, except the very narrow fringes of timber along the borders of the streams. The antelope of the high prairies which we now occasionally saw, is

[2] Cottonwood Fork joins the Neosho below Emporia, Kansas, but the campsite and regular crossing was near present Durham, in Marion County. Gregg's table places it 27 miles beyond Diamond Spring and 12 beyond Lost Spring. According to the survey, it was 29 miles and 40 chains from Diamond Spring. *Ibid.*, 60–61.

sometimes found as far east as Council Grove; and as a few old buffaloes have sometimes been met with about Cottonwood, we now began to look out for this desirable game. Some scattering bulls are generally to be seen first, forming as it would appear the 'van' or 'piquet guards' of the main droves with their cows and calves. The buffalo are usually found much further east early in the spring, than during the rest of the year, on account of the long grass, which shoots up earlier in the season than the short pasturage of the plains.

Our hopes of game were destined soon to be realized; for early on the second day after leaving Cottonwood (a few miles beyond the principal Turkey creek),[3] our eyes were greeted with the sight of a herd amounting to nearly a hundred head of buffalo, quietly grazing in the distance before us. Half of our company had probably never seen a buffalo before (at least in its wild state); and the excitement that the first sight of these 'prairie beeves' occasions among a party of novices, beggars all description. Every horseman was off in a scamper: and some of the wagoners, leaving their teams to take care of themselves, seized their guns and joined the race afoot. Here went one with his rifle or yager—there another with his double-barrelled shot-gun—a third with his holster-pistols—a Mexican perhaps with his lance—another with his bow and arrows—and numbers joined without any arms whatever, merely for the 'pleasures of the chase'—all helter-skelter—a regular John Gilpin race,[4] truly 'neck or naught.' The fleetest of the pursuers were soon in the midst of the game, which scattered in all directions, like a flock of birds upon the descent of a hawk.

A few 'beeves' were killed during the chase; and as soon as our camp was pitched, the bustle of kindling fires and preparing for supper commenced. The new adventurers were curious to taste this prairie luxury; while we all had been so long upon salt provisions— now nearly a month—that our appetites were in exquisite condition to relish fresh meat. The fires had scarcely been kindled when the fumes of broiling meat pervaded the surrounding atmosphere; while

[3] Turkey Creek, a branch of the Little Arkansas, was crossed near present McPherson, Kansas, 25 miles beyond Cottonwood Creek by Gregg's table but only 19 miles and 63 chains by the survey. *Ibid.*, 61.

[4] The reference is to "The Diverting History of John Gilpin," by William Cowper (1731–1800).

all huddled about, anxiously watching their cookeries, and regaling their senses in anticipation upon the savory odors which issued from them.

For the edification of the reader, who has no doubt some curiosity on the subject, I will briefly mention, that the 'kitchen and tableware' of the traders usually consists of a skillet, a frying-pan, a sheet-iron campkettle, a coffee-pot, and each man with his tin cup and a butcher's knife. The culinary operations being finished, the pan and kettle are set upon the grassy turf, around which all take a 'lowly seat,' and crack their gleesome jokes, while from their greasy hands they swallow their savory viands—all with a relish rarely experienced at the well-spread tables of the most fashionable and wealthy.

The insatiable appetite acquired by travellers upon the Prairies is almost incredible, and the quantity of coffee drunk is still more so. It is an unfailing and apparently indispensable beverage, served at every meal—even under the broiling noon-day sun, the wagoner will rarely fail to replenish a second time, his huge tin cup.

Early the next day we reached the 'Little Arkansas,' which, although endowed with an imposing name, is only a small creek with a current but five or six yards wide. But, though small, its steep banks and miry bed annoyed us exceedingly in crossing.[5] It is the practice upon the prairies on all such occasions, for several men to go in advance with axes, spades and mattocks, and by digging the banks and erecting temporary bridges, to have all in readiness by the time the wagons arrive. A bridge over a quagmire is made in a few minutes, by cross-laying it with brush (willows are best, but even long grass is often employed as a substitute), and covering it with earth, across which a hundred wagons will often pass in safety.

We had now arrived at the point nearest to the border, I believe, where any outrages have been perpetrated upon the traders to Santa Fé. One of the early packing companies lost their animals on this spot, and had to send back for a new supply.

[5] The Little Arkansas, flowing southeastward into the Arkansas at present Wichita, was crossed by Gregg a little below the town of Little River, in Rice County, Kansas, 17 miles from his Turkey Creek ford. It was 22 miles and 70 chains between these streams by the surveyed route. K. Gregg (ed.), *Road to Santa Fe*, 62–63.

Next day we reached Cow creek,[6] where all the difficulties encountered at Little Arkansas had to be reconquered: but after digging, bridging, shouldering the wheels, with the usual accompaniment of whooping, swearing and cracking of whips, we soon got safely across and encamped in the valley beyond. Alarms now began to accumulate more rapidly upon us. A couple of persons had a few days before been chased to the wagons by a band of—buffalo; and this evening the encampment was barely formed when two hunters came bolting in with information that a hundred, perhaps of the same 'enemy,' were at hand—at least this was the current opinion afterwards. The hubbub occasioned by this fearful news had scarcely subsided, when another arrived on a panting horse, crying out "Indians, Indians! I've just escaped from a couple, who pursued me to the very camp!" "To arms! to arms!" resounded from every quarter—and just then a wolf, attracted by the fumes of broiling buffalo bones, sent up a most hideous howl across the creek. "Some one in distress!" was instantly shouted: "To his relief!" vociferated the crowd—and off they bolted, one and all, arms in hand, hurly-burly —leaving the camp entirely unprotected; so that had an enemy been at hand indeed, and approached us from the opposite direction, they might easily have taken possession of the wagons. Before they had all returned, however, a couple of hunters came in and laughed very heartily at the expense of the first alarmist, whom they had just chased into the camp.

Half a day's drive after leaving this camp of 'false alarms' brought us to the valley of Arkansas river. This point is about 270 miles from Independence.[7] From the adjacent heights the landscape presents an imposing and picturesque appearance. Beneath a ledge of wave-like yellow sandy ridges and hillocks spreading far beyond, descends the majestic river (averaging at least a quarter of a mile

[6] Cow Creek, emptying into the Arkansas at Hutchinson, Kansas, was generally crossed west of Lyons. Gregg's ford was 20 miles beyond the Little Arkansas. The road commission in 1825 called it Cold Water Creek and encountered it only 9 miles and 21 chains beyond the latter stream. *Ibid.*, 64.

[7] The Arkansas River was usually struck at its Great Bend near Ellinwood, Kansas. Gregg's table places the river 16 miles beyond Cow Creek and 265 from Independence. As the surveyors met it several miles downstream, only 4 miles beyond the creek, there is no correlation between their distance and Gregg's. *Ibid.*, 64–65, 4–5.

in width), bespeckled with verdant islets, thickly set with cotton-wood timber. The banks are very low and barren, with the exception of an occasional grove of stunted trees, hiding behind a swamp or sand-hill, placed there as it were to protect it from the fire of the prairies, which in most parts keeps down every perennial growth. In many places, indeed, where there are no islands, the river is so entirely bare of trees, that the unthinking traveller might approach almost to its very brink, without suspecting its presence.

Thus far, many of the prairies have a fine and productive appearance, though the Neosho river (or Council Grove) seems to form the western boundary of the truly rich and beautiful country of the border. Up to that point the prairies are similar to those of Missouri—the soil equally exuberant and fertile; while all the country that lies beyond, is of a far more barren character—vegetation of every kind is more stinted—the gay flowers more scarce, and the scanty timber of a very inferior quality: indeed, the streams, from Council Grove westward, are lined with very little else than cotton-wood, barely interspersed here and there with an occasional elm or hackberry.

Following up the course of this stream for some twenty miles, now along the valley, and again traversing the points of projecting eminences, we reached Walnut creek.[8] I have heard of a surgical operation performed at this point, in the summer of 1826, which, though not done exactly *secundum artem*, might suggest some novel reflections to the man of science. A few days before the caravan reached this place, a Mr. Broadus,[9] in attempting to draw his rifle from a wagon muzzle foremost, discharged its contents into his arm. The bone being dreadfully shattered, the unfortunate man was advised to submit to an amputation at once; otherwise, it being in the month of August, and excessively warm, mortification would soon ensue. But Broadus obstinately refused to consent to this course, till death began to stare him in the face. By this time, however, the

[8] Walnut Creek enters the Arkansas about 4 miles east of the town of Great Bend, in Barton County, Kansas, and the usual ford was not far from the mouth, near a scattering of walnut and elm trees. In Gregg's table it was only 8 miles from where he met the Arkansas, but it was 37 miles and 38 chains by the survey. *Ibid.*, 64–68.

[9] Probably Andrew Broadus, of Howard County, Missouri, who had been with the survey party as a guard and hunter in 1825. *Ibid.*, 21, 243.

whole arm had become gangrened, some spots having already appeared above the place where the operation should have been performed. The invalid's case was therefore considered perfectly hopeless, and he was given up by all his comrades, who thought of little else than to consign him to the grave.

But being unwilling to resign himself to the fate which appeared frowning over him, without a last effort, he obtained the consent of two or three of the party, who undertook to amputate his arm merely to gratify the wishes of the dying man; for in such a light they viewed him. Their only 'case of instruments' consisted of a handsaw, a butcher's knife and a large iron bolt. The teeth of the saw being considered too coarse, they went to work, and soon had a set of fine teeth filed on the back. The knife having been whetted keen, and the iron bolt laid upon the fire, they commenced the operation: and in less time than it takes to tell it, the arm was opened round to the bone, which was almost in an instant sawed off; and with the whizzing hot iron the whole stump was so effectually seared as to close the arteries completely. Bandages were now applied, and the company proceeded on their journey as though nothing had occurred. The arm commenced healing rapidly, and in a few weeks the patient was sound and well, and is perhaps still living, to bear witness to the superiority of the 'hot iron' over ligatures, in 'taking up' arteries.

On the following day our route lay mostly over a level plain, which usually teems with buffalo, and is beautifully adapted to the chase. At the distance of about fifteen miles, the attention of the traveller is directed to the 'Pawnee Rock,' so called, it is said, on account of a battle's having once been fought hard by, between the Pawnees and some other tribe. It is situated at the projecting point of a ridge, and upon its surface are furrowed, in uncouth but legible characters, numerous dates, and the names of various travellers who have chanced to pass that way.[10]

We encamped at Ash creek,[11] where we again experienced sundry

[10] Pawnee Rock, about two miles northwest of the town of that name, in Pawnee County, Kansas, was a prominent sandstone cliff capped by a mound of stones. The tradition of a Comanche attack on the Pawnees is recited by Cooke in his *Scenes and Adventures in the Army*, 259. Much of the red sandstone face of the cliff, which served as a register for passing travelers, has since been removed by railroad and home builders, but an historical monument has been erected at the site.

alarms in consequence of 'Indian sign,' that was discovered in the creek valley, such as unextinguished fires, about which were found some old moccasins,—a sure indication of the recent retreat of savages from the vicinity. These constant alarms, however, although too frequently the result of groundless and unmanly fears, are not without their salutary effects upon the party. They serve to keep one constantly on the alert, and to sharpen those faculties of observation which would otherwise become blunted or inactive. Thus far also we had marched in two lines only; but, after crossing the Pawnee Fork,[12] each of the four divisions drove on in a separate file, which became henceforth the order of march till we reached the border of the mountains. By moving in long lines as we did before, the march is continually interrupted; for every accident which delays a wagon ahead stops all those behind. By marching four abreast, this difficulty is partially obviated, and the wagons can also be thrown more readily into a condition of defence in case of attack.

Upon encamping the wagons are formed into a 'hollow square' (each division to a side), constituting at once an enclosure (or corral) for the animals when needed, and a fortification against the Indians. Not to embarrass this cattle-pen, the camp fires are all lighted outside of the wagons. Outside of the wagons, also, the travellers spread their beds, which consist, for the most part, of buffalo-rugs and blankets. Many content themselves with a single Mackinaw; but a pair constitutes the most regular pallet; and he that is provided with a buffalo-rug into the bargain, is deemed luxuriously supplied. It is most usual to sleep out in the open air, as well to be at hand in case of attack, as indeed for comfort; for the serene sky of the Prairies affords the most agreeable and wholesome canopy. That deleterious attribute of night air and dews, so dangerous in other climates, is but little experienced upon the high plains: on the contrary, the serene evening air seems to affect the health rather favorably than otherwise. Tents are so rare on these expeditions that, in a caravan of two hundred men, I have not seen a dozen. In time of rain the traveller

[11] Ash Creek, named for the timber on its banks, was crossed by Gregg 19 miles after fording Walnut Creek. The surveyors, calling it Crooked Creek, measured the distance at 17 miles and 58 chains. K. Gregg (ed.), *Road to Santa Fe*, 70–71.

[12] Pawnee River, joining the Arkansas at Larned, Kansas, was forded 6 miles beyond Ash Creek by Gregg, 6 miles and 56 chains by the surveyors. *Ibid.*, 72.

43

resorts to his wagon, which affords a far more secure shelter than a tent; for if the latter is not beaten down by the storms which so often accompany rain upon the prairies, the ground underneath is at least apt to be flooded. During dry weather, however, even the invalid prefers the open air.

Prior to the date of our trip it had been customary to secure the horses by hoppling them. The 'fore-hopple' (a leathern strap or rope manacle upon the fore-legs) being most convenient, was more frequently used; though the 'side-line' (a hopple connecting a fore and a hind leg) is the most secure; for with this an animal can hardly increase his pace beyond a hobbling walk; whereas, with the fore-hopple, a frightened horse will scamper off with nearly as much velocity as though he were unshackled. But, better than either of these is the practice which the caravans have since adopted of tethering the mules at night around the wagons, at proper intervals, with ropes twenty-five or thirty feet in length, tied to stakes fifteen to twenty inches long, driven into the ground; a supply of which, as well as mallets, the wagoners always carry with them.

It is amusing to witness the disputes which often arise among wagoners about their 'staking ground.' Each teamster is allowed, by our 'common law,' a space of about a hundred yards immediately fronting his wagon, which he is ever ready to defend, if a neighbor shows a disposition to encroach upon his soil. If any animals are found 'staked' beyond the 'chartered limits,' it is the duty of the guard to 'knock them up,' and turn them into the *corral*. Of later years the tethering of oxen has also been resorted to with advantage. It was thought at first that animals thus confined by ropes could not procure a sufficient supply of food; but experience has allayed all apprehension on the subject. In fact, as the camp is always pitched in the most luxuriantly clothed patches of prairie that can be selected, a mule is seldom able to dispatch in the course of one night, all the grass within his reach. Again, when animals are permitted to range at liberty, they are apt to mince and nibble at the tenderest blades and spend their time in roaming from point to point, in search of what is most agreeable to their 'epicurean palates'; whereas if they are restricted by a rope, they will at once fall to with earnestness and clip the pasturage as it comes.

Although the buffalo had been scarce for a few days,—frightened off, no doubt, by the Indians whose 'sign' we saw about Ash creek, they soon became exceedingly abundant. The larger droves of these animals are sometimes a source of great annoyance to the caravans, as, by running near our loose stock, there is frequent danger of their causing *stampedes* (or general scamper), in which case mules, horses and oxen have been known to run away among the buffalo, as though they had been a gang of their own species. A company of traders, in 1824, lost twenty or thirty of their animals in this way. Hunters have also been deprived of their horses in the same way. Leaping from them in haste, in order to take a more determinate aim at a buffalo, the horse has been known to take fright, and, following the fleeing game, has disappeared with saddle, bridle, pistols and all—most probably never to be heard of again. In fact, to look for stock upon these prairies, would be emphatically to 'search for a needle in a haystack;' not only because they are virtually boundless, but that being everywhere alive with herds of buffalo, from which horses cannot be distinguished at a distance, one knows not whither to turn in search after the stray animals.

We had lately been visited by frequent showers of rain, and upon observing the Arkansas river, it was found to be rising, which seemed portentous of the troubles which the 'June freshet' might occasion us in crossing it; and, as it was already the 11th of this month, this annual occurrence was now hourly expected. On some occasions caravans have been obliged to construct what is called a 'buffalo-boat,' which is done by stretching the hides of these animals over a frame of poles, or, what is still more common, over an empty wagon-body. The 'June freshets,' however, are seldom of long duration; and, during the greatest portion of the year, the channel is very shallow. Still the bed of the river being in many places filled with quicksand, it is requisite to examine and mark out the best ford with stakes, before one undertakes to cross. The wagons are then driven over usually by double teams, which should never be permitted to stop, else animals and wagons are apt to founder, and the loading is liable to be damaged. I have witnessed a whole team down at once, rendering it necessary to unharness and drag each mule out separately: in fact, more than common exertion is sometimes required to prevent these dumpish animals from drowning in their fright and struggles through the water, though the current be but shallow at the place. Hence it is that oxen are much safer for fording streams than mules. As for ourselves, we forded the river without serious difficulty.[13]

Rattlesnakes are proverbially abundant upon all these prairies, and as there is seldom to be found either stick or stone with which to kill them, one hears almost a constant popping of rifles or pistols among the vanguard, to clear the route of these disagreeable occupants, lest they should bite our animals. As we were toiling up through the sandy hillocks which border the southern banks of the Arkansas, the day being exceedingly warm, we came upon a perfect den of these reptiles. I will not say 'thousands,' though this perhaps were nearer the truth—but hundreds at least were coiled or crawling in every direction. They were no sooner discovered than we were upon them with guns and pistols, determined to let none of them escape.

In the midst of this amusing scramble among the snakes, a wild mustang colt, which had somehow or other, become separated from its dam, came bolting among our relay of loose stock to add to the confusion. One of our mules, evidently impressed with the impertinence of the intruder, sprang forward and attacked it, with the apparent intention of executing summary chastisement; while another mule, with more benignity of temper than its irascible compeer, engaged most lustily in defence of the unfortunate little mustang. As the contest was carried on among the wagons, the teamsters soon became very uproarious; so that the whole, with the snake fracas, made up a capital scene of confusion. When the mule skirmish would have ended, if no one had interfered, is a question which remained undetermined; for some of our company, in view of the consequences that might result from the contest, rather inhumanly took sides with the assailing mule; and soon after they entered the lists, a rifle ball relieved the poor colt from its earthly embarrassments, and the company from further domestic disturbance. Peace once more restored, we soon got under way, and that evening pitched our camp opposite the celebrated 'Caches,'[14] a place where some of the earliest adventurers had been compelled to conceal their merchandise.

[13] See below, chap. IV, n. 1.

The history of the origin of these 'Caches' may be of sufficient interest to merit a brief recital. Beard, of the unfortunate party of 1812, alluded to in the first chapter, having returned to the United States in 1822, together with Chambers, who had descended the Canadian river the year before, induced some small capitalists of St. Louis to join in an enterprise, and then undertook to return to Santa Fé the same fall, with a small party and an assortment of merchandise. Reaching the Arkansas late in the season, they were overtaken by a heavy snow storm, and driven to take shelter on a large island. A rigorous winter ensued, which forced them to remain pent up in that place for three long months. During this time the greater portion of their animals perished; so that, when the spring began to open, they were unable to continue their journey with their goods. In this emergency they made a *cache* some distance above, on the north side of the river, where they stowed away most of their merchandise. From thence they proceeded to Taos, where they procured mules, and returned to get their hidden property.[15]

Few travellers pass this way without visiting these mossy pits, some of which remain partly unfilled to the present day. In the vicinity, or a few miles to the eastward perhaps, passes the hundredth degree of longitude west from Greenwich, which, from the Arkansas to Red River, forms the boundary between the United States and the Mexican, or rather the Texan territory.[16]

The term *cache*, meaning a *place of concealment*, was originally used by the Canadian French trappers and traders. It is made by digging a hole in the ground, somewhat in the shape of a jug, which is lined with dry sticks, grass, or anything else that will protect its contents from the dampness of the earth. In this place the goods to

[14] The Caches were near a prominent mass of conglomerate which the surveyors called Gravel Rocks, about 6 miles west of present Dodge City, Kansas. According to Gregg's table they were 69 miles beyond Pawnee River (having crossed Coon Creek at 33 miles along the way), but the surveyors found the distance 75 miles and 26 chains. K. Gregg (ed.), *Road to Santa Fe*, 72–78.

[15] For this adventure of James Baird and Samuel Chambers, see Chittenden, *American Fur Trade*, III, 502.

[16] As the 100th meridian passes through the eastern edge of Dodge City, it lies east of the Caches, as Gregg presumed. Joseph C. Brown, of the survey party, established the meridian several miles *west* of the Caches, an error which crept into several maps, but not into Gregg's. K. Gregg (ed.), *Road to Santa Fe*, 78–79. The international boundary at the time was established by the treaty of 1819 with Spain.

be concealed are carefully stowed away; and the aperture is then so effectually closed as to protect them from the rains. In *caching*, a great deal of skill is often required, to leave no signs whereby the cunning savage might discover the place of deposit. To this end, the excavated earth is carried to some distance and carefully concealed, or thrown into a stream, if one be at hand. The place selected for a cache is usually some rolling point, sufficiently elevated to be secure from inundations. If it be well set with grass, a solid piece of turf is cut out large enough for the entrance. The turf is afterward laid back, and taking root, in a short time no signs remain of its ever having been molested. However, as every locality does not afford a turfy site, the camp fire is sometimes built upon the place, or the animals are penned over it, which effectually destroys all traces of the cache.

This mode of concealing goods seems to have been in use from the time of the earliest French voyagers in America. Father Hennepin, during his passage down the Mississippi river, in 1680, describes an operation of this kind in the following terms: "We took up the green Sodd, and laid it by, and digg'd a hole in the Earth where we put our Goods, and cover'd them with pieces of Timber and Earth, and then put in again the Green Turf; so that 'twas impossible to suspect that any Hole had been digg'd under it, for we flung the Earth into the River."[17] Returning a few weeks after, they found the cache all safe and sound.

[17] Louis Hennepin, a Belgian missionary, explored in Canada and the Mississippi Valley from 1675 to 1682. The quotation is from the second English translation of his much-disputed revised account of explorations on the Mississippi: *A New Discovery of a Vast Country in America* (London, M. Bentley, *et al.*, 1698). See Reuben Gold Thwaites's edition, I, 193.

CHAPTER IV

A Desert Plain—Preparation for a 'Water-Scrape'—Accident to a French Doctor—Upsetting of a Wagon and its Consequences—A Party of Sioux Warriors—The first real Alarm—Confusion in the Camp—Friendly Demonstrations of the Indians—The Pipe of Peace—Squaws and Papooses—An extemporary Village—Lose our Track—Search after the Lost River—Horrible Prospective—The Cimarron Found at last—A Night of Alarms—Indian Serenade and Thieving—Indian Diplomacy —Hail-stones and Hurricanes—Position of the Captain of a Caravan—His Troubles, his Powers and Want of Powers—More Indians—Hostile Encounter—Results of the Skirmish—The 'Battle-Ground'—Col. Vizcarra and the Gros Ventres.

O UR ROUTE had already led us up the course of the Arkansas river for over a hundred miles, yet the earlier caravans often passed from fifty to a hundred further up before crossing the river; therefore nothing like a regular ford had ever been established.[1] Nor was there a road, not even a trail, anywhere across the famous plain, extending between the Arkansas and Cimarron rivers, a distance of over fifty miles, which now lay before us—the scene of such frequent sufferings in former times for want of water. It having been determined upon, however, to strike across this dreaded desert the following morning, the whole party was busy in preparing for the 'water

[1] According to his table, Gregg later followed the north bank of the Arkansas for 122 miles, fording it 20 miles beyond the Caches, in the vicinity of present Ingalls, in Gray County, Kansas. The surveyors had continued upstream and crossed it 44 miles beyond the Caches. K. Gregg (ed.), *Road to Santa Fe*, 78–86. Other favorites were the so-called Lower Crossing, in the vicinity of Ford, Kansas; the Middle, or Cimarron Crossing, at present Cimarron, in Gray County; an Upper Crossing by way of Chouteau's Island, about 70 miles above Gregg's ford; and another at Bent's Fort, near present La Junta, Colorado.

scrape,' as these drougthy drives are very appropriately called by prairie travellers. This tract of country may truly be styled the grand 'prairie ocean'; for not a single landmark is to be seen for more than forty miles—scarcely a visible eminence by which to direct one's course. All is as level as the sea, and the compass was our surest, as well as principal guide.

In view of this passage, as well as that of many other dry stretches upon the route, the traveler should be apprised of the necessity of providing a water-cask holding at least five gallons to each wagon, in which a supply for drinking and cooking may be carried along to serve in cases of emergency.

The evening before the embarking of a caravan upon this plain, the captain's voice is usually heard above the din and clatter of the camp, ordering to "fill up the water kegs,"—a precaution which cannot be repeated too often, as new adventurers are usually ignorant of the necessity of providing a supply sufficient to meet every contingency that may befall two or more days' journey over this arid region. The cooks are equally engrossed by their respective vocations: some are making bread, others preparing viands, and all tasking their ingenuity to lay by such stores as may be deemed expedient for at least two days' consumption. On the following morning (June 14th), the words 'catch up' again resounded through the camp, and the caravan was once more in motion.

For the first five miles we had a heavy pull among the sandy hillocks; but soon the broad and level plain opened before us. We had hardly left the river's side, however, when we experienced a delay of some hours, in consequence of an accident which came very nigh proving fatal to a French doctor of our company. Fearful lest his stout top-heavy dearborn should upset whilst skirting the slope of a hill, he placed himself below in order to sustain it with his hands. But, in spite of all his exertions, the carriage tumbled over, crushing and mashing him most frightfully. He was taken out senseless, and but little hopes were at first entertained of his recovery. Having revived, however, soon after, we were enabled to resume our march; and, in the course of time, the wounded patient entirely recovered.

The next day we fortunately had a heavy shower, which afforded us abundance of water. Having also swerved considerably toward the south, we fell into a more uneven section of country, where we had to cross a brook swelled by the recent rain, into which one of the wagons was unfortunately overset. This, however, was not a very uncommon occurrence; for unruly oxen, when thirsty, will often rush into a pool in despite of the driver, dragging the wagon over every object in their way, at the imminent risk of turning it topsy-turvy into the water. We were now compelled to make a halt, and all hands flocked to the assistance of the owner of the damaged cargo. In a few minutes about an acre of ground was completely covered with calicoes, and other domestic goods, presenting altogether an interesting spectacle.

All were busily occupied at this work when some objects were seen moving in the distance, which at first were mistaken for buffalo; but were speedily identified as horsemen. Anxiety was depicted in every countenance. Could it be possible that the party of Capt. Sublette,[2] which was nearly a month ahead of us, had been lost in these dreary solitudes? or was it the band of Capt. Bent,[3] who was expected to follow some time after us? This anxious suspense, however, lasted only for a few minutes; and the cry of "Indians!" soon made the welkin ring. Still they appeared to approach too slowly for the western prairie tribes. A little nearer, and we soon perceived that they carried a flag, which turned out to be that of the United States. This welcome sight allayed at once all uneasiness; as it is well known that most savages, when friendly, approach the whites with a hoisted flag, provided they have one. It turned out to be a party of about eighty Sioux, who were on a tour upon the Prairies for the purpose of trading with, stealing from or marauding upon the south-western nations. Our communications were carried on entirely by signals; yet we understood them perfectly to say, that there

[2] William L. Sublette (1799–1845), a Kentuckian, came to the Missouri country in 1818 and soon entered the fur trade. In 1826 he bought General William H. Ashley's holdings in the Rocky Mountain Fur Company, but sold them again in 1830 and entered the Santa Fé trade.

[3] Charles Bent (1797–1847), one of three brothers in the Santa Fé and Indian trade, helped build Bent's Fort on the upper Arkansas, married a New Mexican and resided in Taos, but became a captain of scouts with the American army of occupation in 1846. He was appointed the first American governor of New Mexico, but was murdered shortly afterwards at Taos in an abortive revolt against the American occupation.

were immense numbers of Indians ahead, upon the Cimarron river, whom they described by symbolic language to be Blackfeet and Comanches; a most agreeable prospect for the imagination to dwell upon!

We now moved on slowly and leisurely, for all anxiety on the subject of water had been happily set at rest by frequent falls of rain. But imagine our consternation and dismay, when, upon descending into the valley of the Cimarron, on the morning of the 19th of June, a band of Indian warriors on horseback suddenly appeared before us from behind the ravines—an imposing array of death-dealing savages! There was no merriment in this! It was a genuine alarm—a tangible reality! These warriors, however, as we soon discovered, were only the van-guard of a 'countless host,' who were by this time pouring over the opposite ridge, and galloping directly toward us.

The wagons were soon irregularly 'formed' upon the hill-side: but in accordance with the habitual carelessness of caravan traders, a great portion of the men were unprepared for the emergency. Scores of guns were 'empty,' and as many more had been wetted by the recent showers, and would not 'go off.' Here was one calling for balls— another for powder—a third for flints. Exclamations, such as "I've broke my ramrod"—I've split my caps"—I've rammed down a ball without powder"—"My gun is 'choked'; give me yours"—were heard from different quarters; while a timorous 'greenhorn' would perhaps cry out, "Here, take my gun, you can outshoot me!" The more daring bolted off to encounter the enemy at once, while the timid and cautious took a stand with presented rifle behind the wagons. The Indians who were in advance made a bold attempt to press upon us, which came near costing them dearly; for some of our fiery backwoodsmen more than once had their rusty but unerring rifles directed upon the intruders, some of whom would inevitably have fallen before their deadly aim, had not a few of the more prudent traders interposed. The savages made demonstrations no less hostile, rushing, with ready sprung bows, upon a portion of our men who had gone in search of water; and mischief would, perhaps, have ensued, had not the impetuosity of the warriors been checked by the wise men of the nation.

The Indians were collecting around us, however, in such great numbers, that it was deemed expedient to force them away, so as to resume our march, or at least to take a more advantageous position. Our company was therefore mustered and drawn up in 'line of battle'; and, accompanied by the sound of a drum and fife, we marched towards the main group of the Indians. The latter seemed far more delighted than frightened with this strange parade and music, a spectacle they had, no doubt, never witnessed before, and perhaps looked upon the whole movement rather as a complimentary salute than a hostile array; for there was no interpreter through whom any communication could be conveyed to them. But, whatever may have been their impressions, one thing is certain,—that the principal chief (who was dressed in a long red coat of strouding, or coarse cloth) appeared to have full confidence in the virtues of his calumet; which he lighted, and came boldly forward to meet our warlike corps, serenely smoking the 'pipe of peace.' Our captain, now taking a whiff with the savage chief, directed him by signs to cause his warriors to retire. This most of them did, to rejoin the long train of squaws and papooses with the baggage, who followed in the rear, and were just then seen emerging from behind the hills. Having slowly descended to the banks of the stream, they pitched their wigwams or lodges; over five hundred of which soon bespeckled the ample valley before us, and at once gave to its recently meagre surface the aspect of an immense Indian village. The entire number of the Indians, when collected together, could not have been less than from two to three thousand—although some of our company insisted that there were at least four thousand souls. In such a case they must have mustered nearly a thousand warriors, while we were but little over two hundred strong. Still, our superior arms and the protection afforded by the wagons, gave us considerably the advantage, even supposing an equality in point of valor. However, the appearance of the squaws and children soon convinced us, that, for the present, at least, they had no hostile intentions; so we also descended into the valley and formed our camp a few hundred yards below them. The 'capitanes,' or head men of the whites and Indians, shortly after met, and, again smoking the calumet, agreed to be friends.

Although we were now on the very banks of the Cimarron, even the most experienced traders of our party, whether through fright or ignorance, seemed utterly unconscious of the fact. Having made our descent, far below the usual point of approach, and there being not a drop of water found in the sandy bed of the river, it was mistaken for Sand creek, and we accordingly proceeded without noticing it.[4] Therefore, after our 'big talk' was concluded, and dinner dispatched, we again set out southward, in search of the Cimarron. As we were starting, warriors, squaws and papooses now commenced flocking about us, gazing at our wagons with amazement; for many of them had never, perhaps, seen such vehicles before. A few chiefs and others followed us to our next encampment; but these were sent away at night.

Our guards were now doubled, as a night attack was apprehended; for although we were well aware that Indians never commit outrages with their families at hand, yet it was feared that they might either send them away or conceal them during the night. A little after dark, these fears seemed about to be realized; as a party of thirty or forty Indians were seen coming up towards the encampment. Immediate preparations were made to attack them, when they turned out to be a band of squaws, with merely a few men as gallants—all of whom were summarily turned adrift, without waiting to speculate upon the objects of their visit. The next morning a few others made their appearance, which we treated in precisely the same manner, as a horse was missing, which it was presumed the Indians had stolen.

We continued our march southward in search of the 'lost river.' After a few miles' travel we encountered a ledge of sand-hills, which obstructed our course, and forced us to turn westward and follow their border for the rest of the day. Finding but little water that night, and none at all the next day, we began by noon to be sadly frightened; for nothing is more alarming to the prairie traveller than a 'water-scrape.' The impression soon became general that we were *lost*—lost on that inhospitable desert, which had been the theatre of so many former scenes of suffering! and our course im-

[4] Sand Creek runs north of and parellel to the Cimarron and is joined by Bear Creek near present Ulysses, in Grant County, Kansas, to form the North Fork of the Cimarron. Gregg apparently met the Cimarron below this point, near the boundary between Grant and Haskell counties.

peded by sand-hills! A council of the veteran travellers was called to take our emergency into consideration. It was at once resolved to strike in a northwesterly direction in search of the 'dry ravine' we had left behind us, which was now supposed to have been the Cimarron.

We had just set out, when a couple of Indians approached us, bringing the horse we had lost the night before; an apparent demonstration of good faith which could hardly have been anticipated. It was evidently an effort to ingratiate themselves in our favor, and establish an intercourse—perhaps a traffic. But the outrages upon Major Riley, as well as upon a caravan, not two years before, perpetrated probably by the same Indians, were fresh in the memory of all; so that none of us were willing to confide in their friendly professions. On inquiring by means of signs for the nearest water, they pointed to the direction we were travelling: and finally taking the lead, they led us, by the shortest way, to the valley of the long-sought Cimarron, which, with its delightful green-grass glades and flowing torrent (very different in appearance from where we had crossed it below), had all the aspect of an 'elysian vale,' compared with what we had seen for some time past. We pitched our camp in the valley, much rejoiced at having again 'made a port.'[5]

We were not destined to rest long in peace, however. About midnight we were all aroused by a cry of alarm, the like of which had not been heard since the day Don Quixote had his famous adventure with the fulling-mills; and I am not quite sure but some of our party suffered as much from fright as poor Sancho Panza did on that memorable occasion. But Don Quixote and Sancho only heard the thumping of the mills and the roaring of the waters; while we heard the thumping of the Indian drums, accompanied by occasional yells, which our excited fancies immediately construed into notes of the fearful warsong.

After the whole company had been under arms for an hour or two, finding the cause of alarm approached no nearer, we again re-

---

[5] This must have been near Lower Cimarron Spring, which Gregg's table places at 58 miles from the Arkansas and 8 miles beyond Sand Creek by the best route. The surveyors had continued up the Arkansas to Chouteau's Island and then come almost due south, reaching the Cimarron a little below Lower Spring, 40 miles from the Arkansas. K. Gregg (ed.), *Road to Santa Fe*, 88–89.

tired to rest. But a little before daylight we were again startled by the announcement—"The Indians are coming!—they are upon the very camp!" In a moment every man was up in arms; and several guns were presented to 'salute' the visitors, when, to our extreme mortification, they were found to be but eight or ten in number. They were immediately dispatched, by signs, and directed to remain away till morning—which they did.

On the following day, we had been in motion but a few minutes, when the Indians began flocking around us in large numbers, and by the time we encamped in the evening, we had perhaps a thousand of these pertinacious creatures, males and females, of all ages and descriptions, about us. At night, every means, without resorting to absolute violence, was employed to drive them away, but without entire success. At this time a small band of warriors took the round of our camp, and 'serenaded' us with a monotonous song of *hee-o-hehs*, with the view, I suppose, of gaining permission to remain; hoping, no doubt, to be able to 'drive a fair business' at pilfering during the night. In fact, a few small articles were already missing, and it was now discovered that they had purloined a pig of lead (between fifty and a hundred pounds weight) from one of the cannon-carriages, where it had been carelessly left. This increased the uneasiness which already prevailed to a considerable extent; and many of us would imagine it already moulded into bullets, which we were perhaps destined to receive before morning from the muzzles of their fusils. Some were even so liberal as to express a willingness to pardon the theft, rather than give the Indians the trouble of sending it back in so hasty a manner. After a tedious night of suspense and conjecture, it was no small relief to those whose feelings had been so highly wrought upon, to find, on waking up in the morning, that every man still retained his scalp.

We started at a much earlier hour, this morning, in hopes to leave our Indian tormentors behind; but they were too wide-awake for us. By the time the wagoners had completed the task of gearing their teams, the squaws had 'geared' their dogs, and loaded them with their lodge poles and covers, and other light 'plunder,' and were travelling fast in our wake. Much to our comfort, however, the greatest portion abandoned us before night; but the next day several of the chiefs overtook us again at noon, seeming anxious to renew the 'treaty of peace.' The truth is, the former treaty had never been 'sealed'—they had received no presents, which form an indispensable ratification of all their 'treaties' with the whites. Some fifty or sixty dollars' worth of goods having been made up for them, they now left us apparently satisfied; and although they continued to return and annoy us for a couple of days longer; they at last entirely disappeared.

It was generally supposed at the time that there was a great number of Comanches and Arrapahoes among this troop of savages; but they were principally if not altogether Blackfeet and Gros Ventres.[6] We afterward learned that on their return to the northern mountains, they met with a terrible defeat from the Sioux and other neighboring tribes, in which they were said to have lost more than half their number.

We now encountered a great deal of wet weather; in fact this region is famous for cold protracted rains of two or three days' duration. Storms of hail-stones larger than hen's eggs are not uncommon, frequently accompanied by the most tremendous hurricanes. The violence of the wind is sometimes so great that, as I have heard, two road-wagons were once capsized by one of these terrible thunder-gusts; the rain, at the same time, floating the plain to the depth of several inches. In short, I doubt if there is any known region out of the tropics, that can 'head' the great prairies in 'getting up' thunder-storms, combining so many of the elements of the awful and sublime.

During these storms the guards were often very careless. This was emphatically the case with us, notwithstanding our knowledge of the proximity of a horde of savages. In fact, the caravan was subject to so little control that the patience of Capt. Stanley underwent some very severe trials; so much so that he threatened more than once to resign. Truly, there is not a better school for testing a man's temper, than the command of a promiscuous caravan of independent traders. The rank of captain is, of course, but little more than nomi-

[6] The name Gros Ventres (literally "fat bellies") was applied by the French, followed by others, to two distinct tribes: The Atsina (a detached band of Arapahoes) and the Hidatsa (a Siouian group closely associated with the Mandans and Arikara).

nal. Every proprietor of a two-horse wagon is apt to assume as much authority as the commander himself, and to issue his orders without the least consultation at head-quarters. It is easy then to conceive that the captain has anything but an enviable berth. He is expected to keep order while few are disposed to obey—loaded with execrations for every mishap, whether accidental or otherwise; and when he attempts to remonstrate he only renders himself ridiculous, being entirely without power to enforce his commands. It is to be regretted that some system of 'maritime law' has not been introduced among these traders to secure subordination, which can never be attained while the commander is invested with no legal authority. For my own part, I can see no reason why the captain of a prairie caravan should not have as much power to call his men to account for disobedience or mutiny, as the captain of a ship upon the high seas.

After following the course of the Cimarron for two days longer, we at length reached a place called the 'Willow Bar,'[7] where we took the usual mid-day respite of two or three hours, to afford the animals time to feed, and our cooks to prepare dinner. Our wagons were regularly 'formed,' and the animals turned loose to graze at leisure, with only a 'day-guard' to watch them. Those who had finished their dinners lay stretched upon their blankets, and were just beginning to enjoy the luxury of a siesta—when all of a sudden, the fearful and oft-reiterated cry of "Indians!" turned this scene of repose into one of bustle and confusion.

From the opposite ridge at the distance of a mile, a swarm of savages were seen coming upon us, at full charge, and their hideous whoop and yell soon resounded through the valley. Such a jumbling of promiscuous voices I never expect to hear again. Every one fancied himself a commander, and vociferated his orders accordingly. The air was absolutely rent with the cries of "Let's charge 'em boys!"— "Fire upon 'em, boys!"—"Reserve! don't fire till they come near-

[7] Willow Bar was a well-known campsite in present Cimarron County, Oklahoma. In this stretch the surveyors crossed the meandering Cimarron a dozen times in less than six miles. K. Gregg (ed.), *Road to Santa Fe,* 91. Beyond Lower Spring, Gregg's table lists Middle Spring, 36 miles, and then Willow Bar, 26 miles. The trail followed the north side of the Cimarron Valley and passed from Kansas through the southeast corner of Colorado into the Oklahoma panhandle.

er!"—while the voice of our captain was scarcely distinguishable in his attempts to prevent such rash proceedings. As the prairie Indians often approach their friends as well as enemies in this way, Captain Stanley was unwilling to proceed to extremities, lest they might be peacefully inclined. But a 'popping salute,' and the whizzing of fusil balls over our heads, soon explained their intentions. We returned them several rifle shots by way of compliments, but without effect, as they were at too great a distance.

A dozen cannoniers now surrounded our 'artillery,' which was charged with canister. Each of them had, of course, something to say. "Elevate her; she'll ground," one would suggest. "She'll overshoot, now," rejoined another. At last, after raising and lowering the six-pounder several times, during which process the Indians had time to retreat beyond reach of shot, the match was finally applied, and—bang! went the gun, but the charge grounded mid-way. This was followed by two or three shots with single ball, but apparently without effect; although there were some with sharp eyes, who fancied they saw Indians or horses wounded at every fire. We came off equally unscathed from the conflict, barring a horse of but little value, which ran away, and was taken by the enemy. The Indians were about a hundred in number, and supposed to be Comanches, though they might have been a band of warriors belonging to the party we had just left behind.

The novices were not a little discouraged at these frequent inroads of the enemy, although it is very seldom that any lives are lost in encounters with them. In the course of twenty years since the commencement of this trade, I do not believe there have been a dozen deaths upon the Santa Fé route, even including those who have been killed off by disease, as well as by the Indians.[8]

On the following day we encamped near the 'Battle Ground,' famous for a skirmish which a caravan of traders, in company with a detachment of Mexican troops, under the command of Col. Viz-

[8] A report made only ten years after the Trail was opened states that eight lives had been lost on the Santa Fé road, not counting two fur traders who were killed near it. Wetmore to Secretary of War Lewis Cass, Franklin, Mo., Oct. 11, 1831, in F. F. Stephens (ed.), "Major Alfonso Wetmore's Diary of a Journey to Santa Fe, 1828," *Mo. Hist. Rev.*, Vol. VIII, No. 4 (July, 1914), 180.

carra,[9] had in 1829 with a band of Gros Ventres. The united companies had just encamped on the Cimarron, near the site of the burial catastrophe which occurred the preceding year. A party of about a hundred and twenty Indians soon after approached them on foot; but as the Americans were but little disposed to admit friendly intercourse between them, they passed into the camp of the Mexican commander, who received them amicably—a circumstance not altogether agreeable to the traders. As the Indians seemed disposed to remain till morning, Col. Vizcarra promised that they should be disarmed for the night; but the cunning wretches made some excuse to delay the surrender of their weapons, until the opportunity being favorable for a coup de main, they sprang to their feet, raised a fearful yell, and fired upon the unsuspecting party. Their aim seems chiefly to have been to take the life of the Mexican colonel; and it is said that a Taos Indian who formed one of the Mexican escort, seeing a gun levelled at his commander, sprang forward and received the ball in his own body, from the effects of which he instantly expired! The Indians were pursued for several miles into the hills, and a considerable number killed and wounded. Of the Americans not one received the slightest injury; but of the Mexican dragoons, a captain and two or three privates were killed.

[9] Colonel José Antonio Vizcarra, a native of Chihuahua, came to New Mexico during the Spanish period, served with distinction in the Indian campaigns, became the first governor of the province after independence from Spain, from 1822 to 1825, and served another brief term in 1828. In the latter year, as assistant inspector-general of the army in New Mexico, he led the military escort mentioned by Gregg, and in the following year was promoted to inspector-general, which office he held until 1833. Young, *The First Military Escort*, 142–44; Cooke, *Scenes and Adventures in the Army*, 85–96; Ralph Emerson Twitchell, *Leading Facts of New Mexican History*, II, 16–26.

CHAPTER V

A Beautiful Ravine—'Runners' Starting for Santa Fé—Fourth of July
on the Prairies—The *Cibolero* or Buffalo-hunter—Mournful News of
Captain Sublette's Company—Murder of Captain Smith and another
of the party by the Indians—Carelessness and Risks of Hunters—Captain
Sublette's Peril—Character and Pursuits of the *Ciboleros*—The Art of
Curing Meat—Purity of the Atmosphere—The 'Round Mound'—The
Mirage or False Ponds—Philosophy thereof—Extensive and Interesting
View—Exaggerated Accounts by Travellers of the Buffalo of the Prairies
—Their Decrease—A 'Stampede'—Wagon Repairing—Rio Colorado
or Canadian River—Meeting between old Friends—Mexican Escort—
Disorganizing of the Caravan—Dreadful Thunderstorm—First Symp-
toms of Civilization—San Miguel—Arrival at Santa Fé—Entry of the
Caravan—First Hours of Recreation—Interpreters and Custom-house
Arrangements—A Glance at the Trade, etc.

IT WAS ON THE LAST DAY of June that we arrived at the 'Upper
Spring,' which is a small fountain breaking into a ravine that de-
clines towards the Cimarron some three or four miles to the north.[1]
The scarcity of water in these desert regions, gives to every little
spring an importance which, of course, in more favored countries it
would not enjoy. We halted at noon on the brook below, and then
branched off towards the waters of the Canadian, in an average direction of about thirty degrees south of west. As the wagon-road
passes upon the adjacent ridge a quarter of a mile to the south of
this spring, some of us, to procure a draught of its refreshing water,
pursued a path along the ravine, winding through dense thickets of

---

[1] Upper Spring, about 11 miles north of present Boise City, in Cimarron
County, Oklahoma, is listed in Gregg's table as 18 miles above Willow Bar and 80
miles beyond Lower Spring (75¾ miles according to the surveyors). Here the trail
left the Cimarron river and continued on its west-southwesterly direction. K. Gregg
(ed.), *Road to Santa Fe*, 90–94.

COMMERCE OF THE PRAIRIES

underbrush, matted with green-briers and grape-vines, which, with the wild-currant and plum-bushes, were all bent under their unripe fruit. The wildness of this place, with its towering cliffs, craggy spurs, and deep-cut crevices, became doubly impressive to us, as we reflected that we were in the very midst of the most savage haunts. Often will the lonely traveller, as he plods his weary way in silence, imagine in each click of a pebble, the snap of a firelock, and in every rebound of a twig, the whisk of an arrow. After regaling ourselves with a draught of the delicious beverage which gushed from the pure fountain, we ascended the rugged heights and rejoined the caravan half a mile beyond.

We had now a plain and perfectly distinguishable track before us, and a party of *avant-couriers*, known in the technical parlance of the Prairies as 'runners," soon began to make preparations for pushing forward in advance of the caravans into Santa Fé, though we were yet more than two hundred miles from that city. It is customary for these runners to take their departure from the caravans in the night, in order to evade the vigilance of any enemy that might be lurking around the encampment. They are generally proprietors or agents; and their principal purpose is to procure and send back a supply of provisions, to secure good store-houses, and what is no less important, to obtain an agreeable understanding with the officers of the custom-house.

The second day after the departure of the runners, as we lay encamped at McNees's creek,[2] the Fourth of July dawned upon us. Scarce had gray twilight brushed his dusky brow, when our patriotic camp gave lively demonstrations of that joy which plays around the heart of every American on the anniversary of this triumphant day. The roar of our artillery and rifle platoons resounded from every hill, while the rumbling of the drum and the shrill whistle of the fife, imparted a degree of martial interest to the scene which was well calculated to stir the souls of men. There was no limit to the huzzas and enthusiastic ejaculations of our people; and at every new shout the dales around sent forth a gladsome response. This anniversary

[2] A tributary at the head of the North Canadian River now known as Corrumpa Creek. It was crossed 30 miles beyond Upper Spring, according to Gregg's table, 28½ miles according to the surveyors, who called it Louse Creek. *Ibid.*, 94–98.

is always hailed with heart-felt joy by the wayfarer in the remote desert; for here the strifes and intrigues of party-spirit are unknown: nothing intrudes, in these wild solitudes, to mar that harmony of feeling, and almost pious exultation, which every true-hearted American experiences on this great day.

The next day's march brought us in front of the Rabbit-Ear Mounds,[3] which might now be seen at a distance of eight or ten miles south of us, and which before the present track was established, served as a guide to travellers. The first caravan of wagons that crossed these plains, passed on the south side of these mounds, having abandoned our present route at the 'Cold Spring,'[4] where we encamped on the night of the 1st of July. Although the route we were travelling swerves somewhat too much to the north, that pursued by the early caravans as stated above, made still a greater circuit to the south, and was by far the most inconvenient.

As we were proceeding on our march, we observed a horseman approaching, who excited at first considerable curiosity. His picturesque costume, and peculiarity of deportment, however, soon showed him to be a Mexican *Cibolero* or Buffalo-hunter. These hardy devotees of the chase usually wear leathern trousers and jackets, and flat straw hats; while, swung upon the shoulder of each hangs his *carcage* or quiver of bow and arrows. The long handle of their lance being set in a case, and suspended by the side with a strap from the pommel of the saddle, leaves the point waving high over the head, with a tassel of gay parti-colored stuffs dangling at the tip of the scabbard. Their fusil, if they happen to have one, is suspended in like manner at the other side, with a stopper in the muzzle fantastically tasselled.

The *Cibolero* saluted us with demonstrations of joy; nor were we less delighted at meeting with him; for we were now able to

[3] Rabbit Ear Mounds, so-called from a fancied resemblance, are in eastern Union County, New Mexico, just north of Clayton. As the first prominent elevations seen after crossing the Cimarron plain, they became guides for the caravans between the Cimarron and Canadian rivers. Gregg's table lists a Rabbit Ears Creek (Cieneguilla Creek) as being 20 miles beyond McNees (Corrumpa) Creek (18½ miles according to the surveyors). *Ibid.*, 94–100.

[4] Gregg's table places Cold Spring 5 miles beyond the Upper Spring and indicates that caravans left the Cimarron there. It is probably what the surveyors called Mire Spring, 8 miles from Upper Spring. *Ibid.*, 95.

obtain information from Santa Fé, whence no news had been received since the return of the caravan the preceding fall. Traders and idlers, with equal curiosity, clustered around the new visitor; every one who could speak a word of Spanish having some question to ask:—"What prospects?"—"How are goods?"—"What news from the South?"—while the more experienced traders interested themselves chiefly to ascertain the condition of the custom-house, and who were the present revenue officers; for unpropitious changes sometimes occur during the absence of the caravans.

But whatever joy we at first experienced was soon converted into mourning, by a piece of most melancholy news—the tragical death of a celebrated veteran mountain adventurer. It has already been mentioned that Capt. Sublette and others had started near a month in advance of our company. We had frequently seen their trail, and once or twice had received some vague information of their whereabouts through the Indians, but nothing satisfactory. Our visitor now informed us that a captain of this band had been assassinated by the Indians; and from his description we presumed it to be Capt. Smith,[5] one of the partners,—which was afterwards confirmed, with many particulars of the adventurers of this company.

Capt. Smith and his companions were new beginners in the Santa Fé trade, but being veteran pioneers of the Rocky Mountains, they concluded they could go anywhere; and imprudently set out without out a single person in their company at all competent to guide them on the route. They had some twenty-odd wagons, and about eighty men. There being a plain track to the Arkansas river, they did very well thus far; but from thence to the Cimarron, not a single trail was to be found, save the innumerable buffalo paths, with which these plains are furrowed, and which are exceedingly perplexing to the bewildered prairie traveller. In a great many places which I have observed, they have all the appearance of immense highways, over which entire armies would seem to have frequently passed. They

[5] Jedediah S. Smith (*ca.* 1805–31), one of the greatest of the early explorers of the West, came from New York, joined Ashley's Rocky Mountain Fur Company, and distinguished himself as an Indian fighter, trapper and scout on expeditions to Utah and California, Fort Vancouver, and the northern Rockies. He and his partners, William Sublette and David Jackson, sold their stock in the fur company in 1830 and entered the Santa Fé trade. Maurice S. Sullivan, *The Life of Jedediah Smith, Trader and Trail Breaker*.

generally lead from one watering place to another; but as these reservoirs very often turn out to be dry, the thirsty traveller who follows them in search of water, is liable to constant disappointment.

When Capt. Sublette's party entered this arid plain, it was parched with drought; and they were doomed to wander about for several days, with all the horrors of a death from thirst staring them continually in the face. In this perilous situation, Capt. Smith resolved at last to pursue one of these seductive buffalo paths, in hopes it might lead to the margin of some stream or pond. He set out alone; for besides the temerity which desperation always inspires, he had ever been a stranger to fear; indeed, he was one of the most undaunted spirits that had ever traversed the Rocky Mountains; and if but one-half of what has been told of him be true,—of his bold enterprises—his perilous wanderings—his skirmishings with the savages—his hair-breadth escapes, etc.—he would surely be entitled to one of the most exalted seats in the Olympus of Prairie mythology. But, alas! unfortunate Captain Smith! after having so often dodged the arrow and eluded the snare of the wily Mountain Indian, little could he have thought, while jogging along under a scorching sun, that his bones were destined to bleach upon those arid sands! He had already wandered many miles away from his comrades, when, on turning over an eminence, his eyes were joyfully greeted with the appearance of a small stream meandering through the valley that spread before him. It was the Cimarron. He hurried forward to slake the fire of his parched lips—but, imagine his disappointment, at finding in the channel only a bed of dry sand! With his hands, however, he soon scratched out a basin a foot or two deep, into which the water slowly oozed from the saturated sand. While with his head bent down, in the effort to quench his burning thirst in the fountain, he was pierced by the arrows of a gang of Comanches, who were lying in wait for him! Yet he struggled bravely to the last; and, as the Indians themselves have since related, killed two or three of their party before he was overpowered.

Every kind of fatality seems to have attended this little caravan. Among other calamities, we also learned that a clerk in their company, named Minter, had been killed by a band of Pawnees, before they crossed the Arkansas. This, I believe, is the only instance of loss of life among the traders while engaged in hunting: although the scarcity of accidents can hardly be said to be the result of prudence. There is not a day, from the time a caravan reaches the 'buffalo range,' that hunters do not commit some indiscretion, such as straying at a distance of five and even ten miles from the caravan, frequently alone, and seldom in bands of more than two or three together. In this state, they must frequently be spied by prowling savages; so that the frequency of escape, under such circumstances, must be partly attributed to the cowardice of the Indians: indeed, generally speaking, the latter are very loth to charge upon even a single armed man, unless they can take him at a decided disadvantage. Therefore, it is at all times imprudent to fire at the first approach of Indians; for, seeing their guns empty, the savages would charge upon them; while very small bands of hunters have been known to keep large numbers of the enemy at bay, by presenting their rifles, but reserving their fire, till assistance was at hand.

The companions of Capt. Smith, having descended upon the Cimarron at another point, appear to have remained ignorant of the terrible fate that had befallen him, until they were informed of the circumstances by some Mexican traders, who had ascertained the facts from the murderous savages themselves. Not long after, this band of Capt. Sublette very narrowly escaped a total destruction. They had fallen in with that immense horde of Blackfeet and Gros Ventres, with whom we afterwards met, and, as the traders were literally but a handful among their thousands, they fancied themselves for awhile in imminent peril of being virtually 'eaten up.' But as Capt. Sublette possessed considerable experience, he was at no loss how to deal with these treacherous savages; so that although the latter assumed a menacing attitude, he passed them without any serious molestation, and finally arrived at Santa Fé in safety.

But to return to our *Cibolero*. He was desirous to sell us some provisions, which, by the by, were welcome enough; for most of the company were out of bread, and meat was becoming very scarce, having seen but few buffalo since our first encounter with the Indians on the Cimarron. Our visitor soon retired to his camp hard by, and, with several of his comrades, afterwards brought us an abundance of dry buffalo beef, and some bags of coarse oven-toasted loaves, a kind of hard bread, much used by Mexican travellers. It is prepared by opening the ordinary leavened rolls, and toasting them brown in an oven. Though exceedingly hard and insipid while dry, it becomes not only soft but palatable when soaked in water— or better still in 'hot coffee.' But what we procured on this occasion was unusually stale and coarse, prepared expressly for barter with the Comanches, in case they should meet any: yet bread was bread, emphatically, with us just then.

A word concerning the *Ciboleros* may not be altogether un-interesting. Every year, large parties of New-Mexicans, some pro-vided with mules and asses, others with *carretas* or truckle-carts and oxen, drive out into these prairies to procure a supply of buffalo beef for their families. They hunt, like the wild Indians, chiefly on horse-back, and with bow and arrow, or lance, with which they soon load their carts and mules. They find no difficulty in curing their meat even in mid-summer, by slicing it thin and spreading or suspending it in the sun; or, if in haste, it is slightly barbecued. During the cur-ing operation they often follow the Indian practice of beating or kneading the slices with their feet, which they contend contributes to its preservation.

Here the extraordinary purity of the atmosphere is remarkably exemplified. The caravans cure meat in the same simple manner, except the process of kneading. A line is stretched from corner to corner on each side of a wagon-body, and strung with slices of beef, which remains from day to day till it is sufficiently cured to be stacked away. This is done without salt, and yet it very rarely putrifies. Be-sides, as blowflies are unknown here, there is nothing to favor putre-faction. While speaking of flies, I might as well remark, that, after passing beyond the region of the tall grass, between the Missouri frontier and Arkansas river, the horse-fly also is unknown. Judging from the prairies on our border, we had naturally anticipated a great deal of mischief from these brute-tormentors; in which we were agreeably disappoined.

But I have not yet done with the meat-curing operations. While in the midst of the buffalo range, travellers usually take the precau-tion of laying up a supply of beef for exigencies in the absence of the 'prairie cattle.' We had somewhat neglected this provision in time of abundance, by which we had come near being reduced to extremities. Caravans sometimes lie by a day or two to provide a supply of meat; when numbers of buffalo are slaughtered, and the flesh 'jerked,' or slightly barbecued, by placing it upon a scaffold over a fire. The same method is resorted to by Mexicans when the weather is too damp or cloudy for the meat to dry in the open air.

We were now approaching the 'Round Mound,'[6] a beautiful round-topped cone, rising nearly a thousand feet above the level of the plain by which it is for the most part surrounded. We were yet at least three miles from this mound, when a party set out on foot to ascend it, in order to get a view of the surrounding country. They felt confident it was but half a mile off—at most, three-quarters; but finding the distance so much greater than they had anticipated, many began to lag behind, and soon rejoined the wagons. The optical illusions occasioned by the rarified and transparent atmosphere of these elevated plains, are often truly remarkable, affording another exemplification of its purity. One would almost fancy himself looking through a spy-glass, for objects frequently appear at scarce one-fourth of their real distance—frequently much magnified, and more especially elevated. I have often seen flocks of antelopes mistaken for droves of elks or wild horses, and when at a great distance, even for horsemen; whereby frequently alarms are occasioned. I have also known tufts of grass or weeds, or mere buffalo bones scattered on the prairies, to stretch upward to the height of several feet, so as to present the appearance of so many human beings. Ravens in the same way are not unfrequently taken for Indians, as well as for buffalo; and a herd of the latter upon a distant plain often appear so increased in bulk that they would be mistaken by the inexperienced for a grove of trees. This is usually attended with a continual waving and looming, which often so writhe and distort distant objects as to render them too indistinct to be discriminated. The illusion seems to be occasioned by gaseous vapors rising from the ground while the beaming rays of the sun are darting upon it.

[6] Round Mound may have been any of a number of eminences including Mount Dora, in central Union County, New Mexico. Neither old maps nor those of recent investigators agree on its location. Compare K. Gregg (ed.), *Road to Santa Fe*, 98–101, with Kenyon Riddle, *Records and Maps of the Old Santa Fe Trail*, Plate 4. Gregg's table lists it as 8 miles beyond Rabbit Ear Creek.

But the most curious, and at the same time the most perplexing phenomenon, occasioned by optical deception, is the *mirage*, or, as familiarly called upon the Prairies, the 'false ponds.' Even the experienced traveller is often deceived by these upon the arid plains, where a disappointment is most severely felt. The thirsty wayfarer, after jogging for hours under a burning sky, at length espies a pond —yes, it must be water—it looks too natural for him to be mistaken. He quickens his pace, enjoying in anticipation the pleasure of a refreshing draught: but lo! as he approaches, it recedes or entirely disappears; and when upon its apparent site, he is ready to doubt his own vision—he finds but a parched plain under his feet. It is not until he has been thus a dozen times deceived that he is willing to relinquish the pursuit: and then, perhaps, when he really does see a pond, he will pass it unexamined, for fear of another disappointment.

The philosophy of these 'false ponds' seems generally not well understood. They have usually been attributed to *refraction*, by which a section of the bordering sky would appear below the horizon: but there can be no doubt that they are the effect of *reflection*, upon a gas emanating perhaps from the sun-scorched earth and vegetable matter. Or it may be that a surcharge of carbonic acid, precipitated upon the flats and sinks of those plains, by the action of the sun, produces the effect. At least, it appears of sufficient density, when viewed very obliquely, to reflect the objects beyond: and thus the opposite sky being reflected in the *pond of gas*, gives the appearance of water. As a proof that it is the effect of reflection, I have often observed the distant trees and hilly protuberances which project above the horizon beyond, distinctly inverted in the 'pond;' whereas, were it the result of refraction, these would appear erect, only cast below the surface. Indeed, many are the singular atmospheric phenomena observable upon the plains, which would afford a field of interesting research for the curious natural philosopher.

At last, some of the most persevering of our adventurers succeeded in ascending the summit of the Round Mound, which commands a full and advantageous view of the surrounding country, in some directions to the distance of a hundred miles or more. Looking southward a varied country is seen, of hills, plains, mounds, and sandy undulations; but on the whole northern side, extensive plains

MARCH OF THE CARAVAN

spread out, studded occasionally with variegated peaks and ridges. Far beyond these, to the north-westward, and low in the horizon a silvery stripe appears upon an azure base, resembling a list of chalk-white clouds. This is the perennially snowcapped summit of the eastern spur of the Rocky Mountains.

These immense bordering plains, and even the hills with which they are interspersed, are wholly destitute of timber, except a chance scattering tree upon the margins of the bluffs and ravines, which but scantily serves to variegate the landscape. Not even a buffalo was now to be seen to relieve the dull monotony of the scene; although at some seasons (and particularly in the fall) these prairies are lit-erally strewed with herds of this animal. Then, 'thousands and tens of thousands' might at times be seen from this eminence. But the buffalo is a migratory animal, and even in the midst of the Prairies where they are generally so very abundant, we sometimes travel for days without seeing a single one; though no signs of hunter or Indian can be discovered. To say the truth, however, I have never seen them anywhere upon the Prairies so abundant as some travellers have rep-resented—in dense masses, darkening the whole country. I have only found them in scattered herds, of a few scores, hundreds, or sometimes thousands in each, and where in the greatest numbers, dispersed far and wide; but with large intervals between. Yet they are very sensibly and rapidly decreasing. There is a current notion that the whites frighten them away; but, I would ask, where do they go? To be sure, to use a hunter's phrase, they 'frighten a few out of their skins;' yet for every one killed by the whites, more than a hundred, perhaps a thousand, fall by the hands of the savages. From these, however, there is truly 'nowhere to flee;' for they follow them wheresoever they go: while the poor brutes instinctively learn to avoid the fixed establishments, and, to some degree, the regular travelling routes of the whites.

As the caravan was passing under the northern base of the Round Mound, it presented a very fine and imposing spectacle to those who were upon its summit. The wagons marched slowly in four parallel columns, but in broken lines, often at intervals of many rods be-tween. The unceasing 'crack, crack,' of the wagoners' whips, re-sembling the frequent reports of distant guns, almost made one believe that a skirmish was actually taking place between two hostile parties: and a hostile engagement it virtually was to the poor brutes, at least; for the merciless application of the whip would sometimes make the blood spirt from their sides—and that often without any apparent motive of the wanton *carrettieri,* other than to amuse themselves with the flourishing and loud popping of their lashes!

The rear wagons are usually left without a guard; for all the loose horsemen incline to be ahead, where they are to be seen moving in scattered groups, sometimes a mile or more in advance. As our camp was pitched but a mile west of the Round Mound, those who lingered upon its summit could have an interesting view of the evolutions of 'forming' the wagons, in which the drivers by this time had become very expert. When marching four abreast, the two exterior lines spread out and then meet at the front angle; while the two inner lines keep close together until they reach the point of the rear angle, when they wheel suddenly out and close with the hinder ends of the other two; thus systematically concluding a right-lined quadrangle, with a gap left at the rear corner for the introduction of the animals.

Our encampment was in a beautiful plain, but without water, of which, however, we had had a good supply at noon. Our cattle, as was the usual custom, after having grazed without for a few hours, were now shut up in the pen of the wagons. Our men were all wrapt in peaceful slumber, except the guard, who kept their silent watch around the encampment; when all of a sudden, about the ominous hour of midnight, a tremendous uproar was heard, which caused every man to start in terror from his blanket couch, with arms in hand. Some animal, it appeared, had taken fright at a dog, and by a sudden start, set all around him in violent motion: the panic spread simultaneously throughout the pen; and a scene of rattle, clash, and 'lumbering,' ensued, which far surpassed everything we had yet witnessed. A general 'stampede' (*estampida,* as the Mexicans say) was the result. Notwithstanding the wagons were tightly bound together, wheel to wheel, with ropes or chains, and several stretched across the gaps at the corners of the *corral,* the oxen soon burst their way out; and though mostly yoked in pairs, they went scampering over the plains, as though Tam O'Shanter's 'cutty-sark' Nannie had been at their tails.[7] All attempts to stop them were vain; for it would require 'Auld Clootie' himself to check the headway of a drove of oxen, when once thoroughly frightened. Early the following morning we made active exertions to get up a sufficient quantity of teams to start the caravan. At Rock Creek,[8] a distance of six or seven miles, we were joined by those who had gone in pursuit of the stock. All the oxen were found, except some half a dozen, which were never recovered. No mules were lost: a few that had broken loose were speedily retaken. The fact is, that though mules are generally easiest scared, oxen are decidedly the worst when once started. The principal advantage of the latter in this respect, is, that Indians have but little inducement to steal them, and therefore few attempts would be made upon a caravan of oxen.

We were now entering a region of rough, and in some places, rocky road, as the streams which intervene from this to the mountains are all bordered with fine sandstone. These rugged passes acted very severely upon our wagons, as the wheels were by this time becoming loose and 'shackling,' from the shrink of the wood, occasioned by the extreme dryness and rarity of this elevated atmosphere. The spokes of some were beginning to reel in the hubs, so that it became necessary to brace them with 'false spokes,' firmly bound with 'buffalo tug.' On some occasions, the wagon tires have become so loose upon the felloes as to tumble off while travelling. The most effective mode of tightening slackened tires (at least that most practiced on the plains, as there is rarely a portable forge in company), is by driving strips of hoop-iron around between the tire and felloe—simple wedges of wood are sometimes made to supply the place of iron.[9] During halts I have seen a dozen wheels being repaired at the same time, occasioning such a clitter-clatter of hammers, that one would almost fancy himself in a ship-yard.

Emerging from this region of asperities, we soon passed the

[7] A reference to Robert Burns's "Tam o' Shanter."

[8] Rock Creek, 8 miles beyond Round Mound by Gregg's table, was probably an affluent of Carrizo Creek, a tributary of the Canadian River.

[9] This damage was also repaired by cutting the iron tires and thus reducing them to fit the shrunken wheels. See Lieutenant J. W. Abert's entry for Sept. 26, 1846, in Lieutenant William Hemsley Emory's *Notes on a Military Reconnoissance* (30 Cong., 1 sess., *Senate Executive Document No. 7*), 446.

'Point of Rocks,'[10] as a diminutive 'spur' projecting from the north is called, at the foot of which springs a charming little fount of water. This is but thirty or forty miles from the principal mountains, along whose border, similar detached ridges and hills are frequently to be seen. The next day, having descended from the table plain, we reached the principal branch of the Canadian river, which is here but a rippling brook, hardly a dozen paces in width, though eighty miles from its source in the mountains to the north. The bottom being of solid rock, this ford is appropriately called by the ciboleros, *el Vado de Piedras*. The banks are very low and easy to ascend. The stream is called *Rio Colorado* by the Mexicans, and is known among Americans by its literal translation of *Red River*. This circumstance perhaps gave rise to the belief that it was the head branch of our main stream of this name:[11] but the nearest waters of the legitimate 'Red River of Natchitoches,' are still a hundred miles to the south of this road.

In descending to the Rio Colorado, we met a dozen or more of our countrymen from Taos, to which town (sixty or seventy miles distant) there is a direct but rugged route across the mountains.[12] It was a joyous encounter, for among them we found some of our old acquaintances whom we had not seen for many years. During our boyhood we had 'spelt' together in the same country school, and

[10] Point of Rocks is a southern spur of the Teton Range on the headwaters of Ute Creek, in southern ·Colfax County, New Mexico; 19 miles beyond Rock Creek by Gregg's table (19½ miles, according to the surveyors). K. Gregg (ed.), *Road to Santa Fe*, 101–104.

[11] Previous to the year 1820, this *'Rio Colorado'* seems universally to have been considered as the principal source of *Red River;* but in the expedition of Major Long, during that year, he discovered this to be the head branch of the Canadian. The discovery cost him somewhat dearly too; for striking a branch of the Colorado near the Mountains, he followed down its course, believing it to be of the main Red River. He was not fully undeceived till he arrived at its junction with the Arkansas; whereby he failed in a principal object of the expedition—the exploration of the true sources of "Red River of Natchitoches."—GREGG.

For the expedition of Major Stephen H. Long, see below, Vol. II, chap. 11, n. 8. Gregg met the Río Colorado, or Canadian, about 4 miles above the mouth of Ocaté Creek, 20 miles beyond Point of Rocks. The surveyors found it to be 18 miles, but met it farther upstream. K. Gregg (ed.), *Road to Santa Fe*, 104–105.

[12] This was the route pursued by the road surveyors, who place it 84½ miles from their camp on the Río Colorado, or Canadian. *Ibid.* 105–111. It was the town San Fernando de Taos as distinguished from the Indian pueblo of Taos and the Ranchos de Taos, 4 miles northeast and 4 miles southwest, respectively. Taos was the New Mexican headquarters for most of the American trappers in the southern Rockies.

roamed the wild woods with many a childish glee. They turned about with us, and the remainder of our march was passed in answering their inquiries after their relatives and friends in the United States.

Before reaching the stream, we encountered another party of visitors, being chiefly custom-house agents or clerks, who, accompanied by a military escort, had come out to guard the caravan to the Capital. The ostensible purpose of this escort was to prevent smuggling,—a company of troops being thus dispatched every year, with strict injunctions to watch the caravans. This custom appears since to have nearly grown out of use: and well might it be discontinued altogether, for any one disposed to smuggle would find no difficulty in securing the services of these preventive guards, who, for a trifling *douceur* would prove very efficient auxiliaries, rather than obstacles to the success of any such designs. As we were forming in the valley opposite where the escort was encamped, Col. Vizcarra,[13] the commandant, honored us with a salute from his artillery, which was promptly responded to by our little cannon.

Considering ourselves at last out of danger of Indian hostilities (although still nearly a hundred and forty miles from Santa Fé); and not unwilling to give our 'guard' as much trouble as possible, we abandoned the organization of our cavaran a few miles beyond the Colorado; its members wending their way to the Capital in almost as many detached parties as there were proprietors. The road from this to San Miguel (a town nearly a hundred miles distant), leads in a southwestern direction along the base of, and almost parallel with, that spur of snow-clad mountains, which has already been mentioned, bearing down east of the Rio del Norte.

This region is particularly celebrated for violent showers, hailstorms, and frightful thunder-gusts. The sudden cooling and contraction of the atmosphere which follows these falls of rain, very often reverses the current of the lower stratum of air; so that a cloud

[13] For Colonel José Antonio Vizcarra, see above, chap. 4, n. 9. As to official connivance in smuggling, reports of it reaching Mexico City resulted in an order, in 1835, for the removal of the customs house from Santa Fé to the frontier towns of San Miguel del Vado and Taos; the order, however, was ignored by the New Mexican authorities. Albert William Bork, *Nuevos aspectos del comercio entre Nuevo México y Misuri, 1822–1846,* 45–61.

which has just ceased pouring its contents and been wafted away, is in a few minutes brought back, and drenches the traveller with another torrent. I was deeply impressed with a scene I witnessed in the summer of 1832, about two days' journey beyond the Colorado, which I may be excused for alluding to in this connection. We were encamped at noon, when a murky cloud issued from behind the mountains, and, after hovering over us for a few minutes, gave vent to one of those tremendous peals of thunder which seem peculiar to those regions, making the elements tremble, and leaving us so stunned and confounded that some seconds elapsed before each man was able to convince himself that he had not been struck by lightning. A sulphureous stench filled the atmosphere; but the thunderbolt had skipped over the wagons and lighted upon the *caballada*, which was grazing hard by; some of which were afterward seen stretched upon the plain. It was not a little singular to find an ox lying lifeless from the stroke, while his mate stood uninjured by his side, and under the same yoke.

Some distance beyond the Colorado, a party of about a dozen (which I joined) left the wagons to go ahead to Santa Fé. Fifty miles beyond the main branch of this stream we passed the last of the Canadian waters, known to foreigners as the *Mora*.[14] From thence to the *Gallinas*,[15] the first of the Rio del Norte waters, the road stretches over an elevated plain, unobstructed by any mountainous ridge. At Gallinas creek, we found a large flock of sheep grazing upon the adjacent plain; while a little hovel at the foot of a cliff showed it to be a *rancho*.[16] A swarthy *ranchero* soon made his ap-

[14] As *mora* means mulberry, and this fruit is to be found at the mouth of this stream, one would suppose that it had acquired its name from that fact, did not the Mexicans always call it *Rio de lo de Mora*, thus leaving it to be inferred that the name had originated from some individual called Mora, who had settled upon it.—GREGG.

Gregg forded the Río Mora 59 miles beyond the Río Colorado crossing, having passed Ocaté Creek at 6 miles and Santa Clara Spring at another 21 miles. In 1832 a town was established on the Mora, bearing that name, but it did not thrive.

[15] Called *Río de las Gallinas* by the Mexicans. Though *gallina* is literally *hen*, it is here also applied to the *turkey* (usually with a 'surname,' as *gallina de la tierra*). It is therefore *Turkey* river.—GREGG.

Gregg crossed the Rio de Gallinas 20 miles beyond Mora Creek.

[16] This *rancho* was the first dwelling in present Las Vegas (founded in 1835). The old town is on the west bank of the Río de Gallinas, and the city proper is on the east.

pearance, from whom we procured a treat of goat's milk, with some dirty ewe's milk 'curdle cheese' to supply the place of bread.

Some twenty miles from this place we entered San Miguel,[17] the first settlement of any note upon our route. This consisted of irregular clusters of mud-wall huts, and is stituated in the fertile valley of Rio Pecos, a silvery little river which ripples from the snowy mountains of Santa Fé—from which city this frontier village is nearly fifty miles to the southeast. The road makes this great southern bend, to find a passway through the broken extremity of the spur of mountains before alluded to, which from this point south is cut up into detached ridges and table plains. This mountain section of the road, even in its present unimproved condition, presents but few difficult passes, and might, with little labor, be put into good order.

A few miles before reaching the [capital] city, the road again emerges into an open plain. Ascending a table ridge, we spied in an extended valley to the northwest, occasional groups of trees, skirted with verdant corn and wheat fields, with here and there a square block-like protuberance reared in the midst. A little further, and just ahead of us to the north, irregular clusters of the same opened to our view. "Oh, we are approaching the suburbs!" thought I, on perceiving the cornfields, and what I supposed to be brick-kilns scattered in every direction. These and other observations of the same nature becoming audible, a friend at my elbow said, "It is true those are heaps of unburnt bricks, nevertheless they are *houses*—this is the city of Santa Fé."[18]

Five or six days after our arrival, the caravan at last hove in sight, and, wagon after wagon was seen pouring down the last declivity at about a mile's distance from the city. To judge from the clamorous rejoicings of the men, and the state of agreeable excitement which

[17] San Miguel del Vado, at the ford of the Pecos River, was 23 miles beyond the *rancho* of Las Vegas and 6 miles beyond the Ojo de Bernal, a spring along the road. The town is at the southern extremity of the Trail's bend which skirted the mountains, as does the modern railroad, to reach Santa Fé. Although the Mexican customs house was established at San Miguel by order of the central government, it existed on paper only, the duties being collected at Santa Fé as always until the American occupation in 1846.

[18] According to Gregg's table, Santa Fé was 45 miles beyond San Miguel and a total of 780 from Independence. Pecos village, 23 miles beyond San Miguel, was passed on the way.

the muleteers seemed to be laboring under, the spectacle must have been as new to them as it had been to me. It was truly a scene for the artist's pencil to revel in. Even the animals seemed to participate in the humor of their riders, who grew more and more merry and obstreperous as they descended towards the city. I doubt, in short, whether the first sight of the walls of Jerusalem were beheld by the crusaders with much more tumultuous and soul-enrapturing joy.

The arrival produced a great deal of bustle and excitement among the natives. *"Los Americanos!"*—*"Los carros!"*—*"La entrada de la caravana!"* were to be heard in every direction; and crowds of women and boys flocked around to see the new-comers; while crowds of *léperos* hung about as usual to see what they could pilfer. The wagoners were by no means free from excitement on this occasion. Informed of the 'ordeal' they had to pass, they had spent the previous morning in 'rubbing up;' and now they were prepared, with clean faces, sleek combed hair, and their choicest Sunday suit, to meet the 'fair eyes' of glistening black that were sure to stare at them as they passed. There was yet another preparation to be made in order to 'show off' to advantage. Each wagoner must tie a bran new 'cracker' to the lash of his whip; for, on driving through the streets and the *plaza pública*, every one strives to outvie his comrades in the dexterity with which he flourishes this favorite badge of authority.

Our wagons were soon discharged in the ware-rooms of the custom-house; and a few days' leisure being now at our disposal, we had time to take that recreation which a fatiguing journey of ten weeks had rendered so necessary. The wagoners, and many of the traders, particularly the novices, flocked to the numerous fandangoes, which are regularly kept up after the arrival of a caravan. But the merchants generally were anxiously and actively engaged in their affairs—striving who should first get his goods out of the custom-house, and obtain a chance at the 'hard chink' of the numerous country dealers, who annually resort to the capital on these occasions.

Now comes the harvest for those idle interpreters, who make a business of 'passing goods,' as they term it; for as but a small portion of the traders are able to write the Spanish language, they are obliged to employ these legal go-betweens, who pledge themselves, for a stipulated fee, to make the 'arrangements,' and translate the *manifiestos* (that is, bills of merchandise to be *manifested* at the custom-house), and to act the part of interpreters throughout.

The inspection ensues, but this is rarely carried on with rigid adherence to rules; for an 'actuated sympathy' for the merchants, and a 'specific desire' to promote the trade, cause the inspector to open a few of such packages only, as will exhibit the least discrepancy with the manifest.

The *derechos de arancel* (tariff imposts) of Mexico are extremely oppressive, averaging about a hundred per cent. upon the United States' cost of an ordinary 'Santa Fe assortment.' Those on cotton textures are particularly so. According to the Arancel of 1837 (and it was still heavier before), all plain-wove cottons, whether white or printed, pay twelve and a half cents duty per *vara*, besides the *derecho de consumo* (consumption duty), which brings it up to at least fifteen. But it is scarcely necessary to add that there are believed to be very few ports in the Republic at which these rigid exactions are strictly executed. An 'arrangement'—a compromise is expected, in which the officers are sure at least to provide for themselves. At some ports, a custom has been said to prevail, of dividing the legal duties into three equal parts: one for the officers—a second for the merchants—the other for the government.

For a few years, Gov. Armijo[19] of Santa Fé, established a tariff of *his own*, entirely arbitrary,—exacting five hundred dollars for each wagon-load, whether large or small—of fine or coarse goods! Of course this was very advantageous to such traders as had large wagons and costly assortments, while it was no less onerous to those with smaller vehicles or coarse heavy goods. As might have been anticipated, the traders soon took to conveying their merchandise

---

[19] Manuel Armijo (d. 1853) rose from obscurity to become governor of New Mexico three times (1827–29, 1837–44, and 1845–46). As a boy, legend has it, he herded sheep for a wealthy rancher near Albuquerque and by stealing and selling the animals (often to the original owner), he became rich himself. He was notoriously corrupt in public affairs and dissolute in private life. Most Americans considered him a tyrant, but some found him an easy mark for bribery, and his own investments in the overland trade weighed heavily in his official policy. Upon the approach of the American army in 1846 he prepared elaborate defenses but retreated with his troops without firing a shot. He was tried for treason by the Mexican government but acquitted, and later returned to New Mexico, where he died.

79

only in the largest wagons, drawn by ten or twelve mules, and omitting the coarser and more weighty articles of trade. This caused the governor to return to an *ad valorem* system, though still without regard to the *Arancel general* of the nation. How much of these duties found their way into the public treasury, I will not venture to assert.[20]

The arrival of a caravan at Santa Fé changes the aspect of the place at once. Instead of the idleness and stagnation which its streets exhibited before, one now sees everywhere the bustle, noise and activity of a lively market town. As the Mexicans very rarely speak English, the negotiations are mostly conducted in Spanish.

Taking the circuit of the stores, I found they usually contained general assortments, much like those to be met with in the retail variety stores of the west. The stocks of the inexperienced merchants are apt to abound in unsalable goods—*mulas*, as the Mexicans figuratively term them.

Although a fair variety of dry goods, silks, hardware, etc., is to be found in this market, domestic cottons, both bleached and brown, constitute the great staple, of which nearly equal quantities ought to enter into a 'Santa Fé assortment.' The demand for these goods is such that at least one half of our stocks of merchandise is made up of them. However, although they afford a greater nominal per centum than many other articles, the profits are reduced by their freight and heavy duty. In all the Southern markets, where they enter into competition, there is a decided preference given to the American manufactures over the British, as the former are more heavy and durable. The demand for calicoes is also considerable, but this kind of goods affords much less profit. The quantity in an assortment should be about equal to half that of domestics. Cotton velvets, and drillings (whether bleached, brown or blue, and especially the latter), have also been in much request. But all the coarser cotton goods, whether shirtings, calicoes or drillings, etc., were prohibited by the *Arancel* of 1837; and still continue to be, with some modifications.

[20] Customs reports to the central government show very incomplete returns down to the American capture of the province. The treasury reports indicate that, of the several states, New Mexico was one of the more scandalously inefficient in customs administration. Ministerio de Hacienda, *Memoria de la Hacienda General de la República* for the years 1837–46.

CHAPTER VI

Sketches of the Early History of Santa Fé—First Explorations—Why called New Mexico—Memorial of Oñate—His Colony—Captain Leyva's prior Settlement—Singular Stipulations of Oñate—Incentives presented by the Crown to Colonizers—Enormities of Spanish Conquerors—Progress of the new Colony—Cruel Labors of the Aborigines in the mines—Revolt of the Indians in 1680—Massacre of the Spaniards —Santa Fé Besieged—Battles—Remaining Spanish Population finally evacuate the Province—Paso del Norte—Inhuman Murder of a Spanish Priest—Final Recovery of the Country—Insurrection of 1837—A Prophecy—Shocking Massacre of the Governor and other distinguished Characters—American Merchants, and Neglect of our Government—Governor Armijo: his Intrigues and Success—Second Gathering of Insurgents and their final Defeat.

H AVING RESIDED for nearly nine years in Northern Mexico, and enjoyed opportunities for observation which do not always fall to the lot of a trader, it has occurred to me that a few sketches of the country—the first settlements—the early, as well as more recent struggles with the aboriginal inhabitants—their traditions and antiquities—together with some account of the manners and customs of the people, etc., would not be altogether unacceptable to the reader. The dearth of information which has hitherto prevailed on this subject, is my best apology for travelling out of my immediate track, and trespassing as it were upon the departure of the regular historian.

The province of New Mexico, of which Santa Fé, the capital, was one of the first establishments, dates among the earliest settlements made in America. By some traditions it is related that a small band of adventurers proceeded thus far north shortly after the capture of the city of Mexico by Hernan Cortés. The historian Mariana[1] speaks of some attempts having been made, during the career of this renowned chieftain in America, to conquer and take possession of these regions. This, however, is somewhat doubtful; for it is hardly probable that the Spaniards, with all their mania for gold, would have pushed their conquests two thousand miles into the interior at so early a day,[2] traversing the settlements of hostile savages, and leaving unexplored intermediate regions, not only more beautiful, but far more productive of the precious metals.

Herrera,[3] writing of the events of 1550, mentions New Mexico as a known province lying north of New Galicia, though as yet only inhabited by the aborigines. It was probably called New Mexico from the resemblance of its inhabitants to those of the city of Mexico and its environs.[4] They appear to have assimilated in their habits, their agriculture, their manufactures and their houses; while those of the intermediate country (the Chichimecos, etc.) were in a much ruder state, leading a more wandering life, and possessing much less knowledge of agriculture, arts, etc.

The only paper found in the archives at Santa Fé which gives any clue to the first settlement of New Mexico, is the memorial of one Don Juan de Oñate, a citizen of Zacatecas, dated September 21, 1595,[5] of which I have been furnished with a copy through the polite-

[1] Juan de Mariana. Gregg's reference is to his *Historiae de Rebvs Hispaniae* (Toledo, P. Roderici, 1592), subsequently extended and first translated into Spanish at Toledo in 1601, and into English at London in 1699.

[2] Álvar Núñez Cabeza de Vaca passed through the El Paso region in 1535–36, but the first Spaniard to enter New Mexico proper was Francisco Vázquez de Coronado in 1540.

[3] Antonio de Herrera y Tordesilla's *Historia general de los hechos de los Castellanos en las islas y tierra firma de el Mar Occeano* (4 vols. Madrid, Emprenta Real, 1601), translated into English at London in 1740.

[4] Recent historians agree with Gregg. Hubert Howe Bancroft, *History of New Mexico and Arizona*, 72–91; Twitchell, *Leading Facts of New Mexican History*, I, 283–84.

[5] Juan de Oñate, "Petición al virrey don Luis Velasco para la jornada de descubrimiento . . . y capitulaciones del virrey con don Juan de Oñate, México, 21 de Septiembre de 1595." MS. This document has since disappeared from the archives at Santa Fé, and Gregg's résumé was probably the only English version available for many years. The original was discovered in the Patronato Real section of the Archivo General de las Indias at Seville and is published in Charles W. Hackett (ed.), *Historical Documents Relating to New Mexico, Nueva Vizcaya and Approaches Thereto, to 1773*, I, 224–55.

Juan de Oñate (*fl.* 1595–1622), son of the conquistador and mining baron,

ness of Don Guadalupe Miranda, Secretary of State at Santa Fé.[6] This petition prayed for the permission and assistance of the vice-regal government at Mexico, to establish a colony on the Rio del Norte in the region already known as New Mexico; which having been granted, it was carried into effect, as I infer from the documents, during the following spring.

This appears to have been the first *legal* colony established in the province; yet we gather from different clauses in Oñate's memorial, that an adventurer known as Captain Francisco de Leyva Bonillo had previously entered the province with some followers, without the king's permission, whom Oñate was authorized to arrest and punish.[7] Some historians insist that New Mexico was first visited by a few missionaries in 1581; and there is a tradition in the country which fixes the first settlement in 1583—both having reference no doubt to the party of Leyva.[8]

Oñate bound himself to take into New Mexico two hundred soldiers, and a sufficiency of provisions for the first year's support of the colony; with abundance of horses, black cattle, sheep, etc., as also merchandise, agricultural utensils, tools and materials for me-

Cristóbal de Oñate, was born in Zacatecas. He inherited a fortune from his father, married an heiress of Montezuma, received royal authority to colonize New Mexico in 1595, and eventually, in 1598, led some 400 people, 83 wagons, and 7,000 head of stock into the new province. Besides establishing the first Spanish settlements there, Oñate re-explored lands visited by Coronado from the Gulf of California to the Great Bend of the Arkansas River. George P. Hammond, *Don Juan de Oñate and the Founding of New Mexico.*

[6] Guadalupe Miranda was superintendent of the public school in Santa Fé (1832), *secretario de gobierno* of New Mexico (1839–41), and for a time (1841–46) co-owner of what later became known as the Maxwell Grant. After the American occupation he become a leading citizen in Doña Ana County.

[7] Francisco de Leyva Bonilla, a Portuguese, entered New Mexico illegally in about 1594 and extended his explorations into the Plains. He was murdered by his lieutenant, Antonio Gutiérrez Humaña, who in turn was killed with nearly all his men in a battle with the Indians. Gaspar Castaño de Sosa, governor of Nuevo León, made an unauthorized entry in 1590, received the submission of thirty-three pueblos, and attempted to establish a colony, but he was arrested and taken back to Mexico in 1591.

[8] Gregg is mistaken. The exploration of 1581 was made by a Franciscan friar, Agustín Rodríguez, and his military escort. A relief expedition in 1582 under Father Bernaldino Beltrán and Captain Antonio Espejo arrived too late to save the missionary's life. George P. Hammond and Agapito Rey, "The Rodríguez Expedition into New Mexico, 1581–82," in *N. Mex. Hist. Rev.*, Vol. II, Nos. 3 and 4 (July, October, 1927), 239–68, 334–64; George P. Hammond and Agapito Rey (eds.), *Expeditions into New Mexico Made by Antonio de Espejo, 1582–1583.*

chanics' purposes; and all at his own cost, or rather at the ultimate expense of the colonists.

This adventurer, in the course of his memorial, also stipulates for some extraordinary provisions on the part of the King: such as, artillery and other arms, ammunitions, etc.—six priests, with a full complement of books, ornaments and church accoutrements—a loan of $20,000 from the royal treasury—a grant of thirty leagues square of land wheresoever he might choose to select it, with all the vassals (Indians) residing upon it—his family to be ennobled, with the hereditary title of Marquis—the office of Governor, with the titles of *Adelantado* and the rank of Captain-general for four generations —a salary of 8,000 ducats of Castile per annum—the privilege of working mines exempt from the usual crown-tax—permission to parcel out the aborigines among his officers and men; and besides other favors to his brothers and relatives, to have "Indians recommended to their charge," which, in other words, was the privilege of making slaves of them to work in the mines—with many other distinctions, immunities and powers to himself, sufficient to establish him in an authority far more despotic than any modern monarch of Europe would venture to assume. And although these exorbitant demands were not all conceded, they go to demonstrate by what incentives of pecuniary interest, as well as of honors, the Spanish monarchs sought the *"descubrimiento, pacificacion y conversion,"* as they modestly termed it, of the poor aborigines of America.

The memorial referred to is extremely lengthy, being encumbered with numerous marginal notes, each containing the decree of assent or dissent of the Viceroy. All this, however, serves rather to illustrate the ancient manners and customs of the Spaniards in those feudal days—the formalities observed in undertaking an exploring and christianizing enterprise—than to afford any historical data of the expedition.

In every part of this singular document there may be traced evidences of that sordid lust for gold and power, which so disgraced all the Spanish conquests in America; and that religious fanaticism— that crusading spirit, which martyrized so many thousands of the aborigines of the New World under Spanish authority.

But to return to Oñate: In one article, this adventurer, or contractor, or whatever else we may choose to call him, inquires, "In case the natives are unwilling to come quietly to the acknowledgment of the true Christian faith, and listen to the evangelical word, and give obedience to the king our sovereign, what shall be done with them? that we may proceed according to the laws of the Catholic Church, and the ordinances of his Majesty. And what tributes, that they may be christianly borne, shall be imposed upon them, as well for the crown as for the adventurers?"—showing that these 'missionaries' (as they were wont to call themselves) not only robbed the Indians of their country and treasure, and made menial slaves of them, but exacted tribute beside—promulgated the gospel at the point of the bayonet, and administered baptism by force of arms—compelling them to acknowledge the 'apostolic Roman Catholic faith,' of which they had not the slighest idea. Cervantes, who wrote his Don Quixote about this time, no doubt intended to make a hit at this cruel spirit of religious bigotry, by making his hero command his captives to acknowledge the superiority of his Dulcinea's beauty over that of all others; and when they protest that they have never seen her, he declares, that "the importance consists in this—that without seeing her, you have it to believe, confess, affirm, swear and defend."

It is much to be regretted that there are no records to be found of the wars and massacres, the numberless incidents and wild adventures which one would presume to have occurred during the first three-quarters of a century of the colonization of New Mexico. It is probable, however, that, as the aborigines seem to have been at first of a remarkably pacific and docile character, the conqueror met with but little difficulty in carrying out his original plans of settlement. Quietly acquiescing in both the civil and religious authority of the invaders, the yoke was easily riveted upon them, as they had neither intelligence nor spirit to resist, until goaded to desperation.

The colony had progressed very rapidly, the settlements extending into every quarter of the territory—villages, and even towns of considerable importance were reared in remote sections; of which there now remain but the ruins, with scarce a tradition to tell the fate of the once flourishing population. Many valuable mines were discovered and worked, as tradition relates,[9] the locations of which have been lost, or (as the Mexicans say,) concealed by the Indians, in order to prevent a repetition of the brutal outrages they had suffered in them. Whether this was the case or not, they surely had cause enough for wishing to conceal those with which they were acquainted; for in these very mines they had been forced to perform, under the lash, the most laborious tasks, till human strength could endure no more. Even then, perhaps, they would not have ventured upon resistance, but for the instigations of an eloquent warrior from a distant tribe, who pretended to have inherited the power of Montezuma, of whose subjects all these Indians, even to the present day, consider themselves the descendants. Tecumseh-like, our hero united the different tribes, and laid the plan of a conspiracy and general massacre of their oppressors; declaring that all who did not enter into the plot, should share the fate of the Spaniards. I have been furnished through the kindness of the Secretary of State before mentioned, with an account of this insurrection and consequent massacre of the Spanish population, taken from the journal of Don Antonio de Otermin, governor and commandant at the time, which was preserved in the public archives at Santa Fé.[10]

It appears that the night of the 13th of August, 1680, was the time fixed for a general insurrection of all the tribes and *Pueblos*.[11] At a stated hour the massacre of the Spanish population was to commence. Every soul was to be butchered without distinction of sex or

[9] Tradition exaggerates. Unlike much of northern Mexico, New Mexico had very few mines. The main exports in Spanish times were sheep, wool, Indian blankets, piñon nuts, and animal skins. There was a deplorable shortage of money, and most internal trade was barter. The "once flourishing population" could only have been of Indian towns, several of which were destroyed in the Pueblo Revolt (1680). The Spanish population then was less than 3,000 and concentrated largely at Santa Fé and the rural settlements in the upper Río Grande valley.

[10] Antonio de Otermín, "Salida para El Paso del Norte, 23 de agusto, hasta 5 de octubre de 1680." MS. This, like the Oñate document, was a copy. The original journal of Otermín was sent to the viceroy at Mexico City. A published translation with supporting evidence appears in Charles W. Hackett (ed.), *The Revolt of the Pueblo Indians of New Mexico and Otermin's Attempted Reconquest, 1680–1682*. The revolt, as much religious as economic in origin, was led by Popé, a medicine man of the San Juan pueblo who became a powerful influence from the expulsion of the Spaniards to his death in 1688.

[11] A general term for all the *Catholic Indians* of N. Mexico, and their *villages*. —GREGG.

age—with the exception of such young and handsome females as they might wish to preserve for wives! Although this conspiracy had evidently been in agitation for a great while, such strict secrecy had been maintained, that nothing was known or even suspected, till a few days before the appointed time. It is said that not a single woman was let into the secret, for fear of endangering the success of the cause; but it was finally disclosed by two Indian chiefs themselves to the governor; and about the same time information of the conspiracy was received from some curates and officers of Taos.

Gov. Otermin, seeing the perilous situation of the country, lost no time in dispatching general orders for gathering the people of the south into the Pueblo of Isleta,[12] where the lieutenant-governor was stationed, and those of the north and adjacent districts into Santa Fé. A considerable number collected in the fortifications of Isleta, and many families from the surrounding jurisdictions were able to reach the capital; yet great numbers were massacred on the way; for the Indians, perceiving their plot discovered, did not await the appointed time, but immediately commenced their work of destruction.

General hostilities having commenced, every possible preparation was made for a vigorous defence of the capital. The population of the suburbs had orders to remove to the centre, and the streets were all barricaded. On the evening of the 10th two soldiers arrived from Taos, having with much difficulty escaped the vigilance of the Indians. They brought intelligence that the Pueblos of Taos[13] had all risen; and that on arriving at La Cañada,[14] they had found the Spaniards well fortified, although a great number of them had been assassinated in the vicinity. The governor now sent out a detachment of troops to reconnoitre, instructing them to bring away the citizens who remained at La Cañada. They returned on the 12th, with the

[12] A Tigua town near present Isleta, in Bernalillo County. In his futile attempt to reconquer New Mexico in 1681, Otermín removed some of the inhabitants and established them in a new town, Isleta del Sur, below El Paso. The others fled westward to the Hopi country but returned in the eighteenth century and reoccupied the original pueblo.

[13] San Gerónimo de Taos, the northernmost Tigua pueblo, about 65 miles north of Santa Fé and 4 miles north of San Fernando de Taos, is still occupied.

[14] Santa Cruz de la Cañada, a Spanish town at the site of present Santa Cruz, in northern Santa Fé County.

painful information that they had found many dead bodies on their way—that the temples had been plundered, and all the stock driven off from the *ranchos*.

The massacre of the Spaniards in many neighboring Pueblos, was now unreservedly avowed by the Indians themselves; and as those who remained in Santa Fé appeared in the most imminent danger, the government buildings were converted into a fortification. By this time two friendly Indians who had been dispatched in the direction of Galisteo,[15] came in with the intelligence that 500 warriors of the tribe called *Tagnos*,[16] were marching towards the city, being even then only a league distant. By conversing with the enemy the spies had been able to ascertain their temper and their projects. They seemed confident of success—"For the God of the Christians is dead," said they, "but our god, which is the sun, never dies;" adding that they were only waiting the arrival of the *Teguas*,[17] Taosas and Apaches, in order to finish their work of extermination.

Next morning the savages were seen approaching from the south. On their arrival they took up their quarters in the deserted houses of the suburbs, with the view of waiting for their expected allies, before they laid siege to the city. A parley was soon afterwards held with the chief leaders, who told the Spaniards that they had brought two crosses, of which they might have their choice: one was red, denoting war, the other was white and professed peace, on the condition of their immediately evacuating the province. The governor strove to conciliate them by offering to pardon all the crimes they had committed, provided they would be good Christians and loyal subjects thereafter. But the Indians only made sport of him and laughed heartily at his propositions. He then sent a detachment to dislodge them; but was eventually obliged to turn out in person,

[15] Santa Cruz de Galisteo, a Tanoan pueblo about 20 miles south of Santa Fé and a mile and a half from present Galisteo, in central Santa Fé County. It was abandoned at the close of the eighteenth century.

[16] The Pecos and several other populous *Pueblos* to the southward of Santa Fé were *Tagnos*.—GREGG.

The Tagno, or Tano, is a language stock embracing the Tigua, Tegua, and Togua (Jémez-Pecos) nations. The term is sometimes applied to a branch of the Teguas, whose range includes the Pecos pueblo but whose language is different. For the ethnic groupings, see Adolph F. Bandelier, *Final Report of Investigations Among the Indians of the Southwestern United States.*

[17] These embraced nearly all the *Pueblos* between Santa Fé and Taos.—GREGG.

with all the efficient men he had. The battle continued the whole day, during which a great number of Indians and some Spaniards were killed. But late in the evening the Teguas, Toasas and others, were seen pouring down upon the city from the north, when the troops had to abandon the advantages they had gained, and fly to the defence of the fortifications.

The siege had now continued for nine days, during which the force of the Indians had constantly been on the increase. Within the last forty-eight hours they had entirely deprived the city of water by turning off the stream which had hitherto supplied it; so that the horses and other stock were dying of thirst. The want of water and provisions becoming more and more insupportable every moment, and seeing no chance of rescue or escape, Governor Otermin resolved to make a sortie the next morning, and die with sword in hand, rather than perish so miserably for want of supplies. At sunrise he made a desperate charge upon the enemy, whom, notwithstanding the inferiority of his forces, he was soon able to dislodge. Their ranks becoming entirely disordered, more than three hundred were slain, and an abundance of booty taken, with forty-seven prisoners, who, after some examination as to the origin of the conspiracy, were all shot. The Spaniards, according to their account of the affair, only had four or five men killed, although a considerable number were wounded—the governor among the rest.

The city of Santa Fé, notwithstanding a remaining population of at least a thousand souls, could not muster above a hundred able-bodied men to oppose the multitude that beset them, which had now increased to about three thousand. Therefore Governor Otermin, with the advice of the most intelligent citizens in the place, resolved to abandon the city. On the following day (August 21), they accordingly set out, the greater portion afoot, carrying their own provisions; as there were scarcely animals enough for the wounded. Their march was undisturbed by the Indians, who only watched their movements till they passed Isleta, when nothing more was seen of them. Here they found that those who had been stationed at Isleta had also retreated to the south a few days before. As they passed through the country, they found the Pueblos deserted by the Indians, and the Spaniards who pertained to them all massacred.

They had not continued on their march for many days, when the caravan became utterly unable to proceed; for they were not only without animals, but upon the point of starvation—the Indians having removed from the route everything that could have afforded them relief. In this emergency, Otermin dispatched an express to the lieutenant-governor, who was considerably in advance, and received from his party a few carts with a supply of provisions. Towards the latter end of September, the Governor and his companions in misfortune reached Paso del Norte (about 320 miles south of Santa Fé), where they found the advance party.

The Governor immediately sent an account of the disaster to the Viceroy at Mexico, soliciting reinforcements for the purpose of recovering the lost province, but none arrived till the following year. Meanwhile the refugees remained where they were, and founded, according to the best traditions, the town of *el Paso del Norte,* so called in commemoration of this retreat, or *passage from the north.*[18] This is an extensive and fertile valley, over which were scattered several Pueblos, all of whom remained friendly to the Spaniards, affording them an asylum with provisions and all the necessaries of life.

The following year Governor Otermin was superseded by Don Diego de Vargas Zapata,[19] who commenced the work of reconquering the country. This war lasted for ten years. In 1688, Don Pedro Petrir de Cruzate entered the province and reduced the Pueblo of Zia,[20] which had been famous for its brave and obstinate resistance. In this attack more than six hundred Indians of both sexes were slain, and a large number made prisoners. Among the latter was a warrior named Ojeda, celebrated for valor and vivacity, who spoke good

[18] Nuestra Señora de Guadalupe del Paso del Norte, now Ciudad Juárez, in Chihuahua, Mexico. The name comes from the river's passage through the canyon, or perhaps from the ford, but not from the retreat of 1680. For its history, see Anne E. Hughes, "The Beginning of Spanish Settlement in the El Paso District," in *University of California Publications in History,* Vol. I, 293–333.

[19] Otermín was not replaced until 1683, by Domingo Jironza Petriz de Cruzate, who in turn was succeeded by Diego de Vargas Zapata in 1691. After formally pacifying the Pueblos in 1693, Governor Vargas re-established the colonies, but resistance continued until 1697.

[20] Zia, a Queres town on the Jemez River in present Sandoval County, is one of the oldest pueblos in New Mexico.

Spanish. This Indian gave a graphic account of all that had transpired since the insurrection.[21]

He said that the Spaniards, and especially the priests, had been everywhere assassinated in the most barbarous manner; and particularly alluded to the murder of the curate of Zia, whose fate had been singularly cruel. It appears that on the night of the outbreak, the unsuspecting *padre* being asleep in the convent, the Indians hauled him out, and having stripped him naked, mounted him upon a hog. Then lighting torches, they carried him in that state through the village, and several times around the church, and cemetery, scourging him all the while most unmercifully! Yet, not even contented with this, they placed the weak old man upon all fours, and mounting upon his back by turns, spurred him through the streets, lashing him without cessation till he expired!

The discord which soon prevailed among the different Pueblos, greatly facilitated their second subjugation, which closely followed their emancipation. These petty feuds reduced their numbers greatly, and many villages were entirely annihilated, of which history only furnishes the names.

In 1698, after the country had been for some time completely subdued again by the Spaniards, another irruption took place in which many Pueblos were concerned; but through the energy of Governor Vargas Zapata it was soon quelled.[22]

Since this last effort, the Indians have been treated with more humanity, each Pueblo being allowed a league or two of land, and permitted to govern themselves. Their rancorous hatred for their conquerors, however, has never entirely subsided, yet no further outbreak took place till 1837, when they joined the Mexican insurgents in another bloody conspiracy. Some time before these tragic events took place, it was prophesied among them that a new race was about to appear from the east, to redeem them from the Spanish yoke. I heard this spoken of several months before the subject of the insurrection had been seriously agitated. It is probable that the Pueblos built their hopes upon the Americans, as they seemed as

[21] Bartolomé Ojeda served the Spaniards as a scout, war chief, and governor of the Queres pueblos during the reconquest.

[22] The last revolt occurred in 1696, not 1698. Vargas was removed from the governorship in 1697 and not reinstated until 1703. He died in the following year.

yet to have no knowledge of the Texans. In fact, they have always appeared to look upon foreigners as a superior people, to whom they could speak freely of their discontent and their grievances. The truth is, the Pueblos, in every part of Mexico, have always been ripe for insurrection. It is well known that the mass of the revolutionary chief Hidalgo's army was made up of this class of people. The immediate cause of the present outbreak in the north, however, had its origin among the Hispano-Mexican population. This grew chiefly out of the change of the federal government to that of *Centralismo* in 1835. A new governor, Col. Albino Perez,[23] was then sent from the city of Mexico, to take charge of this isolated department; which was not very agreeable to the 'sovereign people,' as they had previously been ruled chiefly by native governors. Yet while the new form of government was a novelty and did not affect the pecuniary interests of the people, it was acquiesced in; but it was now found necessary for the support of the new organization, to introduce a system of direct taxation, with which the people were wholly unacquainted; and they would sooner have paid a *doblon* through a tariff than a *real*[24] in this way. Yet, although the conspiracy had been brewing for some time, no indications of violence were demonstrated, until, on account of some misdemeanor, an *alcalde*[25] was imprisoned by the *Prefecto* of the northern district, Don Ramon Abreu.[26] His honor of the staff was soon liberated by a mob; an occurrence which seemed as a watchword for a general insurrection.

These new movements took place about the beginning of August, 1837, and an immense rabble was soon gathered at La Cañada (a

[23] Pérez was named governor and commandant of the armed forces in 1835 by President Antonio López de Santa Anna. The centralist regime, established on October 3, 1835, and formalized by the Constitution of 1836, deprived the Mexican states of their autonomy until the return of federalism in 1846.

[24] The *doblón* (Spanish doubloon) was a large gold coin then worth about sixteen American dollars. The *real* was a silver piece worth one-eighth of a dollar, the Mexican *peso* being equivalent to the dollar at that time.

[25] The *alcalde* was a municipal officer with both executive and judicial authority. At one time the office was elective, but it became appointive, and sometimes was purchased or inherited.

[26] By the Constitution of 1836 the Mexican states were reduced to mere departments, each of which was subdivided into districts under prefects appointed by the governor. Ramón Abreu, prefect of the northern district, at one time owned the only printing press in New Mexico.

town some twenty-five miles to the north of Santa Fé), among whom were to be found the principal warriors of all the Northern Pueblos. Governor Perez issued orders to the alcades for the assembling of the militia; but all that could be collected together was about a hundred and fifty men, including the warriors of the Pueblo of Santo Domingo.[27] With this inadequate force, the Governor made an attempt to march from the capital, but was soon surprised by the insurgents who lay in ambush near La Cañada; when his own men fled to the enemy, leaving him and about twenty-five trusty friends to make their escape in the best way they could. Knowing that they would not be safe in Santa Fé, the refugees pursued their flight southward, but were soon overtaken by the exasperated Pueblos; when the Governor was chased back to the suburbs of the city, and savagely put to death. His body was then stripped and shockingly mangled: his head was carried as a trophy to the camp of the insurgents, who made a foot-ball of it among themselves. I had left the city the day before this sad catastrophe took place, and beheld the Indians scouring the fields in pursuit of their victims, though I was yet ignorant of their barbarous designs. I saw them surround a house and drag from it the secretary of state, Jesus Maria Alarid.[28] He and some other principal characters (including Prefect Abreu), who had also taken refuge among the ranchos, were soon afterwards stripped, and finally dispatched *a lanzadas*, that is, pierced through and through with lances, a mode of assassination very common among those demi-civilized savages.

Don Santiago Abreu (brother of the prefect), formerly governor[29] and the most famed character of N. Mexico, was butchered in a still more barbarous manner. They cut off his hands, pulled out his eyes and tongue, and otherwise mutilated his body, taunting him all the while with the crimes he was accused of, by shaking the shorn members in his face. Thus perished nearly a dozen of the most conspicuous men of the obnoxious party, whose bodies lay for several days exposed to the beasts and birds of prey.

[27] A Queres town near the mouth of Galisteo Creek on the Río Grande, about 30 miles southwest of Santa Fé. During its long history it changed its location several times.
[28] Jesús María Alarid had been superintendent of the customs house in 1833.
[29] *Jefe político*, or governor, from 1831 to 1833.

On the 9th of August about two thousand of the insurgent mob, including the Pueblo Indians, pitched their camp in the suburbs of the capital. The horrors of a *saqueo* (or plundering of the city) were now anticipated by every one. The American traders were particularly uneasy, expecting every instant that their lives and property would fall a sacrifice to the ferocity of the rabble. But to the great and most agreeable surprise of all, no outrage of any importance was committed upon either inhabitant or trader. A great portion of the insurgents remained in the city for about two days, during which one of the boldest leaders, José Gonzalez of Taos, a good honest hunter but a very ignorant man, was elected for governor.[30]

The first step of the revolutionists was to seize all the property of their proscribed or murdered victims, which was afterwards distributed among the victors by a decree of the *Asamblea general*—that being the title by which a council summoned together by Governor Gonzalez, and composed of all the alcaldes and principal characters of the territory, was dignified. The families of the unfortunate victims of this revolutionary movement were thus left destitute of everything; and the foreign merchants who had given the officers credit to a large amount upon the strength of their reputed property and salaries, remained without a single resource with which to cover their demands. As these losses were chiefly experienced in consequence of a want of sufficient protection from the general government, the American merchants drew up a memorial setting forth their claims, which, together with a schedule of the various accounts due, was sent to the Hon. Powhattan Ellis, American Minister at Mexico.[31] These demands were certainly of a far more equitable character than many of those which some time after occasioned the French blockade;[32] yet our Government has given the unfortunate claimants no hope of redress. Even Mexico did not dispute the justness of these claims, but, on the contrary, she promptly paid to the order of General Armijo, a note given by the late Governor Perez

[30] The rise and fall of José González was so rapid that almost no biographical details were recorded.

[31] Powhattan Ellis (1794-1844), a Virginian, had been a supreme court justice in Mississippi, a United States senator, and a federal circuit judge. He was appointed chargé d'affaires at Mexico City in 1835 and was minister from 1839 to 1842.

[32] The French blockaded the port of Vera Cruz, bombarded its fortifications, and forced Mexico to recognize certain damage claims in the so-called "Pastry War" (1838-39).

to Mr. Sutton, an American merchant,[33] which Armijo had purchased at a great discount.

In the South, the Americans were everywhere accused of being the instigators of this insurrection, which was openly pronounced another Texas affair.[34] Their goods were confiscated or sequestered, upon the slightest pretexts, or for some pretended irregularity in the accompanying documents; although it was evident that these and other indignities were heaped upon them, as a punishment for the occurrence of events which it had not been in their power to prevent. Indeed, these ill-used merchants were not only innocent of any participation in the insurrectionary movements, but had actually furnished means to the government for the purpose of quelling the disturbances.

As I have observed before, the most active agents in this desperate affair were the Pueblo Indians, although the insurgent party was composed of all the heterogeneous ingredients that a Mexican population teems with. The *rancheros* and others of the lowest class, however, were only the instruments of certain discontented *ricos*, who, it has been said, were in hope of elevating themselves upon the wreck of their enemies. Among these was the present Governor Armijo, an ambitious and turbulent demagogue, who, for some cause or other, seemed anxious for the downfall of the whole administration.

As soon as Armijo received intelligence of the catastrophe, he hurried to the capital, expecting, as I heard it intimated by his own brother, to be elected governor; but, not having rendered any personal aid, the 'mobocracy' would not acknowledge his claim to their suffrages. He therefore retired, Santa-Anna-like, to his residence at Albuquerque,[35] to plot, in imitation of his great prototype, some

[33] Three Santa Fé traders were named Sutton in this period: Jesse, Joseph, and James.

[34] Texas, whose independence from Mexico was instigated and achieved (1835–36) largely by citizens and residents of American origin, claimed all of New Mexico's territory east of the Río Grande.

[35] General Antonio López de Santa Anna (1795–1876), author of the centralist coup of 1835, was the stormy petrel of Mexican politics from 1823 to 1855. His custom was to retire from office whenever the situation became tense and remain in obscurity until "popular demand" summoned him to put things aright. Albuquerque (as it is now spelled) was New Mexico's second city, Armijo's bailiwick, and the center of the Río Abajo, or down-river region.

measures for counteracting the operation of his own intrigues. In this he succeeded so well, that towards September he was able to collect a considerable force in the Rio-Abajo, when he proclaimed a *contra-revolucion* in favor of the federal government. About the same time the disbanded troops of the capital under Captain Caballero,[36] made a similar *pronunciamento*, demanding their arms, and offering their services gratis. The 'mobocratic' dynasty had gone so far as to deny allegiance to Mexico, and to propose sending to Texas for protection: although there had not been any previous understanding with that Republic.

Armijo now marched to Santa Fé with all his force, and Governor Gonzalez being without an army to support him, fled to the north. After his triumphal entrance into the capital, Armijo caused himself to be proclaimed Governor and *Comandante General*, and immediately dispatched couriers to Mexico with a highly colored account of his own exploits, which procured him a confirmation of those titles and dignities for eight years.

In the meanwhile news of the insurrection having reached Mexico, the *Escuadron de Vera Cruz*, from Zacatecas, consisting of about two hundred dragoons, with an equal number of regulars from the *Presidios* of Chihuahua, under the command of Colonel Justiniani,[37] were ordered to New Mexico. Having arrived at Santa Fé, these troops, together with Governor Armijo's little army, marched in January, 1838, to attack the rebels, who, by this time, had again collected in considerable numbers at La Cañada.

The greatest uneasiness and excitement now prevailed at the Capital, lest the rabble should again prove victorious, in which case they would not fail to come and sack the city. Foreign merchants had as usual the greatest cause for fear, as vengeance had been openly vowed against them for having furnished the government party with supplies. These, therefore, kept up a continual watch, and had everything in readiness for a precipitate flight to the United States. But in a short time their fears were completely dispelled by the arrival

[36] Captain José Caballero. The Santa Fé company had been disbanded in 1837 for lack of funds.

[37] Colonel Cayetano Justiniani, later a general, participated in the battle of Brazitos (1846) and was governor of Chihuahua for a short time.

of an express, with the welcome news of the entire defeat of the insurgents.

It appeared that, when the army arrived within view of the insurgent force, Armijo evinced the greatest perturbation. In fact, he was upon the point of retiring without venturing an attack, when Captain Munoz,[38] of the Vera Cruz dragoons, exclaimed, "What's to be done, General Armijo? If your Excellency will but permit me, I will oust that rabble in an instant with my little company alone." Armijo having given his consent, the gallant captain rushed upon the insurgents, who yielded at once, and fled precipitately—suffering a loss of about a dozen men, among whom was the deposed Governor Gonzalez, who, having been caught in the town after the skirmish had ended, was instantly shot, without the least form of trial.

[38] Captain Pedro Muñoz preceded the federal troops advancing from Chihuahua and strengthened Armijo's position by recognizing him as governor. He remained in New Mexico with the Vera Cruz dragoons until late in 1838.

CHAPTER VII

Geographical Position of New Mexico—Absence of navigable Streams—The Rio del Norte—Romantic Chasm—Story of a sunken River—Mr. Stanley's Excursion to a famous Lake—Santa Fé and its Localities—El Valle de Taos and its Fertility—Soil of N. Mexico—The first Settler at Taos and his Contract with the Indians—Salubrity and Pleasantness of the Climate of New Mexico—Population—State of Agriculture—Staple Productions of the Country—Corn-fields and Fences—Irrigation and *Acequias*—*Tortillas* and *Tortilleras*—*Atole, Frijoles,* and *Chile*—Singular Custom—Culinary and Table Affairs—Flax and the Potato indigenous—Tobacco and *Punche*—Fruits—Peculiar Mode of cultivating the Grape—Forest Growths—*Piñon* and *Mezquite*—Mountain Cottonwood—*Palmilla* or Soap-plant—Pasturage.

NEW MEXICO possesses but a few of those natural advantages, which are necessary to anything like a rapid progress in civilization. Though bounded north and east by the territory of the United States, south by that of Texas and Chihuahua, and west by Upper California, it is surrounded by chains of mountains and prairie wilds, extending to a distance of 500 miles or more, except in the direction of Chihuahua, from which its settlements are separated by an unpeopled desert of nearly two hundred miles—and without a single means of communication by water with any other part of the world.

The whole nominal territory, including those bleak and uninhabitable regions with which it is intersected, comprises about 200,000 square miles—considered, of course, according to its original boundaries, and therefore independent of the claims of Texas to the Rio del Norte. To whichsoever sovereignty that section of land may eventually belong, that portion of it, at least, which is inhabited, should remain united. Any attempt on the part of Texas to make the Rio del Norte the line of demarkation would greatly retard her ultimate acquisition of the territory, as it would leave at least one third of the population accustomed to the same rule, and bound by ties of consanguinity and affinity of customs, wholly at the mercy of the contiguous hordes of savages, that inhabit the Cordilleras on the west of them. This great chain of mountains which reaches the borders of the Rio del Norte, not far above El Paso, would, in my opinion, form the most natural boundary between the two countries, from thence northward.[1]

There is not a single navigable stream to be found in New Mexico. The famous Rio del Norte is so shallow, for the most part of the year, that Indian canoes can scarcely float in it. Its navigation is also obstructed by frequent shoals and rippling sections for a distance of more than a thousand miles below Santa Fé. Opposite Taos, especially, for an uninterrupted distance of nearly fifteen miles, it runs pent up in a deep *cañon,* through which it rushes in rapid torrents. This frightful chasm is absolutely impassable; and, viewed from the top, the scene is imposing in the extreme. None but the boldest hearts and firmest nerves can venture to its brink, and look down its almost perpendicular precipice, over projecting crags and deep crevices, upon the foaming current of the river, which, in some places, appears like a small rippling brook; while in others it winds its serpentine course silently but majestically along, through a narrow little valley; with immense plains bordering and expanding in every direction, yet so smooth and level that the course of the river is not perceived till within a few yards of the verge. I have beheld this *cañon* from the summit of a mountain, over which the road passes some twenty miles below Taos, from whence it looks like the mere fissure of an insignificant ravine.

Baron Humboldt[2] speaks of an extraordinary event as having

[1] Under both Spain and Mexico no definite boundary separated Texas from New Mexico, but their Indian trade was usually divided by the Pecos River. On seceding from Mexico in 1836, Texas claimed all westward to the Río Grande including Santa Fé, Albuquerque, and most of the other important towns of New Mexico.

[2] Friedrich Heinrich Alexander von Humboldt. The reference is to his *Essai politique sur le royaume de la Nouvelle-Espagne* (5 vols., Paris, F. Schoell, 1811), which was republished in English (4 vols., London, 1811–22). Humboldt drew this

occurred in 1752, of which he says the inhabitants of Paso del Norte still preserved the recollection in his day. "The whole bed of the river," says the learned historian, "became dry all of a sudden, for more than thirty leagues above and twenty leagues below the Paso: and the water of the river precipitated itself into a newly formed chasm, and only made its reappearance near the *Presidio* of San Eleazeario. . . . At length, after the lapse of several weeks, the water resumed its course, no doubt because the chasm and the subterraneous conductors had filled up." This, I must confess, savors considerably of the marvellous, as not the least knowledge of these facts appears to have been handed down to the present generation. During very great droughts, however, this river is said to have entirely disappeared in the sand, in some places, between San *Elceario* and the Presidio del Norte.[3]

Notwithstanding the numerous tributary streams which would be supposed to pour their contents into the Rio del Norte, very few reach their destination before they are completely exhausted. Rio Puerco,[4] so called from the extreme muddiness of its waters, would seem to form an exception to this rule. Yet this also, although at least a hundred miles in length, is dry at the mouth for a portion of the year. The creek of Santa Fé itself, though a bold and dashing rivulet in the immediate vicinity of the mountains, sinks into insignificance, and is frequently lost altogether before it reaches the main river. Pecos and Conchos, its most important inlets, would scarcely be entitled to a passing remark, but for the geographical error of Baron Humboldt, who set down the former as the head branch of 'Red River of Natchitoches.'[5] These streams may be considered the

particular information from the manuscript diary of Bishop Pedro Tamarón, "Visita del obispo de Durango, 1759–1763," in the official archives at Mexico City (transcript in the Bancroft Library, Berkeley, Calif.).

[3] The Presidio de San Elizario (spelling varies) was situated on the right bank of the Río Grande, about 20 miles downstream from El Paso del Norte. Owing to a change in the river's course, it is now on the Texas side. The Presidio del Norte was at present-day Ojinaga, at the junction of the Conchos and Río Grande rivers, opposite Presidio, Texas.

[4] The Puerco rises near the continental divide in McKinley County and enters the Río Grande 50 miles below Albuquerque.

[5] The Pecos flows from the Sangre de Cristo range in San Miguel County southward into the Río Grande, in Val Verde County, Texas. The Conchos runs eastward from the Sierra Madre range in western Chihuahua to the Río Grande at

first constant-flowing inlets which the Rio del Norte receives from Santa Fé south—say for the distance of five hundred miles! It is then no wonder that this 'Great River of the North' decreases in volume of water as it descends. In fact, above the region of tide-water, it is almost everywhere fordable during most of the year, being seldom over knee-deep, except at the time of freshets. Its banks are generally very low, often less than ten feet above low-water mark; and yet, owing to the disproportioned width of the channel (which is for the most part some four hundred yards), it is not subject to inundations. Its only important rises are those of the annual freshets, occasioned by the melting of the snow in the mountains.

This river is only known to the inhabitants of Northern Mexico as *Rio del Norte,* or North river, because it descends from that direction; yet in its passage southward, it is in some places called *Rio Grande,* on account of its extent; but the name of *Rio Bravo* (Bold or Rapid river), so often given to it on maps, is seldom if ever heard among the people. Though its entire length, following its meanders from its source in the Rocky Mountains to the Gulf of Mexico, must be considerably over two thousand miles, it is hardly navigable to the extent of two hundred miles above its mouth.

The head branch of Pecos, as well as the creeks of Santa Fé and Tezuque, are said to be fed from a little lake which is located on the summit of a mountain about ten miles east of Santa Fé. Manifold and marvellous are the stories related of this lake and its wonderful localities, which although believed to be at least greatly exaggerated, would no doubt induce numbers of travellers to visit this snow-bound elysium, were it not for the laboriousness of the ascent. The following graphic account of a 'pleasure excursion' to this celebrated 'watering place,' is from the memoranda of Mr. E. Stanley, who spent many years in the New Mexican capital.

"The snow had entirely disappeared from the top of the highest mountains, as seen from Santa Fé before the first of May, and on the eighteenth we set off on our trip. All were furnished with arms

Ojinaga. The Red courses eastward from its source in the Texas panhandle to the Mississippi, about midway between Natchez, Mississippi, and Baton Rouge, Louisiana.

and fishing-tackle—well prepared to carry on hostilities both by land and water. Game was said to be abundant on the way—deer, turkeys, and even the formidable grizzly bear, ready to repel an invasion of his hereditary domain. Santa Fé creek, we knew, abounded with trout, and we were in hopes of finding them in the lake, although I have been told by some Mexicans, that there were no fish in it, and that it contained no living thing, except a certain nondescript and hideously misshapen little animal. We travelled up the course of the creek about eight miles, and then began to climb the mountain. Our journey now became laborious, the ascent being by no means gradual—rather a succession of hills—some long, others short—some declivitous, and others extremely precipitous. Continuing in this way for six or seven miles, we came to a grove of aspen, thick as cottonwoods in the Missouri bottoms. Through this grove, which extended for nearly a mile, no sound met the ear; no sign of life—not even an insect was to be seen; and not a breath of air was stirring. It was indeed a solitude to be felt. A mile beyond the grove brought us near the lake. On this last level, we unexpectedly met with occasional snow-banks, some of them still two or three feet deep. Being late, we sought out a suitable encampment, and fixed upon a little marshy prairie, east of the lake. The night was frosty and cold, and ice was frozen nearly an inch thick. Next morning we proceeded to the lake; when, lo—instead of beholding a beautiful sheet of water, we found an ugly little pond, with an area of two or three acres—frozen over, and one side covered with snow several feet deep. Thus all our hope of trout and monsters were at an end; and the *tracks* of a large bear in the snow, were all the *game* we saw during the trip."

Santa Fé, the capital of New Mexico, is the only town of any importance in the province. We sometimes find it written *Santa Fé de San Francisco* (Holy Faith of St. Francis), the latter being the patron, or tutelary saint. Like most of the towns in this section of country it occupies the site of an ancient Pueblo or Indian village, whose race has been extinct for a great many years.[6] Its situation is twelve of fifteen miles east of the Rio del Norte, at the western base

[6] Santa Fé, founded in 1610 by Governor Pedro de Peralta, occupies the site of one or more prehistoric Indian cultures.

of a snow-clad mountain, upon a beautiful stream of small mill-power size, which ripples down in icy cascades, and joins the river some twenty miles to the southwestward. The population of the city itself but little exceeds 3,000; yet, including several surrounding villages which are embraced in its corporate jurisdiction, it amounts to nearly 6,000 souls.[7]

The town is very irregularly laid out, and most of the streets are little better than common highways traversing scattered settlements which are interspersed with corn-fields nearly sufficient to supply the inhabitants with grain. The only attempt at anything like architectural compactness and precision, consists in four tiers of buildings, whose fronts are shaded with a fringe of *portales* or *corredores* of the rudest possible description. They stand around the public square, and comprise the *Palacio*, or Governor's house, the Custom-house, the Barracks (with which is connected the fearful *Calabozo*), the *Casa Consistorial* of the *Alcaldes*, the *Capilla de los Soldados* or Military Chapel, besides several private residences, as well as most of the shops of the American traders.[8]

The population of New Mexico is almost exclusively confined to towns and villages, the suburbs of which are generally farms. Even most of the individual *ranchos* and *haciendas* have grown into villages,—a result almost indispensable for protection against the marauding savages of the surrounding wilderness. The principal of these settlements are located in the valley of the Rio del Norte, extending from nearly one hundred miles north to about one hun-

[7] The latitude of Santa Fé, as determined by various observations, is 35°41' (though it is placed on most maps nearly a degree further north); and the longitude about 106° west from Greenwich. Its elevation above the ocean is nearly 7,000 feet; that of the valley of Taos is no doubt over a mile and a half. The highest peak of the mountain (which is covered with perennial snow) some ten miles to the north-east of the capital, is reckoned about 5,000 feet above the town. Those from Taos northward rise still to a much greater elevation.—GREGG.

Gregg's calculations are substantially correct. Santa Fé is 35°41' N. Lat., 105°54' W. Long., and 6,954 ft. above the sea. The elevation of Taos, however, is only 6,983 and Truchas Peak, 13,110 ft. above the sea, or 6,150 above Santa Fé.

[8] Of these landmarks only the governor's palace and the plaza itself remain. The *palacio*, on the north side of the square, was built in 1610, occupied continuously by the Spanish, Indian, Mexican, and American governors until 1909, and now houses the collections of the Historical Society of New Mexico. Near the plaza is the chapel of San Miguel, built in 1621, and close by is the "oldest house in the United States," of Indian construction and possibly of pre-Spanish age.

dred and forty south of Santa Fé.[9] The most important of these, next to the capital, is *El Valle de Taos*,[10] so called in honor of the *Taosa* tribe of Indians, a remnant of whom still forms a *Pueblo* in the north of the valley. No part of New Mexico equals this valley in amenity of soil, richness of produce and beauty of appearance. Whatever is thrown into its prolific bosom, which the early frosts of autumn will permit to ripen, grows to a wonderful degree of perfection.

Wheat especially has been produced of a superlative quality, and in such abundance, that, as is asserted, the crops have often yielded over a hundred fold. I would not have it understood, however, that this is a fair sample of New Mexican soil; for, in point of fact, though many of the bottoms are of very fertile character, the uplands must chiefly remain unproductive; owing, in part, to the sterility of the soil, but as much, no doubt, to want of irrigations; hence nearly all the farms and settlements are located in those valleys which may be watered by some constant-flowing stream.[11]

The first settler of the charming valley of Taos, since the country was reconquered from the Indians, is said to have been a Spaniard named Pando, about the middle of the eighteenth century. This pioneer of the North, finding himself exposed to the depredations of the Comanches, succeeded in gaining the friendship of that tribe, by promising his infant daughter, then a beautiful child, to one of their chiefs in marriage. But the unwilling maiden having subsequently refused to ratify the contract, the settlement was immediately attacked by the savages, and all were slain except the betrothed damsel who was led into captivity. After living some years with the Comanches on the great prairies, she was bartered away to the Paw-

[9] The settlements *up the river* from the capital are collectively known as *Rio-Arriba*, and those *down the river* as *Rio Abajo*. The latter comprises over a third of the population, and the principal wealth of New Mexico.—GREGG.

[10] The '*Valley of Taos*,' there being no *town* of this name. It includes several villages and other settlements, the largest of which are Fernandez and Los Ranchos, four or five miles apart.—GREGG.

See above, chap. 5, n. 12.

[11] For the generally barren and desolate appearance which the uplands of New Mexico present, some of them have possessed an extraordinary degree of fertility; as is demonstrated by the fact that many of the fields on the undulating lands in the suburbs of Santa Fé, have no doubt been in constant cultivation over two hundred years, and yet produce tolerable crops, without having been once renovated by manure.—GREGG.

nees, of whom she was eventually purchased by a Frenchman of St. Louis. Some very respectable families in that city are descended from her; and there are many people yet living who remember with what affecting pathos the old lady was wont to tell her tale of woe. She died but a few years ago.[12]

Salubrity of climate is decidedly the most interesting feature in the character of New Mexico. Nowhere—not even under the much boasted Sicilian skies, can a purer or a more wholesome atmosphere be found. Bilious diseases—the great scourge of the valley of the Mississippi—are here almost unknown. Apart from a fatal epidemic fever of a typhoid character, that ravaged the whole province from 1837 to 1839, and which, added to the smallpox that followed in 1840, carried off nearly ten per cent. of the population, New Mexico has experienced very little disease of a febrile character; so that as great a degree of longevity is attained there, perhaps, as in any other portion of the habitable world. Persons withered almost to mummies, are to be encountered occasionally, whose extraordinary age is only to be inferred from their recollection of certain notable events which have taken place in times far remote.

A sultry day, from Santa Fé north, is of very rare occurrence. The summer nights are usually so cool and pleasant that a pair of blankets constitutes an article of comfort seldom dispensed with. The winters are long, but not so subject to sudden changes as in damper climates; the general range of the thermometer, throughout the year, being from 10 to 75 degrees above zero, of Fahrenheit.[13] Baron Humboldt was led into as great an error with respect to the climate of New Mexico as to the rivers; for he remarks, that near Santa Fé and a little further north, "the Rio del Norte is sometimes covered for a succession of several years, with ice thick enough to admit the passage of horses and carriages:" a circumstance which would be scarcely less astounding to the New Mexicans, than would

[12] María Rosa Villapando (d. 1830), the daughter of Pablo Villapando, was taken by the Comanches at Taos in August of 1760, ransomed and taken to St. Louis in 1770, and there married to one Jean Baptiste Salle, known as Lajoie. Houck, *The Spanish Regime in Missouri*, II, 381; Bishop Tamarón describes the raid on Taos, which occurred a month after his departure. Tamarón, "Visita del Obispo de Durango."

[13] The mean annual temperature at Santa Fé is now 48.8° F., but extreme temperatures of _13° and 97° have been recorded.

the occurrence of a similar event in the harbor of New York be to her citizens.

The great elevation of all the plains about the Rocky Mountains, is perhaps the principal cause of the extraordinary dryness of the atmosphere. There is but little rain throughout the year, except from July to October—known as the *rainy season;* and as the Missouri traders usually arrive about its commencement, the coincidence has given rise to a superstition, quite prevalent among the vulgar, that the Americans bring the rain with them. During seasons of drought, especially, they look for the arrival of the annual caravans as the harbinger of speedy relief.

There has never been an accurate census taken in New Mexico.[14] Of the results of one which was attempted in 1832, the Secretary of State at Santa Fé speaks in the following terms: "At present (1841) we may estimate the Spanish or white population at about 60,000 souls or more, being what remains of 72,000, which the census taken eight or nine years ago showed there then existed in New Mexico." He supposes that this great diminution resulted from the ravages of the frightful diseases already alluded to. The decrease of population from these causes, however, is thus greatly overrated. The discrepancy must find its explanation in the original inaccuracy of the census referred to.

If we exclude the unsubjugated savages, the entire population of New Mexico, including the Pueblo Indians, cannot be set down, according to the best estimates I have been able to obtain, at more than 70,000 souls. These may be divided as follows: white creoles, say 1,000; Mestizos, or mixed creoles, 59,000; and Pueblos, 10,000. Of naturalized citizens, the number is inconsiderable—scarcely twenty; and if we except transient traders, there are not over double as many alien residents. There are no negroes in New Mexico, and consequently neither mulattoes nor *zambos.* In 1803, Baron Humboldt set down the population of this province at 40,200 so that according to this the increase for forty years has barely exceeded one per cent. per annum.

---

[14] A census was taken in 1827 giving 43,433 as the population of the province (5,160 for Santa Fé). Its tables are reproduced in H. Bailey Carrol and J. Villasana Haggard (eds.), *Three New Mexican Chronicles,* 88.

Agriculture, like almost everything else in New Mexico, is in a very primitive and unimproved state. A great portion of the peasantry cultivate with the hoe alone—their ploughs (when they have any) being only used for mellow grounds, as they are too rudely constructed to be fit for any other service. Those I have seen in use are mostly fashioned in this manner:—a section of the trunk of a tree, eight or ten inches in diameter, is cut about two feet long, with a small branch left projecting upwards, of convenient length for a handle. With this a beam is connected to which oxen are yoked. The block, with its fore end sloped downwards to a point, runs flat, and opens a furrow similar to that of the common shovel-plough. What is equally worthy of remark is, that these ploughs are often made exclusively of wood, without one particle of iron, or even a nail to increase their durability.

The *labores* and *milpas* (cultivated fields) are often, indeed most usually, without any enclosure. The owners of cattle are obliged to keep herdsmen constantly with them, else graze them at a considerable distance from the farms; for if any trespass is committed upon the fields by stock, the proprietor of the latter is bound to pay damages: therefore, instead of the cultivator's having to guard his crop from the cattle as with us, the owners of these are bound to guard them from the crops. Only a chance farm is seen fenced with poles scattered along on forks, or a loose hedge of brush. Mud-fences, or walls of very large *adobes*, are also occasionally to be met with.

The necessity of irrigation has confined, and no doubt will continue to confine agriculture principally to the valleys of the constant-flowing streams. In some places the crops are frequently cut short by the drying up of the streams. Where water is abundant, however, art has so far superseded the offices of nature in watering the farms, that it is almost a question whether the interference of nature in the matter would not be a disadvantage. On the one hand the husbandman need not have his grounds overflowed if he administers the water himself, much less need he permit them to suffer from drought. He is therefore more sure of his crop than if it were subject to the caprices of the weather in more favored agricultural regions.

One *acequia madre* (mother ditch) suffices generally to convey water for the irrigation of an entire valley, or at least for all the fields of one town or settlement. This is made and kept in repair by the public, under the supervision of the alcaldes; laborers being alloted to work upon it as with us upon our county roads. The size of this principal ditch is of course proportioned to the quality of land to be watered. It is conveyed over the highest part of the valley, which, on these mountain streams, is, for the most part, next to the hills. From this, each proprietor of a farm runs a minor ditch, in like manner, over the most elevated part of his field. Where there is not a superabundance of water, which is often the case on the smaller streams, each farmer has his day, or portion of a day allotted to him for irrigation; and at no other time is he permitted to extract water from the *acequia madre*. Then the cultivator, after letting the water into his minor ditch, dams this, first at one point and then at another, so as to overflow a section at a time, and with his hoe, depressing eminences and filling sinks, he causes the water to spread regularly over the surface. Though the operation would seem tedious, an expert irrigator will water in one day his five or six acre field, if level, and everything well arranged; yet on uneven ground he will hardly be able to get over half of that amount.[15]

All the *acequias* for the valley of the Rio del Norte are conveyed from the main stream, except where a tributary of more convenient water happens to join it. As the banks of the river are very low, and the descent considerable, the water is soon brought upon the surface by a horizontal ditch along an inclined bank, commencing at a convenient point of constant-flowing water—generally without dam, except sometimes a wing of stones to turn the current into the canal.

The staple productions of the country are emphatically Indian corn and wheat. The former grain is most extensively employed for making *tortillas*—an article of food greatly in demand among the people, the use of which has been transmitted to them by the aborigines. The corn is boiled in water with a little lime: and when it has been sufficiently softened, so as to strip it of its skin, it is ground

[15] There is no land measure here correspondent to our acres. Husbandmen rate their fields by the amount of wheat necessary to sow them, and thus speak of a *fanega* of land—*fanega* being a measure of about two bushels—meaning an extent which two bushels of wheat will suffice to sow. Tracts are usually sold by the number of *leguas* (leagues), or *varas* front of irrigable lands; for those back from the streams are considered worthless. The *vara* is very nearly 33 English inches, 5,000 of which constitute the Mexican league—under two miles and two-thirds.—GREGG.

A KITCHEN SCENE

into paste upon the *metate*,[16] and formed into a thin cake. This is afterwards spread on a small sheet of iron or copper, called *comal* (*comalli*, by the Indians), and placed over the fire, where, in less than three minutes, it is baked and ready for use. The thinness of the tortilla is always a great test of skill in the maker, and much rivalry ensues in the art of preparation. The office of making tortillas has, from the earliest times, pertained to the women, who appear to be better adapted to this employ than the other sex, both as regards skill and dexterity, in preparing this particular food for the table. I perfectly agree with the historian Clavigero,[17] however, in the opinion that "although this species of corn-bread may be very wholesome and substantial, and well-flavored when newly made, it is unpleasant when cold."

A sort of thin mush, called *atole*, made of Indian meal, is another article of diet, the preparation of which is from the aborigines; and such is its nationality, that in the North it is frequently called *el cafe de los Mexicanos* (the coffee of the Mexicans). How general

[16] From the Indian word *metatl*, a hollowed oblong stone, used as a grinding machine.—GREGG.

[17] Francisco Javier Clavijero, *Storia Antica del Messico* (4 vols., Cessena, G. Biasini, 1780–81), followed by several translations including one in English (London, 1787).

soever the use of coffee among Americans may appear, that of *atole* is still more so among the lower classes of Mexicans. They virtually 'breakfast, dine and sup' upon it. Of this, indeed, with *frijoles* and *chile* (beans and red pepper), consists their principal food. The extravagant use of red pepper among the Mexicans has become truly proverbial. It enters into nearly every dish at every meal, and often so predominates as entirely to conceal the character of the viands. It is likewise ground into a sauce, and thus used even more abundantly than butter. *Chile verde* (green pepper,) not as a mere condiment, but as a salad, served up in different ways, is reckoned by them one of the greatest luxuries. But however much we may be disposed to question their taste in this particular, no one can hesitate to do homage to their incomparable chocolate, in the preparation of which the Mexicans surely excel every other people.

Besides these, many other articles of diet peculiar to the country, and adopted from the aborigines, are still in use—often of rich and exquisite flavor, and though usually not much relished at first by strangers, they are for the most part highly esteemed after a little use.

The rancheros, and all the humbler classes of people, very seldom use any table for their meals, an inconvenience which is very little felt, as the dishes are generally served out from the kitchen in courses of a single plate to each guest, who usually takes it upon his knees. Knives and forks are equally dispensed with, the viands being mostly hashed or boiled so very soft as to be eaten with a spoon. This is frequently supplied by the *tortilla*, a piece of which is ingeniously doubled between the fingers, so as to assist in the disposal of anything, be it ever so rare or liquid. Thus it may well be said, as in the story of the Oriental monarch, that these rancheros employ a new spoon for every mouthful: for each fold of the tortilla is devoured with the substance it conveys to the mouth.

The very singular custom of abstaining from all sorts of beverage during meals, has frequently afforded me a great deal of amusement. Although a large cup of water is set before each guest, it is not customary to drink it off till the repast is finished. Should any one take it up in his hand while in the act of eating, the host is apt to cry out, "Hold, hold! there is yet more to come." I have never been able to ascertain definitely the meaning of this peculiarity; but from the strictness with which it is observed, it is natural to suppose, that the use of any kind of drink whilst eating, is held extremely unwholesome.[18] The New Mexicans use but little wine at meals, and that exclusively of the produce of the Paso del Norte.

But to return to the productions of the soil. *Cotton* is cultivated to no extent, although it has always been considered as indigenous to the country; while the ancient manufactures of the aborigines prove it to have been especially so in this province. *Flax* is entirely neglected, and resembling in every respect that of the *linum usitatissimum*, is to be found in great abundance in many of the mountain valleys. The potato (*la papa*), although not cultivated in this country till very lately, is unquestionably an indigenous plant, being still found in a state of nature in many of the mountain valleys—though of small size, seldom larger than filberts: whence it appears that this luxury had not its exclusive origin in South America, as is the current opinion of the present day. Universal as the use of tobacco is among these people, there is very little of it grown, and that chiefly of a light and weak species, called by the natives *punche*, which is also indigenous, and still to be met with growing wild in some places. What has in a great measure contributed to discourage people from attending to the cultivation of the tobacco plant, is the monopoly of this *indispensable* by the federal government; for although the tobacco laws are not enforced in New Mexico (there being no *Estanquillo*, or public store-house), yet the people cannot carry it anywhere else in the republic for sale, without risk of its being immediately confiscated. A still more powerful cause operating against this, as well as every other branch of agriculture in New Mexico, is the utter want of navigable streams, as a cheap and convenient means of transportation to distant markets.

Famous as the republic of Mexico has been for the quality and variety of its fruits, this province, considering its latitude, is most singularly destitute in this respect. A few orchards of apples, peaches and apricots, are occasionally met with, but even these are of very

---

[18] What also strikes the stranger as a singularity in that country, is that the females rarely ever eat with the males—at least in the presence of strangers—but usually take their food in the kitchen by themselves.—GREGG.

inferior quality, being only esteemed in the absence of something better. A few small vineyards are also to be found in the valley of the Rio del Norte, but the grape does not thrive as at El Paso. The mode of cultivating the grape in these parts is somewhat peculiar, and might, I have no doubt, be practised to great advantage in other countries. No scaffold or support of any kind is erected for the vines, which are kept pruned so as to form a sort of shrubbery. Every fall of the year, these are completely covered with earth, which protects them during the winter. Upon the opening of spring the dirt is scraped away, and the vines pruned again. This being repeated from year to year, the shrubs soon acquire sufficient strength to support the heavy crops of improved and superiorly-flavored grapes which they finally produce.

Indigenous wild fruits are not quite so scarce; a clear evidence that the lack of cultivated fruit is not so much the fault of nature, as the result of indolence and neglect on the part of the people. The prickly pear is found in greatest abundance, and of several varieties: and though neither very wholesome nor savory, it is nevertheless frequently eaten.

There is but little timber in New Mexico, except in the mountains and along the water-courses; the table-plains and valleys are generally all open prairie. The forest growths, moreover, of all the north of Mexico, present quite a limited variety of timber, among which a species of pitch-pine mostly predominates. The tree which appears to be most peculiar to the country, is a kind of scrub pine called piñon,[19] which grows generally to the height of twenty or thirty feet, with leaves ever-green and pine-like, but scarcely an inch long. From the surface of this tree exudes a species of turpentine resembling that of the pitch-pine, but perhaps less resinous. The wood is white and firm, and much used for fuel. The most remarkable appendage of this tree is the fruit it bears, which is also known by the same name. This is a little nut about the size of a kidney-bean, with a rich oily kernel in a thin shell, enclosed in a chestnut-like bur. It is of pleasant flavor and much eaten by the natives, and consider-

[19] The Spanish term *piñón* is applied to several species of pines in the Rocky Mountains and northwestern Mexico including *pinus edulis, pinus monophylla, pinus Parryana,* and *pinus cembroides.*

able quantities are exported annually to the southern cities. It is sometimes used for the manufacture of a certain kind of oil, said to be very good for lamps.

The *mezquite* tree, vulgarly called *muskeet* in Texas, where it has attained some celebrity, grows in some of the fertile valleys of Chihuahua to the height of thirty and forty feet, with a trunk of one to two feet in diameter. The wood makes excellent fuel, but it is seldom used for other purposes, as it is crooked, knotty, and very coarse and brittle, more resembling the honey-locust (of which it might be considered a scrubby species) than the mahogany, as some people have asserted. The fruit is but a diminutive honey-locust in appearance and flavor, of the size and shape of a flattened bean-pod, with the seeds disposed in like manner. This pod, which, like that of the honey-locust, encloses a glutinous substance, the Apaches and other tribes of Indians grind into flour to make their favorite *pinole*. The mezquite seems undoubtedly of the *Acacia Arabica* species;[20] as some physicians who have examined the gum which exudes from the tree, pronounce it genuine Arabic.

On the water-courses there is little timber to be found except cottonwoods, scantily scattered along their banks. Those of the Rio del Norte are now nearly bare throughout the whole range of the settlements, and the inhabitants are forced to resort to the distant mountains for most of their fuel. But nowhere, even beyond the settlements, are there to be seen such dense cottonwood bottoms as those of the Mississippi valley. Besides the common cottonwood there is another to be found upon the mountain streams of New Mexico, which has been called willow-leaf or bitter cottonwood (*populus angustifolia?*) and has been reckoned by some a species of cinchona, yet for no other reason perhaps than that the bark possesses efficacious tonic qualities. Attached to the seeds of this tree is also a cotton similar to that of the sweet cottonwood, or *populus angulata*.

Among the wild productions of New Mexico is the *palmilla*—a species of palmetto, which might be termed the *soap-plant*—whose roots, as well as those of another species known as *palma* (or palm),

[20] The mesquite, or honey locust (*Prosopis juliflora*), is native to the arid regions extending from northern Chile to southwestern United States. The screw-bean, or screw-pod (*Prosopis pubescens*), is an allied species which furnishes fodder for livestock.

when bruised, form a saponaceous pulp called *amole*, much used by the natives for washing clothes, and is said to be even superior to soap for scouring woollens.[21]

But by far the most important indigenous product of the soil of New Mexico is its pasturage. Most of the high table-plains afford the finest grazing in the world, while, for want of water, they are utterly useless for most other purposes. That scanty moisture which suffices to bring forth the natural vegetation, is insufficient for agricultural productions, without the aid of irrigation. The high prairies of all Northern Mexico differ greatly from those of our border in the general character of their vegetation. They are remarkably destitute of the gay flowering plants for which the former are so celebrated, being mostly clothed with different species of a highly nutritious grass called *grama*,[22] which is of a very short and curly quality. The highlands, upon which alone this sort of grass is produced, being seldom verdant till after the rainy season sets in, the grama is only in perfection from August to October. But being rarely nipped by the frost until the rains are over, it cures upon the ground and remains excellent hay—equal if not superior to that which is cut and stacked from our western prairies. Although the winters are rigorous, the feeding of stock is almost entirely unknown in New Mexico; nevertheless, the extensive herds of the country, not only of cattle and sheep, but of mules and horses, generally maintain themselves in excellent condition upon the dry pasturage alone through the cold season, and until the rains start up the green grass again the following summer.

[21] The *Yucca*, from several species of which *amole* is made, belongs to the lily rather than the palm family, though somewhat resembling the latter in appearance.
[22] *Bouteloua*.

CHAPTER VIII

The Mines of New Mexico—Supposed Concealment of them by the Indians—Indian Superstition and Cozenage—Ruins of *La Gran Quivira*—Old Mines—*Placeres* or Mines of Gold Dust—Speculative Theories as to the original Deposites of the Gold—Mode of Working the *Placeres*—Manners and Customs of the Miners—Arbitrary Restrictions of the Mexican Government upon Foreigners—Persecution of a Gachupin—Disastrous Effects of official Interference upon the Mining Interest—Disregard of American Rights and of the U. States Government—*Gambucinos* and their System—Gold found throughout N. Mexico—Silver Mines—Copper, Zinc, and Lead—Sulphurous Springs—Gypsum, and Petrified Trees.

TRADITION SPEAKS of numerous and productive mines having been in operation in New Mexico before the expulsion of the Spaniards in 1680; but that the Indians, seeing that the cupidity of the conquerors had been the cause of their former cruel oppressions, determined to conceal all the mines by filling them up, and obliterating as much as possible every trace of them. This was done so effectually, as is told, that after the second conquest (the Spaniards in the mean time not having turned their attention to mining pursuits for a series of years), succeeding generations were never able to discover them again. Indeed it is now generally credited by the Spanish population, that the Pueblo Indians, up to the present day, are acquainted with the *locales* of a great number of these wonderful mines, of which they most sedulously preserve the secret. Rumor further asserts that the old men and sages of the Pueblos periodically lecture the youths on this subject, warning them against discovering the mines to the Spaniards, lest the cruelties of the original conquest be renewed towards them, and they be forced to toil and suffer in those mines as in days of yore. To the more effectual preservation of secrecy, it is also stated that they have called in the aid of superstition, by promulgating the belief that the Indian who reveals the location of these hidden treasures, will surely perish by the wrath of their gods.

Playing upon the credulity of the people, it sometimes happens that a roguish Indian will amuse himself at the expense of his reputed superiors in intelligence, by proffering to disclose some of these concealed treasures. I once knew a waggish savage of this kind to propose to show a valley where virgin gold could be 'scraped up by the basket-full.' On a bright Sunday morning, the time appointed for the expedition, the chuckling Indian set out with a train of Mexicans at his heels, provided with mules and horses, and a large quantity of meal-bags to carry in the golden stores; but, as the shades of evening were closing around the party, he discovered—that he couldn't find the place.

It is not at all probable, however, that the aborigines possess a tenth part of the knowledge of these ancient fountains of wealth, that is generally attributed to them; but that many valuable mines *were* once wrought in this province, not only tradition but authenticated records and existing relics sufficiently prove. In every quarter of the territory there are still to be seen vestiges of ancient excavations, and in some places, ruins of considerable towns evidently reared for mining purposes.[1]

Among these ancient ruins the most remarkable are those of *La Gran Quivira*, about 100 miles southward from Santa Fé.[2] This appears to have been a considerable city, larger and richer by far than the present capital of New Mexico has ever been. Many walls, particularly those of churches, still stand erect amid the desolation that surrounds them, as if their sacredness had been a shield against which Time dealt his blows in vain. The style of architecture is

---

[1] Although rarely taken in by rumors and tall tales, Gregg is here perpetuating mere legend. The story of lost mines persists throughout the Southwest and almost every other region which the Spaniards first settled. See above, chap. 6. n. 9.

[2] Recent archaeological research has identified Gregg's "La Gran Quivira" as the ruins of Tabirá, a Piro pueblo where the Spaniards established a mission in 1628, on a desolate mesa 150 miles south of Santa Fé between Torrance and Socorro counties.

altogether superior to anything at present to be found north of Chihuahua—being of hewn stone, a building material wholly unused in New Mexico. What is more extraordinary still, is, that there is no water within less than some ten miles of the ruins; yet we find several stone cisterns, and remains of aqueducts eight or ten miles in length, leading from the neighboring mountains, from whence water was no doubt conveyed. And, as there seem to be no indications whatever of the inhabitants' ever having been engaged in agricultural pursuits, what could have induced the rearing of a city in such an arid, woodless plain as this, except the proximity of some valuable mine, it is difficult to imagine. From the peculiar character of the place and the remains of the cisterns still existing, the object of pursuit in this case would seem to have been a *placer*, a name applied to mines of gold-dust intermixed with the earth. However, other mines have no doubt been worked in the adjacent mountains, as many spacious pits are found, such as are usually dug in pursuit of ores of silver, etc.; and it is stated that in several places heaps of scoria are still to be seen.

By some persons these ruins have been supposed to be the remains of an ancient Pueblo or aboriginal city. That is not probable, however; for though the relics of aboriginal temples might possibly be mistaken for those of Catholic churches, yet it is not to be presumed that the Spanish coat of arms would be found sculptured and painted upon their facades, as is the case in more than one instance. The most rational accounts represent this to have been a wealthy Spanish city before the general massacre of 1680, in which calamity the inhabitants perished—all except one, as the story goes; and that their immense treasures were buried in the ruins. Some credulous adventurers have lately visited the spot in search of these long lost coffers, but as yet none have been found.[3]

The mines of *Cerrillos*,[4] twenty miles southward of Santa Fé,

[3] In the same vicinity there are some other ruins of a similar character, though less extensive; the principal of which are those of Abó, Taguique, and Chililí. The last of these is now being resettled by the Mexicans.—GREGG.

The ruins of Abó, in southeastern Torrance County, are of Piro origin; those of Tajique, 10 miles to the north, and of Chililí, 15 miles north of the latter, in eastern Bernalillo County, were Tigua pueblos.

[4] Cerrillos, in southeastern Santa Fé County, is one of the oldest gold mining sites in the United States. Silver, lead, and zinc are also produced there.

although of undoubted antiquity, have, to all appearance, been worked to some extent within the present century; indeed, they have been reopened within the recollection of the present generation; but the enterprise having been attended with little success, it was again abandoned. Among numerous pits still to be seen at this place, there is one of immense depth cut through solid rock, which it is believed could not have cost less than $100,000. In the mountains of Sandía, Abiquiú, and more particularly in those of Picuris and Embudo, there are also numerous excavations of considerable depth.[5] A few years ago an enterprising American undertook to reopen one of those near Picuris; but after having penetrated to the depth of more than a hundred feet, without reaching the bottom of the original excavation (which had probably been filling up for the last hundred and fifty years), he gave it up for want of means. Other attempts have since been made, but with as little success. Whether these failures have been caused by want of capital and energy, or whether the veins of ore were exhausted by the original miners, remains for future enterprise to determine.

The only successful mines known in New Mexico at the present day, are those of gold, the most important one of which is that originally incorporated as *El Real de Dolores,* but generally known by the significant name of *El Placer.* This mine lies in a low detached spur of mountains, at a distance of twenty-seven miles south of the capital. In 1823, a *Sonoreño* who was in the habit of herding his mules in that vicinity, being one day in pursuit of some that had strayed into the mountains, happened to pick up a stone, which he soon identified as being of the same class that was to be found in the gold regions of Sonora. Upon a little further examination, he detected sundry particles of gold, which did not fail to occasion some degree of excitement in the country. Although the amount procured from these mines, was, for the first two or three years, very insignificant, yet it answered the purpose of testing the quality of the metal, which was found to be of uncommon purity. A market was therefore very soon opened with foreign merchants.

[5] The Sandía Mountains are in southeastern Sandoval and northeastern Bernalillo counties; those around Abiquiú in southeastern Rio Arriba County; those near Picurís in Taos County; and those near Embudo in Rio Arriba County.

The quantity of gold extracted between the years 1832 and '35 could not have amounted to less than from $60,000 to $80,000 per annum. Since this time, however, there has been a considerable falling off, some seasons producing but $30,000 or $40,000. It is believed, notwithstanding, that the entire aggregate yield since the first discovery has exceeded half a million of dollars. The reduction in profit during the last few years has been caused more by want of energy and enterprise, than by exhaustion of the precious metal, as only a very small portion of the 'gold region' has as yet been dug; and experience has shown that the 'dust' is about as likely to be found in one part of it as in another. All the best 'diggings' in the immediate vicinity of the water, however, seem pretty well excavated: in some places the hills and valleys are literally cut up like a honey-comb.

It has been the impression of some persons, that the gold of this region was originally accumulated in some particular deposit, and that it has thus been spread over the surface of the country by some volcanic eruption.

The dust and grains obtained at this mine, are virgin gold, and, as before remarked, of very fine quality, producing at the United States Mint an average of at least $19 70 to the ounce troy after melting, or about $19 30 gross. It was at first bought by the traders at the rate of fifteen dollars per ounce, but in consequence of the competition which was afterwards excited among the dealers, its price was raised for a short time above its maximum at the Mint, although it has since settled down at about $17 30 per ounce troy.

During the process of these excavations, when such a depth has been reached as to render a ladder indispensable, a pole ten or fifteen feet long is cut full of notches for that purpose, and set diagonally in the orifice. In proportion as the pit becomes deeper, others are added, forming a somewhat precarious zigzag staircase, by which the agile miner descends and ascends without even using his hands to assist himself, although with a large load of earth upon his shoulders. It is in this way that most of the rubbish is extracted from these mines, as windlasses or machinery of any kind are rarely used.

The winter season is generally preferred by the miners, for the facilities it affords of supplying the gold-washers with water in the

GOLD WASHING

immediate neighborhood of their operations; for the great scarcity
of water about the mining regions is a very serious obstacle at other
seasons to successful enterprise. Water in winter is obtained by melting a quantity of snow thrown into a sink, with heated stones. Those
employed as washers are very frequently the wives and children of
the miners. A round wooden bowl called *batea*, about eighteen inches
in diameter, is the washing vessel, which they fill with the earth, and
then immerse it in the pool, and stir it with their hands, by which
operation the loose dirt floats off, and the gold settles to the bottom.
In this manner they continue till nothing remains in the bottom of
the *batea* but a little heavy black sand mixed with a few grains of
gold, the value of which (to the trayful) varies from one to twelve
cents, and sometimes, in very rich soils, to twenty-five or more. Some
attempts have been made to wash with machinery, but as yet without
success; partly owing to the scarcity of water, but as much perhaps to
a lack of perseverance, and to the arbitrary restrictions imposed upon
foreigners, who, after all, are the only persons that have ever attempted any improvements of the kind. An instance or two will fully
illustrate the embarrassments and disadvantages to which foreigners
are subject, in embarking capital in mining enterprises in this country.
When the Placer was in its greatest *bonanza*—yielding very large

profits to those engaged in the business—the 'mining fever' rose to such a tremendous pitch among the New Mexicans, particularly the government officers, that every one fancied he saw a door opened for the accumulation of a princely fortune.

About the commencement of this gold mania, a very arbitrary and tyrannical measure was adopted in order to wrest from a persecuted *Gachupin*[6] his interest in a mine, in which he had made a very propitious commencement. This mine, different from the rest of the *Placer*, consisted of a vein of gold in a stratum of rock, which it was necessary to grind and separate with quicksilver; and as it belonged to a native named Ortiz who knew nothing of this operation, the latter formed a partnership with Don Dámaso Lopez, the Gachupin before alluded to, who had some experience and skill in mining operations and the extraction of metals. The partners went vigorously to work, and at the close of the first month found that their net profits amounted to several hundred dollars, consisting in a few balls of gold. At the sight of these, Ortiz was so overjoyed that he must needs exhibit his valuable acquisitions to the governor and other officers and magnates of the capital, who, with characteristic cupidity, at once begrudged the Gachupin his prospective fortune. A compact was thereupon entered into between the *oficiales* and the acquiescent Ortiz, to work the mine on their joint account, and to exclude Lopez altogether. This they effected by reviving the old decree of expulsion (spoken of in another place), which had virtually become obsolete. The unfortunate victim of this outrageous conspiracy was accordingly ordered to the frontier, as the patriotic officers alleged that they "could no longer connive at his residence so near the capital in contravention of the laws."

The new company now commenced operations with additional zeal and earnestness. But they were destined to expiate their ill conduct in a way they had least anticipated. The ores collected during the first month, had been ground and impregnated with quicksilver, and the amalgamation being supposed complete, all the partners in the concern were summoned to witness the splendid results of the new experiments. Yet, after the most diligent examination, not a grain of gold appeared! The fact is, that they were all ignorant of

[6] A term used to designate European Spaniards in America.—GREGG.

mining operations, and knew nothing of the art of separating the metals from the ores. The mine had therefore soon to be abandoned, and Ortiz found himself prostrated by his losses—a victim to the unprincipled rapacity of his new associates.

Lest foreigners generally should share the wealth which was being developed in these mountains, an order was subsequently issued prohibiting all except natives from working at the mines. Some who had commenced operations at the Placer, and incurred considerable expense, were compelled suddenly to break up, with an entire loss of all their labor and outlays.

Acts of political oppression like these have discouraged Americans from making any further attempts, although the decree of prohibition has ceased to be enforced. Could any dependence be placed in the integrity of the government, I have no doubt that, with sufficient capital and the aid of machinery (such as is used in the mines of Georgia and Carolina), the old mines of this province might be reopened, and a great number of the *placeres* very extensively and profitably worked. But as New Mexico is governed at present, there is no security in an enterprise of the kind. The progress of a foreign adventurer is always liable to be arrested by the jealousy of the government, upon the first flattering *bonanza*, as the cited instances abundantly demonstrate. Americans in particular would have little to hope for in the way of redress; for our government has shown itself so tardy in redressing or revenging injuries done its citizens by foreign states, that they would be oppressed, as they have been, with less scruple because with more impunity than the subjects of any other nation.

The gold regions are, for the most part, a kind of common property, and have been wrought chiefly by an indigent class of people, known familiarly as *gambucinos*, a name applied to petty miners who work 'on their own hook.' Among these one very seldom finds any foreigners; for according to the present simple method of working, the profit is too small and too precarious to entice the independent American laborer, who is seldom willing to work for less than a dollar a day, clear of all expenses; while the Mexican *gambucino* is content with two or three *reales*, most of which is required to furnish him food. Therefore these poor miners lead a miserable life after all. When short of means they often support themselves upon only a *real* each per day, their usual food consisting of bread and a kind of coarse cake-sugar called *piloncillo*, to which is sometimes added a little crude ranchero cheese; yet they seem perfectly satisfied.

To prevent collisions among such heterogeneous multitudes as are to be found at the mining places, some municipal provisions have been established, in pursuance of which any person may open a *labor* or pit on unoccupied ground not nearer than ten paces to another, and is entitled to the same extent in every direction, not interfering with prior claims— his *labor* being confirmed for a small fee by application to the alcalde. But if the proprietor abandon his *labor* for a certain time, any one that chooses may take possession.

Besides the Placer of which I have already spoken, others have lately been discovered in the same ledge of mountains towards the south, one of which is now extensively worked, being already filled with retail shops of every description, where all the gold that is extracted, is either sold or bartered. The *gambucinos* being generally destitute of all other resources, are often obliged to dispose of their gold daily—and very frequently in driblets of but a few cents value. *Placers* of gold have also been discovered in the mountains of Abiquiú, Taos and elsewhere, which have been worked to some extent. In truth, as some of the natives have justly remarked, New Mexico is almost one continuous *placer;* traces of gold being discoverable over nearly the whole surface of the country. The opinion formerly entertained that gold is only to be found in southern climates, seems fully confuted here; for at a point called Sangre de Cristo, considerably north of Taos, (above the 37th degree of latitude), and which from its location among the snowy mountains of that region, is ice-bound over half the year, a very rich *placer* has been discovered; yet owing to the peculiarly exposed situation in which it lies, it has been very little worked.[7]

For the last century no *silver* mines have been in successful operation in New Mexico. A few years ago there was discovered

[7] Several mines are now operated in this region. The Sangre de Cristo range extends from Taos and Colfax counties northward into Colorado.

near the village of Manzano, in the mountains of Tomé,[8] a vein of silver which bid fair to prove profitable; but when the ore came to be tested, the rock was found to be so hard that the pursuit has been entirely abandoned.

In addition to gold and silver, there are also to be found, in many isolated spots, ores of copper, zinc, and lead; although the latter is so mixed up with copper and other hard metals, as to be almost unfit for ordinary purposes. The copper obtained in the province has frequently been found to contain a slight mixture of the precious metals, well worth extracting. Iron is also abundant.

Besides the mines of metals which have been discovered, or yet remain concealed in the mountains of New Mexico, those of *Salt* (or *salt lakes*, as they would perhaps be called), the *Salinas*, are of no inconsiderable importance. Near a hundred miles southward from the capital, on the high table-land between the Rio del Norte and Pecos, there are some extensive salt ponds, which afford an inexhaustible supply of this indispensable commodity, not only for the consumption of this province, but for portions of the adjoining departments. The largest of these *Salinas* is five or six miles in circumference. The best time to collect the salt is during the dry season, when the lakes contain but little water; but even when flooded, salt may be scooped up from the bottom, where it is deposited in immense beds, in many places of unknown depth; and, when dried, much resembles the common alum salt. The best, however, which is of superior quality, rises as a scum upon the water. A great many years ago, a firm causeway was thrown up through the middle of the principal lake, upon which the *carretas* and mules are driven, and loaded with salt still dripping with water. The *Salinas* are public property, and the people resort to them several times a year,—in caravans, for protection against the savages of the desest in which they are situated. Although this salt costs nothing but the labor of carrying it away, the danger from the Indians and the privations experienced in an expedition to the *Salinas* are such, that it is seldom sold in the capital for less than a dollar per bushel. On the same great plain still a hundred miles further south, there is another *Salina* of the same character.[9]

[8] The Manzano Mountains, in western Torrance County.

While I am on this subject, I cannot forbear a brief notice of the mineral springs of New Mexico. There are several warm springs (*ojos calientes*), whose waters are generally sulphurous, and considered as highly efficacious in the cure of rheumatisms and other chronic diseases. Some are bold springs, and of a very agreeable temperature for bathing; but there is one in the west of the province, which does not flow very freely, but merely escapes through the crevices of the rocks, yet it is hot enough to cook any article of food. It is a curious phenomenon, that, within a few paces of it, as in the case of the hot springs of Arkansas, there is another spring perfectly cold.

New Mexico affords many interesting geological productions, of which the most useful to the natives is *yeso* or gypsum, which abounds in many places. Being found in foliated blocks, composed of laminae, which are easily separated with a knife into sheets from the thickness of paper to that of window-glass, and almost as transparent as the latter, it is used to a great extent in the ranchos and villages for window-lights, for which indeed it is a tolerable substitute.

In several places about the borders of the *mesas* are to be found some beautiful specimens of petrified trees. One lies between Santa Fé and the Placer, broken into blocks since its petrifaction, which shows every knot, crack and splinter almost as natural as in its ligneous state. It is said that there are some of these arboreous petrifactions in the vicinity of Galisteo, still standing erect.

[9] The northern salt beds are east of the Manzano Mountains in Torrance County; the southern ones east of the San Andres Mountains in southeastern Socorro County.

CHAPTER IX

Domestic Animals and their Condition—Indifference on the subject of Horsebreeding—*Caballos de Silla*—Popularity and Usefulness of the Mule—Mode of harnessing and lading Mules for a Journey—*Arrieros* and their System—The *Mulera* or Bell-mare—Surprising feats of the Muleteers and *Vaqueros*—The *Lazo* and its uses—Ridiculous Usages of the country in regard to the Ownership of Animals—Anecdote of a Mexican Colonel—The *Burro* or domestic ass and its Virtues—Shepherds and their Habits—The Itinerant Herds of the Plains—Sagacity of the Shepherds' Dogs—The Sheep Trade—Destruction of Cattle by the Indians—Philosophical notions of the Marauders—Excellent Mutton—Goats and their Utility—Wild Animals and their Character—A 'Bear Scrape'—Wolves, Panthers, Wild Birds and Reptiles—The Honey-bee, etc.

NOTHING that has come within my sphere of observation in New Mexico, has astonished me more than the little attention that is paid to the improvement of domestic animals. While other nations have absolutely gone mad in their endeavors to better their breeds of horses, and have ransacked the four quarters of the world for the best blood and purest pedigrees, the New Mexicans, so justly celebrated for skilful horsemanship, and so much devoted to equestrian exercise, that they have been styled a race of centaurs, leave the propagation of their horses exclusively to chance; converting their best and handsomest steeds into saddle-horses.

Their race of *horses* is identical with that which is found running wild on the Prairies, familiarly known by the name of *mustang*. Although generally very small, they are quick, active and spirited: and were they not commonly so much injured in the breaking, they would perhaps be as hardy and long-lived as any other race in existence. Some of their *caballos de silla*, or saddle-horses are so remarkably well trained, that they will stop suddenly upon the slightest check, charge against a wall without shrinking, and even attempt to clamber up its sides. In addition to this, a complete riding horse should have a peculiar up-and-down gait, affording all the exercise of the most violent trotter, while he gets over the ground so slowly as to enable the *caballero* to enjoy the 'pleasures' of a fatiguing ride of hours, without losing sight of his mistress's balcony.

The little attention paid to the breeding of horses in New Mexico, may perhaps be accounted for from the fact that, until lately, when the continued depredations of the hostile Indians discouraged them from their favorite pursuit, the people of the country had bestowed all their care in the raising of *mules*. This animal is in fact to the Mexican, what the camel has always been to the Arab—invaluable for the transportation of freight over sandy deserts and mountainous roads, where no other means of conveyance could be used to such advantage. These mules will travel for hundreds of miles with a load of the most bulky and unwieldy articles, weighing frequently three or four hundred pounds.

The *Aparejo* (or pack-saddle, if it can be so styled), is a large pad, consisting of a leathern case stuffed with hay, which covers the back of the mule and extends half way down on both sides. This is secured with a wide sea-grass bandage, with which the poor brute is so tightly laced as to reduce the middle of its body to half its natural size. During the operation of lacing, the corseted quadruped stands trembling in perfect agony, not an inapt emblem of some fashionable exquisites who are to be met with lounging on tip-toe, in all the principal thoroughfares of large cities.

The muleteers contend that a tightly laced beast, will travel, or at least support burdens, with greater ease; and though they carry this to an extreme, still we can hardly doubt that a reasonable tension supports and braces the muscles. It is necessary too for the *aparejo* to be firmly bound on to prevent its slipping and chafing the mule's back; indeed, with all these precautions, the back, withers and sides of the poor brute are often horribly mangled—so much so that I have seen the rib-bones bare, from day to day, while carrying a usual load of three hundred pounds! The *aparejo* is also furnished with a huge crupper, which often lacerates the tail most shockingly.

It is this packing that leaves most of the lasting cicatrices and marks so common upon Mexican mules.

The *carga*, if a single package, is laid across the mule's back, but when composed of two, they are placed lengthwise, side by side; and being coupled with a cord, they are bound upon the aparejo with a long rope of sea-grass or raw-hide, which is so skilfully and tensely twined about the packages as effectually to secure them upon the animal. The mule is at first so tightly bound that it seems scarcely able to move; but the weight of the pack soon settles the aparejo, and so loosens the girths and cords as frequently to render it necessary to tighten them again soon after getting under way. It keeps most of the muleteers actively employed during the day, to maintain the packs in condition; for they often lose their balance and sometimes fall off. This is done without detaining the *atajo* (drove of pack-mules), the rest of which travel on while one is stopped to adjust its disordered pack. Indeed it is apt to occasion much trouble to stop a heavily laden *atajo;* for, if allowed a moment's rest, the mules are inclined to lie down, when it is with much difficulty they can rise again with their loads. In their efforts to do so they sometimes so strain their loins as to injure them ever after. The day's travel is made without a nooning respite; for the consequent unloading and reloading would consume too much time: and as a heavily-packed atajo should rarely continue *en route* more than five or six hours, the *jornada de recua* (day's journey of a pack-drove) is usually but twelve or fifteen miles.

It is truly remarkable to observe with what dexterity and skill the *Arrieros,* or muleteers, harness and adjust the packs of merchandise upon their beasts. Half a dozen usually suffice for forty or fifty mules. Two men are always engaged at a time in the dispatch of each animal, and rarely occupy five minutes in the complet adjustment of his *aparejo* and *carga*. In this operation they frequently demonstrate a wonderful degree of skill in the application of their strength. A single man will often seize a package, which, on a 'dead lift,' he could hardly have raised from the ground, and making a fulcrum of his knees and a lever of his arms and body, throw it upon the mule's back with as much apparent ease as if the effort cost him but little exertion. At stopping-places the task of unpacking is executed with still greater expedition. The packages are piled in a row upon the ground, and in case of rain the aparejos are laid upon them, over which is stretched a covering of *mantas de guangoche* (sheets of sea-grass texture), which protects the goods against the severest storms; a ditch also being cut around the pile, to prevent the water from running underneath. In this way freights are carried from point to point, and over the most rugged mountain passes at a much cheaper rate than foreigners can transport their merchandise in wagons, even through a level country. The cheapness of this mode of transportation arises from the very low wages paid to the *arrieros*, and the little expense incurred to feed both them and the mules. The salary of the muleteer ranges from two to five dollars per month; and as their food seldom consists of anything else except corn and *frijoles*, it can be procured at very little cost. When the arrieros get any meat at all, it is generally at their own expense.

An *atajo* is conducted in a very systematic manner, each *arriero* having his appropriate sphere of action allotted to him. They have also their regulations and technicalities, which, if not as numerous, are about as unintelligible to the uninitiated as sailors' terms. One person, called the *savanero*, has the charge of the mules at night, which are all turned loose without tether or hopple, with the *mulera* or bell-mare, to prevent them from straying abroad. Although the attachment of the mules to the mulera appears very great, it seems to be about as much for the bell as for the animal. What the queen-bee is to a hive, so is the *mulera* to an *atajo*. No matter what may be the temper of a mule, it can seldom be driven away from her; and if she happen to be taken from among her associates, the latter immediately become depressed and melancholy, and ramble and whinny in every direction, as if they were completely lost. In addition to preparing food for the party, it is the office of the *madre* (or mother, as the cook of the company is facetiously called) to lead the mulera ahead, during the journey, after which the whole pack follows in orderly procession.[1]

[1] Similar descriptions of the pack-train appear in Kendall, *The Texan Santa Fé Expedition*, II, 169–72, and George Frederick Augustus Ruxton, *Life in the Far West*, 170–72, 180–82. The Mexican techniques for loading, the nomenclature of the apparatus, and the mule itself were adopted by the United States Army. H. W. Daly, *Manual of Pack Transportation*, 16, *et passim.*

MEXICAN ARRIEROS WITH AN ATAJO OF PACK-MULES

The muleteers, as well as the *vaqueros* (cow-herds), are generally mounted upon swift and well-trained horses, and in their management of the animals will often perform many surprising feats, which would grace an equestrian circus in any country; such, for instance, as picking up a dollar from the ground at every pass with the horse at full gallop. But the greatest display of skill and agility consists in their dextrous use of the *lazo* or *lareat*,[2] which is usually made of horse-hair, or sea-grass tightly twisted together, with a convenient noose at one end. Their aim is always more sure when the animal to be caught is running at full speed, for then it has no time to dodge the *lareat*. As soon as the noose is cast, the *lazador* fetches the end of his *lazo* a turn around the high pommel of his saddle, and by a quick manoeuvre the wildest horse is brought up to a stand or topsy-turvy at his pleasure. By this process, the head of the animal is turned towards his subduer, who, in order to obtain the mastery over him more completely, seldom fails to throw a *bozal* (or half-hitch, as boatmen would say) around the nose, though at full rope's length.

If the object of pursuit happens to be a cow or an ox, the *lazo* is usually thrown about the horns instead of the neck. Two *vaqueros*, each with his rope to the horns, will thus subject the wildest and most savage bull, provided they are mounted upon well-trained steeds. While the infuriated animal makes a lunge at one of his pursuers, the other wheels round and pulls upon his rope, which always brings the beast about in the midst of his career; so that between the two he is jerked to and fro till he becomes exhausted and ceases to make any further resistance. The use of the lazo is not confined to the *arrieros* and *vaqueros*, although these generally acquire most skill in that exercise: it prevails in every rank of life; and no man, especially among the rancheros, would consider his education complete until he had learned this national accomplishment. They acquire it in fact from infancy; for it forms one of the principal rural sports of children, who may daily be seen with their *lazitos*, noosing the dogs and chickens about the yards, in every direction.

[2] *Lasso* and *lariat*, as most usually written, are evidently corruptions of the Spanish *lazo* and *la reata* (the latter with the article *la* compounded), both meaning kinds of rope. I have therefore preferred retaining the orthography indicated by their etymology.—GREGG.

The lazo is often employed also as a 'weapon' both offensive and defensive. In skirmishes with the Indians, the mounted *vaquero*, if haplessly without arms, will throw this formidable object round the neck or the body of his enemy, who, before he has time to disencumber himself, is jerked to the ground and dragged away at full speed; when, if his brains are not beaten out against the stones, roots, or trees, he becomes at least so stunned and disabled that the *lazador* can dispatch him at his leisure. The panther, the bear, and other ferocious animals of the mountains and prairies, are also successfully attacked in this manner.

The laws and customs of the country with regard to the ownership of animals are very annoying to the inexperienced foreign traveler. No matter how many proprietors a horse or mule may have had, every one marks him with a huge hieroglyphic brand, which is called the *fierro*, and again, upon selling him, with his *venta*, or sale-brand; until at last these scars become so multiplied as to render it impossible for persons not versed in this species of 'heraldry,' to determine whether the animal has been properly *vented* or not: yet any *fierro* without its corresponding *venta* lays the beast liable to the claim of the brander. Foreigners are the most frequently subjected to this kind of imposition; and when a party of *estrangeros* enters any of the southern towns, they are immediately surrounded by a troop of loungers, who carefully examine every horse and mule; when, should they by chance discover any *unvented* brand, they immediately set to work to find some one with a branding-iron of the same shape, by which the beast is at once claimed and taken; for in all legal processes the only proof required of the claimant is his *fierro*, or branding-iron, which, if found to assimilate in shape with the mark on the animal, decides the suit in his favor.[3] A colonel in Chihuahua once claimed a mule of me in this manner, but as I was convinced that I had bought it of the legitimate owner, I refused to

[3] This occasioned a major legal hazard for American traders. As the Apaches were generally at war with Chihuahua and at peace with New Mexico, it was their custom to steal horses and mules from the inhabitants of the former and sell them to those of the latter. Thus, Americans passing through New Mexico unknowingly purchased stolen animals and were duly relieved of them on entering Chihuahua at El Paso del Norte. For the experience of James Josiah Webb in this respect, see Ralph P. Bieber (ed.), *Adventures in the Santa Fe Trade, 1844–1847*, 191–93.

give it up. The officer, unwilling to lose his prize, started immediately for the alcalde, in hopes of inducing that functionary to lend him the aid of the law; but during his absence I caused the shoulder of the animal to be shorn, so that the *venta* became distinctly visible. As soon as the discovery was made known to the colonel and his judge, they made a precipitate exit, as though conscious of detected fraud.

But while I fully acknowledge the pretensions of the mule, as an animal of general usefulness, I must not forget paying a passing tribute to that meek and unostentatious member of the brute family, the 'patient ass;' or, as it is familiarly called by the natives, *el burro*. This docile creature is here emphatically the 'poor man's friend,' being turned to an infinite variety of uses, and always submissive under the heaviest burdens. He is not only made to carry his master's grain, his fuel, his water, and his luggage, but his wife and his children. Frequently the whole family is stowed away together upon one diminutive donkey. In fact, the chief riding animal of the peasant is the *burro*, upon which saddle, bridle, or halter, is seldom used. The rider, seated astride his haunches instead of his back, guides the docile beast with a bludgeon which he carries in his hand.

Nothing, perhaps, has been more systematically attended to in New Mexico than the raising of *sheep*. When the territory was at the zenith of its prosperity, *ranchos* were to be met with upon the borders of every stream, and in the vicinity of every mountain where water was to be had. Even upon the arid and desert plains, and many miles away from brook or pond, immense flocks were driven out to pasture, and only taken to water once in two or three days. On these occasions it is customary for the shepherds to load their burros with *guages* filled with water, and return again with their folds to the plains. The *guage* is a kind of gourd, of which there are some beautiful specimens with two bulbs; the intervening neck serving to retain the cord by which it is carried.

These itinerant herds of sheep generally pass the night wherever the evening finds them, without cot or enclosure. Before nightfall the principal shepherd sallies forth in search of a suitable site for his *hato*, or temporary sheep-fold; and building a fire on the most convenient spot, the sheep generally draw near it of their own accord.

Should they incline to scatter, the shepherd then seizes a torch and performs a circuit or two around the entire fold, by which manoeuvre, in their efforts to avoid him, the heads of the sheep are all turned inwards; and in that condition they generally remain till morning, without once attempting to stray. It is unnecessary to add that the flock is well guarded during the night by watchful and sagacious dogs against prowling wolves or other animals of prey. The well-trained shepherd's dog of this country is indeed a prodigy: two or three of them will follow a flock of sheep for a distance of several miles as orderly as a shepherd, and drive them back to the pen again at night, without any other guidance than their own extraordinary instincts.

In former times there were extensive proprietors who had their *ranchos* scattered over half the province, in some cases amounting to from three to five hundred thousand head of sheep. The custom has usually been to farm out the ewes to the rancheros, who make a return of twenty per cent. upon the stock in merchantable *carneros* —a term applied to sheep generally, and particularly to wethers fit for market.

Sheep may be reckoned the staple production of New Mexico, and the principal article of exportation. Between ten and twenty years ago, about 200,000 head were annually driven to the southern markets; indeed, it is asserted, that, during the most flourishing times, as many as 500,000 were exported in one year. This trade has constituted a profitable business to some of the *ricos* of the country. They would buy sheep of the poor rancheros at from fifty to seventy-five cents per head, and sell them at from one to two hundred per cent. advance in the southern markets. A large quantity of wool is of course produced, but of an inferior quality. Inconsiderable amounts have been introduced into the United States via Missouri, which have sometimes been sold as low as fifteen cents per pound.[4] It is bought, however, at the New Mexican ranchos at a very low rate—three or four cents per pound, or (as more generally sold) per fleece, which will average, perhaps but little over a pound. Yet, from

[4] Gregg and Sutton imported a cargo of New Mexican wool valued at $3,000 in the fall of 1834. Ralph P. Bieber (ed.), "Letters of James and Robert Aull," in *Missouri Historical Society Collection*, Vol. V, 286-87.

the superiority of the pasturage and climate, New Mexico might doubtless grow the finest wool in the world. In conformity with their characteristic tardiness in improvement, however, the natives have retained their original stocks, which are wretchedly degenerate. They formerly sheared their flocks chiefly for their health, and rarely preserved the fleece, as their domestic manufactures consumed but a comparatively small quality.

But the *ganado menor*, or small beasts of pasture (that is, sheep and goats in general), have of late been very much reduced in quantity: having suffered to a deplorable extent from the frequent inroads of the aboriginal 'lords of the soil,' who, every now and then, whenever hunger or caprice prompts them, attack the ranchos, murder the shepherds, and drive the sheep away in flocks of thousands. Indeed, the Indians have been heard to observe, that they would long before this have destroyed every sheep in the country, but that they prefer leaving a few behind for breeding purposes, in order that their Mexican shepherds may raise them new supplies!

The sheep of New Mexico are exceedingly small, with very coarse wool, and scarcely fit for anything else than mutton, for which, indeed, they are justly celebrated. Their flesh has a peculiarly delicious flavor, and is reckoned by epicures to be far superior to our best venison; owing probably in part to the excellence of the grass upon which they feed. The flesh of the sheep is to the New Mexican what that of the hog is to the people of our Western States,—while pork is but seldom met with in Northern Mexico. The sheep there are also remarkable for horny appendages, which frequently branch out in double or triple pairs, giving the head a very whimsical and grotesque appearance. I have seen some of them with at least six separate horns, each pointing in a different direction.

Although the raising of *goats* has not been made so much of a business as the raising of sheep, the former are nevertheless to be found in great abundance. Their milk is much more generally used than that of the cow, not only because it is sweeter and richer, but because the goat, like the *burro*, sustains itself upon the mere rubbish that grows in the mountain passes, and on the most barren hills, where cows could not exist without being regularly fed. The flesh of the goat is coarse, but wholesome, and being cheaper than mutton or beef, it is very freely used by the poor. That of the kid is hardly surpassed for delicacy and sweetness.

With regard to domestic *fowls*, it may be worthy of remark, that there is not to be found, as I believe, in all New Mexico, a single species (saving half a dozen turkeys perhaps, and a few pigeons), except the common hen, of which, however, there is a sufficient abundance. The goose, the duck, the peacock, etc., are altogether unknown.

Of wild animals there is not so great a variety as in the southern districts of the republic, where they are found in such abundance. The *black* and *grizzly* bear, which are met with in the mountains, do not appear to possess the great degree of ferocity, however, for which the latter especially is so much famed further north. It is true they sometimes descend from the mountains into the corn-fields, and wonderful stories are told of dreadful combats between them and the *labradores;* but judging from a little adventure I once witnessed, with an old female of the grizzly species, encountered by a party of us along the borders of the great prairies, I am not disposed to consider either their ferocity or their boldness very terrible.

Our company had just halted at noon, to take refreshments, when we perceived a group of these interesting animals,—a dam with a few cubs fully as large as common wolves,—busily scratching among the high grass in an adjacent valley, as if in search of roots or insects. Some of our party immediately started after the brutes, in hopes of getting a shot at them, in which, however, they were disappointed. One or two 'runners,' who had followed on horseback, then made a desperate charge upon the enemy, but the old monster fled to the thickets, without even so much as turning once upon her pursuers, although one of her cubs was killed, and the remainder were scattered in different directions, during the general scamper.

The sequel of the adventure served to confirm me in the opinion I had of the exaggerated stories in regard to these much dreaded animals. We had in our company a giant blacksmith and general repairer of wagons, named Campbell, who measured full six feet eight in his stockings,[5] and was besides, elegantly proportioned. In-

5 Probably Andrew Campbell, described in his safe-conduct pass for 1845 as 33 years old and 6 ft. 3 in. tall. MS in the National Archives at Washington, Miscel-

dependent of his universal utility as 'Jack-of-all-trades,' our colossal friend was in such constant requisition, that he might well have given origin to the western phrase of one's being 'a whole team;' for if a wagon happened to be in the mire, he was worth more than the whole team to extract it. He was, in short, the most appropriate subject for a regular grizzly-bear scrape. On the occasion I speak of, Campbell had laid himself down under the shade of a bush, upon the brink of a precipice about ten feet high, and was taking a comfortable snooze, while his companions were sporting in the neighborhood. During the chase, one of the young bears, which had been scared from its mother, was perceived loping down the trail towards our camp, apparently heedless of the company. Several of us seized our guns, and as it sprang across the ravine through a break near the spot where Campbell lay, we gave it a salute, which caused it to tumble back wounded into the branch, with a frightful yell. Campbell being suddenly roused by the noise, started up with the rapidity of lightning, and tumbled over the precipice upon the bear. "Whauh!" growled master bruin—"Murder!" screamed the giant—"Clinch it, Campbell, or you're gone!" exclaimed his comrades; for no one could venture to shoot for fear of killing the man. The latter, however, had no notion of closing clutches with his long-clawed antagonist, but busied himself in vain attempts to clamber up the steep bank; while the bear rising upon his hinder legs, and staring a moment at the huge frame of the blacksmith, soon made up his mind as to the expediency of 'turning tail,' and finally succeeded in making his escape, notwithstanding a volley of shot that were fired after him.

The large *gray wolf* of the Prairies is also to be found in great abundance in Northern Mexico. They sometimes make dreadful havoc among the cattle, frequently killing and devouring even mules and horses; but they never extend their rapacity as far as to attack human beings, unless urged by starvation. There are other animals of prey about the mountains, among which the panther is most conspicuous.

Elk and deer are also to be met with, but not in large quantities.

laneous Record Books of the American Consulate-General at Mexico City, Vol. III, 123.

Of the latter, the species known as the *black-tailed* deer is the most remarkable. It differs but little from the common buck, except that it is of darker color and its tail is bordered with black, and that, though its legs are shorter, its body is larger. The *carnero cimarron* or bighorn of the Rocky Mountains—the *berrendo* or antelope and the *tuza* or prairie dog of the plains—hares, polecats, and other animals of lesser importance, may also be considered as denizens of these regions.

Of wild *birds*, the water fowls are the most numerous; the ponds and rivers being literally lined at certain seasons of the year with myriads of geese, ducks, cranes, etc. In some of the mountains, wild turkeys are very numerous; but partridges and quails are scarce. There is to be found in Chihuahua and other southern districts a very beautiful bird called *paisano* (literally 'countryman'),[6] which when domesticated, performs all the offices of a cat in ridding the dwelling-houses of mice and other vermin. It is also said to kill and devour the rattlesnake; a reptile, however, which seems much less vicious here than elsewhere. Scorpions, tarantulas and centipedes also, although found in this province, are almost harmless, and very little dreaded by the natives. Another indigenous reptile is the horned-frog of the Prairies, known here by the name of *camaleon* (or chameleon), of which it is probably a species, as its color has been observed to vary a little in accordance with the character of the soil it inhabits.

The *honey-bee* would appear to have originated exclusively from the east, as its march has been observed westward, but none have yet reached this portion of the Mexican dominion. According to ancient historians, different species were indigenous to the south of the republic; but in the north, the only insect of the kind more resembles the bumble-bee than that of our hives; and builds in rocks and holes in the ground, in some parts of the mountains. They unite in but small numbers (some dozens together), and seldom make over a few ounces of honey, which is said, however, to be of agreeable flavor.

As to *flies*, like the high plains, this dry climate is but little infested—particularly with the more noxious kinds. Fresh meats are

[6] The chaparral cock, or road-runner (*Geococcyx californianus*).

preserved and dried in mid-summer without difficulty, as there are very few blow-flies. Horse-flies are not seen except sometimes in the mountains: the prairie-fly, so tormenting to stock with us in the West, is unknown.

CHAPTER X

Condition of the Arts and Sciences in New Mexico—Neglect of Education—Primary Schools—Geographical Ignorance—Female Accomplishments—Imported Refinements—Peculiarities of Language, etc.—Condition of the Public Press—State of Medical Science—The Mechanical Arts—Carpentry and Cabinet Work—State of Architecture—Dwelling Houses and their Peculiarities—Rustic Furniture—Curiously constructed Vehicles—Manufacture of Blankets—Other Fabrics—Want of Machinery.

THERE IS NO PART of the civilized globe, perhaps, where the Arts have been so much neglected, and the progress of Science so successfully impeded as in New Mexico. Reading and writing may fairly be set down as the highest branches of education that are taught in the schools; for those pedants who occasionally pretend to teach arithmetic, very seldom understand even the primary rules of the science of numbers. I should perhaps make an exception in favor of those ecclesiastics, who have acquired their education abroad; and who, from their vocation, are necessarily obliged to possess a smattering of Latin. Yet it is a well known fact that the majority of this privileged class, even, are lamentably deficient in the more important branches of familiar science. I have been assured by a highly respectable foreigner, who has long resided in the country, that the questions were once deliberately put to him by a curate—whether Napoleon and Washington were not *one* and the *same* person, and whether Europe was not a province of Spain!

From the earliest time down to the secession of the colonies, it was always the policy of the Spanish Government as well as of the papal hierarchy, to keep every avenue of knowledge closed against their subjects of the New World;[1] lest the lights of civil and religious liberty should reach them from their neighbors of the North. Although a system of public schools was afterwards adopted by the republic, which, if persevered in, would no doubt have contributed to the dissemination of useful knowledge, yet its operations had to be suspended about ten years ago, for want of the necessary funds to carry out the original project. It is doubtful, however, whether the habitual neglect and utter carelessness of the people, already too much inured to grope their way in darkness and in ignorance, added to the inefficiency of the teachers, would not eventually have neutralized all the good that such an institution was calculated to effect. The only schools now in existence, are of the lowest primary class, supported entirely by individual patronage, the liberal extension of which, may be inferred from the fact, that at least three-fourths of the present population can neither read nor write. To illustrate the utter absence of geographical information among the humbler classes, it is only necessary to mention that I have been asked by persons, who have enjoyed a long intercourse with Americans, whether the United States was as large a place as the town of Santa Fé!

Female education has, if possible, been more universally neglected than that of the other sex; while those who have received any instruction at all, have generally been taught in private families. Indeed, until very lately, to be able to read and write on the part of a woman, was considered an indication of very extraordinary talent; and the fair damsel who could pen a billet-doux to her lover, was looked upon as almost a prodigy. There is, however, to be found among the higher classes a considerable sprinkling of that superficial refinement which is the bane of fashionable society everywhere, and which consists, not in superiority of understanding, not in acquired knowledge, but in that peculiar species of assumption, which has happily been styled "the flowing garment with which Ignorance decks herself."

[1] Gregg is mistaken. There were more than twenty universities in the Spanish colonies, and although certain categories of books were banned, large amounts of this literature actually passed port inspection, while education of the Indians far surpassed that of Anglo-America. In New Mexico, however, there were no such attainments. Clarence H. Haring, *The Spanish Empire in America*, 230; Irving A. Leonard, *Books of the Brave*, 166–82.

Yet, notwithstanding this dreadful state of ignorance on all those subjects which it behooves man to be acquainted with, it is truly astonishing to notice the correctness with which the common people speak their mother tongue, the Spanish. The application of words out of their classical sense may occasionally occur, but a violation of the simple grammatical rules (which is so common among the illiterate who use the English language), is extremely rare. In pronunciation, the only material difference between them and the Castilian race, consists in the adoption of certain provincialisms, which can hardly be ranked as defects. Thus, instead of giving *c* before *e* and *i*, and *z* in all cases, the Castilian lisp of *th* as in *thin*, they sound both like *s* in *sin;* and instead of pronouncing *ll* as the Italian liquid *gl* in *seraglio*, they sound this double letter precisely like *y* in *yes;* and in writing, frequently confound the *ll* and *y* indiscriminately together. These may be considered as their only peculiarities of pronunciation, and they prevail through most sections of the republic. In fact, this point of difference is looked upon by many with national pride, as distinguishing their language from that of their former oppressors. They have also adopted many significant Indian words from their aboriginal predecessors and neighbors, which serve to embellish and amplify this already beautiful and copious language.

In nothing is the deplorable state of things already noticed made more clearly manifest, than in the absence of a public press. There has never been a single newspaper or periodical of any kind published in New Mexico, except in the year 1834, when a little foolscap sheet (entitled *El Crepúsculo*) was issued weekly, for about a month, to the tune of fifty subscribers, and was then abandoned, partially for want of patronage and partially because the editor had accomplished his object of procuring his election to Congress. Indeed, the only printing press in the country is a small affair which was brought the same year across the prairies from the United States,[2] and is now employed occasionally in printing billets, primers and Catholic catechisms. This literary negligence is to be attributed, not more to the limited number of reading people, than to those injudicious

[2] This press was brought to New Mexico by Gregg and his partner. *Manifiesto de José Sutton y Josias Gregg, Santa Fé, 29 de Julio de 1834*, MS in Archivo Histórico de Hacienda (Mexico City), Legajo 176-3.

restrictions upon that freedom of the press, which is so essential to its prosperity. An editor attempting to arraign the conduct of public functionaries, or to oppose 'the powers that be' is sure to subject himself to persecution, and most probably suspension, a tyrannical course of proceeding which has checked the career of two or three papers even among the more enlightened inhabitants of Chihuahua; where a miserable organ of the Government is still occasionally issued from the office of the *Imprenta del Gobierno*, or Government Press. No wonder then that the people of Northern Mexico are so much behind their neighbors of the United States in intelligence, and that the pulse of national industry and liberty beats so low!

Medical science is laboring under similar disadvantages; there being not a single native physician in the province[3]; although a great multitude of singular cures are daily performed with indigenous roots and herbs that grow in abundance all over the country. But lest a knowledge of this scarcity of doctors should induce some of the Esculapian faculty to strike for Santa Fé in quest of fortune, I would remark that the country affords very poor patronage. Foreign physicians who have visited New Mexico, have found the practice quite unprofitable; not more for the want of patients, than on account of the poverty of the people. Nine-tenths of those who are most subject to disease, are generally so destitute of means, that the only return they can make, is *"Dios se lo pague"* (May God pay you!) Even the more affluent classes do not hesitate sometimes to liquidate their bills in the same currency. A French doctor of Santa Fé, who had been favored with too many payments of this description, was wont to rebuke their *"Dios se lo pague"* with a *"No señor, su bolsa me lo pagará"*—No, sir, your purse shall pay me!

The mechanical arts have scarcely risen above the condition they were found in among the aborigines. Gold and silversmiths are perhaps better skilled in their respective trades than any other class of artisans whatever; as the abundance of precious metals in former days, and the ruling passion of the people for ostentatious show, gave a very early stimulus to the exercise of this peculiar talent. Some mechanics of this class have produced such singular specimens of in-

---

[3] Neither is there a professed lawyer in New Mexico: a fact which at least speaks favorably of the state of litigation in the country.—GREGG.

genious workmanship, that on examining them, we are almost unwilling to believe that rude art could accomplish so much. Even a bridle-bit or a pair of spurs it would no doubt puzzle the 'cutest' Yankee to fashion after a Mexican model—such as I have seen manufactured by the commonest blacksmiths of the country.

In carpentry and cabinet-work the mechanic has to labor to great disadvantage, on account of a want of tools and scarcity of suitable timber. Their boards have to be hewed out with the axe—sawed lumber being absolutely unknown throughout New Mexico, except what is occasionally cut by foreigners. The axe commonly used for splitting and hewing is formed after the model of those clumsy hatchets known as 'squaw-axes' among Indian traders. Yet this is not unfrequently the only tool of the worker in wood: a cart or a plough is often manufactured without even an auger, a chisel, or a drawing-knife.

In architecture, the people do not seem to have arrived at any great perfection, but rather to have conformed themselves to the clumsy style which prevailed among the aborigines, than to waste their time in studying modern masonry and the use of lime. The materials generally used for building are of the crudest possible description; consisting of unburnt bricks, about eighteen inches long by nine wide and four thick, laid in mortar of mere clay and sand. These bricks are called *adobes*, and every edifice, from the church to the palacio, is constructed of the same stuff. In fact, I should remark, perhaps, that though all Southern Mexico is celebrated for the magnificence and wealth of its churches, New Mexico deserves equal fame for poverty-stricken and shabby-looking houses of public worship.

The general plan of the Mexican dwellings is nearly the same everywhere. Whether from motives of pride, or fear of the savages, the wealthier classes have adopted the style of Moorish castles; so that all the larger buildings have more the appearance of so many diminutive fortifications, than of private family residences. Let me add, however, that whatever may be the roughness of their exterior, they are extremely comfortable inside. A tier of rooms on each side of a square, comprising as many as the convenience of the occupant may require, encompass an open *patio* or court, with but one door opening into the street,—a huge gate, called *la puerta del zaguan*, usually large enough to admit the family coach. The back tier is generally occupied with the *cocina, dispensa, granero* (kitchen, provision-store, and granary), and other offices of the same kind. Most of the apartments, except the winter rooms, open into the *patio;* but the latter are most frequently entered through the *sala* or hall, which, added to the thickness of their walls and roofs, renders them delightfully warm during the cold season, while they are perfectly cool and agreeable in summer. In fact, hemmed in as these apartments are with nearly three feet of earth, they may be said to possess all the pleasant properties of cellars, with a freer circulation of air, and nothing of the dampness which is apt to pervade those subterranean regions.

The roofs of the houses are all flat *azoteas* or terraces, being formed of a layer of earth two or three feet in thickness, and supported by stout joists or horizontal rafters. These roofs, when well packed, turn the rain off with remarkable effect, and render the houses nearly fire-proof.[4] The *azotea* also forms a pleasant promenade, the surrounding walls rising usually so high as to serve for a balustrade, as also a breastwork, behind which, in times of trouble, the combatants take their station, and defend the premises.

The floors are all constructed of beaten earth 'slicked over' with soft mortar, and covered generally with a coarse carpet of domestic manufacture. A plank floor would be quite a curiosity in New Mexico; nor have I met with one even in Chihuahua, although the best houses in that city are floored with brick or squares of hewn stone. The interior of each apartment is roughly plastered over with a clay mortar unmixed with lime, by females who supply the place of trowels with their hands. It is then white washed with calcined *yeso* or gypsum, a deleterious stuff, that is always sure to engraft its affections upon the clothing of those who come in contact with it. To obviate this, the parlors and family rooms are usually lined with

---

[4] During a residence of nearly nine years in the country, I never witnessed but one fire, and that was in the mining town of Jesus Maria. There a roof of pine clapboards is usually extended over the *azotea*, to protect it against the mountain torrents of rain. This roof was consumed, but the principal damage sustained, in addition, was the burning of a huge pile of corn and some bags of flour, which were in the garret: the body of the building remained nearly *in statu quo.*—GREGG.

wall-paper or calico, to the height of five or six feet. The front of the house is commonly plastered in a similar manner, although not always white washed. In the suburbs of the towns, and particularly in the villages and ranchos, a fantastic custom prevails of painting only a portion of the fronts of the houses, in the shape of stripes, which imparts to the landscape a very striking and picturesque appearance.

Wood buildings of any kind or shape are utterly unknown in the north of Mexico, with the exception of an occasional picket-hut in some of the ranchos and mining-places. It will readily be perceived, then, what a flat and uncouth appearance the towns of New Mexico present, with houses that look more like so many collections of brick-kilns prepared for burning than human abodes.

The houses of the villages and ranchos are rarely so spacious as those of the capital, yet their construction is much the same. Some very singular subterrene dwellings are to be found in a few places. I was once passing through the village of Casa Colorada,[5] when I observed some noisy urchins just before me, who very suddenly and mysteriously disappeared. Upon resorting to the spot, I perceived an aperture under a hillock, which, albeit considerably larger, was not very unlike the habitations of the little prairie dogs.

The immense expense attending the purchase of suitable furniture and kitchen-ware, indeed, the frequent impossibility of obtaining these articles at any price, caused the early settlers of Northern Mexico to resort to inventions of necessity, or to adopt Indian customs altogether, many of which have been found so comfortable and convenient, that most of those who are now able to indulge in luxuries, feel but little inclination to introduce any change. Even the few pine-board chairs and settees that are to be found about the houses are seldom used; the prevailing fashion being to fold mattresses against the walls, which, being covered over with blankets, are thus converted into sofas. Females, indeed, most usually prefer accommodating themselves, *á l'Indienne,* upon a mere blanket spread simply upon the floor.

Wagons of Mexican manufacture are not to be found; although

[5] Casa Colorado, 40 miles below Albuquerque on the east bank of the Río Grande, belonged to the hacienda of the same name.

a small number of American-built vehicles, of those introduced by the trading caravans, have grown into use among the people.[6] Nothing is more calculated to attract the curiosity of strangers than the unwieldy *carretas* or carts of domestic construction, the massive wheels of which are generally hewed out of a large cottonwood. This, however, being rarely of sufficient size to form the usual diameter, which is about five feet, an additional segment or felloe is pinned upon each edge, when the whole is fashioned into an irregular circle. A crude pine or cottonwood pole serves for the axle-tree, upon which is tied a rough frame of the same material for a body. In the construction of these *carretas* the use of iron is, for the most part, wholly dispensed with; in fact, nothing is more common than a cart, a plough, and even a mill, without a particle of iron or other metal about them. To this huge truckle it is necessary to hitch at least three or four yokes of oxen; for even a team of six would find it difficult to draw the load of a single pair with an ordinary cart. The labor of the oxen is much increased by the Mexican mode of harnessing, which appears peculiarly odd to a Yankee. A rough pole serves for a yoke, and, with the middle tied to the cart-tongue, the extremities are placed across the heads of the oxen behind the horns, to which they are firmly lashed with a stout rawhide thong. Thus the head is maintained in a fixed position, and they pull, or rather push by the force of the neck, which, of course, is kept continually strained upwards.

Rough and uncouth as these *carretas* always are, they constitute nevertheless the 'pleasure-carriages' of the rancheros, whose families are conveyed in them to the towns, whether to market, or to *fiestas*, or on other joyful occasions. It is truly amusing to see these rude vehicles bouncing along upon their irregularly rounded wheels, like a limping bullock, and making the hills and valleys around vocal with the echo of their creaking and frightful sounds.

The New Mexicans are celebrated for the manufacture of coarse blankets, which is an article of considerable traffic between them and the southern provinces, as also with the neighboring Indians, and on

[6] By 1843 more than a hundred American wagons had been purchased in Chihuahua alone. Governor José Mariano Monterde to the Minister of Interior, Chihuahua, May 19, 1843, MS in the Archivo General y Pública de la Nación (Mexico City), Fomento-Caminos, XIII, Expediente 283.

some occasions with the United States. The finer articles are curiously woven in handsome figures of various colors. These are of different qualities, the most ordinary being valued at about two dollars apiece, while those of the finest texture, especially their imitations of the *Sarape Navajó,* will sell for twenty dollars or more. There have also been made in New Mexico a few imitations of the *Sarape Saltillero,* —the blanket of Saltillo, a city of the south celebrated for the manufacture of the most splendid fancy blankets, singularly figured with all the colors of the rainbow. These are often sold for more than fifty dollars each. What renders the weaving of the fancy blankets extremely tedious, is, that the variegation of colors is all effected with the shuttle, the texture in other respects being perfectly plain, without even a twill. An additional value is set upon the fine sarape on account of its being a fashionable substitute for a cloak. Indeed, the inferior *sarape* is the only overdress used by the peasantry in the winter.

Besides blankets, the New Mexicans manufacture a kind of coarse twilled woollen stuff, called *gerga,* which is checkered with black and white, and is used for carpets, and also by the peasantry for clothing, which, in fact, with some other similar domestic stuffs, together with buckskin, constituted almost the only article of wear they were possessed of, till the trade from Missouri furnished them with foreign fabrics at more reasonable prices than they had been in the habit of paying to the traders of the southern provinces. Their domestic textures are nearly all of wool, there being no flax or hemp[7] and but little cotton spun. The manufacture even of these articles is greatly embarrassed for want of good spinning and weaving machinery. Much of the spinning is done with the *huso* or *malacate* (the whirligig spindle), which is kept whirling in a bowl with the fingers while the thread is drawn. The dexterity with which the females spin with this simple apparatus is truly astonishing.

[7] Hemp is unknown in this province, and flax, as has before been remarked, though indigenous, is nowhere cultivated. "The court of Spain (as Clavigero tells, speaking of Michuacan, New Mexico, and Quivira, where he says flax was to be found in great abundance), informed of the regions adapted to the cultivation of this plant, sent to those countries about the year 1778, twelve families from the valley of Granada, for the purpose of promoting so important a branch of agriculture." The enterprise seems never to have been prosecuted, however—at least in New Mexico.—GREGG.

CHAPTER XI

Style of Dress in New Mexico—Riding-dress of the Caballero—Horse Trappings—The *Rebozo*—Passion for Jewelry—Apparel of the Female Peasantry—'Wheeled Tarantulas'—General Appearance of the People —Tawny Complexion—Singular Mode of Painting the Human Face— Striking Traits of Character—Alms-giving—Beggars and their Tricks —Wonderful Cure of Paralysis—Lack of Arms and Officers—Traits of Boldness among the Yeomanry—Politeness and Suavity of the Mexicans—Remarks of Mr. Poinsett—Peculiarities observed in epistolary Intercourse—Salutations—*La Siesta.*

THE BEST SOCIETY in the interior of New Mexico is fast conforming to European fashion, in the article of dress, with the exception of the peculiar riding costume, which is still worn by many *caballeros*. This generally consists of a *sombrero*—a peculiarly shaped low crowned hat with wide brim, covered with oil-cloth and surmounted with a band of tinsel cord nearly an inch in diameter: a *chaqueta* or jacket of cloth gaudily embroidered with braid and fancy barrel-buttons: a curiously shaped article called *calzoneras*, intended for pantaloons, with the outer part of the legs open from hip to ankle—the borders set with tinkling filigree buttons, and the whole fantastically trimmed with tinsel lace and cords of the same materials. As suspenders do not form a component part of a regular Mexican costume, the nether garment is supported by a rich sash which is drawn very tightly around the body, and contributes materially to render the whole appearance of the *caballero* extremely picturesque. Then there are the *botas* which somewhat resemble the leggins worn by the bandits of Italy, and are made of embossed leather, embroidered with fancy silk and tinsel thread and bound around the

149

knee with curiously tasselled garters. The *sarape* saltillero (a fancy blanket) completes the picture. This peculiarly useful as well as ornamental garment is commonly carried dangling carelessly across the pommel of the saddle, except in bad weather, when it is drawn over the shoulders, after the manner of a Spanish cloak, or as is more frequently the case, the rider puts his head through a slit in the middle, and by letting it hang loosely from the neck, his whole person is thus effectually protected.

The steed of the caballero is caparisoned in the same pompous manner, the whole of the saddle trappings weighing sometimes over a hundred pounds. First of all we have the high pommel of the saddle-tree crowned with silver, and the 'hinder tree' garnished with the same, and a quilted cushion adjusted to the seat. The *coraza* is a cover of embossed leather embroidered with fancy silk and tinsel, with ornaments of silver, and is thrown loose over the cushion and *fuste* or saddle-tree, the extremities of which protrude through appropriate apertures. Then comes the *cola de pato*, literally 'duck's tail' (it were more appropriately called 'peacock's tail'), a sort of leathern housing, also gaudily ornamented to correspond with the *coraza*, attached to the hind-tree, and covering the entire haunches of the animal. The *estribos* or stirrups are usually made either of bent or mortised wood, fancifully carved, over which are fastened the *tapaderas* or coverings of leather to protect the toes. Formerly the stirrups constituted a complete slipper, mortised in a solid block of wood, which superseded the use of *tapaderas*. But one of the most costly articles of the saddle-suit is perhaps the bridle, which is sometimes of entire silver, or otherwise heavily ornamented with silver buckles, slides and stars. To this is appended a massive bit, sometimes of pure silver, but more commonly of iron, most singularly wrought. The spurs are generally of iron, though silver spurs are very frequent. The shanks of the *vaquero* spurs are three to five inches long, with rowels sometimes six inches in diameter. I have in my possession a pair of these measuring over ten inches from one extremity to another, with rowels five and three-fourths inches in diameter, weighing two pounds and eleven ounces. Last, not least, there are the *armas de pelo,* being a pair of shaggy goat skins (richly trimmed across the top with embroidered leather), dangling from the pom-

mel of the saddle for the purpose of being drawn over the legs in case of rain, or as a protection against brush and brambles. The *corazas* of travelling saddles are also provided with several pockets called *coginillos*—a most excellent contrivance for carrying a lunch or bottle, or anything to which convenient access may be desired.

In former times there was a kind of harness of leather attached to the saddle behind, covering the hinder parts of the horse as low as mid-thighs, with its lower border completely fringed with jingling iron tags, but these are now seldom met with in the North. Even without this noisy appendage, however, a Mexican caballero of the present day, with full equestrian rigging, his clink and his rattle, makes altogether a very remarkable appearance.

Though the foregoing description refers particularly to the chivalrous caballero of the South—the *rico* of the country, yet similar modes of costume and equipage, but of coarser material, are used by the lower classes. Nor are they restricted among these to the riding-dress, but are very generally worn as ordinary apparel. Common velveteens, fustians, blue drillings and similar stuffs, are very much in fashion among such rancheros and *villageois* as are able to wear anything above the ordinary woollen manufactures of the country. Coarse wool hats, or of palm-leaf (*sombreros de petate*), all of low crowns, are the kind generally worn by the common people.

As I have already observed, among the better classes the Euro-

pean dress is now frequently worn; although they are generally a
year or two behind our latest fashions. The ladies, however, never
wear either hat, cap or bonnet, except for riding; but in lieu of it,
especially when they walk abroad, the *rebozo* (or scarf), or a large
shawl, is drawn over the head. The *rebozo* is by far the most fashionable: it is seven or eight feet in length by nearly a yard in width,
and is made of diverse stuffs—silk, linen or cotton, and usually variegated and figured in the warp by symmetrically disposed threads
waved in the dying. It is certainly a beautiful specimen of domestic
manufacture. The finest articles are valued at fifty to a hundred
dollars in the North; but the ordinary cotton *rebozo* ranges at from
one to five dollars, and is generally worn by the lower classes. A
Mexican female is scarcely ever seen without her rebozo or shawl,
except when it is laid aside for the dance. In-doors, it is loosely
thrown about her person, but in the promenade it is coquettishly
drawn over the head, and one end of it brought round, and grace-
fully hooked over the opposite shoulder. As a favorite modern
authoress[1] justly remarks, however, in speaking of the rebozo and
the sarape, an important objection to their use, in this unsettled
society, is the facility they afford for the concealment of the person,
as well as secret weapons of the wearer. Pistols, knives, and even
swords are carried unsuspected under the sarape, while a lady
fashionably muffled with a rebozo, may pass a crowd of familiar
acquaintances without being recognized.

The ordinary apparel of the female peasantry and the *rancheras,*
is the *enaguas* or petticoat of home-made flannel; or, when they are
able to procure it, of coarse blue or scarlet cloth, connected to a wide
list of some contrasting-colored stuff, bound around the waist over a
loose white chemise, which is the only covering for the body, except
the rebozo. Uncouth as this costume may appear at first, it constitutes
nevertheless a very graceful sort of undress—in which capacity it
is used even by ladies of rank.

The New Mexican ladies are all passionately fond of jewelry;
and they may commonly be seen, with their necks, arms and fingers
loaded with massive appendages of a valuable description. But as
there has been so much imposition with regard to foreign jewelry,

[1] Frances Erskine Calderón de la Barca. See below, Vol. I, chap. 12, n. 18.

articles of native manufacture, some of which are admirably executed, without alloy or counterfeit, are generally preferred.

In New Mexico, *coches de paseo* of any kind are very rare; occasionally, however, one of those huge, clumsy, old-fashioned vehicles of Mexican manufacture, so abundant in the southern cities, and often nick-named 'wheeled tarantulas,' by strangers, may be seen. Such an apparition in a Yankee city would excite as much curiosity as a caravan of the rarest animals. The coach alone is a load for two mules, therefore the vehicle is usually drawn by four and sometimes six, and invariably driven by postillions.

The stature of both sexes in New Mexico is commonly below medium: but they are mostly well proportioned, of athletic make, and sound, healthy constitutions. Their complexion is generally dark; but every variety of shade is found among them, from the lightest European tint to the swarthiest hue. Their darkness has resulted partly from their original Moorish blood, but more from intermarriages with the aborigines. An occasional Indian, and sometimes an entire village, have abandoned their wonted seclusion, and become identified with their conquerors. In the North, the system of Indian slavery has contributed still more to the same result. They buy the captive children of both sexes of the wild tribes, taken prisoners among each other, or by the Pueblos in their petty wars with the former—and indeed by the Mexicans themselves—who are generally held in bondage to the age of twenty-one years, and some, from ignorance, their whole lives. Such as resume their liberty, intermarry with the race of their masters, becoming Mexican citizens, often undistinguishable from many of the already dark-hued natives. The present race of New Mexicans has thus become an amalgam, averaging about equal parts of the European and aboriginal blood. The peasantry, as well from a more general intermixture with the Indian, as from exposure, are the darkest; yet the tawny complexion pervades all classes—the rich as well as the poor.

The females, although many of them are about as broad-featured as the veriest Indian, not unfrequently possess striking traits of beauty. They are remarkable for small feet and handsome figures, notwithstanding their profound ignorance of the 'refined art' of lacing. The belles of the ranchos and villages have a disgusting habit of besmearing their faces with the crimson juice of a plant or fruit called *alegría,* which is not unlike blood; as also with clay and starch. This is not intended, as some travellers have supposed, as a beautifying appendage, but for the purpose of protecting the skin from the sun. A country beauty will often remain in this filthy condition for a whole fortnight, in order to appear to advantage at some favorite feast or ball; when, by washing off the paint, the cheeks look as fresh and ruddy as the natural darkness of their skin will permit.

The New Mexicans appear to have inherited much of the cruelty and intolerance of their ancestors, and no small portion of their bigotry and fanaticism. Being of a highly imaginative temperament and of rather accommodating moral principles—cunning, loquacious, quick of perception and sycophantic, their conversation frequently exhibits a degree of tact—a false glare of talent, eminently calculated to mislead and impose. They have no stability except in artifice; no profundity except for intrigue: qualities for which they have acquired an unenviable celebrity. Systematically cringing and subservient while out of power, as soon as the august mantle of authority falls upon their shoulders, there are but little bounds to their arrogance and vindictiveness of spirit. While such are the general features of the character of the Northern Mexicans, however, I am fain to believe and acknowledge, that there are to be found among them numerous instances of uncompromising virtue, good faith and religious forbearance.

But taking the Northern Mexicans without distinction of class or degree, there is scarcely a race of people on the face of the earth more alive to the dictates of charity—that is, almsgiving; which is more owing perhaps to the force of religious instruction than to real sympathy for the sufferings of the indigent and the helpless. The law making no provision for paupers, there is no country perhaps more infested with beggars, especially from Chihuahua south. In the large cities, Saturday is the alms-giving day by custom; and on such occasions the *limosneros* (as the mendicant race is called), may be seen promenading the streets in gangs of thirty or forty, or in smaller numbers, performing genuflections at every nook and corner of the town, each croaking aloud his favorite set of orisons and inviting the blessings of heaven upon every man, woman or child, who may have been so fortunate as to propitiate the benison by casting a few *clacos*[2] into his outstretched hand. In some sections of the country, this system of begging has proved so successful that parents have actually been known to maim and deform their children, during the earliest stages of infancy, in order to fit them for the trade, and thereby secure to themselves a constant source of emolument for the remainder of their lives. Persons affecting diseases and frequently malformation for the purpose of exciting the commiseration of the wayfarer, are also extremely numerous. I had often observed in Chihuahua a robust-looking fellow, who, to all appearance, had partially lost the use of his lower extremities, sliding about the streets from door to door upon a sort of cushion, asking alms. One fine day, a furious bull, pursued by some *vaqueros*, came plunging down in the direction where he sat, moaning and grieving most piteously; when, forgetting his physical disabilities he sprang to his feet with the agility of a dancing master, and incontinently betook himself to his heels.

The Northern Mexicans have often been branded with cowardice: a stigma which may well be allowed to rest upon the wealthier classes, and the city-bred caballeros, from whose ranks are selected the military leaders who decide the fate of battles. But the rancheros, or as they might be still more appropriately styled—the yeomanry of the country, inured as they are from their peculiar mode of life to every kind of fatigue and danger, possess a much higher calibre of moral courage. Their want of firmness in the field, is partially the result of their want of confidence in their commanders; while the inefficacy and worthlessness of their weapons are alone sufficient to inspire even a valiant heart with dismal forebodings. It is true that most of the regular troops are provided with English muskets, which, by the way, they are generally too ignorant to keep in order; but a great portion of the militia are obliged to use the clumsy old-fashioned *escopeta*, or firelock of the sixteenth century; while others have nothing but the bow and arrow, and sometimes the lance, which is in fact a weapon very much in use throughout the country. I have

[2] The *claco* (properly *tlaco*) was a copper coin worth one-eighth of a *real* or approximately one and a half cents.

seen persons of the lower class do things, however, which would really seem to indicate a superlative degree of courage. Some of them will often perform journeys alone through wildernesses teeming with murderous savages; but as they not unfrequently embark upon these perilous jaunts unarmed, it is evident they depend greatly upon good luck and swiftness of limbs, and still more upon the protection of their favorite saint, *la Vírgen de Guadalupe.*

The Mexicans, like the French, are remarkable for their politeness and suavity of manners. You cannot visit a friend but he assures you that, *"Está V. en su casa, y puede mandar,"* etc. (You are in your own house, and can command, etc.), or, *"Estoy enteramente á su disposicion"* (I am wholly at your disposal), without, however, meaning more than an expression of ordinary courtesy. Nor can you speak in commendation of any article, let its value be what it may, but the polite owner immediately replies, *"Tómelo, V. Señor; es suyo* (Take it, sir; it is yours), without the slightest intention or expectation that you should take him at his word.—Mr. Poinsett[3] observes, "Remember, when you take leave of a Spanish grandee, to bow as you leave the room, at the head of the stairs, where the host accompanies you; and after descending the first flight, turn round and you will see him expecting a third salutation, which he returns with great courtesy, and remains until you are out of sight; so that as you wind down the stairs, if you catch a glimpse of him, kiss your hand, and he will think you a most accomplished cavalier." Graphic as this short sketch is, it hardly describes the full measure of Mexican politeness; for in that country, when the visitor reaches the street, another tip of the hat, and another inclination of the head, will be expected by the attentive host, who gently waves, with his hand, a final *'á dios'* from a window.

In epistolary correspondence, the ratio of respect is generally indicated by the width of the left margin. If the letter is addressed to an equal, about one-fourth of the page is occupied for that purpose; but when extraordinary respect is intended to be shown to a

[3] Joel R. Poinsett (1779–1851), of South Carolina, was a special United States emissary in South America during its wars for independence, congressman (1821–25), a special emissary (1822) and later minister to Mexico (1825–29), and secretary of war under President Van Buren (1837–41). Gregg's reference is to an observation in his *Notes on Mexico Made in 1822* (Philadelphia, Carey & Lea, 1824).

superior, nearly one-half of the page is left a blank. There are other marks of civility and respect peculiar to the country, which among us would be accounted servility.

In their salutations, the ancient custom of close embrace, not only between individuals of the same sex, but between those of different sexes, is almost universal. It is quite a luxury to meet a pretty señorita after some absence. The parties approach, shake hands in a cordial manner, and without loosening the grasp, the left arm of each is brought about the other's waist; and while a gentle embrace brings their persons closer to each other, the contact of the cheeks becomes inevitable—without admitting a kiss, however, which would be held as decidedly indelicate. In short, it is worth while absenting oneself, for the gratification of a first meeting with the prettier of one's female friends upon the return.

Among the least unpleasant customs of this country is that of the *siesta* or afternoon nap; a species of indulgence in which all classes are prone to share. The stores, private and public offices, are, by common consent, generally closed at one o'clock (that being the usual dinner hour), and not reopened till three. During that interval nearly every kind of business and labor is suspended. The streets are comparatively deserted; the rich and the poor retire to their respective couches, and remain wrapped in slumber, or 'thinking o' nothing,' till the loud peal of the three o'clock bell warns them to resume their occupations.

CHAPTER XII

Government of New Mexico—The Administration of Justice—Judicial Corruption—Prejudices Against Americans—Partiality for the English —Anecdote of Governor Armijo and a Trapper—Outrage upon an American Physician—Violence suffered by the American Consul and others—Arbitrary Impositions upon Foreigners—*Contribucion de Guerra* —The Alcaldes and their System—The *Fueros*—Mode of punishing Delinquents and Criminals—Mexican System of Slavery—Thieves and Thieveries—Outrage upon an American Merchant—Gambling and Gambling-houses—Game of Monte—Anecdote of a Lady of Fashion —*Chuza*—Cockpits—*Correr el gallo*—*El Coleo*—Fandangoes— *Cigarritos.*

Prior to the adopting of the *Sistema Central* in the Mexican republic, the province of New Mexico was under a territorial government. The executive was called *Gefe Político* (political chief), and the *Diputacion Provincial* very inefficiently supplied the place of a legislature. Under the present system, however, New Mexico being a *department*, the names of these powers have been changed, but their functions remain very nearly the same. The *Gobernador* (governor) is appointed by the President for eight years. The legislative power is nominally vested in a *Junta Departmental*, a kind of state council, with very circumscribed powers, somewhat analogous to, and certainly not more extensive than, those of a board of aldermen with us. But even this shadow of popular representation was 'prorogued' by Gov. Armijo soon after his accession to power (five or six years ago), and has never since been convened; so that its functions have been arbitrarily exercised by the governor ever since.

The administration of the laws in Northern Mexico constitutes one of the most painful features of her institutions. Justice, or rather judgments, are a common article of traffic; and the hapless litigant who has not the means to soften the claws of the alcalde with a 'silver unction,' is almost sure to get severely scratched in the contest, no matter what may be the justice of his cause, or the uprightness of his character. It is easy to perceive, then, that the poor and the humble stand no chance in a judicial contest with the wealthy and consequential, whose influence, even apart from their facilities for corrupting the court and suborning witnesses, is sufficient to neutralize any amount of plebian testimony that might be brought against them.

The evil consequences arising from maladministration of justice in New Mexico are most severely felt by foreigners, against whom a strong prejudice prevails throughout the South. Of these, the citizens of the United States are by far the most constant sufferers; an inevitable result of that sinister feeling with which the 'rival republic' views the advancement and superiority of her more industrious neighbors. It is a notorious fact, that while the English are universally treated with comparative consideration and respect, the Americans residing in the southern parts of the republic are frequently taunted with the effeminacy of their government and its want of decision. So openly has this preference for British subjects been manifested, and so thoroughly conscious have the Americans become of the humiliating fact, that when a mercantile firm, consisting of an American and an Englishman, has occasion to present a memorial of any description, or to sue either for an act of favor or of justice from the nation, the application is sure to be made in the name of the latter, knowing it will thus be more likely to command proper attention.

Few men, perhaps, have done more to jeopard the interests of American traders, or to bring the American character itself into contempt, than Armijo, the present arbitrary governor of New Mexico. I am happy to say, however, that in the midst of his many oppressions, he was once at least obliged to 'knock under' to one of those bold and daring spirits of the Rocky Mountains whom obstacles rather energize than subdue. This was about the year 1828, during

Armijo's previous governorship. A law was then in existence which had been enacted by the general Congress prohibiting foreigners from trapping beaver in the Mexican territory, under penalty of confiscation, etc.; but as there were no native trappers in New Mexico, Gov. Baca and his successor (Narbona)[1] thought it expedient to extend licenses to foreigners, in the name of citizens, upon condition of their taking a certain proportion of Mexicans to learn the art of trapping. In pursuance of this disposition, Gov. Narbona extended a license to one Ewing Young,[2] who was accompanied by a Mr. Sublette, brother of Capt. Wm. Sublette, and almost equally celebrated for his mountain adventures.[3] Previous to the return of this party from their trapping expedition, Armijo had succeeded Narbona in office, and they were informed that it was his intention to seize their furs. To prevent this, they deposited them at a neighboring village, where they were afterwards discovered, seized, and confiscated. The furs being damp, they were spread out in the sun before the *Guardia*, in Santa Fé, when Sublette, perceived two packs of beaver which had been his own property, got by honest labor, instantly seized them and carried them away before the eyes of the whole garrison, and concealed both them and his own person in a house opposite. The entire military force was immediately put in requisition, and a general search made for the offender and his prize; but in vain: indeed, if the truth must be spoken, the troops seemed to have as little desire to find Sublette as the latter had of being found; for his character was too well known to leave any room for hope that his capture could be effected without a great deal of trouble. In the meanwhile, Armijo raved, and threatened the Americans for not ferreting out their countryman and delivering him over to justice. Failing to produce

[1] Bartolomé Baca, a militia officer since 1808, was governor from 1823 to 1825. Antonio Narbona, his successor, came from Chihuahua to fight the Navajos in 1805, was governor from 1825 to 1827, and as commandant of New Mexico's troops, led an expedition against the Apaches of Arizona in 1843.

[2] Ewing Young (d. 1841), of Tennessee, was a prominent trader, trapper, and explorer. He accompanied Becknell to Santa Fé in 1821, went to California in 1828, where he helped the mission padres suppress an Indian revolt, returned in 1829 and married at Taos, and went to California again in 1831. In 1834 he established one of the first American settlements in Oregon and set up grist and lumber mills.

[3] Milton J. Sublette (d. 1836) was a younger brother of William Sublette but reputedly the most enterprising and daring of his family.

any impression by blustering, however, he caused a couple of cannons to be pointed at the house where the offender was supposed to be concealed, declaring at the same time that he would batter it down; but all to no purpose. Mr. Sublette finally conveyed his furs in safety to the frontier, and thence to the United States.[4]

The following anecdote affords another illustration of Armijo's summary mode of dealing with Americans. In the fall of 1840, a gross outrage was committed upon a physician from Massachusetts[5] (said to be a gentleman of unexceptionable deportment), who was travelling through the country for his health. He had loaned nine hundred dollars to a person of the name of Tayon,[6] who afterwards borrowed the same amount of another foreigner[7] and repaid this debt. The doctor then left for the South, where he intended to pass the winter, being afflicted with a pulmonary disease. But the individual who had lent Tayon the money, being informed that he was insolvent, applied to Gov. Armijo for an order to compel the doctor to return, expecting thereby to make him reimburse the money. The order overtook him at the village of Algodones,[8] near forty miles from Santa Fé, where he was at once arrested by the alcalde, and detained some time, ignorant even of the offence for which he was doing penance. In the meantime, the American Consul at Santa Fé,[9] having been informed of what had taken place, procured a counter-order from the governor for the release of the prisoner. When the alcalde of Algodones received this document, he determined at once that so extraordinary an act of justice should cost the foreigner some trifle. Accordingly, another order was forged on the spot, commanding that he should be taken to the capital—yet a 'gentle hint' was given, that his liberty might be purchased by the payment of two hundred dollars. Being in a land of strangers, among whom he had but little hope of receiving fair play, the doctor resolved to pay the amount demanded, and fly to Chihuahua, where he would at least

[4] A fuller account of this incident, from a transcript of the official record, appears in Cleland, *This Reckless Breed of Men*, 218–25.

[5] Dr. J. H. Lyman.

[6] François Valentine Tayon, of St. Louis, Missouri.

[7] Stephen Lewis Lee, also of St. Louis.

[8] A community of several hundred persons on the east bank of the Río Grande, about 23 miles above Albuquerque.

[9] Manuel Alvarez. See below, this chapter, n. 13.

be safe from Armijo's clutches. Having been informed, however, of the fraud practiced by the alcalde, before he had proceeded far on his journey, he returned and made an attempt to bring the delinquent officer to justice, but altogether without success.[10]

But perhaps the most glaring outrages upon American citizens were committed in 1841, upon the occasion of the capture of the Texan Santa Fé Expedition. In Taos, a poor deaf and dumb U. S. creole Frenchman was beaten to death in open day.[11] In San Miguel, the alcalde, at the head of a mob, entered the store of a Mr. Rowland, whom he robbed of a considerable amount of merchandise.[12] At the same time, the greatest excitement raged in Santa Fé against Americans, whose lives appeared in imminent danger; and a most savage attack was made upon our excellent Consul, Manuel Alvarez, Esq.,[13] who had always taken an active interest in the welfare of American citizens.

A few minutes after the governor had departed for San Miguel, to encounter the Texans, a fellow named Martin,[14] his nephew and confidential agent, aided by a band of ferocious *sans culottes,* and armed with a large knife, secretly entered the house of the Consul, who perceived him in time, however, to avert the blow; yet he re-

[10] By his own admission Lyman paid fifty dollars to bribe the *alcalde* of Algodones, but, although none of the officials involved were brought to justice, the money was restored to him. J. H. Lyman to Manuel Alvarez, Santa Fé, December 7, 1840, MS in the B. M. Read Collection of the Historical Society of New Mexico at Santa Fé, Folder L, No. 174. In a subsequent letter from Rancho de Taos, August 8, 1841, Lyman frantically appealed to the consul to bribe an official into pre-dating an authorization for his safe passage to the South. *Ibid.,* Folder L, No. 175.

[11] François Lacompe. He was killed resisting arrest.

[12] Thomas Rowland, of Pennsylvania, had married in New Mexico and resided there for several years. His brother, John Rowland, a merchant at Taos as early as 1825 and a trapper before that, was appointed to the Texas commission (along with William Workman and William G. Dryden) seeking an amicable reception for the Texan Santa Fé expedition. This latter circumstance led to the hasty departure of John Rowland and other Americans for California and probably also to the difficulties of Thomas Rowland.

[13] Manuel Alvarez (1794–1856), a native of Spain, came to the United States in 1823 and to New Mexico in the following year, where he operated a store for over thirty years. He became United States consul at Santa Fé in 1839, an American citizen in 1842, and lieutenant governor of the Territory in 1850. For the details of the incidents described by Gregg, see Alvarez's Memorial to the Secretary of State, Washington City, February 2, 1842, MS in the National Archives, Consular Dispatches, Santa Fé, Vol. I.

[14] Tomás Martín, an ensign in the militia.

ceived a severe wound in the face during the scuffle that ensued: the rabble running in at the same time, and vociferating, *"Sáquenlo afuera! mátenlo!"*—Drag him out! kill him! Mr. Alvarez doubtless owed his preservation partially to the consternation with which the failure of their clandestine attempt at his life inspired the cowardly ruffians. Instead of being punished for this diabolical act, the principal assassin, on the contrary, was soon after promoted in the army.

The outrage did not end here, however; for on the Consul's demanding his passport for the United States, it was refused for nearly a month; thus detaining him until the cold season had so far advanced, that, of his party (about fifteen in number), two perished from the cold; and not one arrived without being more or less frostbitten—some very severely—besides suffering a loss of about fifty animals from the same cause.

Although these and other daring outrages have been duly represented to our Government, it does not appear that any measures of redress have yet been taken.

With a view of oppressing our merchants, Gov. Armijo had, as early as 1839, issued a decree exempting all the natives from the tax imposed on store-houses, shops, etc., throwing the whole burden of impost upon foreigners and naturalized citizens; a measure clearly and unequivocally at variance with the treaties and stipulations entered into between the United States and Mexico. A protest was presented without effect;[15] when our Consul, finding all remonstrances useless, forwarded a memorial to the American Minister at Mexico, who, although the vital interests of American citizens were at stake, deemed the affair of too little importance, perhaps, and therefore appears to have paid no attention to it. But this system of levying excessive taxes upon foreigners, is by no means an original invention of Gov. Armijo. In 1835, the government of Chihuahua having levied a *contribucion de guerra* for raising means to make war upon the savages, who were laying waste the surrounding country, foreign merchants, with an equal disregard for their rights and

[15] The memorial, addressed to Governor Armijo, Santa Fé, Dec. 2, 1839, was signed somewhat bilingually by Josias Gregg, John Scholly, Juan Fournier, J. K. Dormston, Manuel Alvarez, Carlos Blummer, and Benito Wilson. MS copy in the National Archives, Consular Dispatches, Santa Fé, Vol. I.

the obligations of treaties, were taxed twenty-five dollars each per month; while the native merchants, many of whom possessed large haciendas, with thousands of stock, for the especial protection of which these taxes were chiefly imposed, paid only from five to ten dollars each. Remonstrances were presented to the governor, but in vain. In his official reply, that functionary declared, *"que el gobierno cree arreglado el reparto de sus respectivas contribuciones,"* the government believes your respective contributions in accordance with justice—which concluded the correspondence, and the Americans paid their twenty-five dollars per month.

The only tribunals of 'justice' in New Mexico are those of the ordinary *alcaldes* or justices of the peace; and an appeal from them is carried to the Supreme Court in the department of Chihuahua. The course of litigation is exceedingly simple and summary. The plaintiff makes his verbal complaint or demand before the alcalde, who orders him to summon the defendant, which is done by simply saying, *"Le llama el alcalde"* (the alcalde calls you) into his presence, the applicant acting thus in the double capacity of constable and complainant. The summons is always verbal, and rarely for a future time—instant attendance being expected. Should the defendant refuse to obey this simple mandate (which, by the bye, is a very rare occurrence), the alcalde sends his *baston de justicia*, his staff of justice, an ordinary walking-cane, distinguished only by a peculiar black silk tassel. This never fails to enforce compliance, for a refusal to attend after being shown the staff, would be construed into a contempt of court, and punished accordingly. The witnesses are sometimes sworn upon a cross cut on the *baston de justicia*, or more frequently, perhaps, upon a cross formed with the finger and thumb. Generally speaking, however, the process of examination is gone through without a single oath being administered; and in the absence of witnesses, the alcalde often proceeds to sentence upon the single statements of the contending parties. By a species of mutual agreement, the issue of a suit is sometimes referred to *hombres buenos* (arbitrators), which is the nearest approximation that is made to trial by jury. In judicial proceedings, however, but little, or rather no attention is paid to any code of laws; in fact, there is scarcely one alcalde in a dozen who knows what a law is, or who ever saw a law-book. Their decisions when not influenced by corrupt agencies, are controlled by the prevailing customs of the country.

In the administration of justice, there are three distinct and privileged jurisdictions, known as *fueros:* the *eclesiástico,* which provides that no member of the clergy, at least of the rank of curate and upwards, shall ever be arraigned before a civil tribunal, but shall be tried by their superiors in the order; the *militar,* which makes a similar provision in favor not only of commissioned officers, but of every common soldier from the ranks; and the *civil* or ordinary courts, for all cases in which the defendants are laymen. These *fueros* have hitherto maintained the ecclesiastical and military classes in perfect independence of the civil authorities. The *civil,* in fact, remains in some degree subordinate to the other two *fueros;* for it can, under no circumstances, have any jurisdiction whatever over them; while the lay plaintiff, in the privileged tribunals of these, may, if unsuccessful, have judgment entered up against him: a consequence that can never follow the suits of the ecclesiastical or military orders before the civil tribunals. The judgments of the latter, in such cases, would be void. It is no wonder, then, that the cause of freedom in Mexico has made so little progress.[16]

Imprisonment is almost the only sort of punishment resorted to in the North. For debt, petit larceny, highway robbery, and murder, the usual sentence is *"A la cárcel"* (to jail), where a person is likely to remain about as long for inability to pay *dos reales,* as for the worst of crimes: always provided he has not the means to pacify the offended majesty of the law. I never heard of but one execution for murder in New Mexico, since the declaration of independence. The most desperate and blood-stained criminals escape with impunity, after a few weeks of incarceration, unless the prosecutor happens to be a person of great influence; in which case, the prisoner is detained in the *calabozo* at will, even when the offence committed has been of a trivial character. Notwithstanding this laxity in the execution of the laws, there are few murders of any kind commited.

In case of debt, as before remarked, the delinquent is sent to

16 The special judicial privilege of the military and ecclesiastical services were abolished by the Juárez Law of November 24, 1855, which was incorporated into the Constitutions of 1857 and 1917.

jail—provided the creditor will not accept his services. If he will, however, the debtor becomes *nolens volens* the servant of the creditor till the debt is satisfied; and, serving, as he does, at very reduced wages, his expenses for clothing, and other necessaries, but too often retain him in perpetual servitude. This system does not operate, however, upon the higher classes, yet it acts with terrible severity upon the unfortunate poor, whose condition is but little better, if not worse indeed than that of the slaves of the South. They labor for fixed wages, it is true; but all they can earn is hardly sufficient to keep them in the coarsest clothing and pay their contingent expenses. Men's wages range from two to five dollars a month, and those of women from fifty cents to two dollars; in payment of which, they rarely receive any money, but instead thereof, articles of apparel and other necessaries at the most exorbitant prices. The consequence is that the servant soon accumulates a debt which he is unable to pay— his wages being often engaged for a year or two in advance. Now, according to the usages, if not the laws of the country, he is bound to serve his master until all arrearages are liquidated; and is only enabled to effect an exchange of masters, by engaging another to pay his debt, to whom he becomes in like manner bound.

As I have already remarked, capital crimes and highway robberies are of comparatively rare occurrence in the North, but in small delinquencies, such as pilfering and petty rogueries of every shade and description, the common classes can very successfully compete with any other people. Nothing indeed can be left exposed or unguarded without great danger of its being immediately stolen. No husbandman would think of leaving his axe or his hoe, or anything else of the slightest value, lying out over night. Empty wagons are often pillaged of every movable piece of iron, and even the wheels have been carried away. Pieces of merchandise are frequently purloined from the shelves, when they happen to be in reach. In Chihuahua, goods have actually been snatched from the counter while being exposed to the inspection of a pretended purchaser. I once had a trick of this kind played upon me by a couple of boys, who made their escape through a crowd of spectators with their booty exposed. In vain I cried *"Agarren á los ladrones!"* (catch the thieves!) not a single individual moved to apprehend them. I then proffered the goods stolen, to any person who might succeed in bringing the rogues to me, but to no purpose. In fact there seems to exist a great deal of repugnance, even among the better classes, to apprehending thieves; as if the mere act of informing against them was considered dishonorable. I heard a very respectable caballero once remark that he had seen a man purloin certain articles of merchandise, but he could not be induced to give up his name; observing, "O, I can't think of exposing the poor fellow!"

The impunity with which delinquencies of this description are every day committed is perhaps in some degree, the consequence of those severe enactments, such as the *Leyes de las Indias* (the laws of the Indies), which rendered many thefts and robberies punishable with death[17]. The magistracy contracted the habit of frequently winking at crime, rather than resort to the barbarous expedients prescribed by the letter of the law. The utmost that can be gained now by public prosecution, is the recovery of the stolen property, if that be anywhere to be found, and occasionally a short period of imprisonment for the culprit. This is more particularly the case when the prosecutor happens to be a foreigner; while on the other hand, if he be the party accused, he is likely to be subjected to very severe treatment. A remarkable circumstance of this kind occurred in Chihuahua in the year 1835. One of our most respectable Missouri merchants had bought a mule of a stranger, but the animal was soon after claimed by a third person, who proved that it had been stolen from him. The Missourian would have been perfectly satisfied to lose the mule, and end the matter there; but to the surprise of all, he was directly summoned before an alcalde, and forthwith sentenced to jail: the partial judge having labored to fix the theft upon the innocent purchaser, while the real culprit, who was a native, was permitted to go at large.

The love of gambling also deserves to be noticed as a distinguishing propensity of these people. Indeed it may well be said, without any undue stretch of imagination, that shoplifting, pocket-picking, and other elegant pastimes of the same kindred, are the legitimate

[17] Although harsh by nineteenth century standards, this code was relatively enlightened for its time in protecting the native population. First published as *Recopilación de leyes de los reynos de Indias* (4 vols., Madrid, Ivlian de Paredes, 1681), it was reissued for the fourth and final time in 1791.

offspring, especially among the lower classes, of that passion for gaming, which in Mexico more than anywhere else—to use Madame Calderon's language—"is impregnated with the constitution—in man, woman, and child."[18] It prevails in the lowly hut, as well as in the glittering saloon; nor is the sanctity of the gown nor the dignity of station sufficient proof against the fascinations of this exciting vice. No one considers it a degradation to be seen frequenting a *monte bank:* the governor himself and his lady, the grave magistrate and the priestly dignity, the gay caballero and the titled señora may all be seen staking their doubloons upon the turn of a card; while the humbler ranchero, the hired domestic and the ragged pauper, all press with equal avidity to test their fortune at the same shrine. There are other games at cards practiced among these people, depending more upon skill; but that of *el monte,* being one exclusively of chance, seems to possess an all-absorbing attraction, difficult to be conceived by the uninitiated spectator.

The following will not only serve to show the light in which gambling is held by all classes of society, but to illustrate the purifying effects of wealth upon character. Some twelve or fifteen years ago there lived (or rather roamed) in Taos a certain female of very loose habits, known as *La Tules.* Finding it difficult to obtain the means of living in that district, she finally extended her wanderings to the capital. She there became a constant attendant on one of those pandemoniums where the favorite game of *monte* was dealt *pro bono publico.* Fortune, at first, did not seem inclined to smile upon her efforts, and for some years she spent her days in lowliness and misery. At last her luck turned, as gamblers would say, and on one occasion she left the bank with a spoil of several hundred dollars! This enabled her to open a bank of her own, and being favored by a continuous run of good fortune, she gradually rose higher and higher in the scale of affluence, until she found herself in possession of a very handsome fortune. In 1843, she sent to the United States some ten thousand dollars to be invested in goods. She still continues her favorite 'amusement,' being now considered the most

[18] Frances Erskine Calderón de la Barca (1804–82), the Scottish wife of a Spanish minister to the United States and later to Mexico. Her lively letters, published as *Life in Mexico* (London, Chapman & Hall, 1843), constitute an excellent commentary on Mexican manners and customs of the time.

expert 'monte dealer' in all Santa Fé. She is openly received in the first circles of society: I doubt, in truth, whether there is to be found in the city a lady of more fashionable reputation than this same Tules, now known as Señora Doña Gertrudes Barceló.[19]

Among the multitude of games which seem to constitute the real business of life in New Mexico, that of *chuza* evidently presents the most attractions to ladies; and they generally lay very heavy wagers upon the result. It is played with little balls, and bears some faint resemblance to what is called *roulette*. Bull-baiting and cock-fighting, about which so much has been said by every traveler in Mexico, are also very popular 'amusements' in the North, and generally lead to the same excesses and the same results as gaming. The cock-pit rarely fails to be crowded on Sundays and other feast days; on which occasions the church, the ball-room, the gambling-house, and the cock-pit look like so many opposite establishments; for nothing is more common than to see people going from one place to another by alternate fits, just as devotional feeling or love of pleasure happens to prompt them.

One of the most attractive sports of the rancheros and the peasantry, and that which, more than any other, calls for the exercise of skill and dexterity, is that called *correr el gallo*, practised generally on St. John's day. A common cock or hen is tied by the feet to some swinging limb of a tree, so as to be barely within the reach of a man on horseback: or the fowl is buried alive in a small pit in the ground leaving only the head above the surface. In either case, the racers, passing at full speed, grapple the head of the fowl, which being well greased, generally slips out of their fingers. As soon as some one, more dextrous than the rest, has succeeded in tearing it loose, he clasps spurs to his steed, and endeavors to escape with the prize. He is hotly pursued, however, by the whole sporting crew, and the first who overtakes him tries to get possession of the fowl,

[19] Gertrudes Barcelo (d. *ca.* 1851) became a favorite with the Mexican and later American officers. According to rumor, she loaned a thousand dollars to the United States Army to meet its requirements after the supply officer agreed to escort her to the military ball. Susan Magoffin in 1846 described her as "a stately dame of a certain age, the possessor of a portion of that shrewd sense and fascinating manner necessary to allure the wayward, inexperienced youth to the hall of final ruin." Drumm (ed.), *Down the Santa Fe Trail*, 119–20.

when a strife ensues, during which the poor chicken is torn into atoms. Should the holder of the trophy be able to outstrip his pursuers, he carries it to a crowd of fair spectators and presents it to his mistress, who takes it to the fandango which usually follows, as a testimony of the prowess of her lover.

Among the vaqueros, and even among persons of distinction, *el coleo* (tailing) is a much nobler exercise than the preceding, and is also generally reserved for days of festivity. For this sport the most untractable ox or bull is turned loose upon a level common, when all the parties who propose to join in the amusement, being already mounted, start off in pursuit of him. The most successful rider, as soon as he gets near enough to the bull, seizes him by the tail, and with a sudden manoeuvre, whirls him topsy-turvy upon the plain—to the no little risk of breaking his own neck, should his horse stumble or be tripped by the legs of the falling bull.

Respecting *fandangos,* I will observe that this term, as it is used in New Mexico, is never applied to any particular dance, but is the usual designation for those ordinary assemblies where dancing and frolicking are carried on; *baile* (or ball) being generally applied to those of a higher grade. The former especially are very frequent; for nothing is more general, throughout the country, and with all classes than dancing. From the gravest priest to the buffoon—from the richest nabob to the beggar—from the governor to the ranchero —from the soberest matron to the flippant belle—from the grandest *señora* to the *cocinera*—all partake of this exhilarating amusement. To judge from the quantity of tuned instruments which salute the ear almost every night in the week, one would suppose that a perpetual carnival prevailed everywhere. The musical instruments used at the *bailes* and *fandangos* are usually the fiddle and *bandolin,* or *guitarra,* accompanied in some villages by the *tombé* or little Indian drum. The musicians occasionally acquire considerable proficiency in the use of these instruments. But what most oddly greets, and really outrages most Protestant ears, is the accompaniment of divine service with the very same instruments, and often with the same tunes.

Of all the petty vices practised by the New Mexicans, the *vicio inocente* of smoking among ladies, is the most intolerable; and yet it is a habit of which the loveliest and the most refined equally partake. The *puro* or *cigarro*[20] is seen in the mouths of all: it is handed round in the parlor, and introduced at the dinner table—even in the ball-room it is presented to ladies as regularly as any other species of 'refreshment;' and in the dance the señorita may often be seen whirling round with a lighted *cigarrito* in her mouth. The belles of the Southern cities are very frequently furnished with *tenazitas de oro* (little golden tongs), to hold the cigar with, so as to prevent their delicate fingers from being polluted either with the stain or scent of tobacco; forgetting at the same time its disagreeable effects upon the lips and breath.

Notwithstanding their numerous vices, however, I should do the New Mexicans the justice to say that they are but little addicted to inebriety and its attendant dissipations. Yet this doubtlessly results to a considerable degree from the dearness of spirituous liquors, which virtually places them beyond the reach of the lower classes.

[20] The *puro* is a common cigar of *pure* tobacco; but the term *cigarro* or *cigarrito* is applied to those made of cut tobacco rolled up in a strip of paper or corn-husk. The latter are by far in the most general use in New Mexico, even among men, and are those only smoked by the females. In this province cigarros are rarely sold in the shops, being generally manufactured by everyone just as they are needed. Their expertness in this 'accomplishment' is often remarkable. The mounted vaquero will take out his *guagito* (his little tobacco-flask), his packet of *hojas* (or prepared husks), and his flint, steel, etc.,—make his cigarrito, strike fire and commence smoking in a minute's time—all while at full speed: and the next minute will perhaps lazo the wildest bull without interrupting his smoke.—GREGG.

CHAPTER XIII

Military Hierarchy of Mexico—Religious Superstitions—Legend of *Nuestra Señora de Guadalupe*—A profane version of the Story—A curious Plan for manufacturing Water—Saints and Images—Processions—How to make it Rain—The Sacred Host—Fanaticism and Murder—Honors paid to a Bishop—Servility to Priests—Attendance at Public Worship—New Mexicans in Church—The Vesper Bells—Passion Week and the Ceremonies pertaining thereto—Ridiculous *Penitencia*—Whitewashing of Criminals—Matrimonial Connexions and Mode of Contracting them—Restrictions upon Lovers—Onerous Fees paid for Marriages and Burials—Anecdote of a *Ranchero*—Ditto of a Servant and a Widow, illustrative of Priestly Extortion—Modes of Burial, and Burial Ground of the Heretics.

T HE MEXICANS seem the legitimate descendants of the subjects of 'His Most Catholic Majesty;' for the Romish faith is not only the religion established by law, but the only one tolerated by the constitution: a system of republican liberty wholly incomprehensible to the independent and tolerant spirits of the United States. Foreigners only of other creeds, in accordance with treaty stipulations, can worship privately within their own houses. The Mexicans, indeed, talk of a 'union of Church and State:' they should rather say a 'union of Church and Army;' for, as has already been shown, the civil authority is so nearly merged in the military and the ecclesiastical, that the government, if not a military hierarchy, is something so near akin that it is difficult to draw the distinction. As Mr. Mayer[1] very appropriately remarks, you are warned of the double dominion of the

---

[1] Brantz Mayer (1809–97), of Baltimore, was secretary of the United States legation at Mexico City, a noted author, and founder of the Maryland Historical Society. Gregg is quoting from his *Mexico as It Was and as It Is* (New York, J. Winchester, *et al.*, 1844).

army and the church "by the constant sound of the drum and the bell, which ring in your ears from morn to midnight, and drown the sounds of industry and labor."

In the variety and grossness of popular superstitions, Northern Mexico can probably compete with any civilized country in the world. Others may have their extravagant traditions, their fanatical prejudices, their priestly impostures, but here the popular creed seems to be the embodiment of as much that is fantastic and improbable in idolatrous worship, as it is possible to clothe in the garb of a religious faith. It would fill volumes to relate one-half of the wonderful miracles and extraordinary apparitions said to have occurred during and since the conquest of the Indian Pueblos and their conversion to the Romish faith. Their character may be inferred from the following national legend of *La Maravillosa Aparicion de Nuestra Señora de Guadalupe—anglicè*, the marvellous apparition of Our Lady of Guadalupe,—which in some one of its many traditionary shapes, is generally believed throughout the republic. I have seen some half a dozen written versions of this celebrated tradition, and heard about as many oral ones; but no two agree in all the particulars. However, that which has received most currency informs us, that, on the 12th of December, 1531, an Indian called Juan Diego, while passing over the barren hill of Tepeyacac (about a league northward from the city of Mexico), in quest of medicinal herbs, had his attention suddenly arrested by the fragrance of flowers, and the sound of delightful music; and on looking up, he saw an angelic sort of figure directly before him. Being terrified he attempted to flee; but the apparition calling to him by name, "Juan Diego," said she, "go tell the bishop to have me a place of worship erected on this very spot." The Indian replied that he could nòt return, as he was seeking *remedios* for a dying relative. But the figure bade him to do as commanded, and have no further care about his relative—that he was then well. Juan Diego went to the city, but being unable to procure an audience from the bishop, he concluded he had been acting under a delusion, and again set off for his *remedios*. Upon ascending the same hill, however, the apparition again accosted him, and hearing his excuse, upbraided him for his want of faith and energy; and said, "Tell the bishop that it is Guadalupe, the Virgin

173

Mary, come to dwell amongst and protect the Mexicans, who sends thee." The Indian, returning again to the city, forced his way into the presence of the bishop, who, like a good sensible man, received the messenger with jeers, and treated him as a maniac; telling him finally to bring some sign, which, if really the Mother of God, his directress could readily furnish.

The perplexed Indian left the bishop's presence resolved to avoid further molestation from his spiritual acquaintance, by taking another route; yet, when near the place of his first meeting, he again encountered the apparition, who, hearing the result of his mission, ordered him to climb a naked rock hard by, and collect a bouquet of flowers which he would find growing there. Juan Diego, albeit without faith, obeyed, when, to his surprise he found the flowers referred to, and brought them to the Virgin, who, throwing them into his *tilma*, commanded him to carry them to the bishop; saying, "When he sees these he will believe, as he well knows that flowers do not bloom at this season, much less upon that barren rock." The humble messenger now with more courage sought the bishop's presence, and threw out the blooming credentials of his mission before him; when lo! to the astonishment of all, and to the entire conviction of his *Señoría ilustrísima*, the perfect image of the apparition appeared imprinted on the inside of the *tilma*.[2]

The reverend Prelate now fully acknowledged the divinity of the picture, and in a conclave of ecclesiastics convened for the purpose, he pronounced it the image of *La verdadera Virgen* and protectress of Mexico. A splendid chapel was soon after erected upon the spot designated in the mandate, in which the miraculous painting was deposited, where it is preserved to the present day. In the suburbs of every principal city in the republic, there is now a chapel specially dedicated to *Nuestra Señora de Guadalupe*, where coarse resemblances of the original picture are to be seen. Rough paintings of the same, of various dimensions, are also to be met with in nearly every dwelling, from the palace to the most miserable hovel. The

[2] This is a kind of mantle or loose covering worn by the Indians, which, in the present instance, was made of the coarse filaments of a species of maguey, and a little resembled the common coffee sacks. The painting, as it necessarily must be on such material, is said to be coarse, and represents the Virgin covered with a blue robe bespangled with stars.—GREGG.

image, with an adapted motto, has also been stamped upon medals, which are swung about the necks of the faithful.[3]

As a further confirmation of the miracle, it is also told, that when Juan Diego returned to his home, he found his relative in good health—that he had suddenly risen from the last extremity about the time of the former's meeting with the Virgin.

Now comes the profane version of the story, which the skeptical have set afloat, as the most reasonable one; but against which, in the name of orthodoxy, I feel bound to enter my protest. To the better understanding of this 'explanatory tradition,' it may be necessary to premise that the name of Guadalupe was already familiar to the Spaniards, the Virgin Mary having, it is said, long before appeared in Spain, under the same title; on which occasion an order of monks, styled *Frailes Guadalupanos,* had been instituted. One of these worthy fathers who had been sent as a missionary to Mexico, finding the Indians rather stubborn and unyielding, conceived the plan of flattering their national vanity by fabricating a saint suited for the occasion. The Guadalupano had a poor friend who was an

[3] The accompanying cut represents both sides of a medal of *"Nuestra Señora de Guadalupe de Mexico,"* of which, as I have been informed, 216,000 were struck at Birmingham in the year 1831, designed for the Mexican market. Similar medals are worn by nearly nine-tenths of the population of Northern Mexico. On one side, as will be seen, the Virgin is represented in her star-spangled robe, supported by a cherub and the moon under her feet: a design, which, it has been suggested, was most probably drawn from Revelation xii, I. The date, "A. 1805," is that perhaps of some one of the innumerable miracles, which, according to fame in Mexico, have been wrought by the Virgin Guadalupe. The motto, *"Non fecit taliter omni nationi"* (She "hath not dealt so with any nation") which is found on the reverse of the medal, is extracted from Psalm cxlvii. 20.—GREGG.

excellent painter, to whom he said, one day, "Take this tilma"—presenting him one of the coarsest and most slazy texture (a sort of *manta de guangoche*); "paste it upon the canvass, and paint me thereon the handsomest effigy of Nuestra Señora de Guadalupe that your fancy can portray." When this was done according to order, and the tilma separated from the canvass, the picture appeared somewhat miraculous. Viewed very closely, it showed exceedingly dim; but upon receding to some distance, so that the eye could embrace a larger field of the open texture, it appeared quite distinct and beautiful. This effect is often alluded to at the present day, and easily as it might be accounted for upon philosophical principles, I have heard many an ignorant Mexican declare, that *la Santísima Vírgen* concealed herself from such as profaned her shrine by a too near approach, and only shone forth in all her brilliancy to those who kept at a respectful distance. But, in conclusion, the story relates, that a suitable damsel being selected and decked out to represent the Virgin, the affair was played off as it has been narrated.

As regards the miracle of the fresh flowers in December the *profanos* say, that there was nothing very wonderful about it, as flowers were known to bloom in the lowlands, and only a few leagues from the spot where the affair took place, at all seasons of the year; implying that these had been engrafted upon the rock for the occasion. There are some who go so far as to insinuate that the bishop and other ecclesiastics were privy to the whole affair, and that every precaution had been taken to see the Indian who played first fiddle in the matter, provided with a tilma, similar to the one on which the image of the Virgin was painted, and that this was artfully slipped in the place of the former, which the Indian had doffed when he climbed the rock after the flowers.—I have not seen the original portrait, but most of the copies and imitations I have met with, represent the Virgin with that peculiarly tawny complexion which was probably deemed indispensable to conciliate the prejudices of the aborigines.

The reader may reconcile the foregoing discrepancies in the best way he can: all that I have to add is, that the apparition having been canonized by the Pope, a belief in it now constitutes as much as part of the religious faith of the Mexicans, as any article of the Apostolic

Creed. To judge from the blind and reverential awe in which the Virgin Guadalupe is held by the lowly and the ignorant, one would suppose her to be the first person in the Divinity; for to her their vows are directed, their prayers offered up, and all their confessions made.

Among the many traditions implicitly believed in by the people, and which tend to obstruct the advancement of knowledge, there is one equally as amusing and extravagant as the foregoing, which has been gravely recounted by the present Vicar of New Mexico and ex-delegate to Congress. During the memorable insurrection of 1680, the Pueblo of San Felipe was about the only one that remained faithful to the Spaniards in all the North.[4] It was during that exciting period that the padre of another Pueblo took refuge among them. Being besieged by their neighbors and their communication with the water entirely cut off, they applied for advice to the reverend padre, who bade them not despair, as he had it in his power to supply them with water. He then began to pray very fervently after which he opened a vein in each of his arms, from whence there flowed two such copious streams of water that all fears of being reduced by thirst were completely allayed!

It is a part of the superstitious blindness of these people to believe that every one of their legion of canonized saints possesses the power of performing certain miracles; and their aid is generally invoked on all occasions of sickness and distress. The kindest office, therefore, that the friends of a sick person can perform, is to bring forward the image of some of those saints whose healing powers have been satisfactorily tested. The efficacy of these superstitious remedies will not be difficult to account for, when the powerful influence of the imagination upon disease is taken into consideration.

The images of patron saints are never put in such general requisition, however, as in seasons of severe drought. The priests, being generally expert at guessing the approach of a pluvial period, take good care not to make confident promises till they have substantial reason to anticipate a speedy fulfilment of their prophecies. When

---

[4] San Felipe was not besieged during the Revolt of 1680, but its inhabitants took part in risings at Santo Domingo and elsewhere. It is a Queres pueblo which, after having been moved four times during the last four centuries, is now on the west bank of the Río Grande in Sandoval County, opposite Tuerto Creek.

the fitting season draws nigh, they carry out the image of Nuestra Señora de Guadalupe, or that of some other favorite saint, and parade about the streets, the fields and the meadows, followed by all the men, women, and children of the neighborhood, in solemn procession. Should the clouds condescend to vouchsafe a supply of rain within a week or two of this general humiliation, no one ever thinks of begrudging the scores of dollars that have been paid to the priests for bringing about so happy a result.

Speaking of processions, I am reminded of another peculiar custom so prevalent in Mexico, that it never fails to attract the attention of strangers. This is the passage of the Sacred Host to the residence of persons dangerously ill, for the purpose of administering to them the Extreme Unction. In New Mexico, however, this procession is not attended with so much ostentatious display as it is in the South, the paradise of ecclesiastics, where it is conveyed in a black coach drawn by a pair of black mules, accompanied by armed soldiers and followed by crowds of *léperos* of all sexes and ages. During the procession of the Host, two church-bells of different tones are kept sounding by alternate strokes. Also the carriage is always preceded by a bell-man tinkling a little bell in regular time, to notify all within hearing of its approach, that they may be prepared to pay it due homage. When this bell is heard, all those that happen to be within sight of the procession, though at ever so great a distance, instantly kneel and remain in that position till it has passed out of sight. On these occasions, if an American happens to be within hearing, he endeavors to avoid the *cortège*, by turning the corner of a street or entering a shop or the house of a friend; for although it may be expedient, and even rational, to conform with the customs and ceremonies of those countries we are sojourning in, very few Protestants would feel disposed to fall on their knees before a coach freighted with frail mortals pretending to represent the Godhead: I am sorry to say that non-compliants are frequently insulted and sometimes pelted with stones by the rabble. Even a foreign artisan was once massacred in the Mexican metropolis because he refused to come out of his shop, where he was kneeling, and perform the act of genuflexion in the street!

This abject idoltry sometimes takes a still more humiliating aspect, and descends to the worship of men in the capacity of religious rulers. On the occasion of the Bishop of Durango's visit to Santa Fé in 1833, an event which had not taken place for a great many years, the infatuated population hailed his arrival with as much devotional enthusiasm as if it had been the second advent of the Messiah. Magnificent preparations were made everywhere for his reception: the streets were swept, the roads and bridges on his route repaired and decorated; and from every window in the city there hung such a profusion of fancy curtains and rich cloths that the imagination was carried back to those glowing descriptions of enchanted worlds which one reads of in the fables of necromancers. I must observe, however, that there is a custom in all the towns of Mexico (which it would not be safe to neglect), providing that whenever a religious procession takes place, all the doors and windows facing the street along which it is to pass, shall be decorated with shawls, carpets, or fancy cloths, according to the means and capabilities of the proprietor. During the bishop's sojourn in Santa Fé, which, to the great joy of the inhabitants, lasted for several weeks, he never appeared in the streets, but that 'all true Catholics' who were so fortunate as to obtain a glimpse of his *Señoría Ilustrísima* immediately dropped upon their knees, and never moved from that position till the mitred priest had either vouchsafed his benediction or had disappeared. Even the principal personages of the city would not venture to address him till they had first knelt at his feet and kissed his 'pastoral ring.' This, however, is only a heightened picture of what occurs every day in the intercourse between the rancheros and the common padres of the country. The slavish obsequiousness of the lower classes towards these pampered priests is almost incredible.

No people are more punctual in their attendance upon public worship, or more exact in the performance of the external rites of religion, than the New Mexicans. A man would about as soon think of venturing in twenty fathoms of water without being able to swim, as of undertaking a journey without hearing mass first. These religious exercises, however, partake but seldom of the character of true devotion; for people may be seen chattering or tittering while in the act of crossing themselves, or muttering some formal prayer. Indeed, it is the common remark of strangers, that they are wont to wear much graver countenances while dancing at a fandango than during their devotional exercises at the foot of the altar. In nothing, however, is their observance of the outward forms of religion more remarkable than in their deportment every day towards the close of twilight, when the large bell of the *Parroquia*[5] peals for *la oracion,* or vespers. All conversation is instantly suspended—all labor ceases —people of all classes, whether on foot or on horseback, make a sudden halt—even the laden porter, groaning under the weight of an insupportable burden, stops in the midst of his career and stands still. An almost breathless silence reigns throughout the town, disturbed only by the occasional sibilations of the devout multitude: all of which, accompanied by the slow heavy peals of a large sonorous bell, afford a scene truly solemn and appropriate. At the expiration of about two minutes the charm is suddenly broken by the clatter of livelier-toned bells; and a *buenas tardes* (good evening) to those present closes the ceremony: when *presto,* all is bustle and confusion again—the colloquial chit-chat is resumed—the smith plies upon his anvil with redoubled energy—the clink of the hammer simultaneously resounds in every direction—the wayfarers are again in motion,—both pleasure and business, in short, assume their respective sway.

Although the Catholics have a saint for each day in the year, the number of canonized *fiestas* in which labor is prohibited has been somewhat reduced in Mexico. *La Semana Santa,* or Passion Week, is perhaps the period when the religious feeling, such as it is, is most fully excited: *Viernes Santo* (Good Friday), especially, is observed with great pomp and splendor. An image of Christ large as life, nailed to a huge wooden cross, is paraded through the streets, in the midst of an immense procession, accompanied by a glittering array of carved images, representing the Virgin Mary, Mary Magdalene, and several others; while the most notorious personages of antiquity, who figured at that great era of the World's history,—the centurion with a band of guards, armed with lances, and apparelled in the costume supposed to have been worn in those days,—may be seen bestriding splendidly caparisoned horses, in the breathing reality of flesh and blood. Taking it all in all, this spectacle,—the cere-

[5] The present St. Francis cathedral (built in 1869) incorporates the Parroquia building, which dates from 1622.

monies and manoeuvres which attend its career through the densely crowded and ornamented streets,—are calculated to produce impressions of a most confused description, in which regret and melancholy may be said to form no inconsiderable share.

It has been customary for great malefactors to propitiate Divine forgiveness by a cruel sort of *penitencia*, which generally takes place during the *Semana Santa*. I once chanced to be in the town of Tomé[6] on Good Friday, when my attention was arrested by a man almost naked, bearing, in imitation of Simon, a huge cross upon his shoulders, which, though constructed of the lightest wood, must have weighed over a hundred pounds. The long end dragged upon the ground, as we have seen it represented in sacred pictures, and about the middle swung a stone of immense dimensions, appended there for the purpose of making the task more laborious. Not far behind followed another equally destitute of clothing, with his whole body wrapped in chains and cords, which seemed buried in the muscles, and which so cramped and confined him that he was scarcely able to keep pace with the procession. The person who brought up the rear presented a still more disgusting aspect. He walked along with a patient and composed step, while another followed close behind belaboring him lustily with a whip, which he flourished with all the satisfaction of an amateur; but as the lash was pointed only with a tuft of untwisted sea-grass, its application merely served to keep open the wounds upon the penitent's back, which had been scarified, as I was informed, with the keen edge of a flint, and was bleeding most profusely. The blood was kept in perpetual flow by the stimulating juice of certain herbs, carried by a third person, into which the scourger frequently dipped his lash. Although the actors in this tragical farce were completely muffled, yet they were well known to many of the by-standers, one of whom assured me that they were three of the most notorious rascals in the country. By submitting to this species of penance, they annually received complete absolution of their past year's sins, and, thus 'purified,' entered afresh on the old career of wickedness and crime.[7]

[6] On the east bank of the Río Grande 26 miles below Albuquerque. In the seventeenth century it was an hacienda belonging to Thomé Domínguez.

[7] Gregg here describes the rites of Los Hermanos de Penitencia, or the Penitentes, a society of flagellants introduced into Spanish America in the sixteenth and seven-

In New Mexico, the institution of marriage changes the legal rights of the parties, but is scarcely affects their moral obligations. It is usually looked upon as a convenient cloak for irregularities, which society less willingly tolerates in the lives of unmarried women. Yet when it is considered that the majority of matches are forced and ill-assorted, some idea may be formed of the little incitement that is given to virtue. There are very few parents who would stoop to consult a young lady's wishes before concluding a marriage contract, nor would maidens, generally, ever dream of a matrimonial connexion unless proposed first by the father. The lover's proposals are, upon the same principle, made in writing direct to the parents themselves, and without the least deference to the wishes or inclinations of the young lady whose hand is thus sought in marriage. The tender emotions engendered between lovers during walks and rambles along the banks of silent streams, are never experienced in this country; for the sexes are seldom permitted to converse or be together alone. In short, instances have actually occurred when the bethrothed couple have never seen each other till brought to the altar to be joined in wedlock.

Among the humbler classes, there are still more powerful causes calculated to produce irregularity of life; not the least of which is the enormous fee that must be paid to the curate for tying the matrimonial knot. This system of extortion is carried so far as to amount very frequently to absolute prohibition: for the means of the bridegroom are often insufficient for the exigency of the occasion; and the priests seldom consent to join people in wedlock until the money has been secured to them. The curates being without control, the marriage rates are somewhat irregular, but they usually increase in proportion to the character of the ceremonies and to the circumstances of the parties. The lowest (about twenty dollars) are adapted to the simplest form, solemnized in church at mass; but with the excuse of any extra service and ceremonies, particularly if performed at a private house, the fees are increased often as high as several hundred

---

teenth centuries (into New Mexico in the early nineteenth century), whose practices reached their worst stages between 1850 and 1890. Although ordered by the archbishop of Santa Fé to disband in 1889, the society still prevails on a reduced scale. *The Catholic Encyclopedia*, XI, 635-36.

dollars: I have heard of $500 being paid for a marriage ceremony. The following communication, which appeared in a Chihuahua paper under the signature of *"Un Ranchero,"* affords some illustration of the grievances of the plebeians in this respect. Literally translated it runs thus:

"Messrs. Editors of the Noticioso de Chihuahua:

"Permit me, through your paper, to say a few words in print, as those of my pen have been unsuccessfully employed with the *curas* of Allende and Jimenez, to whom I applied the other day for the purpose of ascertaining their legal charge to marry one of my sons. The following simple and concise answer is all that I have been able to elicit from either of these ecclesiastics:—'*The marriage fees are a hundred and nineteen dollars.*' I must confess that I was completely suffocated when I heard this outrageous demand upon my poor purse; and did I not pride myself on being a true Apostolic Roman Catholic, and were it not that the charming graces of my intended daughter-in-law have so captivated my son that nothing but marriage will satisfy him, I would assuredly advise him to contrive some other arrangement with his beloved, which might not be so ruinous to our poor purse; for reflect that $119 are the life and all of a poor ranchero. If nothing else will do, I shall have to sell my few cows (*mis vaquitas*) to help my son out of this difficulty." The 'Ranchero' then appeals to the Government to remedy such evils, by imposing some salutary restrictions upon the clergy; and concludes by saying, "If this is not done, I will never permit either of my remaining three sons to marry."

This article was certainly an effort of boldness against the priesthood, which may have cost the poor 'Ranchero' a sentence of excommunication. Few of his countrymen would venture on a similar act of temerity; and at least nine-tenths profess the most profound submission to their religious rulers. Being thus bred to look upon their priests as infallible and holy samples of piety and virtue, we should not be so much surprised at the excesses of the 'flock' when a large portion of the *pastores,* the padres themselves, are foremost in most of the popular vices of the country: first at the fandango—first at the gaming table—first at the cock-pit—first at bacchanalian orgies—and by no means last in the contraction of those *liaisons* which are so emphatically prohibited by their vows.

The baptismal and burial fees (neither of which can be avoided without incurring the charge of heresy) are also a great terror to the candidates for married life. "If I marry," says a poor yeoman, "my family must go unclad to baptize my children; and if any of them should die, we must starve ourselves to pay the burial charges." The fee for baptism, it is true, is not so exorbitant, and in accordance to custom, is often paid by the *padrino* or sponsor; but the burial costs are almost equally extravagant with those of marriage, varying in proportion to the age and circumstances of the deceased. A faithful Mexican servant in my employ at Chihuahua, once solicited forty dollars to bury his mother. Upon my expressing some surprise at the exorbitancy of the amount, he replied—"That is what the cura demands, sir, and if I do not pay it my poor mother will remain unburied!" Thus this man was obliged to sacrifice several months' wages, to pamper the avarice of a vicious and mercenary priest. On another occasion, a poor widow in Santa Fé, begged a little medicine for her sick child: "Not," said the disconsolate mother, "that the life of the babe imports me much, for I know the *angelito* will go directly to heaven; but what shall I do to pay the priest for burying it? He will take my house and all from me—and I shall be turned desolate into the street!—and so saying, she commenced weeping bitterly.

Indigent parents are thus frequently under the painful necessity of abandoning and disowning their deceased children, to avoid the responsibility of burial expenses. To this end the corpse is sometimes deposited in some niche or corner of the church during the night; and upon being found in the morning, the priest is bound to inter it gratis, unless the parent can be discovered, in which case the latter would be liable to severe castigation, besides being bound to pay the expenses.

Children that have not been baptized are destined, according to the popular faith, to a kind of negative existence in the world of spirits, called *Limbo*, where they remain forever without either suffering punishment or enjoying happiness. Baptized infants, on the other hand, being considered without sin, are supposed to enter at once into the joys of heaven. The deceased child is then denominated an *angelito* (a little angel), and is interred with joy and mirth instead of grief and wailing. It is gaudily bedecked with fanciful attire and ornaments of tinsel and flowers; and being placed upon a small bier, it is carried to the grave by four children as gaily dressed as their circumstances will allow; accompanied by musicians using the instruments and playing the tunes of the fandangos; and the little procession is nothing but glee and merriment.

In New Mexico the lower classes are very rarely, if ever, buried in coffins: the corpse being simply wrapped in a blanket, or some other covering, and in that rude attire consigned to its last home. It is truly shocking to a sensitive mind to witness the inhuman treatment to which the remains of the dead are sometimes subjected. There being nothing to indicate the place of the previous graves, it not unfrequently happens that the partially decayed relics of a corpse are dug up and forced to give place to the more recently deceased, when they are again thrown with the earth into the new grave with perfect indifference. The operation of filling up the grave especially, is particularly repulsive; the earth being pounded down with a large maul, as fast as it is thrown in upon the unprotected corpse, with a force sufficient to crush a delicate frame to atoms.

As the remains of heretics are not permitted to pollute either the church-yard or *Campo Santo,* those Americans who have died in Santa Fé, have been buried on a hill which overlooks the town to the northward. The corpses have sometimes been disinterred and robbed of the shroud in which they were enveloped; so that, on a few occasions, it has been deemed expedient to appoint a special watch for the protection of the grave.

CHAPTER XIV

The Pueblos—Their Character for Sobriety, Honesty, and Industry—
Traditional Descent from Montezuma—Their Languages—Former
and present Population—The Pueblo of Pecos—Singular Habits of that
ill-fated Tribe—Curious Tradition—Montezuma and the Sun—Legend
of a Serpent—Religion and Government—Secret Council—Laws and
Customs—Excellent Provisions against Demoralization—Primitive Pastimes of the Pueblos—Their Architecture—Singular Structures of Taos,
and other novel Fortifications—Primitive state of the Arts among the
Pueblos—Style of Dress, Weapons, etc.—Their Diet—The *Guayave.*

ALLUSION has so frequently been made to the aboriginal tribes of
New Mexico, known as *Los Pueblos,* that I think I shall not be
trespassing too much upon the patience of the reader, in glancing
rapidly at some of the more conspicuous features of their national
habits and character.

Although the term *Pueblo* in Spanish literally means the *people,*
and their *towns,* it is here specifically applied to the *Christianized
Indians* (as well as their villages)—to those aborigines whom the
Spaniards not only subjected to their laws, but to an acknowledgment
of the Romish faith, and upon whom they forced baptism and the
cross in exchange for the vast possessions of which they robbed them.
All that was left them was, to each Pueblo a league or two of land
situated around their villages, the conquerors reserving to themselves at least ninety-nine hundredths of the whole domain as a re-
quital for their generosity.

When these regions were first discovered it appears that the inhabitants lived in comfortable houses and cultivated the soil, as they
have continued to do up to the present time. Indeed, they are now

considered the best horticulturists in the country, furnishing most of
the fruits and a large portion of the vegetable supplies that are to be
found in the markets. They were until very lately the only people in
New Mexico who cultivated the grape. They also maintain at the
present time considerable herds of cattle, horses, etc. They are, in
short, a remarkably sober and industrious race, conspicuous for
morality and honesty, and very little given to quarrelling or dissipation, except when they have had much familiar intercourse with the
Hispano-Mexican population.

Most of these Pueblos call themselves the descendants of Montezuma, although it would appear that they could only have been
made acquainted with the history of that monarch, by the Spaniards;
as this province is nearly two thousand miles from the ancient kingdom of Mexico. At the time of the conquest they must have been a
very powerful people—numbering near a hundred villages, as existing ruins would seem to indicate; but they are now reduced to about
twenty, which are scattered in various parts of the territory.

There are but three or four different languages spoken among
them, and these, indeed, may be distantly allied to each other. Those
of Taos, Picuris, Isleta, and perhaps some others, speak what has
been called the *Piro* language. A large portion of the others, viz.,
those of San Juan, Santa Clara, Nambé, Pojuaque, Tezuque, and
some others, speak *Tegua*, having all been originally known by this
general name; and those of Cochití, Santo Domingo, San Felipe,
and perhaps Sandía, speak the same tongue, though they seem formerly to have been distinguished as *Queres*. The numerous tribes that
inhabited the highlands between Rio del Norte and Pecos, as those
of Pecos, Ciénega, Galisteo, etc., were known anciently as *Tagnos*,
but these are now all extinct; yet their language is said to be spoken
by those of Jemez and others of that section.[1] Those further to the
westward[2] are perhaps allied to the Navajoes. Though all these

[1] Gregg's classification is inaccurate. His Piro grouping is actually Tigua (or
Tiwa) and includes the Sandía pueblo, which he identifies tentatively as Queres (or
Keres). The true Piro (now extinct) occupied the southernmost pueblos of New
Mexico. Tagno (or Tano) is not a separate language but the generic term for the
Tigua, Tegua, and Togua (or Towa). Gregg is correct, however, in identifying the
widely separated pueblos of Pecos and Jémez as being of the same (Togua) lan-
guage.
[2] Of these, the Pueblo of Zuñi has been celebrated for honesty and hospitality.

Pueblos speak their native languages among themselves, a great many of them possess a smattering of Spanish, sufficient to carry on their intercourse with the Mexicans.

The population of these Pueblos will average nearly five hundred souls each (though some hardly exceed one hundred), making an aggregate of nine or ten thousand. At the time of the original conquest, at the close of the sixteenth century, they were, as has been mentioned, much, perhaps ten-fold, more numerous. Ancient ruins are now to be seen scattered in every quarter of the territory: of some, entire stone walls are yet standing, while others are nearly or quite obliterated, many of them being now only known by their names which history or tradition has preserved to us. Numbers were no doubt destroyed during the insurrection of 1680, and the petty internal strifes which followed.[3]

Several of these Pueblos have been converted into Mexican villages, of which that of *Pecos*[4] is perhaps the most remarkable instance. What with the massacres of the second conquest, and the inroads of the Comanches, they gradually dwindled away, till they found themselves reduced to about a dozen, comprising all ages and sexes; and it was only a few years ago that they abandoned the home of their fathers and joined the Pueblo of Jemez.

Many curious tales are told of the singular habits of this ill-fated tribe, which must no doubt have tended to hasten its utter annihilation. A tradition was prevalent among them that Montezuma had

The inhabitants mostly profess the Catholic faith, but have now no curate. They cultivate the soil, manufacture, and possess considerable quantities of stock. Their village is over 150 miles west of the Rio del Norte, on the waters of the Colorado of the West, and is believed to contain between 1,000 and 1,500 souls. The "seven pueblos of Moqui" (as they are called) are a similar tribe living a few leagues beyond. They formerly acknowledged the government and religion of the Spaniards, but have long since rejected both, and live in a state of independence and paganism. Their dwellings, however, like those of the Zuñi, are similar to those of the interior Pueblos, and they are equally industrious and agricultural, and still more ingenious in their manufacturing. The language of the *Moquis* or *Moquinos* [i. e. Hopis] is said to differ but little from that of the Navajoes.—GREGG.

[3] For the current (*ca.* 1840) Pueblo population, Gregg's estimate is much below the 1827 census, and his pre-Spanish figure is four times what archaeologists now compute. Bandelier, *Final Report*, III, 121–36. Gregg failed to realize that many Indian towns were in ruins before the Spaniards came.

[4] About 30 miles southeast of Santa Fé. At the close of the seventeenth century, Pecos was the largest New Mexican pueblo (pop. 2,000).

kindled a holy fire, and enjoined their ancestors not to suffer it to be extinguished until he should return to deliver his people from the yoke of the Spaniards. In pursuance of these commands, a constant watch had been maintained for ages to prevent the fire from going out; and, as tradition further informed them, that Montezuma would appear with the sun, the deluded Indians were to be seen every clear morning upon the terraced roofs of their houses, attentively watching for the appearance of the 'king of light,' in hopes of seeing him 'cheek by jowl' with their immortal sovereign. I have myself descended into the famous *estufas*, or subterranean vaults, of which there were several in the village, and have beheld this consecrated fire, silently smouldering under a covering of ashes, in the basin of a small altar. Some say that they never lost hope in the final coming of Montezuma until, by some accident or other, or a lack of a sufficiency of warriors to watch it, the fire became extinguished; and that it was this catastrophe that induced them to abandon their villages, as I have before observed.

The task of tending the sacred fire was, it is said, allotted to the warriors. It is further related, that they took the watch by turns for two successive days and nights, without partaking of either food, water, or sleep; while some assert, that instead of being restricted to two days, each guard continued with the same unbending severity of purpose until exhaustion, and very frequently death, left their places to be filled by others. A large portion of those who came out alive were generally so completely prostrated by the want of repose and the inhalation of carbonic gas that they very soon died; when, as the vulgar story asseverates, their remains were carried to the den of a monstrous serpent, which kept itself in excellent condition by feeding upon these delicacies. This huge snake (invented no doubt by the lovers of the marvellous to account for the constant disappearance of the Indians) was represented as the idol which they worshipped, and as subsisting entirely upon the flesh of his devotees: live infants, however, seemed to suit his palate best. The story of this wonderful serpent was so firmly believed in by many ignorant people, that on one occasion I heard an honest ranchero assert, that upon entering the village very early on a winter's morning, he saw the huge trail of the reptile in the snow, as large as that of a dragging ox.

This village, anciently so renowned, lies twenty-five miles eastward of Santa Fé, and near the *Rio Pecos,* to which it gave name. Even so late as ten years ago, when it contained a population of fifty to a hundred souls, the traveller would oftentimes perceive but a solitary Indian, a woman, or a child, standing here and there like so many statues upon the roofs of their houses, with their eyes fixed on the eastern horizon, or leaning against a wall or a fence, listlessly gazing at the passing stranger; while at other times not a soul was to be seen in any direction, and the sepulchral silence of the place was only disturbed by the occasional barking of a dog, or the cackling of hens.

No other Pueblo appears to have adopted this extraordinary superstition: like Pecos, however, they have all held Montezuma to be their perpetual sovereign. It would likewise appear that they all worship the sun; for it is asserted to be their regular practice to turn the face towards the east at sunrise. They profess the Catholic faith, however, of which, nevertheless, they cannot be expected to understand anything beyond the formalities; as but very few of their Mexican neighbors and teachers can boast of more.

Although nominally under the jurisdiction of the federal government, as Mexican citizens, many features of their ancient customs are still retained, as well in their civil rule as in their religion. Each Pueblo is under the control of a *cacique* or *gobernadorcillo,* chosen from among their own sages, and commissioned by the governor of New Mexico. The cacique, when any public business is to be transacted, collects together the principal chiefs of the Pueblo in an *estufa,* or cell, usually under ground, and there lays before them the subjects of debate, which are generally settled by the opinion of the majority. No Mexican is admitted to these councils, nor do the subjects of discussion ever transpire beyond the precincts of the cavern. The council has also charge of the interior police and tranquility of the village. One of their regulations is to appoint a secret watch for the purpose of keeping down disorders and vices of every description, and especially to keep an eye over the young men and women of the village. When any improper intercourse among them is detected, the parties are immediately carried to the council, and the cacique intimates to them that they must be wedded forthwith.

Should the girl be of bad character, and the man, therefore, unwilling to marry her, they are ordered to keep separate under penalty of the lash. Hence it is, that the females of these Pueblos are almost universally noted for their chastity and modest deportment.

They also elect a *capitan de guerra,* a kind of commander-in-chief of the warriors, whose office it is to defend their homes and their interests both in the field and in the council chamber. Though not very warlike, these Pueblos are generally valiant, and well skilled in the strategies of Indian warfare; and although they have been branded with cruelty and ferocity, yet they can hardly be said to surpass the Mexicans in this respect: both, in times of war, pay but little regard either to age or sex. I have been told that when the Pueblos return from their belligerent expeditions, instead of going directly to their homes, they always visit their council cell first. Here they undress, dance, and carouse, frequently for two days in succession before seeing their families.

Although the Pueblos are famous for hospitality and industry, they still continue in the rudest state of ignorance, having neither books nor schools among them, as none of their languages have been reduced to rules, and very few of their children are ever taught in Spanish. A degree of primitiveness characterizes all their amusements, which bear a strong similarity to those of the wilder tribes. Before the New Mexican government had become so much impoverished, there was wont to be held in the capital on the 16th of September of every year, a national celebration of the declaration of Independence, to which the Pueblos were invited. The warriors and youths of each nation with a proportionate array of dusky damsels would appear on these occasions, painted and ornamented in accordance with their aboriginal customs, and amuse the inhabitants with all sorts of grotesque feats and native dances. Each Pueblo generally had its particular uniform dress and its particular dance. The men of one village would sometimes disguise themselves as elks, with horns on their heads, moving on all-fours, and mimicking the animal they were attempting to personate. Others would appear in the garb of a turkey, with large heavy wings, and strut about in imitation of that bird. But the Pecos tribe, already reduced to seven men, always occasioned most diversion. Their favorite exploit was, each to put on the skin of a buffalo, horns, tail, and all, and thus accoutred scamper about through the crowd, to the real or affected terror of all the ladies present, and to the great delight of the boys.

The Pueblo villages are generally built with more regularity than those of the Mexicans, and are constructed of the same materials as were used by them in the most primitive ages. Their dwelling-houses, it is true, are not so spacious as those of the Mexicans, containing very seldom more than two or three small apartments upon the ground floor, without any court-yard, but they have generally a much loftier appearance, being frequently two stories high and sometimes more. A very curious feature in these buildings, is, that there is most generally no direct communication between the street and the lower rooms, into which they descend by a trap-door from the upper story, the latter being accessible by means of ladders. Even the entrance to the upper stories is frequently at the roof. This style of building seems to have been adopted for security against their marauding neighbors of the wilder tribes, with whom they were often at war. When the family had all been housed at night, the ladder was drawn up, and the inmates were thus shut up in a kind of fortress, which bid defiance to the scanty implements of warfare used by the wild Indians.

Though this was their most usual style of architecture, there still exists a Pueblo of Taos, composed, for the most part, of but two edifices of very singular structure—one on each side of a creek, and formerly communicating by a bridge. The base-story is a mass of near four hundred feet long, a hundred and fifty wide, and divided into numerous apartments, upon which other tiers of rooms are built, one above another, drawn in by regular grades, forming a pyramidal pile of fifty or sixty feet high, and comprising some six or eight stories. The outer rooms only seem to be used for dwellings, and are lighted by little windows in the sides, but are entered through trap-doors in the *azoteas* or roofs. Most of the inner apartments are employed as granaries and store-rooms, but a spacious hall in the centre of the mass, known as the *estufa*, is reserved for their secret councils. These two buildings afford habitations, as is said, for over six hundred souls. There is likewise an edifice in the Pueblo of Picuris[5] of the same class, and some of those of Moqui are also said to be similar.

Some of these villages were built upon rocky eminences deemed almost inaccessible: witness for instance the ruins of the ancient Pueblo of San Felipe,[6] which may be seen towering upon the very verge of a precipice several hundred feet high, whose base is washed by the swift current of the Rio del Norte. The still existing Pueblo of Acoma[7] also stands upon an isolated mound whose whole area is occupied by the village, being fringed all around by a precipitious *ceja* or cliff. The inhabitants enter the village by means of ladders, and by steps cut into the solid rock upon which it is based.

At the time of the conquest, many of these Pueblos manufactured some singular textures of cotton and other materials; but with the loss of their liberty, they seem to have lost most of their arts and ingenuity; so that the finer specimens of native fabrics are now only to be met with among the Moquis and Navajoes, who still retain their independence. The Pueblos, however, make some of the ordinary classes of blankets and *tilmas*,[8] as well as other woollen stuffs. They also manufacture, according to their aboriginal art, both for their own consumption, and for the purposes of traffic, a species of earthenware not much inferior to the coarse crockery of our common potters. The pots made of this material stand fire remarkably well, and are the universal substitutes for all the purposes of cookery, even among the Mexicans, for the iron castings of this country, which are utterly unknown there. Rude as this kind of crockery is, it nevertheless evinces a great deal of skill, considering that it is made entirely without lathe or any kind of machinery. It is often fancifully painted with colored earths and the juice of a plant called *guaco*,[9] which brightens by burning. They also work a singular kind of wicker-ware, of which some bowls (if they may be so called) are so closely platted, that, once swollen by dampness, they serve to hold

[5] A Tigua town in Taos County, about 70 miles north of Santa Fé.

[6] Not to be confused with the more recent town at the base of the mesa mentioned above (chap. 13, n. 4). During the Pueblo Revolt, San Felipe was on the summit of this mesa.

[7] A western Queresan pueblo in Valencia County, on an isolated mesa 350 feet above the plain, about 70 miles southwest of Santa Fé.

[8] The *tilma* of the North is a sort of small but durable blanket, worn by the Indians as a mantle.—GREGG.

[9] The common Rocky Mountain bee plant (*Cleome serrulata*).

liquids, and are therefore light and convenient vessels for the purposes of travellers.

The dress of many of the Pueblos has become assimilated in some respects to that of the common Mexicans; but by far the greatest portion still retain most of their aboriginal costume. The Taosas and others of the north somewhat resemble the prairie tribes in this respect; but the Pueblos to the south and west of Santa Fé dress in a different style, which is said to be similar in many respects to that of the aboriginal inhabitants of the city of Mexico. The moccasin is the only part of the prairie suit that appears common to them all, and of both sexes. They mostly wear a kind of short breeches and long stockings, the use of which they most probably acquired from the Spaniards. The *saco*, a species of woollen jacket without sleeves, completes their exterior garment; except during inclement seasons, when they make use of the tilma. Very few of them have hats or head-dress of any kind; and they generally wear their hair long— commonly fashioned into a *queue*, wrapped with some colored stuff. The squaws of the northern tribes dress pretty much like those of the Prairies; but the usual costume of the females of the southern and western Pueblos is a handsome kind of small blanket of dark color, which is drawn under one arm and tacked over the other shoulder, leaving both arms free and naked. It is generally worn with a cotton chemise underneath and is bound about the waist with a girdle. We rarely if ever see a thorough-bred Pueblo woman in Mexican dress.

The weapons most in use among the Pueblos are the bow and arrow, with a long-handled lance and occasionally a fusil. The rawhide shield is also much used, which, though of but little service against fire-arms, serves to ward off the arrow and lance.

The aliment of these Indians is, in most respects, similar to that of the Mexicans; in fact, as has been elsewhere remarked, the latter adopted with their utensils numerous items of aboriginal diet. The *tortilla*, the *atole*, the *pinole*,[10] and many others, together with the

[10] *Pinole* is in effect the *cold-flour* of our hunters. It is the meal of parched Indian corn, prepared for use by stirring it up with a little cold water. This food seems also to have been of ancient use among the aborigines of other parts of America. Father Charlevoix, in 1721, says of the savages about the northern lakes, that they "reduce [the maize] to Flour which they call *Farine froide* (cold Flour), and this is the best Provision that can be made for Travellers."—GREGG.

Gregg's reference is to Pierre François Xavier de Charlevoix's *Histoire et*

use of *chile,* are from the Indians. Some of the wilder tribes make a peculiar kind of *pinole,* by grinding the bean of the mezquite tree into flour, which is then used as that of corn. And besides the tortilla they make another singular kind of bread, if we may so style it, called *guayave,* a roll of which so much resembles a 'hornets' nest,' that by strangers it is often designated by this title. It is usually made of Indian corn prepared and ground as for tortillas, and diluted into a thin paste. I once happened to enter an Indian hut where a young girl of the family was baking *guayaves.* She was sitting by a fire, over which a large flat stone was heating, with a crock of prepared paste by her side. She thrust her hand into the paste, and then wiped it over the heated stone. What adhered to it was instantly baked and peeled off. She repeated this process at the rate of a dozen times or more per minute. Observing my curiosity, the girl handed me one of the 'sheets,' silently; for she seemed to understand but her native tongue. I found it pleasant enough to the taste; though when cold, as I have learned by experience, it is, like the cold tortilla, rather tough and insipid. They are even thinner than wafers; and some dozens, being folded in a roll, constitute the laminate composition before mentioned. Being thus preserved, they serve the natives for months upon their journeys.

description générale de la Nouvelle France (6 vols., Paris, Chez le veuve Ganeau, 1744) or to one of the English translations (1769, ff.)

CHAPTER XV

The wild Tribes of New Mexico—Speculative Theories—Clavigero and the *Azteques*—Pueblo Bonito and other Ruins—Probable Relationship between the *Azteques* and tribes of New Mexico—The several Nations of this Province—*Navajoes* and *Azteques*—Manufactures of the former —Their Agriculture, Religion, etc.—Mexican Cruelty to the Indians and its Consequences—Inroads of the Navajoes—Exploits of a Mexican Army—How to make a Hole in a Powder-keg—The *Apaches* and their Character—Their Food—Novel Mode of settling Disputes—Range of their marauding Excursions—Indian Traffic and imbecile Treaties— Devastation of the Country—Chihuahua Rodomontades—Juan José, a celebrated Apache Chief, and his tragical End, etc.—Massacre of Americans in Retaliation—A tragical Episode—*Proyecto de Guerra* and a 'gallant' Display—The *Yutas* and their Hostilities—A personal Adventure with them, but no blood shed—Jicarillas.

ALL THE INDIANS of New Mexico not denominated Pueblos—not professing the Christian religion—are ranked as *wild tribes*, although these include some who have made great advances in arts, manufactures and agriculture. Those who are at all acquainted with the ancient history of Mexico, will recollect that, according to the traditions of the aborigines, all the principal tribes of Anahuac descended from the North: and that those of Mexico, especially the Azteques, emigrated from the north of California, or northwest of New Mexico. Clavigero, the famous historian heretofore alluded to, speaking of this emigration, observes, that the *Azteques*, or Mexican Indians, who were the last settlers in the country of Anahuac, lived until about the year 1160 of the Christian era in Aztlan, a country situated to the north of the Gulf of California; as is inferred from the route of their peregrinations, and from the information afterwards acquired by the Spaniards in their expeditions through those countries. He then proceeds to show by what incentives they were probably induced to abandon their native land; adding that whatever may have been the motive, no doubt can possibly exist as to the journey's having actually been performed. He says that they travelled in a southeastwardly direction towards the Rio Gila,[1] where they remained for some time—the ruins of their edifices being still to be seen, upon its banks. They then struck out for a point over two hundred and fifty miles to the northwest of Chihuahua in about 29° of N. latitude, where they made another halt. This place is known by the name of *Casas Grandes* (big houses),[2] on account of a large edifice which still stands on the spot, and which, according to the general tradition of those regions, was erected by the Mexican Indians, during their wanderings. The building is constructed after the plan of those in New Mexico, with three stories, covered with an *azotea* or terrace, and without door or entrance into the lower story. A hand ladder is also used as a means of communication with the second story.

Even allowing that the traditions upon which Clavigero founded his theoretical deductions are vague and uncertain, there is sufficient evidence in the ruins that still exist to show that those regions were once inhabited by a far more enlightened people than are now to be found among the aborigines. Of such character are the ruins of *Pueblo Bonito*,[3] in the direction of Navajo, on the borders of the Cordilleras; the houses being generally built of slabs of fine-grit sand-stone, a material utterly unknown in the present architecture of the North. Although some of these structures are very massive and spacious, they are generally cut up into small, irregular rooms, many of which yet remain entire, being still covered, with the *vigas*

[1] The Gila, rising in the Elk Mountains and Black Range of Catron County, New Mexico, flows into the Colorado River near Yuma, Arizona.

[2] The Casas Grandes de Moctezuma, on the river of the same name in northwestern Chihuahua, are distinct from the Casa Grande ruins in Pinal County, Arizona, but share the same (now discredited) legend of Aztec origin. Compare Gregg's description with those of John Russell Bartlett, *Personal Narrative of Explorations and Incidents in Texas, New Mexico, California, Sonora and Chihuahua*, II, 339–65; Hubert Howe Bancroft, *Native Races of the Pacific States*, IV, 604–14; and Carmen Alessio Robles, *La región arqueológica de Casas Grandes de Chihuahua*.

[3] In Chaco Canyon National Monument, San Juan County, New Mexico.

or joists remaining nearly sound under the *azoteas* of earth; and yet their age is such that there is no tradition which gives any account of their origin. But there have been no images or sculptured work of any kind found around them. Besides these, many other ruins (though none so perfect) are scattered over the plains and among the mountains. What is very remarkable is, that a portion of them are situated at a great distance from any water; so that the inhabitants must have depended entirely upon rain, as is the case with the Pueblo of Acoma at the present day.

The general appearance of Pueblo Bonito, as well as that of the existing buildings of Moqui in the same mountainous regions, and other Pueblos of New Mexico, resembles so closely the ruins of Casas Grandes, that we naturally come to the conclusion that the founders of each must have descended from the same common stock. The present difference between their language and that of the Indians of Mexico, when we take into consideration the ages that have passed away since their separation, hardly presents any reasonable objection to this hypothesis.

The principal wild tribes which inhabit or extend their incursions or peregrinations upon the territory of New Mexico, are the *Navajoes*, the *Apaches*, the *Yutas*, the *Caiguas* or Kiawas, and the *Comanches*. Of the latter I will speak in another place. The two first are from one and the same original stock, there being, even at the present day, no very important differences in their language. The Apaches are divided into numerous petty tribes, of one of which an insignificant band, called Jicarillas, inhabiting the mountains north of Taos, is an isolated and miserable remnant.

The *Navajoes* are supposed to number about 10,000 souls, and though not the most numerous, they are certainly the most important, at least in a historical point of view, of all the northern tribes of Mexico. They reside in the main range of Cordilleras, 150 to 200 miles west of Santa Fé, on the waters of Rio Colorado of California, not far from the region, according to historians, from whence the Azteques emigrated to Mexico; and there are many reasons to suppose them direct descendants from the remnant, which remained in the North, of this celebrated nation of antiquity. Although they mostly live in rude *jacales*, somewhat resembling the wigwams of the Pawnees, yet, from time immemorial, they have excelled all others in their original manufactures: and, as well as the Moquis, they are still distinguished for some exquisite styles of cotton textures, and display considerable ingenuity in embroidering with feathers the skins of animals, according to their primitive practice. They now also manufacture a singular species of blanket, known as the *Sarape Navajo*, which is of so close and dense a texture that it will frequently hold water almost equal to gum-elastic cloth. It is therefore highly prized for protection against the rains. Some of the finer qualities are often sold among the Mexicans as high as fifty or sixty dollars each.

Notwithstanding the present predatory and somewhat unsettled habits of the Navajoes, they cultivate all the different grains and vegetables to be found in New Mexico. They also possess extensive herds of horses, mules, cattle, sheep and goats of their own raising, which are generally celebrated as being much superior to those of the Mexicans; owing, no doubt to greater attention to the improvement of their stocks.

Though Baron Humboldt tells us that some missionaries were established among this tribe prior to the general massacre of 1680, but few attempts to christianize them have since been made. They now remain in a state of primitive paganism—and not only independent of the Mexicans, but their most formidable enemies.[4]

After the establishment of the national independence, the government of New Mexico greatly embittered the disposition of the neighboring savages, especially the Navajoes, by repeated acts of cruelty and ill-faith well calculated to provoke hostilities. On one occasion, a party consisting of several chiefs and warriors of the Navajoes assembled at the Pueblo of Cochití,[5] by invitation of the government, to celebrate a treaty of peace; when the New Mexicans, exasperated no doubt by the remembrance of former outrages, fell upon them unawares and put them all to death. It is also related, that about the same period, three Indians from the northern moun-

---

[4] The Navajos, an Athapascan tribe, befriended the Spaniards until about 1700, when their raids began. Intermittent war continued and became most intense during the early 1800's.

[5] The northernmost Queresan town, almost due west of Santa Fé, on the west bank of the Río Grande.

tains having been brought as prisoners into Taos, they were peremptorily demanded by the Jicarillas, who were their bitterest enemies; when the Mexican authorities, dreading the resentment of this tribe, quietly complied with the barbarous request, suffering the prisoners to be butchered in cold blood before their very eyes! No wonder, then, that the New Mexicans are so generally warred upon by their savage neighbors.

About fifteen years ago, the Navajoes were subjected by the energy of Col Vizcarra,[6] who succeeded in keeping them in submission for some time; but since that officer's departure from New Mexico, no man has been found of sufficient capacity to inspire this daring tribe either with respect or fear; so that for the last ten years they have ravaged the country with impunity, murdering and destroying just as the humor happened to prompt them. When the spring of the year approaches, terms of peace are generally proposed to the government at Santa Fé, which the latter never fails to accept. This amicable arrangement enables the wily Indians to sow their crops at leisure, and to dispose of the property stolen from the Mexicans during their marauding incursions, to advantage; but the close of their agricultural labors is generally followed by a renewal of hostilities, and the game of rapine and destruction is played over again.

Towards the close of 1835, a volunteer corps, which most of the leading men in New Mexico joined, was raised for the purpose of carrying war into the territory of the Navajoes. The latter hearing of their approach, and anxious no doubt to save them the trouble of so long a journey, mustered a select band of their warriors, who went forth to intercept the invaders in a mountain pass, where they lay concealed in an ambuscade. The valiant corps, utterly unconscious of the reception that awaited them, soon came jogging along in scattered groups, indulging in every kind of boisterous mirth; when the war-whoop, loud and shrill, followed by several shots, threw them all into a state of speechless consternation. Some tumbled off their horses with fright, others fired their muskets at random; a terrific panic had seized everybody, and some minutes elapsed before they could recover their senses sufficiently to betake themselves to their heels. Two or three persons were killed in this ridiculous

[6] See above, chap. 4, n. 9.

engagement, the most conspicuous of whom was Capt. Hinófos,[7] who commanded the regular troops.

A very curious but fully authentic anecdote may not be inappropriately inserted here, in which this individual was concerned. On one occasion, being about to start on a belligerent expedition, he directed his orderly-sergeant[8] to fill a powder-flask from an unbroached keg of twenty-five pounds. The sergeant, having bored a hole with a gimlet, and finding that the powder issued too slowly, began to look about for something to enlarge the aperture, when his eyes haply fell upon an iron poker which lay in a corner of the fire-place. To heat the poker and apply it to the hole in the keg was the work of but a few moments; when an explosion took place which blew the upper part of the building into the street, tearing and shattering everything else to atoms. Miraculous as their escape may appear, the sergeant, as well as the captain who witnessed the whole operation, remained more frightened than hurt, although they were both very severely scorched and bruised. This ingenious sergeant was afterwards Secretary of State of Gov. Gonzalez, of revolutionary memory and has nearly ever since held a clerkship in some of the offices of state, but is now captain in the regular army.

I come now to speak of the *Apaches*, the most extensive and powerful, yet the most vagrant of all the savage nations that inhabit the interior of Northern Mexico. They are supposed to number some fifteen thousand souls, although they are subdivided into various petty bands, and scattered over an immense tract of country. Those that are found east of the Rio del Norte are generally known as *Mezcaleros*, on account of an article of food much in use among them, called *mezcal*;[9] but by far the greatest portion of the nation is located in the west, and is mostly known by the sobriquet of *Coyoteros*, in consequence, it is said, of their eating the *coyote* or prairie-wolf. The Apaches are perhaps more given to itinerant habits

[7] Captain Blas Hinojos, of the Santa Fé company.

[8] Sergeant Donaciano Vigil (1802–77), later secretary of the departmental assembly under Governor González, military secretary under Governor Armijo, territorial secretary under Governor Bent, acting-governor in 1847, and subsequently territorial legislator.

[9] *Mezcal* is the baked root of the maguey (*agave Americana*) and of another somewhat similar plant.—GREGG.

than any other tribe in Mexico. They never construct houses, but live in the ordinary wigwam, or tent of skins and blankets. They manufacture nothing—cultivate nothing: they seldom resort to the chase, as their country is destitute of game—but depend almost entirely upon pillage for the support of their immense population, some two or three thousand of which are warriors.

For their food, the Apaches rely chiefly upon the flesh of the cattle and sheep they can steal from the Mexican rancheros and haciendas. They are said, however, to be more fond of the meat of the mule than that of any other animal. I have seen about encampments which they had recently left, the remains of mules that had been slaughtered for their consumption. Yet on one occasion I saw their whole trail, for many miles, literally strewed with the carcasses of these animals, which, it was evident, had not been killed for this purpose. It is the practice of the Apache chiefs, as I have understood, whenever a dispute arises betwixt their warriors relative to the ownership of any particular animal, to kill the brute at once, though it be the most valuable of the drove; and so check all further cavil. It was to be inferred from the number of dead mules they left behind them, that the most harmonious relations could not have existed between the members of the tribe, at least during this period of their journeyings. Like most of the savage tribes of North America, the Apaches are passionately fond of spirituous liquors, and may frequently be seen, in times of peace, lounging about the Mexican villages, in a state of helpless inebriety.

The range of this marauding tribe extends over some portions of California, most of Sonora, the frontiers of Durango, and at certain seasons it even reaches Coahuila: Chihuahua, however, has been the mournful theatre of their most constant depredations. Every nook and corner of this once flourishing state has been subjected to their inroads. Such is the imbecility of the local governments, that the savages, in order to dispose of their stolen property without even a shadow of molestation, frequently enter into partial treaties of peace with one department while they continue to wage a war of extermination against the neighboring states. This arrangement supplies them with an ever-ready market, for the disposal of their booty and the purchase of munitions wherewith to prosecute their work of destruction. In 1840, I witnessed the departure from Santa Fé of a large trading party freighted with engines of war and a great quantity of whiskey, intended for the Apaches in exchange for mules and other articles of plunder which they had stolen from the people of the south. This traffic was not only tolerated but openly encouraged by the civil authorities, as the highest public functionaries were interested in its success—the governor himself not excepted.

The Apaches, now and then, propose a truce to the government of Chihuahua, which is generally accepted very nearly upon their own terms. It has on some occasions been included that the marauders should have a *bona fide* right to all their stolen property. A *venta* or quit-claim brand, has actually been marked by the government upon large numbers of mules and horses which the Indians had robbed from the citizens. It is hardly necessary to add that these truces have rarely been observed by the wily savages longer than the time necessary for the disposal of their plunder. As soon as more mules were needed for service or for traffic—more cattle for beef—more scalps for the war-dance—they would invariably return to their deeds of ravage and murder.

The depredations of the Apaches have been of such long duration, that, beyond the immediate purlieus of the towns, the whole country from New Mexico to the borders of Durango is almost entirely depopulated. The haciendas and ranchos have been mostly abandoned, and the people chiefly confined to towns and cities. To such a pitch has the temerity of those savages reached, that small bands of three or four warriors have been known to make their appearance within a mile of the city of Chihuahua in open day, killing the laborers and driving off whole herds of mules and horses without the slightest opposition. Occasionally a detachment of troops is sent in pursuit of the marauders, but for no other purpose, it would seem, than to illustrate the imbecility of the former, as they are always sure to make a precipitate retreat, generally without even obtaining a glimpse of the enemy.[10] And yet the columns of a little

[10] It has been credibly asserted that, during one of these 'bold pursuits,' a band of Comanches stopped in the suburbs of a village on Rio Conchos, turned their horses into the wheat-fields, and took a comfortable *siesta*—desirous, it seemed, to behold their pursuers face to face; yet, after remaining most of the day, they departed without enjoying that pleasure.—GREGG.

weekly sheet published in Chihuahua always teem with flaming accounts of prodigious feats of valor performed by the 'army of operations' against *los bárbaros:* showing how "the enemy was pursued with all possible vigor"—how the soldiers "displayed the greatest bravery, and the most unrestrainable desire to overhaul the dastards," and by what extraordinary combinations of adverse circumstances they were "compelled to relinquish the pursuit." Indeed, it would be difficult to find a braver race of people than the *Chihua-hueños*[11] contrive to make themselves appear upon paper. When intelligence was received in Chihuahua of the famous skirmish with the French, at Vera Cruz, in which Santa Anna acquired the glory of losing a leg, the event was celebrated with uproarious demonstrations of joy; and the next number of the *Noticioso*[12] contained a valiant fanfaronade, proclaiming to the world the astounding fact, that one Mexican was worth four French soldiers in battle: winding up with a *"Cancion Patriótica,"* of which the following exquisite verse was the *refrain:*

> *"Chihuahuenses, la Patria gloriosa*
> *Otro timbre á su lustre ha añadido;*
> *Pues la ɪuʌɪɔʇɐ, ɪɐ Ɔɐɪıɐ ɪupoɯɐqlǝ*
> AL VALOR MEXICANO *ha cedido."*

Literally translated:

> Chihuahuenses! our glorious country
> Another ray has added to her lustre;
> For the *invincible, indomitable Gallia*
> Has succumbed to Mexican valor.

By the inverted letters of *"invicta, la Galia indomable,"* in the third line, the poet gives the world to understand that the kingdom of the Gauls had at length been whirled topsy-turvy, by the glorious achievements of *el valor Mexicano!*

From what has been said of the ravages of the Apaches, one would be apt to believe them an exceedingly brave people; but the Mexicans themselves call them cowards when compared with the

[11] Of *Chihuahuenses*, citizens of Chihuahua.—GREGG.
[12] *Noticioso de Chihuahua* of December 28, 1838.—GREGG.

Comanches; and we are wont to look upon the latter as perfect specimens of poltroonery when brought in conflict with the Shawnees,
Delawares, and the rest of our border tribes.

There was once a celebrated chief called Juan José at the head
of this tribe, whose extreme cunning and audacity caused his name
to be dreaded throughout the country. What contributed more than
anything else to render him a dangerous enemy, was the fact of his
having received a liberal education at Chihuahua, which enabled
him, when he afterwards rejoined his tribe, to outwit his pursuers,
and, by robbing the mails, to acquire timely information of every
expedition that was set on foot against him. The following account
of the massacre in which he fell may not be altogether uninteresting to the reader.

The government of Sonora, desirous to make some efforts to
check the depredations of the Apaches, issued a proclamation, giving
a sort of *carte blanche* patent of 'marque and reprisal,' and declaring
all the booty that might be taken from the savages to be the rightful
property of the captors. Accordingly, in the spring of 1837, a party
of some 20 men composed chiefly of foreigners, spurred on by the
love of gain, and never doubting but the Indians, after so many years
of successful robberies, must be possessed of a vast amount of property, set out with an American as their commander, who had long
resided in the country.[13] In a few days they reached a *ranchería* of
about fifty warriors with their families, among whom was the famous
Juan José himself, and three other principal chiefs. On seeing the
Americans advance, the former at once gave them to understand,
that, if they had come to fight, they were ready to accommodate
them; but on being assured by the leader, that they were merely bent
on a trading expedition, a friendly interview was immediately established between the parties. The American captain having determined
to put these obnoxious chiefs to death under any circumstances, soon
caused a little field-piece which had been concealed from the Indians
to be loaded with chain and canister shot, and to be held in readiness
for use. The warriors were then invited to the camp to receive a
present of flour, which was placed within range of the cannon. While
they were occupied in dividing the contents of the bag, they were

[13] James Johnson, later a resident of California.

fired upon and a considerable number of their party killed on the spot! The remainder were then attacked with small arms, and about twenty slain, including Juan José and the other chiefs. Those who escaped became afterwards their own avengers in a manner which proved terribly disastrous to another party of Americans, who happened at the time to be trapping on Rio Gila not far distant. The enraged savages resolved to take summary vengeance upon these unfortunate trappers; and falling upon them, massacred them every one![14] They were in all, including several Mexicans, about fifteen in number.[15]

The projector of this scheme had probably been under the impression that treachery was justifiable against a treacherous enemy. He also believed, no doubt, that the act would be highly commended by the Mexicans who had suffered so much from the depredations of these notorious chiefs. But in this he was sadly mistaken; for the affair was received with general reprehension, although the Mexicans had been guilty of similar deeds themselves, as the following brief episode will sufficiently show.

In the summer of 1839, a few Apache prisoners, among whom was the wife of a distinguished chief, were confined in the calabozo of Paso del Norte. The bereaved chief, hearing of their captivity, collected a band of about sixty warriors, and, boldly entering the town, demanded the release of his consort and friends. The commandant of the place wishing to gain time, desired them to return

[14] Benjamin Davis Wilson seems to have escaped as he relates this adventure in his memoirs: "Observations on Early Days in California and New Mexico" (MS, 1877, in the Bancroft Library), 3–15. Gregg's information may have come from Wilson, for on his return from this adventure he was Gregg's storekeeper (1835–37) at Santa Fé. *Ibid.*, 17. Wilson, however, errs in dating these events.

[15] The Apaches, previous to this date, had committed but few depredations upon foreigners—restrained either by fear or respect. Small parties of the latter were permitted to pass the highways of the wilderness unmolested, while large caravans of Mexicans suffered frequent attacks. This apparent partiality produced unfounded jealousies, and the Americans were openly accused of holding secret treaties with the enemy, and even of supplying them with arms and ammunition. Although an occasional foreigner engaged in this clandestine and culpable traffic, yet the natives themselves embarked in it beyond comparison more extensively, as has been noted in another place. This unjust impression against Americans was partially effaced as well by the catastrophes mentioned in the text, as by the defeat and robbery (in which, however, no American lives were lost), of a small party of our people, about the same period, in *La Jornada del Muerto*, on their way from Chihuahua to Santa Fé.—GREGG.

the next morning, when their request would be granted. During the night the forces of the country were concentrated; notwithstanding, when the Apaches reappeared, the troops did not show their faces, but remained concealed, while the Mexican commandant strove to beguile the Indians into the prison, under pretence of delivering to them their friends. The unsuspecting chief and twenty others were entrapped in this manner, and treacherously dispatched in cold blood: not, however, without some loss to the Mexicans, who had four or five of their men killed in the fracas. Among these was the commandant himself, who had no sooner given the word, *"Maten á los carajos!"* (kill the scoundrels!) than the chief retorted, *"Entónces morirás tu primero,* carajo!" (then you shall die first, carajo!) and immediately stabbed him to the heart!

But as New Mexico is more remote from the usual haunts of the Apaches, and, in fact, as her scanty ranchos present a much less fruitful field for their operations than the abundant haciendas of the South, the depredations of this tribe have extended but little upon that province. The only serious incursion that has come within my knowledge, was some ten years ago. A band of Apache warriors boldly approached the town of Socorro[16] on the southern border, when a battle ensued between them and the Mexican force, composed of a company of regular troops and all the militia of the place. The Mexicans were soon completely routed and chased into the very streets, suffering a loss of thirty-three killed and several wounded. The savages bore away their slain, yet their loss was supposed to be but six or seven. I happened to be in the vicinity of the catastrophe the following day, when the utmost consternation prevailed among the inhabitants, who were in hourly expectation of another descent from the savages.

Many schemes have been devised from time to time, particularly by the people of Chihuahua, to check the ravages of the Indians, but generally without success. Among these the notorious *Proyecto de Guerra,* adopted in 1837, stands most conspicuous. By this famous 'war-project' a scale of rewards was established, to be paid out of a

[16] Originally a Piro pueblo but after the Revolt of 1680 a Spanish town, the natives being removed to a new site, Socorro del Sur, below El Paso. Socorro is on the west side of the Río Grande about 75 miles below Albuquerque.

fund raised for that purpose. A hundred dollars reward were offered for the scalp of a full grown man, fifty for that of a squaw, and twenty-five for that of every papoose! To the credit of the republic, however, this barbarous *proyecto* was in operation but a few weeks, and never received the sanction of the general government; although it was strongly advocated by some of the most intelligent citizens of Chihuahua. Yet, pending its existence, it was rigidly complied with. I saw myself, on one occasion, a detachment of horsemen approach the Palacio in Chihuahua, preceded by their commanding officer, who bore a fresh scalp upon the tip of his lance, which he waved high in the air in exultation of his exploit! The next number of our little newspaper contained the official report of the affair. The soldiers were pursuing a band of Apaches, when they discovered a squaw who had lagged far behind in her endeavors to bear away her infant babe. They dispatched the mother without commiseration and took her scalp, which was the one so 'gallantly' displayed as already mentioned! The officer concluded his report by adding, that the child had *died* not long after it was made prisoner.

The *Yutas* (or *Eutaws*, as they are generally styled by Americans) are one of the most extensive nations of the West, being scattered from the north of New Mexico to the borders of Snake river and Rio Colorado, and numbering at least ten thousand souls. The habits of the tribe are altogether itinerant. A band of about a thousand spend their winters mostly in the mountain valleys northward of Taos, and the summer season generally in the prairie plains to the east, hunting buffalo. The vernacular language of the Yutas is said to be distantly allied to that of the Navajoes, but it has appeared to me much more guttural, having a deep sepulchral sound resembling ventriloquism. Although these Indians are nominally at peace with the New Mexican government, they do not hesitate to lay the hunters and traders who happen to fall in with their scouring parties under severe contributions; and on some occasions they have been known to proceed even to personal violence. A prominent Mexican officer[17] was scourged not long ago by a party of Yutas, and yet the government has never dared to resent the outrage. Their hostilities,

[17] Don Juan Andrés Archuleta, who commanded at the capture of Gen. McLeod's division of the Texans.—GREGG.

however, have not been confined to Mexican traders, as will be perceived by the sequel.

In the summer of 1837, a small party of but five or six Shawnees fell in with a large band of Yutas near the eastern borders of the Rocky Mountains, south of Arkansas river. At first they were received with every demonstration of friendship; but the Yutas, emboldened no doubt by the small number of their visitors, very soon concluded to relieve them of whatever surplus property they might be possessed of. The Shawnees, however, much to the astonishment of the marauders, instead of quietly surrendering their goods and chattels, offered to defend them; upon which a skirmish ensued that actually cost the Yutas several of their men, including a favorite chief; while the Shawnees made their escape unhurt toward their eastern homes.

A few days after this event, and while the Yutas were still bewailing the loss of their people, I happened to pass near their *ranch-erías* (temporary village) with a small caravan which mustered about thirty-five men. We had hardly pitched our camp, when they began to flock about us—men, squaws, and papooses—in great numbers; but the warriors were sullen and reserved, only now and then muttering a curse upon the Americans on account of the treatment they had just received from the Shawnees, whom they considered as half-castes, and our allies. All of a sudden, a young warrior seized a splendid steed which belonged to our party, and leaping upon his back, galloped off at full speed. Being fully convinced that, by acquiescing in this outrage, we should only encourage them to commit others, we resolved at once to make a peremptory demand for the stolen horse of their principal chief. Our request being treated with contumely, we sent in a warlike declaration, and forthwith commenced making preparations for descending upon the *rancherías*. The war-whoop resounded immediately in every direction; and as the Yutas bear a very high character for bravery and skill, the readiness with which they seemed to accept our challenge began to alarm our party considerably. We had defied them to mortal combat merely by way of bravado, without the least expectation that they would put themselves to so much inconvenience on our account. It was too late, however, to back out of the scrape.

No sooner had the alarm been given than the *rancherías* of the Indians were converted into a martial encampment; and while the mounted warriors were exhibiting their preliminary feats of horsemanship, the squaws and papooses flew like scattered partridges to the rocks and clefts of a contiguous precipice. One-third of our party being Mexicans, the first step of the Indians was to proclaim a general *indulto* to them, in hopes of reducing our force, scanty as it was already. "My Mexican friends," exclaimed in good Spanish, a young warrior who daringly rode up within a few rods of us, "we don't wish to hurt *you:* so leave those Americans, for we intend to kill every one of *them*." The Mexicans of our party to whom this language was addressed, being rancheros of some mettle, only answered, "*Al diablo!* we have not forgotten how you treat us when you catch us alone: now that we are with Americans who will defend their rights, expect ample retaliation for past insults." In truth, these rancheros seemed the most anxious to begin the fight,—a remarkable instance of the effects of confidence in companions.

A crisis seemed now fast approaching: two swivels we had with us were levelled and primed, and the matches lighted. Every man was at his post, with his rifle ready for execution, each anxious to do his best, whatever might be the result; when the Indians, seeing us determined to embrace the chances of war, began to open negotiations. An aged squaw, said to be the mother of the principal chief, rode up and exclaimed, "My sons! the Americans and Yutas have been friends, and our old men wish to continue so: it is only a few impetuous and strong-headed youths who want to fight." The stolen horse having been restored soon after this harangue, peace was joyfully proclaimed throughout both encampments, and the *capitanes* exchanged ratifications by a social smoke.

The little tribe of Jicarillas also harbored an enmity for the Americans, which, in 1834, broke out into a hostile *rencontre*. They had stolen some animals of a gallant young backwoodsman from Missouri, who, with a few comrades, pursued the marauders into the mountains and regained his property; and a fracas ensuing, an Indian or two were killed. A few days afterward all their warriors visited Santa Fé in a body, and demanded of the authorities there, the delivery of the American offenders to their vengeance. Though the former showed quite a disposition to gratify the savages as far as practicable, they had not helpless creatures to deal with, as in the case of the Indian prisoners already related. The foreigners, seeing their protection devolved upon themselves, prepared for defence, when the savages were fain to depart in peace.

CHAPTER XVI

Incidents of a Return Trip from Santa Fé—Calibre of our Party—Return Caravans—Remittances—Death of Mr. Langham—Burial in the Desert—A sudden Attack—Confusion in the Camp—A Wolfish Escort—Scarcity of Buffalo—Unprofitable Delusion—Arrival—Table of Camping Sites and Distances—Condition of the Town of Independence—The Mormons—Their Dishonesty and Immorality—Their highhanded Measures, and a Rising of the People—A fatal Skirmish—A chivalrous Parade of the Citizens—Expulsions of the Mormans—The Meteoric Shower, and Superstition, etc.—Wanderings and Improprieties of the 'Latter-day Saints'—Gov. Boggs' Recipe—The City of Nauvoo—Contemplated Retribution of the Mormons.

I DO NOT PROPOSE to detain the reader with an account of my journeyings between Mexico and the United States, during the seven years subsequent to my first arrival at Santa Fé. I will here merely remark, that I crossed the plains to the United States in the falls of 1833 and 1836, and returned to Santa Fé with goods each succeeding spring. It was only in 1838, however, that I eventually closed up my affairs in Northern Mexico, and prepared to take my leave of the country, as I then supposed, forever. But in this I was mistaken, as will appear in the sequel.

The most usual season for the return of the caravans to the United States is the autumn, and not one has elapsed since the commencement of the trade which has not witnessed some departure from Santa Fé with that destination. They have also crossed occasionally in the spring, but without any regularity or frequency, and generally in very small parties. Even the 'fall companies,' in fact, are small when compared with the outward-bound caravans; for besides the numbers who remain permanently in the country, many of those who trade southward return to the United States *via* Matamoros or some other Southern port.[1] The return parties of autumn are therefore comparatively small, varying in number from fifty to a hundred men. They leave Santa Fé some four or five weeks after their arrival—generally about the first of September. In these companies there are rarely over thirty or forty wagons; for a large portion of those taken out by the annual caravans are disposed of in the country.

Some of the traders who go out in the spring, return the ensuing fall, because they have the good fortune to sell off their stock promptly and to advantage: others are compelled to return in the fall to save their credit; nay, to preserve their homes, which, especially in the earlier periods, have sometimes been mortgaged to secure the payment of the merchandise they carried out with them. In such cases, their goods were not unfrequently sold at great sacrifice, to avoid the penalties which the breaking of their engagements at home would involve. New adventurers, too, are apt to become discouraged with an unanticipated dullness of times, and not unfrequently sell off at wholesale for the best price they can get, though often at a serious loss. But those who are regularly engaged in this trade usually calculate upon employing a season—perhaps a year, in closing an enterprise—in selling off their goods and making their returns.

The wagons of the return caravans are generally but lightly laden: one to two thousand pounds constitute the regular return cargo for a single wagon; for not only are the teams unable to haul heavy loads, on account of the decay of pasturage at this season, but the approaching winter compels the traders to travel in greater haste; so that this trip is usually made in about forty days. The amount of freight, too, from that direction is comparatively small. The remittances, as has already been mentioned, are chiefly in specie, or gold and silver bullion. The gold is mostly *dust*, from the Placer or gold mine near Santa Fé: the silver bullion is all from the mines

[1] From Missouri west to New Mexico, south to Chihuahua, east through Coahuila, Nuevo León and Tamaulipas, to Matamoros (at the mouth of the Río Grande) was estimated as three thousand miles over tolerable wagon roads. At Matamoros packet boats from New Orleans picked up the wagons and returned them to Missouri. Maj. Wetmore to Sec. of War Cass, Franklin, Oct. 11, 1831, in *Mo. Hist. Rev.*, VIII, (July, 1914), 181–82.

of the South—chiefly from those of Chihuahua. To these returns may be added a considerable number of mules and asses—some buffalo rugs, furs, and wool,—which last barely pays a return freight for the wagons that would otherwise be empty. Coarse Mexican blankets, which may be obtained in exchange for merchandise, have been sold in small quantities to advantage on our border.

On the 4th of April, 1838, we departed from Santa Fé. Our little party was found to consist of twenty-three Americans, with twelve Mexican servants. We had seven wagons, one dearborn, and two small field-pieces, besides a large assortment of small-arms. The principal proprietors carried between them about $150,000 in specie and bullion, being for the most part the proceeds of the previous year's adventure.

We moved on at a brisk and joyous pace until we reached Ocaté creek, a tributary of the Colorado,[2] a distance of a hundred and thirty miles from Santa Fé, where we encountered a very sudden bereavement in the death of Mr. Langham,[3] one of our most respected proprietors. This gentleman was known to be in weak health, but no fears were entertained for his safety. We were all actively engaged in assisting the more heavily laden wagons over the miry stream, when he was seized with a fit of apoplexy and expired instantly. As we had not the means of giving the deceased a decent burial, we were compelled to consign him to the earth in a shroud of blankets. A grave was accordingly dug on an elevated spot near the north bank of the creek, and on the morning of the 13th, ere the sun had risen in the east, the mortal remains of this most worthy man and valued friend were deposited in their last abode,—without a tomb-stone to consecrate the spot, or an epitaph to commemorate his virtues. The deceased was from St. Louis, though he had passed the last eleven years of his life in Santa Fé, during the whole of which period he had seen neither his home nor his relatives.

The melancholy rites being concluded, we resumed our line of march. We now continued for several days without the occurrence of any important accident or adventure. On the 19th we encamped in the Cimarron valley, about twelve miles below the Willow Bar.

[2] Ocaté Creek joins the Canadian (Río Colorado) in northeastern Mora County.
[3] John J. Langham, of St. Louis, a New Mexican resident since 1825.

214

The very sight of this desolate region, frequented as it is by the most savage tribes of Indians, was sufficient to strike dismay into the hearts of our party; but as we had not as yet encountered any of them, we felt comparatively at ease. Our mules and horses were 'staked' as usual around the wagons, and every man, except the watch, betook himself to his blanket, in anticipation of a good night's rest. The hour of midnight had passed away, and nothing had been heard except the tramping of the men on guard, and the peculiar grating of the mules' teeth, nibbling the short grass of the valley. Ere long, however, one of our sentinels got a glimpse of some object moving stealthily along, and as he was straining his eyes to ascertain what sort of apparition it could be, a loud Indian yell suddenly revealed the mystery. This was quickly followed by a discharge of fire-arms, and the shrill note of the 'Pawnee whistle,' which at once made known the character of our visitors. As usual, the utmost confusion prevailed in our camp: some, who had been snatched from the land of dreams, ran their heads against the wagons—others called out for their guns while they had them in their hands. During the height of the bustle and uproar, a Mexican servant was observed leaning with his back against a wagon, and his fusil elevated at an angle of forty-five degrees, cocking and pulling the trigger without ceasing, and exclaiming at every snap, *"Carajo, no sirve!"*—Curse it, it's good for nothing.

The firing still continued—the yells grew fiercer and more frequent; and everything betokened the approach of a terrible conflict. Meanwhile, a number of persons were engaged in securing the mules and horses which were staked around the encampment; and in a few minutes they were all shut up in the *corral*—a hundred head or more in a pen formed by seven wagons. The enemy failing in their principal object—to frighten off our stock, they soon began to retreat; and in a few minutes nothing more was to be heard of them. All that we could discover the next morning was, that none of our party had sustained any injury, and that we had not lost a single animal.

The Pawnees have been among the most formidable and treacherous enemies of the Santa Fé traders. But the former have also suffered a little in turn from the caravans. In 1832, a company of traders were approached by a single Pawnee chief, who commenced a parley with them, when he was shot down by a Pueblo Indian of New Mexico, who happened to be with the caravan. Though this cruel act met with the decided reprobation of the traders generally, yet they were of course held responsible for it by the Indians.

On our passage this time across the 'prairie ocean' which lay before us, we ran no risk of getting bewildered or lost, for there was now a plain wagon trail across the entire stretch of our route, from the Cimarron to Arkansas river.

This track, which has since remained permanent, was made in the year 1834. Owing to continuous rains during the passage of the caravan of that year, a plain trail was then cut in the softened turf, on the most direct route across this arid desert, leaving the Arkansas about twenty miles above the 'Caches.' This has ever since been the regular route of the caravans; and thus a recurrence of those distressing sufferings from thirst, so frequently experienced by early travellers in that inhospitable region, has been prevented.

We forded the Arkansas without difficulty, and pursued our journey to the Missouri border with comparative ease; being only now and then disturbed at night by the hideous howlings of wolves, a pack of which had constituted themselves into a kind of 'guard of honor,' and followed in our wake for several hundred miles—in fact to the very border of the settlements. They were at first attracted no doubt by the remains of buffalo which were killed by us upon the high plains, and afterwards enticed on by an occasional fagged animal, which we were compelled to leave behind, as well as by the bones and scraps of food, which they picked up about our camps. Not a few of them paid the penalty of their lives for their temerity.

Had we not fortunately been supplied with a sufficiency of meat and other provisions, we might have suffered of hunger before reaching the settlements; for we saw no buffalo after crossing the Arkansas river. It is true that, owing to their disrelish for the long dry grass of the eastern prairies, the buffalo are rarely found so far east in autumn as during the spring; yet I never saw them so scarce in this region before. In fact, at all seasons, they are usually very abundant as far east as our point of leaving the Arkansas river.

Upon reaching the settlements, I had an opportunity of experiencing a delusion which had been the frequent subject of remark by travellers on the Prairies before. Accustomed as we had been for some months to our little mules, and the equally small-sized Mexican ponies, our sight became so adjusted to their proportions, that when we came to look upon the commonest hackney of our frontier horses, it appeared to be almost a monster. I have frequently heard exclamations of this kind from the new arrivals:—"How the Missourians have improved their breed of horses!"—"What a huge gelding!"—"Did you ever see such an animal!" This delusion is frequently availed of by the frontiersmen to put off their meanest horses to these deluded travellers for the most enormous prices.

On the 11th of May we arrived at Independence, after a propitious journey of only thirty-eight days.[4] We found the town in a

[4] Having crossed the Prairies between Independence and Santa Fé six times, I can now present a table of the most notable camping sites, and their respective intermediate distances, with approximate accuracy—which may prove acceptable to some future travellers. The whole distance has been variously estimated at from 750 to 800 miles, yet I feel confident that the aggregate here presented is very nearly the true distance.

From INDEPENDENCE to	M.	Agg.		M.	Agg.
Round Grove,	35		Sand Cr. (leav. Ark. r.)	50	442
Narrows,	30	65	Cimarron r. (Lower sp.)	8	450
110-mile Creek,	35[a]	100[a]	Middle Spr. (up Cim. r.)	36	486
Bridge Cr.,	8	108	Willow Bar,	26	512
Big John Spring,			Upper Spring,	18	530
(crossing sev'l Crs.)	40	148	Cold spr. (leav. Cim. r.)	5	535
Council Grove,	2	150	M'Nees's Cr.,	25	560
Diamond Spring,	15	165	Rabbit-ear Cr.,	20	580
Lost Spring,	15	180	Round Mound	8	588
Cottonwood Cr.,	12	192	Rock Creek	8	596
Turkey Cr.,	25	217	Point of Rocks,	19	615
Little Arkansas,	17	234	Rio Colorado,	20	635
Cow Creek,	20	254	Ocaté	6	641
Arkansas River,	16	270	Santa Clara Spr.,	21	662
Walnut Cr. (up Ark. r.)	8	278	Rio Mora,	22	684
Ash Creek,	19	297	Rio Gallinas (Vegas),	20	704
Pawnee Fork,	6	303	Ojo de Bernal (spr.),	17	721
Coon Creek,	33	336	San Miguel,	6	727
Caches,	36	372	Pecos village,	23	750[b]
Ford of Arkansas,	20	392	SANTA FÉ,	25	775[b]

—GREGG.

[a] In the second edition these distances were reduced by five miles and the subsequent aggregate distances down to San Miguel were reduced by the same amount.

[b] In the second edition the aggregate distance to Pecos village is given as 755 miles and the total distance to Santa Fé as 780, an obvious error of ten miles having occurred in adding 23 to 722, getting 755 instead of 745 miles.

thriving condition, although it had come very near being laid waste a few years before by the Mormons, who had originally selected this section of the country for the site of their New Jerusalem. In this they certainly displayed far more taste and good sense than they are generally supposed to be endowed with: for the rich and beautiful uplands in the vicinity of Independence might well be denominated the 'garden spot' of the Far West. Their principal motive for preferring the border country, however, was no doubt a desire to be in the immediate vicinity of the Indians, as the reclamation of the 'Lost tribes of Israel' was a part of their pretended mission.

Prior to 1833, the Mormons, who were then flocking in great swarms to this favored region, had made considerable purchases of lots and tracts of land both in the town of Independence and in the adjacent country. A general depot, profanely styled the 'Lord's Store,' was established, from which the faithful were supplied with merchandise at moderate prices; while those who possessed any surplus of property were expected to deposit it in the same, for the benefit of the mass. The Mormons were at first kindly received by the good people of the country, who looked upon them as a set of harmless fanatics, very susceptible of being moulded into good and honest citizens. This confidence, however, was not destined to remain long in the ascendant, for they soon began to find that the corn in their cribs was sinking like snow before the sun-rays, and that their hogs and their cattle were by some mysterious agency rapidly disappearing. The newcomers also drew upon themselves much animadversion in consequence of the immorality of their lives, and in particular their disregard for the sacred rites of marriage.

Still they continued to spread and multiply, not by conversion but by immigration, to an alarming extent; and in proportion as they grew strong in numbers, they also became more exacting and bold in their pretensions. In a little paper printed at Independence under their immediate auspices,[5] everything was said that could provoke hostility between the 'saints' and their 'worldly' neighbors, until at last they became so emboldened by impunity, as openly to boast of their determination to be the sole proprietors of the 'Land of Zion;' a revelation to that effect having been made to their prophet.

[5] *The Evening and Morning Star*, which began publication in June, 1832.

The people now began to perceive, that, at the rate the intruders were increasing, they would soon be able to command a majority of the county, and consequently the entire control of affairs would fall into their hands. It was evident, then, that one of the two parties would in the course of time have to abandon the country; for the old settlers could not think of bringing up their families in the midst of such a corrupt state of society as the Mormons were establishing. Still the nuisance was endured very patiently, and without any attempt at retaliation, until the 'saints' actually threatened to eject their opponents by main force. This last stroke of impudence at once roused the latent spirit of the honest backwoodsmen, some of whom were of the pioneer settlers of Missouri, and had become familiar with danger in their terrific wars with the savages. They were therefore by no means appropriate subjects for yielding what they believed to be their rights. Meetings were held for the purpose of devising means of redress, which only tended to increase the insolence of the Mormons. Finally a mob was collected, which proceeded at once to raze the obnoxious printing establishment to the ground, and to destroy all the materials they could lay hands upon. One or two of the Mormon leaders who fell into the hands of the people, were treated to a clean suit of 'tar and feathers,' and otherwise severely punished. The 'Prophet Joseph,'[6] however, was not then in the neighborhood. Having observed the storm-clouds gathering apace in the frontier horizon, he very wisely remained in Ohio, whence he issued his flaming mandates.

These occurrences took place in the month of October, 1833, and I reached Independence from Santa Fé while the excitement was raging at its highest. The Mormons had rallied some ten miles west of the town, where their strongest settlements were located. A hostile encounter was hourly expected: nay, a skirmish actually took place shortly after, in which a respectable lawyer of Independence, who had been an active agent against the Mormons, was killed. In short, the whole country was in a state of dreadful fermentation.

[6] Joseph Smith (1805–44), of Vermont, was the founder (1830) of the Church of Jesus Christ of Latter Day Saints, based upon his revelation in 1827 and discovery, near Palmyra, N. Y., of the golden plates of the *Book of Mormon*, which he translated from hieroglyphics. Smith remained head of the church through its years of persecution and peregrinations until arrested, jailed, and then lynched at Carthage, Illinois.

Early on the morning after the skirmish just referred to, a report reached Independence that the Mormons were marching in a body towards the town, with the intention of sacking and burning it. I had often heard the cry of "Indians!" announcing the approach of hostile savages, but I do not remember ever to have witnessed so much consternation as prevailed at Independence on this memorable occasion. The note of alarm was sounded far and near, and armed men, eager for the fray, were rushing in from every quarter. Officers were summarily selected without deference to rank or station: the 'spirit-stirring drum' and the 'ear-piercing fife' made the air resound with music; and a little army of as brave and resolute a set of fellows as ever trod a field of battle, was, in a very short time, paraded through the streets. After a few preliminary exercises, they started for a certain point on the road where they intended to await the approach of the Mormons. The latter very soon made their appearance, but, surprised at meeting with so formidable a reception, they never even attempted to pull a trigger, but at once surrendered at discretion. They were immediately disarmed, and subsequently released upon condition of their leaving the country without delay.

It was very soon after their affair that the much talked of phenomenon of the meteoric shower (on the night of November 12th) occurred. This extraordinary visitation did not fail to produce its effects upon the superstitious minds of a few ignorant people, who began to wonder whether, after all, the Mormons might not be in the right; and whether this was not a sign sent from heaven as a remonstrance for the injustice they had been guilty of towards that chosen sect.[7] Sometime afterward, a terrible misfortune occurred which was in no way calculated to allay the superstitious fears of the ignorant. As some eight or ten citizens were returning with the ferryboat which had crossed the last Mormons over the Missouri river, into Clay county, the district selected for their new home, the craft filled with water and sunk in the middle of the current; by which accident three or four men were drowned! It was owing perhaps to

[7] In Northern Mexico, as I learned afterwards, the credulity of the superstitious was still more severely tried by this celestial phenomenon. Their Church had been deprived of some important privileges by the Congress but a short time before, and the people could not be persuaded but that the meteoric shower was intended as the curse upon the nation in consequence of that sacrilegious act.—GREGG.

the craziness of the boat, yet some persons suspected the Mormons of having scuttled it by secretly boring auger-holes in the bottom just before they had left it.

After sojourning a few months in Clay county, to the serious annoyance of the inhabitants (though, in fact, they had been kindly received at first), the *persecuted* 'Latter day Saints' were again compelled to shift their quarters further off. They now sought to establish themselves in the new county of Caldwell, and founded their town of Far West,[8] where they lingered in comparative peace for a few years. As the county began to fill up with settlers, however, quarrels repeatedly broke out, until at last, in 1838, they found themselves again at open war with their neighbors. They appear to have set the laws of the state at defiance, and to have acted so turbulently throughout, that Governor Boggs[9] deemed it necessary to order out a large force of state militia to subject them: which was easily accomplished without bloodshed. From that time the Mormons have harbored a mortal enmity towards the Governor: and the attempt which was afterwards made to assassinate him at Independence, is generally believed to have been instigated, if not absolutely perpetrated, by that deluded sect.

Being once more forced to emigrate, they passed into Illinois, where they founded the famous 'City of Nauvoo.' It would seem that their reception from the people of this state was even more strongly marked with kindness and indulgence than it had been elsewhere, being generally looked upon as the victims of persecution on account of their religious belief; yet it appears that the good people of Illinois have since become about as tired of them as were any of their former neighbors. It seems very clear then, that fanatical delusion is not the only sin which stamps the conduct of these people with so much obliquity, or they would certainly have found permanent friends somewhere; whereas it is well known that a general aversion has prevailed against them wherever they have sojourned.

[8] Founded in 1836, its population was 12,000 by 1838.

[9] Lilburn W. Boggs (1798–1852), of Kentucky, was an Indian trader in Missouri before entering politics. He became lieutenant-governor in 1832 and governor in 1836, his administration being distinguished for its anti-Mormon policy. In 1846 Boggs went to California, where he became *alcalde* of Sonoma and later a member of the constitutional convention.

Before concluding this chapter, it may be proper to remark, that the Mormons have invariably refused to sell any of the property they had acquired in Missouri, but have on the contrary expressed a firm determination to reconquer their lost purchases. Of these, a large lot, situated on an elevated point at Independence, known as the 'Temple Lot,' upon which the 'Temple of Zion' was to have been raised,—has lately been 'profaned,' by cultivation, having been converted into a cornfield!

COMMERCE OF THE PRAIRIES

VOLUME II

GREGG'S MAP OF 1844
(MODIFIED)

OF THE INDIAN TERRITORY IN
NORTHERN TEXAS AND
NEW MEXICO

SCALE IN MILES
0   20   40   60

EXPLANATION

⊛ Towns   ▲ Campsites and Springs
• Villages and Forts   × Ruins

———— Route of Santa Fe Caravan
———— Chihuahua Road
—·—·— Captain Pike's Route, 1806
—··—·· Major Long's Route, 1820
———— J. Gregg's Route to Santa Fe, 1839
———— J. Gregg's Return Route, 1840
———— Route of Caravan from Chihuahua to
        Arkansas, 1839
·········· Route of Caravan from Arkansas to
        Chihuahua, 1840
———— Route of Texan–Santa Fe Expedition, 1841

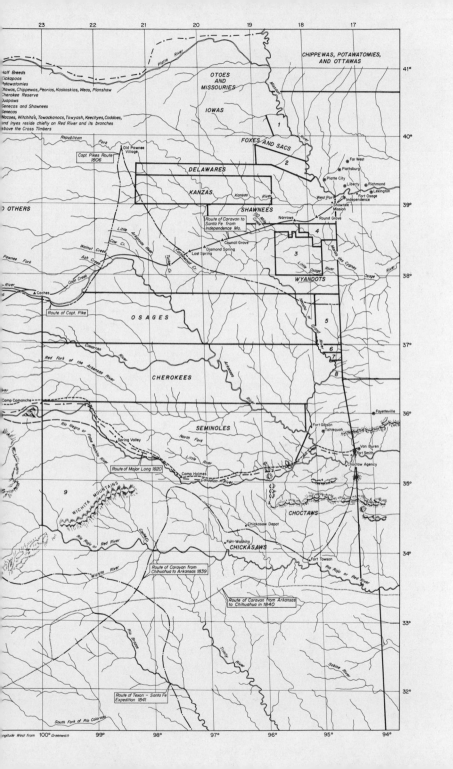

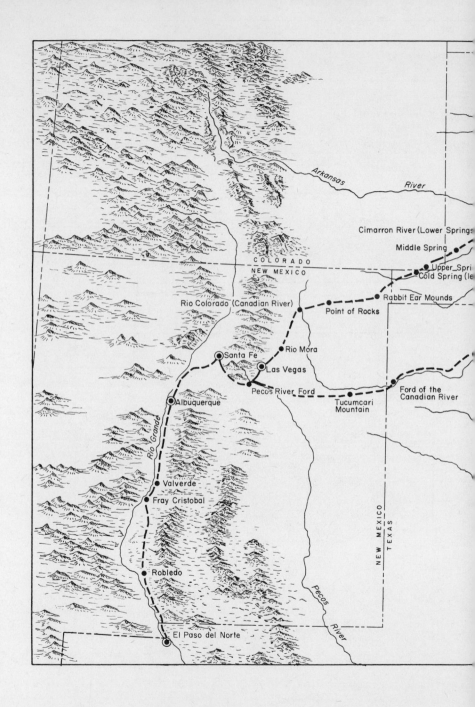

Arkansas River

Cimarron River (Lower Springs)

Middle Spring

Upper Spri
Cold Spring (le

COLORADO
NEW MEXICO

Rabbit Ear Mounds

Rio Colorado (Canadian River)

Point of Rocks

Rio Mora

Santa Fe

Las Vegas

Pecos River Ford

Ford of the
Canadian River

Tucumcari
Mountain

Albuquerque

Rio Grande

Valverde

Fray Cristobal

NEW MEXICO
TEXAS

Robledo

Pecos River

El Paso del Norte

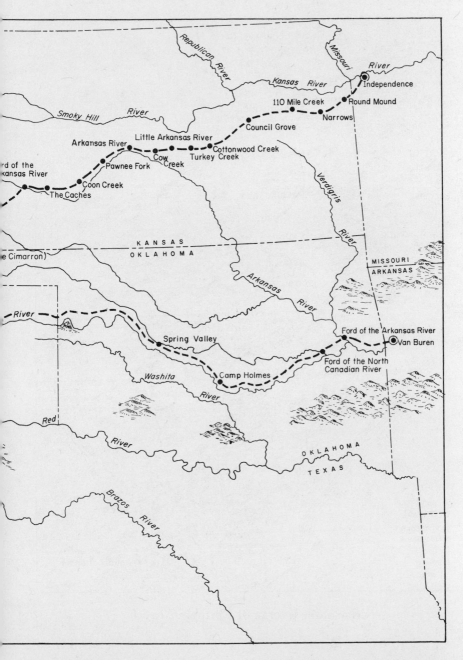

Map of Gregg's Routes from Independence and Van Buren to
Santa Fe

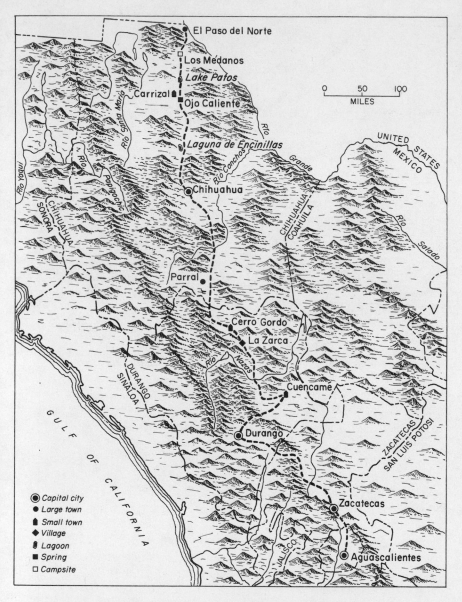

Map of the Interior of Northern Mexico

CHAPTER I

A Return to Prairie Life—Abandonment of the regular Route—The Start—A Suicide—Arrest of a Mulatto for Debt—Cherokee 'Bankrupt Law'—Chuly, the Creek Indian—The Muster and the Introduction—An 'Olla Podrida'—Adventure of a 'Down-Easter'—Arrival of U.S. Dragoons—Camp Holmes, and the Road—A Visit from a Party of Comanches—Tabba-quena, a noted Chief—His extraordinary Geographical Talent—Indians set out for the 'Capitan Grande,' and we through an Unexplored Region—Rejoined by Tabba-quena and his 'suite'—Spring Valley—The Buffalo Fever—The Chase—A Greenhorn Scamper—Prairie Fuel.

AN UNCONQUERABLE PROPENSITY to return to prairie life inclined me to embark in a fresh enterprise. The Blockade of the Mexican ports by the French also offered strong inducements for undertaking such an expedition in the spring of 1839; for as Chihuahua is supplied principally through the sea-ports, it was now evident that the place must be suffering from great scarcity of goods. Being anxious to reach the market before the ports of the Gulf were reopened, we deemed it expedient to abandon the regular route from Missouri for one wholly untried, from the borders of Arkansas, where the pasturage springs up nearly a month earlier. It is true, that such an attempt to convey heavily laden wagons through an unexplored region was attended with considerable risk; but as I was familiar with the general character of the plains contiguous to the north, I felt little or no apprehension of serious difficulties, except from what might be occasioned by regions of sandy soil. I have often been asked since, why did we not steer directly for Chihuahua, as our trade was chiefly destined for that place, instead of taking the circuitous route via Santa Fé. I answer, that we dreaded a journey across the southern prairies on account of the reputed aridity of the country in that direction, and I had no great desire to venture directly into a southern port in the present state of uncertainty as to the conditions of entry.[1]

Suitable arrangements having been made, and a choice stock of about $25,000 worth of goods shipped to Van Buren on the Arkansas river, we started on the evening of the 21st of April, but made very little progress for the first eight days. While we were yet but ten or fifteen miles from Van Buren, an incident occurred which was attended with very melancholy results. A young man named Hays, who had driven a wagon for me for several months through the interior of Mexico, and thence to the United States in 1838, having heard that this expedition was projected, was desirous of engaging in the same employ. I was equally desirous to secure his services, as he was well-tried, and had proved himself an excellent fellow on those perilous journeys. But soon after our outset, and without any apparent reason, he expressed an inclination to abandon the trip. I earnestly strove to dissuade him from his purpose, and supposed I had succeeded. What was my surprise, then, upon my return after a few hours' absence in advance of the company, to learn that he had secretly absconded! I was now led to reflect upon some of his eccentricities, and bethought me of several evident indications of slight mental derangement. We were, however, but a few miles from the settlements of the whites, and in the midst of the civilized Cherokees, where there was little or no danger of his suffering; therefore, there seemed but little occasion for serious uneasiness on his account. As it was believed he had shaped his course back to Van Buren, I immediately wrote to our friends there, to have search made for him. However, nothing could be found of him till the next day, when his hat and coat were discovered upon the bank of the Arkansas, near

[1] Four American merchants in Chihuahua (George East, John Patton, Lucien Thurston, and Riley Jackson) tried to open a direct southern route in 1838; but their funds proved inadequate, and the Mexican government refused to grant them special exemption from import duties. Finally, when a group of Mexican merchants made the round trip from Chihuahua to Arkansas at more expense than profit, as Gregg describes below, the project was abandoned. The correspondence on this subject is in the Archivo General y Público de la Nación, Fomento-Caminos, Tomo 11, Expediente 225.

Van Buren, which were the last traces ever had of the unfortunate Hays! Whether intentionally or accidentally, he was evidently drowned.

On the 28th of April we crossed the Arkansas river a few miles above the mouth of the Canadian fork.[2] We had only proceeded a short distance beyond, when a Cherokee shop-keeper came up to us with an attachment for debt against a free mulatto, whom we had engaged as teamster. The poor fellow had no alternative but to return with the importunate creditor, who committed him at once to the care of 'Judge Lynch' for trial. We ascertained afterwards that he had been sentenced to 'take the benefit of the bankrupt law' after the manner of the Cherokees of that neighborhood. This is done by stripping and tying the victim to a tree; when each creditor, with a good cow-hide or hickory switch in his hand, scores the amount of the bill due upon his bare back. One stripe for every dollar due is the usual process of 'whitewashing;' and as the application of the lash is accompanied by all sorts of quaint remarks, the exhibition affords no small merriment to those present, with the exception, no doubt, of the delinquent himself. After the ordeal is over, the creditors declare themselves perfectly satisfied: nor could they, as is said, ever be persuaded thereafter to receive one red cent of the amount due, even if it were offered to them. As the poor mulatto was also in our debt, and was perhaps apprehensive that we might exact payment in the same currency, he never showed himself again.

On the 2d of May we crossed the North Fork of the Canadian about a mile from its confluence with the main stream. A little westward of this there is a small village of Creek Indians, and a shop or two kept by American traders.[3] An Indian who had quarrelled with his wife, came out and proposed to join us, and, to our great surprise, carried his proposal into execution. The next morning his repentant consort came to our camp and set up a most dismal weeping and howling after her truant husband, who, notwithstanding, was neither to be caught by tears nor softened by entreaties, but persisted in his determination to see foreign countries. His name was Echú-eleh-hadjó (or *Crazy-deer-foot*), but, for brevity's sake, we always called

[2] Between Sequoyah and Muskogee counties in present Oklahoma.
[3] The Creek town was Eufaula, now the seat of McIntosh County, Oklahoma.

him *Chuly*. He was industrious, and possessed many clever qualities, though somewhat disposed to commit excesses whenever he could procure liquor, which fortunately did not occur until our arrival at Santa Fé. He proved to be a good and willing hand on the way, but as he spoke no English, our communication with him was somewhat troublesome. I may as well add here, that, while in Santa Fé, he took another freak and joined a volunteer corps, chiefly of Americans, organized under one James Kirker[4] to fight the Navajo and Apache Indians; the government of Chihuahua having guaranteed to them all the spoils they should take. With these our Creek found a few of his 'red brethren'—Shawnees and Delawares, who had wandered thus far from the frontier of Missouri. After this little army was disbanded, Chuly returned home, as I have been informed, with a small party who crossed the plains directly from Chihuahua.

We had never considered ourselves as perfectly *en chemin* till after crossing the Arkansas river; and as our little party experienced no further change, I may now be permitted to introduce them collectively to the reader. It consisted of thirty-four men, including my brother John Gregg[5] and myself. These men had all been hired by us except three, two of whom were Eastern-bred boys—a tailor and a silversmith—good natured, clever little fellows, who had thought themselves at the 'jumping-off place' when they reached Van Buren, but now seemed nothing loth to extend their peregrinations a thousand miles or so further, in the hope of 'doing' the 'Spaniards,' as the Mexicans are generally styled in the West, out of a little surplus of specie. The other was a German peddler, who somewhat resembled the Dutchman's horse, "put him as you vant, and he ish alvays tere;"

---

[4] James Kirker (1793–*ca*. 1852) was a notorious borderland adventurer. He came to Santa Fé in 1825, operated the Santa Rita copper mine in 1827, ran afoul the New Mexican government while leading a band of Shawnees in 1839, and in 1840 with a party of Americans (including Shawnees and Delawares) contracted with the governor of Chihuahua to exterminate the Apaches of that state. After several forays Kirker collected more scalps (some allegedly were not Apache) than the governor could pay for. He returned to his family at Correlitos (Sonora), but in 1846 joined Colonel Doniphan's regiment as a scout. After the war he went to California, where he died.

[5] John Gregg (b. 1800), Josiah's favorite brother, had been to Santa Fé as early as 1825 and was in Chihuahua in 1826. "*Estado de Estranjeros*," MS in Archivo de la Secretaría de Relaciones Exteriores (Mexico City), L–E–1005, pp. 149–50.

for he did nothing during the whole journey but descant on the value of a chest of trumperies which he carried, and with which he calculated, as he expressed it, to "py a plenty of te Shpanish tollar." The trip across the Prairies cost these men absolutely nothing, inasmuch as we furnished them with all the necessaries for the journey, in consideration of the additional strength they brought to our company.

It is seldom that such a variety of ingredients are found mixed up in so small a compass. Here were the representatives of seven distinct nations, each speaking his own native language, which produced at times a very respectable jumble of discordant sounds. There was one Frenchman whose volubility of tongue and curious gesticulations, contrasted very strangely with the frigidity of two phlegmatic wanderers from Germany; while the calm eccentricity of two Polish exiles, the stoical look of two sons of the desert (the Creek already spoken of, and a Chickasaw), and the pantomimic gestures of sundry loquacious Mexicans, contributed in no small degree to heighten the effects of the picture. The Americans were mostly backwoodsmen, who could handle the rifle far better than the whip, but who nevertheless officiated as wagoners.

We had fourteen road-wagons, half drawn by mules, the others by oxen (eight of each to the team); besides a carriage and a Jersey wagon. Then we had two swivels mounted upon one pair of wheels; but one of them was attached to a movable truckle, so that, upon stopping, it could be transferred to the other side of the wagons. One of these was a long brass piece made to order, with a calibre of but an inch and a quarter, yet of sufficient metal to throw a leaden ball to the distance of a mile with surprising accuracy. The other was of iron, and a little larger. Besides these, our party was well supplied with small arms. The Americans mostly had their rifles and a musket in addition, which they carried in their wagons, always well charged with ball and buckshot. Then my brother and myself were each provided with one of Colt's repeating rifles, and a pair of pistols of the same, so that we could, if necessary, carry thirty-six ready-loaded shots apiece; which alone constituted a capacity of defence rarely matched even on the Prairies.

Previous to our departure we had received a promise from the war department of an escort of U. S. Dragoons, as far as the borders of the Mexican territory; but, upon sending an express to Gen. Arbuckle at Fort Gibson[6] to that effect, we were informed that in consequence of some fresh troubles among the Cherokees, it was doubtful whether the force could be spared in time. This was certainly no very agreeable news, inasmuch as the escort would have been very serviceable in assisting to search out a track over the unexplored wilderness we had to pass. It was too late, however, to recede; and so we resolved at all hazards to pursue our journey.

We had advanced beyond the furthest settlements of the Creeks and Seminoles,[7] and pitched our camp on a bright balmy evening, in the border of a delightful prairie, when some of the young men, attracted by the prospect of game, shouldered their rifles and wended their steps through the dense forests which lay contiguous to our encampment. Among those that went forth, there was one of the 'down-easters' already mentioned, who was much more familiar with the interior of a city than of a wilderness forest. As the shades of evening were beginning to descend and all the hunters had returned except him, several muskets and even our little fieldpieces were fired, but without effect. The night passed away, and the morning dawned upon the encampment, and still he was absent. The firing was then renewed; but soon after he was seen approaching, very sullen and dejected. He came with a tale of perilous adventures and 'hairbreadth 'scapes' upon his lips, which somewhat abated the storm of ridicule by which he was at first assailed. It seemed that he had heard our firing on the previous evening, but believed it to proceed from a contrary direction—a very common mistake with persons who have become bewildered and lost. Thus deceived and stimulated by the fear of Indians (from a party of whom he supposed the firing to proceed), he continued his pathless wanderings till dark, when, to render his situation still more critical, he was attacked by a 'painter'— *anglicè*, panther—which he actually succeeded in beating off with

---

[6] Fort Gibson was built in 1824 on the left bank of the Neosho, or Grand, near its confluence with the Arkansas in present Muskogee County, Oklahoma. It was abandoned in 1857. Matthew Arbuckle (1776–1851) entered the army in 1799, was breveted brigadier-general in 1830, and died at Fort Smith after more than twenty years of service in Indian Territory. The Arbuckle Mountains of south-central Oklahoma are named for him.

[7] At this time the Creek and Seminole settlements extended westward to Little River in present Seminole County, Oklahoma.

the breech of his gun, and then betook himself to the topmost extremity of a tree, where, in order to avoid a similar intrusion, he passed the remainder of the night. From a peculiar odor with which the shattered gun was still redolent, however, it was strongly suspected that the 'terrific painter' was not many degrees removed, in affinity, from a—polecat.

We had just reached the extreme edge of the far-famed 'Cross Timbers,'[8] when we were gratified by the arrival of forty dragoons, under the command of Lieut. Bowman,[9] who had orders to accompany us to the supposed boundary of the United States. On the same evening we had the pleasure of encamping together at a place known as Camp Holmes, a wild romantic spot in latitude 35° 5′, and but a mile north of the Canadian river.[10] Just at hand there was a beautiful spring, where, in 1835, Colonel Mason with a force of U.S. troops, had a 'big talk' and still bigger 'smoke' with a party of Comanche and Witchita Indians.[11] Upon the same site Col. Chouteau[12] had also caused to be erected not long after, a little stockade fort, where a considerable trade was subsequently carried on with the Comanches and other tribes of the southwestern prairies. The place had now been abandoned, however, since the preceeding winter.

[8] A belt of woods in present Oklahoma and Texas separating the prairie from the arid plains to the west. Gregg describes them at length below, in chap. 10.

[9] James Monroe Bowman (d. 1839), of Pennsylvania, graduated from West Point, became a lieutenant in the mounted rangers in 1832, and was transferred to the dragoons in 1833. Gregg mentions his death at Fort Gibson in the next chapter.

[10] Camp Holmes, better known as Camp Mason, was on the old course of Chouteau Creek (now diverted), near present Lexington, in Cleveland County, Oklahoma, and is distinct from Fort Holmes, near the confluence of Little River and the Canadian in Hughes County. The latitude of Camp Mason was more nearly 35° than 35° 5′

[11] The treaty, signed August 24, 1835, was a peace and friendship pact between the Comanches, Wichitas (Taovayas), and associated bands, on the one part, and the Cherokees, Creeks, Choctaws, Osages, Senecas, and Quapaws, all recently removed to Indian territory, on the other. General Arbuckle and Montford Stokes were the federal commissioners. Richard Barnes Mason (1797–1850), a Virginian, was a major when the treaty was signed and not a colonel until 1846. He became the first United States governor of California after its official acquisition.

[12] Auguste Pierre Chouteau (1787–1838), of St. Louis, the eldest son of Pierre Chouteau, Sr. and brother of the Pierre Chouteau of Missouri Fur Company renown. He attended West Point, joined the infantry as an ensign, resigned in 1809, and took charge of the Arkansas branch of the fur trade until his death at Fort Gibson. For his adventures on the Arkansas and in New Mexico, see above, Vol. I, chap. 1, n. 22.

From the Arkansas river to Chouteau's Fort, our route presented an unbroken succession of grassy plains and fertile glades, intersected here and there with woody belts and numerous rivulets, most of which, however, are generally dry except during the rainy season. As far as Camp Holmes, we had a passable wagon road, which was opened upon the occasion of the Indian treaty before alluded to, and was afterwards kept open by the Indian traders. Yet, notwithstanding the road, this stretch gave us more trouble—presented more rugged passes, miry ravines and steep ascents—than all the rest of our journey put together.

We had not been long at the Fort, before we received a visit from a party of Comanches, who having heard of our approach came to greet us a welcome, on the supposition that it was their friend Chouteau returning to the fort with fresh supplies of merchandise. Great was their grief when we informed them that their favorite trader had died at Fort Gibson, the previous winter. On visiting their wigwams and inquiring for their *capitan*,[13] we were introduced to a corpulent, squint-eyed old fellow, who certainly had nothing in his personal appearance indicative of rank or dignity. This was Tábba-quena[14] (or the Big Eagle), a name familiar to all the Comanche traders. As we had frequently heard that he spoke Spanish fluently, we at once prepared ourselves for a social chit-chat; but, on accosting him in that tongue, and inquiring whether he could talk Spanish, he merely replied '*Poquito*,' putting at the same time his forefinger to his ear, to signify that he merely understood a little —which proved true to a degree, for our communication was chiefly by signs. We were now about to launch upon an unknown region— our route lay henceforth across that unexplored wilderness, of which I have already spoken, without either pilot or trail to guide us for nearly 500 miles. We had to depend entirely upon our knowledge of the geographical position of the country for which we were steering, and the indications of a compass and sextant. This was emphatically a pioneer trip; such a one also as had, perhaps, never before been undertaken—to convey heavily laden wagons through a

[13] Most of the prairie Indians seem to have learned this Spanish word, by which, when talking to the whites, all their chiefs are designated.—GREGG.

[14] Gregg later named a favorite pony after this chief. Letter to John Gregg, Saltillo, May 15, 1848, in *Diary & Letters*, II, 216.

country almost wholly untrod by civilized man, and of which *we*, at least, knew nothing. We were therefore extremely anxious to acquire any information our visitors might be able to give us; but Tábba-Quena being by no means experienced in wagon tactics, could only make us understand, by gestures, mixed with a little wretched Spanish, that the route up the Canadian presented no obstacles according to *his* mode of traveling. He appeared, however, very well acquainted with the whole Mexican frontier, from Santa Fé to Chihuahua, and even to the Gulf, as well as with all the Prairies. During the consultation he seemed occasionally to ask the opinions of other chiefs who had huddled around him. Finally, we handed him a sheet of paper and a pencil, signifying at the same time a desire that he would draw us a map of the Prairies. This he very promptly executed; and although the draft was somewhat rough, it bore, much to our astonishment, quite a map-like appearance, with a far more accurate delineation of all the principal rivers of the plains—the road from Missouri to Santa Fé and the different Mexican settlements, than is to be found in many of the engraved maps of those regions.

Tábba-quena's party consisted of about sixty persons, including several squaws and papooses, with a few Kiawa chiefs and warriors, who, although of a tribe so entirely distinct, are frequently found domiciled among the Comanches. As we were about to break up the camp they all started for Fort Gibson, for the purpose, as they informed us, of paying a visit to the 'Capitan Grande'—a Spanish phrase used by many prairie tribes, and applied, in their confused notions of rank and power, not only to the President of the United States himself, but to the seat of the federal government. These they are again apt to confound with Fort Gibson and the commanding officer of that station.

On the 18th of May, we set out from Chouteau's fort. From this forward our wagons were marched in two lines, and regularly 'formed' at every camp, so as to constitute a fortification and a *corral* for the stock. This is different from the 'forming' of the large caravans. The two front wagons are driven up, side by side, with their 'tails' a little inclined outward. About half of the rest are drawn up in the same manner, but each stopped with the fore-wheel a little back of the hind-wheel of the next ahead. The remainder are similarly brought up, but inclined inward behind, so as nearly to close again at the rear of the pen; leaving a gap through which to introduce the stock. Thus the *corral* remains of an ovate form. After the drivers become expert the whole is performed in a very short time.

On the following day we were again joined by old Tábba-quena, and another Comanche chief, with five or six warriors, and as many squaws, including Tab's wife and infant son. As we were jogging along in the afternoon, I held quite a long conversation in our semi-mute language with the squinting old chief. He gave me to understand, as well as he could, that his comrades[15] had proceeded on their journey to see the Capitan Grande, but that he had concluded to return home for better horses. He boasted in no measured terms of his friendship for the Americans, and promised to exert his influence to prevent the turbulent and unruly spirits of his nation from molesting us. But he could not disguise his fears in regard to the Pawnees and Osages, who, he said, would be sure to run off with our stock while we were asleep at night. When I informed him that we kept a strict night-watch, he said *"Está bueno"* (that's good), and allowed that our chances for safety were not so bad after all.

These friendly Indians encamped with us that night, and on the following morning the old chief informed us that some of his party had a few "mulas para *swap*" (mules to trade; for having learned the word *swap* of some American traders, he very ingeniously tacked it at the tail of his little stock of Spanish). A barter for five mules was immediately concluded upon, much to our advantage, as our teams were rather in a weak condition. Old Tab and his party then left us to join his band, which, he said, was located on the Faux Ouachittâ river,[16] and we never saw aught of them more.

After leaving the Fort we generally kept on the ridge between the Canadian and the North Fork, crossing sometimes the tributary brooks of the one and sometimes those of the others. Having travelled in this manner for about eighty miles, we entered one of the

[15] Some of these (principally Kiawas, as I afterwards learned), reached Fort Gibson, and received a handsome reward of government presents for their visit.— GREGG.

[16] The Washita, or False Washita (to distinguish it from the Ouachita in Arkansas and Louisiana), runs from the Texas panhandle to the Red River (now Lake Texoma) in Marshall County, Oklahoma.

most charming prairie vales that I have ever beheld, and which in the plenitude of our enthusiasm, we named 'Spring Valley,' on account of the numerous spring-fed rills and gurgling rivulets that greeted the sight in every direction; in whose limpid pools swarms of trout and perch were carelessly playing. Much of the country, indeed, over which we had passed was somewhat of a similar character—yet nowhere quite so beautiful. I must premise, however, that westward of this, it is only the valleys immediately bordering the streams that are at all fit for cultivation: the high plains are too dry and sandy. But here the soil was dark and mellow, and the rich vegetation with which it was clothed plainly indicated its fertility. 'Spring Valley' gently inclines towards the North Fork, which was at the distance of about five miles from our present route.[17] It was somewhere along the border of this enchanting vale that a little picket fort was erected in 1822, by an unfortunate trader named McKnight, who was afterwards betrayed and murdered by the faithless Comanches.[18] The landscape is beautifully variegated with stripes and fringes of timber: while the little herds of buffalo that were scattered about in fantastic groups imparted a degree of life and picturesqueness to the scene, which it was truly delightful to contemplate.

It was three days previous that we had first met with these 'prairie cattle.' I have often heard backwoodsmen speak of the 'buck ague,' but commend me to the 'buffalo fever' of the Prairies for novelty and amusement. Very few of our party had ever seen a buffalo before in its wild state; therefore at the first sight of these noble animals the excitement surpassed anything I had ever witnessed before. Some of our dragoons, in their eagerness for sport, had managed to frighten away a small herd that were quietly feeding at some distance, before our 'still hunters,' who had crawled towards them, had been able to get within rifle-shot of them. No sooner were

[17] Gregg's mileage from Chouteau's post and his graphic description would place 'Spring Valley' between present Geary and Greenfield, in Blaine County, Oklahoma. There a wide valley sloping toward the North Canadian is watered by numerous spring-fed streams, the largest of which is Horse Creek.

[18] John McKnight, brother of Robert McKnight of the ill-fated Santa Fé expedition of 1812 described above, Vol. I, chap. 1, n. 9. For his final expedition and death, in 1823, see the memoirs of his associate: Thomas James, *Three Years among the Indians and Mexicans*, ed. by Walter B. Douglas, 98. The picket fort on the Canadian may have been that established by General James in 1822.

the movements of our mounted men perceived, than the whole extent of country, as far as the eye could reach, became perfectly animate with living objects, fleeing and scampering in every direction. From the surrounding valleys sprang up numerous herds of these animals which had hitherto been unobserved, many of which, in their indiscriminate flight, passed so near the wagons, that the drivers, carried away by the contagious excitment of the moment, would leave the teams and keep up a running fire after them. I had the good fortune to witness the exploits of one of our Northern greenhorns, who, mounted upon a sluggish mule, and without any kind of weapon, amused himself by chasing every buffalo that came scudding along, as if he expected to capture him by laying hold of his tail. Plying spur and whip, he would gallop after one division till he was left far behind: and then turn to another and another, with the same earnestness of purpose, until they had all passed out of sight. He finally came back disheartened and sullen, with his head hanging down like one conscious of having done something supremely ridiculous; but still cursing his lazy mule, which, he said, might have caught the buffalo, if it had had a mind to.

The next day the buffalo being still more numerous, the chase was renewed with greater zest. In the midst of the general hurly-burly which ensued, three persons on foot were perceived afar off, chasing one herd of buffalo and then another, until they completely disappeared. These were two of our cooks, the one armed with a pistol, the other with a musket, accompanied by Chuly (the Creek), who was happily provided with a rifle. We travelled several miles without hearing anything of them. At last, when we had almost given them up for lost, Frank, the French cook, came trudging in, and his rueful countenance was no bad index of the doleful tale he had to relate. Although he had been chasing and shooting all day, he had, as he expressed it, "no killet one," till eventually he happened to stumble upon a wounded calf, which he boldly attacked; but as ill luck would have it, the youngster took it into his head to give him battle. "Foutre de varment! be butt me down," exclaimed the exasperated Frenchman,—"Sacré! me plentee scart; but me kill him for all." Chuly and the other cook came in soon after, in equally dejected spirits; for, in addition to his ill luck in hunting, the latter had been lost. The Indian had perhaps killed buffalo with his rifle, but he was in no humor to be communicative in his language of signs; so nothing was ever known of his adventures. One thing seemed certain, that they were all cured of the 'buffalo fever.'

On the night after the first buffalo scamper, we encamped upon a woodless ravine, and were obliged to resort to 'buffalo chips' (dry ordure) for fuel. It is amusing to witness the bustle which generally takes place in collecting this offal. In dry weather it is an excellent substitute for wood, than which it even makes a hotter fire; but when moistened by rain, the smouldering pile will smoke for hours before it condescends to burn, if it does at all. The buffalo meat which the hunter roasts or broils upon this fire, he accounts more savory than the steaks dressed by the most delicate cooks in civilized life.

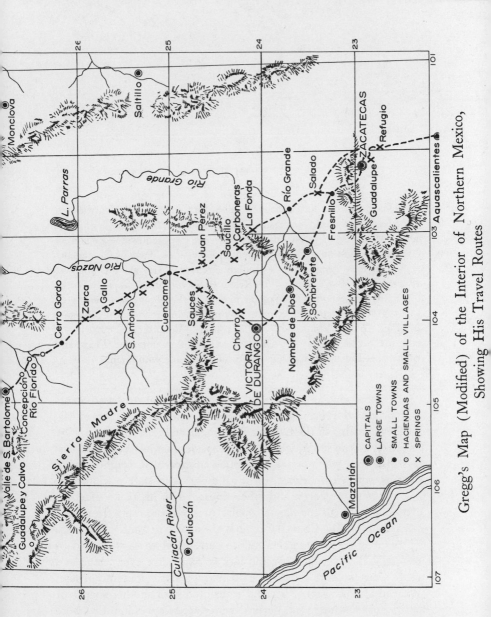

Gregg's Map (Modified) of the Interior of Northern Mexico, Showing His Travel Routes

CHAPTER II

Travelling out of our Latitude—The Buffalo-gnat—A Kiawa and Squaw—Indian *crim. con.* Affair—Extraordinary Mark of Confidence in the White Man—A Conflagration—An Espy Shower—Region of Gypsum—Our Latitude—A Lilliputian Forest—A Party of Comanches —A Visit to a 'Dog Town'—Indian Archery—Arrival of Comanche Warriors—A 'Big Talk,' and its Results—Speech of the *Capitan Mayor* —Project of bringing Comanche Chiefs to Washington—Return of Lieut. Bowman, and our March resumed—Melancholy Reflections— Another Indian Visit—Mexican Captives—Voluntary Captivity—A sprightly Mexican Lad—Purchase of a Captive—Comanche Trade and Etiquette—Indians least dangerous to such as trade with them.

As it now appeared that we had been forced at least two points north of the course we had originally intended to steer, by the northern bearing of the Canadian, we made an effort to cross a ridge of timber to the south, which, after considerable labor, proved successful. Here we found a multitude of gravelly, bright-flowing streams, with rich bottoms, lined all along with stately white oak, black-walnut, mulberry, and other similar growths, that yielded us excellent materials for wagon repairs, of which the route from Missouri, after passing Council Grove, is absolutely in want.

Although we found the buffalo extremely scarce westward of Spring Valley, yet there was no lack of game; for every nook and glade swarmed with deer and wild turkeys, partridges and grouse. We had also occasion to become acquainted with another species of prairie-tenant whose visits generally produced impressions that were anything but agreeable. I allude to a small black insect generally known to prairie travellers as the 'buffalo-gnat'. It not only attacks the face and hands, but even contrives to insinuate itself under the clothing, upon the breast and arms, and other covered parts. Here it fastens itself and luxuriates, until completely satisfied. Its bite is so poisonous as to give the face, neck, and hands, or any other part of the person upon which its affectionate caresses have been bestowed, the appearance of a pustulated varioloid. The buffalo-gnat is in fact a much more annoying insect than the mosquito, and also much more frequently met with on the prairie streams.

We now continued our line of march between the Canadian and the timbered ridge with very little difficulty. Having stopped to 'noon' in a bordering valley, we were quite surprised by the appearance of an Indian with no other protection than his squaw. From what we could gather by their signs, they had been the victims of a 'love scrape.' The fellow, whom I found to be a Kiowa, had, according to his own account, stolen the wife of another, and then fled to the thickets, where he purposed to lead a lonely life, in hopes of escaping the vengeance of his incensed predecessor. From this, it would appear that affairs of gallantry are not evils exclusively confined to civilization. Plausible, however, as the Indian's story seemed to be, we had strong suspicions that others of his band were not far off; and that he, with his 'better half,' had only been skulking about in hopes of exercising their 'acquisitiveness' at our expense; when, on finding themselves discovered, they deemed it the best policy fearlessly to approach us. This singular visit afforded a specimen of that confidence with which civilization inspires even the most untutored savages. They remained with us, in the utmost nonchalance, till the following morning.

Shortly after the arrival of the visitors, we were terribly alarmed at a sudden prairie conflagration. The old grass of the valley in which we were encamped had not been burned off, and one of our cooks having unwittingly kindled a fire in the midst of it, it spread at once with wonderful rapidity; and a brisk wind springing up at the time, the flames were carried over the valley, in spite of every effort we could make to check them. Fortunately for us, the fire had broken out to the leeward of our wagons, and therefore occasioned us no danger; but the accident itself was a forcible illustration of the danger that might be incurred by pitching a camp in the midst of dry grass, and the advantages that might be taken by hostile savages in such a locality.

After the fire had raged with great violence for a few hours, a cloud suddenly obscured the horizon, which was almost immediately followed by a refreshing shower of rain: a phenomenon often witnessed upon the Prairies after an extensive conflagration; and affording a practical exemplification of Professor Espy's celebrated theory of artificial showers.[1]

We now continued our journey without further trouble, except that of being still forced out of our proper latitude by the northern bearing of the Canadian. On the 30th of May, however, we succeeded in 'doubling' the spur of the Great North Bend.[2] Upon ascending the dividing ridge again, which at this point was entirely destitute of timber, a 'prairie expanse' once more greeted our view. This and the following day, our route lay through a region that abounded in gypsum, from the finest quality down to ordinary plaster. On the night of the 31st we encamped on a tributary of the North Fork, which we called Gypsum creek,[3] in consequence of its being surrounded with vast quantities of that substance.

Being compelled to keep a reckoning of our latitude, by which our travel was partly governed, and the sun being now too high at noon for the use of artificial horizon, we had to be guided entirely by observations of the meridian altitude of the moon, planets, or fixed stars. At Gypsum creek our latitude was 36° 10'—being the utmost northing we had made. As we were now about thirty miles north of the parallel of Santa Fé, we had to steer, henceforth, a few degrees south of west in order to bring up on our direct course.

The following night we encamped in a region covered with sandy hillocks, where there was not a drop of water to be found: in

[1] James Pollard Espy (1785–1860), the noted meteorologist whose daily records of atmospheric conditions led to the establishment of the United States Weather Bureau. His theory was that storms could be produced artificially by heating the atmosphere with sustained fires. See his *Philosophy of Storms* (Boston, Little & Brown, 1841).

[2] This bend of the Canadian extends five miles above the 36th parallel, just north of Taloga, in Dewey County, Oklahoma.

[3] Persimmon Creek, which enters the North Canadian near Richmond, in Woodward County, or one of its tributaries. Gregg has here reached the second line of gypsum hills in Oklahoma.

fact, an immense sand-plain was now opening before us, somewhat variegated in appearance, being entirely barren of vegetation in some places, while others were completely covered with an extraordinarily diminutive growth which has been called *shin-oak*, and a curious plum-bush of equally dwarfish stature. These singular-looking plants (undistinguishable at a distance from the grass of the prairies) were heavily laden with acorns and plums, which, when ripe, are of considerable size, although the trunks of either were seldom thicker than oat-straws, and frequently not a foot high. We also met with the same in many other places on the Prairies.

Still the most indispensable requisite, water, was nowhere to be found, and symptoms of alarm were beginning to spread far and wide among us. When we had last seen the Canadian and the North Fork, they appeared to separate in their course almost at right angles, therefore it was impossible to tell at what distance we were from either. At last my brother and myself, who had been scouring the plains during the morning without success, finally perceived a deep hollow leading in the direction of the Canadian, where we found a fine pool of water, and our wagons 'made port' again before midday; thus quieting all alarm.

Although we had encountered but very few buffalo since we left Spring Valley, they now began to make their appearance again, though not in very large droves; together with the deer and the fleet antelope, which latter struck me as being much more tame in this wild section of the Prairies than I had seen it elsewhere. The graceful and majestic mustang would also now and then sweep across the naked country, or come curvetting and capering in the vicinity of our little caravan, just as the humor prompted him. But what attracted our attention most were the little dog settlements, or, as they are more technically called, 'dog towns,' so often alluded to by the prairie travellers. As we were passing through their 'streets,' multitudes of the diminutive inhabitants were to be seen among the numerous little hillocks which marked their dwellings, where they frisked about, or sat perched at their doors, yelping defiance, to our great amusement—heedless of the danger that often awaited them from the rifles of our party: for they had perhaps never seen such deadly weapons before.

On the 5th day of June, we found ourselves once more travelling on a firm rolling prairie, about the region, as we supposed,[4] of the boundary between the United States and Mexico; when Lieut. Bowman, in pursuance of his instruction, began to talk seriously of returning. While the wagons were stopped at noon, a small party of us, including a few dragoons, advanced some miles ahead to take a survey of the route. We had just ascended the highest point of the ridge to get a prospect of the country beyond, when we descried a herd of buffalo in motion and two or three horsemen in hot pursuit. "Mexican Ciboleros!" we all exclaimed at once; for we supposed we might now be within the range of the buffalo hunters of New Mexico. Clapping spurs to our horses. we set off towards them at full speed. As we might have expected, our precipitate approach frightened them away and we soon lost sight of them altogether. On reaching the spot where they had last been seen, we found a horse and two mules saddled, all tied to the carcass of a slain buffalo which was partly skinned. We made diligent search in some copses of small growth, and among the adjacent ravines, but could discover no further traces of the fugitives. The Indian rigging of the animals, however, satisfied us that they were not Mexicans.

We were just about giving up the pursuit, when a solitary Indian horseman was espied upon a ridge about a mile from us. My brother and myself set out towards him, but on seeing us approach, he began to manifest some fear, and therefore my brother advanced alone. As soon as he was near enough he cried out *"Amigo!"* to which the Indian replied *"Comantz!"* and giving himself a thump upon the breast, he made a graceful circuit, and came up at full speed, presenting his hand in token of friendship. Nothing, however, could induce him to return to his animals with us, where the rest of our party had remained. He evidently feared treachery and foul play. Therefore we retraced our steps to the wagons, leaving the Indian's property just as we had found it, which, we subsequently discovered, was taken away after our departure.

In the afternoon of the same day, five more Indians (including a squaw), made their appearance, and having been induced by friend-

[4] From subsequent observations, this point appears to have been some miles west of the 100th degree of longitude.—GREGG.

ly tokens to approach us, they spent the night at our encampment. The next morning, we expressed a desire, by signs, to be conducted to the nearest point on our route where good pasturage and water might be found. A sprightly young chief, armed with only his bow and arrows, at once undertook the task, while his comrades still travelled along in our company. We had not progressed far before we found ourselves in the midst of another large 'dog-town.'

The task of describing the social and domestic habits of these eccentric little brutes, has been so graphically and amusingly executed by the racy and popular pen of G. Wilkins Kendall, that any attempt by me would be idle; and I feel that the most agreeable service I can do my readers is to borrow a paragraph from his alluring "Narrative," describing a scene presented by one of these prairie commonwealths.[5]

"In their habits they are clannish, social, and extremely convivial, never living alone like other animals, but, on the contrary, always found in villages or large settlements. They are a wild, frolicsome, madcap set of fellows when undisturbed, uneasy and ever on the move, and appear to take especial delight in chattering away the time, and visiting from hole to hole to gossip and talk over each other's affairs—at least so their actions would indicate. . . . . . On several occasions I crept close to their villages, without being observed, to watch their movements. Directly in the centre of one of them I particularly noticed a very large dog, sitting in front of the door or entrance to his burrow, and by his own actions and those of his neighbors it really seemed as though he was the president, mayor, or chief—at all events, he was the 'big dog' of the place. For at least an hour I secretly watched the operations in this community. During that time the large dog I have mentioned received at least a dozen visits from his fellow-dogs, which would stop and chat with him a few moments, and then run off to their domiciles. All this while he never left his post for a moment, and I thought I could discover a gravity in his deportment not discernible in those by which he was surrounded. Far is it from me to say that the visits he received were upon business, or had anything to do with the local government of

[5] Kendall, *Narrative of the Texan Santa Fé Expedition*, I, 192. For Gregg's own description of the prairie dogs, see below, chap. 11.

CAMP COMANCHE

the village; but it certainly appeared so. If any animal has a system of laws regulating the body politic, it is certainly the prairie dog."

As we sat on our horses, looking at these 'village transactions,' our Comanche guide drew an arrow for the purpose of cutting short the career of a little citizen that sat yelping most doggedly in the mouth of his hole, forty or fifty paces distant. The animal was almost entirely concealed behind the hillock which encompassed the entrance of his apartment, so that the dart could not reach it in a direct line; but the Indian had resort to a manoeuvre which caused the arrow to descend with a curve, and in an instant it quivered in the body of the poor little quadruped. The slayer only smiled at his feat, while we were perfectly astounded. There is nothing strange in the rifleman's being able to hit his mark with his fine-sighted barrel; but the accuracy with which these savages learn to shoot their feathered missiles, with such random aim, is almost incomprehensible. I had at the same time drawn one of Colt's repeating pistols, with a view of paying a similar compliment to another dog; when, finding that it excited the curiosity of the chief, I fired a few shots in quick succession, as an explanation of its virtues. He seemed to comprehend the secret instantly, and, drawing his bow once more, he discharged a number of arrows with the same rapidity, as a palpable intimation that he could shoot as fast with his instrument as we could with our patent fire-arms. This was not merely a vain show: there was more of reality than of romance in his demonstration.

Shortly after this we reached a fresh brook, a tributary of the North fork, which wound its silent course in the midst of a picturesque valley, surrounded by romantic hills and craggy knobs. Here we pitched our camp: when three of our visitors left us for the purpose of going to bring all the 'capitanes' of their tribe, who were said to be encamped at no great distance from us.

Our encampment, which we designated as 'Camp Comanche,' was only five or six miles from the North Fork,[6] while, to the southward, the main Canadian was but a little more distant.

After waiting anxiously for the arrival of the Comanche chiefs,

[6] Gregg mistook Wolf Creek for the North Canadian, which was now 50 miles north of his course. His 'Camp Comanche' (judging from the landscape and distance travelled) was probably in the watershed of Northup Creek, a tributary of the Wolf, just west of the Lipscomb-Ochiltree county line, in the Texas panhandle.

until our patience was well nigh exhausted, I ascended a high knoll just behind our camp, in company with the younger of the two chiefs who had remained with us, to see if anything could be discovered. By and by, the Comanche pointed anxiously towards the northwest, where he espied a party of his people, though at such a great distance, that it was some time before I could discern them. With what acuteness of vision are these savages endowed! Accustomed to the open plains, and like the eagle to look out for their prey at immense distances, their optical perception is scarcely excelled by that of the king of birds.

The party, having approached still nearer, assembled upon an eminence as if for the purpose of reconnoitring; but our chief upon the knoll hoisting his blanket, which seemed to say, 'come ahead,' they advanced slowly and deliberately—very unlike the customary mode of approach among all the prairie tribes.

The party consisted of about sixty warriors, at the head of whom rode an Indian of small stature and agreeable countenance, verging on the age of fifty. He wore the usual Comanche dress, but instead of moccasins, he had on a pair of long white cotton hose, while upon his bare head waved a tall red plume,—a mark of distinction which proclaimed him at once the *capitan mayor*, or principal chief. We addressed them in Spanish, inquiring if they had brought an interpreter, when a lank-jawed, grum-looking savage announced his readiness to officiate in that capacity. *"Sabes hablar en Español, amigo?"* (can you talk Spanish, friend?) I inquired. *"Sí"* (yes), he gruffly replied. "Where are your people?" "Encamped just above on yonder creek," "How many of you are there?" "Oh, a great many—nearly all the Comanche nation; for we are *en junta* to go and fight the Pawnees." "Well, can you tell us how far it is to Santa Fé?"—But the surly savage cut short my inquiries by observing—*"Ahí platicarémos despues"*—"We will talk about that hereafter."

We then showed them a spot a few rods from us, where they might encamp so as not to intermix their animals with ours; after which all the *capitanes* were invited to our camp to hold a 'big talk.' In a very short time we had ten chiefs seated in a circle within our tent, when the pipe, the Indian token of peace, was produced: but, doubting perhaps the sincerity of our professions, they at first refused to smoke. The interpreter, however, remarked as an excuse for their conduct that it was not their custom to smoke until they had received some presents: but a few Mexican *cigarritos* being produced, most of them took a whiff, as if under the impression that to smoke cigars was no pledge of friendship.

Lieut. Bowman now desired us to broach the subject of peace and amity betwixt the Comanches and our people, and to invite them to visit the 'Capitan Grande' at Washington, and enter into a perpetual treaty to that effect; but they would not then converse on the subject. In fact, the interpreter inquired, "Are we not at war?—how can we go to see the Capitan Grande?" We knew they held themselves at war with Mexico and Texas, and probably had mistaken us for Texans, which had no doubt caused the interpreter to speak so emphatically of their immense numbers. Upon this we explained to them that the United States was a distinct government and at peace with the Comanches. As an earnest of our friendly disposition, we then produced some scarlet cloth, with a small quantity of vermilion, tobacco, beads, etc., which being distributed among them, they very soon settled down into a state of placidness and contentment. Indeed, it will be found, that, with wild Indians, presents are always the corner-stone of friendship. "We are rejoiced," at last said the elder chief with a ceremonious air, "our hearts are glad that you have arrived among us: it makes our eyes laugh to see Americans walk in our land. We will notify our old and young men—our boys and our maidens—our women and children,—that they may come to trade with you. We hope you will speak well of us to your people, that more of them may hunt the way to our country, for we like to trade with the white man." This was delivered in Comanche, but translated into Spanish by the interpreter, who, although a full Indian, had lived several years among the Mexicans and spoke that language tolerably well. Our 'big talk' lasted several hours, after which the Indians retired to sleep. The next morning, after renewing their protestations of friendship, they took their departure, the principal chief saying, "Tell the Capitan Grande that when he pleases to call us we are all ready to go to see him."

The project of bringing some of the chiefs of these wild prairie tribes to Washington city, had been entertained, but never yet carried into effect. The few who have penetrated as far as Fort Gibson, or perhaps to a frontier village, have probably left with more unfavorable impressions than they had before. Believing the former to be our great Capital, and the most insignificant among the latter, our largest cities, they have naturally come to the conclusion that they surpass us in numbers and power, if not in wealth and grandeur. I have no doubt that the chiefs of the Comanches and other prairie tribes, if rightly managed, might be induced to visit our veritable 'Capitan Grande," and our large cities, which would doubtless have a far better effect than all the treaties of peace that could be concluded with them for an age to come. They would then 'see with their own eyes and hear with their own ears' the magnificence and power of the whites, which would inspire them at once with respect and fear.

This was on the 7th of June. About noon, Lieut. Bowman and his command finally took leave of us, and at the same time we resumed our forward march. This separation was truly painful: not so much on account of the loss we were about to experience, in regard to the protection afforded us by the troops (which, to say the truth, was more needed now than it had ever been before), as for the necessity of parting with a friend, who had endeared himself to us all by his affable deportment, his social manners and accommodating disposition. Ah! little did we think then that we should never see that gallant officer more! So young, so robust, and so healthy, little did we suspect that the sound of that voice which shouted so vigorously in responding to our parting salute in the desert, would never greet our ears again! But such was Fate's decree! Although he arrived safely at Fort Gibson, in a few short weeks he fell a victim to disease.

There were perhaps a few timid hearts that longed to return with the dragoons, and ever and anon a wistful glance would be cast back at the receding figures in the distance. The idea of a handful of thirty-four men having to travel without guide or protection through a dreary wilderness, peopled by thousands of savages who were just as likely to be hostile as friendly, was certainly very little calculated to produce agreeable impressions. Much to the credit of our men, however, the escort was no sooner out of sight than the timorous regained confidence, and all seemed bound together by stronger ties than before. All we feared were ambuscades or surprise; to guard against which, it was only necessary to redouble our vigilance.

On the following day, while we were enjoying our noon's rest upon a ravine of the Canadian, several parties of Indians, amounting altogether to about three hundred souls, including women and children, made their appearance. They belonged to the same band of Comanches with whom we had had so agreeable an intercourse, and had brought several mules in the expectation of driving a trade with us. The squaws and papooses were so anxious to gratify their curiosity, and so very soon began to give such striking manifestations of their pilfering propensities, that at the request of the chiefs, we carried some goods at a little distance, where a trade was opened, in hopes of attracting their attention. One woman, I observed, still lingered among the wagons, who, from certain peculiarities of features, struck me very forcibly as not being an Indian. In accordance with this impression I addressed her in Spanish, and was soon confirmed in all my suspicions. She was from the neighborhood of Matamoros, and had been married to a Comanche since her captivity. She did not entertain the least desire of returning to her people.

Similar instances of voluntary captivity have frequently occurred. Dr. Sibley,[7] in a communication to the War Department, in 1805, relates an affecting case, which shows how a sensitive female will often prefer remaining with her masters, rather than encounter the horrible ordeal of ill-natured remarks to which she would inevitably be exposed on being restored to civilized life.[8] The Comanches, some twenty years previous, having kidnapped the daughter of the Governor-General of Chihuahua, the latter transmitted $1000 to a trader to procure her ransom. This was soon affected, but to the astonishment of all concerned, the unfortunate girl refused to leave the Indians. She sent word to her father, that they had disfigured her by tattooing; that she was married and perhaps *enceinte;* and that she would be more unhappy by returning to her father under these circumstances than by remaining where she was.

[7] Dr. John Sibley (1757–1837), of Massachusetts, father of George C. Sibley of the Santa Fé road survey, was Indian agent at Natchitoches from 1804 to 1814 and subsequently a member of the Louisiana legislature.

[8] The incident is described by Dr. Sibley in his report of April 5, 1805. *American State Papers*, V, *Indian Affairs*, I, 724.

My attention was next attracted by a sprightly lad, ten or twelve years old, whose nationality could scarcely be detected under his Indian guise. But, though quite 'Indianized,' he was exceedingly polite. I inquired of him in Spanish, "Are you not a Mexican?" "Yes, sir,— I once was." "What is your name?" "Bernardino Saenz, sir, at your service." "When and where were you taken?" "About four years ago, at the Hacienda de las Animas, near Parral." "Shan't we buy you and take you to your people?—we are going thither." At this he hesitated a little and then answered in an affecting tone. *"No, señor; ya soy demasiado bruto para vivir entre los Cristianos"* (O, no, sir; I am now too much of a brute to live among Christians); adding that his owner was not there, and that he knew the Indian in whose charge he came would not sell him.

The Hacienda de las Animas is in the department of Chihuahua, some fifteen miles from the city of Parral, a much larger place than Santa Fé. Notwithstanding this, about three hundred Comanches made a bold inroad into the very heart of the settlements—laid waste the unfortunate hacienda, killing and capturing a considerable number—and remained several days in the neighborhood, committing all sorts of outrages. This occurred in 1835. I happened to be in Chihuahua at the time, and very well remember the bustle and consternation that prevailed. A thousand volunteers were raised, commanded by the governor himself, who 'hotly pursued' the enemy during their tardy retreat; but returned with the usual report—*"No les pudimos alcanzar,"*—we could not overtake them.

Out of half a dozen Mexican captives that happened to be with our new visitors, we only met with one who manifested the slightest inclination to abandon Indian life. This was a stupid boy about fifteen years of age, who had probably been roughly treated on account of his laziness. We very soon struck a bargain with his owner, paying about the price of a mule for the little outcast, whom I sent to his family as soon as we reached Chihuahua. Notwithstanding the inherent stupidity of my *protégé*, I found him abundantly grateful— much to his credit be it spoken—for the little service I had been able to render him.

We succeeded in purchasing several mules which cost us between ten and twenty dollars worth of goods apiece. In Comanche trade the main trouble consists in fixing the price of the first animal. This being settled by the chiefs, it often happens that mule after mule is led up and the price received without further cavil. Each owner usually wants a general assortment; therefore the price must consist of several items, as a blanket, a looking-glass, an awl, a flint, a little tobacco, vermillion, beads, etc.

Our trade with the new batch of Comanches being over, they now began to depart as they had come, in small parties, without bidding us adieu, or even informing us of their intention, it being the usual mode of taking leave among Indians, to depart *sans cérémonie*, and as silently as possible.

The Santa Fé caravans have generally avoided every manner of trade with the wild Indians, for fear of being treacherously dealt with during the familiar intercourse which necessarily ensues. This I am convinced is an erroneous impression; for I have always found, that savages are much less hostile to those with whom they trade, than to any other people. They are emphatically fond of traffic, and, being anxious to encourage the whites to come among them, instead of committing depredations upon those with whom they trade, they are generally ready to defend them against every enemy.

CHAPTER III

Ponds and Buffalo Wallows—Valley of the Canadian, and romantic Freaks of Nature—Melancholy Adventure of a Party of Traders in 1832 —Fears of being lost—Arrival of a Party of *Comancheros,* and their wonderful Stories—Their Peculiarities and Traffic—Bitter Water, and the *Salitre* of New Mexico—Avant-couriers for Santa Fé—Patent Fire-arms and their Virtues—Ranchero Ideas of Distance, and their Mode of giving Directions—The Angostura, and erroneous Notions of the Texans —A new Route revealed—Solitary Travel—Supply of Provisions sent back—Arrival at Santa Fé—Gov. Armijo, etc.—A 'Flare-up' with His Excellency.

THE COMANCHES having all disappeared, we resumed our march, and soon emerged into an open plain or *mesa* which was one of the most monotonous I have ever seen, there being not a break, not a hill nor valley, nor even a shrub to obstruct the view. The only thing which served to turn us from a direct course pursued by the compass, was the innumerable ponds which bespeckled the plain, and which kept us at least well supplied with water. Many of these ponds seem to have grown out of 'buffalo wallows,'—a term used on the Prairies to designate a sink made by the buffalo's pawing the earth for the purpose of obtaining a smooth dusty surface to roll upon.

After three or four days of weary travel over this level plain, the picturesque valley of the Canadian burst once more upon our view, presenting one of the most magnificent sights I had ever beheld. Here rose a perpendicular cliff, in all the majesty and sublimity of its desolation;—there another sprang forward as in the very act of losing its balance and about to precipitate itself upon the vale below; —a little further on, a pillar with crevices and cornices so curiously

formed as easily to be mistaken for the work of art; while a thousand
other objects grotesquely and fantastically arranged, and all shaded
in the sky-bound perspective by the blue ridge-like brow of the *mesa*
far beyond the Canadian, constituted a kind of chaotic space where
nature seemed to have indulged in her wildest caprices. Such was the
confusion of ground-swells and eccentric cavities, that it was altogether impossible to determine whereabouts the channel of the
Canadian wound its way among them.[1]

It would seem that these mesas might once have extended up to
the margin of the stream, leaving a *cañon* or chasm through which
the river flowed, as is still the case in some other places. But the basis
of the plain not having been sufficiently firm to resist the action of
the waters, these have washed and cut the bordering *cejas* or brows
into all the shapes they now present. The buffalo and other animals
have no doubt assisted in these transmutations. Their deep-worn
paths over the brows of the plains, form channels for the descending
rains; which are soon washed into the size of ravines—and even
considerable creeks. The beds of these continue to be worn down
until veins of lasting water are opened, and constant-flowing streams
thus established. Numerous were the embryo rivulets which might
be observed forming in this way along the borders of those streams.
The frequent isolated benches and mounds, whose tabular summits
are on a level with the adjacent plains, and appear entirely of a similar formation, indicate that the intermediate earth has been washed
away, or removed by some other process of nature—all seeming to
give plausibility to our theory.

It was somewhere in this vicinity that a small party of Americans
experienced a terrible calamity in the winter of 1832–3, on their way
home; and as the incident had the tendency to call into play the most
prominent features of the Indian character, I will disgress so far here
as to relate the facts.

The party consisted of twelve men, chiefly citizens of Missouri.
Their baggage and about ten thousand dollars in specie were packed
upon mules. They took the route of the Canadian river, fearing to

---

[1] Having traveled three or four days on the high plain with the brow of the
Canadian Escarpment visible in the west, Gregg must have met the canyon of the
Canadian near the 102nd meridian, in Moore County, Texas.

venture on the northern prairies at that season of the year. Having left Santa Fé in December, they had proceeded without accident thus far, when a large body of Comanches and Kiawas were seen advancing towards them. Being well acquainted with the treacherous and pusillanimous disposition of those races, the traders prepared at once for defence; but the savages having made a halt at some distance, began to approach one by one, or in small parties, making a great show of friendship all the while, until most of them had collected on the spot. Finding themselves surrounded in every direction, the travellers now began to move on, in hopes of getting rid of the intruders: but the latter were equally ready for the start; and, mounting their horses, kept jogging on in the same direction. The first act of hostility perpetrated by the Indians proved fatal to one of the American traders named Pratt, who was shot dead while attempting to secure two mules which had become separated from the rest. Upon this, the companions of the slain man immediately dismounted and commenced a fire upon the Indians, which was warmly returned, whereby another man of the name of Mitchell was killed.

By this time the traders had taken off their packs and piled them around for protection; and now falling to work with their hands they very soon scratched out a trench deep enough to protect them from the shot of the enemy. The latter made several desperate charges, but they seemed too careful of their own personal safety, notwithstanding the enormous superiority of their numbers, to venture too near the rifles of the Americans. In a few hours all the animals of the traders were either killed or wounded, but no personal damage was done to the remaining ten men, with the exception of a wound in the thigh received by one, which was not at the time considered dangerous.

During the siege, the Americans were in great danger of perishing from thirst, as the Indians had complete command of all the water within reach. Starvation was not so much to be dreaded; because, in case of necessity, they could live on the flesh of their slain animals, some of which lay stretched close around them. After being pent up for thirty-six hours in this horrible hole, during which time they had seldom ventured to raise their heads above the surface without being shot at, they resolved to make a bold *sortie* in the night, as any death was preferable to the fate which awaited them there. As there was not an animal left that was at all in a condition to travel, the proprietors of the money gave permission to all to take and appropriate to themselves whatever amount each man could safely undertake to carry. In this way a few hundred dollars were started with, of which, however, but little ever reached the United States. The remainder was buried deep in the sand, in hopes that it might escape the cupidity of the savages; but to very little purpose, for they were afterwards seen by some Mexican traders making a great display of specie, which was without doubt taken from this unfortunate *cache*.

With every prospect of being discovered, overtaken, and butchered, but resolved to sell their lives as dearly as possible, they at last emerged from their hiding-place, and moved on silently and slowly until they found themselves beyond the purlieus of the Indian camps. Often did they look back in the direction where from three to five hundred savages were supposed to watch their movements, but, much to their astonishment, no one appeared to be in pursuit. The Indians, believing no doubt that the property of the traders would come into their hands, and having no amateur predilection for taking scalps at the risk of losing their own, appeared willing enough to let the spoliated adventurers depart without further molestation.

The destitute travellers having run themselves short of provisions, and being no longer able to kill game for want of materials to load their rifles with, they were soon reduced to the necessity of sustaining life upon roots, and the tender bark of trees. After travelling for several days in this desperate condition, with lacerated feet, and utter prostration of mind and body, they began to disagree among themselves about the route to be pursued, and eventually separated into two distinct parties. Five of these unhappy men steered a westward course, and after a succession of sufferings and privations which almost surpassed belief, they reached the settlements of the Creek Indians, near the Arkansas river, where they were treated with great kindness and hospitality. The other five wandered about in the greatest state of distress and bewilderment, and only two finally succeeded in getting out of the mazes of the wilderness. Among those who were abandoned to their fate, and left to perish thus miserably, was a Mr. Schenck, the same individual who had been shot in the thigh; a gentleman of talent and excellent family connections, who was a brother, as I am informed of the Hon. Mr. Schenck, at present a member of Congress from Ohio.[2]

But let us resume our journey. We had for some days, while travelling along the course of the Canadian, been in anxious expectation of reaching a point from whence there was a cart-road to Santa Fé, made by the Ciboleros; but being constantly baffled and disappointed in this hope, serious apprehensions began to be entertained by some of the party that we might after all be utterly lost. In this emergency, one of our Mexicans who pretended to be a great deal wiser than the rest, insisted that we were pursuing a wrong direction, and that every day's march only took us further from Santa Fé. There appeared to be so much plausibility in his assertion, as he professed a perfect knowledge of all the country around, that many of our men were almost ready to mutiny,—to take the command from the hands of my brother and myself and lead us southward in search of the Colorado, into the fearful *Llano Estacado*,[3] where we would probably have perished. But our observations of the latitude, which

[2] Essentially the same details appeared in the newspaper at St. Louis shortly after the first survivors arrived. The attack (which began about January 1, 1833, and lasted 32 hours) occurred on the Canadian about 200 miles from Santa Fé, and the survivors were 42 days in reaching the first white settlement. Pratt is identified as a tinner who had resided for some time in Santa Fé and Mitchell only as being from Boone County, Missouri. St. Louis *Missouri Republican*, March 5, 1833.

Other details are supplied by the Kiowas, who recorded the incident as the "Winter they captured the money." The traders (being beyond the United States border and far off the regular Santa Fé Trail) were mistaken for Texans by a Kiowa war party under "Lame-old-man." In the attack "several" whites and only one Indian, "Black Wolf," were killed. The Kiowas carried off a few silver coins but, learning from some Comanches the value of silver, returned and unearthed the full cache. Gregg's description of the locality of the attack agrees with the Kiowa version, that it was near the Canadian River, a short distance below "Skunkberry-bush creek" (Skunk Arroyo in central Oldham County, Texas). James Mooney, "Calendar History of the Kiowas," in the Bureau of American Ethnology, *Seventeenth Annual Report, 1895–96*, Part 1, 254–57.

[3] The Llano Estacado, traversed by Coronado in 1541, is the high, barren plain bordered by sculptured rim-rock in southeastern New Mexico and northwestern Texas. The Spanish name is most frequently translated as "Staked Plains," but Bolton argues convincingly for "Stockaded Plains" or "Palisaded Plains," as the bordering escarpment presents a palisade-like appearance. Herbert E. Bolton, *Coronado: Knight of Pueblo and Plains*, 282–88.

we took very frequently, as well as the course we were pursuing, completely contradicted the Mexican wiseacre. A few days afterwards we were overtaken by a party of *Comancheros,* or Mexican Comanche traders, when we had the satisfaction of learning that we were in the right track.

These men had been trading with the band of Comanches we had lately met, and learning from them that we had passed on, they had hastened to overtake us, so as to obtain our protection against the savages, who, after selling their animals to the Mexicans, very frequently take forcible possession of them again, before the purchasers have been able to reach their homes. These parties of *Comancheros* are usually composed of the indigent and rude classes of the frontier villages, who collect together, several times a year, and launch upon the plains with a few trinkets and trumperies of all kinds, and perhaps a bag of bread and may-be another of *pinole,* which they barter away to the savages for horses and mules. The entire stock of an individual trader very seldom exceeds the value of twenty dollars, with which he is content to wander about for several months, and glad to return home with a mule or two, as the proceeds of his traffic.

These Mexican traders had much to tell us about the Comanches; saying, that they were four or five thousand in number, with perhaps a thousand warriors, and that the fiery young men had once determined to follow and attack us; but that the chiefs and sages had deterred them, by stating that our cannons could kill to the distance of many miles, and shoot through hills and rocks and destroy everything that happened to be within their range. The main object of our visitors, however, seemed to be to raise themselves into importance by exaggerating the perils we had escaped from. That they had considered themselves in great jeopardy, there could be no doubt whatever, for, in their anxiety to overtake us, they came very near killing their animals.

It was a war-party of this band of Comanches that paid the 'flying visit' to Bent's Fort on the Arkansas river, to which Mr. Farnham alludes in his trip to Oregon.[4] A band of the same Indians also fell

[4] Thomas Jefferson Farnham (1804–48), New England lawyer, traveler, and writer. His *Travels in the Great Western Prairie, the Anahuac and Rocky Mountains, and in the Oregon Territory* (cited above, Vol. I, chap. 2, n. 4) was popularly read but much maligned by critical historians. Bent's Fort, or Fort William, was

in with the caravan from Missouri, with whom they were for a while upon the verge of hostilities.

The next day we passed the afternoon upon a ravine where we found abundance of water, but to our great surprise our animals refused to drink. Upon tasting the water, we found it exceedingly nauseous and bitter; far more repugnant to some palates than a solution of Epsom salts. It is true that the water had been a little impregnated with the same loathsome substance for several days; but we had never found it so bad before. The salinous compound which imparts this savor, is found in great abundance in the vicinity of the tableplain streams of New Mexico, and is known to the natives by the name of *salitre*.[5] We had the good fortune to find in the valley a few sinks filled by recent rains, so that actually we experienced no great inconvenience from the want of fresh water. As far as our own personal necessities were concerned, we were abundantly supplied; it being an unfailing rule with us to carry in each wagon a five-gallon keg always filled with water, in order to guard against those frightful contingencies which so frequently occur on the Prairies. In truth upon leaving one watering place, we never knew where we would find the next.

On the 20th of June we pitched our camp upon the north bank of the Canadian or Colorado, in latitude 35° 24′ according to a meridian altitude on Saturn.[6] On the following day, I left the caravan, accompanied by three Comancheros, and proceeded at a more rapid pace towards Santa Fé. This was rather a hazardous journey, inasmuch as we were still within the range of the Pawnee and Comanche war-parties, and my companions were men in whom I could not repose the slightest confidence, except for piloting; being fully convinced that in case of meeting with an enemy, they would either for-

begun in 1829 and completed in 1832 by Colonel William Bent, his brother Charles, and Céran St. Vrain. It was on the northern bank of the Arkansas between the present towns of La Junta and Las Animas, Colorado. For twenty years it was important as a trading post and as a way station on the mountain branch of the Santa Fé Trail. It was destroyed in 1852.

[5] Literally *saltpetre;* but the *salitre* of New Mexico is a compound of several other salts besides nitre.—GREGG.

[6] The Canadian reaches this latitude a few miles east of the present New Mexico border. Gregg's own map shows the trail crossing the Canadian in this vicinity and departing from it for the last time.

sake or deliver me up, just as it might seem most conducive to their own interest and safety. All I had to depend upon were my fire-arms, which could hardly fail to produce an impression in my favor; for, thanks to Mr. Colt's invention,[7] I carried thirty-six charges ready-loaded, which I could easily fire at the rate of a dozen per minute. I do not believe that any band of those timorous savages of the western prairies would venture to approach even a single man, under such circumstances. If, according to an old story of the frontier, an Indian supposed that a white man fired both with his tomahawk and scalping knife, to account for the execution done by a brace of pistols, thirty-six shots discharged in quick succession would certainly over-awe them as being the effect of some great medicine.

As we jogged merrily along, I often endeavored to while away the time by catechising my three companions in relation to the topography of the wild region we were traversing; but I soon found, that, like the Indians, these ignorant rancheros have no ideas of distances, except as compared with time or with some other distance. They will tell you that you may arrive at a given place by the time the sun reaches a certain point: otherwise, whether it be but half a mile or half a day's ride to the place inquired for, they are as apt to apply *está cerquita* (it is close by), or *está lejos* (it is far off), to the one as to the other, just as the impression happens to strike them, when compared with some other point more or less distant. This often proves a source of great annoyance to foreign travellers, as I had an opportunity of experiencing before my arrival. In giving directions, these people—in fact, the lower classes of Mexicans generally—are also in the habit of using very odd gesticulations, altogether peculiar to themselves. Instead of pointing with their hands and fingers, they generally employ the mouth, which is done by thrusting out the lips in the direction of the spot, or object, which the inquirer wishes to find out—accompanied by *aquí* or *allí está*. This habit of substituting labial gestures for the usual mode of indicating, has grown from the use of the *sarape*, which keeps their hands and arms perpetually confined.

[7] Samuel Colt (1814–62), of Connecticut, invented the revolver to which Gregg makes frequent reference, securing patent in England in 1835 and in the United States in 1836.

From the place where we left the wagons, till we reached the *Angostura,* or narrows[8] (a distance of 60 miles), we had followed a plain cart-road, which seemed everywhere passable for wagons. Here, however, we found the point of a table plain projecting abruptly against the river, so as to render it impossible for wagons to pass without great risk. The huge masses of solid rock, which occur in this place, and the rugged cliffs or brows of the table lands which rise above them, appear to have been mistaken by a detachment of the Texan Santa Fé expedition, for spurs of the Rocky Mountains; an error which was rational enough, as they not unfrequently tower to the height of two thousand feet above the valley, and are often rocky and rough as the rudest heads of trap-rock can make them. By ascending the main summit of these craggy promontories, however, the eastern ridge of the veritable Rocky Mountains may be seen, still very far off in the western horizon, with a widespread and apparently level table plain, intervening and extending in every direction as far as the eye can reach; for even the deep-cut chasms of the intersecting rivers are rarely visible except one be upon their very brink.

Upon expressing my fears that our wagons would not be able to pass the *Angostura* in safety, my companions informed me that there was an excellent route, of which no previous mention had been made, passing near the *Cerro de Tucumcari,* a round mound plainly visible to the southward.[9] After several vain efforts to induce some of the party to carry a note back to my brother, and to pilot the caravan through the Tucumcari route, one of them, known as Tio Baca, finally proposed to undertake the errand for a bounty of ten dollars, besides high wages till they should reach the frontier. His conditions being accepted, he set out after breakfast, not, however, without previously recommending himself to the Virgin Guadalupe, and all

[8] The Narrows in the Canadian canyon were about 8 miles below the junction of the Conchos (now Conchos Dam Reservoir), in eastern San Miguel County, New Mexico.

[9] Tucumcari Mountain (elev. 4,967 ft.) is immediately to the southeast of the present city of Tucumcari, in Quay County, New Mexico, and about 10 miles south of the Canadian River. The route Gregg mentions was an old Comanchero trail swinging around the southeast side of Mount Tucumcari and then westward to the valley of the Pecos which was followed by the wagons of the Texan Santa Fé party in 1841. Kendall, *Narrative of the Texan Santa Fé Expedition,* I, 260–62.

the saints in the calendar, and desiring us to remember him in our prayers. Notwithstanding his fears, however, he arrived in perfect safety, and I had the satisfaction of learning afterward that my brother found the new route everything he could have desired.

I continued my journey westward with my two remaining companions; but, owing to their being provided with a relay of horses, they very soon left me to make the balance of the travel alone— though yet in a region haunted by hostile savages. On the following day, about the hour of twelve, as I was pursuing a horse-path along the course of the Rio Pecos, near the frontier settlements, I met with a shepherd, of whom I anxiously inquired the distance to San Miguel. "O, it is just there," responded the man of sheep. "Don't you see the point of mesa yonder? It is just beyond that." This welcome information cheered me greatly; for, owing to the extraordinary transparency of the atmosphere, it appeared to me that the distance could not exceed two or three miles. *"Está cerquita,"* exclaimed the shepherd as I rode off; *"ahora está V. allá"*—"it is close by; you will soon be there."

I set off at as lively a pace as my jaded steed could carry me, confident of taking dinner in San Miguel. Every ridge I turned I thought must be the last, and thus I jogged on, hoping and anticipating my future comforts till the shades of evening began to appear; when I descended into the valley of the Pecos, which, although narrow, is exceedingly fertile and beautifully lined with verdant fields, among which stood a great variety of mud cabins. About eight o'clock, I called at one of these cottages and again inquired the distance to San Miguel; when a swarthy-looking ranchero once more saluted mine ears with *"Está cerquita; ahora está V. allá."* Although the distance was designated in precisely the same words used by the shepherd eight hours before, I had the consolation at least of believing that I was something nearer. After spurring on for a couple of miles over a rugged road, I at last reached the long-sought village.

The next day, I hired a Mexican to carry some flour back to meet the wagons; for our party was by this time running short of provisions. In fact, we should long before have been in danger of starvation, had it not been for our oxen; for we had not seen a buffalo since the day we first met with the Comanches. Some of our cattle being in good plight, and able, as we were, to spare a few from our teams, we made beef of them when urged by necessity: an extra advantage in ox-teams on these perilous expeditions.

On the 25th of June I arrived safely at Santa Fé,—but again rode back to meet the wagons, which did not reach the capital till the 4th of July. We did not encounter a very favorable reception from 'his majesty,' Gov. Armijo. He had just established his arbitrary impost of $500 per wagon,[10] which bore rather heavily upon us; for we had an overstock of coarse articles which we had merely brought along for the purpose of increasing the strength of our company, by adding to the number of our wagons.

But these little troubles in a business way, were entirely drowned in the joyful sensation arising from our safe arrival, after so long and so perilous an expedition. Considering the character and our ignorance of the country over which we had travelled, we had been exceedingly successful. Instances are certainly rare of heavily-laden wagons' having been conducted, without a guide, through an unexplored desert; and yet we performed the trip without any important accident—without encountering any very difficult passes—without suffering for food or for water.

We had hoped that at least a few days of rest and quiet recreation might have been allowed us after our arrival; for relaxation was sorely needed at the end of so long a journey and its concomitant privations; but it was ordered otherwise. We had scarcely quartered ourselves within the town before a grand 'flare-up' took place between Gov. Armijo and the foreigners[11] in Santa Fé, which, for a little while, bid fair to result in open hostilities. It originated in the following circumstances.

In the winter of 1837–8, a worthy young American, named Daley,[12] was murdered at the Gold Mines, by a couple of villains, solely for plunder. The assassins were arrested, when they confessed their guilt; but, in a short time, they were permitted to run at large

[10] See above, Vol. I, chap. 5.

[11] Among the New Mexicans, the term *foreigner* and American are synonymous: indeed, the few citizens of other nations to be found there identify themselves with those of the United States. All foreigners are known there as *Americanos*; but south of Chihuahua they are indiscriminately called *Los Ingleses*, the English.—GREGG.

[12] Andrew W. Daley, a Santa Fé trader since at least 1834.

again, in violation of every principle of justice or humanity. About this time they were once more apprehended, however, by the interposition of foreigners; and, at the solicitation of the friends of the deceased, a memorial from the Americans in Santa Fé was presented to Armijo, representing the injustice of permitting the murderers of their countrymen to go unpunished; and praying that the culprits be dealt with according to law. But the governor affected to consider the affair as a conspiracy; and, collecting his ragamuffin militia, attempted to intimidate the petitioners. The foreigners were now constrained to look to their defence, as they saw that no justice was to be expected. Had Armijo persisted, serious consequences might have ensued; but seeing the 'conspirators' firm, he sent an apology, affecting to have misconstrued their motives, and promising that the laws should be duly executed upon the murderers.

Besides the incentives of justice and humanity, foreigners felt a deep interest in the execution of this promise. But a few years previous, another person had been assassinated and robbed at the same place; yet the authorities having taken no interest in the matter, the felons were never discovered: and now, should these assassins escape the merited forfeit of their atrocious crime, it was evident there would be no further security for our lives and property. But the governor's *due execution of the laws* consisted in retaining them a year or two in nominal imprisonment, when they were again set at liberty. Besides these, other foreigners having been murdered in New Mexico with equal impunity:—all which contrasts very strikingly with the manner our courts of justice have since dealt with those who killed Chavez, in 1843, on the Santa Fé road.[13]

[13] See below, chap. 9, n. 7.

CHAPTER IV

Preparations for a Start to Chihuahua—Ineptness of Married Men for the Santa Fé Trade—The Chihuahua Trade—Annoying Custom-house Regulations—Mails in New Mexico—Insecurity of Correspondence— Outfit and Departure—*Derecho de Consumo*—Ruins of Valverde— 'Towns without Houses'—La Jornada del Muerto—Laguna and Ojo del Muerto—A Tradition of the *Arrieros*—Laborious Ferrying and Quagmires—Arrival at Paso del Norte—Amenity of the Valley—*Sierra Blanco* and *Los Organos*—Face of the Country—Sea-grass—An accidental River—Laguna de Encinillas—Southern Haciendas—Arrival— Character of the Route and Soil.

AFTER PASSING the custom-house ordeal, and exchanging some of our merchandise for 'Eagle Dollars'—an operation which occupied us several weeks, I prepared to set out for the Chihuahua market, whither a portion of our stock had been designed. Upon this expedition I was obliged to depart without my brother, who was laboring under the 'home fever,' and anxious to return to his family. "He that hath wife and children," says Lord Bacon, "hath given hostages to fortune; for they are impediments to great enterprises, either of virtue or mischief."[1] Men under such bonds are peculiarly unfitted for the chequered life of a Santa Fé trader. The domestic hearth, with all its sacred and most endearing recollections, is sure to haunt them in the hour of trial, and almost every step of their journey is apt to be attended by melancholy reflections of home and domestic dependencies.

Before starting on this new journey I deem it proper to make a few observations relative to the general character of the *Chihuahua Trade*. I have already remarked, that much surprise has frequently

[1] Francis Bacon (1561–1626), "Of Marriage and Single Life," in *Essayes*.

been expressed by those who are unacquainted with all the bearings of the case, that the Missouri traders should take the circuitous route to Santa Fé, instead of steering direct for Chihuahua, inasmuch as the greatest portion of their goods is destined for the latter city. But as Chihuahua never had any port of entry for foreign goods till the last six or eight years, the market of that department had to be supplied in a great measure from Santa Fé. By opening the ports of El Paso and Presidio del Norte, the commercial interest was so little affected, that when Santa Anna's decree for closing them again was issued, the loss was scarcely felt at all.[2]

The mode of transmitting merchandise from the ports to the interior, is very different from what it is in the United States. It is not enough to have to pass the tedious ordeal of custom-houses on the frontier, and we have not only to submit to a supervision and repayment of duty on arriving at our point of destination but our cargo is subject to scrutiny at every town we have to pass through on our journey. Nor would it be advisable to forsake the main route in order to avoid this tyrannical system of vexation; because, according to the laws of the country, every *cargamento* which is found out of the regular track (except in cases of unavoidable necessity), is subject to confiscation, although accompanied by the necessary custom-house documents.

There are also other risks and contingencies very little dreamed of in the philosophy of the inexperienced trader. Before setting out, the entire bill of merchandise has to be translated into Spanish; when, duplicates of the translation being presented to the custom-house, one is retained, while the other, accompanied by the *guia* (a sort of clearance or mercantile passport),[3] is carried along with the

[2] El Paso del Norte and Presidio del Norte were made ports of entry in Chihuahua on October 20, 1835, along with San Miguel del Vado and San Fernando de Taos in New Mexico, but judging by succeeding orders, enforcement was not immediate, and so neither San Miguel nor Santa Fé were affected by the closure decree of August 7, 1843. Manuel Dublán and José María Lozano (compilers), *Legislación mexicana ó colección completa de las disposiciones legislativas expedidas desde la independencia de la república*, III, 507.

[3] The *guia*, a printed form, required the following information: place and date of issue, serial number, bearer's name, number of packages, origin and value of goods, destination, consignee, days allowed to reach destination, days allowed for return of delivery certification (the *tornaguia*), and signature of the customs administrator. A sample *guia* is in the Twitchell Collection (Doc. 7757) of the Historical Society of New Mexico at Santa Fé.

cargo by the conductor. The trader can have three points of destination named in his *guia,* to either of which he may direct his course, but to no others: while in the drawing up of the *factura,* or invoice, the greatest care is requisite, as the slightest mistake, even an accidental slip of the pen, might, according to the terms of the law, subject the goods to confiscation.[4]

The *guia* is not only required on leaving the ports for the interior, but is indispensable to the safe conveyance of goods from one department of the republic to another: nay, the simple transfer of property from town to town, and from village to village, in the same department, is attended by precisely the same proportion of risk, and requires the same punctilious accuracy in the accompanying documents. Even the produce and manufactures of the country are equally subject to these embarrassing regulations. New Mexico has no internal custom-houses, and is therefore exempt from this rigorous provision; but from Chihuahua south every village has its revenue officers; so that the same stock of merchandise sometimes pays the internal duty at least half-a-dozen times before the sale is completed.

Now, to procure this same *guia,* which is the cause of so much difficulty and anxiety in the end, is no small affair. Before the authorities condescend to draw a single line on paper, the merchant must produce an endorser for the *tornaguia,* which is a certificate from the custom-house to which the cargo goes directed, showing that the goods have been legally entered there. A failure in the return of this document within a prescribed limit of time subjects the endorser to a forfeiture equal to the amount of the impost. Much inconvenience and not a little risk are also occasioned on this score by the irregularity—I may say, insecurity of the mails.

Speaking of mails, I beg leave to observe, that there are no conveniences of this kind in New Mexico, except on the route from Santa Fé to Chihuahua, and these are very irregular and uncertain.

---

[4] In confirmation of this it is only necessary to quote the following from the *Pauta de Comisos,* II, Art. 22: 'Ni las guias ni las facturas, ni los pases, en todos los casos de que trata este decreto han de contener enmendadura, raspadura, ni entrerenglonadura alguna' ["Neither the consignment papers nor the invoices, nor the passes, in any case covered by this decree, may contain any emendation, erasure, or interlineation."]—and this under penalty of confiscation.—GREGG.

Before the Indians had obtained such complete possession of the highways through the wilderness, the mails between these two cities were carried semi-monthly;[5] but now they are much less frequent, being mere expresses, in fact, dispatched only when an occasion offers. There are other causes, however, besides the dread of marauding savages, which render the transportation of the mails in New Mexico very insecure: I mean the dishonesty of those employed in superintending them. Persons known to be inimical to the postmaster, or to the 'powers that be,' and wishing to forward any communication to the South, most generally either wait for a private conveyance, or send their letters to a post-office (the only one besides that of Santa Fé in all New Mexico) some eighty miles on the way; thus avoiding an overhauling at the capital. Moreover, as the postrider often carries the key of the mail bag (for want of a supply at the different offices), he not unfrequently permits whomsoever will pay him a trifling *douceur*, to examine the correspondence. I was once witness to a case of this kind in the Jornada del Muerto, where the entire mail was tumbled out upon the grass, that an individual might search for letters, for which luxury he was charged by the accommodating carrier the moderate price of one dollar.

The *derecho de consumo* (the internal or consumption duty) is an impost averaging nearly twenty per cent on the United States cost of the bill.[6] It supplies the place of a direct tax for the support of the departmental government, and is decidedly the most troublesome if not the most oppressive revenue system that ever was devised for internal purposes. It operates at once as a drawback upon the commercial prosperity of the country, and as a potent incentive to fraudulent practices. The country people especially have resort to every species of clandestine intercourse, to escape this galling burden; for, every article of consumption they carried to market, whether fish, flesh or fowl, as well as fruit and vegetables, is taxed more

[5] The rider was scheduled to leave Chihuahua on the first and fifteenth of each month, meeting and exchanging mail pouches with the rider from Santa Fé at El Brazito, about 35 miles north of El Paso del Norte. José Antonio Escudero, *Noticias Estadísticas de Chihuahua*, 186.

[6] This rate was in force for only a week (November 26 to December 2, 1839). It was 3 per cent in 1824, 5 per cent in 1829, 6 per cent in 1832, 20 per cent and 5 per cent in 1839, and 15 per cent in 1843. Dublán and Lozano (compilers), *Legislación Mexicana*, I, 748–49; II, 151, 435; III, 667, 673; IV, 641.

or less; while another impost is levied upon the goods they purchase with the proceeds of their sales. This system, so beautifully entangled with corruptions, is supported on the ground that it supersedes direct taxation, which, in itself, is an evil that the 'free and independent' people of Mexico would never submit to. Besides the petty annoyances incidental upon the laxity of custom-house regulations, no one can travel through the country without a passport,[7] which, to free-born Americans, is a truly insupportable nuisance.

Having at last gone through with all the vexatious preparations necessary for our journey, on the 22d of August we started for Chihuahua. I fitted out myself but six wagons for this market, yet joining in company with several other traders, our little caravans again amounted to fourteen wagons, with about forty men. Though our route lay through the interior of Northern Mexico, yet, on account of the hostile savages which infest most of the country through which we had to pass, it was necessary to unite in caravans of respectable strength, and to spare few of those precautions for safety which are required on the Prairies.

The road we travelled passes down through the settlements of New Mexico for the first hundred and thirty miles, on the east side of the Rio del Norte. Nevertheless, as there was not an inn of any kind to be found upon the whole route, we were constrained to put up with very primitive accommodations. Being furnished from the outset, therefore, with blankets and buffalo rugs for bedding, we were prepared to bivouac, even in the suburbs of the villages, in the open air; for in this dry and salubrious atmosphere it is seldom that travellers go to the trouble of pitching tents.[8] When travelling alone, however, or with but a comrade or two, I have always experienced a great deal of hospitality from the rancheros and villageois of the country. Whatever sins these ignorant people may have to answer for, we must accord to them at least two glowing virtues—gratitude

[7] Gregg obviously means a safe-conduct pass (*carta de seguridad*), which foreign travelers were required to obtain each year through their consuls.

[8] How scant soever our outfit of 'camp comforts' might appear, our Mexican muleteers were much more sparely supplied. The exposure endured by this hardy race is really surprising. Even in the coldest winter weather, they rarely carry more than one blanket apiece—the *sarape*, which serves as a cloak during the day, and at night is their only 'bed and bedding.'—GREGG.

and hospitality. I have suffered like others, however, from one very disagreeable custom which prevails among them. Instead of fixing price for the services they bestow upon travellers, they are apt to answer, *"Lo que guste,"* or *"Lo que le dé la gana"* (whatever you please, or have a mind to give), expecting, of course, that the liberal foreigner will give more than their consciences would permit them to exact.

In about ten days' drive we passed the southernmost settlements of New Mexico,[9] and twenty or thirty miles further down the river we came to the ruins of Valverde. This village was founded about twenty years ago, in one of the most fertile valleys of the Rio del Norte. It increased rapidly in population, until it was invaded by the Navajoes, when the inhabitants were obliged to abandon the place after considerable loss, and it has never since been repeopled.[10] The bottoms of the valley, many of which are of rich alluvial loam, have lain fallow ever since, and will perhaps continue to be neglected until the genius of civilization shall have spread its beneficent influences over the land. This soil is the more valuable for cultivation on account of the facilities for irrigation which the river affords; as it too frequently happens that the best lands of the settlements remain unfruitful for want of water.

Our next camping place deserving of mention was *Fray Cristóbal*, which, like many others on the route, is neither town nor village, but a simple isolated point on the river-bank—a mere *parage*, or camping-ground.[11] We had already passed San Pascual, El Contadero, and many others, and we could hear Aleman, Robledo,[12]

[9] La Joya de Sevilleta (107 miles south of Santa Fé) and La Parida (17 miles further south) on the east bank and Socorro (3 miles below La Parida) on the west.

[10] Valverde (18 miles below Socorro but on the east bank) was settled temporarily in 1820 and again in 1825. In 1846 it was the rendezvous for Doniphan's regiment and some 300 merchant wagons on their march to Chihuahua and in 1862 was a Civil War battlefield.

[11] At the foot of Fray Cristóbal Mountain, about 22 miles below Valverde and 167 from Santa Fé. The name was attached at least as early as the seventeenth century.

[12] San Pascual was a Piro pueblo (abondoned in the seventeenth century) just north of San Pascual Mountain and about 17 miles above Fray Cristóbal camp. El Paso del Contadero was a winding road of about 8 miles through the hills mid-way between San Pascual and Fray Cristóbal. La Cruz de Alemán was a seventeenth-century grave, and a regular camp on the Jornada del Muerto (about 45 miles south of Fray Cristóbal), and now a railroad station. For Robledo, see below, this chapter, n. 17.

and a dozen such spoken of on the way, leading the stranger to imagine that the route was lined with flourishing villages. The arriero will tell one to hasten—"we must reach San Diego[13] before sleeping." We spur on perhaps with redoubled vigor, in hopes to rest at a town; but lo! upon arriving, we find only a mere watering-place, without open ground enough to graze the *caballada*. Thus every point along these wilderness highways used as a camping-site, has received a distinctive name, well known to every muleteer who travels them. Many of these *parages*, without the slightest vestige of human improvement, figure upon most of the current maps of the day as towns and villages. Yet there is not a single settlement (except of very recent establishment) from those before mentioned to the vicinity of El Paso, a distance of near two hundred miles.

We arrived at Fray Cristóbal in the evening, but this being the threshold of the famous Jornada del Muerto, we deemed it prudent to let our animals rest here until the following afternoon. The road over which we had hitherto been travelling, though it sometimes traverses upland ridges and undulating sections, runs generally near the border of the river, and for the most part in its immediate valley: but here it leaves the river and passes for nearly eighty miles over a table-plain to the eastward of a small ledge of mountains, whose western base is hugged by the circuitous channel of the Rio del Norte.[14] The craggy cliffs which project from these mountains render the eastern bank of the river altogether impassable. As the direct route over the plain is entirely destitute of water, we took the precaution to fill all our kegs at Fray Cristóbal, and late in the afternoon we finally set out. We generally find a great advantage in travelling through these arid tracts of land in the freshness of the evening, as the mules suffer less from thirst, and move on in better spirits—particularly in the season of warm weather.

Early the next morning we found ourselves at the *Laguna del Muerto*, or 'Dead Man's Lake,'[15] where there was not even a ves-

[13] A camp about 72 miles south of Fray Cristóbal, to the west of San Diego Mountain, where the Río Grande returns from its westward bend and resumes its southward course.

[14] The river is separated from the northern half of the road by the Fray Cristóbal Range and from the southern half by the Caballo Mountains. It is now dammed at two places, forming Elephant Butte and Caballo reservoirs.

[15] About 26 miles south of Fray Cristóbal.

tige of water. This lake is but a sink in the plain of a few rods in diameter, and only filled with water during the rainy season. The *marshes,* which are said by some historians to be in this vicinity, are nowhere to be found: nothing but the firmest and driest table land is to be seen in every direction. To procure water for our thirsty animals, it is often necessary to make a halt here, and drive them to the *Ojo del Muerto* (Dead Man's Spring), five or six miles to the westward, in the very heart of the mountain ridge that lay between us and the river. This region is one of the favorite resorts of the Apaches, where many a poor arriero has met with an untimely end. The route which leads to the spring winds for two or three miles down a narrow cañon or gorge, overhung on either side by abrupt precipices, while the various clefts and crags, which project their gloomy brows over the abyss below, seem to invite the murderous savage to deeds of horror and blood.

There is a tradition among the arrieros from which it would appear that the only road known in ancient time about the region of the *Jornada,* wound its circuitous course on the western side of the river. To save distance, an intrepid traveller undertook to traverse this desolate tract of land in one day, but having perished in the attempt, it has ever after borne the name of *La Jornada del Muerto,* 'the Dead Man's Journey,' or, more strictly, 'the Day's Journey of the Dead Man.'[16] One thing appears very certain, that this dangerous pass has cost the life of many travellers in days of yore; and when we at last reached Robledo,[17] a camp-site upon the river, where we found abundance of wood and water, we felt truly grateful that the arid *Jornada* had not been productive of more serious consequences to our party. We now found ourselves within the department of Chihuahua, as the boundary betwixt it and New Mexico passes not far north of Robledo.

[16] This story is probably apocryphal, for the Oñate caravan took this road. On May 25, 1598, its scouts found a dry creek in the mountains to the west which they called Arroyo de los Muertos. This may have been the origin of the name. For Oñate's "Ytinerario," see Joaquín F. Pacheco, Francisco de Cárdenas and Luís Torres de Mendoza (eds.), *Colección de documentos inéditos relativos al descubrimiento, conquista y colonización de las posesiones españoles en América,* XVI, 249.

[17] About 85 miles south of Fray Cristóbal (68 north of El Paso del Norte), opposite Robledo Mountain on the west bank. The camp was named for the grave of Pedro de Robledo, who was buried by the Oñate party on May 21, 1598. *Ibid.,* XVI, 247.

We were still some sixty miles above Paso del Norte, but the balance of the road now led down the river valley or over the low bordering hills. During our journey between this and El Paso we passed the ruins of several settlements,[18] which had formerly been the seats of opulence and prosperity, but which have since been abandoned in consequence of the marauding incursions of the Apaches.

On the 12th of September we reached the usual ford of the Rio del Norte, six miles above El Paso; but the river being somewhat flushed we found it impossible to cross over with our wagons. The reader will no doubt be surprised to learn that there is not a single ferry on this 'Great River of the North' till we approach the mouth. But how do people cross it? Why, during three-fourths of the year it is everywhere fordable, and when the freshet season comes on, each has to remain on his own side or swim, for canoes even are very rare. But as we could neither swim our wagons and merchandise, nor very comfortably wait for the falling of the waters, our only alternative was to unload the vehicles, and ferry the goods over in a little 'dug-out' about thirty feet long and two feet wide, of which we were fortunate enough to obtain possession.

We succeeded in finding a place shallow enough to haul our empty wagons across: but for this good fortune we should have been under the necessity of taking them to pieces (as I had before done), and of ferrying them on the 'small craft' before mentioned. Half of a wagon may thus be crossed at a time, by carefully balancing it upon the canoe, yet there is of course no little danger of capsizing during the passage.

This river even when fordable often occasions a great deal of trouble, being, like the Arkansas, embarrassed with many quicksand mires. In some places, if a wagon is permitted to stop in the river but for a moment, it sinks to the very body. Instances have occurred when it became necessary, not only to drag out the mules by the ears and to carry out the loading package by package, but to haul out the wagon piece by piece—wheel by wheel.

[18] Probably the *ranchos of* Canutillo, Abalos, Montes, Gallega, and Brazito, which were stops on the mail route between El Paso del Norte and Robledo in the 1830's. Escudero, *Noticias Estadísticas de Chihuahua,* 184.

On the 14th we made our entrance into the town of *El Paso del Norte*,[19] which is the northernmost settlement in the department of Chihuahua. Here our cargo had to be examined by a stern, surly officer, who, it was feared, would lay an embargo on our goods upon the slightest appearance of irregularity in our papers; but notwithstanding our gloomy forebodings, we passed the ordeal without any difficulty.

The valley of El Paso is supposed to contain a population of about four thousand inhabitants, scattered over the western bottom of the Rio del Norte to the length of ten or twelve miles. These settlements are so thickly interspersed with vineyards, orchards, and cornfields, as to present more the appearance of a series of plantations than of a town: in fact, only a small portion at the head of the valley, where the *plaza pública* and parochial church are located, would seem to merit this title. Two or three miles above the *plaza* there is a dam of stone and brush across the river, the purpose of which is to turn the current into a dike or canal, which conveys nearly half the water of the stream, during a low stage, through this well cultivated valley, for the irrigation of the soil. Here we were regaled with the finest fruits of the season: the grapes especially were of the most exquisite flavor. From these the inhabitants manufacture a very pleasant wine, somewhat resembling Malaga. A species of *aguardiente* (brandy) is also distilled from the same fruit, which, although weak, is of very agreeable flavor. These liquors are known among Americans as 'Pass wine' and 'Pass whiskey,' and constitute a profitable article of trade, supplying the markets of Chihuahua and New Mexico.[20]

[19] This place is often known among Americans as 'The Pass.' It has been suggested in another place [Vol. I, chap. 6, n. 18], that it took its name from the *passing* thither of the refugees from the massacre of 1680; yet many persons very rationally derive it from the *passing* of the river *(el paso del Rio del Norte)* between two points or mountains which project against it from each side, just above the town.—GREGG.

[20] There is very little wine or legitimate *aguardiente* manufactured in New Mexico. There was not a distillery, indeed in all the province until established by Americans some fifteen or twenty years ago. Since that period, considerable quantities of whiskey have been made there, particularly in the vicinity of Taos,—distilled mainly from wheat, as this is the cheapest grain the country affords.—GREGG.

The distillery near Taos was established in 1825 by James Baird, Samuel Chambers, Thomas L. ("Peg-Leg") Smith, and one Stevens. K. Gregg (ed.), *Road to Santa Fe*, 267.

As I have said before, the road from Santa Fé to El Paso leads partly along the margin of the Rio del Norte, or across the bordering hills and plains; but the *sierra* which separates the waters of this river and those of the Rio Pecos was always visible on our left. In some places it is cut up into detached ridges, one of which is known as *Sierra Blanca*, in consequence of its summit's being covered with snow till late in the spring, and having all the appearance of a glittering white cloud. There is another still more picturesque ridge further south, called *Los Organos*, presenting an immense cliff of basaltic pillars, which bear some resemblance to the pipes of an *organ*, whence the mountain derived its name. Both these sierras are famous as being the strongholds of the much-dreaded Apaches.

The mountains from El Paso northward are mostly clothed with pine, cedar, and a dwarfish species of oak. The valleys are timbered with cottonwood, and occasionally with *mezquite*, which, however, is rarely found higher up than the lower settlements of New Mexico. In the immediate vicinity of El Paso there is another small growth called *tornillo* (or screw-wood),[21] so denominated from a spiral pericarp, which, though different in shape, resembles that of the mezquite in flavor. The plains and highlands generally are of a prairie character, and do not differ materially from those of all Northern Mexico, which are almost everywhere completely void of timber.

One of the most useful plants to the people of El Paso is the *lechuguilla*,[22] which abounds on the hills and mountain sides of that vicinity, as well as in many other places from thence southward. Its blades, which resemble those of the palmilla, being mashed, scraped and washed, afford very strong fibres like the common Manilla sea-grass, and equally serviceable for the manufacture of ropes, and other purposes.

After leaving El Paso, our road branched off at an angle of about two points to the westward of the river, the city of Chihuahua being situated nearly a hundred miles to the west of it. At the distance of about thirty miles we reached *Los Médanos*, a stupendous ledge of sand-hills, across which the road passes for about six miles.

[21] *Prosopis pubescens.*
[22] *Agave lechuguilla.*

As teams are never able to haul the loaded wagons over this region of loose sand, we engaged an *atajo* of mules at El Paso, upon which to convey our goods across. These Médanos consist of huge hillocks and ridges of pure sand, in many places without a vestige of vegetation. Through the lowest gaps between the hills, the road winds its way.[23]

What renders this portion of the route still more unpleasant and fatiguing, is the great scarcity of water. All that is to be found on the road for the distance of more than sixty miles after leaving El Paso, consists in two fetid springs or pools,[24] whose water is only rendered tolerable by necessity. A little further on, however, we very unexpectedly encountered, this time, quite a superabundance of this necessary element. Just as we passed Lake Patos,[25] we were struck with astonishment at finding the road ahead of us literally overflowed by an immense body of water, with a brisk current, as if some great river had suddenly been conjured into existence by the aid of supernatural arts. A considerable time elapsed before we could unravel the mystery. At last we discovered that a freshet had lately occurred in the streams that fed Lake Patos, and caused it to overflow its banks, which accounted for this unwelcome visitation. We had to flounder through the mud and water for several hours, before we succeeded in getting across.

The following day we reached the *acequia* below Carrizal, a small village with only three or four hundred inhabitants, but somewhat remarkable as being the site of a *presidio* (fort),[26] at which is stationed a company of troops to protect the country against the ravages of the Apaches, who, notwithstanding, continue to lay waste

[23] About 35 miles south of Ciudad Juárez (formerly El Paso del Norte) the modern highway passes over a high sandy plain for 12 miles, but the highest dunes appear at a considerable distance east of the road. In Gregg's time loaded wagons avoided the worst part of the Médanos by continuing down the river from El Paso del Norte for 30 or 40 miles, skirting the dunes on the sheltered side of the Sierra del Presidio, and returning to the direct route near the Lago de Patos.

[24] Ojo de Samalayuca (at 33 miles) and Ojo de Lucero (36 miles beyond).

[25] Lago de Patos is 70 miles south of El Paso del Norte by the direct road and 96 miles by the one avoiding the sand dunes.

[26] San Fernando de las Amarillas del Carrizal (about 18 miles south of Lago de Patos and 8 west of the modern highway) was occupied early in the eighteenth century by *ranchos* and became a garrison town in 1758.

the ranchos in the vicinity, and to depredate at will within the very sight of the fort.

About twelve miles south of Carrizal there is one of the most charming warm springs called Ojo Caliente,[27] where we arrived the next day. It forms a basin some thirty feet long by about half that width, and just deep and warm enough for a most delightful bath at all seasons of the year. Were this spring (whose outlet forms a bold little rivulet) anywhere within the United States, it would doubtless soon be converted into a place of fashionable resort. There appears to be a somewhat curious phenomenon connected with this spring. It proceeds, no doubt, from the little river of Cármen which passes within half a mile, and finally discharges itself into the small lake of Patos before mentioned. During the dry season, this stream disappears in the sand some miles above the spring; and what medium it traverses in its subterranean passage to impart to it so high a temperature, before breaking out in this fountain, would afford to the geologist an interesting subject of inquiry.

After fording the Rio Cármen,[28] which, though usually without a drop of water in its channel, we now found a very turbulent stream, we did not meet with any object particularly worthy of remark, until we reached the *Laguna de Encinillas*.[29] This lake is ten or twelve miles long by two or three in width, and seems to have no outlet even during the greatest freshets, though fed by several small constantly-flowing streams from the surrounding mountains. The water of this lake during the dry season is so strongly impregnated with nauseous and bitter salts, as to render it wholly unpalatable to man and beast. The most predominant of these noxious substances is a species of alkali, known there by the title of *tequesquite*. It is often seen oozing out from the surface of marshy grounds, about the table plains of all Northern Mexico, forming a grayish crust, and is extensively used in the manufacture of soap, and sometimes by the bakers even for raising bread. Here we had another evidence of the alarming effects of the recent flood, the road for several miles along the margin of the lake being completely inundated. It was, however,

[27] About 5 miles west of Ojo Caliente station on the Mexican National Railroad.
[28] About one mile south of Ojo Caliente, by the old road.
[29] Approximately 67 miles south of Ojo Caliente (67 north of Chihuahua) and to the west of the road. The size of the lagoon varies considerably with the seasons.

in the city of Chihuahua itself that the disastrous consequences of the freshet were most severely felt. Some inferior houses of *adobe* were so much soaked by the rains, that they tumbled to the ground, occasioning the loss of several lives.

The valley of Encinillas is very extensive and fertile, and is the locale of one of those princely estates which are so abundant further south, and known by the name of *Haciendas*. It abounds in excellent pasturage, and in cattle of all descriptions. In former times, before the Apaches had so completely devastated the country, the herds which grazed in this beautiful valley presented much the appearance of the buffalo of the plains, being almost as wild and generally of dark color. Many of the proprietors of these princely haciendas pride themselves in maintaining a uniformity in the color of their cattle: thus some are found stocked with black, others red, others white—or whatsoever shade the owner may have taken a fancy to.

As we drew near to Chihuahua, our party had more the appearance of a funeral procession than of a band of adventurers, about to enter into the full fruition of 'dancing hopes,' and the realization of 'golden dreams.' Every one was uneasy as to what might be the treatment of the revenue officers. For my own part, I had not quite forgotten sundry annoyances and trials of temper I had been made to experience in the season of 1837, on a similar occasion. Much to our surprise, however, as well as delight, we were handled with a degree of leniency by the custom-house deities, on our arrival, that was almost incomprehensible. But the charm which operated in our favor, when understood, was very simple. A caravan had left Chihuahua direct for the United States the spring previous, and was daily expected back.[30] The officers of the custom-house were already compromised by certain cogent arguments to receive the proprietors of this caravan with striking marks of favor, and the *Señor Administrador de Rentas*, Zuloaga himself,[31] was expecting an *ancheta* of goods. Therefore, had they treated us with their wonted severity, the contrast would have been altogether too glaring.

We arrived at Chihuahua on the first of October, after a trip of forty days, with wagons much more heavily laden than when we

[30] See below, chap. 9, n. 4.
[31] Luís Zuloaga, later governor pro tem of Chihuahua (1853).

started from the United States. The whole distance from Santa Fé to Chihuahua is about 550 miles,—being reckoned 320 to Paso del Norte, and 230 from thence to Chihuahua.[32] The road from El Paso south is mostly firm and beautiful, with the exception of the sand-hills before spoken of; and is only rendered disagreeable by the scarcity and occasional ill savor of the water. The route winds over an elevated plain among numerous detached ridges of low mountains—spurs, as it were, of the main Cordilleras, which lie at a considerable distance to the westward. Most of these extensive intermediate plains, though in many places of fertile looking soil, must remain wholly unavailable for agricultural purposes, on account of their natural aridity and a total lack of water for irrigation.

[32] By the modern highway it is 235 miles. Gregg describes the city of Chihuahua below, in chap. 6.

CHAPTER V

Trip from Chihuahua to Aguascalientes, in 1835—Southern Trade and
Ferias—Hacienda de la Zarca, and its innumerable Stock—Rio Nazas,
and Lakes without outlet—Perennial Cotton—Exactions for Water and
Pasturage—Village of Churches—City of Durango and its Peculiarities
—Persecution of Scorpions—Negroship in the ascendant—Robbers and
their *modus operandi*—City of Aguascalientes—Bathing Scene—Haste to
return to the North—Mexican Mule-shoeing—Difficulties and Perplexities—A Friend in time of need—Reach Zacatecas—City Accommodations—Hotels unfashionable—*Locale,* Fortifications, etc. of the City of
Zacatecas—Siege by Santa Anna and his easy-won Victory—At Durango
again—Civil Warfare among the 'Sovereigns'—Hair-breadth 'scapes—
Troubles of the Road—Safe Arrival at Chihuahua—Character of the
Southern Country.

T HE PATIENT reader who may have accompanied me thus far,
without murmuring at the dryness of some of the details, will
perhaps pardon me for presenting here a brief account of a trip
which I made to *Aguascalientes,* in the interior of Northern Mexico,[1]
in the year 1835, and which the arrangement I have adopted has
prevented me from introducing before, in its chronological order.

The trade to the South constitutes a very important branch of the
commerce of the country, in which foreigners, as well as natives, are
constantly embarking. It is customary for most of those who maintain
mercantile establishments in Chihuahua, to procure assortments of
Mexican fabrics from the manufactories of Leon, Aguascalientes, and
other places of the same character in the more southern districts of
the republic. At certain seasons of the year, there are held regular

---

[1] Aguascalientes (founded 1575), capital of the state of the same name, is 745
miles south of Chihuahua by the main highway.

ferias, at which the people assemble in great numbers, as well of sellers as of purchasers. There are some eight or ten of these annual fairs held in the republic, each of which usually lasts a week or more. It was about as much, however, from a desire to behold the sunny districts of the South, as for commercial purposes, that I undertook this expedition in 1835; and as my engagements have not permitted me to revisit this section since, the few notes of interest I was then able to collect, seem to come more appropriately in this part of my work than in any other place that I could readily select.

I set out from Chihuahua on the 26th of February, 1835. My party consisted of four men (including myself) and two empty wagons—not a very formidable escort to protect our persons as well as specie and bullion (the only transmissible currency of the country) against the bands of robbers which at all times infest that portion of our route that lay south of Durango. From Chihuahua to that city the road was rendered still more perilous by the constant hostilities of the Indians. On the 7th of March, however, we arrived, without accident, at the town of Cerro Gordo, the northernmost settlement in the department of Durango;[2] and the following day we reached La Zarca, which is the principal village of one of the most extensive haciendas in the North. So immense is the amount of cattle on this estate, that, as it was rumored, the proprietor once offered to sell the whole hacienda, stock, etc., for the consideration alone of fifty cents for each head of cattle found on the estate; but that no person has ever yet been able or willing to muster sufficient capital to take up the offer. It is very likely, however, that if such a proposition was ever made, the proprietor intended to include all his stock of rats and mice, reptiles and insects—in short, every genus of 'small cattle' on his premises. This estate covers a territory of perhaps a hundred miles in length, which comprises several flourishing villages.

In two days more, we reached Rio Nazas, a beautiful little river that empties into Lake Cayman.[3] Rio Nazas has been celebrated for the growth of cotton, which, owing to the mildness of the climate,

[2] Cerro Gordo (now Villa Hidalgo, Durango) was an important garrison town in colonial times, 283 miles southeast of Chihuahua by the old road.

[3] The numerous little lakes throughout the interior of Mexico, without outlets yet into which rivers are continually flowing, present a phenomenon which seems quite singular to the inhabitants of our humid climates. But the wastage in the

is sometimes planted fresh only every three or four years. The light frosts of winter seldom destroy more than the upper portion of the stalks, so that the root is almost perennial. About twenty-five miles further, we stopped at the mining village of La Noria, where we were obliged to purchase water for our mules—a novel expense to the American traveller, but scarcely to be complained of, inasmuch as the water had to be drawn from wells with a great deal of labor. It is not unusual, also, for the proprietors of haciendas to demand remuneration for the pasturage on the open plains, consumed by the animals of travellers—a species of exaction which one never hears of further north.

Our next stopping-place was Cuencamé,[4] which may well be called the Village of Churches: for, although possessing a very small population, there are five or six edifices of this description. As I had business to transact at Durango,[5] which is situated forty or fifty miles westward of the main Southern road. I now pursued a direct route for that city, where I arrived on the 16th of March.

Durango is one of the handsomest cities in the North, with a population of about 20,000. It is situated in a level plain, surrounded in every direction by low mountains. It presents two or three handsome squares, with many fine edifices and some really splendid churches. The town is supplied with water for irrigating the gardens, and for many other ordinary purposes, by several open aqueducts, which lead through the streets, from a large spring, a mile or two distant; but as these are kept filthy by the offal that is thrown into them, the inhabitants who are able to buy it, procure most of their water for drinking and culinary purposes, from the *aguadores*, who pack it, on asses, usually in large jars, from the spring.

This is the first Northern city in which there is to be found any evidence of that variety of tropical fruits, for which Southern Mexico is so justly famed. Although it was rather out of season, yet the

sand, and still greater evaporation in those elevated dry regions, is such that there are no important rises in the lakes except during unusual freshets.—GREGG.
Gregg's Lake Cayman is now called Laguna de Mayrán and Laguna de Parras. The Nazas was crossed about 75 miles beyond Cerro Gordo.

[4] Cuencamé (established as a convent in 1589) was about 31 miles southeast of the Río de las Nazas ford.

[5] Durango (founded 1565) is about 75 miles southwest of Cuencamé.

market actually teemed with all that is most rich and exquisite in this kind of produce. The *maguey*, from which is extracted the popular beverage called *pulque*,[6] is not only cultivated extensively in the fields, but grows wild everywhere upon the plains. This being the height of the pulque season, a hundred shanties might be seen loaded with jugs and goblets filled with this favorite liquor, from its sweetest unfermented state to the grade of 'hard cider;' while the incessant cries of "Pulque! pulque dulce! pulque bueno!" added to the shrill and discordant notes of the fruit venders, created a confusion of sounds amidst which it was impossible to hear oneself talk.

Durango is also celebrated as being the head-quarters, as it were, of the whole scorpion family. During the spring, especially, so much are the houses infested by these poisonous insects, that many people are obliged to have resort to a kind of mosquito-bar, in order to keep them out of their beds at night. As an expedient to deliver the city from this terrible pest, a society has actually been formed, which pays a reward of a *cuartilla* (three cents) for every *alacran* (or scorpion) that is brought to them. Stimulated by the desire of gain, the idle boys of the city are always on the look-out: so that, in the course of a year, immense numbers of this public enemy are captured and slaughtered. The body of this insect is of the bulk and cast of a medium spider, with a jointed tail one to two inches long, at the end of which is a sting whose wounds are so poisonous as often to prove fatal to children, and are very painful to adults.

The most extraordinary peculiarity of these scorpions is, that they are far less dangerous in the North than in the South, which in some manner accounts for the story told Capt. Pike, that even those of Durango lose most of their venom as soon as they are removed a few miles from the city.[7]

---

[6] Also from the *Pulque* is distilled a spiritous liquor called *mezcal*. The *maguey* (*Agave americana*) is besides much used for hedging. It here performs the double purpose of a cheap and substantial fence, and of being equally valuable for *pulque*. When no longer serviceable in these capacities, the pulpy stalk is converted, by roasting, into a pleasant item of food, while the fibrous blades, being suitably dressed, are still more useful. They are manufactured into ropes, bags, etc., which resemble those made of the common sea-grass, though the fibres are finer. There is one species (which does not produce pulque, however), whose fibres, known in that country as *pita*, are nearly as fine as dressed hemp, and are generally used for sewing shoes, saddlery, and similar purposes.—GREGG.

Although we were exceedingly well armed, yet so many fearful stories of robberies said to be committed, almost daily, on the Southern roads, reached my ears, that before leaving Durango, I resolved to add to my 'weapons of defence' one of those peculiarly terrible dogs which are sometimes to be found in this country, and which are very serviceable to travellers situated as I was. Having made my wishes known to a free negro from the United States, named George, he recommended me to a custom-house officer, and a very particular friend of his, as being possessed of the very article I was in search of. I accordingly called at the house of that functionary, in company with my sable informant, and we were ushered into a handsome parlor, where two or three well-dressed señoritas sat discussing some of the fruitful topics of the day. One of them—the officer's wife, as it appeared, and a very comely dame she was—rose immediately, and, with a great deal of ceremonious deference, saluted *Señor Don Jorge,* inviting him at the same time to a seat, while I was left to remain perfectly unnoticed in my standing position. George appeared considerably embarrassed, for he had not quite forgotten the customs and manners of his native country, and was even yet in the habit of treating Americans not only with respect but with humility. He therefore declined the tendered distinction, and remarked that *'el señor'* had only come to purchase their dog. Upon this, the lady pointed to a kennel in a corner, when the very first glimpse of the ferocious animal convinced me that he was precisely the sort of a customer I wanted for a companion. Having therefore paid down six dollars, the stipulated sum of purchase, I bowed myself out of the presence of the ladies, not a little impressed with my own insignificance, in the eyes of these fair *doñas,* contrasted with the grandeur of my sable companion. But the popularity of negroes in Northern Mexico has ceased to be a matter of surprise to the traveller.

With regard to *Don Jorge,* if I was surprised at the marks of attention paid him by a white lady, I had cause to be much more astonished shortly after. As the sooty don was lounging about my wagons, a clever-visaged youth approached and placed in his hands a

---

[7] The scorpion of Durango is identified as *Androctomus biaculeatus* and Gregg's explanation of Pike's comment is endorsed by Elliott Coues, in *Expeditions of Zebulon Montgomery Pike,* II, 763, n.

satin stock, with the compliments of his sister (the officer's wife), hoping that he would accept that trifle, wrought by her own hand, as a token of her particular regard! But, notwithstanding these marks of distinction (to apply no harsher epithet), George was exceedingly anxious to engage in my employ, in whatsoever capacity I might choose to take him; for he had discovered that such honors were far from affording him a livelihood: yet I did not then need his services, and have never heard of him since.

On the 22d we left Durango, and after a few days' march found ourselves once more in the *camino real* that led from Chihuahua to Zacatecas. All the frightful stories I had heard about robbers now began to flash upon my memory, which made me regard every man I encountered on the road with a very suspicious eye. As all travellers go armed, it is impossible to distinguish them from banditti;[8] so that the unsuspecting traveller is very frequently set upon by the very man he had been consorting with in apparent good-fellowship, and either murdered on the spot, or dragged from his horse with the lazo, and plundered of all that is valuable about him.

I have heard it asserted that there is a regular bandit trade organized throughout the country, in which some of the principal officers of state (and particularly of the judicial corps) are not unfrequently engaged. A capital is made up by shares, as for any other enterprise, bandits are fitted out and instructed where to operate, and at stated periods of the year a regular dividend is paid to the stockholders. The impunity which these 'gentlemen of the order' almost everywhere enjoy in the country, is therefore not to be marvelled at. In Durango, during my sojourn there, a well dressed caballero was frequently in the habit of entering our *meson*,[9] whom mine host soon pointed out to me as a notorious brigand. "Beware of him," said the honest publican; "he is prying into your affairs"— and so it turned out; for my muleteer informed me that the fellow had been trying to pump from him all the particulars in regard to

[8] Travellers on these public highways not only go 'armed to the teeth,' but always carry their weapons exposed. Even my wagoners carried their guns and pistols swung upon the pommels of their saddles. At night, as we generally camped out, they were laid under our heads, or close by our sides.—GREGG.

[9] The *mesón*, a roadhouse providing food and shelter for travelers and their animals, was common on the public road from Chihuahua on south but nonexistent to the north.

our condition and destination. Yet this worthy was not only suffered to prowl about unmolested by the authorities, but appeared to be on familiar terms with many of the principal dignitaries of the city. Notwithstanding all our apprehensions, however, we arrived at our place of destination without even the novelty of an incident to swell our budget of gossip.

The city of Aguascalientes is beautifully situated in a level plain, and would appear to contain about twenty thousand inhabitants, who are principally engaged in the manufacture of *rebozos* and other textures mostly of cotton. As soon as I found myself sufficiently at leisure, I visited the famous warm spring (*ojo caliente*) in the suburbs, from which the city derives its euphonious name. I followed up the *acequia* that led from the spring—a ditch four or five feet wide, through which flowed a stream three or four feet in depth. The water was precisely of that agreeable temperature to afford the luxury of a good bath, which I had hoped to enjoy; but every few paces I found men, women, and children, submerged in the acequia; and when I arrived at the basin, it was so choked up with girls and full-grown women, who were paddling about with all the nonchalance of a gang of ducks, that I was forced to relinquish my long-promised treat.

It had been originally my intention to continue on to Leon, another manufacturing town some seventy or eighty miles from Aguascalientes; but, hearing that Santa Anna had just arrived there with a large army, on his way to Zacatecas to quell an insurrection, I felt very little curiosity to extend my rambles further. Having, therefore, made all my purchases in the shortest possible time, in a few days I was again in readiness to start for the North.

That my mules might be in condition for the hard travel before me, it was necessary to have them shod: a precaution, however, which is seldom used in the north of Mexico, either with mules or horses. Owing a little to the peculiar breed, but more still no doubt to the dryness of the climate, Mexican animals have unusually hard hoofs. Many will travel for weeks, and even months, over the firm[10] and

[10] Some of these table-plain highways, though of but a dry sandy and clayey soil, are as firm as a brick pavement. In some places, for miles, I have remarked that the nail-heads of my shod animals would hardly leave any visible impression. —GREGG.

often rocky roads of the interior (the pack-mules carrying their huge loads), without any protection whatever to the feet, save that which nature has provided. But most of mine being a little tender-footed, I engaged Mexican *herreros* to fit them out in their own peculiar style. Like almost everything else of their manufacture, their mule-shoes are of a rather primitive model—broad thin plates, tacked on with large club-headed nails. But the expertness of the shoers compensated in some degree for the defects of the *herraduras.* It made but little odds how wild and vicious the mule—an assistant would draw up his foot in an instant, and soon place him *hors de combat;* and then fixing a nail, the shoer would drive it to the head at a single stroke, standing usually at full arm's length, while the assistant held the foot. Thus in less than half the time I had ever witnessed the execution of a similar job before, they had completely shod more than twenty of the most unruly brutes—without once resorting to the expedient so usual in such cases, of throwing the animals upon the ground.

Just as the process of shoeing my mules had been completed, a person who proved to be a public officer entered the *corral,* and pointing to the mules, very politely informed me that they were wanted by the government to transport troops to Zacatecas. "They will be called for to-morrow afternoon," he continued; "let them not be removed!" I had of course to bow acquiescence to this imperative edict, well knowing that all remonstrance would be vain; yet fully determined to be a considerable distance on the road northward before that 'morrow' should be very far advanced.

But a new difficulty now presented itself. I must procure a *guia* or passport for my cargo of merchandise, with a *responsible endorser,* —an additional imposition I was wholly unprepared for, as I was then ignorant of any law to that effect being in force, and had not a single acquaintance in the city. I was utterly at a loss what to do: under any other circumstances I might have left the amount of the *derecho de consumo* in deposit, as others have been obliged to do on similar occasions; but unfortunately I had laid out the last dollar of my available means.

As I left the custom-house brooding over these perplexities, one of the principal clerks of the establishment slipped a piece of paper into my hand containing the following laconic notice:—"Aguárdeme afuera" (wait for me without);—an injunction I passively obeyed, although I had not the least idea of its purport. The clerk was soon with me, and remarked, "You are a stranger in the city, and ignorant of our severe revenue laws: meet me in an hour from this at my lodgings, and we will devise some remedy for your difficulties." It may be well supposed that I did not fail to be punctual. I met the obliging officer in his room with a handful of blank custom-house *pases*. It should be understood that a *pase* only differs from a *guia* in requiring no endorser, but the former can only be extended for amounts of goods not exceeding fifty dollars. Taking my bill, he very soon filled me up a *pase* for every package, directing each to a different point in the North. "Now," observed my amiable friend, "if you are disposed to do a little smuggling, these will secure your safety, if you avoid the principal cities, till you reach the borders of Chihuahua: if not, you may have a friend on the way who will endorse your *guia*." I preferred the latter alternative. I had formed an acquaintance with a worthy German merchant in Durango, who, I felt convinced, would generously lend his signature to the required document.

As the revenue officers of Northern Mexico are not celebrated for liberality and disinterestedness, I took it for granted that my friend of the custom-house was actuated by selfish motives, and therefore proffered him a remuneration for the trouble he had taken on my account; but to my surprise, he positively refused accepting anything, observing that he held it the duty of every honest man to assist his fellow creatures in case of difficulty. It is truly a pleasant task to bear record of such instances of disinterestedness, in the midst of so many contaminating influences.

While speaking of *guias*, I may as well remark that they are also frequently required for specie and always for bullion. This is often very annoying to the traveller, not only because it is sometimes inconvenient to find an endorser, but because the robbers are thus enabled to obtain precise and timely information of the funds and route of every traveller; for they generally have their agents in all the principal cities, who are apt to collude with some of the custom-house clerks, and thus procure regular reports of the departures, with the amounts of valuables conveyed.

I was not long in taking leave of Aguascalientes, and heard nothing more of the impressment of my mules. It was not my good fortune, however, to remain for any length of time out of trouble. Being anxious to take the city of Zacatecas in my route without jeoparding my goods, I took passage by the *diligencia*, while my wagons continued on in the *camino real* or main road. On my arrival at Zacatecas, I very soon discovered that by leaving 'my bed and board' behind with the wagons, I had doomed myself to no small inconvenience and privation. It was with the greatest difficulty I could obtain a place to lie upon, and clean victuals with which to allay my hunger. I could get a room, it is true, even for a *real* per day, in one of those great barn-like *mesones* which are to be met with in all these cities, but not one of them was at all furnished. There is sometimes, in a corner, a raised platform of mud, much resembling a common blacksmith's hearth, which is to supply the place of a bedstead, upon which the traveller may spread his blankets, if he happens to have any. On this occasion I succeeded in borrowing one or two of the stage-driver who was a Yankee, and so made out 'pretty comfortably' in the sleeping way. These *mesones* are equally ill-prepared to furnish food for the traveller, unless he is willing to put up with a dish of *frijoles* and *chile guisado* with *tortillas*, all served up in the most filthy manner. I therefore sought out a public *fonda* kept by an Italian, where I procured an excellent supper. Fondas, however, are mere *restaurants*, and consequently without accommodations for lodging.

Strange as the fact may appear, one may travel fifteen hundred miles, and perhaps more, on the main public highway through Northern Mexico, without finding a single tavern with general accommodations. This, however, may be accounted for, by taking into consideration the peculiar mode of travelling of the country, which renders resorts of this kind almost unnecessary. *Arrieros* with their *atajos* of pack-mules always camp out, being provided with their cooks and stock of provisions, which they carry with them. Ordinary travellers generally unite in little caravans, for security against robbers and marauders; and no caballero ever stirs abroad without a train of servants, and a pack-mule to carry his *cantinas* (a pair of large wallets or leathern boxes), filled with provisions, on the top of which is lashed a huge machine containing a mattress and all the other 'fixings' for bed furniture. Thus equipped, the caballero snaps his fingers at all the *hotels garnis* of the universe, and is perfectly independent in every movement.

The city of Zacatecas,[11] as my readers are doubtless aware, is celebrated for its mining interests. Like all other Mexican towns of the same class, it originated in small, insignificant settlements on the hillsides, in the immediate vicinity of the mines, until it gradually grew up to be a large and wealthy city, with a population of some 30,000 inhabitants. Its locale is a deep ravine formed among rugged mountain ridges; and as the houses are mostly built in rows, overtopping one another, along the hillsides, some portions of the city present all the appearance of a vast amphitheatre. Many of the streets are handsomely paved, and two of the squares are finely ornamented with curiously carved *jets-d'eau*, which are supplied with water raised by mule power, from wells among the adjacent hills. From these the city is chiefly furnished with water.

I have already mentioned, that General Santa Anna was at this time marching against Zacatecas with a large force. It may be remembered that after the General's accession to the supreme authority of Mexico (upon the establishment of *Centralismo*), he deemed it expedient to issue a decree abolishing the state militia, known as *Civicos*, as being dangerous to the liberties of——the *dictador*. Zacatecas, so far from obeying this despotic mandate, publicly called on the Cívicos to defend their rights, and Santa Anna was now descending upon them with an army double that which the city could raise, to enforce their obedience. The *Zacatecanos*, however, were not idle. The militia was pouring in from the surrounding villages, and a degree of enthusiasm prevailed throughout the city, which seemed to be the presage of successful defence. In fact, the city itself, besides being from its location almost impregnable, was completely protected by artificial fortifications. The only accessible point was

[11] Zacatecas (established in 1546 as a mining camp) was 177 miles southeast of Durango by the stage road taken by Gregg.

by the main road, which led from the south immediately up the narrow valley of the ravine. Across this a strong wall had been erected some years before, and the road passed through a large gate, commanded by a bastion upon the hillside above, whence a hundred men well supplied with arms and ammunition, might easily cut off thousands upon thousands, as fast as they advanced. The city was therefore deemed impregnable, and being supplied with provisions for a lengthy siege, the patriots were in high spirits. A foreign engineer or two had been engaged to superintend the fortifications.

Santa Anna reached Zacatecas a few days after my departure. As he had no idea of testing the doubtful mettle of his army, by an attempt to storm the place, which presented so formidable an appearance, he very quietly squatted himself down at the village of Guadalupe, three miles below. From this point he commenced his operations by throwing 'missiles' into the city—not of lead, or cast-iron, or any such cruel agents of warfare, but *bombs of paper,* which fell among the besieged, and burst with gentle overtures to their commanding officers. This novel 'artillery' of the dictator produced a perfectly electric effect; for the valor of the commandant of the Cívicos rose to such a pitch, that he at once marched his forces out of the fortifications, to attack the besiegers in the open field—face to face, as true bravery required. But on the very first onset, this valiant officer, by some mysterious agency which could not be accounted for, was suddenly seized with a strange panic, and, with all his forces, made a precipitate retreat, fleeing helter-skelter, as if all the engines of destruction that were ever invented, had been brought to bear upon them; when the victorious army of Santa Anna marched into the city without further opposition.

This affair is a pretty just sample of most of the successful battles of this 'great general.' The treacherous collusion of the principal Zacatecas officers was so apparent, that they deemed it prudent to fly the city for safety, lest the wrath of their incensed fellow-citizens should explode upon them. Meanwhile the soldiery amused themselves by sacking the city, and by perpetrating every species of outrage that their mercenary and licentious appetites could devise. Their savage propensities were particularly exercised against the few foreigners that were found in the place.

Meanwhile I was journeying very leisurely towards Durango, where I arrived on the 21st of April. As the main wagon road to the north does not pass through that city, it was most convenient and still more prudent for me to leave my wagons at a distance: their entrance would have occasioned the confiscation of my goods, for the want of the 'necessary documents,' as already alluded to. But I now procured a *guia* without further difficulty; which was indeed a principal object of my present visit to that city.

Before leaving Durango I witnessed one of those civil broils which are so common in Mexico. I was not even aware that any difficulty had been brewing, till I was waked on the morning of the 25th by a report of fire-arms. Stepping out to ascertain what was the matter, I perceived the *azotea* of the parochial church occupied by armed men, who seemed to be employed in amusing themselves by discharging their guns at random upon the people in the streets. These *bravos*, as I was afterwards informed, belonged to the bishop's party, or that of the *Escoceses*, which was openly at war with the liberalists, anti-hierarchists, or *Yorkinos*,[12] and were resorting to this summary mode of proceeding, in order to bring about a change of affairs; for at this time the liberal party had the ascendency in the civil government of Durango.

Being somewhat curious to have a nearer view of what was going on, I walked down past the church, towards a crowd which was assembled in a *plaza* beyond. This movement on my part was rather inconsiderate: for foreigners were in extremely bad odor with the belligerents; nor had I mingled with the multitude many minutes, before a sober-looking citizen plucked me by the sleeve, and advised me, if I valued my two ears, and did not wish to have my career of usefulness cut short prematurely, to stay within doors. Of course I needed no further persuasion, and returned at once to my lodgings, where I made immediate preparations for a speedy departure. As I was proceeding through the streets soon afterwards, with a cargo of goods, I received, just after leaving the custom-house, a very warm salutation from the belligerents, which made the dust start

[12] The *Escoceses* followed the Scottish Rite masonic lodge which in Mexico was encouraged by Henry G. Ward, the first British chargé d'affaires; the *Yorkinos*, supporters of the York Rite lodge, sponsored by Joel R. Poinsett, the first American envoy.

from almost under my very feet. The *cargadores* who were carrying my packages were no doubt as much frightened as myself. They supposed the reason of their shooting at us to be because they imagined we were carrying off the *parque* (ammunition) of the government, which was deposited in the building we had just left.

We were soon under way, and very little regret did I feel when I fairly lost sight of the city of scorpions. But I was not yet wholly beyond the pale of difficulties. Owing to the fame of the Indian hostilities in the North, it was almost impossible to procure the services of Mexican muleteers for the expedition. One I engaged, took the first convenient opportunity to escape at night, carrying away a gun with which I had armed him; yet I felt grateful that he did not also take a mule, as he had the whole *caballada* under his exclusive charge: and soon after, a Mexican wagoner was frightened back by the reports of savages.

After a succession of such difficulties, and still greater risks from the Indians that infested the route, I was of course delighted when I reached Chihuahua, on the 14th of May, in perfect safety.[13]

[13] The distance from Chihuahua to Durango is about five hundred miles, and from thence to Aguascalientes it is nearly three hundred—upon the route we travelled, which was very circuitous. All the intermediate country resembles in its physical features, that lying immediately north of Chihuahua, which has already been described.—GREGG.

CHAPTER VI

Visit to the Mining Town of Jesus-Maria—Critical Roads—Losing Speculations—Mine of Santa Juliana—Curious mining Operations—Different Modes of working the Ore—The Crushing-mill, etc.—*Barras de Plata*—Value of Bullion—The Silver Trade—Return to Chihuahua—Resumption of the regular Narrative—Curious Wholesales—Money Table—Redundancy of Copper Coin—City of Chihuahua and its Peculiarities—Ecclesiastical Architecture—Hidalgo and his Monument—Public Works, and their present Declension—*Fête* in honor of Iturbide—Illiberality towards Americans—Shopping Mania—Anti-Masonic *Auto de Fe*.

BEFORE RESUMING my regular narrative, I trust the reader will pardon me for introducing here a brief account of an excursion which I made in the fall of the year 1835, to the mining town of Jesus-Maria, one of the most important mineral districts in the department of Chihuahua,[1] situated about a hundred and fifty miles west of the city, in the very heart of the great Cordilleras.

I had long been desirous of visiting some of the mining establishments of Mexico, and seeing a favorable opportunity of embarking in a profitable enterprise, I set out from Chihuahua on the 15th of October. My party consisted of but one American comrade, with a Mexican muleteer—and three or four mules freighted with specie to be employed in the *silver trade:* a rather scanty convoy for a route subject to the inroads both of savages and robbers. For transportation, we generally pack our specie in sacks made of raw beefhide, which shrinks upon drying, and thus presses the contents so closely

[1] Jesús María (now Mineral de Ocampo) was established in 1821, on the headwaters of the Río Mayo, in southwestern Chihuahua.

as to prevent friction. A pair of these packages, usually containing between one and two thousand dollars each, constitutes an ordinary mule-load on the mountain routes.

The road in this direction leads through the roughest mountain passes; and, in some places, it winds so close along the borders of precipices, that by a single misstep an animal might be precipitated several hundred feet. Mules, however, are very sure-footed; and will often clamber along the most craggy cliffs with nearly as much security as the goat. I was shown the projecting edge of a rock over which the road had formerly passed. This shelf was perhaps thirty feet in length by only two or three in width. The road which leads into the town of Jesus-Maria from the west side of the mountain is also extremely perilous and steep, and seems almost to overhang the houses below. Heavily laden mules have sometimes slipped off the track, and tumbled headlong into the town. This place is even more pent up between ridges than Zacatecas: the valley is narrower and the mountains much higher; while, as is the case with that remarkable city, the houses are sometimes built in successive tiers, one above another; the *azoteas* of the lower ones forming the yard of those above.

The first mine I visited consisted of an immense horizontal shaft cut several hundred feet into a hill-side, a short distance below the town of Jesus-Maria, upon which the proprietors had already sunk, in the brief space of one year, the enormous sum of one hundred and twenty thousand dollars! Such is often the fate of the speculative miner, whose vocation is closely allied to gaming, and equally precarious.

The most important mine of Jesus-Maria at this time was one called Santa Juliana, which had been the means of alternately making and sinking several splendid fortunes. This mine had then reached a depth of between eight and nine hundred feet, and the operations were still tending downwards. The materials were drawn up by mule power applied to a windlass: but as the rope attached to it only extended half way down, another windlass had been erected at the distance of about four hundred feet from the mouth of the cavern, which was also worked by mules, and drew the ores, etc., from the bottom. On one occasion, as I was standing near the aper-

ture of this great pit watching the ascent of the windlass-rope, expecting every moment the appearance of the large leathern bucket which they employ for drawing up the minerals as well as the rubbish and water[2] from the bottom, what should greet my vision but a mule, puffing and writhing, firmly bound to a huge board constructed for the purpose, and looking about as demure upon the whole as a sheep under shears. On being untied, the emancipated brute suddenly sprang to his feet, and looked around him at the bright scenes of the upper world with as much astonishment as Rip Van Winkle may be supposed to have felt after waking up from his twenty years' sleep.

The ore which is obtained from these mines, if sufficiently rich to justify the operation, is transferred to the smelting furnaces, where the pure metal is melted down and extracted from the virgin fossil. If, on the contrary, the ore is deemed of inferior quality, it is then submitted to the process of amalgamation.

The *moliendas,* or crushing-mills (*arrastres,* as called at some mines), employed for the purpose of grinding the ores, are somewhat singular machines. A circular (or rather annular) cistern of

2 Water has sometimes accumulated so rapidly in this mine as to stop operations for weeks altogether.—GREGG.

some twenty or thirty feet in diameter is dug in the earth, and the sides as well as the bottom are lined with hewn stone of the hardest quality. Transversely through an upright post which turns upon its axis in the centre of the plan, passes a shaft of wood, at each end of which are attached by cords one or two grinding-stones with smooth flat surfaces, which are dragged (by mules fastened to the extremities of the shaft) slowly around upon the bottom of the cistern, into which the ore is thrown after being pounded into small pieces. It is here ground, with the addition of water, into an impalpable mortar, by the constant friction of the dragging stones against the sides and bottom of the cistern. A suitable quantity of quicksilver is perfectly mixed with the mortar; to which are added different mineral salts,[3] and other chemical substances, to facilitate the amalgamation. The compound is then piled up in small heaps, and not disturbed again until this process is supposed to be completed, when it is transferred to the washing-machine. Those I have observed are very simple, consisting of a kind of stone tub, into which a stream of water is made to flow constantly, so as to carry off all the lighter matter, which is kept stirred up by an upright studded with pegs, that revolves in the centre, while the amalgamated metals sink to the bottom. Most of the quicksilver is then pressed out, and the silver submitted to a burning process, by which the remaining portion of mercury is expelled.[4]

The silver which is taken from the furnace, generally contains an intermixture of gold, averaging from ten to thirty per cent.; but what is extracted by amalgamation is mostly separated in the washing. While in a liquid state, the gold, from its greater specific gravity, mostly settles to the bottom; yet it usually retains a considerable alloy of silver. The compound is distinguished by the name of *oroche*. The main portion of the silver generally retains too little gold to make it worth separating.

Every species of silver is moulded into *barras* or ingots, weighing from fifty to eighty pounds each, and usually worth between one and two thousand dollars. These are assayed by an authorized agent

[3] "To which are added some muriate sulphates," in Gregg's second edition.

[4] Gregg is describing the famous "*patio* process," introduced at Pachuca in 1556, which tremendously increased the yield of gold and silver mines in the New World.

of the government, and stamped with their weight and character, which enables the holder to calculate their value by a very simple rule. When the bullion is thus stamped, it constitutes a species of currency, which is much safer for remittances than coin. In case of robbery, the *barras* are easily identified, provided the robbers have not had time to mould them into some other form. For this reason, people of wealth frequently lay up their funds in ingots; and the cellars of some of the *ricos* of the South, are often found teeming with large quantities of them, presenting the appearance of a winter's supply of firewood.

As the charge for parting the gold and silver at the Mexican mints, is generally from one to two dollars, and coinage about fifty cents, per pound, this assayed bullion yields a profit upon its current value of nearly ten per cent. at the United States Mint; but, if un-assayed, it generally produces an advance of about double that amount upon the usual cost at the mines. The exportation of bullion, however, is prohibited, except by special license from the general government.[5] Still a large quantity is exported in this way, and considerable amounts smuggled out through some of the ports.

A constant and often profitable business in the 'silver trade' is carried on at these mines. As the miners rarely fail being in need of ready money, they are generally obliged to sell their bullion for coin, and that often at a great sacrifice, so as to procure available means to prosecute their mining operations. To profit by this trade, as is already mentioned, was a principal object of my present visit. Having concluded my business transactions, and partially gratified my curiosity, I returned to Chihuahua, where I arrived, November 24, 1835, without being molested either by robbers or Indians, though the route is sometimes infested by both of these classes of independent gentry.

But, as it is now high time I should put an end to this digression, I will once more resume my narrative, where it was interrupted at my arrival in Chihuahua, on the first of October, 1839.

It is usual for each trader, upon his arrival in that city, to engage a store-room, and to open and exhibit his goods, as well for the

[5] Executive order of September 9, 1835. Dublán and Lozano (compilers), *Legislación Mexicana*, III, 71–72.

purpose of disposing of them at wholesale as retail. His most profitable custom is that of the petty country merchants from the surrounding villages. Some traders, it is true, continue in the retail business for a season or more, yet the greater portion are transient dealers, selling off at wholesale as soon as a fair bargain is offered.

The usual mode of selling by the lot in Chihuahua is somewhat singular. All such cottons as calicoes and other prints, bleached, brown and blue domestics both plain and twilled, stripes, checks, etc., are rated at two or three *reales*[6] per *vara*, without the least reference to quality or cost, and the 'general assortment' at 60 to 100 per cent. upon the bills of cost, according to the demand. The *varage* is usually estimated by adding eight per cent. to the yardage, but the *vara* being thirty-three inches (nearly), the actual difference is more than nine. In these sales, cloths—indeed all measurable goods, except ribands and the like, sometimes enter at the *varage* rate. I have heard of some still more curious contracts in these measurement sales, particularly in Santa Fé, during the early periods of the American trade. Everything was sometimes rated by the vara—not only all textures, but even hats, cutlery, trinkets, and so on! In such cases, very singular disputes would frequently arise as to the mode of measuring some particular articles: for instance, whether pieces of riband should be measured in bulk, or unrolled, and yard by yard; looking-glasses, cross or lengthwise; pocket-knives, shut or open; writing-paper, in the ream, in the quire, or by the single sheet; and then, whether the longer or shorter way of the paper; and so of many others.

Before the end of October, 1839, I had an opportunity of selling out my stock of goods to a couple of English merchants, which relieved me from the delays, to say nothing of the inconveniences

---

[6] The Mexican money table is as follows: 12 *granos* make 1 *real*; 8 *reales*, 1 *peso*, or dollar. These are the divisious used in computation, but instead of *granos*, the copper coins of Chihuahua and many other places, are the *claco* or *jola* (⅛ real) and the *cuartilla* (¼ real). The silver coins are the *medio* (6¼ cents), the *real* (12½ cents), the *peseta* (2 reales), the *toston* or half dollar, and the *peso* or dollar. The gold coins are the *doblon* or *onza* (doubloon), with the same subdivisions as the silver dollar, which are also of the same weight. The par value of the doubloon is sixteen dollars; but, as there is no kind of paper currency, gold, as the most convenient remittance, usually commands a high premium—sometimes so high, indeed, that the doubloon is valued in the North at from eighteen to twenty dollars.—GREGG.

attending a retail trade: such, for, instance, as the accumulation of copper coin, which forms almost the exclusive currency in petty dealings. Some thousands of dollars' worth are frequently accumulated upon the hands of the merchant in this way, and as the copper of one department is worthless in another, except for its intrinsic value, which is seldom more than ten per cent. of the nominal value, the holders are subjected to a great deal of trouble and annoyance.

With regard to the city, there is but little to be said that is either very new or unusually interesting. When compared with Santa Fé and all the towns of the North, Chihuahua might indeed be pronounced a magnificent place; but, compared with the nobler cities of *tierra afuera*, it sinks into insignificance. According to Capt. Pike, the city of Chihuahua was founded in 1691.[7] The ground-plan is much more regular than that of Santa Fé, while a much greater degree of elegance and classic taste has been exhibited in the style of the architecture of many buildings; for though the bodies be of *adobe*, all the best houses are cornered with hewn stone, and the doors and windows are framed in the same. The streets, however, remain nearly in the same state as Nature formed them, with the exception of a few roughly-paved side-walks. Although situated about a hundred miles east of the main chain of the Mexican Cordilleras, Chihuahua is surrounded on every side by detached ridges of mountains, but none of them of any great magnitude. The elevation of the city above the ocean is between four and five thousand feet; its latitude is 28° 36';[8] and its entire population numbers about ten thousand souls.

The most splendid edifice in Chihuahua is the principal church, which is said to equal in architectural grandeur anything of the sort in the republic. The steeples, of which there is one at each front corner, rise over a hundred feet above the azotea. They are composed of very fancifully-carved columns; and in appropriate niches of the frontispiece, which is also an elaborate piece of sculpture, are to be seen a number of statues, as large as life, the whole forming a complete representation of Christ and the twelve Apostles. This

[7] Chihuahua was not founded until 1705, as a mining camp. It became a town in 1718 and a city in 1823. Nombre de Dios, a nearby mission, dates from 1697.

[8] The elevation is now given as 4,690 ft., the latitude as 28°30'12".

church was built about a century ago, by contributions levied upon the mines (particularly those of Santa Eulalia, fifteen or twenty miles from the city), which paid over a per centage on all the metal extracted therefrom; a *medio*, I believe, being levied upon each *marco* of eight ounces. In this way, about a million of dollars was raised and expended in some thirty years, the time employed in the construction of the building.[9] It is a curious fact, however, that, notwithstanding the enormous sums of money expended in outward embellishments, there is not a church from thence southward, perhaps, where the interior arrangements bear such striking marks of poverty and neglect. If, however, we are not dazzled by the sight of those costly decorations for which the churches of Southern Mexico are so much celebrated, we have the satisfaction of knowing that the turrets are well provided with bells, a fact of which every person who visits Chihuahua very soon obtains auricular demonstration. One, in particular, is so large and sonorous that it has frequently been heard, so I am informed, at the distance of twenty-five miles.

A little below the *Plaza Mayor* stands the ruins (as they may be called) of San Francisco—the mere skeleton of another great church of hewn-stone, which was commenced by the Jesuits previous to their expulsion in 1767, but never finished. By the outlines still traceable amid the desolation which reigns around, it would appear that the plan of this edifice was conceived in a spirit of still greater magnificence than the Parroquia which I have been describing. The abounding architectural treasures that are mouldering and ready to tumble to the ground, bear sufficient evidence that the mind which had directed its progress was at once bold, vigorous and comprehensive.

This dilapidated building has since been converted into a sort of state prison, particularly for the incarceration of distinguished prisoners. It was here that the principals of the famous Texan Santa Fé Expedition were confined, when they passed through the place, on their way to the city of Mexico. This edifice has also acquired considerable celebrity as having received within its gloomy embraces several of the most distinguished patriots, who were taken prisoners

[9] The tax was a *real* on each ingot of gold or silver and the fund finally amounted to $1,500,000, a surplus of $300,000 remaining after completion of the building, according to Pike. Coues (ed.), *Expeditions of Zebulon Montgomery Pike*, II, 766.

during the first infant struggles for Mexican independence. Among these was the illustrious ecclesiastic, Don Miguel Hidalgo y Costilla, who made the first declaration at the village of Dolores, September 16, 1810. He was taken prisoner in March, 1811, some time after his total defeat at Guadalaxara; and being brought to Chihuahua, he was shot on the 30th of July following, in a little square back of the prison, where a plain white monument of hewn stone has been erected to his memory. It consists of an octagon base of about twenty-five feet in diameter, upon which rises a square, unornamented pyramid to the height of about thirty feet. The monument indeed is not an unapt emblem of the purity and simplicity of the curate's character.

Among the few remarkable objects which attract the attention of the traveller is a row of columns supporting a large number of stupendous arches which may be seen from the heights, long before approaching the city from the north. This is an aqueduct of considerable magnitude which conveys water from the little river of Chihuahua, to an eminence above the town, whence it is passed through a succession of pipes to the main public square, where it empties itself into a large stone cistern; and by this method the city is supplied with water. This and other public works to be met with in Chihuahua, and in the southern cities, are glorious remnants of the prosperous times of the Spanish empire. No improvements on so exalted a scale have ever been made under the republican government. In fact, everything in this benighted country now seems to be on the decline, and the plain honest citizen of the old school is not unfrequently heard giving vent to his feelings by ejaculation "Ojalá por los dias felices del Rey!"—Oh, for the happy days of the King! In short, there can be no doubt, that the common people enjoyed more ease—more protection against the savages—more security in their rights and property—more liberty, in truth, under the Spanish dynasty than at present.

No better evidence can be found of the extensive operations which have been carried on in this the greatest mining district of Northern Mexico, than in the little mountains of *scoria* which are found in the suburbs of the city. A great number of poor laborers make a regular business of hammering to pieces these metallic excrescences, from which they collect silver enough to buy their daily bread. An opinion has often been expressed by persons well acquainted with the subject, that a fair business might be done by working this same scoria over again. There are still in operation several furnaces in the city, where silver ores extracted from the mines of the surrounding mountains are smelted. There is also a rough mint in Chihuahua (as there is indeed in all the mining departments), yet most of its silver and all of its gold have been coined in the cities further south.[10]

When I arrived at Chihuahua, in 1839, a great fête had just come off for the double purpose of celebrating the anniversary of the Emperor Iturbide's birth day (Sept. 27, 1783), and that of his triumphal entrance into the city of Mexico in 1821. It will be remembered, that, after Mexico had been struggling for independence several years, General Iturbide, who had remained a faithful officer of the crown, and an active agent in persecuting the champions of Mexican liberty, finding himself, about the close of 1820, at the head of a large division of the royal army sent against the patriot Guerrero,[11] suddenly turned over his whole force to the support of the republican cause, and finally succeeded in destroying the last vestige of Spanish authority in Mexico. How he was afterwards crowned emperor, and subsequently dethroned, outlawed by a public decree and eventually executed, is all matter of history.[12] But it is not generally known, I believe, that this unfortunate soldier has since received the honors of the Father of the Republic, a dignity to which he was probably as much entitled as any one else—absurd though the adoption of such a hero as the 'champion of liberty,' may appear to 'republicans of the Jefferson school.' A *grande fête d'hilarité* takes place annually, in honor of his political canonization, which 'comes off' at the date already mentioned. To this great ball, however, no Americans were invited, with the exception of a Mexicanized denizen or

[10] No gold had been minted for lack of machinery, but between 1832 and 1840 $1,700,915 worth of silver and $50,428 worth of copper were coined at Chihuahua. *Memoria de la Hacienda Nacional* (1846), Doc. 4.

[11] Vicente Guerrero (1782–1831), the most active leader of guerrilla resistance to the royalists after 1815. His collaboration with Iturbide in 1821 established Mexico's independence, and he became president in 1829.

[12] See above, Vol. I, chap. 1, n. 8.

two, whose invitation ticket informed the *honored party* that the price of admission to this famous feast,—a ball given by the governor and other magnates of the land, in honor of the hero of independence,—was twenty-five dollars.

Balls or reunions of this kind, however, seem not as frequent in Chihuahua as in New Mexico: and to those we hear of, claiming the title of 'fashionable,' Americans are very rarely invited. There is, in fact, but little social intercourse between foreigners and the natives, except in a business way, or with a certain class of the former, at the gambling-table. This want of hospitable feelings is one of the worst traits in the character of the Chihuahueños, and when placed in contrast with the kind and courteous treatment those who visit the United States invariably experience from the lawgivers of fashion among us, their illiberality will appear a hundred fold more ungracious. These exclusive laws are the more severely felt in Chihuahua, because in that city there are no *cafés*, nor reading rooms, nor in short any favorite public resorts, except of a gambling character, at which gentlemen can meet to lounge or amuse themselves.

Besides the cock-pit, the gaming-table, and the *Alameda,* which is the popular promenade for the wealthy and the indolent, one of the most favorite pastimes of the females generally is shopping; and the most fashionable time for this is by candle-light, after they have partaken of their chocolate and their *cigarritos.* The streets and shops are literally filled from dusk till nine or ten o'clock; and many a time have I seen the counter of a store actually lined till a late hour, with the fairest and most fashionable señoritas of the city. On such occasions it is not a little painful as well as troublesome to be compelled to keep a strict eye to the rights of property, not that the dealers are all dishonest, but because there never fail to be some present who are painfully afflicted with the self-appropriating mania, even among the fairest-looking señoritas. This, with other purposes no less culpable, has no doubt tended to establish the custom of nightshopping.

It may already be generally known perhaps, that the predominant party, in Mexico, (and particularly in the North), is decidedly anti-masonic. During my stay in Chihuahua I had an opportunity to test their antipathy for that mysterious brotherhood. This was evinced in the seizure of a dozen or two cotton handerchiefs, which, unknown to myself, happened to bear the stamp of the 'masonic carpet.' These obnoxious articles having attracted the attention of some lynx-eyed friar, one day, much to my consternation, my store was suddenly invaded by the alcalde and some ecclesiastics. The handkerchiefs were seized without ceremony, and by an *auto de fe*, condemned to be publicly burned.

CHAPTER VII

Departure for Santa Fé—Straitened for Food—Summary Effort to procure Beef—Seizure of one of our Party—Altercation with a *Rico*—His
pusillanimous Procedure—Great Preparations in Chihuahua for our Arrest—Arrival of Mexican Troops—A polite Officer—Myself with three
of my Men summoned back to Chihuahua—Amiable Conduct of Señor
Artalejo—*Junta Departmental* and Discussion of my Affair—Writ of
Habeas Corpus not in vogue—The Matter adjusted and Passport granted
—The *Morale*—Impunity of savage Depredators—Final Start—Company of *Paseños* with their Fruits and Liquors—Arrival at Santa Fé.

HAVING CLOSED all my affairs in Chihuahua and completed my
preparations for departing, I took my leave of that city for the
North, on the 31st of October, 1839. I was accompanied by a caravan
consisting of twenty-two wagons (all of which save one belonged
to me), and forty odd men, armed to the teeth, and prepared for any
emergency we might be destined to encounter: a precaution altogether necessary, in view of the hordes of hostile savages which at
all times infested the route before us.

We also set out provided with an ample stock of bread and other
necessaries; for, from the suburbs of Chihuahua to the village of
Carrizal, a distance of nearly a hundred and fifty miles, there are
no settlements on the route, from whence to procure supplies. To
furnish the party with meat, I engaged twenty sheep, to be delivered
a few miles on the way, which were to be driven along for our daily
consumption. But the contractor having failed, we found ourselves
entering the wilderness without a morsel of meat. The second day
our men began to murmur—it was surely 'dry living' upon mere
bread and coffee: in fact, by the time we entered the 'territory' of

the Hacienda de Encinillas,[1] spoken of in another chapter, they were clearly suffering from hunger. I was therefore under the necessity of sending three Mexican muleteers of our party to *lazo* a beef from a herd which was grazing at some distance from where we had pitched our camp; being one of those buffalo-like droves which run so nearly wild upon this extensive domain. It had been customary, from time immemorial, for travellers when they happened to be distressed for meat, to supply their wants out of the wild cattle which nominally belonged to this hacienda, reserving to themselves the privilege of paying a reasonable price afterwards to the proprietor for the damage committed. I must say, however, that, although I had travelled over the same road nine times, I had never before resorted to this summary mode of procuring food; nor should I, on the present occasion, have deviated from my regular practice, though thus partially authorized by a custom of the country, but for the strait in which we found ourselves, and the fact that I was confident I should meet either with a *mayordomo* or some of the *vaqueros*, to whom I could pay the value of the beef, before passing beyond the purlieus of the hacienda, upon the lands of which we had yet to travel for sixty or eighty miles.

The muleteers had just commenced giving chase to the cattle, when we perceived several horsemen emerge from behind a contiguous eminence, and pursue them at full speed. Believing the assailants to be Indians, and seeing them shoot at one of the men, chase another, and seize the third, bearing him off prisoner, several of us prepared to hasten to the rescue, when the other two men came running in and informed us that the aggressors were Mexican vaqueros. We followed them, notwithstanding, to the village of Torreon, five or six miles to the westward,[2] where we found a crowd of people already collected around our poor friend, who was trembling from head to foot, as though he had really fallen into the hands of savages. I immediately inquired for the mayordomo, when I was

[1] The Hacienda de Encinilla (established in the late 1600's by Benito Pérez) was one of the largest private estates in Mexico during the nineteenth century. The walled town itself was to the west of the road, on the southwest edge of the Laguna de Encinillas.

[2] Torreón, on the right bank of the Río Sacramento, was far to the south of the village of Encinillas.

informed that the proprietor himself, Don Angel Trias,[3] was present. Accordingly I addressed myself to *su señoria,* setting forth the innocence of my servant, and declaring myself solely responsible for whatever crime had been committed. Trias, however, was immovable in his determination to send the boy back to Chihuahua to be tried for robbery, and all further expostulation only drew down the grossest and coarsest insults upon myself, as well as my country, of which he professed no inconsiderable knowledge.[4]

The altercation was at first conducted solely in Spanish; but the princely señor growing weary of hearing so many unpalatable truths told of himself in the vernacular of his own humble and astounded menials, he stepped out from among the crowd, and addressed me in English,—a language in which he had acquired some proficiency in the course of his travels. The change of language by no means altered his views, nor abated his pertinacity. At last, finding there was nothing to be gained by this war of words, I ordered the boy to mount his horse and rejoin the wagons. "Beware of the consequences!" vociferated the enraged Trias. "Well, let them come," I replied; "here we are." But we were suffered to depart in peace with the prisoner.

That the reader may be able to form some idea of the pusillanimity of this lordly *haciendero,* it is only necessary to add, that when the altercation took place we were inside of the fortifications,

[3] Angel Trías (d. 1867), owner also of the Hacienda del Peñol, was a member of the Chihuahua city council, a colonel in the state militia, and a justice on the state supreme court. Later he became a brigadier general, member of congress, and for five short terms between 1845 and 1864, governor of his state. John Kendall Bartlett, of the United States Boundary Commission described him as follows: "He is very well versed in several European languages, and speaks English with great correctness. Of English literature, he told me he was very fond; and he considered that no native appreciated the beauties of Shakespeare and Milton better than he. There is no doubt that General Trias detests the Americans as a people; yet American gentlemen and officers who stop at Chihuahua are always treated by him with great politeness and attention." Bartlett, *Personal Narrative,* II, 426–27. Compare with Gregg's comment, n. 4, made twelve years earlier.

[4] Trias, while yet a youth, was dispatched by his adopted father to take the tour of Europe and the United States. He was furnished for 'pocket money' (as I have been told) with nearly a hundred *barras de plata,* each worth a thousand dollars or upwards. This money he easily got rid of during his travels, but retained most of his bigotry and self-importance: and, with his knowledge of the superiority of the people among whom he journeyed, grew his hatred for the foreigners. —GREGG.

from which our egress might easily have been prevented by simply closing the outer gate. We were surrounded by the whole population of the village, besides a small detachment of regular troops, whose commandant took a very active part in the controversy, and fought most valiantly with his tongue. But the valor of the illustrious Señor Don Angel knew a much safer course than to vent itself where there was even a remote chance of personal risk. His influence could not fail to enlist the public in his behalf, and he thought no doubt that his battles might just as well be fought by the officers of justice as by himself.

Yet ignorant of his designs, and supposing the matter would end at this, we continued our march the next day, and by the time night approached we were full twenty miles from the seat of our late troubles. While at breakfast on the following morning we were greatly surprised by the appearance of two American gentlemen direct from Chihuahua, who had ridden thus far purposely to apprise us of what was brewing in the city to our detriment. It appeared that Trias had sent an express to the governor accusing me of rescuing a culprit from the hands of justice by force of arms, and that great preparations were accordingly being made to overtake and carry me back. That the reader may be able to understand the full extent and enormity of my offence, he has only to be informed that the proprietor of an hacienda is at once governor, justice of the peace, and everything besides which he has a mind to fancy himself—a perfect despot within the limits of his little dominion. It was, therefore, through contempt for *his* 'excellency' that I had insulted the majesty of the laws!

Having expressed my sentiment of gratitude to my worthy countrymen for the pains they had taken on my account, we again pursued our journey, determined to abide the worst. This happened on the 3rd of November: on the 5th we encamped near the Ojo Caliente, a hundred and thirty miles from Chihuahua. About eleven o'clock at night, a large body of men were seen approaching. They very soon passed us, and quietly encamped at a distance of several hundred yards. They were over a hundred in number.

Nothing further occurred till next morning when, just as I had risen from my pallet, a soldier approached and inquired if I was up.

In a few minutes he returned with a message from *El Señor Capitan* to know if he could see me. Having answered in the affirmative, a very courteous and agreeable personage soon made his appearance, who, after bowing and scraping until I began to be seriously afraid that his body would break in two, finally opened his mission by handing me a packet of letters, one of which contained an order from the Governor for my immediate presence in Chihuahua, together with the three muleteers whom I had sent after the cattle; warning me, at the same time, not to give cause, by my resistance, for any other measure, which might be unpleasant to my person. The next document was from Señor Trias himself, in which he expressed his regret at having carried the matter to such an extreme, and ended with the usual offer of his services to facilitate an adjustment. Those, however, which most influenced my course, were from Don José Artalejo (*Juez de Hacienda*, Judge of the Customs, of Chihuahua), who offered to become responsible for a favorable issue if I would peaceably return; and another from a Mr. Sutton, with whom I had formerly been connected in business.[5] The manly and upright deportment of this gentleman inspired me with the greatest confidence, and therefore caused me to respect his opinions. But, besides my obligation to submit to a mandate from the government, however arbitrary and oppressive, another strong motive which induced me to return, in obedience to the Governor's order, was a latent misgiving lest any hostile movement on my part, no matter with what justice or necessity, might jeopardize the interest if not the lives of many of my countrymen in Chihuahua.

With regard to ourselves and our immediate safety, we would have found but very little difficulty in fighting our way out of the country. We were all well-armed, and many appeared even anxious to have a brush with the besiegers. However, I informed the capitan that I was willing to return to Chihuahua, with the three 'criminals,' provided we were permitted to go armed and free, as I was not aware of having committed any crime to justify an arrest. He rejoined that this was precisely in accordance with his orders, and politely tendered me an escort of five or six soldiers, who should be placed under my

---

[5] Jesse B. Sutton. Gregg was his bookkeeper at Santa Fé in 1831 and later his partner.

command, to strengthen us against the Indians, that were known to infest our route. Thanking him for his favor, I at once started for Chihuahua, leaving the wagons to continue slowly on the journey, and the amiable captain with his band of *valientes* to retrace their steps at leisure towards the capital.

Late on the evening of the third day, I reached the city, and put up at the American Fonda,[6] where I was fortunate enough to meet with my friend Artalejo, who at once proposed that we should proceed forthwith to the Governor's house.[7] When we found ourselves in the presence of his excellency, my valued friend began by remarking that I had returned according to orders, and that he would answer for me with his person and property; and then, without even waiting for a reply, he turned to me and expressed a hope that I would make his house my residence while I remained in the city. I could not, of course, decline so friendly an invitation, particularly as I thought it probable that, being virtually my bail, he might prefer to have me near his person. But, as soon as we reached the street, he very promptly removed that suspicion from my mind. "I invite you to my house," said he, "as a friend, and not as a prisoner. If you have any business to transact, do not hold yourself under the least restraint. To-morrow I will see the affair satisfactorily settled."

The *Junta Departamental*, or State Council, of which Señor Artalejo was an influential member, was convened the following day. Meanwhile, every American I met with expressed a great deal of surprise to see me at liberty, as, from the excitement which had existed in the city, they expected I would have been lodged in the safest calabozo. I was advised not to venture much into the streets, as the rabble were very much incensed against me; but, although I afterwards wandered about pretty freely, no one offered to molest me; in fact, I must do the 'sovereigns of the city' the justice to say, that I was never more politely treated than during this occasion. Others suggested that, as Trias was one of the most wealthy and influential citizens of Chihuahua, I had better try to pave my way out of the difficulty with *plata*, as I could stand no chance in law against

[6] A hotel operated by Benjamin Riddells, for some time the American consul, and a partner named Stephens.

[7] At this time the governor was José María Irigoyen de la O.

him. To this, however, I strenuously objected. I felt convinced that I had been ordered back to Chihuahua mainly for the purposes of extortion, and I was determined that the *oficiales* should be disappointed. I had unbounded confidence in the friendship and integrity of Don José Artalejo, who was quite an exception to the general character of his countrymen. He was liberal, enlightened and honorable, and I shall ever remember with gratitude the warm interest he took in my affair, when he could have had no other motive for befriending me except what might spring from the consciousness of having performed a generous action.

At first, when the subject of my liberation was discussed in the *Junta Departamental*, the symptoms were rather squally, as some bigoted and unruly members of the Council seemed determined to have me punished, right or wrong. After a long and tedious debate, however, my friend brought me the draft of a petition which he desired me to copy and sign, and upon the presentation of which to the Governor, it had been agreed I should be released. This step, I was informed, had been resolved upon, because, after mature deliberation, the Council came to the conclusion that the proceedings against me had been extremely arbitrary and illegal, and that, if I should hereafter prosecute the Department, I might recover heavy damages. The wholesome lesson which had so lately been taught the Mexicans by France, was perhaps the cause of the fears of the Chihuahua authorities. A clause was therefore inserted in the petition, wherein I was made to renounce all intention on my part of ever troubling the Department on the subject, and became myself a suppliant to have the affair considered as concluded.

This petition I would never have consented to sign, had I not been aware of the arbitrary power which was exercised over me. Imprisonment, in itself, was of but little consequence; but the total destruction of my property, which might have been the result of further detention, was an evil which I deemed it necessary to ward off, even at a great sacrifice of feeling. Moreover, being in duress, no forced concession would, of course, be obligatory upon me after I resumed my liberty. Again, I felt no very great inclination to sue for redress where there was so little prospect of procuring anything. I might certainly have represented the matter to the Mexican government, and even have obtained perhaps the acknowledgment of my claims against Chihuahua for damages; but the payment would have been extremely doubtful. As to our own Government, I had too much experience to rely for a moment upon her interposition.

During the progress of these transactions, I strove to ascertain the character of the charges made against me; but in vain. All I knew was, that I had offended a *rico*, and had been summoned back to Chihuahua at his instance; yet whether for 'high treason,' for an attempt at robbery, or for contempt to his *señoría*, I knew not. It is not unusual, however, in that 'land of liberty,' for a person to be arrested and even confined for weeks without knowing the cause. The writ of *Habeas Corpus* appears unknown in the judicial tribunals of Northern Mexico.

Upon the receipt of my petition, the Governor immediately issued the following decree, which I translate for the benefit of the reader, as being not a bad specimen of Mexican grand eloquence:

"In consideration of the memorial which you have this day directed to the Superior Government, His Excellency, the Governor, has been pleased to issue the following decree:

" 'That, as Don Angel Trias has withdrawn his prosecution, so far as relates to his personal interests, the Government, using the equity with which it ought to look upon faults committed without a deliberate intention to infringe the laws, which appears presumable in the present case, owing to the memorialist's ignorance of them, the grace which he solicits is granted to him; and, in consequence, he is at liberty to retire when he chooses: to which end, and that he may not be interrupted by the authorities, a copy of this decree will be transmitted to him.'

"In virtue of the above, I inclose the said decree to you, for the purpose intended.

"God and Liberty. Chihuahua, Nov. 9, 1839.

"AMADO DE LA VEGA, Sec.

"To Don Josiah Gregg."

Thus terminated this 'momentous' affair. The moral of it may be summed up in a few words. A citizen of the United States who, under the faith of treaties, is engaged in his business, may be seized and harassed by the arbitrary authorities of Chihuahua with perfect impunity, because experience has proved that the American Government winks at almost every individual outrage, as utterly unworthy of its serious consideration. At the same time, the Indians may enter, as they frequently do, the suburbs of the city,—rob, plunder, and destroy life, without a single soldier being raised, or an effort made to bring the savage malefactors within the pale of justice. But a few days before the occasion of my difficulty at Torreon, the Apaches had killed a ranchero or two in the immediate neighborhood of the same village; and afterwards, at the very time such a bustle was being made in Chihuahua to raise troops for my 'special benefit,' the Indians entered the corn-fields in the suburbs of the city, and killed several *labradores* who were at work in them. In neither of these cases, however, were there any troops at command to pursue and chastise the depredators—though a whole army was in readiness to persecute our party. The truth is, they felt much less reluctance to pursue a band of civil traders, who, they were well aware, could not assume a hostile attitude, than to be caught in the wake of a band of savages, who would as little respect their lives as their laws and their property.

Early on the morning of the 10th, I once more, and for the last time, and with anything but regret, took my leave of Chihuahua, with my companions in trouble. Towards the afternoon we met my old friend the captain, with his valiant followers, whom I found as full of urbanity as ever—so much so, indeed, that he never even asked to see my passport.

On the evening of the next day, now in the heart of the savage haunts, we were not a little alarmed by the appearance of a large body of horsemen in the distance. They turned out, however, to be *Paseños*, or citizens of the Paso del Norte. They were on their way to Chihuahua with a number of pack-mules laden with apples, pears, grapes, wine, and *aguardiente*—proceeds of their productive orchards and vineyards. It is from El Paso that Chihuahua is chiefly supplied with fruits and liquors, which are transported on mules or in carretas. The fruits, as well fresh as in a dried state, are thus carried to the distant markets. The grapes, carefully dried in the shade make excellent *pasas* or raisins, of which large quantities are annually prepared for market by the people of that delightful town of vineyards and orchards, who, to take them altogether, are more sober and industrious than those of any other part of Mexico I have visited; and are happily less infested by the extremes of wealth and poverty.

On the 13th, I overtook my wagons a few miles south of El Paso, whence our journey was continued, without any additional casualty, and on the 6th of December we reached Santa Fé, in fine health and spirits.

CHAPTER VIII

Preparations for returning Home—Breaking out of the Smallpox—The Start—Our Caravan—Manuel the Comanche—A New Route—The Prairie on fire—Danger to be apprehended from these Conflagrations—A Comanche Buffalo-chase—A Skirmish with the Pawnees—An intrepid Mexican—The Wounded—Value of a thick Skull—Retreat of the Enemy and their Failure—A bleak Northwester—Loss of our Sheep—The Llano Estacado and Sources of Red River—The Canadian River—Cruelties upon Buffalo—Feats at 'Still-hunting'—Mr. Wethered's Adventure—Once more on our own Soil—The False Washita—Enter our former Trail—Character of the Country over which we had travelled—Arrival at Van Buren—The two Routes to Santa Fé—Some Advantages of that from Arkansas—Restlessness of Prairie Travellers in civilized life, and Propensity for returning to the Wild Deserts.

ABOUT THE BEGINNING of February, 1840, and just as I was making preparations to return to the United States, the small-pox broke out among my men, in a manner which at first occasioned at least as much astonishment as alarm. One of them, who had been vaccinated, having travelled in a district where the small-pox prevailed, complained of a little fever, which was followed by slight eruptions, but so unlike true variolous pustules, that I treated the matter very lightly; not even suspecting a varioloid. These slight symptoms having passed off, nothing more was thought of it until eight or ten days after, when every unvaccinated member of our company was attacked by that fell disease, which soon began to manifest very malignant features. There were no fatal cases, however; yet much apprehension was felt, lest the disease should break out again on the route; but, to our great joy, we escaped this second scourge.

A party that left Santa Fé for Missouri soon afterward, was much more unfortunate. On the way, several of their men were attacked by the small-pox: some of them died, and, others retaining the infection till they approached the Missouri frontier, they were compelled to undergo a 'quarantine' in the bordering prairie, before they were permitted to enter the settlements.

On the 25th of February we set out from Santa Fé: but owing to some delays, we did not leave San Miguel till the 1st of March. As the pasturage was yet insufficient for our animals, we here provided ourselves with over six hundred bushels of corn, to feed them on the way. This time our caravan consisted of twenty-eight wagons, two small cannons, and forty-seven men, including sixteen Mexicans and a Comanche Indian who acted in the capacity of guide.[1] Two gentlemen of Baltimore, Messrs. S. Wethered and J. R. Ware,[2] had joined our caravan with one wagon and three men, making up the aggregate above mentioned. We had also a caballada of more than two hundred mules, with nearly three hundred sheep and goats. The sheep were brought along partially to supply us with meat in case of emergency: the surplusage, however, could not fail to command a fair price in the United States.

Instead of following the trail of the year before, I determined to seek a nearer and better route down the south side of the Canadian river, under the guidance of the Comanche; by which movement, we had again to travel a distance of four hundred miles over an entirely new country.[3] We had just passed the Laguna Colorado,

[1] Manuel *el Comanche* was a full Indian, born and bred upon the great prairies. Long after having arrived at the state of manhood, he accompanied some Mexican *Comancheros* to the frontier village of San Miguel, where he fell in love with a Mexican girl—married her—and has lived in that place, a sober, 'civilized' citizen for the last ten or twelve years—endowed with much more goodness of heart and integrity of purpose than a majority of his Mexican neighbors. He had learned to speak Spanish quite intelligibly, and was therefore an excellent Comanche interpreter; and being familiar with every part of the prairies, he was very serviceable as a guide.—GREGG.

[2] Samuel Wethered and James R. Ware were partners in the Santa Fé trade for several years.

[3] According to Gregg's preliminary draft of this chapter, he left Santa Fé on a rough and crooked road through the mountains. The route was E. 35° S. for about 45 miles to San Miguel; E. 6 miles to Ojo de Bernal; E. 35° S. 20 miles to Ojo de los Chupaines; E. 10° S. 10 miles to Gallinas Creek; E. 40° S. 15 miles to the Esteros, a watering place on a tributary of the Pecos; E. 30° S. 15 miles to Cuerbito

where, the following year, a division of Texan volunteers, under General McLeod, surrendered to Col. Archuleta,[4] when our fire was carelessly permitted to communicate with the prairie grass. As there was a head-wind blowing at the time, we very soon got out of reach of the conflagration: but the next day, the wind having changed, the fire was again perceived in our rear approaching us at a very brisk pace. The terror which these prairie conflagrations are calculated to inspire, when the grass is tall and dry, as was the case in the present instance, has often been described, and though the perils of these disasters are not unfrequently exaggerated, they are sometimes sufficient to daunt the stoutest heart. Mr. Kendall relates a frightful incident of this kind which occurred to the Texan Santa Fé Expedition; and all those who have crossed the Prairies have had more or less experience as to the danger which occasionally threatens the caravans from these sweeping visitations. The worst evil to be apprehended with those bound for Santa Fé is from the explosion of gunpowder, as a keg or two of twenty-five pounds each, is usually to be found in every wagon. When we saw the fire gaining so rapidly upon us, we had to use the whip very unsparingly; and it was only when the lurid flames were actually rolling upon the heels of our teams, that we succeeded in reaching a spot of short-grass prairie, where there was no further danger to be apprehended.

The head way of the conflagration was soon after checked by a small stream which traversed our route; and we had only emerged fairly from its smoke, on the following day (the 9th), when our Comanche guide returned hastily from his accustomed post in advance, and informed us that he had espied three buffaloes, not far off. They were the first we had met with, and, being heartily anxious for a change from the dried beef with which we were provided, I

Creek, a tributary of the Canadian; E. 7° N. 12 miles to Pajarito Creek; E. 10 miles to the Laguna Colorado; E. 10° S. 15 miles to the headwaters of Arroyo de Monte Revuelto; and E. 25° N. 12 miles to a camp 4 or 5 miles southeast of Cerro de Tucumcari on the same creek. For most of this distance Gregg had followed the route taken by his wagons the previous year, but he was now without either road or trail. *Diary & Letters*, I, 45–46.

[4] Colonel Juan Andrés Archuleta, not to be confused with Colonel Diego Archuleta, who was involved in the revolt against the American occupation in 1846–47. Laguna Colorado, near the head of Tucumcari Creek, was about 12 miles west of Mount Tucumcari in western Quay County, New Mexico.

directed the Comanche, who was by far our surest hunter, to prepare at once for the *chasse*. He said he preferred to hunt on horseback and with his bow and arrow; and believing my riding-horse the fleetest in company (which, by the by, was but a common pony, and thin in flesh withal), I dismounted and gave him the bridle, with many charges to treat him kindly, as we still had a long journey before us. "Don't attempt to kill but one—that will serve us for the present!" I exclaimed, as he galloped off. The Comanche was among the largest of his tribe—bony and muscular—weighing about two hundred pounds: but once at his favorite sport, he very quickly forgot my injunction, as well as the weakness of my little pony. He soon brought down two of his game—and shyly remarked to those who followed in his wake, that, had he not feared a scolding from me, he would not have permitted the third to escape.

On the evening of the 10th our camp was pitched in the neighborhood of a ravine in the prairie,[5] and as the night was dark and dreary, the watch tried to comfort themselves by building a rousing fire, around which they presently drew, and commenced 'spinning long yarns' about Mexican fandangoes, and black-eyed damsels. All of a sudden the stillness of the night was interrupted by a loud report of fire-arms, and a shower of bullets came whizzing by the ears of the heedless sentinels. Fortunately, however, no one was injured; which must be looked upon as a very extraordinary circumstance, when we consider what a fair mark our men, thus huddled round a blazing fire, presented to the rifles of the Indians. The savage yells, which resounded from every part of the ravine, bore very satisfactory testimony that this was no false alarm; and the 'Pawnee whistle' which was heard in every quarter, at once impressed us with the idea of its being a band of that famous prairie banditti.

Every man sprang from his pallet with rifle in hand; for, upon the Prairies, we always sleep with our arms by our sides or under our heads. Our Comanche seemed at first very much at a loss what to do. At last, thinking it might possibly be a band of his own nation he began a most boisterous harangue in his vernacular tongue, which he continued for several minutes; when finding that the enemy took no notice of him, and having been convinced also, from an occa-

[5] Between present Endee and Glenrio, in Quay County, New Mexico.

sional Pawnee word which he was able to make out, that he had been wasting breath with the mortal foes of his race, he suddenly ceased all expostulations, and blazed away with his rifle, with a degree of earnestness which was truly edifying, as if convinced that that was the best he could do for us.

It was now evident that the Indians had taken possession of the entire ravine, the nearest points of which were not fifty yards from our wagons: a warning to prairie travellers to encamp at a greater distance from whatsoever might afford shelter for an enemy. The banks of the gully were low, but still they formed a very good breast-work, behind which the enemy lay ensconced, discharging volleys of balls upon our wagons, among which we were scattered. At one time we thought of making an attempt to rout them from their forti-fied position; but being ignorant of their number, and unable to dis-tinguish any object through the dismal darkness which hung all around, we had to remain content with firing at random from behind our wagons, aiming at the flash of their guns, or in the direction whence any noise appeared to emanate. Indeed their yelling was almost continuous, breaking out every now and then in the most hideous screams and vociferous chattering, which were calculated to appal such timorous persons as we may have had in our caravan. All their screeching and whooping, however, had no effect—they could not make our animals break from the enclosure of the wagons, in which they were fortunately shut up; which was no doubt their principal object for attacking us.

I cannot forbear recording a most daring feat performed by a Mexican muleteer, named Antonio Chavez, during the hottest of the first onset. Seeing the danger of my two favorite riding horses, which were tethered outside within a few paces of the savages, he rushed out and brought safely in the most valuable of the two, though fusil-balls were showering around him all the while. The other horse broke his halter and made his escape.

Although sundry scores of shots had been fired at our people, we had only two men wounded. One, a Mexican,[6] was but slightly injured in the hand, but the wound of the other, who was an Italian,[7]

[6] Nacifor Palacio, a wagoner. *Diary & Letters*, I, 49.
[7] Giovanni Elmini, one of the men accompanying Wethered and Ware. *Ibid.*

bore a more serious aspect, and deserves especial mention. He was a short, corpulent fellow, and had been nicknamed 'Dutch'—a loquacious chicken-hearted *fainéant*, and withal in the daily habit of gorging himself to such an enormous extent, that every alternate night he was on the sick list. On this memorable occasion, Dutch had 'foundered' again, and the usual prescription of a double dose of Epsom salts had been his supper potion. The skirmish had continued for about an hour, and although a frightful groaning had been heard in Dutch's wagon for some time, no one paid any attention to it, as it was generally supposed to be from the effects of his dose. At length, however, some one cried out, "Dutch is wounded!" I immediately went to see him, and found him writhing and twisting himself as if in great pain, crying all the time that he was shot. "Shot! —where?" I inquired. "Ah! in the head, sir?" "Pshaw! Dutch, none of that; you've only bumped your head in trying to hide yourself." Upon lighting a match, however, I found that a ball had passed through the middle of his hat, and that, to my consternation, that the top of his head was bathed in blood. It turned out, upon subsequent examination, that the ball had glanced upon the skull, inflicting a serious-looking wound, and so deep that an inch of sound skin separated the holes at which the bullet had entered and passed out. Notwithstanding I at first apprehended a fracture of the skull, it very soon healed, and Dutch was 'up and about' again in the course of a week.

Although teachers not unfrequently have cause to deplore the thickness of their pupils' skulls, Dutch had every reason to congratulate himself upon possessing such a treasure, as it had evidently preserved him from a more serious catastrophe. It appeared he had taken shelter in his wagon at the commencement of the attack, without reflecting that the boards and sheets were not ball-proof: and as Indians, especially in the night, are apt to shoot too high, he was in a much more dangerous situation than if upon the ground.

The enemy continued the attack for nearly three hours, when they finally retired, so as to make good their retreat before daylight. As it rained and snowed from that time till nine in the morning, their 'sign' was almost entirely obliterated, and we were unable to discover whether they had received any injury or not. It was evidently a foot party, which we looked upon as another proof of their being Pawnees; for these famous marauders are well known to go forth on their expeditions of plunder without horses, although they seldom fail to return well mounted.

Their shot had riddled our wagons considerably: in one we counted no less than eight bullet-holes. We had the gratification to believe, however, that they did not get a single one of our animals: the horse which broke away at the first onset, doubtless made his escape; and a mule which was too badly wounded to travel, was dispatched by the muleteers, lest it should fall into the hands of the savages, or into the mouths of the wolves; and they deemed it more humane to leave it to be eaten dead than alive. We also experienced considerable damage in our stock of sheep, a number of them having been devoured by wolves. They had been scattered at the beginning of the attack; and, in their anxiety to fly from the scene of action, had jumped, as it were, into the very jaws of their ravenous enemies.

On the 12th of March, we ascended upon the celebrated *Llano Estacado*, and continued along its borders for a few days. The second night upon this dreary plain, we experienced one of the strongest and bleakest 'northwesters' that ever swept across those prairies; during which, our flock of sheep and goats, being left unattended, fled over the plain, in search of some shelter, it was supposed, from the furious element. Their disappearance was not observed for some time, and the night being too dark to discern anything, we were obliged to defer going in pursuit of them till the following morning. After a fruitless and laborious search, during which the effects of the mirage proved a constant source of annoyance and disappointment, we were finally obliged to relinquish the pursuit, and return to the caravan without finding one of them.

These severe winds are very prevalent upon the great western prairies, though they were seldom quite so inclement. At some seasons, they are about as regular and unceasing as the 'trade winds' of the ocean. It will often blow a gale for days, and even weeks together, without slacking for a moment, except occasionally at night. It is for this reason, as well as on account of the rains, that percussion guns are preferable upon the Prairies, particularly for those who understand their use. The winds are frequently so severe as to sweep away both sparks and priming from a flint lock, and thus render it wholly ineffective.

The following day we continued our march down the border of the Llano Estacado. Knowing that our Comanche guide was about as familiar with all those great plains as a landlord with his premises, I began to question him, as we travelled along, concerning the different streams which pierced them to the southward. Pointing in that direction, he said there passed a water-course, at the distance of a hard day's ride, which he designated as a *cañada* or valley, in which there was always water to be found at occasional places, but that none flowed in its channel except during the rainy season. This cañada[8] he described as having its origin in the Llano Estacado some fifty or sixty miles east of Rio Pecos, and about the same distance south of the route we came, and that its direction was a little south of east, passing to the southward of the northern portion of the Witchita mountains, known to Mexican Ciboleros and Comancheros as *Sierra Jumanes*. It was, therefore, evident that this was the principal northern branch of Red River. The False Washita, or *Rio Negro*, as the Mexicans call it, has its rise, as he assured me, between the Canadian and this cañada, at no great distance to the southeastward of where we were then travelling.

On the 15th, our Comanche guide, being fearful lest we should find no water upon the plain, advised us to pursue a more northwardly course, so that, after a hard day's ride, we again descended the *ceja* or brow of the Llano Estacado, into the undulating lands which border the Canadian; and, on the following day, we found ourselves upon the southern bank of that stream.[9]

Although, but a few days' travel above where we now were, the Canadian runs pent up in a narrow channel, scarcely four rods across, we here found it spread out to the width of from three to six hundred yards, and so full of sand-bars (only interspersed with narrow rills) as to present the appearance of a mere sandy valley instead of the bed of a river. In fact, during the driest seasons, the water wholly disappears in many places. Captain Boone, of the U. S. Dragoons,[10]

[8] Palo Duro Canyon, in Randall, Armstrong, and Briscoe counties, Texas.
[9] At or very near the present-day Hutchinson-Roberts county line, Texas, judging by the direction and distance travelled.

being upon an exploring expedition in the summer of 1843, came to the Canadian about the region of our western boundary, where he found the channel perfectly dry. Notwithstanding it presents the face of one of the greatest rivers of the west during freshets, yet even then it would not be navigable on account of its rapidity and shallowness. It would appear almost incredible to those unacquainted with the prairie streams, that a river of about 1500 miles in length, and whose head wears a cap of perennial snow (having its source in the Rocky Mountains), should scarcely be navigable, for even the smallest craft, over fifty miles above its mouth.

We pursued our course down the same side of the river for several days, during which time we crossed a multitude of little streams which flowed into the Canadian from the adjoining plains, while others presented nothing but dry beds of sand. One of these was so remarkable, on account of its peculiarity and size, that we named it 'Dry River.'[11] The bed was at least 200 yards wide, yet without a vestige of water; notwithstanding, our guide assured us that it was a brisk-flowing stream some leagues above: and from the drift-wood along its borders, it was evident that, even here, it must be a considerable river during freshets.

While travelling down the course of the Canadian, we sometimes found the buffalo very abundant. On one occasion, two or three hunters, who were a little in advance of the caravan, perceiving a herd quietly grazing in an open glade, they 'crawled upon' them after the manner of the 'still hunters.' Their first shot having brought down a fine fat cow, they slipped up behind her, and, resting their guns over her body, shot two or three others, without occasioning any serious disturbance or surprise to their companions; for, extraordinary as it may appear, if the buffalo neither see nor smell the hunter, they will pay but little attention to the crack of guns, or to the mortality which is being dealt among them.

The slaughter of these animals is frequently carried to an excess,

[10] Nathan Boone (1780–1857), the youngest son of Daniel Boone, came to Missouri from Kentucky, entered the regular army as a captain in 1832 and retired in 1853 as a lieutenant colonel.

[11] Red Deer Creek, which joins the Canadian River at Canadian, the seat of Hemphill County, Texas. The name "Dry River" or "Dry Creek" persisted on the maps for several years.

which shows the depravity of the human heart in very bold relief. Such is the excitement that generally prevails at the sight of these fat denizens of the prairies, that very few hunters appear able to refrain from shooting as long as the game remains within reach of their rifles; nor can they ever permit a fair shot to escape them. Whether the mere pleasure of taking life is the incentive of these brutal excesses, I will not pretend to decide; but one thing is very certain, that the buffalo killed yearly on these prairies far exceeds the wants of the traveller, or what might be looked upon as the exigencies of rational sport.[12]

But in making these observations, I regret that I cannot give to my precepts the force of my own example: I have not always been able wholly to withstand the cruel temptation. Not long after the incident above alluded to, as I was pioneering alone, according to my usual practice, at a distance of a mile or two ahead of the wagons, in search of the best route, I perceived in a glade, a few rods in front of me, several protuberances, which at first occasioned me no little fright, for I took them, as they loomed dimly through the tall grass, for the tops of Indian lodges. But I soon discovered they were the huge humps of a herd of buffalo, which were quietly grazing.

[12] The same barbarous propensity is observable in regard to wild horses. Most persons appear unable to restrain this wanton inclination to take life, when a mustang approaches within rifle-shot. Many a stately steed thus falls a victim to the cruelty of man.—GREGG.

I immediately alighted, and approached unobserved to within forty or fifty yards of the unsuspecting animals. Being armed with one of Cochran's nine-chambered rifles, I took aim at one that stood broad-side, and 'blazed away.' The buffalo threw up their heads and looked about, but seeing nothing (for I remained concealed in the grass), they again went on grazing as though nothing had happened. The truth is, the one I had shot was perhaps but little hurt; for, as generally happens with the inexperienced hunter—and often with those who know better, the first excitement allowing no time for reflection—I no doubt aimed too high, so as to lodge the ball in the hump. A buffalo's heart lies exceedingly low, so that to strike it the shot should enter not over one-fourth of the depth of the body above the lower edge of the breast bone.

The brutes were no sooner quiet, than I took another and more deliberate aim at my former victim, which resulted as before. But believing him now mortally wounded, I next fired in quick succession at four others of the gang. It occurred to me, by this time, that I had better save my remaining three shots; for it was possible enough for my firing to attract the attention of strolling savages, who might take advantage of my empty gun to make a sortie upon me—yet there stood my buffalo, some of them still quietly feeding.

As I walked out from my concealment, a party of our own men came galloping up from the wagons, considerably alarmed. They had heard the six shots, and, not recollecting my repeating rifle, supposed I had been attacked by Indians, and therefore came to my relief. Upon their approach the buffalo all fled, except three which appeared badly wounded—one indeed soon fell and expired. The other two would doubtless have followed the example of the first, had not a hunter, anxious to dispatch them more speedily, approached too near; when, regaining strength from the excitement, they fled before him, and entirely escaped, though he pursued them a considerable distance.

A few days after this occurrence, Mr. Wethered returned to the camp one evening with seven buffalo tongues (the hunter's usual trophy) swung to his saddle. He said that, in the morning, one of the hunters had ungenerously objected to sharing a buffalo with him; whereupon Mr. W. set out, vowing he would kill buffalo for himself, and 'no thanks to any one.' He had not been out long when he spied a herd of only seven bulls, quietly feeding near a ravine; and slipping up behind the banks, he shot down one and then another, until they all lay before him; and their seven tongues he brought in to bear testimony of his skill.

Not long after crossing Dry River, we ascended the high grounds, and soon found ourselves upon the high ridge which divides the waters of the Canadian and False Washita, whose 'breaks' could be traced descending from the Llano Estacado far to the southwest.

By an observation of an eclipse of one of Jupiter's satellites, on the night of the 25th of March, in latitude 35° 51' 30", I found that we were very near the 100th degree of longitude west from Greenwich.[13] On the following day, therefore, we celebrated our entrance into the United States territory. Those who have never been beyond the purlieus of the land of their nativity, can form but a poor conception of the joy which the wanderer in distant climes experiences on treading once more upon his own native soil! Although we were yet far from the abodes of civilization, and further still from home, nevertheless the heart within us thrilled with exhilarating sensations; for we were again in our own territory, breathed our own free atmosphere, and were fairly out of reach of the arbitrary power which we had left behind us.

As we continued our route upon this narrow dividing ridge, we could not help remarking how nearly these streams approach each other: in one place they seemed scarcely five miles apart. On this account our Comanche guide, as well as several Mexicans of our party, who had some acquaintance with these prairies, gave it as their opinion that the Washita or *Rio Negro* was in fact a branch of the Canadian; for its confluence with Red River was beyond the bounds of their peregrinations.

As the forest of Cross Timbers was now beginning to be seen

[13] Gregg miscalculates. He had crossed the 100th meridian on March 23 and camped 5 miles beyond it, near the Upper Mound of the "Boundary Mountains" (the Antelope Hills in Roger Mills County, Oklahoma). The next day he overtook the Canadian beyond its northern bend around these hills and continued along its course for another 11 miles. *Diary & Letters*, I, 59–60. On the night of March 25, when he thought himself very near the 100th meridian, he was actually 33 miles east of it.

in the distance, and fearing we might be troubled to find a passway through this brushy region, south of the Canadian, we forded this river on the 29th,[14] without the slightest trouble, and very soon entered our former trail, a little west of Spring Valley. This gave a new and joyful impulse to our spirits; for we had been travelling over twenty days without even a trail, and through a region of which we knew absolutely nothing, except from what we could gather from our Comanche pilot. This trail, which our wagons had made the previous summer, was still visible, and henceforth there was an end to all misgivings.

If we take a retrospective view of the country over which we travelled, we shall find but little that can ever present attractions to the agriculturist. Most of the low valleys of the Canadian, for a distance of five hundred miles, are either too sandy or too marshy for cultivation; and the upland prairies are, in many places, but little else than sand-hills. In some parts, it is true, they are firm and fertile, but wholly destitute of timber, with the exception of a diminutive branch of the Cross Timbers, which occupies a portion of the ridge betwixt the Canadian and the North Fork. The Canadian river itself is still more bare of timber than the upper Arkansas. In its whole course through the plains, there is but little except cottonwood, and that very scantily scattered along its banks—in some places, for leagues together, not a stick is to be seen. Except it be near the Mountains, where the valleys are more fertile, it is only the little narrow bottoms which skirt many of its tributary rivulets that indicate any amenity. Some of these are rich and beautiful in the extreme, timbered with walnut, mulberry, oak, elm, hackberry, and occasionally cedar about the bluffs.

We now continued our journey without encountering any further casualty, except in crossing the Arkansas river, where we lost several mules by drowning; and on the 22d of April we made our entrance into Van Buren. This trip was much more tedious and protracted than I had contemplated—owing in the first part of the journey, to the inclemency of the season, and a want of pasturage for our animals; and, towards the conclusion, to the frequent rains, which kept the route in a miserable condition.

[14] About 3 miles west of present Fay, in Dewey County, Oklahoma.

Concerning this expedition, I have only one or two more remarks to offer. As regards the two different routes to Santa Fé, although Missouri, for various reasons which it is needless to explain here, can doubtless retain the monopoly of the Santa Fé trade, the route from Arkansas possesses many advantages. Besides its being some days' travel shorter,[15] it is less intersected with large streams; there are fewer sandy stretches, and a greater variety of wood-skirted brooks, affording throughout the journey very agreeable camping-places. Also, as the grass springs up nearly a month earlier than in Upper Missouri, caravans could start much sooner, and the proprietors would have double the time to conduct their mercantile transactions. Moreover, the return companies would find better pasturage on their way back, and reach their homes before the season of frost had far advanced. Again, such as should desire to engage in the 'stock trade' would at once bring their mules and horses into a more congenial climate—one more in accordance with that of their nativity; for the rigorous winters of Missouri often prove fatal to the unacclimated Mexican animals.

This was my last trip across the Plains, though I made an excursion, during the following summer, among the Comanche Indians, and other wild tribes, living in the heart of the Prairies, but returned without crossing to Mexico. The observations made during this trip will be found incorporated in the notices, which are to follow, of the Prairies and their inhabitants.

Since that time I have striven in vain to reconcile myself to the even tenor of civilized life in the United States; and have sought in its amusements and its society a substitute for those high excitements which have attached me so strongly to Prairie life. Yet I am almost ashamed to confess that scarcely a day passes without my experiencing a pang of regret that I am not now roving at large upon those western plains. Nor do I find my taste peculiar; for I have hardly known a man, who has ever become familiar with the kind of life

[15] The latitude of Independence, Mo., is 39°8′, while that of Van Buren is 35°26′,—within a few miles of the parellel of Santa Fé; and being on about the same meridian as Independence, the distance of course is considerably shorter.— GREGG.

The latitudes of Independence and Van Buren are now given as 39°5′ and 35°25′, respectively, and that of Santa Fe as 35°40′.

which I have led for so many years, that has not relinquished it with regret.

There is more than one way of explaining this apparent incongruity. In the first place—the wild, unsettled and independent life of the Prairie trader, makes perfect freedom from nearly every kind of social dependence an absolute necessity of his being. He is in daily, nay, hourly exposure of his life and property, and in the habit of relying upon his own arm and his own gun both for protection and support. Is he wronged? No court or jury is called to adjudicate upon his disputes or his abuses, save his own conscience; and no powers are invoked to redress them, save those with which the God of Nature has endowed him. He knows no government—no laws, save those of his own creation and adoption. He lives in no society which he must look up to or propitiate. The exchange of this untrammelled condition—this sovereign independence, for a life in civilization, where both his physical and moral freedom are invaded at every turn, by the complicated machinery of social institutions, is certainly likely to commend itself to but few,—not even to all those who have been educated to find their enjoyments in the arts and elegancies peculiar to civilized society;—as is evinced by the frequent instances of men of letters, of refinement and of wealth, voluntarily abandoning society for a life upon the Prairies, or in the still more savage mountain wilds.

A 'tour on the Prairies' is certainly a *dangerous* experiment for him who would live a quiet contented life at home among his friends and relatives: not so dangerous to life or health, as prejudicial to his domestic habits. Those who have lived pent up in our large cities, know but little of the broad, unembarrassed freedom of the Great Western Prairies. Viewing them from a snug fireside, they seem crowded with dangers, with labors and with sufferings; but once upon them, and these appear to vanish—they are soon forgotten.

There is another consideration, which, with most men of the Prairies, operates seriously against their reconciliation to the habits of civilized life. Though they be endowed naturally with the organs of taste and refinement, and though once familiar with the ways and practices of civilized communities, yet a long absence from such society generally obliterates from their minds most of those common laws of social intercourse, which are so necessary to the man of the world. The awkwardness and the *gaucheries* which ignorance of their details so often involves, are very trying to all men of sensitive temperaments. Consequently, multitudes rush back to the Prairies, merely to escape those criticisms and that ridicule, which they know not how to disarm.

It will hardly be a matter or surprise then, when I add, that this passion for Prairie life, how paradoxical soever it may seem, will be very apt to lead me upon the plains again, to spread my bed with the mustang and the buffalo, under the broad canopy of heaven,—there to seek to maintain undisturbed my confidence in men, by fraternizing with the little prairie dogs and wild colts, and the still wilder Indians—the *unconquered Sabaeans* of the Great American Deserts.

CHAPTER IX
CONCLUSION OF THE SANTA FÉ TRADE

Decline of Prices—Statistical Table—Chihuahua Trade—Its Extent—
Different Ports through which Goods are introduced to that Market—
Expedition between Chihuahua and Arkansas—The more recent Inci-
dents of the Santa Fé Caravans—Adventures of 1843—Robbery and
Murder of Chavez—Expedition from Texas—Defeat of Gen. Armijo's
Van-guard—His precipitate Retreat—Texan Grievances—Unfortunate
Results of Indiscriminate Revenge—Want of Discipline among the
Texans—Disarmed by Capt. Cook—Return of the Escort of U. S.
Dragoons, and of the Texans—Demands of the Mexican Government—
Closing of the Santa Fé Trade.

BEFORE PROCEEDING to the graver matters to be presented in the
succeeding chapters, a few words to those who are curious about
the history of the Santa Fé trade intervening between the conclusion
of my personal narrative and the closing of the trade by the Mexican government, in 1843, may not be amiss.

The Santa Fé trade, though more or less fluctuating from its
origin, continued to present an average increase and growth down to
the year 1831. During the same period, the prices of goods continued to go down in even a more rapid ratio. Since 1831, the rates of
sales have continued steadily to fall, to the latest period of the trade,
although there has been no average increase in the number of adventurers, or amount of merchandise.[1]

From 1831 to the present date, prices have scarcely averaged, for

[1] Some general statistics of the Santa Fé trade may prove not wholly without
interest to the mercantile reader. With this view, I have prepared the following
table of the probable amounts of merchandise invested in the Santa Fé trade, from
1822 to 1843 inclusive, and about the proportion of the same transferred to the

Southern markets (chiefly Chihuahua) during the same period; together with the approximate number of wagons, men and proprietors engaged each year:

Years	Amt.Mdse.	W'gs.	Men	Pro's.	T'n to Ch'a.	Remarks
1822	15,000		70	60	[9,000][a]	Pack-animals only used.[b]
1823	12,000		50	30	[3,000][a]	do. do.
1824	35,000	26	100	80	3,000	do. and wagons.
1825	65,000	37	130	90	5,000	do. do.
1826	90,000	60	100	70	7,000	Wagons only henceforth.
1827	85,000	55	90	50	8,000	
1828	150,000	100	200	80	20,000	3 men killed, being the first.
1829	60,000	30	50	20	5,000	1st U. S. Es.—1 trader killed.
1830	120,000	70	140	60	20,000	First oxen used by traders.
1831	250,000	130	320	80	80,000	Two men killed.
1832	140,000	70	150	40	50,000	{ Party defeated on Canadian.
1833	180,000	105	185	60	80,000	{ 2 men killed, 3 perished.
1834	150,000	80	160	50	70,000	2d U. S. Escort.
1835	140,000	75	140	40	70,000	
1836	130,000	70	135	35	60,000[c]	
1837	150,000	80	160	35	80,000[d]	
1838	90,000	50	100	20	40,000[e]	
1839	250,000	130	250	40	100,000	Arkansas Expedition.
1840	50,000	30	60	5	10,000	Chihuahua Expedition.
1841	150,000	60	100	12	80,000	Texan Santa Fé Expedition.
1842	160,000	70	120	15	90,000	
1843	450,000	230	350	30	300,000	3d U. S. Es.—Ports closed.

[a] Left blank in first edition.

[b] Three wagons used by Becknell in this year. See above, Vol. I, chap. 1, notes 13, 14.

[c] Changed to 50,000 in the second edition.

[d] Changed to 60,000 in the second edition.

[e] Changed to 80,000 in the second edition.

The foregoing table is not given as perfectly accurate, yet it is believed to be about as nearly so as any that could be made out at the present day. The column marked "Pro's." (Proprietors), though even less precise than the other statistics, presents, I think, about the proportions of the whole number engaged each year who were owners. At first, as will be seen, almost every individual of each caravan was a proprietor, while of late the capital has been held by comparatively few hands. In 1843, the greater portion of the traders were New Mexicans, several of whom, during the three years previous, had embarked in this trade, of which they bid fair to secure a monopoly.

The amount of merchandise transported to Santa Fé each year, is set down at its probable cost in the Eastern cities of the United States. Besides freights and insurance to Independence, there has been an annual investment, averaging nearly twenty-five per cent. upon the cost of the stocks, in wagons, teams, provisions, hire of hands, &c., for transportation across the Prairies. A large portion of this remaining unconsumed, however, the ultimate loss on the outfit has not been more than half of the above amount. Instead of purchasing outfit, some traders prefer employing freighters, a number of whom are usually to be found on the frontier of Missouri, ready to transport goods to Santa Fé, at ten to twelve cents per pound. From thence to Chihuahua the price of freights is six to eight cents—upon mules, or in wagons.

The average gross returns of the traders has rarely exceeded fifty per cent. upon medium calicoes, thirty-seven cents, and for plain domestic cottons thirty-one cents per yard. Taking assortments round, 100 per cent. upon United States costs were generally considered excellent sales: many stocks have been sold at a much lower rate. The average prices of Chihuahua are equally low, yet a brisker demand has rendered this the most agreeable and profitable branch of the trade.

The first attempt to introduce American goods into the more southern markets of Mexico from Santa Fé, was made in the year 1824. The amounts were very small, however, till towards the year 1831. For a few of the first years, the traders were in the habit of conveying small lots to Sonora and California; but this branch of the trade has, I believe, latterly ceased altogether.[2] Yet the amounts transferred to Chihuahua have generally increased; so that for the last few years, that trade has consumed very nearly half of the entire imports by the Missouri Caravans.

The entire consumption of foreign goods in the department of Chihuahua, has been estimated by intelligent Mexican merchants, at from two to three millions annually;[3] the first cost of which might be set down at nearly one half. Of this amount the Santa Fé trade, as will be seen from the accompanying table, has not furnished a tenth part; the balance being introduced through other ports, viz.:

the cost of their merchandise, leaving a net profit of between twenty and forty per cent.; though their profits have not unfrequently been under ten per cent.: in fact, as has been mentioned, their adventures have sometimes been losing speculations.*—GREGG.

* Those who are familiar with Mr. Mayer's very interesting work on Mexico [see above, Vol. I, chap. 13, n. 1] will observe that a portion of the preceding table corresponds substantially with one presented on page 318 of that work. In justice to myself, I feel compelled to state, that, in 1841, I published in the Galveston "Daily Advertiser," a table of the Santa Fé trade from 1831 to 1840 inclusive, of which that of Mr. Mayer embraces an exact copy. I have since made additions, and corrected it to some extent, but still the correspondence is such as seemed to require of me this explanation.—GREGG.

[2] A road between Santa Fé and Los Angeles was opened by a party of traders under Antonio Armijo in 1829-30. An annual caravan trade developed, but except for a few "mountain men" who bought and stole horses from the California missions, this commerce was monopolized by the New Mexicans. Cleland, *This Reckless Breed of Men*, 247-75. According to Gregg's revised table, the Southern markets were reached as early as 1822.

[3] Only $920,200 in 1833, according to official statistics. Pedro Garcia Conde, "Ensayo Estadístico sobre el estado de Chihuahua," in *Boletin de la Sociedad Mexicana de Geografia y Estadistica*, Vol. V (Mexico City, 1857), 297.

Matamoros, whence Chihuahua has received nearly half of its supplies—*Vera Cruz* via the city of Mexico, whence considerable amounts have been brought to this department—*Tampico* on the Gulf of Mexico, and *Mazatlan* on the Pacific, via Durango, whence the imports have been of some importance—while nearly all the west of the department, and especially the heavy consumption of the mining town of Jesus-Maria, receives most of its supplies from the port of *Guaymas* on the Gulf of California; whence, indeed, several stocks of goods have been introduced as far as the city of Chihuahua itself. In 1840, a large amount of merchandise was transported directly from the Red River frontier of Arkansas to Chihuahua; but no other expedition has ever been made in that direction.[4]

[4] With a view to encourage adventurers, the government of Chihuahua agreed to reduce impost duties to a very low rate, in favor of a pioneer enterprise; and to furnish an escort of dragoons for the protection of the traders.

The expedition was undertaken chiefly by Mexicans; but one American merchant, Dr. H. Connelly,[a] having invested capital in it. I obtained from this intelligent gentleman a very interesting sketch of the adventures of this pioneer party, which I regret that my plan will not permit me to present in detail.

The adventurers set out from Chihuahua on the 3d of April, 1839, amidst the benisons of the citizens, and with the confident hope of transferring the valuable trade of the North to their city. The caravan (including fifty dragoons), consisted of over a hundred men, yet only about half a dozen of the number were proprietors. Though they had but seven wagons, they brought about seven hundred mules, and two or three hundred thousand dollars in specie and bullion, for the purposes of their adventure.

They took the Presidio del Norte in their route, and then proceeding northwesterly [!], finally arrived at Fort Towson[b] after a protracted journey of three months; but without meeting with any hostile savages, or encountering any serious casualty, except getting bewildered, after crossing Red River, which they mistook for the Brazos. This caused them to shape their course thence nearly north, in search of the former stream, until they reached the Canadian River, where they met with some Delaware Indians, of whom they obtained the first correct information of their whereabouts; and by whom they were piloted safely to Fort Towson.

It had been the intention of these adventurers to return to Chihuahua the ensuing fall; but from various accidents and delays, they were unable to get ready until the season had too far advanced; which, with an incessant series of rains that followed, prevented them from travelling till the ensuing spring. Learning that the Texans were friendly disposed toward them, they now turned their course through the midst of the northern settlements of that republic. Of the kind treatment they experienced during their transit, Dr. Connelly speaks in the following terms: "I have never been more hospitably treated, or had more efficient assistance, than was given me by the citizens of Red River. All seemed to vie with each other in rendering us every aid in their power; and our Mexican friends, notwithstanding the hostile attitude in which the two countries stood towards each other, were treated with a kindness which they still recollect with the warmest feelings of gratitude." This

By far the greatest portion of the introductions through the seaports just alluded to, have been made by British merchants. It is chiefly the preference given to American manufactures, which has enabled the merchandise of the Santa Fé adventurers to compete in the Southern markets, with goods introduced through the sea-ports, which have had the benefit of the draw-back. In this last respect our traders have labored under a very unjust burden.

It is difficult to conceive any equitable reason why merchants conveying their goods across the Prairies in wagons, should not be as much entitled to the protection of the Government, as those who transport them in vessels across the ocean. This assistance (with the

forms a very notable contrast with the treatment which the Texan traders, who afterwards visited Santa Fé, received at the hands of the Mexicans.

The caravan now consisted of sixty or seventy wagons laden with merchandise, and about two hundred and twenty-five men, including their escort of Mexican dragoons. They passed the Texan border early in April, and expected to intersect their former track beyond the Cross Timbers, but that trail having been partially obliterated, they crossed it unobserved, and were several days lost on the waters of the Brazos river. Having turned their course south for a few days, however, they fortunately discovered their old route at a branch of the Colorado.

After this they continued their journey without further casualty; for notwithstanding they met with a large body of Comanches, they passed them amicably, and soon reached the Rio Pecos. Though very narrow, this stream was too deep to be forded, and they were compelled to resort to an expedient characteristic of the Prairies. There being not a stick of timber anywhere to be found, of which to make even a raft, they buoyed up a wagon-body by binding several empty water-kegs to the bottom, which served them the purpose of a ferry-boat.

When they reached Presidio del Norte again, they learned that Gov. Irigóyen, with whom they had celebrated the contract for a diminution of their duties, had died during their absence. A new corps of officers being in power,[c] they were now threatened with a charge of full tariff duties. After a delay of forty-five days at the Presidio, however, they made a compromise, and entered Chihuahua on the 27th of August, 1840.

The delays and accumulated expenses of this expedition caused it to result so disastrously to the interests of all who were engaged in it, that no other enterprise of the kind his since been undertaken.—GREGG.

[a] Henry Connelly (1800–66), of Kentucky, received a medical degree from Transylvania University, began to practice medicine at Liberty, Mo., but joined a party bound for Santa Fé and Chihuahua, all in 1828. He became a store clerk for Ludwell Powell in Chihuahua, bought him out, married a Mexican lady, and continued in the overland trade until the close of the Mexican War, when he moved to New Mexico. There he established several mercantile houses and became territorial governor, appointed in 1861 and again in 1864.

[b] At the present town of Fort Towson, in Choctaw County, Oklahoma.

[c] Governor José María Irigóyen de la O. was succeeded by Pedro Olivares on May 20, 1840. Final arrangements must have been made with Governor Francisco García Conde, who succeeded Olivares on July 6, 1840.

reopening of the ports) might enable our merchants to monopolize the rich trade of Chihuahua; and they would obtain a share of the still richer departments of Durango and Zacatecas, as well as some portion of the Sonora and California trade. Then rating that of Chihuahua at two millions, half that of Durango at the same, and a million from Zacatecas, Sonora, etc., it would ascend to the clever amount of some five millions of dollars per annum.[5]

In point of revenue, the Santa Fé trade has been of but little importance to the government of Mexico. Though the amount of duties collected annually at this port has usually been fifty to eighty thousand dollars, yet nearly one-half has been embezzled by the officers of the customs, leaving an average net revenue of perhaps less than forty thousand dollars per annum.[6]

It is not an unimportant fact to be known, that, since the year 1831, few or none of the difficulties and dangers which once environed the Santa Fé adventurer have been encountered. No traders have been killed by the savages on the regular route, and few animals stolen from the caravans. On the whole, the rates of insurance upon adventures in this trade should hardly be as high as upon marine adventures between New York and Liverpool. While I declare, however, the serious dangers and troubles to have been in general so slight, I ought not to suppress at least an outline of the difficulties that occurred on the Prairies in 1843, which were attended with very serious consequences.

[5] In his preface to the second edition (September, 1845), Gregg calls attention to the partial realization of these anticipations: "Even without any government assistance, our enterprising merchants are beginning to extend their trade into the Departments of Durango, Zacatecas, and even further south. Last year, a large amount of goods introduced at Santa Fé, found their way to the *Feria de San Juan* (some 800 miles south of Chihuahua, and nearly 1400 from Santa Fé), and were sold to advantage. When our merchandise can thus successfully compete, through such an extent of the richest interior of Northern Mexico, with the importations *via* the ports of the Mexican Gulf, and the Pacific Ocean, a new market is opened, which ten times the amount ever taken across the Prairies in one season could not overstock: nay, ten millions a year would not suffice to supply."

[6] According to official statistics, the customs revenue from Santa Fé between 1825 and 1837 amounted to $241,380, or an annual average of only $18,568. There were no reports (and presumably no revenues) from Santa Fé for the years 1838, 1839, and 1840, but the average annual revenue from 1841 to 1843 was $52,177, which was not far from Gregg's estimate. *Memoria de la Hacienda Nacional*, issues of 1826 to 1844, *passim*.

It had been reported in Santa Fé as early at November, 1842, that a party of Texans were upon the Prairies, prepared to attack any Mexican traders who should cross the Plains the succeeding spring; and as some Americans were accused of being spies, and in collusion with the Texans, many were ordered to Santa Fé for examination, occasioning a deal of trouble to several innocent persons. Than this, however, but little further attention was paid to the report, many believing it but another of those rumors of Texan invasion which had so often spread useless consternation through the country.

So little apprehension appeared to exist, that, in February, 1843, Don Antonio José Chavez,[7] of New Mexico, left Santa Fé for Independence, with but five servants, two wagons, and fifty-five mules. He had with him some ten or twelve thousand dollars in specie and gold bullion, besides a small lot of furs. As the month of March was extremely inclement, the little party suffered inconceivably from cold and privations. Most of them were frost-bitten, and all their animals, except five, perished from the extreme severity of the season; on which account Chavez was compelled to leave one of his wagons upon the Prairies. He had worried along, however, with his remaining wagon and valuables, till about the tenth of April, when he found himself near the Little Arkansas; at least a hundred miles within the territory of the United States. He was met there by fifteen men from the border of Missouri, professing to be Texan troops, under the command of one John M'Daniel. This party had been collected, for the most part, on the frontier, by their leader, who was recently from Texas, from which government he professed to hold a captain's commission. They started no doubt with the intention of joining one Col. Warfield (also said to hold a Texan commission), who had been upon the Plains near the Mountains, with a small party, for several months—with the avowed intention of attacking the Mexican traders.[8]

[7] Son of Francisco Javier Chávez (acting governor, 1823) and brother of Mariano Chávez (acting governor, 1835), not to be confused with José Antonio Chávez (governor, 1823-31).

[8] Charles A. Warfield, a Missourian residing in New Mexico, was commissioned (August 16, 1842) by the Texas secretary of war to raise an expedition against New Mexico. This project was abandoned near Bent's Fort at the end of May, 1843, but

Upon meeting Chavez, however, the party of M'Daniel at once determined to make sure of the prize he was possessed of, rather than take their chances of a similar booty beyond the U.S. Boundary. The unfortunate Mexican was therefore taken a few miles south of the road, and his baggage rifled. Seven of the party then left for the settlements with their share of the booty, amounting to some four or five hundred dollars apiece; making the journey on foot, as their horses had taken a *stampede* and escaped. The remaining eight, soon after the departure of their comrades, determined to put Chavez to death,—for what cause it would seem difficult to conjecture, as he had been, for two days, their unresisting prisoner. Lots were accordingly cast to determine which four of the party should be the cruel executioners; and their wretched victim was taken off a few rods and shot down in cold blood. After his murder a considerable amount of gold was found about his person, and in his trunk. The body of the unfortunate man, together with his wagon and baggage, was thrown into a neighboring ravine; and a few of the lost animals of the marauders having been found, their booty was packed upon them and borne away to the frontier of Missouri.

Great exertions had been made to intercept this lawless band at the outset; but they escaped the vigilance even of a detachment of dragoons that had followed them over a hundred miles. Yet the honest citizens of the border were too much on the alert to permit them to return to the interior with impunity. However, five of the whole number (including three of the party that killed the man) effected their escape, but the other ten were arrested, committed, and sent to St. Louis for trial before the United States Court. It appears that those who were engaged in the killing of Chavez have since been convicted of murder; and the others, who were only concerned in the robbery, were found guilty of larceny, and sentenced to fine and imprisonment.[9]

Warfield took over Colonel Snively's forces as Gregg relates. John McDaniels was commissioned by Warfield without consultation with the government of Texas, which later disavowed his acts. Warfield later settled in Texas, became a legislator (1859–61), and moved to California in 1866, where he was still living in 1883.

[9] McDaniel and his brother David were executed. For the names of the others involved, see *Niles' Weekly Register*, Vol. LXIV (Baltimore, May 22, 1843), 195.

About the first of May of the same year, a company of a hundred and seventy-five men, under one Col. Snively,[10] was organized in the north of Texas, and set out from the settlements for the Santa Fé trace. It was at first reported that they contemplated a descent upon Santa Fé; but their force was evidently too weak to attempt an invasion at that crisis. Their prime object, therefore, seems to have been to attack and make reprisals upon the Mexicans engaged in the Santa Fé trade, who were expected to cross the Prairies during the months of May and June.

After the arrival of the Texans upon the Arkansas, they were joined by Col. Warfield with a few followers. This officer, with about twenty men, had some time previously attacked the village of Mora, on the Mexican frontier, killing five men (as was reported) and driving off a number of horses. They were afterwards followed by a party of Mexicans, however, who *stampeded* and carried away, not only their own horses, but those of the Texans. Being left afoot, the latter burned their saddles, and walked to Bent's Fort, where they were disbanded; whence Warfield passed to Snively's camp, as before mentioned.

The Texans now advanced along the Santa Fé road, beyond the sand hills south of the Arkansas, when they discovered that a party of Mexicans had passed towards the river. They soon came upon them, and a skirmish ensuing, eighteen Mexicans were killed, and as many wounded, five of whom afterwards died. The Texans suffered no injury, though the Mexicans were a hundred in number. The rest were all taken prisoner except two, who escaped and bore the news to Gen. Armijo, encamped with a large force at the Cold Spring, 140 miles beyond. As soon as the General received notice of the defeat of his vanguard, he broke up his camp most precipitately, and retreated to Santa Fé. A gentleman of the caravan which passed shortly afterward, informed me that spurs, lareats and other scraps of equipage, were found scattered in every direction about Armijo's

[10] Jacob Snively (*ca.* 1808–71), probably of Pennsylvania, came to Texas in 1835 as a surveyor for the Mexican government, remained as a colonist, joined the Texas army in 1836 as a lieutenant, became a colonel in 1837, but retired to serve in the government. A few years after the expedition of 1843, which Gregg describes, he engaged in prospecting and mining in California, Texas, and Arizona. He was killed by Apaches near Vulture, Arizona.

camp—left by his troops in the hurly-burly of their precipitate retreat.[11]

Keeping beyond the territory of the United States, the right of the Texans to harass the commerce of Mexicans will hardly be denied, as they were at open war; yet another consideration, it would seem, should have restrained them from aggressions in that quarter. They could not have been ignorant that but a portion of the traders were Mexicans—that many American citizens were connected in the same caravans. The Texans assert, it is true, that the lives and property of Americans were to be respected, *provided* they abandoned the Mexicans. But did they reflect upon the baseness of the terms they were imposing? What American, worthy of the name, to save his own interests, or even his life, could deliver up his travelling companions to be sacrificed? Then, after having abandoned the Mexicans, or betrayed them to their enemy—for such an act would have been accounted treachery—where would they have gone? They could not then have continued on into Mexico; and to have returned to the United States with their merchandise, would have been the ruin of most of them.

The inhuman outrages suffered by those who were captured in New Mexico in 1841, among whom were many of the present party, have been pleaded in justification of this second Texan expedition. When we take their grievances into consideration, we must admit that they palliate, and indeed justify almost any species of revenge consistent with the laws of Nature and of nations: yet whether, under the existing circumstances, this invasion of the Prairies was proper or otherwise, I will leave for others to determine, as there seems to be a difference of opinion on the subject. The following considerations, however, will go to demonstrate the unpropitious consequences which are apt to result from a system of indiscriminate revenge.

The unfortunate Chavez (whose murder, I suppose, was perpetrated under pretext of the cruelties suffered by the Texans, in the name of whom the party of M'Daniel was organized) was of the most wealthy and influential family of New Mexico, and one that was anything but friendly to the ruling governor, Gen. Armijo. Don

[11] Additional details of this expedition appear in Henderson K. Yoakum, *History of Texas*, II, 399–405.

Mariano Chavez, a brother to the deceased, is a gentleman of very amiable character, such as is rarely to be met with in that unfortunate land. It is asserted that he furnished a considerable quantity of provisions, blankets, etc., to Col. Cooke's division of Texan prisoners.[12] Señora Chavez (the wife of Don Mariano), as is told, crossed the river from the village of Padillas, the place of their residence, and administered comforts to the unfortunate band of Texans. Though the murder of young Chavez was evidently not sanctioned by the Texans generally, it will, notwithstanding, have greatly embittered this powerful family against them—a family whose liberal principles could not otherwise have been very unfavorable to Texas.[13]

The attack upon the village of Mora, though of less important results, was nevertheless an unpropitiatory movement. The inhabitants of that place are generally very simple and innocent rancheros and hunters, and, being separated by the snowy mountains from the principal settlements of New Mexico, their hearts seem ever to have been inclined to the Texans. In fact, the village having been founded by some American Denizens, the Mexican inhabitants appear in some degree to have imitated their character.

The defeat of Armijo's vanguard was attended by still more disastrous consequences, both to the American and Texan interest. That division was composed of the militia of the North—from about Taos—many of them Taos Pueblos. These people had not only remained embittered against Gov. Armijo since the revolution of 1837, but had always been notably in favor of Texas. So loth were they to fight the Texans, that, as I have been assured, the governor found it necessary to bind a number of them upon their horses, to prevent their escape, till he got them fairly upon the prairies. And yet the poor fellows were compelled to suffer the vengeance which was due to their guilty general!

When the news of their defeat reached Taos, the friends and rel-

[12] Colonel William G. Cooke (1808–47) came to Texas from Virginia. As one of the commissioners appointed to negotiate with the New Mexicans, he was unsuspectingly maneuvered into surrendering his party to Damasio Salazar at Antón Chico and was held until June 16, 1842. Returning to Texas, he became adjutant general of the militia until his death.

[13] This family is very distinct from one Manuel Chávez (who, though Gov. Armijo's nephew, is a very low character), a principal agent in the treacheries practised upon the Texan Santa Fé expedition.—GREGG.

atives of the slain—the whole population indeed, were incensed beyond measure; and two or three naturalized foreigners who were supposed to favor the cause of Texas, and who were in good standing before, were now compelled to flee for their lives; leaving their houses and property a prey to the incensed rabble. Such appears to have been the reaction of public sentiment resulting from the catastrophe upon the Prairies!

Had the Texans proceeded differently—had they induced the Mexicans to surrender without battle, which they might no doubt easily have accomplished, they could have secured their services, without question, as guides to Gen. Armijo's camp, and that unmitigated tyrant might himself have fallen into their hands. The difficulty of maintaining order among the Texans was perhaps the cause of many of their unfortunate proceedings. And no information of the caravan having been obtained, a detachment of seventy or eighty men left, to return to Texas.

The traders arrived soon after, escorted by about two hundred U. S. Dragoons under the command of Capt. Cook.[14] Col. Snively with a hundred men being then encamped on the south side of the Arkansas river, some ten to fifteen miles below the point called the 'Caches,' he crossed the river and met Capt. Cook, who soon made known his intention of disarming him and his companions,—an intention which he at once proceeded to put into execution. A portion of the Texans, however, deceived the American captain in this wise. Having concealed their own rifles, which were mostly Colt's repeaters, they delivered to Capt. Cook the worthless fusils they had taken from the Mexicans; so that, when they were afterwards released, they still had their own valuable arms; of which, however, so far as the caravan in question was concerned, they appear to have had no opportunity of availing themselves.

These facts are mentioned merely as they are said to have occurred. Capt. Cook has been much abused by the Texans, and accused of having violated a friendly flag—of having taken Col. Snively prisoner while on a friendly visit. This is denied by Capt. Cook, and by other persons who were in company at the time. But apart from the means employed by the American commander (the

[14] Philip St. George Cooke. See above, Vol. I, chap. 1, n. 26.

propriety or impropriety of which I shall not attempt to discuss), the act was evidently the salvation of the Santa Fé caravan, of which a considerable portion were Americans. Had he left the Texans with their arms, he would doubtless have been accused by the traders of escorting them to the threshold of danger, and then delivering them over to certain destruction, when he had it in his power to secure their safety.

Capt. Cook with his command soon afterward returned to the United States,[15] and with him some forty of the disarmed Texans, many of whom have been represented as gentlemen worthy of a better destiny. A large portion of the Texans steered directly home from the Arkansas river; while from sixty to seventy men, who elected Warfield their commander, were organized for the pursuit and capture of the caravan, which had already passed on some days in advance towards Santa Fé. They pursued in the wake of the traders, it is said, as far as the Point of Rocks (twenty miles—east of the crossing of the Colorado or Canadian), but made no attempt upon them whence they returned direct to Texas. Thus terminated the 'Second Texan Santa Fé Expedition,' as it has been styled; and though not so disastrous as the first, it turned out nearly as unprofitable.

Although this expedition was composed wholly of Texans, or persons not claiming to be citizens of the United States, and organized entirely in Texas—and, notwithstanding the active measures adopted by the United States government to defend the caravans, as well of Mexicans as of Americans, against their enemy— Señor Bocanegra, Mexican Minister of Foreign Relations,[16] made a formal demand upon the United States (as will be remembered), for dam-

[15] As U. S. troops cannot go beyond our boundary, which, on this route is the Arkansas river, these escorts afford but little protection to the caravans. Such an extensive, uninhabitable waste as the great prairies are, ought certainly to be under maritime regulations. Some international arrangements should be made between the United States and Texas or Mexico (accordingly as the proprietorship of the region beyond our boundary may be settled), whereby the armies of either might indiscriminately range upon this desert, as ships of war upon the ocean.—GREGG.

[16] José María Bocanegra, a Liberal, came into power with President Guerrero. He was minister of interior and foreign affairs and acting president in 1829, minister of the treasury in 1833, and minister of foreign affairs again in 1842.

ages resulting from this invasion. In a rejoinder to Gen. Thompson[17] (alluding to Snively's company), he says, that "Independence, in Missouri, was the starting point of these men." The preceding narrative will show the error under which the honorable secretary labored.

A portion of the party who killed Chavez was from the frontier of Missouri; but witness the active exertions on the border to bring these depredators to justice—and then let the contrast be noted betwixt this affair and the impunity with which robberies are every day committed throughout Mexico, where well-known highwaymen often run at large, unmolested either by the citizens or by the authorities. What would Señor Bocanegra say if every other government were to demand indemnity for all the robberies committed upon their citizens in Mexico?

But the most unfortunate circumstance attending this invasion of the Prairies—unfortunate at least to the United States and to New Mexico—was the closing of the Northern ports to foreign commerce, which was doubtless, to a great degree, a consequence of the beforementioned expedition, and, which of course terminated the Santa Fé Trade, at least for the present.[18]

I am of the impression, however, that little apprehension need be entertained, that this decree of Gen. Santa Anna will be permitted much longer to continue,[19] unless our peaceful relations with Mexico should be disturbed; an event, under any circumstances, seriously to

[17] Waddy Thompson (1798–1868), a South Carolina legislator, member of Congress, and (1842–44) United States minister to Mexico. On his return to the United States he published his *Recollections of Mexico* (New York, Wiley & Putnam, 1846).

[18] The following is the substance of Santa Anna's decree, dated at his palace of Tacubaya, August 7, 1843:

"Article 1st. The frontier custom-houses of Taos, in the department of New Mexico, Paso del Norte and Presidio del Norte in that of Chihuahua, are entirely closed to all commerce.

"Art. 2d. This decree shall take effect within forty-five days after its publication in the capital of the Republic."

It should be understood that the only port in New Mexico for the introduction of foreign goods was nominally Taos, though the custom-house was at Santa Fé, where all the entrances were made.—GREGG.

[19] These northern ports have since been reopened by decree of March 31, 1844; and about ninety wagons, with perhaps $200,000 cost of goods, (and occupying 150 to 200 men), crossed the plains to Santa Fé, during the following summer and fall.—GREGG.

be deprecated. With the continuation of peace between us, the Mexicans will certainly be compelled to open their northern frontier ports, to avoid a revolution in New Mexico, with which they are continually threatened while this embargo continues. Should the obnoxious decree be repealed, the Santa Fé Trade will doubtless be prosecuted again with renewed vigor and enterprise.

CHAPTER X

GEOGRAPHY OF THE PRAIRIES

Extent of the Prairies—Mountains—*Mesas* or Table-lands—*El Llano Estacado*—*Cañones*—Their annoyance to the early Caravans—Immense Gullies—Coal Mines and other geological Products—Gypsum—Metallic Minerals—Salines—Capt. Boone's Exploration—'Salt Plain' and 'Salt Rock'—Mr. Sibley's Visit—Saline Exudations—Unhabitableness of the high Prairies—Excellent Pasturage—Rich border Country sufficient for two States—Northern Texas—Rivers of the Prairies—Their Unfitness for Navigation—Timber—Cross Timbers—Encroachments of the Timber upon the Prairies—Fruits and Flowers—Salubrity of Climate.

WHILE I HAVE ENDEAVORED in the preceding pages to give the reader some general idea of life upon the Prairies, I feel that I have wholly failed thus far to convey any adequate notions of their natural history. I propose in the following pages to repair this deficiency as far as I am able, and to present a rapid sketch of the vastness of those mighty territories; of their physical geography; and of the life, as well vegetable as animal, which they sustain. It is to be regretted that this ample field for observation should have received so little of the consideration of scientific men; for there is scarcely a province in the whole wide range of Nature's unexplored domains, which is so worthy of study, and yet has been so little studied by the natural philosopher.

If we look at the Great Western Prairies, independently of the political powers to which portions of them respectively belong, we shall find them occupying the whole of that extensive territory lying between the spurs of the Rocky Mountains on the north, and the rivers of Texas on the south—a distance of some seven or eight hundred miles in one direction; and from the frontiers of Missouri and Arkansas on the east to the eastern branches of the southern Rocky Mountains on the west—about six hundred miles in the transverse direction: the whole comprising an area of about 400,000 square miles, some 30,000 of which are within the original limits of Texas, and 70,000 in those of New Mexico (if we extend them east to the United States boundary,) leaving about 300,000 in the territory of the United States.

This vast territory is not interrupted by any important mountainous elevations, except along the borders of the great western sierras, and by some low, craggy ridges about the Arkansas frontier —skirts of the Ozark mountains. There is, it is true, high on the dividing ridge between Red River and the False Washita, a range of hills, the southwestern portion of which extends about to the 100th degree of longitude west from Greenwich; that is, to the United States boundary line. These are generally called the Witchita mountains, but sometimes *Towyash* by hunters, perhaps from *tóyavist*, the Comanche word for mountain.[1] I inquired once of a Comanche Indian how his nation designated this range of mountains, which was then in sight of us. He answered, "*Tóyavist*." "But this simply means a mountain," I replied. "How do you distinguish this from any other mountain?" "There are no other mountains in the Comanche territory," he rejoined—"none till we go east to your country, or south to Texas, or west to the land of the Mexican."

With these exceptions, there are scarcely any elevations throughout these immense plains which should be dignified by the title of mountains. Those seen by the Texan Santa Fé Expedition about the sources of Red River, were without doubt the *cejas* or brows of the elevated table plains with which the Prairies abound, and which, when viewed from the plain below, often assume the appearance of formidable mountains; but once upon their summit, the spectator sees another vast plain before him.

These *table-lands*, or *mesas*, as the Mexicans term them, of which

[1] More likely from the Taovayas. The Wichita Mountains (in southwestern Oklahoma were known first as the Jumano and later as the Towyash, all three names having also been applied to the Taovayas (Pawnee Pict) Indians.

there are many thousands of square miles lying between the frontier of the United States and the Rocky Mountains, are level plains, elevated a considerable distance above the surrounding country, and may be likened to the famous steppes of Asia. They are cut up with numerous streams, the largest of which are generally bordered for several miles back by hilly uplands, which are for the most part sandy, dry and barren.

The most notable of the great *plateaux* of the Prairies is that known to Mexicans as *El Llano Estacado,* which is bounded on the north by the Canadian river—extends east about to the United States boundary, including the heads of the False Washita and other branches of Red River—and spreads southward to the sources of Trinity, Brazos and Colorado rivers, and westward to Rio Pecos. It is quite an elevated and generally a level plain, without important hills or ridges, unless we distinguish as such the craggy breaks of the streams which border and pierce it. It embraces an area of about 30,000 square miles, most of which is without water during three-fourths of the year; while a large proportion of its few perennial streams are too brackish to drink of.

I have been assured by Mexican hunters and Indians, that, from Santa Fé southeastward, there is but one route upon which this plain can be safely traversed during the dry season; and even some of the watering-places on this are at intervals of fifty to eighty miles, and hard to find. Hence the Mexican traders and hunters, that they might not lose their way and perish from thirst, once staked out this route across the plain, it is said; whence it has received the name of *El Llano Estacado,* or the Staked Plain.[2]

In some places the brows of these *mesas* approach the very borders of the streams. When this occurs on both sides, it leaves deep chasms or ravines between, called by the Mexicans *cañones,* and which abound in the vicinity of the mountains. The Canadian river flows through one of the most remarkable of these cañones for a distance of more than fifty miles—extending from the road of the Missouri caravans downward—throughout the whole extent of which the gorge is utterly impassable for wagons, and almost so for animals.

[2] See above, Vol. II, chap. 3, n. 3.

Intersecting the direct route from Missouri, this cañon was a source of great annoyance to some of the pioneers in the Santa Fé trade. In 1825, a caravan with a number of wagons reached it about five miles below the present ford. The party was carelessly moving along, without suspecting even a ravine at hand, as the bordering plains were exceedingly level, and the opposite margins of equal height, when suddenly they found themselves upon the very brink of an immense precipice, several hundred yards deep, and almost perpendicular on both sides of the river. At the bottom of those cliffs, there was, as is usually the case, a very narrow but fertile valley, through which the river wound its way, sometimes touching the one bluff and sometimes the other.

Ignorant of a ford so near above, the caravan turned towards the crossing of the former traders. "We travelled fifty miles," says Mr. Stanley, who was of the caravan, "the whole of which distance the river is bound in by cliffs several hundred feet high, in many places nearly perpendicular. We at length came to the termination of the table land; but what a scene presented itself! The valley below could only be reached by descending a frightful cliff of from 1200 to 1500 feet, and more or less precipitous. After a search of several hours, a practicable way was found; and, with the greatest fatigue and exertion, by locking wheels, holding on with ropes, and literally lifting the wagons down in places, we finally succeeded in reaching the bottom.[3] . . . . How did the Canadian and other streams in New Mexico sink themselves to such immense depths in the solid rock? It seems impossible that the water should have worn away the rock while as hard as in its present state. What a field of speculation for the geologist, in the propositions—Were the chasms made for the streams, or did the streams make the chasms? Are they not of volcanic origin?"

Nor are the flat prairies always free from this kind of annoyance to travellers. They are not unfrequently intersected by diminutive chasms or water-cuts, which, though sometimes hardly a rod in width, are often from fifty to a hundred feet deep. These little cañones are washed out by the rains, in their descent to the bordering

[3] In the vicinity of present Conchas Dam Reservoir, San Miguel County, New Mexico.

streams, which is soon effected after an opening is once made through the surface; for though the clayey foundation is exceedingly firm and hard while dry, it seems the most soluble of earths, and melts almost as rapidly as snow under the action of water. The tenacious turf of the 'buffalo grass,' however, retains the marginal surface, so that the sides are usually perpendicular—indeed, often shelving inward at the base, and therefore utterly impassable. I have come unsuspectingly upon the verge of such a chasm; and though, to a stranger, the appearance would indicate the very head of the ravine, I would sometimes be compelled to follow its meandering course for miles without being able to double its 'breaks.' These I have more especially observed high on the borders of the Canadian.

The geological constitution of the Prairies is exceedingly diversified. Along the eastern border, especially towards the north, there is an abundance of limestone, interspersed with sandstone, slate, and many extensive beds of bituminous coal. The coal is particularly abundant in some of the regions bordering the Neosho river; where there are also said to be a few singular bituminous or 'tar springs,'[4] as they are sometimes called by the hunters. There are also many other mineral, and particularly sulphur springs, to be met with.

Further westward, the sandstone prevails; but some of the table plains are based upon strata of a sort of friable calcareous rock, which has been denominated 'rotten limestone:' yet along the borders of the mountains the base of the plains seems generally to be of trap and greenstone. From the waters of Red River to the southwest corner of Missouri, throughout the range of the Ozark mountains, granite, limestone, flint and sandstone prevail. But much of the middle portion of the Prairies is without any apparent rocky foundation—we sometimes travel for days in succession without seeing even as much as a pebble.

On passing towards Santa Fé in 1839, and returning in 1840, I observed an immense range of plaster of Paris, both north and south of the Canadian river, and between thirty and fifty miles east of the United States western boundary. The whole country seemed based upon this fossil, and cliffs and huge masses of it were seen in every

---

[4] One such is on Tar Creek, 2 miles south of Picher, in Ottawa County, Oklahoma. Bituminous coal is now mined in several eastern Oklahoma counties.

direction. It ranges from the coarsest compact sulphate of lime or ordinary plaster, to the most transparent gypsum or selenite, of which last there is a great abundance. By authentic accounts from other travellers, this range of gypsum extends, in a direction nearly north, almost to the Arkansas river.

Of metallic minerals, iron, lead, and perhaps copper, are found on the borders of the Prairies; and it is asserted that several specimens of silver ores have been met with on our frontier, as well as about the Witchita and the Rocky Mountains. Gold has also been found, no doubt, in different places; yet it is questionable whether it has anywhere been discovered in sufficient abundance to render it worth the seeking. Some trappers have reported an extensive gold region about the sources of the Platte river; yet, although recent search has been made, it has not been discovered.

The most valuable perhaps, and the most abundant mineral production of the Prairies is *Salt*. In the Choctaw country, on the waters of Red River, there are two salt-works in operation; and in the Cherokee nation salt springs are numerous, three or four of which are now worked on a small scale; yet a sufficient quantity of salt might easily be produced to supply even the adjoining States. The *Grand Saline*, about forty miles above Fort Gibson, near the Neosho river,[5] was considered a curiosity of its kind, before its natural beauties were effaced by 'improvements.' In the border of a little valley, a number of small salt springs break out, around the orifice of each of which was formed, in the shape of a pot, a kind of calcareous saline concretion. None of the springs are very bold, but the water is strong, and sufficiently abundant for extensive works.

There have been several *Salines*, or mines (if we may so term them) of pure salt, discovered in different parts of the Prairies. The most northern I have heard of, is fifty or sixty miles west of the Missouri river, and thirty or forty south of the Platte, near a tributary called the Saline;[6] where the Otoes and other Indians procure salt. It is described as resembling the *salinas* of New Mexico, and the quantity of salt is inexhaustible. South of the Arkansas river and

[5] On the east bank of the Neosho (Grand River) and about 2 miles southwest of Salina, in Mayes County, Oklahoma.
[6] In Saline County, Nebraska.

a degree or two further westward, there are several of these salines, which are perhaps still more extensive.

I have been favored with some extracts from the journal of Capt. Nathan Boone[7] of the United States' Dragoons, who made an exploring tour through those desolate regions during the summer of 1843. In his journey, between the Canadian and Upper Arkansas, he found efflorescent salt in many places, as well as a superabundance of strongly impregnated salt-water; but, besides these, he visited two considerable salines.

Of the first, which he calls the 'Salt Plain,'[8] he remarks, that "the approach was very gratifying, and from the appearance one might expect to find salt in a solid mass, for the whole extent of the plain, of several feet in thickness." This is situated in the forks of the Salt Fork of the Arkansas. The plain is described as being level as a floor, and evidently sometimes overflowed by the streams which border it. Yet the extent of salt, it would seem, did not realize Capt. Boone's anticipations, as he remarks that it was covered "with the slightest possible film of crystallized salt on the surface, enough to make it white." But he explored only a small portion of the plain, which was very extensive.

However, the most wonderful saline is the great *Salt Rock*, which he found further to the southwestward on the main Red Fork.[9] "The whole cove on the right of the two forks of the river," says Capt. Boone, "appears to be one immense salt spring of water so much concentrated, that, as soon as it reaches the point of breaking forth, it begins depositing its salt. In this way a large crust, or rock is formed all over the bottom for perhaps 160 acres. Digging through the sand for a few inches anywhere in this space, we could find the solid salt, so hard that there was no means in our power of getting up a block of it. We broke our mattock in the attempt. In

[7] Capt. Boone is a son of the late Col. Daniel Boone, the celebrated pioneer of the West. Being of practical habits, and of extensive experience upon those deserts, much weight is due to his observations.—GREGG.

[8] The Great Salt Plain, south of the Salt Fork of the Arkansas in Alfalfa County, Oklahoma, is now a reservoir and the environs a wildlife refuge.

[9] The Great Salt Rock is a thick crust of salt along the Cimarron River (formerly known as the Red Fork of the Arkansas) in Woodward and Harper counties, Oklahoma. In the same vicinity is Salt Spring, a station on the Atchison, Topeka and Santa Fe Railroad.

many places, through this rock-salt crust the water boiled up as clear as crystal . . . . . . but so salt that our hands, after being immersed in it and suffered to dry, became as white as snow. Thrusting the arm down into these holes, they appeared to be walled with salt as far down as one could reach. The cliffs which overhang this place are composed of red clay and gypsum, and capped with a stratum of the latter. . . . . . . We found this salt a little bitter from the impurities it contained, probably Epsom salts principally." As it is overhung with sulphate of lime, and perhaps also based upon the same, might not this 'salt-rock' be heavily impregnated with this mineral, occasioning its excessive hardness? Capt. Boone also speaks of gypsum in various other places, both north and south of this, during his travel.

Mr. Sibley[10] (then of Fort Osage), who was quite familiar with the western prairies, visited a saline, over thirty years ago, which would seem to be the 'Salt Plain' first mentioned by Capt. Boone. The former, it is true, found the salt much more abundant than as described by the latter; but this may be owing to Capt. Boone's not having penetrated as far as the point alluded to by Mr. Sibley,—whose description is in the following language:[11]

"The Grand Saline is situated about 280 miles southwest of Fort Osage, between two forks of a small branch of the Arkansas, one of which washes its southern extremity, and the other, the principal one, runs nearly parallel, within a mile of its opposite side. It is a hard level plain of reddish colored sand, and of an irregular or mixed figure. Its greatest length is from northwest to southeast, and its circumference about thirty miles. From the appearance of the driftwood that is scattered over, it would seem the whole plain is at times inundated by the overflowing of the streams that pass near it. This plain is entirely covered in dry hot weather, from two to six inches deep with a crust of beautiful cléan white salt, of a quality rather superior to the imported blown salt. It bears a striking resemblance to a field of brilliant snow after a rain, with a light crust on its top."

This is, in extent and appearance, nearly as described by several hunters and Indian traders with whom I have conversed. Col. Lo-

[10] George C. Sibley. See above, Vol. I, chap. 2, n. 9.

[11] Brackenbridge's [sic] Voyage up the Missouri River, p. 205.—GREGG.
[Henry Marie Brackenridge, *Journal of a Voyage up the River Missouri in 1811* (Baltimore, Coale & Maxwell, 1815), 205.]

gan, a worthy former agent of the Creek Indians,[12] visited no doubt the same, not far from the same period; and he describes it in a similar manner—only representing the depth of the salt as greater. Everywhere that he dug through the stratum of earth about the margin, at the depth of a few inches he came to a *rock of solid salt*, which induced him to believe that the whole country thereabouts was based upon a stratum of 'rock salt.' This was of a reddish cast, partaking of the color of the surface of the surrounding country. Mr. Sibley remarks that "the distance to a navigable branch of Arkansas is about eighty miles"—referring perhaps to the Red Fork; though the saline is no doubt at a still less distance from the main stream.

With such inexhaustible mines of salt within two or three days' journey of the Arkansas river, and again within the same distance of the Missouri, which would cost no further labor than the digging it up and the transportation of it to boats for freighting it down those streams, it seems strange that they should lie idle, while we are receiving much of our supplies of this indispensable commodity from abroad.

Besides the *salines* already mentioned, there is one high on the Canadian river, some two hundred miles east of Santa Fé. Also, it is said, there are some to be found on the waters of Red River; and numerous others are no doubt scattered throughout the same regions, which have never been discovered.

Many of the low valleys of all the western streams (Red River as well as Arkansas and its branches), are impregnated with salinous qualities, and, during wet weather, ooze saltish exudations, which effloresce in a thin scum. This is sometimes pure salt, but more frequently compounded of different salts—not only of the muriate, but of the sulphate of soda, and perhaps magnesia; often strongly tinctured with nitre. Some of the waters of these sections (particularly when stagnant) are so saturated with this compound during dry weather, that they are insupportable even for brutes—much to the consternation of a forlorn traveller. In these saline flats nothing grows but hard wiry grass, which a famished beast will scarcely eat.

[12] Colonel James Logan was agent for the Creeks in Indian Territory from about 1838 to 1842 and from 1844 to 1849.

It is from these exudations, as well as from the salines or salt plains before mentioned, that our western waters, especially from Arkansas to Red River, acquire their brackishness during the low seasons; and not from the mountains, as some have presumed. Such as issue from thence are there as pure, fresh and crystalline as snow-fed rills and icy fountains can make them.

It will now readily be inferred that the Great Prairies from Red River to the western sources of the Missouri, are, as has before been intimated, chiefly uninhabitable—not so much for want of wood (though the plains are altogether naked), as of soil and of water; for though some of the plains appear of sufficiently fertile soil, they are mostly of a sterile character, and all too dry to be cultivated. These great steppes seem only fitted for the haunts of the mustang, the buffalo, the antelope, and their migratory lord, the prairie Indian. Unless with the progressive influence of time, some favorable mutation should be wrought in nature's operations, to revive the plains and upland prairies, the occasional fertile valleys are too isolated and remote to become the abodes of civilized man.

Like the table plains of Northern Mexico, these high prairies could at present only be made available for grazing purposes, and that in the vicinity of the water-courses. The grass with which they are mostly clothed, is of a superior quality. The celebrated 'buffalo grass' is of two kinds, both of which are species of the *grama* of New Mexico, and equally nutritious at all seasons. It is the same, I believe, that is called 'mezquite grass' in Texas, from the mezquite tree which grows there in the same dry regions with it.[13] Of this unequalled pasturage the great western prairies afford a sufficiency to graze cattle for the supply of all the United States. It is particularly adapted to sheep-raising, as is shown by example of the same species in New Mexico.

But from the general sterility and unhabitableness of the Prairies is excepted, as will be understood, that portion, already alluded to, which borders our western frontier. The uplands from the Arkansas boundary to the Cross Timbers, are everywhere beautifully interspersed with isolated prairies and glades, many of which are fertile,

[13] The so-called mesquite grasses include the grama *(Bouteloua oligostachya)*, but buffalo grass *(Buchloë dactyloides)* is of another genus.

though some are too flat, and consequently inclined to be marshy. The valleys of the streams are principally of a rich loam, rather subject to inundations, but mostly tillable. The timbered uplands are mostly of fair quality, except on the broken ridges and mountainous sections before referred to. Some of the uplands, however, known usually as 'post-oak flats,' like the marshy prairies, seem to be based upon quick-sand. The soil is of a dead unproductive character, and covered with small lumps or mounds of various sizes, and of irregular shapes.

The country lying west of Missouri, which includes the sources of the Neosho, the Verdigris, the Marais-des-Cygnes and other branches of the Osage, and the lower sections of the Kansas river, vies with any portion of the Far West in the amenity of its upland prairies—in the richness of its alluvial bottoms—in the beauty and freshness of its purling rills and rivulets—and in the salubrity of its atmosphere.

We have here, then, along the whole border, a strip of country, averaging at least two hundred miles wide by five hundred long—and even more if we extend it up the Missouri river—affording territory for two States, respectable in size, and though more scant in timber, yet more fertile, in general, than the two conterminous States of Missouri and Arkansas. But most of this delightful region has been ceded to the different tribes of the Frontier Indians.

Concerning that portion of the Prairies which lies south of Red River, in Northern Texas, I learn from some interesting memoranda, politely furnished me by Dr. Henry Connelly, one of the principals of the pioneer expedition from Chihuahua to Arkansas, of which I have already spoken, that, besides some beautiful lands among the Cross Timbers, there is a great deal of delightful country still further west, of a part of which that gentleman holds the following language:—"Between the Brazos and Red River, there is surely the most beautiful and picturesque region I have ever beheld. I saw some of the finest timber, generally oak—not that scrubby oak which characterizes so much of the Texan territory—but large black and bur-oak; such as would answer all the purposes for which the largest timber is useful. Between those two rivers, no doubt there is destined to be one of the most dense and prosperous settlements.

The fertility of the soil is not exceeded by any I have seen; and, from the high and undulating character of the country, there can be no doubt of its being very healthy."

To the westward of Rio Brazos, and south of some sandy and saline regions which border the upper portions of this stream, the same enterprising traveller represents many of the valleys as rich and beautiful, and the uplands as being in many places sparsely timbered with mezquite trees. This is particularly the case on the sources of the Colorado,[14] where the country is delightfully watered. But immediately north of this sets in that immense desert region of the Llano Estacado.

The chief natural disadvantage to which the Great Western Prairies are exposed, consists in the absence of navigable streams. Throughout the whole vast territory which I have been attempting to describe, there is not a single river, except the Missouri, which is navigable during the whole season. The remaining streams, in their course through the plains, are and must continue to be, for all purposes of commerce, comparatively useless.

The chief of these rivers are the Missouri, the Arkansas, and Red River, with their numerous tributaries. The principal western branches of the Missouri are the Yellow Stone, the Platte and the Kansas. Small 'flats' and 'buffalo boats' have passed down the two former for a considerable distance, during high water; but they are never navigable to any extent by steamboats.

The *Arkansas* river penetrates far into the the Rocky Mountains, its ramifications, interlocking with some of the waters of the Missouri, Columbia, San Buenaventura,[15] Colorado of the West, and Rio del Norte. The channel of this stream, in its course through the Prairies, is very wide and shallow, with banks in many places hardly five feet above low water. It will probably measure nearly 2000 miles in length, from its source to the frontier of Arkansas. It is called *Rio Napeste* by the Mexicans; but among the early French voyagers it

---

[14] The Colorado River of Texas, not to be confused with the Red or the Canadian, which were sometimes called by the same name.

[15] A mythical river of which Gregg probably read in Pike's Journal. It is described as emptying into the Pacific north of California but is mapped as running into an unnamed salt lake, in the vicinity of Lake Sevier, Utah. Coues (ed.), The *Expeditions of Zebulon Montgomery Pike*, II, 733, n. 18.

acquired the name of *Arkansas,* or rather *Akansa,*[16] from a tribe of the Dahcotah or Osage stock, who lived near its mouth. This river has numerous tributaries, some of which are of great length, yet there is not one that is at all navigable, except the Neosho from the north, which has been descended by small boats for at least a hundred miles.

Red River is much shorter and narrower from the frontier westward than the Arkansas, bearing but little over half the volume of water. Even in its serpentine course it can hardly exceed 1200 miles from the Arkansas boundary to its source. This river rises in the table plains of the Llano Estacado, and has not, as I have been assured by traders and hunters, any mountainous elevations about its source of any consequence;[17] although we are continually hearing the inhabitants of its lower borders speak of the *"June freshets* produced by the melting of the snow in the mountains."

The upper portions of this river, and emphatically from the mouth of the False Washita (or Faux Ouachittâ) upward, present little or no facilities for navigation; being frequently spread out over sand-bars to the width of several hundred yards. A very credible Indian trader, who had been on Red River some two hundred miles above the False Washita, informed me, that, while in some places he found it not over fifty yards wide, in others it was at least five hundred. This and most other prairie streams have commonly very low banks with remarkably shallow channels, which, during droughts, sometimes go dry in their transit through the sandy plains.[18]

It would be neither interesting nor profitable to present to my

[16] A stranger would be led to suppose we were without a system of orthography, from the fact of our so generally adopting the French spelling of Indian names, whereby all sight is soon lost of the original. The French first corrupt them, and we, by adapting our pronunciation to their orthography, at once transform them into new names. Thus 'polite usage' has converted into *Arkan'sas* the plural of the primitive *Arkansa* or *Arkonsah;* though an approximate *Ar'kansaw,* is still the current 'vulgar' pronunciation. *Osage* and a great many others have suffered similar metamorphoses.—GREGG.

[17] Gregg was one of the first writers to locate the headwaters of the Red River correctly.

[18] Of all the rivers of this character, the Cimarron, being on the route from Missouri to Santa Fé, has become the most famous. Its water disappears in the sand and reappears again, in so many places, that some travellers have contended that it 'ebbs and flows' periodically. This is doubtless owing to the fact, that the little

readers a detailed account of all the tributaries of the three principal rivers already mentioned. They may be found for the most part laid down, with their bearings and relative magnitudes, upon the map which accompanies this work. It is only necessary to say in addition, that none of them can ever be availed of to any considerable extent for purposes of navigation.

With regard to the productions of the soil of these regions, the reader will probably have formed, in the main, a tolerably correct idea already; nevertheless a few further specifications may not be altogether unacceptable.

The timber of that portion of the United States territory which is included between the Arkansas frontier and the Cross Timbers, throughout the highlands, is mostly oak of various kinds, of which black-jack and post-oak predominate, as these, and especially the former, seem only capable of withstanding the conflagrations to which they are exposed, and therefore abound along the prairie borders. The black-jack presents a blackened, scrubby appearance, with harsh rugged branches—partly on account of being so often scorched and crisped by the prairie fires. About the streams we find an intermixture of elm, hackberry, paccan (or pecan), ash, walnut, mulberry, cherry, persimmon, cottonwood, sycamore, birch, etc., with varieties of hickory, gum, dogwood, and the like. All of the foregoing, except paccan, gum and dogwood, are also found west of

current which may flow above the sand in the night, or in cloudy weather, is kept dried up, in an unshaded channel, during the hot sunny days. But in some places the sand is so porous that the river never flows above it, except during freshets.

I was once greatly surprised upon encountering one of these sandy sections of the river after a tremendous rain-storm. Our caravan was encamped at the 'Lower Cimarron Spring:' and, a little after night-fall, a dismal, murky cloud was seen gathering in the western horizon, which very soon came lowering upon us, driven by a hurricane, and bringing with it one of those tremendous bursts of thunder and lightning, and rain, which render the storms of the Prairies, like those of the tropics, so terrible. Hail-stones, as large as turkeys' eggs, and torrents of rain soon drenched the whole country; and so rapidly were the banks of the river overflowed, that the most active exertions were requisite to prevent the mules that were 'staked' in the valley from drowning. Next morning, after crossing the neck of a bend, we were, at the distance of about three miles, upon the river-bank again; when, to our astonishment, the wetted sand, and an occasional pool, fast being absorbed, were the only vestiges of the recent flood—no water was flowing there!

In these sandy stretches of the Cimarron, and other similar 'dry streams,' travellers procure water by excavating basins in the channel, a few feet deep, into which the water is filtrated from the saturated sand.—GREGG.

Missouri, where, although the uplands are almost wholly prairie, the richest growths predominate in the valleys.

In many of the rich bottoms from the Canadian to Red River, for a distance of one or two hundred miles west of the frontier, is found the celebrated *bois-d'arc* (literally, *bow-wood*),[19] usually corrupted in pronunciation to *bowdark*. It was so named by the French on account of its peculiar fitness for *bows*. This tree is sometimes found with a trunk two or three feet in diameter, but, being much branched, it is rarely over forty or fifty feet high. The leaves are large, and it bears a fruit a little resembling the orange in general appearance, though rougher and larger, being four or five inches in diameter; but it is not used for food. The wood is of a beautiful light orange color, and, though course, is susceptible of polish. It is one of the hardest, firmest and most durable of timbers, and is much used by wagon-makers and millwrights, as well as by the wild Indians, who make bows of the younger growths.

On the Arkansas and especially its southern tributaries as far west as the Verdigris, and up those of Red River nearly to the False Washita, the bottoms are mostly covered with cane. And scattered over all the south to about the same distance westward, the sassafras abounds, which grows here in every kind of soil and locality.

The celebrated *Cross Timbers*, of which frequent mention has been made, extend from the Brazos, or perhaps from the Colorado of Texas, across the sources of Trinity, traversing Red River above the False Washita, and thence west of north, to the Red Fork of Arkansas,[20] if not further. It is a rough hilly range of country, and, though not mountainous, may perhaps be considered a prolongation of that chain of low mountains which pass to the northward of Bexar and Austin city in Texas.[21]

The Cross Timbers vary in width from five to thirty miles, and entirely cut off the communication betwixt the interior prairies and those of the great plains. They may be considered as the 'fringe' of the great prairies, being a continuous brushy strip, composed of

[19] *Maclura aurantiaca*, also known as Osage orange.
[20] The Cimarron.
[21] San Antonio de Béjar (founded 1718), formerly called Béjar or Béxar, is the present San Antonio, Texas. Austin (founded 1839) was made the capital of the republic and later the state.

various kinds of undergrowth; such as black-jacks, post-oaks, and in some places hickory, elm, etc., intermixed with a very diminutive dwarf oak, called by the hunters 'shin-oak.' Most of the timber appears to be kept small by the continual inroads of the 'burning prairies;' for, being killed almost annually, it is constantly replaced by scions of undergrowth; so that it becomes more and more dense every reproduction. In some places, however, the oaks are of considerable size, and able to withstand the conflagrations. The underwood is so matted in many places with grape-vines, green-briars, etc., as to form almost impenetrable 'roughs,' which served as hiding-places for wild beasts, as well as wild Indians; and would, in savage warfare, prove almost as formidable as the hammocks of Florida.

South of the Canadian, a branch of these Cross Timbers projects off westward, extending across this stream, and up its course for 100 miles or so, from whence, it inclines northwest beyond the North Fork, and ultimately ceases, no doubt, in the great sandy plains in that direction.

The region of the Cross Timbers is generally well-watered; and is interspersed with romantic and fertile tracts. The bottoms of the tributaries of Red River, even for some distance west of the Cross Timbers (perhaps almost to the U. S. boundary), are mostly very fertile, and timbered with narrow stripes of elm, hackberry, walnut, hickory, mulberry, bur-oak and other rich growths.

But further north, and west of the Cross Timbers, even the streams are nearly naked. The Cimarron river for more than a hundred miles is absolutely without timber; and the Arkansas, for so large a stream, is remarkably scant. The southern border, being protected from the prairie fires by a chain of sand-hills, which extends for two hundred miles along it, is not so bare as the northern bank; though even here it is only skirted with occasional sparsely set groves of cottonwood in the nooks and bends. It is upon the abundance of islands which intersperse its channel, that the greatest quantity of timber (though purely cottonwood) is to be found; yet withal, there are stretches of miles without a tree in view. The banks of the Canadian are equally naked; and, having fewer islands, the river appears still more barren. In fact, there is scarce anything else but cottonwood, and that very sparsely scattered along the streams, throughout most of the far-western prairies.

It is unquestionably the prairie conflagrations that keep down the woody growth upon most of the western uplands. The occasional skirts and fringes which have escaped their rage, have been protected by the streams they border. Yet may not the time come when these vast plains will be covered with timber? It would seem that the prairie region, long after the discovery of America, extended to the very banks of the Mississippi. Father Marquette, in a voyage down this river, in 1673, after passing below the mouth of the Ohio, remarks:—"The banks of the river began to be covered with high trees, which hindered us from observing the country as we had done all along; but we judged from the bellowing of the oxen (buffalo) that the meadows are very near."[22]—Indeed, there are parts of the southwest now thickly set with trees of good size, that, within the remembrance of the oldest inhabitants, were as naked as the prairie plains; and the appearance of the timber in many other sections indicates that it has grown up within less than a century. In fact, we are now witnessing the encroachment of the timber upon the prairies, wherever the devastating conflagrations have ceased their ravages.

The high plains seem too dry and lifeless to produce timber; yet might not the vicissitudes of nature operate a change likewise upon the seasons? Why may we not suppose that the genial influences of civilization—that extensive cultivation of the earth—might contribute to the multiplication of showers, as it certainly does of fountains? Or that the shady groves, as they advance upon the prairies, may have some effect upon the seasons? At least, many old settlers maintain that the droughts are becoming less oppressive in the West. The people of New Mexico also assure us that the rains have much increased of latter years, a phenomenon which the vulgar superstitiously attribute to the arrival of the Missouri traders. Then may we not hope that these sterile regions might yet be thus revived and fertilized, and their surface covered one day by flourishing settlements to the Rocky Mountains?

[22] Jacques Marquette (1635–75), whose journal was first published in Melchisédech Thévenot's *Recueil de Voyages* (Paris, E. Michallet, 1681). For this quotation see Reuben G. Thwaites (ed.), *The Jesuit Relations and Allied Documents*, LIX, 149.

With regard to fruits, the Prairies are of course not very plentifully supplied. West of the border, however, for nearly two hundred miles, they are covered, in many places, with the wild strawberry; and the groves lining the streams frequently abound in grapes, plums, persimmons, mulberries, paccans, hackberries, and other 'sylvan luxuries.' The high prairies beyond, however, are very bare of fruits. The prickly pear[23] may be found over most of the dry plains; but this is neither very palatable nor wholesome, though often eaten by travellers for want of other fruits. Upon the branches of the Canadian, North Fork, and Cimarron, there are, in places, considerable quantities of excellent plums, grapes, choke-cherries, gooseberries, and currants—of the latter there are three kinds, black, red, and white. About the ravines and marshy grounds (particularly towards the east) there are different kinds of small onions, with which the traveller may season his fresh meats. On the plains, also, I have met with a species resembling garlic in flavor.

But the flowers are among the most interesting products of the frontier prairies. These gay meadows wear their most fanciful piebald robes from the earliest spring till divested of them by the hoary frosts of autumn. When again winter has fled, but before the grassy green appears, or other vegetation has ventured to peep above the earth, they are bespeckled in many places with a species of *erythronium*, a pretty lilaceous little flower, which springs from the ground already developed, between a pair of lanceolate leaves, and is soon after in full bloom.[24] But the floriferous region only extends about two hundred miles beyond the border: the high plains are nearly as destitute of flowers as they are of fruits.

The *climate* of most parts of the Prairies is no doubt healthy in the extreme; for a purer atmosphere is hardly to be found. But the cold rains of the 'wet season,' and the colder snows of winter, with the annoying winds that prevail at nearly all times, often render it very unpleasant. It can hardly be said, it is true, that the Prairies have their regular 'dry and rainy seasons;' yet the summers are often so droughty, that, unless some change should be effected in nature's functions, cultivators would generally find it necessary, no doubt, to

[23] A species of *Opuntia*.
[24] Commonly known as the dog-tooth violet.

resort to irrigation. That portion, however, which is conterminous with our western border, and to the distance of nearly two hundred miles westward, in every respect resembles the adjacent States of Missouri and Arkansas in climate. The south is a little disposed to chills and fevers; but the northern portion is as healthy as the most salubrious uplands of Missouri.

CHAPTER XI
ANIMALS OF THE PRAIRIES

The Mustang or Wild Horse—Capturing him by 'Creasing,' and with the Lazo—Horse-flesh—The Buffalo—Its Appearance—Excellence of its Meat—General Utility to the Indian and Traveller—Prospect of its Extinction—Hunting the Buffalo with Bow and Arrows, the Lance, etc. —'Still-hunting'—The Buffalo ferocious only when wounded—Butchering, etc.—The Gray Wolf—Its Modes of killing Buffalo—Their great Numbers—A 'Wolf-scrape'—The Prairie Wolf, or 'Jackal of the Prairies'—Elk, Deer and Bear—The Antelope—The Bighorn—The Prairie Dog—Owls and Rattlesnakes—The Horned Frog—Fowls— Bees, etc.

THE ZOOLOGY of the Prairies has probably attracted more attention than any other feature of their natural history. This has not arisen altogether from the peculiar interest the animals of the Prairie possess; but they constitute so considerable a portion of the society of the traveller who journeys among them, that they get to hold somewhat the same place in his estimation that his fellow-creatures would occupy if he were in civilization. Indeed, the animals are *par éminence* the communities of the Prairies.

By far the most noble of these, and therefore the best entitled to precedence in the brief notice I am able to present of the animals of those regions, is the *mustang*[1] or wild horse of the Prairies. As he is descended from the stock introduced into America by the first Spanish colonists, he has no doubt a partial mixture of Arabian blood.

---

[1] *Mustang* would most naturally seem a corruption of the Spanish adjective *mostrenco* (without owner), but the Mexicans call wild horses *mesteñas*, a synonyme in one of its senses with *mostrenco*.—GREGG.

Being of domestic origin, he is found of various colors, and sometimes of a beautiful piebald.

It is a singular fact in the economy of nature, that all *wild* animals of the same species should have one uniform color (with only occasional but uniform differences between males and females); while that of the *domestic* animals, whether quadruped or fowl, is more or less diversified.

The beauty of the mustang is proverbial. One in particular has been celebrated by hunters, of which marvellous stories are told. He has been represented as a medium-sized stallion of perfect symmetry, milk-white, save a pair of black ears—a natural 'pacer,' and so fleet, it has been said, as to leave far behind every horse that had been tried in pursuit of him, without breaking his 'pace.' But I infer that this story is somewhat mythical, from the difficulty which one finds in fixing the abiding place of its equine hero. He is familiarly known, by common report, all over the great Prairies. The trapper celebrates him in the vicinity of the northern Rocky Mountains; the hunter, on the Arkansas, or in the midst of the Plains; while others have him pacing at the rate of half a mile a minute on the borders of Texas. It is hardly a matter of surprise, then, that a creature of such an ubiquitary existence should never have been caught.

The wild horses are generally well-formed, with trim and clean limbs; still their elegance has been much exaggerated by travellers, because they have seen them at large, abandoned to their wild and natural gaiety. Then, it is true, they appear superb indeed; but when caught and tamed, they generally dwindle down to ordinary ponies. Large droves are very frequently seen upon the Prairies, sometimes of hundreds together, gambolling and curvetting within a short distance of the caravans. It is sometimes difficult to keep them from dashing among the loose stock of the traveller, which would be exceedingly dangerous; for, once together, they are hard to separate again, particularly if the number of mustangs is much the greatest. It is a singular fact, that the gentlest wagon-horse (even though quite fagged with travel), once among a drove of mustangs, will often acquire in a few hours all the intractable wildness of his untamed companions.

The mustang is sometimes taken by the cruel expedient of 'creasing,' which consists of shooting him through the upper *crease* of the neck, above the cervical vertebrae; when, the ball cutting a principal nerve, he falls as suddenly as if shot in the brain, and remains senseless for a few minutes, during which he is secured with a rope. He soon recovers from the shock, however, and springs to his feet, but finds himself deprived of his liberty. He is easily tamed after this, and the wound heals without leaving any physical injury. But 'creasing' is so nice an operation that many are killed in the attempt. If the ball pass a little low, it fractures a vertebra and kills the poor brute instantly.

But the most usual mode, among the Mexicans and Indians, of taking the *mesteña* (as the former call these animals), is with the lazo. They pursue them on fleet horses, and great numbers are thus noosed and tamed. The mustang has been taken in Texas in considerable numbers by preparing a strong pen at some passway or crossing of a river, into which they are frightened and caught.

Upon the plains, I once succeeded in separating a gay-looking stallion from his herd of *mesteñas*, upon which he immediately joined our *caballada*, and was directly lazoed by a Mexican. As he curvetted at the end of the rope, or would stop and gaze majestically at his subjecters, his symmetrical proportions attracted the attention of all; and our best jockeys at once valued him at five hundred dollars. But it appeared that he had before been tamed, for he soon submitted to the saddle, and in a few days dwindled down to scarce a twenty-dollar hackney.

Prairie travellers have often been reduced to the necessity of eating the flesh of the mustang; and, when young and tender, it has been accounted savory enough; but, when of full age, it is said to be exceedingly rancid, particularly when fat. They are sometimes hunted by Mexicans for their oil, which is used by the curriers.

The *buffalo*, though making no pretensions to the elegance and symmetry of the mustang, is by far the most important animal of the Prairies to the traveller. It is sufficiently well known that these animals bear but little resemblance to the buffalo of India; but that they are a species of bison, or *bos Americanus*, according to naturalists.

They are called *Cíbolos* by the Mexicans; and it would certainly have prevented ambiguity, had they been distinguished by some other name than buffalo with us.

Their dusky black color becomes much paler during the season of long hair.[2] The phenomenon of a white buffalo has frequently been remarked upon the Prairies; but as the white skin is said to have been used in the mystic ceremonies of many of the northern tribes of Indians, this probably created such a demand for them, that they have become nearly extinct. Their unusual color has commonly been considered a *lusus naturae*, yet it is probable that they stand in about the same relation to the black or brown buffalo that black sheep do to white ones. The horns of the buffalo are short and black, and almost concealed under the frightfully shaggy frontlets of long woolly hair that crown the foreheads of the bulls; which, with the goat-like beard, and ill-shapen hump, form the chief distinction between them and the domestic cattle: in fact, they are so nearly of the same species that they will breed together; though the offspring, like the mule, is said to be unfruitful. Between the males and females there is still a greater disproportion in size than among the domestic cattle. A buffalo cow is about as heavy as a common ox, while a large fat bull will weigh perhaps double as much.

These are very gregarious animals. At some seasons, however, the cows rather incline to keep to themselves; at other times they are mostly seen in the centre of the gang, while the bulls are scattered around, frequently to a considerable distance, evidently guarding the cows and calves. And on the outskirts of the buffalo range, we are apt to meet with small gangs of bulls alone, a day or two's travel distant, as though performing the office of 'piquet guards' for the main herds.

The flesh of the buffalo is, I think, as fine as any meat I ever tasted: the old hunter will not admit that there is anything equal to it. Much of its apparent savoriness, however, results perhaps from our sharpened 'prairie appetites,' and our being usually upon salt provisions awhile before obtaining it. The flesh is of coarser texture than beef, more juicy, and the fat and lean better distributed. This

---

[2] The bulls usually shed in the spring, from the shoulders back, but not in front, which imparts to them quite a lion-like appearance.—GREGG.

meat is also very easy of digestion,[3] possessing even aperient qualities. The circumstance that bulls of all ages, if fat, make good beef, is a further proof of the superiority of buffalo meat. These are generally selected for consumption in the winter and early spring, when the cows, unless barren, are apt to be poor; but during most of the year, the latter are the fattest and tenderest meat. Of these, the udder is held as hardly second to the tongue in delicacy. But what the tail of the beaver is to the trapper, the tongue of the buffalo is to the hunter. Next to this are 'marrow-bones,' the tender-loins, and the hump-ribs. Instead of a gristly substance, as sometimes stated, the hump is produced by a convex tier of vertical ribs, which project from the spine, forming a gradual curve over the shoulders: those of the middle being sometimes nearly two feet in length. The 'veal' is rarely good, being generally poor, owing to the scanty supply of milk which their dams afford, and to their running so much from hunters and wolves.

This animal furnishes almost the exclusive food of the prairie Indians, as well as covering for their wigwams and most of their clothing; also their bedding, ropes, bags for their meat, etc.; sinews for bow-strings, for sewing moccasins, leggins, and the like; besides sustenance for the numerous travellers and trappers who range upon their grazing regions. Were they only killed for food, however, their natural increase would perhaps replenish the loss: yet the continual and wanton slaughter of them by travellers and hunters, and the still greater havoc made among them by the Indians, not only for meat, but often for the skins and tongues alone (for which they find a ready market among their traders), are fast reducing their numbers, and must ultimately effect their total annihilation from the continent. It is believed that the annual 'export' of *buffalo rugs*[4] from the Prairies and bordering 'buffalo range,' is about a hundred thousand: and the number killed wantonly, or exclusively for meat, is no doubt still greater, as the skins are fit to dress scarcely half the year. The vast extent of the prairies upon which they now pasture is no argument against the prospect of their total extinction, when we

---

[3] It has often been remarked by travellers, that however much buffalo meat one may eat, no inconvenience is ever suffered from it.—GREGG.

[4] Often, but it would seem improperly, called 'buffalo *robes*.'—GREGG.

take into consideration the extent of country from which they have already disappeared; for it is well known, that, within the recollection of our oldest pioneers, they were nearly as abundant east of the Mississippi as they now are upon the western prairies; and from history we learn, that they once ranged to the Atlantic coast. Even within thirty years, they were abundant over much of the present States of Missouri and Arkansas; yet they are rarely seen within two hundred miles of the frontier. Indeed, upon the high plains they have sensibly decreased within the last ten years. Nevertheless, the number of buffalo upon the Prairies is still immense. But, as they incline to migrate *en masse* from place to place, it sometimes happens, that, for several days' travel together, not a single one is to be met with; but, in other places, many thousands are often seen at one view.

The Indians, as well as Mexicans, hunt the buffalo mostly with the bow and arrows. For this purpose they train their fleetest horses to run close beside him; and, when near enough, with almost unerring aim, they pierce him with their arrows, usually behind the short ribs, ranging forward, which soon disables and brings him to the ground. When an arrow has been ill-directed, or does not enter deep enough, and even sometimes when it has penetrated a vital part, but is needed to use again, the hunter sometimes rides up and draws it out while the animal is yet running. An athletic Indian will not unfrequently discharge his darts with such force, that I have seen them (30 inches long) wholly buried in the body of a buffalo: and I have been assured by hunters that the arrows, missing the bones, have been known to pass entirely through the huge carcass and fall upon the ground.

The dexterity acquired by these wild hunters in shooting the buffalo, is very surprising. On one occasion, upon the prairies, a party of Witchita Indians were encamped near us; and a drove of buffalo passing in the vicinity, I requested a chief to take my horse and kill one 'upon the shares.' He delighted in the sport: so, gathering his arrows, he mounted the pony, which was slow, and withal very lean, and giving chase, in a few minutes he had two buffaloes lying upon the plain, and two others went off so badly wounded, that, with a little exertion, they might have been secured.

But the dexterity of the Comanches in the buffalo chase is perhaps superior to that of any other tribe. The Mexican *Ciboleros*, however, are scarcely if at all inferior to the Indians in this sport. I once went on a hunting expedition with a Cibolero, who carried no arms except his bow and arrows and a butcher's knife. Espying a herd of buffalo, he put spurs to his horse, and, though I followed as fast as a mule I rode could trudge, when I came up with him, after a chase of two or three miles, he had the buffalo partly skinned! This was rather unusual dispatch, to be sure, for the animal oftener lingers awhile after receiving the fatal dart.

In the chase, the experienced hunter singles out the fattest buffalo as his victim, and having given him a mortal wound, he in like manner selects another, and so on, till the plain is sometimes literally strewed with carcasses.

It seems that Capt. Bonneville[5] marvelled greatly that some Indians, during his peregrinations in the Rocky Mountains, should have killed buffalo "without guns or arrows, and with only an old spear;" and he was no doubt mistaken in supposing "that they had chased the herds of buffalo at full speed, until they tired them down, when they easily dispatched them with the spear." For both Indians and Mexicans often chase with a long-handled spear or lance, which, if the horse be well trained, is still a more expeditious mode of killing them than with the bow and arrow. An expert lancer will enter a drove, and drawing up alongside, will pierce buffalo after buffalo until several are brought down.

In default of bow or lance, they chase with the fusil, but seldom so successfully as with the former weapons. The Americans generally prefer 'running' with the horseman's pistol; yet the Indian is apt to kill double as many with his arrows or lance.

In all these modes of hunting, the buffalo is sometimes dangerous; for, becoming enraged from his wounds, he will often make

[5] Benjamin Louis Eulalie de Bonneville (1796–1878) came to the United States from France, graduated from West Point (1819), and after army duty on the frontier, fur-traded and explored as far west as the Columbia River. He later participated in the Seminole, Mexican, and Civil Wars, being breveted brigadier general in 1865. Gregg refers to the narrative of his exploration as rewritten by Washington Irving, *Rocky Mountains, or Scenes, Incidents and Adventures in the Far West* (2 vols., Philadelphia, Carey, Lea & Blanchard, 1837).

desperate lunges at his pursuer; and, if the horse be not well trained, he may be himself disembowelled, leaving his rider at the mercy of the buffalo, as has happened on some occasions. But if the steed understand his business, he will dodge the animal with the expertness of a fencer.

Buffalo calves (but not full-grown buffalo) are often taken with the lazo by Mexicans and Indians; yet, being separated from their dams and the droves during chases, these simple little creatures not unfrequently take up with the riding animals of the hunters, and follow them to the camp as tamely as though they were their dams. If provided with domestic cows, they may be raised without much difficulty.

Some of the northern Indians, particularly the Assinaboins, are said to practice still a distinct mode of taking the buffalo. A staunch pound is erected at some convenient point, and, after a course of mystic rites by their medicine-men, they start upon the enterprise. A gang of buffalo is frightened towards the pen, while an Indian, covered with one of their woolly skins, runs at a distance ahead. Being seen by the animals, they mistake him for one of their kind, and follow him into the pen. Once secured in the enclosure, they leisurely dispatch them with their arrows, as they are said to believe it would offend the Great Spirit and render future hunts unpropitious to use fire arms in killing their imprisoned game.

However, of all other modes, our backwoodsmen prefer 'still-hunting'—that is stealing upon their game afoot with the rifle. Buffalo are much more easily approached than deer. When the hunter perceives a herd at rest, or quietly feeding, he crawls upon them behind a bank, a shrub, or a tuft of grass, with the greatest facility, provided he 'has the wind of them,' as hunters say—that is, if the wind blows from the buffalo; but if the reverse, he will find it impossible to approach them, however securely he may have concealed himself from their sight. In fact, their scent being acute, they seem to depend more upon it than their sight; for if a gang of buffalo be frightened, from any quarter whatever, they are apt to shape their course against the wind, that they may scent an enemy in their way.

If the hunter succeed in 'bringing down' his first shot, he may frequently kill several out of the same herd; for, should the game neither see nor smell him, they may hear the rifle-cracks, and witness their companions fall one after another, without heeding, except to raise their heads, and perhaps start a little at each report. They would seem to fancy that the fallen are only lying down to rest, and they are loth to leave them. On one occasion, upon the Cimarron river, I saw some ten or a dozen buffaloes lying upon a few acres of ground, all of which had been shot from the same herd by a couple of our hunters. Had not the gang been frightened by the approaching caravan, perhaps a dozen more of them might have fallen.

A dextrous hunter will sometimes 'crawl upon' a gang of buffalo, on a perfectly level plain. As their sight is at best not acute, and is always more or less obscured by the shaggy hair of their foreheads, they will hardly observe an approaching enemy when they are feeding, unless the wind bears them the scent. The hunter is, therefore, careful to 'have the wind' of them, and crawls slowly and closely upon the ground, until within gun-shot. If he bring down the first, the others will perhaps retire a little, when he may sometimes approach behind the fallen buffalo, and shoot several others.

The tenacity of these animals for life is often very extraordinary. When one receives even a mortal shot, he frequently appears not hurt—he seems to disdain to flinch—but will curl his tail and step about as though he neither felt nor feared anything! If left undisturbed however, he begins to stagger, and in a few moments expires: but if provoked, he might run for miles before he would fall. I have seen a party of hunters around a wounded and enraged bull, fire at a few paces distance, a dozen or two shots, aimed at his very heart, without their seeming to have any effect till his anger cooled, when in an instant he would lie lifeless upon the ground. In such cases, the inexperienced hunter often aims to shoot them in the brain, but without success. Owing not only to the thickness of the scull, but to the matted wool upon it, I have never witnessed an instance of a rifleball's penetrating to the brain of a buffalo bull.

The 'still-hunter' must needs be upon his guard; for the wounded buffalo is prone to make battle, upon the too near approach of his enemy. With a little presence of mind, however, his attacks are easily shunned. If he make a lunge, the pedestrian hunter has only to wheel abruptly to one side; for the animal is apt to pass on in a direct line. I have never heard of a serious accident of the kind; yet some frightful though amusing incidents have occurred in such cases.

The buffalo never attacks, however, except when wounded. Even the largest droves (the opinion of some travellers to the contrary notwithstanding), though in the wildest career, are easily turned from their course by a single man who may intercept their way. I have crouched in the tall grass in the direct route of a frighted gang, when, firing at them on their near approach, they would spread in consternation to either side. Still their advance is somewhat frightful —their thundering rumble over the dry plain—their lion-like fronts and dangling beards—their open mouths and hanging tongues—as they come on, puffing like a locomotive engine at every bound, does at first make the blood settle a little heavy about the heart.

The gait of these animals is a clumsy gallop, and any common pony can overtake them in the chase; though, as the hunter would express it, they 'lumber' over the ground rather deceivingly. The cows are usually much faster than the bulls. It has been the remark of travellers that the buffalo jumps up from the ground differently from any other animal. The horse rises upon his fore feet first, and the cow upon her hind feet, but the buffalo seems to spring upon them all at once.

American hunters, as well as Indians, to butcher the buffalo, generally turn it upon the belly, and commence on the back. The hump-ribs, tender-loins, and a few other choice bits being appropriated, the remainder is commonly left for the wolves. The skin is chiefly used for buffalo rugs, but for which it is only preserved by the Indians during fall and winter (and then rarely but from the cows and bullocks), when the hair is long and woolly. I have never seen the buffalo hide tanned, but it seems too porous and spongy to make substantial leather. Were it valuable, thousands of hides might be saved that are annually left to the wolves upon the Prairies.

Although the buffalo is the largest, he has by no means the control among the prairie animals: the sceptre of authority has been lodged with the large *gray wolf*. Though but little larger than the wolf of the United States, he is much more ferocious. The same species abound throughout the north of Mexico, where they often kill horses, mules and cattle of all sizes; and on the Prairies they make considerable havoc among the buffalo.

Many curious tales are told of the wiles and expedients practised by these animals to secure their prey. Some assert that they collect in companies, and chase a buffalo by turns, till he is fatigued, when they join and soon dispatch him: others, that, as the buffalo runs with the tongue hanging out, they snap at it in the chase till it is torn off which preventing him from eating, he is reduced by starvation, and soon overpowered: others, that, while running, they gnaw and lacerate the legs and ham-strings till they disable him, and then he is killed by the gang. Be this as it may, certain it is that they overcome many of the largest buffaloes, employing perhaps different means of subduing them, and among these is doubtless the last mentioned, for I have myself seen them with the muscles of the thighs cruelly mangled—a consequence no doubt of some of these attacks. Calves are constantly falling victims to the rapacity of these wolves; yet, when herds of buffalo are together, they defend their offspring with great bravery.

Though the color of this wolf is generally a dirty gray, it is sometimes met with nearly white. I am of opinion, however, that the diversity of color originates chiefly from the different ages of the hair, and the age and condition of the animal itself. The few white wolves I have seen, have been lean, long-haired, and apparently very old. There are immense numbers of them upon the Prairies. Droves are frequently to be seen following in the wake of caravans, hunting companies, and itinerant Indian bands, for weeks together— not, like the jackal, so much to disinter the dead (though this they sometimes do), as to feast upon the abandoned carcasses of the buffalo which are so often wantonly killed and wasted. Unless in these cases, they are rarely seen, except in the neighborhood of buffalo; therefore, when the hungry traveller meets with wolves, he feels some assurance that supplies of his favorite game are at hand.

I have never known these animals, rapacious as they are, [to] extend their attacks to man, though they probably would, if very hungry and a favorable opportunity presented itself. I shall not soon forget an adventure with one of them, many years ago, on the frontier of Missouri. Riding near the prairie border, I perceived one of the largest and fiercest of the gray species, which had just descended from the west, and seemed famished to desperation. I at once prepared for a chase; and, being without arms, I caught up a cudgel, when I betook me valiantly to the charge, much stronger, as I soon discovered, in my cause than in my equipment. The wolf was in no humor to flee, however, but boldly met me full half-way. I was soon disarmed, for my club broke upon the animals head. He then 'laid to' my horse's legs, which, not relishing the conflict, gave a plunge and sent me whirling over his head, and made his escape, leaving me and the wolf at close quarters. I was no sooner upon my feet than my antagonist renewed the charge; but, being without weapon, or any means of awakening an emotion of terror, save through his imagination, I took off my large black hat, and using it for a shield, began to thrust it towards his gaping jaws. My *ruse* had the desired effect; for, after springing at me a few times, he wheeled about and trotted off several paces, and stopped to gaze at me. Being apprehensive that he might change his mind and return to the attack, and conscious that, under the compromise, I had the best of the bargain, I very resolutely—took to my heels, glad of the opportunity of making a drawn game, though I had myself given the challenge.

There is a small species called the *prairie wolf* on the frontier, and *coyote*[6] by the Mexicans, which is also found in immense numbers on the Plains. It is rather smaller than an ordinary dog, nearly

[6] *Canis latrans,* a distinction to which its noisiness emphatically entitles it. Clavigero says of this animal: "El *coyotl, ó coyote,* como dicen los Españoles, es una fiera semejante al lobo en la voracidad, á la zorra en la astucia, al perro en la forma, y en otras propriedades al *adive, ó chacal;* por lo que algunos escritores Megicanos lo han numerado entre varias de aquellas especias; pero es indudable que se diferencia de todas ellas," etc. *Hist. Ant. de Meg. Tom. I, p. 40.*[a]

A similar propensity is observable among us to refer nearly all American animals to European species, whereas but very few that are legitimately indigenous to this continent, agree in every particular to those of the Old World. It would surely have contributed to the copiousness and euphony of the language, as well as to perspicuity in the distinction of species, had we, like the Mexicans, retained the Indian names of our indigenous animals.—GREGG.

[a] "The *coyotl,* or *coyote,* as the Spanish call it, is an animal similar to the wolf in voracity, to the fox in cunning, to the dog in shape, and in other propensities to the *adive,* or *jackal;* for which reason some Mexican writers have counted it among several of these species; but it undoubtedly is different from all of them," etc. *Historia Antigua de Méjico,* I, 40. (Original Italian edition cited above, Vol. I, chap. 7, n. 17.)

the color of the common gray wolf, and though as rapacious as the larger kind, it seems too cowardly to attack stout game. It therefore lives upon the remains of buffalo killed by hunters and by the large wolves, added to such small game as hares, prairie dogs, etc., and even reptiles and insects. It will lie for hours beside a 'dog-hole,' watching for the appearance of the little animal, which no sooner peeps out than the enemy pounces upon it.

The coyote has been denominated the 'jackal of the Prairies;' indeed, some have reckoned it really a species of that animal, yet it would seem improperly, as this creature partakes much less of the nature of the jackal than of the common wolf. Still, however noisy the former may be, he cannot exceed the prairie wolf. Like ventriloquists, a pair of these will represent a dozen distinct voices in such succession—will bark, chatter, yelp, whine, and howl in such variety of note, that one would fancy a score of them at hand. This, added to the long and doleful bugle-note of the large wolf, which often accompanies it, sometimes makes a night upon the Prairies perfectly hideous.—Some hunters assert that the coyote and the dog will breed together. Be this as it may, certain it is that the Indian dogs have a wonderfully wolfish appearance.

The *elk* as well as the *deer* is found somewhat abundant upon the Arkansas river, as high as the Santa Fé road, but from thence westward they are both very scarce; for these animals do not resort to the high prairie plains. Further south, however, in the prairies bordering the brushy tributaries of the Canadian and Red River, deer are exceedingly plenty—herds of hundreds are sometimes seen together; but in these southern regions there are but few elks.

About the thickety streams above-mentioned, as well as among the Cross Timbers, the *black bear* is very common, living chiefly upon acorns and other fruits. The grape vines and the branches of the scrubby oaks, and plum-bushes, are in some places so torn and broken by the bear in pursuit of fruits, that a stranger would conclude a violent hurricane had passed among them.

That species of gazelle known as the *antelope* is very numerous upon the high plains. This beautiful animal, though reckoned a link between the deer and goat, is certainly much nearest the latter. It is about the size and somewhat of the figure of a large goat. Its horns also resemble those of the latter, being likewise persistent; but they are more erect, and have a short prong projecting in front. The ground of this animal's color a little resembles that of the common deer, but it is variegated with a whitish section or two on each side.

The antelope is most remarkable for its fleetness: not bounding like the deer, but skimming over the ground as though upon skates. The fastest horse will rarely overtake them. I once witnessed an effort to catch one that had a hind-leg broken, but it far out-stripped our fleetest 'buffalo horse.' It is, therefore, too swift to be hunted in the chase. I have seen dogs run after this animal, but they would soon stop and turn about, apparently much ashamed of being left so far behind.

The flesh of the antelope is, like that of the goat, rather coarse, and but little esteemed: consequently, no great efforts are made to take them. Being as wild as fleet, the hunting of them is very difficult, except they be entrapped by their curiosity. Meeting a stranger, they seem loth to leave him until they have fully found him out. They will often take a circuit around the object of their curiosity, usually approaching nearer and nearer, until within rifle-shot—frequently stopping to gaze. Also, they are often decoyed with a scarlet coat, or a red handkerchief attached to the tip of a ramrod. which will sometimes allure them within reach of the hunter's aim. But this interesting animal, like the buffalo, is now very rarely seen within less than 200 miles of the frontier: though early voyagers tell us that it once frequented as far east as the Mississippi.

The *bighorn* (*carnero cimarron,* as called by Mexicans, and sometimes known to trappers as the mountain sheep), so abundant in most of the Rocky Mountain chain, is found in the spurs and table-plain cliffs about the sources of the Cimarron river (whence this stream acquired its name), as well as in the highland gorges, and other parts of those mountain borders. Its flesh is said to be excellent, and is preferred by many hunters to venison. It is larger than a common sheep, and covered with brownish hair instead of wool—darker than the deer, but whitish on the belly. It is most remarkable for its huge spiral horns, resembling in shape and curvature those of the sheep, but sometimes over three feet long, and four to six inches in diameter at the base.[7]

The bighorn is quite celebrated for its agility, and its habit of secluding itself among the most inaccessible mountain crags. It seems to delight in perching and capering upon the very verge of the most frightful precipices and overhanging cliffs, and in skipping from rock to rock, regardless of the yawning chasms, hundreds of feet in depth, which intervene. In fact, when pursued, it does not hesitate, as I have been assured, to leap from a cliff into a valley a hundred or more feet below, where, lighting upon its huge horns, it springs to its feet uninjured; for the neck is so thick and strong as to support the greatest shock the animal's weight can bring upon it. Being exceedingly timorous, it rarely descends to the valleys, but feeds and sleeps about such craggy fastnesses as are inaccessible to the wolves and other animals of prey. This animal seems greatly to resemble the *moufflon* or Buffon, in color, figure and horns, but the *chamois* in habits.

But of all the prairie animals, by far the most curious, and by no means the least celebrated, is the little *prairie dog*. This singular quadruped is but little larger than a common squirrel, its body being nearly a foot long, with a tail of three or four inches. The color ranges from brown to a dirty yellow. The flesh, though often eaten by travellers, is not esteemed savory. It was denominated the 'barking squirrel,' the 'prairie ground-squirrel,' etc., by early explorers, with much more apparent propriety than the present established name. Its yelp, which resembles that of the little toy-dog, seems its only canine attribute. It rather appears to occupy a middle ground betwixt the rabbit and squirrel—like the former in feeding and burrowing—like the latter in frisking, flirting, sitting erect, and somewhat so in its barking.

The prairie dog has been reckoned by some naturalists a species of the marmot (*arctomys ludoviciana*); yet it seems to possess scarce any other quality in common with this animal except that of burrowing. Some have supposed, it is true, that like the marmot, they lie torpid during the cold season; and it is observed in 'Long's Expedition,' that, "as they pass the winter in a lethargic state, they lay

[7] Mr. Irving furnishes the following dimensions of a male of this species: "From the nose to the base of the tail, five feet; length of the tail, four inches; girth of the body, four feet; height, three feet eight inches," etc.—*Rocky Mts., Vol. I, p. 48.*—GREGG.

"DOG-TOWN," OR, A SETTLEMENT OF PRAIRIE DOGS

up no provisions," etc.:[8] but this is no doubt erroneous; for I have the concurrent testimony of several persons, who have been upon the Prairies in winter, that, like rabbits and squirrels, they issue from their holes every soft day; and therefore lay up no doubt a hoard of 'hay' (as there is rarely anything else to be found in the vicinity of their towns) for winter's use.

A collection of their burrows has been termed by travellers a 'dog-town,' which comprises from a dozen or so, to some thousands in the same vicinity; often covering an area of several square miles. They generally locate upon firm dry plains, coated with fine short grass, upon which they feed; for they are no doubt exclusively herbivorous. But even when tall coarse grass surrounds, they seem commonly to destroy this within their 'streets,' which are nearly always found 'paved' with a fine species suited to their palates. They must need but little water, if any at all, as their 'towns' are often, indeed generally, found in the midst of the most arid plains—unless we suppose they dig down to subterranean fountains. At least they evidently burrow remarkably deep. Attempts either to dig or drown them out of their holes have generally proved unsuccessful.

Approaching a 'village,' the little dogs may be observed frisking about the 'streets'—passing from dwelling to dwelling apparently on visits—sometimes a few clustered together as though in council —here feeding upon the tender herbage—there cleansing their 'houses,' or brushing the little hillock about the door—yet all quiet. Upon seeing a stranger, however, each streaks to its home, but is apt to stop at the entrance, and spread the general alarm by a succession of shrill yelps, usually sitting erect. Yet at the report of a gun or the too near approach of the visitor, they dart down and are seen no more till the cause of alarm seems to havè disappeared.

Two other animals appear to live in communion with the prairie

[8] Dr. Edwin James, *An Account of an Expedition from Pittsburgh to the Rocky Mountains* (3 vols., Philadelphia, Carey & Lea, 1823). Major Stephen H. Long (1784–1864), of New Hampshire, entered the army in 1814 and became famous as a military explorer and engineer. His most celebrated exploration was his search (1819–20) for the headwaters of the Red and Arkansas rivers, the boundaries of the United States as established in the treaty of 1819 with Spain. He mistook the Canadian for the Red and followed it to its mouth, as described by Gregg above, Vol. I, chap. 5, n. 11.

dogs—the *rattle-snake* and a small *owl;*[9] but both are no doubt intruders, resorting to these burrows for shelter, and to feed, it is presumed, upon the 'pups' of the inmates.

Rattle-snakes are exceedingly abundant upon these plains: scores of them are sometimes killed in the course of a day's travel; yet they seem remarkably harmless, for I have never witnessed an instance of a man's being bitten, though they have been known to crawl even into the beds of travellers.[10] Mules are sometimes bitten by them, yet very rarely, though they must daily walk over considerable numbers.

The *horned frog,* as modern travellers have christened it, or horned lizard,[11] as those of earlier times more rationally called it, is the most famed and curious reptile of the plains. Like the prairie dog, it is only found in the dry regions, often many miles from water. It no doubt lives nearly, if not wholly, without drink. Its food probably consists chiefly of ants and other insects; though many Mexicans will have it, that the *camaleon* (as they call it) *vive del aire*—lives upon the air. It has been kept several months without partaking of a particle of aliment. I once took a pair of them upon the far-western plains, which I shut up in a box and carried to one of the eastern cities, where they were kept for several months before they died,—without having taken food or water, though repeatedly offered them.

The whole length of the horned frog is from two to five inches—body flatted horizontally, oval-shaped, and between one and two inches wide in the middle. The back is beautifully variegated, with white and brown, and sometimes a yellowish purple. The belly is whitish and covered with brown specks. It acquired its name from a pair of short horns projecting from the top of the head—with other

[9] This has been called the *Coquimbo owl.* Its note, whether natural or imitative, much resembles that of the prairie dog.—GREGG.

This is the *Speotyto cunicularia.*

[10] Though I never saw it tried, it has been said that snakes will not crawl over a hair-rope stretched upon the ground, and that consequently these form good barriers to keep these reptiles out of a bed.—GREGG.

[11] Orbicular lizard, as it has been technically denominated. It would seem a species of chameleon, having apparently some, though very little, variability in color.—GREGG.

This is the common horned toad *(Phyrnosoma cornutum).*

smaller horny protuberances upon the head and body. It has a short tail, which gives it a lizard-like appearance. It is a very inoffensive creature, and may be handled with perfect impunity, notwithstanding its uncouth appearance, and sometimes vicious demonstrations.

As birds mostly incline to the timbered regions, there is but a scant variety to be met with upon the plains. About the Cross Timbers and indeed on all the brushy creeks, especially to the southward, are quantities of wild *turkeys*, which are frequently seen ranging in large flocks in the bordering prairies. That species of American grouse, known west as the *prairie-hen*, is very abundant on the frontier, and is quite destructive, in autumn, to the prairie corn-fields. This fowl is rarely seen over two hundred miles beyond the border. *Partridges* are found about as far west; but their number is quite limited anywhere beyond the precincts of the settlements. About the streams there are different species of geese and ducks, as well as both sandhill and white cranes: also flocks of a species of plover and curlew. Add to these numbers of hawks and ravens, and we have most of the fowls of the Prairies. Flocks of the latter follow in the wake of the caravans with even greater constancy than wolves.

The *bee*, among Western pioneers, is the proverbial precursor of the Anglo-American population: in fact, the aborigines of the frontier have generally corroborated the notion; for they used to say, they knew the whites were not far behind, when bees appeared among them. This partial coincidence, I suppose, is the result of their emigration westward being at nearly an even pace with that of the settlers. As yet no honey-bees seem to have been discovered as far westward as any part of the Rocky Mountains. They are scattered, however, to the distance of two or three hundred miles west of the Missouri and Arkansas frontier, where there is timber affording them suitable habitations. On the Santa Fé route but few have been found beyond the Council Grove.

CHAPTER XII
ABORIGINES OF AMERICA

Indian Cosmogony—Traditions of Origin—Identity of Religious Notions—Adoration of the Sun—Shawnee Faith—Anecdote of Tecumseh—Legendary Traditions—Missionaries, and Success of the Catholics—The Indian's Heaven—Burial Customs—Ancient Accounts—Depositing the Dead on Scaffolds—Superstition and Witchcraft—Indian Philosophy—Polygamy and other Matrimonial Affairs—Abhorrence of Incest—Difference in Character—Indian Hospitality—Traits of the Ancient Asiatics—Names—Relationship of Different Tribes—Dreadful Decrease of the Indians.

IT WILL HARDLY BE EXPECTED from a work making so little pretension as this to scientific accuracy and completeness, that the remarks which my plan necessarily leads me to make concerning the aborigines of western America, should be either critical or comprehensive. Neither can I feel that it is a topic which I am at liberty wholly to disregard. The opportunities which I have enjoyed for obtaining a knowledge of the character and habits of the western Indians have been such, that I trust that a brief account of them may prove in some measure new, and not altogether uninteresting to a portion of my readers. Impressed with this belief, I propose, in the few following pages, to record such facts as shall seem to be most novel, and to corroborate, in my humble measure, occasional others which have before been related. With this view, I shall proceed to notice, in the present chapter, such leading characteristics of the aborigines generally, as shall seem most note-worthy; and then, in those that follow, ask the reader's attention to many peculiarities which make the most conspicuous differences between them.

No aboriginal nation or people has ever yet been discovered, to my knowledge, which has not professed to have a mysterious ancestry of a mythical character. It is interesting to mark the analogies and the differences between their various systems. Although among some tribes who have lived much in communication with the whites, their cosmogony has been confounded very much with the Mosaic or Scripture account, so that it is now often difficult to distinguish clearly the aboriginal from the imported, yet all the Americo-Indian tribes have more or less preserved their traditions on this subject. The old full-blood Choctaws, for instance, relate that the first of their tribe issued from a cave in Nunnewaya or Bending Mountain, in the 'Old Nation,' east of the Mississippi; yet this tradition has but little currency among the young men and mixed-bloods of the tribe.[1] The minute account of this supposed origin cannot now be readily procured; yet some idea may be formed of it from a kindred tradition among the Mandans which has been preserved to us by Lewis and Clark,[2] and is thus related:

"The whole nation resided in one large village under ground near a subterraneous lake: a grape vine extended its roots down to their habitation and gave them a view of the light: some of the most adventurous climbed up the vine, and were delighted with the sight of the earth, which they found covered with buffalo, and rich with every kind of fruits: returning with the grapes they had gathered, their countrymen were so pleased with the taste of them that their whole nation resolved to leave their dull residence for the charms of the upper regions; men, women and children ascended by means of the vine; but when about half the nation had reached the surface of the earth, a corpulent woman who was clambering up the vine broke

[1] Another legend is that the Choctaws, migrating from the west, established their first formal government at Nanih Waya. A large mound about 10 miles southeast of Noxapater, in Winston County, Mississippi, was long known by the Choctaws as Nanih Waya, and their first capital in Indian Territory (about a mile and a half west of Tuskahoma in present Pushmataha County, Oklahoma) received the same name. Muriel H. Wright, *A Guide to the Indian Tribes of Oklahoma*, 100, 105.

[2] Meriwether Lewis (1774-1809) and William Clark (1770-1838) visited the Mandans on the Missouri River a little above present Bismarck, North Dakota, in October, 1804, during their celebrated exploration for President Jefferson. The first published record of the expedition was Patrick Gass's *Journal of the Voyages and Travels of a Corps of Discovery* (Pittsburgh, Z. Cramer, 1807). Several others followed, the most complete being Reuben G. Thwaites (ed.), *Original Journals of the Lewis and Clark Expedition, 1804-1806*. (7 vols. and an atlas, New York, Dodd, Mead, 1904-1905). For the portion quoted by Gregg, see Vol. V, 347.

it with her weight, and closed upon herself and the rest of the nation, the light of the sun."

Besides the Mandans it seems that other neighboring tribes had somewhat analogous notions of their origin. An early explorer relates that the Osages believed that their forefathers grew from a snail, which, having become a man, married the daughter of a beaver, whence sprang the present race.

The resemblance of the American Indians to each other, however, is not more conspicuous in anything than in their religious opinions. They seem to have no well-defined creeds: yet there are very few but profess a faith in some sort of First Cause—a Great Spirit, a Master of Life, who rules the destinies of the world. Though the different nations have not always typified their deity by the same objects, yet by far the greater number seem to have fixed upon the sun as the fit object of their adoration. "Next to *Virachocha*, or their supreme God." says Father Acosta,[3] speaking of the Indians of Peru, "that which most commonly they have and do adore amongst the Infidells is the Sunne." Many of the Mexican Tribes[4] professed the same faith, and particularly those of New Mexico, as has already been mentioned. This seems also the most current among the Comanches and other wild tribes of the Prairies: and the Choctaws and several other nations of the frontier appear at least to have held the sun in great veneration.

But of all the Indian tribes, none appear to have ascribed to the 'fountain of light' more of the proper attributes of deity than the Shawnees. They argue, with some plausibility, that the sun animates everything—therefore, he is clearly the Master of Life, or the Great Spirit; and that everything is produced originally from the bosom of the earth—therefore, she is the mother of creation. The following

[3] José de Acosta (1539–1600), author of *Historia natural y moral de las Indias* (Sevilla, Iuan de León, 1590). It would appear from the spelling that Gregg quotes from the first English edition (London, 1604), or a reprint thereof.

[4] Clavigero asserts of the Indians of Mexico, that their first heaven (that of the warriors, etc.) they called *"la casa del sol"* (the house of the sun), which luminary they worshipped every morning at sunrise.—GREGG.

[5] I have since met with the same, in substance, related by Mr. Schoolcraft.—GREGG.

Henry Rowe Schoolcraft (1793–1864), a long-time agent for the Indians at Mackinac, wrote and published extensively on Indian subjects.

anecdote[5] (as told to me by a gentleman of integrity), which transpired upon the occasion of an interview of Tecumseh with Gen. Harrison,[6] is as illustrative of the religious opinions of the Shawnees, as it is characteristic of the hauteur and independent spirit of that celebrated Shawnee chief. The General, having called Tecumseh for a 'talk,' desired him to take a seat, saying, "Come here, Tecumseh, and sit by your father." "You my father?" replied the chief, with a stern air—"No! yonder sun is my father (pointing towards it), and the earth is my mother; so I will rest on her bosom"—and immediately seated himself upon the ground, according to Indian custom.

But though the Shawnees consider the sun the type, if not the essence, of the Great Spirit, many also believe in an evil genius, who makes all sorts of bad things, to counterbalance those made by the Good Spirit. For instance, when the latter made a sheep, a rose, wholesome herbs, etc., the bad spirit matched them with a wolf, a thorn, poisonous plants, and the like. They also appear to think there is a kind of purgatory in which the spirits of the wicked may be cleansed before entering into their elysium.

The worship of all the aborigines seems to consist chiefly in feasting and dancing. A worthy missionary among the Shawnees related to me the following legendary tradition, as explanatory of their ideas of another world, and the institution of their worship, which may serve as a fair sample of the traditions of many other tribes.

In days of yore (say the Shawnees), there lived a pious brother and an affectionate sister, who were inordinately attached to each other. It came to pass that the sister sickened and died, and was carried to the world of spirits. The good brother was inconsolable, and for a while refused to eat or drink, or to partake of any kind of nourishment: he wished to follow his beloved sister. At length he resolved to set out in search of her; so he commenced his pilgrimage toward the setting sun. Steadily pursuing the same course for days and moons together, he at last came to where the sky and earth meet; and finding an opening, he ascended into the upper regions. He now turned his course towards the rising sun, which he continued, above

[6] William Henry Harrison (1773–1841), then governor of Indiana Territory and commander of the troops which defeated the followers of Tecumseh (1768–1813) in the battle of Tippecanoe (1811). He was later president of the United States, dying after one month in office.

the sky, till he came to the abode of his grandfather—which seems but another name for one of the good spirits. This sage, knowing his errand, gave him 'medicine' to transform him into a spirit, that he might pass through the celestial courts. He also gave him instructions how to proceed, and where he would find his sister. He said she would be at a dance; and when she rose to join in the amusement, he must seize and ensconce her in the hollow of a reed with which he was furnished, and cover the orifice with the end of his finger.

After an arduous peregrination through the land of spirits, the brother found and secured his sister as directed. He returned with his charge to the habitation of his grandfather, who gave another 'medicine' to transform them both into material beings again, that they might revisit their brothers on earth. The sage also explained to them the mysteries of heaven and the sacred rites of worship, that they might instruct their tribe therein. When about to start back, the venerable spirit told them that the route by which the brother had come was very circuitous—there was a much nearer way; and opening a trap-door through the sky, they beheld their native town just below them. So the good brother and sister descended; and returning home, a great feast was celebrated, accompanied by a solemn dance—in accordance with the grandfather's instructions. Thus originated, as they say, the sacred dance and other religious ceremonies now in practice.

As they believe the Indian heaven separate, and essentially different and distinct from that of the whites, and as they do not wish their people divided, this has often occasioned a serious opposition to the labor of the missionaries.[7] For the purpose of thwarting the

[7] The Shawnees have four missionary establishments among them, viz. a Methodist, Baptist, Moravian, and Quaker. There are also missionaries of different sects among most of the tribes of the border, the labors of whom have been attended with some degree of success. There is, I believe, but one Catholic Mission upon the frontier, which is among the Pottawatomies, about a thousand of whom have embraced this faith. The Catholics, however, appear to have succeeded better than most other denominations, in their missionary efforts. It is so in Mexico, so in Canada, and appears so everywhere else that they have undertaken the Christianization of the heathen. I would not be understood to attribute this to any intrinsic superiority of their religion, but to the peculiarities of its forms and ceremonies. The pageantry of their worship, the palpable representation of the divine mysteries by the introduction of images, better accords with their pristine idolatry, than a more spiritual faith. Catholics, indeed, have had the sagacity to permit the Indians (at least in some countries) to interweave many of their own heathen ceremonies with the sacred Christian

measures of these, a noted anti-christian sage 'played off,' a few years ago, the following 'vision.' Being very ill (as they relate), this sage, to all appearance, died, and became stiff and cold, except a spot upon his breast, which still retained the heat of life. In this state he remained a day or more, when he again breathed and returned among the living; and calling his friends about him, he related the scenes he had witnessed. He had ascended to the Indian's heaven, he said, which he described as usual: a fine country, abounding in all sorts of game, and everything an Indian could desire. There he met with his grandfather, who said to him. "It is meet, my son, that thou return to the earth, and warn thy brothers against the dangers that await them. Tell them to beware of the religion of the white man: that every Indian who embraces it is obliged to take the road to the white man's heaven; and yet no red man is permitted to enter there, but will have to wander about forever without a resting place."

The identity of the notions which the different tribes have conceived of a future existence, and the character of the 'world of spirits,' seems still more general. They fancy heaven but another material world, superior, it is true, yet resembling this—a kind of elysian vale, or paradise—a 'happy hunting-ground,' abounding in game and all their comforts of life, which may be procured without labor. This elysium they generally seem to locate 'upon the sky,' which they fancy a material solid vault. It appears impossible for them, in their pristine barbarism, to conceive of a spiritual existence, or of a world differing materially from that which they see around them.

Father Hennepin (writing about 1680) relates, that the northern Indians inquired about the manner of living in heaven, and remarks: "When I made answer that they live there without eating or drinking, 'We will not go thither,' said they, 'because we must not eat;' and when I have added that there would be no occasion for food there, they clapt their hands to their mouths, as a sign of admiration, and said *'Thou art a great liar!—is there anything can live without eating?'* "[8]

rites, forming a singular *mêlée* of Romish and pagan worship, which is especially the case in Mexico. Also the less rigid Catholic creed and customs do not debar them from their wonted favorite amusements, not to say vices. It is therefore that whole tribes sometimes simultaneously embrace this imposing creed.—GREGG.

[8] See Thwaites (ed.), *Hennepin's New Discovery*, II, 537–38.

Similar opinions, among many different tribes, I have heard declared in direct terms; yet, did we want further testimony, some of their burial customs and funeral rites would seem to indicate their ideas of the future state. The Cherokees, Choctaws, Creeks, Kansas, and kindred tribes, besides many others, or perhaps most others of the frontier, have been accustomed to inter the most valuable property of the deceased and many necessaries with them. "Their whole property was buried with them,"[9] says an intelligent Cherokee, in some manuscript notes concerning his ancestors, I have in my possession: and I have been assured by credible natives, that, within their recollection, they have seen, at these burials, provisions, salt, and other necessaries, interred with the dead for their long journey.

There are very few of the prairie Indians but practise something of this kind: many kill the favorite hunting-horses, and deposite the arms, etc., of the deceased, for his use in the chase, when he arrives at the 'happy hunting ground.' We are also informed by Capt. Bonneville, and other travellers, that this is practised by some, if not all, of the natives beyond the Rocky Mountains. The same is told of the Navajoes, Apaches, and other uncatholicized tribes of the north of Mexico.

Peter Martyr, a learned and celebrated protestant divine,[10] who wrote his "Decades of the Newe Worlde" towards the middle of the sixteenth century, observes that, "in many places of the firme lande, when any of the kynges dye, all his householde servauntes, as well women as men which have continually served hym, kyl themselves, beleavynge, as they are taught by the devyl *Tuyra*, that they which kyll themselves when the kynge dyeth, go with hym to heaven and serve hym in the same place and office as they dyd before on the earth whyle he lyved.[11] And that all that refuse so to doo, when

[9] Adair, who resided forty years with the southern Indians, previous to 1775, speaks of the same among them all.—GREGG.

James Adair, *The History of the American Indians* (London, E. & C. Dilly, 1775).

[10] Not Pietro Martire Vermigli (1500–62), the Protestant, but Pietro Martire d'Anghiera (*ca.* 1457–1526), the very Catholic tutor of the children of Ferdinand and Isabel of Spain. Gregg used the 1555 English edition of his *De rebus oceanicis et novo orbe decades* (Compluti, Michaele d'Egina, 1530).

[11] Also Clavigero speaks of similar beliefs and practices among the Mexican Indians, particularly in the obsequies of the kings; and adds—"El número de víc-

after they dye by theyr naturall death or otherwyse, theyr soules to dye with theyr bodyes, and to bee dissolved into ayer and become nothynge as do the soules of hogges, byrdes or fysshes, or other brute beastes."[12] In corroboration of a similar custom among the natives along the Mississippi, in 1542, Herrera relates, that, after the death of Fernando de Soto, and his party had set out westward, they were joined by a youth, who stated that he had fled to escape being buried with his lord who had died; which was the practise in that country. Travellers from the upper lakes to the Mississippi speak of similar customs, at an early day, among the tribes of that quarter.

It would appear that they believe everything, both animate and inanimate—beasts, arms, ornaments, etc.—to possess immortal attributes, subject to resurrection in the world of spirits. However, did not their motives seem so well defined by the direct allusions to their notions of futurity, we might suppose, as is frequently urged, that the burying of property, slaves, etc., with the deceased, was only intended as a mark of respect; which, indeed, is hardly more irrational than the custom of interring costly garniture and appendages with the dead among us.

Some of the modes of burial adopted by the American aborigines are different I believe, from those of any other people. Though, as among civilized nations, even the wildest tribes sometimes inter in ordinary graves, yet they frequently deposit their dead, in a sitting and even in a standing posture, in pits, caves, and hollow trees; and occasionally, they lay the corpse out upon scaffolds suspended from the branches of trees, or resting upon them where they will admit of it, so as to be out of reach of the wolves and other beasts.

I was once, with a little caravan, travelling up the course of the Arkansas river, when, a thunder-storm coming up suddenly, and night drawing near, we turned the wagons, as soon as we could, to the river-bank, to encamp. The bustle of ungearing and securing the

timas correspondía á la grandeza del funeral, y segun algunos autores, llegaban á veces á doscientas."—GREGG.

["The number of victims corresponded to the grandeur of the funeral, and according to some authors, reached at times two hundred."]

[12] Edition of 1555, translated from the Latin, fol. 181.—In another place, the same author also says they buried corn, etc., with the dead, for their use in the world to come.—GREGG.

teams before they should be frightened by the tempest, was hardly over, when he discovered a platform suspended above our heads, upon the branches of a cottonwood, which, upon examination, was found to contain an Indian corpse, from whose bones the putrid flesh had not yet separated!

This mode of disposing of the dead would seem once to have been quite extensive; for, as well as upon the western prairies, it formerly prevailed among the Potawatomies of the north, and the Choctaws of the south, as least while on their expeditions. In this case, if practicable, they would leave a band of aged men, known as 'bone-pickers,' to clean the bones, when the flesh decayed, and carry them to their village for interment.

Barbarians are generally superstitious to an extreme, believing in hobgoblins, witchcraft, legerdemain and all sorts of mummeries.[13] Like many grandmothers in backwoods life, they delight in recounting the extraordinary apparitions, transmigrations, sorceries, etc., which they pretend to have witnessed. Nothing seems too absurd for their belief. Among many other cases of similar cast, an intelligent Potawatomie once assured me that he had witnessed the death of one of his nation, who had received a stab in his side with a knife (probably in some illicit adventure); and it being unknown to his friends how the wound had been inflicted, it was currently reported and believed, that from their present home on the frontier of Missouri, he had visited the 'Old Nation' in Michigan, poisoned an enemy there, received the fatal stab, and returned and died, all in one day.

[13] The Indians often so imposed upon the credulous ancients as to make them believe that they had direct communication with Satan. The learned divine, Peter Martyr, has a whole chapter "Of the familiarie which certeyne of the Indians have with the devyll, and howe they receave answere of hym of thynges to come:" and very seriously and philosophically concludes that, "the devyll beynge so auncient an Astronomer, nowethe the tymes of thynges, and seeth howe they are naturally directed:" to which he appends numerous instances of the evil spirit's revelations of the "tymes of thynges to coome" to his ministers, the magi. And even as late as 1721, Father Charlevoix gravely says, an instance he relates, and many others that he "knows, which are equally certain, prove that the Devil is sometimes concerned in the magic of the Savages." The Choctaws, and perhaps some others, used to punish witchcraft with all the rigor of our own ancestors, putting poor creatures to death upon the slightest proof of their tampering with the black art: but this barbarity is now prohibited by their more civilized laws. Yet, the more barbarous tribes still have their conjurors and medicine men, who deal in auguries and mystic ceremonies; which, with their dances, constitutes the greater part of their worship.—GREGG.

If you tell an Indian that such things are absurd and impossible, he is apt to answer, "It may be so with the white man, but how do you know it to be impossible with the Indian? You tell us many strange things which happened to your fathers—we don't contradict them, though we believe such things never could have happened to the red man." Or, they will reply, perhaps, as they did to Father Hennepin in a similar case: "Fie, thou knowest not what thou sayest; thou may'st know what has passed in thy own Country, for thy Ancestors have told thee of them; but thou canst not know what has passed in ours before the Spirits (that is to say the Europeans) came hither."

In their matrimonial customs there is also a similarity among most of the American savages. Polygamy seems once to have been universal; and I believe still is so among the uncivilized tribes. Every man takes as many wives as he can obtain, or is able to support. The squaws, however, the more willingly consent to this multiplicity, as it affords additional helpmates in their labors. Polygamy among these savages would appear, indeed, not altogether an unwise provision. At least it seems palliated with such a belligerent people, who lose so many males in their continual wars, leaving a great surplus of females; and where the duties of the latter are so numerous and so severe.

The custom of buying wives, or at least making large presents to their parents, has always been very general; and still exists, not only among the more savage, but even with many of the partially civilized nations. Yet, notwithstanding their depravity in other respects, there is one thing truly remarkable in their marriages. All modern observers seem to agree with the ancient authors, that they universally abhor incestuous connections. Among the Creeks, even the marrying of cousins was punished by cutting off the ears. The Cherokees (according to some manuscript notes which I have of an intelligent member of the tribe) were prohibited from marrying in their own clans (i. e. kindred) under penalty of death; and their clans themselves were their executioners. But, although the Indians thus so strictly prohibit marriage within the degrees of consanguinity, it is not so with those of affinity among many tribes. The Otoes, Kansas, and others of the same stock, will not only marry several sisters, but their deceased brothers' wives; in fact, this last seems considered a duty, so that the orphan children of the brothers may not be without a protector.[14]

While the aborigines of the New World have been noted above almost every other uncivilized nation in history, for their vindictiveness and cruelty towards their enemies, there are, in these attributes, wide differences apparent among them. The Indians along the Pacific coast, as well as in most of Mexico, were always more mild and peaceable than those of the United States. Hence it is, in fact, that the Spaniards did not meet with that formidable resistance to their conquests which they encountered among the fiery tribes of Florida, or that relentless and desperate hostility which the Anglo-Americans experienced in the first settlement of most parts of the United States.

But in the common trait of hospitality to strangers all the western tribes are alike distinguished. The traveller who is thrown upon their charity, is almost universally received and treated with the greatest kindness; and, though they might pilfer him to the skin, and even place his person in jeopardy, if he show want of confidence in them, and endeavor to conceal his effects, yet his property is generally secure when under their charge; they appear to consider a breach of confidence one of the greatest crimes.

Among the wild tribes, as well as among most of the unadulterated border Indians, to set something to eat before a friend, and even a stranger, immediately upon his arrival at a lodge or a cabin, is deemed not only an act of hospitality but of necessary etiquette; and a refusal to partake is looked upon as an unfriendly token—an insult, in fact, to the family. Travellers are often severely taxed to preserve the good feeling of their hosts in this particular, especially among the prairie Indians. One at all fastidious in matters of diet, would find it hard to relish food from a greasy horn-spoon which every urchin had been using; and then to ladle it out of a pot which had been common for all the papooses and pups of the premises: or to partake from a slice rolled up in a musty skin, or a dirtier blanket.

---

[14] Clavigero remarks of the Indians of Mexico, "Estaba severemente prohibido . . . todo enlace matrimonial, entre parientes en primer grado de consanguinidad, ó de afinidad, excepto entre cuñados."—GREGG.

[". . . All matrimonial alliances between relatives of the first degree of consanguinity, or affinity, except among in-laws, is severely prohibited."]

And yet an apology even of having already dined half-a-dozen times would scarcely palliate the insult of a refusal. Though one visit fifty lodges in the course of a day, he must taste the food of every one.

The Indian system of chiefs, which still prevails, and is nearly the same everywhere, except with the Cherokees, Choctaws, Chickasaws, and the Creeks to a degree, seems to bear a strong resemblance to that of the patriarchs of old; which, with their clans so analogous to those of our forefathers, perhaps affords as strong a proof as any other of their Asiatic origin.[15] To this might be added their mode

[15] The origin of the American Indians has been discussed by too many able writers for me to enter into it here; nor will I attempt to show the general traits of similarity that are to be observed in their various languages: yet it may interest an occasional reader to be informed of the relations of consanguinity which subsist between many of the different Indian tribes. They may be arranged principally under the following heads: I. The Dahcotah stock, which is by far the most extensive of those indigenous west of the Mississippi. It embraces the Arkansas (of which the Quapaws are now the only remnant), the Osages, Kansas or Kaws, Iowas, Winnebagoes, Otoes, Missouries, Omahas, Poncas, and the various bands of the Sioux: all of whom speak a language still traceable to the same origin though some of them have been separated for several centuries. I call these indigenous to the West, because most of them have been so from the period of the earliest explorers on the Mississippi; yet the tradition among them is that they came from about the northern lakes; which appears corroborated by the fact that the language of the Naudowessies, Assiniboins, and perhaps others in that quarter, shows them to be of the same family.—2. The different bands of the Comanches and Shoshonies or Snakes, constitute another extensive stock, speaking one language.—3. The Blackfeet, Gros Ventres, or Minnatarees, Crows and Arrapahoes, speak dialects of another. —4. The Pawnees and Rickaras of the north, and the Wacoes, Witchitas, Towockanoes, Towyash and Keechyes, of Red River, are of the same origin. The Cheyennes, originally from near Lake Winnipeg, and the Kiawas (or Caiguas, according to Mexican orthography), appear unallied to any of the foregoing nations.—5. Of those from the north and east, the Algonquin stock appears most extensive,—embracing the Potawatomies, Ottawas, Chippewas, Knisteneaux, Crees, Sacs and Foxes; with whom the Delawares have also been classed, though their language would now appear very distinct.—6. The Wyandots, Senecas, and others of the Six Nations, are of the Huron or Iroquois.—7. The Shawnees and Kickapoos are of one stock. —8. The Kaskaskias, Piorias, Piankeshaws and Weaws, are descendants of the Miamies.—9. The Choctaws and Chickasaws are nearly the same people.—10. The Creeks and Seminoles—though old authors speak of the Creeks as being akin to the Choctaws, yet there is now but little relationship to be traced in their language; while that of the Cherokees appears entirely *sui generis*.—GREGG.

Gregg's classification is remarkably perceptive, but he fails to show the common Algonquin root of his groups 3, 5, 7, and 8 and the Muskogean root of his groups 9 and 10. The Crow and one tribe of the Gros Ventres (the Hidatsa) properly belong to his Dahcotah (Siouan) group. He is quite correct in classifying the Kiowa as a separate language stock, but the Cheyenne are Algonquin and the Cherokee, Iroquoyan. See Frederick Webb Hodge (ed.), *Handbook of American Indians North of Mexico*, Bureau of American Ethnology *Bulletin No. 30.*

of naming; for the Indians universally apply names significant of acts, qualities, beasts, birds, etc., to their offspring,—a practice which seems to have prevailed generally among the ancient Asiatics.[16] Surnames have only been adopted by educated families and mixed-bloods of the border nations, and are generally taken from their missionaries or some favorite friends; except they inherit surnames from parents of white extraction.

That the Indians of America are decreasing in numbers is very well known, but many are dwindling away, perhaps, at a more rapid pace than is generally suspected. The number of the Osages, it is confidently believed, has diminished fifty per cent. within the last ten years: the once powerful tribe of Missouries is now reduced to a mere remnant; while the Mandans, as a nation, have become entirely extinct: and others have shared or bid fair soon to share the same fate. This has resulted partially from the ravages of the small-pox and other diseases, yet as much no doubt from the baneful effects of intoxicating liquors. On this account, their diminution has generally been less in proportion as they are more remote from the whites. But the 'red man' has suffered from his intercourse with the whites not in this respect alone. The incentives to luxury and avarice continually presented by them, have had a very pernicious influence. Formerly the savages were contented with the indispensables of life —generally sober, just and charitable; but now they will sacrifice their comfort—risk their lives, and commit the most atrocious outrages, to gratify their vanity and lusts—to bedeck themselves with gewgaws and finery.

[16] The *tribes* often take the names of the seceding chiefs who originate them, or are called from some circumstance attending their separation; but frequently they assume a name from an important word in their language; thus *Choctaw* and *Chickasaw* are said to have been the name of chiefs; *Seminole* (or *Seminóleh*) and *Pioria* imply runaways or seceders; while *Illinois*, in the language of that ancient tribe, and *Lunnapáe*, by which the Delawares distinguish themselves, signify *man*. This last is perhaps most common; for, as each nation holds itself superior to all others, its members call themselves *men*, in contradistinction to *boys* or *squaws*, as they are wont to denominate their enemies.—GREGG.

CHAPTER XIII
THE FRONTIER INDIANS

Causes of Removal West—Annuities, etc.—Dissatisfaction of the Indians—Their Melioration by the Change—Superiority of their present Location—Lands granted to them—Improvements, Agriculture, etc.—Their Slaves—Manufactures—Style of Living, Dress, etc.—Literary Opportunities and Improvements—Choctaw Academy—Harpies and Frauds—Games—Systems of Government—Polygamy—Ancient Laws and Customs—Intemperance—Preventive Measures—A Choctaw Enactment—Marriage and Funeral Customs of the Choctaws—The Creeks—Their Summary Executions—Mourning—Indian Titles—The Northern Tribes—Census of the Frontier Nations.

FOR THE PURPOSE of a somewhat more discriminating notice of the Indian tribes beyond our western border—for it is to those I intend my remarks, in these pages, to be strictly confined—I will distinguish them, according to the prevailing classification of the West, as 'Frontier' or 'Border Indians,' which title includes those occupying that district lying west of and immediately adjoining Arkansas and Missouri, and known as the *Indian Territory;* and the 'Wild Tribes' or 'Prairie Indians,' by which are meant those who are found west of the others, and who range those immense plains from the borders of the Indian Territory to the Rocky Mountains. Of these I will speak in their order.

The most important of the frontier tribes, as is well known, are the Cherokees, Choctaws and Chickasaws, Creeks and Seminoles, Shawnees, Delawares, etc. It is equally well known that most of these tribes were removed from within the States, not less because of the vicious propensities which they contracted and the imposition to which they were continually exposed, than on account of the difficulty of maintaining peaceful relations between them and our own citizens, while they remained in their midst. Their situation within the States certainly presented quite an anomaly in government—independent powers within the limits of others claiming sovereign jurisdiction.[1]

A mistaken philanthropy—mistaken for want of a full knowledge of all the bearings of the subject—among some people, has occasioned much censure upon this branch of the policy of our government. But were we to take into consideration the treatment of other nations towards the aborigines of America, that of the United States, when placed in contrast, would certainly present a very benevolent aspect. They have always been removed by their own consent, obtained through their chiefs and councils; and have not only been given equal amounts of land, west of the border, but have generally been removed and furnished a year's subsistence at the expense of the government, and received valuable equivalents beside, in utensils and other necessaries, and in regular annuities. These are sums, generally in money, annually paid, for a series of years, to the several tribes, proportioned usually to the size of the tribe and the amount of territory acquired from it. This institution of annuities, however, though intended as the most charitable, has doubtless been the most injurious branch of the policy of the United States towards the Indians. Being thus afforded the means of living without much labor, they have neglected manufactures, and even agriculture, to a considerable degree, and many of them have acquired confirmed habits of indolence and dissipation; and now that their annuities are growing short, they are being left destitute, without the energy, the industry, or the means wherewith to procure a livelihood.

But, notwithstanding the constant efforts of the general government to make them comfortable, and the immense sums of money

[1] In the face of increasing pressure from white settlement, detached parties of Choctaw migrated west of the Mississippi as early as 1805, and bands of other tribes followed suit. A general removal (recommended by President Monroe in 1824) was carried out under President Jackson beginning in 1830. Land grants having already been made in Arkansas to some of the tribes, Indian Territory, to the west, was created in 1832. The Choctaws, Chickasaws and Creeks were forcibly removed to the latter (1836–38) as were the Seminoles after a bloody war of resistance (1835–42). Grant Foreman, *Indian Removal*.

398

which have been paid them, and their being located in regions far better suited to their wants and their habits of life than those they abandoned, many of them appear greatly dissatisfied with the change and with the government; which seems painfully demonstrative of that perverse, restless disposition, which appears ever to have characterized the conduct of half-civilized nations.

One ostensible reason for their unwillingness to remove, has been a reluctance to abandon their native homes and the 'graves of their fathers.' Many fabulous legends are told of the attachment of the Indian to his native soil, yet but few who are acquainted with their habitudes, will place much stress on this. Their own traditions, as well as experience, have shown, that, when left to themselves, they incline to migrate; of which the Azteques of Mexico, and the Osages, with others of our border, afford striking examples: in fact, there is scarcely a tribe on the frontier which has not its traditions of migrations at some period. The Shawnees say their fore-fathers emigrated from the south to the regions north of the Ohio—the Creeks, as well as many of the Choctaws, that they were originally from west of the Mississippi—besides many other cases.

But, with regard to this passage of our country's history, I will merely say, in addition, that, so far as I am able to judge, the condition of the 'red man' has been very materially bettered by the change. The lands they at present occupy are, for the most part, of a more fertile character than those which they have left. The climate is equally, or perhaps more healthy, in general; notwithstanding the dreadful mortality which afflicted many of them shortly after their removal—a calamity which was attributable, primarily, to the change of climate, as well as to the change of habits which their new dwelling-places involved; and secondarily, to the too abundant use of spirituous liquors, with which they were frequently provided by both native and white peddlers and traders, before any measures, efficient enough to check the evil, were taken either by themselves or by the general government. But, although the latter cause still prevails to some degree, I have little doubt that the average mortality among the frontier tribes, at present, is less than it was before their removal.

To each tribe has generally been granted a greater number of acres, with definite metes and boundaries, than had been ceded by them east of the Mississippi. It is deemed unnecessary, however, to swell this brief notice with a statement of the several amounts of land given to each tribe, and their localities, as these may be seen with sufficient accuracy and definiteness by consulting the map which accompanies this work.

The lands of each tribe are the property of the Indian commonwealth; and, therefore, even among the most civilized of them, the settler has a title only in his improvement, which he holds by occupancy, and can sell at pleasure. To prevent collisions in improvements, the first occupant is entitled to a certain distance in every direction. Among the Cherokees, no one can build within a quarter of a mile of the house or field of another: so, to extend their possessions, the more wealthy sometimes make several isolated improvements, scattered in different directions, within half a mile of each other.

The game in the interspersed forests having now become scarce, and that of the western prairies being too remote, the frontier Indians have generally turned their attention to agriculture, and to the raising of stock; and most of them have large numbers of horses, cattle, and hogs.

Some of these Indians, particularly of the southern nations, have very extensive farms: but the mass of their population extend their culture no further than they seem compelled by necessity. The traveller, passing through the Cherokee Nation, is struck with the contrast between an occasional stately dwelling, with an extensive farm attached, and the miserable hovels of the indigent, sometimes not ten feet square, with a little patch of corn, scarce large enough for a family garden. In fact, among all the tribes who have no slaves, what little there is of cultivation, is mostly the work of the women. Scattered through the country, one continually encounters dilapidated huts with trifling improvements, which have been abandoned by the owners for some fancy they may have taken to some other location at a distance, better adapted, as they think, to the promotion of their comfort, and upon which they may live with less labor.

Most of the labor among the wealthier classes of Cherokees, Choctaws, Chickasaws, Creeks, and Seminoles, is done by negro slaves; for they have all adopted substantially the Southern system of slavery.[2] Some individuals of these nations own over fifty slaves each: but they are the only slaveholders of the frontier tribes, except very few among the Shawnees.

With some tribes, and particularly among the lower classes of the Creek, they are inclined to settle in 'towns,' as they are called,—making large fields, which are cultivated in common, and the produce proportionally distributed. But these 'towns' are rather settlements than villages, being but sparse clusters of huts without any regularity. Indeed, there is not, I believe, a regularly laid out town in all the Indian country, nor a place that could even merit the name of a village; except Doaksville near Fort Towson, and perhaps Park Hill in the Cherokee nation.

Besides agriculture, most of the frontier tribes attend a little to manufactures, though with no greater energy. The women have generally learned to spin, weave and sew, at which they occupy themselves, occasionally during recess from the labors of the field. But very few of the men acquire mechanical arts or follow trades of any kind: their carpenter, wheelwright and smith work is done by a few mechanics provided the several tribes in accordance with treaty stipulations. To each tribe is furnished in particular one or more blacksmiths from the United States.

These frontier Indians for the most part live in cabins of logs, like those of our backwoods settlers; and many of them are undistinguishable, except in color, language, and to some degree in costume, from the poorer classes of their white neighbors. Even in dress and language the more civilized are fast conforming to the latter. In many families, especially of the Cherokees, the English tongue only is spoken; and great numbers of these, as well as of the Choctaws and Chickasaws, dress according to the American fashions: but the ruder portions of even these, the most enlightened nations, as is also the case with nearly all of the northern tribes, wear the hunting-shirt, sometimes of buckskin, but now more commonly of calico, cotton plaid or linsey. Instead of using hats, they wreathe about their heads

[2] The civilized tribes held slaves before their removal to Indian Territory. At the outbreak of the Civil War the Cherokees sided with the Confederacy, but a majority of their troops having gone over to the Union, they abolished slavery by law early in 1863 and permanently ended it by constitutional amendment in 1866. See *Constitution and Laws of the Cherokee Nation*.

a fancy-colored shawl or handkerchief. Neither do the women of these classes wear bonnets, but leave their heads exposed, or protected only with a shawl, somewhat after the manner of the Mexican females; to the lower classes of whom, indeed, the mixed-bloods of these Indians bear a strong resemblance. Their most usual dress is a short petticoat of cotton goods, or as frequently with the tribes of the north, of coarse red or blue broad-cloth.

The literary opportunities afforded to the border tribes are so important in their consequences as to deserve some notice. To each tribe has been granted, by the United States, a school fund, generally somewhat proportioned to the extent of the tribe. The Cherokees and Choctaws seem to have availed themselves of this provision to the greatest advantage. These funds are for the most part invested in American stocks, and the proceeds appropriated to educational uses, establishing schools, etc.[3] The tuition is, I believe, in every case, free to the Indians; and yet it is painful to know that comparatively few of the common classes will send their children.

The most extensive literary institution which has ever been in operation, for the benefit of the 'red man', was the 'Choctaw Academy,' established in Kentucky, and supported by a common fund of several different tribes. It was not as successful, however, as was anticipated by its projectors; and is now being transferred and merged into an academy near Fort Towson, in the Choctaw country, wholly supported out of the Choctaw fund.[4] This Academy proved very unsatisfactory to many of the tribes concerned. They said, with

[3] Their schools are mostly conducted in English, yet among some tribes they are often taught in their native languages. As in other respects, the Cherokees have made the greatest advancement in a literary point. Their singular system of characters representing syllables, invented by an illiterate native, is no doubt known to most of my readers. In these characters, a considerable number of books have been printed in their vernacular tongue. Many Cherokees, however, as well as Choctaws, have received good English educations. In the language of the latter also a great number of books have been published, but in which the common letter is used. A few books have also been printed in the languages of the Creeks, Wyandots, Potawatomies, and Ottawas, Shawnees, Delawares, and some in the different dialects of Osage, Kansas, Otoes, etc. There is now a printing-office in operation at Park Hill, in the Cherokee Nation, and another among the Shawnees at the Baptist Mission. —GREGG.

The Cherokee syllabary, completed after twelve years in 1821, was the work of George Guess (1760–1843), a half-blood subsequently called Sequoyah, who introduced it to the western Cherokees in 1822.

[4] Spencer Academy, at present Spencerville, Choctaw County, Oklahoma.

apparent justice, that their boys, educated there, forgot all their customs, their language, their relatives, their national attachments; and, in exchange, often acquired indolent and effeminate, if not vicious habits; and were rendered unfit to live among their people, or to earn a maintenance by labor. There seems but little doubt that the funds of each tribe might be employed to a much better advantage in their own country. The influence of the institutions would there be more likely to extend to all classes; and by gradual, the only practicable means, a change might be wrought upon the nation.

It is one of the calamities incident to the state of ignorance in which most of these poor Indians remain, and their close, indeed political connection with the more civilized people of the United States, that they are continually preyed upon by the unprincipled harpies who are ever prowling through their country, ready to seize every opportunity of deceiving and defrauding them out of their money or effects.[5] The most depraving agencies employed to this end are the ministration of intoxicating drinks, and gaming, of both which the Indians are passionately fond, and by which they are frequently robbed of their money as soon almost as received.

Apart from the usual games at cards, dice, etc., the Indians of the border have some peculiar games of their own, as well at cards as

[5] By no means the least considerable of the frauds practised upon the frontier Indians, have been by contractors and government agents. The character of these impositions may be inferred from the following instance, as it is told and very generally believed, upon the southwestern frontier.

It had been pretty well known, that some of those who had been in the habit of contracting to furnish with subsistence several of the southern tribes, in the year 1838 *et seq.*, had been imposing grossly upon the Indians as well as the Government, in the way of 'short rations' and other delinquencies, which resulted in the gain of a very large sum to the parties concerned. About the close of their operation, one of the *employés*, who was rather more cunning than the principals, took it in his head, on account of some ill-treatment he had suffered, to make an *exposé* of their transactions. He happened to hold a letter of instructions (which were of course of a confidential character), wherein were set forth the processes by which these frauds were to be practised. And to turn the affair to his particular profit, he threatened the parties with a complete exposure, unless a satisfactory *gratification* should interpose. A compromise being indispensible to the welfare of 'all whom it concerned,' a negotiation was soon set on foot: but the 'noisy customer' was not silenced, until he was paid $13,000 in cash; whereupon he delivered up the obnoxious 'papers,' and agreed to abscond. Some notice of the facts in this case are said to have been brought to the knowledge of the Government; and how it has escaped an investigation—and, more especially, how it escaped the attention of the Superintendent of that immediate district, have been matters of great surprise to those who had a knowledge of the particulars.—GREGG.

otherwise. Among these the most celebrated is the 'Ball Play,' which resembles, in some respects, the old-fashioned game of *bandy*. The wagers are usually laid upon beating the majority of a given number, a dozen or more of these games; and large amounts in horses, blankets, and other goods, and even money, are frequently staked upon the result.

Besides the ball play, *dancing* is a most favorite amusement of these tribes, indeed of all the frontier as well as prairie Indians. They formerly had many kinds of dances,—the green-corn dance, the medicine, the eagle, the scalp and the war dances. But these are now only practiced by the ruder portions of the border nations and the less improved tribes; among whom may still be witnessed frequently their genuine aboriginal frolics.

The green-corn dance generally lasts several days, commencing when the new crop begins to ripen. A large arbor of green branches is usually prepared, and numerous parties of both sexes dance in a body to their native songs and rude instrumental music, accompanied by their monotonous "heh! heh! heh!" with a chorus of yells at intervals; and their movements are attended with the most comical gesticulations. Having passed through a course of 'purification' by drinking a decoction of certain stimulant herbs, prepared by their medicine-men, and put out all the fires, they strike fire anew by rubbing sticks together; and a quantity of corn, pulse and other fruits of the season, being cooked with the 'new fire,' the dance is closed with a general feast. Each family, as it is said, then takes a supply from the 'new breed' of fire. A more interesting and salutary influence of this custom, which is said to prevail among some tribes at this festival, is the cancelling or composing of all old difficulties and disputes.

The most advanced of these border nations, the *Cherokees* and the united tribes of the *Choctaws* and *Chickasaws*, have adopted systems of government, which are based upon the constitutions of our States. The Cherokee being the most complete, some account of it may not be out of place in this connection.

A council or convention of the wise men of the nation was convened on the first of July, 1839, who framed a constitution, of which the following are the general features, it being somewhat similar to one previously adopted in the 'Old Nation.' The three powers, legislative, executive and judicial, are distinguished and established. The legislative consists of a National Committee and Council. The former is composed of two and the latter of three members from each of the eight or ten districts into which the nation was to be divided—elected for two years by the people. They convene annually on the first Monday in October, and each house elects a presiding officer out of its own body. Bills are introduced, discussed and passed according to parliamentary usage.

The executive, called Principal Chief, and an assistant chief, are elected for four years by the people. The executive has the usual veto and pardoning power. He is assisted by an 'Executive Council' of five, and the common cabinet of secretaries. The judiciary consists of a Supreme and Circuit Court, and the ordinary justices of the peace. Trial by jury is secured; and the common law of England appears to have been generally adopted. Religious toleration is guaranteed, but no person can hold a civil office who denies the existence of a God, and a future state of rewards and punishments.[6]

According to laws subsequently enacted by the same council, the punishment for murder is death; and for an attempt to kill, a fine correspondent to the damage, for a benefit of the injured party: for rape, a hundred lashes—but for infanticide, only twenty-five to fifty![7] Whipping seems the punishment for all inferior crimes; which is the same with the Choctaws and Creeks, among whom the executioners are called the 'light-horse,' a kind of police-guard, also formerly in use by the Cherokees, but now their place is supplied by a common sheriff and *posse*.

As is to be inferred from their institution, the Cherokees stand first among the 'red men' in refinement, though in industry, morality, and sobriety, they are no doubt excelled by the Choctaws and Chickasaws, who are reckoned the most quiet and Christian-like Indians of the border.

No laws have yet been passed to enforce the payment of debts, except by the Cherokees; and these found it necessary to suspend their operation for two years. Even the most improved have not

---

[6] See *Constitution and Laws of the Cherokee Nation.*

[7] By 1875 these laws had been changed to correspond with those of the United States. *Ibid.*, arts. ii, iv, vi, x.

prohibited polygamy by any law; though, from the example of the whites and of the more civilized among them, as well as the exertions of the missionaries, it is growing out of repute with most of the border nations. It is still occasionally practiced, however; and the ruder classes among them all, I believe, sometimes still take any number of wives, and divorce them at pleasure. But the more enlightened are married by preachers, or authorized civil officers.

With the united nation of Choctaws and Chickasaws, the executive power is vested in four chiefs, called in Choctaw *mingoes,* who are selected one from each of the districts into which the country is divided, and of which the Chickasaw tribe constitutes one.[8] These chiefs are vested with the usual veto and pardoning powers, and are elected for four years. Most of their other constitutional provisions resemble those of the Cherokees. The Choctaws, as well as the Creeks, punish the crime of murder with death by shooting, which is generally executed immediately after trial, by the 'light-horse.'

It has become evident, however, that written laws and courts of justice, judges and juries, are still rather in advance of the state of civilization of the ruder classes, even among these most enlightened tribes. It has been found very difficult to bring them under their subordination. They have had, notwithstanding, a salutary effect in many cases, as especially with regard to murder. Among most of these nations (as well as the wild tribes), it was formerly the custom to leave the punishment of homicide to the relatives of the murdered. With the Choctaws and Cherokees, in particular, the entire clan or family of the murderer were held responsible for the crime; and though the real offender might escape, the bereaved family had a right to kill any one of his nearest relatives that could be found, up to the most remote kindred. There seemed no exceptions for accidental homicide, or killing in self-defence: the Mosaic precept of 'life for life' must be fulfilled, unless satisfactorily commuted. This savage custom had at least one salutary effect, however: the relatives themselves, instead of assisting the escape, as so often occurs in civilized life, were generally the first to apprehend and bring the fugitive criminal to justice.

[8] The Chickasaw Nation was established separately in 1855, adopting a new constitution (1867) modeled on that of the United States.

But among the Choctaws, at least, any one might take the place of the murderer, and in the death of the substitute the law was satisfied, and the true criminal remained exempt. An intelligent and creditable Choctaw related to me an affecting incident, for the truth of which he vouched. An Indian had remained responsible for the appearance, on a certain day, of his brother, who had killed a man. When the day arrived, the murderer exhibited some reluctance to fulfil the pledge, when the other said to him: "My brother, you are no brave—you are afraid to die—stay here and take care of my family—I will die in your place:" whereupon he immediately attended the appointed spot, and was executed accordingly.

The highest honor known among them, in fact, being that of a 'great brave,' it reflected the greatest credit to meet death boldly. Instead of being visited by his tribe with infamy for the crime he had committed, it rather tended to make his name illustrious, if he met the consequences without fear or flinching: whereas, any effort to avoid death was attributed to cowardice. It would have been esteemed quite as ignominious for the murderer to flee the established forfeit of his life, as for a 'gentleman' under the 'civilized code of honor,' to back out from a duel.

But among most of the frontier, as also the wild tribes, a commutation, though not honorable to the perpetrator, was and still is permitted, except by the Cherokees and Choctaws. Any recompense which would satisfy the bereft family, released the murderer from further penalty.

There is scarcely any temptation which the Indian tribes have to encounter so frequently and so seriously fatal to their social improvement, as intemperance. Of this they are conscious themselves, and most of them have adopted measures for prohibiting the introduction of ardent spirits among them, and for checking the propensity to use them, with various degrees of success. Among the Choctaws, a law was passed upon this subject, which, though not entirely, was measurably successful; and the spirit which effected its passage was worthy of the most exalted state of civilization.

It seems that the tribe had generally become sensible of the pernicious influences of strong drinks upon their prosperity and happiness, and had attempted various plans for its suppression, without success. At last, it was determined by the chiefs, captains, and head men, to strike a blow which should reach the very root of the evil at once. A council was called, and many and long were the speeches which were made, and much enthusiasm was created against the monster 'Whiskey,' and all his brood of compound enormities. Still every one seemed loth to move his arrest and execution. Finally, a captain of more than ordinary temerity arose, and offered a resolution that each and every individual who should thenceforward dare to introduce any of the liquid curses into their country, should be punished with a hundred lashes on his bare back, and the liquor be poured out. This was passed, after some slight changes, by acclamation: but, with a due sense of the injustice of *ex-post-facto* restrictions, all those who had liquors on hand were permitted to sell them. The council adjourned; but the members soon began to canvass among each other the pernicious consequences which might result from the protracted use of the whiskey already in the shops, and therefore concluded the quicker it was drank up, the more promptly would the evil be over: so, falling to, in less than two hours Bacchus never mustered a drunker troop than were these same temperance legislators. The consequences of their determination were of lasting importance to them. The law, with some slight improvements, has ever since been rigorously enforced.

Among most of the Indian tribes the daughter has very little to do with the selection of her husband. The parents usually require to be satisfied first, and their permission being secured the daughter never presumes to offer any important resistance. There is a post-nuptial custom peculiar to the full-blood Indians of the Choctaws, which deserves particular notice. For years, and perhaps for life, after the marriage of her daughter, the mother is forbidden to look upon her son-in-law. Though they converse together, he must be hidden from her by a wall, a tent, a curtain, or, when nothing else offers, by covering the eyes. During their emigration, it is said these poor superstitious matrons were put to infinite trouble so as not to infract this custom. While travelling, or in camp often without tents, the mother-in-law was afraid to raise her head or open her eyes, lest they should meet the interdicted object.

It is another peculiarity, which they have in common with some of the more northern tribes, that the Choctaw wife, of the 'old school,' can never call her husband by name. But if they have offspring— she calls him "my son's father;" or, more commonly using the child's name, when, if Ok-le-no-wa, for instance, she calls the husband "Ok-le-no-wa's father." And yet another oddity regarding names: the ignorant Choctaw seems to have a superstitious aversion to telling his own name: indeed it appears impossible to get it from him, unless he have an acquaintance present, whom he will request to tell it for him.

In burials, the civilized Choctaws follow the customs of the whites, but the ruder classes still preserve their aboriginal usages. According to these, a painted pole with a flag is stuck up at the grave, which usually remains three months. During this period they have regular mourning exercises every morning and evening; and are always prompt to avail themselves, at any hour of the day, of the assistance of any friend who may visit them to help them to weep. At the end of the prescribed term, the friends of the bereft family attend a feast at their house, and, after dancing all night, the next morning visit the grave and pull down the pole; which is called 'the pole-pulling.' After this all mourning ceases, and the family is permitted to join in the usual amusements and festivities of the tribe, which was not allowable before.

Though the *Creeks*[9] are generally a very industrious people, raising an abundance of corn and vegetables, yet they are quite behind their neighbors, of whom I have been speaking, as well politically as in a social and literary view. Their executive consists of two principal chiefs, and their legislature or council of about forty minor chiefs or captains, who are also, *ex officio,* justices of the peace. They have no trial by jury, and their judicial proceedings are exceedingly summary—frequently without witnesses; for the warriors are generally too proud to deny a charge, lest it be construed into cowardice. Executions sometimes take place within an hour after the commencement of trial. Murder, rape and a third conviction of stealing are punished with death, usually by shooting; but, in case of homicide,

[9] These Indians called themselves Muscogee or Muscóhgeh. They acquired the name of *Creeks,* by the whites, from the great number of small streams that intersect the country which they formerly inhabited—being first called "Indians of the country of *creeks.*"—GREGG.

if claimed by the relatives of the deceased, the criminal is executed with the same kind of weapon, or, if possible, the very same, with which he committed the murder.

Most inferior crimes, as has been mentioned, are punished by whipping: for the first offence of stealing, fifty lashes; for the second, a hundred and ears cropped. Adultery is punished by cutting off both the nose and ears of the adulteress; but the husband has a right to say if the law shall be executed: in fact, he is generally the executioner, and that often without trial. Notwithstanding the severity of these laws, they are for the most part rigorously enforced: though a commutation satisfactory to the aggrieved is still permitted to release the offender. Their laws, in cases of accidental homicide, are still more barbarously rigid than those of the other nations.

The obsequies of the Creeks are peculiar in this,—that at the moment an Indian expires, a gun is discharged. Their graves are generally under the floors of their dwellings, and a husband's is apt to be under the bed of his widow. The fate of the unfortunate relict is miserable enough in any country, but among the Creeks her doom is barbarously rigorous. She remains in strict mourning for four years,[10] with dishevelled hair and without combing,—unless the relatives of the deceased interfere; whereby it is sometimes put an end to in a few months, provided the sincerity of her grief be evident and her conduct meritorious. In their mourning, however, they do not weep and cry with such clamorous vehemence as the Choctaws and others. But the Shawnees and Delawares are still more celebrated for quiet mourning. As warlike nations, they appear to disdain to mourn and wail aloud, as is the practice among the greater portion of the savage tribes.

Though these people have no family names, they generally take a kind of honorary title or *sobriquet*, as is also the case with the wild tribes, upon the occurrence of any important incident, or the performance of a meritorious feat.—A singular mode of *inheritance* prevails among the Cherokees, the Creeks, and perhaps others. Though the

[10] This custom seems to have descended from antiquity. Adair, prior to 1775, writes that "The Muscohge widows are obliged to live a chaste single life for the space of four years; and the Chikkasah women, for the term of three, at the risk of the law of adultery being executed against the recusants." But I have not heard the custom spoken of among the Chickasaws at the present day.—GREGG.

women in other respects are mostly held as very inferior beings, the clans are all reckoned by them: the children pertain to the mother, and the estates descend through the female branch of the family. They say it is easy enough to verify the mothers of families, but it is difficult to identify the fathers.

The remaining tribes, inhabiting the more northern frontier, as well as the Seminoles who are located among the Creeks, possess so few distinct or striking characteristics, and, indeed, are mostly so few in number, that a particular notice of them seems hardly to be required. Suffice it to say, that all of them, as I believe, still retain their ancient systems of arbitrary chiefs and councils of sages and braves, nearly in their primitive state; and that the greater portion of them live in log huts, and cultivate the soil to a considerable extent. Though the Shawnees, Delawares, and Kickapoos, are among the most agricultural of the northern Indians, yet a few of these spend the greater portion of their time on the Prairies in hunting and in trading with the wild tribes.[11]

[11] No complete census has been taken of the frontier Indians since their removal; but the aggregate population of those settled west of the border, exclusive of the Osages, Kansas, and others of the north (who are more appropriately ranked among the Prairie Indians), is 81,541, according to the report of the Commissioner of Indian Affairs for the year 1843. Of these there are reckoned of Cherokees, 25,911; Choctaws, 15,177; Chickasaws, 4,930; Creeks, 24,594; Seminoles, or Florida Indians, 3,824; Senecas from Sandusky, 251; Senecas and Shawnees, 211; Quawpaws, 476; Wyandots, 664; Potawatomies, Chippewas, and Ottawas, located on the waters of the Osage, 2,350; Kaskaskias and Piorias, 150; Piankeshaws, 98; Weaws, 176; Shawnees, 887; Delawares, 1,059; Stockbridges, Munsees, etc., 278; Kickapoos, 505. In addition to these there still remain east of the Mississippi, of Cherokees, 1000; Choctaws, 3,323;[a] Chickasaws, 80; Creeks, 744; Potawatomies, etc., 500; Weaws, 30; besides some entire remnant tribes.

Many of the foregoing amounts, however, have been standing numbers in the tables of the reports of the Indian Department, ever since the removal of these tribes, and as it is known that most of them have been on the decline, the above aggregate is no doubt excessive. For instance, instead of 25,911, as given in the report for the Cherokees, their very intelligent agent, Governor Butler, reckoned them in 1842, at only about 18,000; the Creeks in place of 24,594, have, in like manner, been set down at about 20,000; and in the 'Choctaw Almanac' for 1843, I find the population of that nation rated as 12,690, instead of 15,177, as stated in the Commissioner's report.—GREGG.

[a] In his second edition, Gregg notes here that these Choctaw were in January, 1845, "in progress of emigration," and revises all census figures in keeping with the Indian Commission's report for 1844.

CHAPTER XIV
INDIANS OF THE PRAIRIES

System of Chiefs—Mode of Warfare—War-Council—The Scalp-dance
—The Calumet or Pipe of Peace—Treaties—Public News-criers—Arms
of the Indians—Bow and Arrows, etc.—Hunting—Dancing—Language of Signs—Telegraphs—Wigwams or Lodges—Pack-dogs—Costumes—Painting, Tattooing, etc.—Indian Dandies—Manufactures, and
Dressing the Buffalo Rug—Indian Diet, Feasting etc.—Primitive Thomsonians—Their domestic Animals, the Dog and the Horse—Wampum—
Their Chronology.

THOSE SAVAGE HORDES which may be considered as the Prairie Indians proper, have made little or no perceptible progress in civilization. They mostly live by plunder and the chase: a few eke out a
subsistence by agriculture. They consist of various distinct tribes, but
among whom there is a greater diversity of language than of habitudes. I would not have it understood, however, that all the customs
of every band are entirely similar: it is this assumption, together
with the practice of setting down as standing customs what they have
observed on some particular occasions, that has frequently created
such a discrepancy between the accounts of transient travellers.

There is scarcely a prairie tribe, however limited in numbers, but
is subdivided into petty bands, each under the immediate control of
its own chief. Their systems of government are frequently compounded of the patriarchal and military. The most influential heads
of families exercise a petty rule, which often extends beyond their
own household to a circle of adherents. Several of these clans, bound
by the ties of consanguinity or friendship, are apt to come under the
control, by common consent, of some more influential chief, who
may have gained celebrity in their wars; but a regular hereditary

descent seems rarely established. These petty bands seldom unite under one general leader, except for the common defence, when threatened with danger. Occasionally there springs up a master spirit—a great brave and a great sage, who is able to unite his whole tribe, in which he is generally aided by a sufficient knack at sorcerous tricks to give him the character of a great 'medicine-man.'

War seems to be the element of the prairie Indians, notwithstanding but few possess much intrinsic bravery. They are, in fact, the most cowardly savages east of the Rocky Mountains, bearing but little similitude in this respect to the aborigines of the interior of the United States. They rarely attack an enemy except with a decided advantage; for the prospect of losing even a single warrior will often deter them from undertaking the most flattering adventure. It is true that, in addition to their timidity, they are restrained by the fact that the loss of a man often casts a gloom upon the most brilliant victory, and throws a whole clan into mourning. On this account they generally attack by surprise, and in the night, when all are presumed to be asleep; having care, if against a formidable enemy, that it be long enough before the morning dawn to allow them to retire beyond reach of pursuit before daylight. When the moon rises at a late hour, just before she appears, is a favorite time; for then they will have a gleam of light by which to collect and drive off the prize of stock which they may be able to frighten away. These prowling parties around a camp sometimes employ a species of signals in imitation of wolves, owls and other nocturnal animals, by which they communicate with each other—mimicking so to the life as not to give alarm to unsuspecting travellers.

War is seldom concluded upon, or even a campaign undertaken, without a general council, in which all the chiefs and most distinguished braves and sages assemble. After all are seated in a circle, the pipe is passed around until their brains are sufficiently soothed to enable them to consult the Great Spirit, and take freely into advisement the important matters under consideration. Therefore the tobacco smoke is usually blown upwards, as a propitiatory incense to the invoked spirits or genii who dwell 'upon the sky.' In this operation the smoke is generally inhaled into the lungs, and discharged in murky streams from the olfactories. If a council be preparatory to a campaign, the warriors sometimes catch the tobacco smoke in the hand, anointing their bodies with it; which they fancy renders them, if not invulnerable, at least far more secure from the darts of their enemies.

Although in their warfare they employ every wile and stratagem, and faithless subterfuge, to deceive their enemies, and in battle are relentless and cruel in the extreme, yet they seldom resort to those horrid punishments and tortures upon their prisoners which were wont to be inflicted by the savages of the interior of the United States, during their early wars with the whites. The practice of burning their captives alive, said to have prevailed many years ago among some prairie tribes, seems now to have grown quite out of use.

Upon returning from a campaign after a defeat, the village resounds for many days with the lamentations, the shrieks and wailings of the women and children; in which, not only the bereft families, but all the relatives and most of the friends of the deceased join. If, on the contrary, the warriors have been successful, and bring home scalps of their enemies, all join in their most famous festival, the scalp-dance. In this fête the savage trophies are usually elevated upon a pole in the centre of the dance; or perhaps the brave captors retain them in their hands, tossing and swinging them about their heads; at the same time vehemently apostrophizing these ghastly representatives of their enemies, with the most taunting and insulting bravadoes; branding the nation with cowardice and effeminacy; daring them to come forward and revenge the blood of their slain; then concluding with scoffs and exulting yells at the dastardly silence of their enemies, whom they represent as afraid to whisper a note of vengeance against their superiors and masters, the triumphing conquerors. After the warriors have become fatigued, the squaws and children generally continue the barbarous festivity; in the midst of which some vainglorious brave will rise perhaps, and repeat the apostrophic fanfaronades, representing that the very squaws and papooses hold them in cowering submission, and that henceforth these only will be sent to subdue them; their warriors being reserved for more noble enemies. These brutal rites and rodomontades being concluded, the scalps are handed to their owners, who cure and paint them for future war-dances and other kindred ceremonies.

When a tribe wishes to celebrate a treaty of peace with an enemy, a number of their warriors, as ambassadors, or perhaps a whole band, move to the neighborhood, and send the calumet or pipe of peace, which supplies the place of the flag of truce among civilized nations:[1] though, when the embassy is to the whites, a flag usually accompanies, as they have learned that this is our token of peace. The overture being accepted, the chiefs and principals of each band meet in council, sometimes in a wigwam, if there be a suitable one, else in the open air, taking their seats, as usual, upon their haunches in a circle proportioned to the number. If there be presents—and these are an indispensable earnest of friendship from the whites—the essence, the seal of the treaty, without which negotiation is vain—these are laid in the centre. A personage in the capacity of an orderly sergeant then lights the calumet, which he hands to a principal chief, who, before smoking, usually points the stem towards the four cardinal points, and towards the heavens and the earth—then takes a certain number of whiffs (generally about three), and passing it to the next, who draws an equal number of whiffs, it thus continues around the circle, in the direction of the sun, each sending fumid currents upward from the nozzle. It seems looked upon as sacrilege for a person to pass before the pipe while the chiefs are smoking; and the heedless or impudent are sometimes severely punished for the act. The 'big talk' follows, and the presents are distributed by a chief who exercises the office of commissary. But in the petty truces among

[1] This seems to have been of ancient and general use among the savages of North America. "I must speak here of the *Calumet*," remarks Father Marquette, "the most mysterious thing in the world. The sceptres of our kings are not so much respected; for the savages have such a deference for this pipe, that one may call it *the god of peace and war, and the arbiter of life and death*. One, with this calumet, may venture amongst his enemies, and in the hottest engagement they lay down their arms before this sacred pipe." The deference is perhaps not so great at the present day, though the 'pipe of peace' is still very much respected. Even the ashes from the calumet seem to he beld sacred; for usually after smoking, the pipe is emptied in some corner of the lodge specially allotted for the purpose. But as they have generally learned that smoking is not practised by the whites on these occasions, it is now not commonly held important for us to smoke with them; but presents are expected instead. Anciently, however, they were more strict; for, in another place, the same author (in 1673) relates:—"As soon as we sat down, they presented us, according to custom, their *calumet*, which one must needs accept, for else he should be lookt upon as an enemy, or a meer brute; however, it is not necessary to smoak, and provided one puts it to his mouth, it is enough."—GREGG.

Marquette's quotations appear in Thwaites (ed.), *Jesuit Relations*, LIX, 117–19,131.

each other, presents are scarcely expected, except they be claimed by the more powerful party as a matter of tribute.

Travellers and hunters are generally obliged to hold a treaty or 'big talk' with every band of prairie Indians they may encounter, if they wish to maintain friendly relations with them. Treaties have also been held, at different periods, with most of the wild tribes, by agents of the U.S. Government, yet for the most part with but very little effect—they generally forget or disregard them by the time the presents they may have received are consumed.

These treaties, as well as other council deliberations, are generally promulgated by a sort of public crier, who proclaims the stipulations and resolutions from lodge to lodge; and the event is preserved in the memory of the sages to future generations. Among some of the tribes their memory is assisted by the famous 'wampum belt,' which is a list or belt made of wampum beads, so interwoven in hieroglyphic figures as to form a record of important events. Others preserve the same by hieroglyphic paintings on their buffalo rugs, and the like.

The *arms* of the wild Indians are chiefly the bow and arrows, with the use of which they become remarkably expert. A dextrous savage will lay a wager, at short shots, against many riflemen. Indeed, there is hardly any more effective weapon than the bow and arrow in the hands of an expert archer. While the musketeer will load and fire once, the bowman will discharge a dozen arrows, and that, at distances under fifty yards, with an accuracy nearly equal to the rifle. In a charge, they are eminently serviceable; for the Indian seems to discharge his arrows with about as much certainty when running at full speed as when standing.

The usual length of the Indian bow is about three feet, though it is sometimes as much as four. It is generally made of elastic wood, yet elk's horn is occasionally used. Those of the latter are made of two of the longest and straightest shafts, which, being shaved down to the necessary proportions, are united by lapping their ends together and binding them firmly with sinew. Bows have also been made, in the same manner, of a pair of buffalo ribs; but as well these as those of elk-horn, are rather items of curiosity than of service: at least, they are not equal to the bows of the bois-d'arc tree. Even the backs of the *wooden* bows are often lined the whole length with a broad strip of sinew, and the whole wrapped with shreds of the same. The arrows are generally about thirty inches long, and pointed with iron, though the primitive flint points are still met with among some of the wildest tribes.

Besides these, the lance or spear, the use of which they may have learned from the Mexicans, is an effective weapon in the charge as well as the chase. Many are also provided with the Northwestern fusil, and some have rifles. Very few, however, have acquired the dexterity of our frontier Indians with this deadly weapon. But no Indian deems his equipage complete without a 'scalping-knife;' yet among the western prairie Indians the tomahawk is but little known. These employ, in its stead, the war-club or 'warhawk,' which are bludgeons with an encased stone for a head in the former, and with a transverse blade or spike in its place in the latter. Many are provided with shields of raw buffalo or elk skin, upon which are frequently painted some rude hieroglyphical devices representing the enemies they have slain, as well as any other notable exploits of which they can boast. Such as are without these have their titles to renown recorded commonly upon the handles of their hatchets, their war-clubs, or perhaps tattooed upon their breasts or arms.

Besides war, *hunting* seems the only creditable employment in which a warrior can engage. Every other labor is put upon the squaws; and even when a party of hunters set out, they generally provide themselves with enough of these 'menials' to take charge of the meat: the Indian only deigns to shoot down the game; the squaws not only have it to cure and pack, but to skin and dress.

Except such tribes as are expert with the rifle, very few of the prairie Indians hunt other game than the buffalo: not, as some have presumed, because they deem all small game too ignoble for them, but because the former is at once easiest taken, and affords the most bounteous supply of food. The antelope is too wild and fleet for their mode of hunting, and is only occasionally taken by stratagem; while the deer, as difficult to take in the chase, is less easily entrapped. But, mounted upon their trained steeds, and with the arrow or lance, they are not to be excelled in the chase. A few of them, let loose among a herd of buffalo, will soon have the plain strewed with their carcasses.

Among the amusements of the Indians generally, *dancing*, is perhaps the most favorite. Besides a war accompaniment, it is practised as a recreation, and often connected with their worship. Their social frolics, in which the squaws are commonly permitted to join, are conducted with less ferocity of manner than their war dances; though even these are accompanied with the wildest and most comical gesticulations, and songs full at once of mirth and obscenity. In these, as well as in the war and scalp dances, a sort of little drum and a shrill squeaking pipe are their common instruments of music.

As so many tongues, entirely different, are spoken by the prairie Indians, a 'language of signs' has become the general medium of communication between the different nations. This system of signs has been brought to such perfection among them, that the most intricate correspondence seems to be intelligibly conducted by such as have acquired a proficiency in this 'dumb language.'

Their systems of telegraphs are very peculiar, and though they might seem impracticable at first, yet so thoroughly are they understood by the savages, that it is availed of frequently to immense advantage. The most remarkable is by raising smokes, by which many important facts are communicated to a considerable distance—and made intelligible by the manner, size, number or repetition of the smokes, which are commonly raised by firing spots of dry grass. When travelling, they will also pile heaps of stones upon mounds or conspicuous points, so arranged as to be understood by their passing comrades; and sometimes they set up the bleached buffalo heads, which are everywhere scattered over those plains, to indicate the direction of their march, and many other facts which may be communicated by those simple signs.

Almost every tribe has some peculiarity in the construction of their lodges or wigwams, in the manner of arranging their camps, and in the different items of dress, by any or all which peculiarities the experienced traveller is able to recognize the tribe of their owner. If a moccasin, or other article of apparel be found, he at once designates the nation to which it belongs—even a track is often sufficient to identify them.[2] Also by the 'sign,' and especially the remains of fires,

[2] As many tribes make their moccasins of different shapes—some with hooked toes, others broad—some with the seam on the bottom, etc., there is always a palpable difference in the tracks.—GREGG.

he determines the interval elapsed since their departure, with remarkable accuracy.

The lodges are composed of a frame of small poles or rods, covered usually with buffalo skins, which receive but little further preparation than the currying off of the hair. Some give their lodges a round wagon-top shape, as those of the Osages, which commonly consist of a frame of bent rods, resembling wagon-bows, and covered with skins, the bark of trees, or, as is generally the case in their villages, with grass and earth. Again, some dispose the poles in two parallel lines, and incline them against a ridge-pole, which gives the wigwam the shape of a house-roof: others, planting small rods in a circle, so twine the points together as to resemble, in some degree, when covered, a rounded hay-mow: but by far the most general style, among the wild tribes, of constructing their wigwams, is by planting the lodge-poles so as to enclose a circular area of from ten to twenty feet in diameter (the size depending upon the number of the family); and the tops being brought together, it forms a conical frame, which is closely covered with skins, except an aperture in the apex for the escape of the smoke. This is the style of the Comanches and most other tribes of the great plains. The doors of the lodges being closed with a skin, they are kept very comfortable in winter with but little fire. This is kindled in the centre, and the smoke is discharged so freely through the hole in the vertex of the apartment, that the interior is but little infected by it.

These lodges are always pitched or set up by the squaws, and with such expedition, that, upon the stopping of an itinerant band, a town springs up in a desert valley in a few minutes, as if by enchantment. The lodge-poles are often neatly prepared, and carried along from camp to camp. In conveying them, one end frequently drags on the ground; whereby the trail is known to be that of a band with families, as war parties never carry lodge-poles. The Chayennes, Sioux and some other northern tribes, often employ dogs for carrying and dragging their lodge covers and poles; indeed for conveying most of their light baggage: but, for ordinary travelling purposes and packing their more weighty baggage, they use horses. So few navigable waters traverse the Prairies, that none of the Indians of the high plains have learned the use of canoes or water-craft of any kind.

There is some variety in the dress in vogue among the different tribes; though they all use moccasins, leggins, flap or breech-clout, and, when not in active pursuits, they generally wrap their bodies in buffalo rugs, blankets or mantles of strouding, according to their wealth or opportunities. Some of the northern tribes display considerable ingenuity and taste in the manufacture of moccasins. But this is the work of the women, who often embroider them with beads and colored porcupine quills, in a most beautiful manner. The *leggin* is a buckskin or cloth covering for the leg and thigh, as of the pantaloon. A superfluous list is usually left outside the seam, which, if of skin, is slitted into long tassels, or if of cloth, the wide border remains entire, to dangle and flap upon the exterior of the legs. A strip of strouding (that is, coarse broad-cloth) about a foot in width and a yard or more long, constitutes the most usual flap; which being passed betwixt the legs, the ends are secured under the belt around the waist, whence the leggins are suspended. As the flap is sometimes near two yards long, a surplusage of half a yard or more at each end is sometimes left dangling down before and behind.

The Indians use no head-dress, but support the bleakest rains and hottest suns of those bare plains with naked heads. Nevertheless, their coarse black hair seems 'fertilized' by exposure; for they rarely become gray till an exceeding old age; and I do not recollect to have ever seen a bald Indian. Their eyesight also, they retain in extraordinary vigor, notwithstanding the want of protection even of the eye-lashes and brows (which are plucked out), and in spite of the constant use of apparently deleterious paints around the edges of the lids. Though using no regular head-dress, they sometimes wear, as a temporary ornament, a fantastic cap of skins; and it is not unusual to see a brave with the entire shaggy frontlet of a buffalo, horns and all, set upon his head, which, with his painted face, imparts a diabolic ferocity to his aspect.

The Indians of the Plains, almost without exception, wear long hair, which dangles in clotted tresses over the shoulders—besmeared with gum, grease and paints, and ornamented with feathers and trinkets. But most of those intermediate tribes nearer our border, trim their hair in a peculiar manner.

Vermillion seems almost indispensable to the Indian's toilet;

but in default of this they paint with colored earths. When going to war, they bedaub their bodies with something black—mud, charcoal or gunpowder, which gives them a frightful appearance. But 'ornamental' painting is much more gay and fanciful. The face, and sometimes arms and breasts are oddly striped and chequered, interspersed with shades of yellow and white clay, as well as occasional black, though the latter is chiefly appropriated to war. Especial pains are taken to tip the eyelids most gaily with vermillion.

Besides painting, most of the tribes tattoo—some sparingly, while others make their faces, breasts, and particularly their arms, perfectly piebald. This seems practised to some extent by all the savages from the Atlantic to the Pacific. Figures are pierced in the skin with any sharp pointed instrument—even the keen prickles of the cactus—and pulverized charcoal or gunpowder, or sometimes the coloring juice of a plant, is rubbed into the fresh punctures, which leaves a lasting stain.

The most usual female dress is of the style worn by the Comanche squaws, which is described in speaking of that nation. With respect to dress and other ornaments, however, the order of the civilized world is reversed among the Indians. The 'fair sex' paint less than the men—use fewer ornaments generally, and particularly, wear no pendants in the ears. While a savage beauty pays but little attention to her person, a 'brave' will spend as much time at his toilet as a French belle, in the adjustment of his ornaments—his paint, trinkets, beads and other gewgaws. A mirror is his idol: no warrior is equipped without this indispensable toilet companion, which he very frequently consults. He usually takes it from its original case, and sets it in a large fancifully carved frame of wood, which is always carried about him. He is also rarely without his tweezers whether of a fold of tin, of hardened wood, or of spirally twisted wire, with which he carefully eradicates, not only his beard, eyelashes and brows, but every villous particle from his body, as fast as it appears; for everything of the kind is considered as extremely unbecoming a warrior. It is on this account that Indians have frequently been represented as naturally beardless.

All Indians are passionately fond of beads, trinkets and gewgaws of every kind. The men often cut up the rim of the ears in a frightful manner to admit their pendants of beads, plate, shells, etc.; and even strips of lead are sometimes twined around the separated rim, by the weight of which the detached portion of the ear is frequently swagged down some inches. It is not unusual to see near half a pound even of beads and 'jewelry' swung to each ear; and among some tribes, also a large quantity to the nose. The hair is likewise garnished with the same, and the neck with strings of beads, bear's claws, and the like; while the arms are profusely ornamented with bracelets of wire or plated metal. The 'braves' are those who commonly deck themselves with the most gaudy trappings, and would usually be taken by a stranger for the chiefs of the band, who, on the other hand, are often apparelled in the most ordinary manner.

The squaws are, in every sense of the word, the slaves of the men. They are called upon to perform every toilsome service—to carry wood and make fires—to skin and dress the meat and prepare the food—to herd, drive up, saddle and unsaddle their lords' horses —to pitch and strike the lodges—to pack up the baggage, and often indeed to carry heavy loads during travel—in short, everything else pretty much but fight and hunt, which the Indian boasts of, as being his peculiar, if not his sole vocations.

What little of manufacturing is done among the Indians is also the work of the women. They prepare the different articles of apparel. In embroidering moccasins and their leathern petticoats, etc., their greatest skill, particularly among the northern tribes, is exhibited. But the most extensive article of their manufacture is the *buffalo rug*, which they not only prepare for their own use, but which constitutes the largest item of their traffic with the Indian traders. These are dressed and cured exclusively by the squaws.

To dress a buffalo rug, the first step is to 'flesh' the skin, or neatly scrape from the inner surface every carneous particle. This is generally done with an instrument of bone, cut something in the shape of a small adz, with a serrate edge. For this operation the skin is sometimes suspended in a frame upon the branch of a tree, or a fork of the lodge—though more commonly, perhaps, stretched with pegs upon the smooth ground, with the flesh-side up. After it dries, the spongy surface of the skin is neatly curried off with another adz-shaped bone or handle of wood, with a flat bit of iron transversely set for the blade, which is edged after the manner of a currier's instrument. The surface is then besmeared with brains (which the Canadians call *mettre à la cervelle*), and rolled up with the flesh-side in, in which condition it is left for two or three days. The brains of the same animals are generally used; those of a buffalo being more than sufficient to dress his own hide. The pores of the skin being fully penetrated by the brains, it is again wetted, and softened by continual working and rubbing till it dries. To facilitate this last operation, it is sometimes stretched in a frame and suspended before a fire, when the inner surface is scraped with the serrated adz before mentioned, and finished off by assiduous rubbing with a pumice-stone, if that article can be had; if not, by passing the skin by small sections rapidly back and forth over a slack cord.

Buffalo rugs are often observed with a seam in the middle. This is caused by cutting them in two, partly for convenience in dressing them, and partly to take out the hollow occasioned by the hump, particularly of the bulls. The hump of the cow being less, their skins generally bear dressing without being cut. The hide is frequently split in two, however, in skinning the animal, the Indians preferring to commence on the back.

The buffalo skin is often dressed without the wool. To this end the hide is soaked in water till the hair is loosened, when it is 'curried' and 'brained,' and softened as above. Of these dressed buffalo skins (known among Mexicans as *anta blanca*) is made a considerable portion of the Indian clothing for both sexes—even the petticoats of the females; though these prefer buckskin when they can procure it.

The chief aliment of the Prairie Indians is flesh, though in default of this they often sustain themselves for weeks together upon roots, herbs and fruits. The buffalo are the common herds of these savages, affording them 'food, raiment and shelter.' It seems there were anciently occasional cannibal tribes[3] in those regions, but not a vestige of cannibalism, as I believe, now remains; except such an inhuman appetite may be ascribed to some of the more savage war-

[3] A diminutive tribe on the Texas border, called Tonkewas, made food of human flesh within the present century, and, it may be of late years, though I have not heard it mentioned.—GREGG.

Cannibalism among the Tonkawas, though often rumored, has never been verified to the satisfaction of modern authorities.

riors, who, as I have heard, in the delirium of exulted victory, have been known to devour the hearts of their bravest victims, at once to satiate their blood-thirsty propensities, and to appropriate to themselves, as they fancy, the valor of the slain enemy.

However, they make food of nearly every animal of their country, and often of insects and even the filthiest vermin. By some tribes, grasshoppers, locusts and the like are collected and dried for future use. Among nearly all the northern tribes, the flesh of the dog[4] is considered as the greatest delicacy; so much so, indeed, that when a favorite visitor is expected to dine, they are sure to have served up for him the choicest pieces from some one of the many fat whelps which pertain to every lodge. In this way travellers have often been constrained to eat Indian dog-meat, and which, prejudice apart, is by no means an unsavory viand; but the flesh of the wolf, and even the American dog, is generally said to be ill-flavored and sometimes insupportable. The polecat is also a favorite food among the Indians; and though the celebrated Irving, during a "Tour on the Prairies," seems to claim a deal of credit for having "plumped into the river" a dressed polecat, whereby he prevented an Osage from "disgracing" their fire by the cooking of it, yet all travellers who have tasted the flesh of this animal have pronounced it fine, and of exquisite relish. "The flesh of the skunk," observes Dr. James, in his account of Maj. Long's Expedition, "we sometimes had dressed for dinner, and found it remarkably rich and delicate food."

These wild tribes are without other kitchen utensils than an occasional kettle. They sometimes broil their meats, but often eat them raw. A savage will feast upon the warm carcass of the buffalo; selecting bits of the tenderloin, liver, etc., and it is not uncommon to see him use the gall as sauce! Feasting is one of their favorite enjoyments; though their ability to endure hunger almost exceeds belief. They will fast a week and yet retain their strength and vigor; but when they do procure food again, it seems as if they never would be satiated.

---

[4] Dogs seem always to have been a favorite food among the aborigines of different parts. Father Marquette, in his voyage down the Mississippi in 1673, remarks of an Indian feast, "The third service was a huge Dog, whom they killed on purpose," etc.—GREGG.

The Indians of the Prairies have become acquainted with the medical virtues of many of their indigenous plants, which are often used in connection with the vapor sweat, and cold bath: wherefore we may consider them as the primitive Thomsonians.[5] After a profuse sweating, assisted by decoctions of sudorific herbs, in a tight lodge filled with vapor by pouring water over heated stones, and while still dripping, they will leap into a pool of cold water, and afterwards wrap themselves in a buffalo rug. This course has proved successful in some diseases, and extraordinary cures have thus been performed: but in other cases, and especially in the small-pox, it has been attended with horrible fatality. They frequently let blood for disease, which is oftenest performed with the keen edge of a flint: and though they sometimes open a vein, they more commonly make their incisions indiscriminately. They have great faith in their 'medicine men,' who pretend to cure the sick with conjurations and charms; and the Comanches and many others often keep up an irksome, monotonous singing over the diseased person, to frighten away the evil spirit which is supposed to torment him: all of which, from its effect upon the imagination, often tends, no doubt, to hasten recovery.

These Indians keep no domestic animals, except horses, mules, and dogs. With the latter every lodge is abundantly supplied; yet, as has already been shown, they are more useful appendages than the annoying packs which so often infest the country cabins, and frequently the villages, in the United States. Horses, however, constitute the chief wealth of the prairie Indian. These are the incentives to most of the predatory excursions. The tribes of the north in particular, as well as the white trappers, frequently maintain their horses, during winter, upon the tender bark of the sweet cottonwood, the *populus angulata* of the Mississippi valley.

The western savages know nothing of the value of money. The wampum bead, it is true, among a few tribes, somewhat resembles a currency: for, being generally esteemed, it acquires a value in proportion to size, and sometimes passes from hand to hand, in exchange for necessaries. The legitimate wampum is only of shells, and was

[5] Followers of Samuel Thomson (1769–1843), a New England physician who devised and advocated the treating of fevers and similar distresses with steam.

of aboriginal manufacture; being small long tubes with an ovate surface, or sometimes simply cylindrical; and handsomely polished: but imitations of glass or porcelain seem now the most common. The color is generally white, though sometimes blue or striped.

These Indians have no knowledge of the division of time, except by palpable distinctions; as days, moons and years; which last they commonly represent as so many springs, or falls of the leaves, or as often by winters, that is, frosts or snows. Distances are represented by days' journey, which are often designated by camps or 'sleeps.' When a day's journey is spoken of in general terms, it is meant that of a band in regular travel, which rarely exceeds twenty miles.

CHAPTER XV
INDIANS OF THE PRAIRIES

Intermediate Tribes—Their Wigwams and their Hunting Excursions—
Dress and Cut of their Hair—The Pawnees—The Osages—Their
Roguery—Matrimonial Customs—Accomplished Mourners—Their
Superstitions—The Indian Stature—The 'Pawnee Picts'—Wild Tribes
—Census—The Comanches—Their Range—Their Sobriety—Their
Chiefs, etc.—Female Chastity—Comanche Marriage—Costumes—
Horsemanship—Comanche Warfare—Predatory Forays—Martial Cer-
emonies—Treatment of Captives—Burial and Religious Rites.

THE TRIBES inhabiting near the borders of the frontier Indians
differ from those that range the far-western prairies in several
traits of general character. The former have their fixed villages, and,
for the most part, combine the pursuits of agriculture and the chase.
They form, indeed, a sort of intermediate class between the frontier
and the wild tribes, resembling the one or the other in all important
particulars. I will merely notice in this place a few of the characteristics by which the more conspicuous of these tribes are distinguished.

Their village wigwams differ from the lodges of the wilder
tribes, in their being much more substantial, and usually covered
with grass and earth instead of skins. The Indians commonly remain
in their villages during the inclement portion of the winter; yet
most of them spend the early spring upon the Prairies in buffalo-
hunting; as well as such portions of the summer and autumn as are
not occupied in the cultivation and gathering of their crops, which
they secure in caches till their return.

In dress they differ but little from the wilder tribes, except that,
having more communication with the whites, they make greater use

of our fabrics—blankets, coarse cloths, calicoes and the like. Their most striking peculiarity consists in the cut of their hair. Most of them, instead, like the Indians of the Plains, of wearing the hair long, trim and arrange it in the most fantastic style. In the care bestowed upon this part of their toilet, they cannot be excelled by the most *soigneux* of civilized dandies. They shave a large portion of the head, but leave a fanciful lock upon the crown as a scalp-crest (an indispensable trophy for the enemy), which is in general gorgeously bedecked with painted feathers and gewgaws.

The *Pawnees*, who now have their principal village on the Loup Fork of the Platte river, are perhaps the most famous of these tribes. Small bands of their war-parties roam on foot through every portion of the Prairies, often to the Mexican frontier, though they generally contrive to return well mounted. When upon these expeditions, they may properly enough be considered the Ishmaelites of the Prairies—their hands are against every man, and every man's hand is against them. They will skulk about in the vicinity of a prize of mules or horses for several days unsuspected, till a favorable opportunity offers to pounce upon them.

This nation is divided into four principal bands, the Grand Pawnees (or *Grand Pans,* as called by the Canadians), the Republics, the Mahas or Loups, and the Tapage or Noisy Pawnees. Their relatives, the Rickaras, are now considered a distinct tribe.[1]

The *Osages* are at present the most important western branch of the Dahcotah stock, after the Sioux. There are two bands of them, the Big and Little Osages. Though the Pawnees stand most prominent as prairie marauders, these are unsurpassed in simple rogueries. Expertness at stealing appears indeed to constitute a part of their faith, and an all-important branch of education, in which degrees are conferred in true 'academic order;' for I have been assured, that, in their councils, the claims of the candidates to the honors of rogueship are duly considered, and to the most proficient is awarded an honorary badge—the right to wear a fancy feather stuck athwart his scalp-crest.

[1] Both the Pawnee and the Arikara are linguistically Caddoan, but the Arikara, being the northernmost of this stock, are closely associated with Siouan tribes (the Mandan and Hidatsa).

The habitudes of the Osages do not appear to have undergone any material change, notwithstanding the exertions of the government and the missionaries to civilize and to christianize them. Some of their matrimonial customs are very curious and rather peculiar. The eldest daughter seems not only 'heiress apparent,' but, when married, becomes absolute owner of the entire property and household of her parents—family and all. While single, however, she has no authority, but is herself held as a piece of merchantable property, estimated somewhat as in civilized life, in proportion to her 'charms,' and to the value of her 'hereditaments.' She is therefore kept under the strictest watch by her parents, that she may not diminish her worth by any improper conduct.

When some warrior 'beau' has taken a fancy to the heiress and wishes to possess her and her estate of sisters, dogs, rugs and household, he takes his finest horses, (and if she be a 'belle' he need not attempt it unless he have some of the noblest), and tying them at her lodge door departs without saying a word; leaving them, like a slow-match, silently to effect his purpose. After the 'pretender' has disappeared, the matron of the premises and her lord inspect the valuables, the 'demure damsel' barely venturing a sly peep through some crevice of the wigwam. If the offer be found unworthy, the horses are sent back to the owner as silently as they came, or maybe with some apology, provided he be a warrior whom they are afraid of offending. But if accepted, the father takes instead some of his own horses and ties them at the door of the proposer, as a token of admission. If the parties be without horses some other valuables are employed in lieu. After this the marriage is solemnized with a joyous fête, and their primitive ceremonies.

But now the son-in-law is fully indemnified for his heavy 'disbursement' in the *purchase* of his bride; for he at once becomes possessor of the entire wealth of his father-in-law—master of the family-lodge and all the household: if there be a dozen younger daughters, they are all his *de droit*—his wives or slaves as we may choose to consider them: in fact, the 'heiress' herself seems in the same predicament, and the wife among them all who may have the tact to gain the husband's affections, generally becomes mistress of the 'harem.' From the refuse of this estate of 'fair ones' the indigent warriors and inferior Indians who are not able to purchase an 'heiress' are apt to supply themselves with wives upon a cheaper scale.[2]

The Osages bury their dead according to the usual Indian mode; and, though it seems always to have been the custom among most savage nations, to keep up a chorus of hideous cries and yells for a long while after the death of a relative, yet the Osages are by far the most accomplished mourners of them all. Being once encamped near a party of them, I was wakened at the dawn of day by the most doleful, piteous, heart-rending howls and lamentations. The apparently distressed mourner would cry with a protracted expiration till completely out of breath. For some instants he seemed to be in the very last agonies: then he would recover breath with a smothered, gurgling inspiration: and thus he continued for several minutes, giving vent to every variety of hideous and terrific sounds. Looking around, I perceived the weeper standing with his face towards the faint gleam which flitted from the still obscured sun. This was perhaps his idol; else he was standing thus because his deceased relation lay in that direction. A full 'choir' of these mourners (which is always joined by the howls and yelps of their myriads of dogs), imparts the most frightful horror to a wilderness camp.

It is considered among these as well as other 'crying' tribes, quite a merit to be a graceful weeper: it becomes even a profitable vocation to those whose eyes and lungs are most capacious of such things. If you tell an Osage that you have lost a kinsman or friend for whom

[2] The custom of taking all the sisters of a family is also said to be common among the Kansas, Omahas and other kindred tribes; indeed it appears to have prevailed from the earliest ages among all the Dahcotah family as well as many Algonquins and most other tribes about the great Lakes. Mons. La Salle, in his trip from these to the Mississippi in 1673, remarks of the savages of those regions: "They marry several Wives, and commonly all Sisters, if they can, thinking they agree better in their Family." Hennepin, Charlevoix and others speak of the same custom. Murray also mentions something of the kind among the Pawnees. Forbes alludes to the same in California. But I am uninformed, whether, in these several instances, the husband's right was only *de facto*, or *de jure* as among the Osages, to all the younger sisters.—GREGG.

The quotation ascribed to René Robert Cavelier de la Salle (1643–87) appears in the second English edition (1698) of Hennepin's account. Thwaites (ed.), *Hennepin's New Discovery*, II, 631. Hennepin's own comment is in *ibid.*, II, 482. The works of Charlevoix and Murray have been previously cited, and the remaining reference is to Alexander Forbes, *California: A History of Upper and Lower California from Their First Discovery to the Present Time* (London, Smith & Elder, 1839).

you wish him to mourn, he will undertake the service for a trifling reward—and acquit himself with more 'credit'—more to the spirit than the best tragic actor. He will mimic every exterior indication of grief and the most heart-felt wailing, till the tears trickle in torrents down his cheeks.

The Osages seem generally to worship a good and evil spirit, and to believe in the most usual Indian paradise. No people can have more implicit faith in witchcraft and all kinds of sorcery and superstitions—such as holding converse with deceased friends or relations —appointing a time to die, etc.: and instances are related of their fancying themselves thus called to the world of spirits, which would so powerfully affect the imagination as to cause them to pine away, and sometimes die even to the appointed day.

Owing partially, no doubt, to the burdensome life they lead, the squaws of all the tribes are, for the most part, much more inclined to corpulency than the men. They are generally chubby and ill-favored, while the males are usually tall, erect, well-turned and active. For their proverbial straightness, however, the Osages are perhaps more famous than any of the other prairie Indians.

The *Wacoes, Witchitas* and their kindred tribes on Red River, are, for the most part, a very indigent race. They are chiefly remarkable for their profuse tattooing, whereby they have sometimes acquired the title of 'Pawnee Picts:' the females particularly make a perfect calico of the whole under-jaw, breast and arms, and the mammae are fancifully ornamented with rings and rays. The tattoo, in fact, seems to constitute the chief female ornament of these tribes; for their only gown consists of about a yard and a half of strouding or else a small dressed skin, suspended from the waist, and constituting a sort of primitive petticoat. The upper portion of the body remains uncovered, except by a blanket or small skin, thrown loosely over the shoulders. The men are often without any other vesture than the flap, and sometimes a buffalo rug or blanket.

As the remaining tribes of this intermediate class present few or no distinctive characteristics, we will pass at once to the consideration of the *wild tribes* proper of the Great Western Prairies.[3] These

[3] The population of the intermediate tribes, according to the Report of the Commissioner of Indian Affairs, for 1842, is as follows: Pawnees, 12,500 souls

neither cultivate the soil nor live in fixed villages, but lead a roving life in pursuit of plunder and game, and without ever submitting themselves to that repose—to those fixed habits, which must always precede any progress in civilization. But as the *Comanches* are the only tribe of these 'wandering Arabs' of the Plains which present any distinguishing features of interest—any prominent points of national character—the remarks that follow will be devoted almost exclusively to them.

The relationship of the Comanches to the Snakes or Shoshonies, shows them to have descended from the north: in fact, it is but half a century since their range was from the Arkansas river northward; but at present this stream is their *ultima Thule*. Yet they even now acknowledge no boundaries, but call themselves the lords of the entire Prairies—all others are but 'tenants at will.' They lead a wandering sort of life, betaking themselves whithersoever the seasons or the habits of the buffalo, their chief object of pursuit, may lead them. Although during summer they are not unfrequently found as far north as the Arkansas river, their winters they usually pass about the head branches of the Brazos and Colorado rivers of Texas.

In their domestic habits, these Indians, for the most part, resemble the other wild tribes; yet in some respects they differ materially. One of the most interesting traits of difference is to be found in their distaste for ardent spirits; but few of them can be induced to taste a drop of intoxicating liquors; thus forming an exception, I believe, to the entire race of the 'red man,' who appears to have a constitutional appetite for strong drinks. The frontier as

---

(though some experienced traders rate them at only about 5,000); Rickaras, 1,200; Chippewas, Potawatomies and Ottawas of the North, 2,298; Sacs and Foxes, 2,348; Winnebagoes, 2,183; Iowas, 470; Poncas, 800; Omahas, 1,600; Otoes and Missouries, 931; Kansas, 1,588; Osages, 4,102;—besides of Caddoes and Inyes about 500; Wacoes, Witchitas, Towockanoes, Towyashes and Keechyes, 1,000; who maintain themselves chiefly in Northern Texas. The wild tribes proper of the Prairies, are, the Comanches, consisting of about 10,000 souls; Kiawas, 2,000; Apaches, 100; Arrapahoes, 2,000; Chayennes, 2,000; besides many others to the north and westward, who rarely descend within the regions to the notice of which these pages are confined. As these tribes would doubtless average at least three-fifth females, they could hardly turn out one-fifth of their numbers in warriors, though this is the usual rule of estimating them by men of Indian experience.—GREGG.

In Gregg's second edition the figures are revised to conform with the Indian Commission's report for 1844.

well as the prairie tribes—the Mexican as well as the Mountain Indians—all are equally slaves to their use.

The Comanches are divided into numerous petty bands, each under the control of its own particular chief. When a chief becomes old and care-worn, he exercises but the 'civil authority' of his clan; while his son, if deemed worthy, otherwise some distinguished brave, assumes, by 'common consent,' the functions of war-chief. As is the case with all barbarous tribes, their chiefs assume every judicial and executive authority. Complaints are made to them and sentence summarily pronounced, and often as summarily executed. For most offences, the chief, if he considers his authority sufficiently well established, freely uses the rod upon his subjects. He rarely attempts this, however, upon noted warriors or 'braves,' whose influence and resentment he may have reason to fear. The punishment of murder among these, as among most of the savage nations, devolves upon the bereaved relatives, who are free to pursue and punish the perpetrators according to their own liking, which is seldom short of death. But the offended party, if disposed to compromise, has also the privilege of accepting a commutation and releasing the murderer.

The husband seems to have complete power over the destinies of his wife and children. For adultery, his punishment is most usually to cut off the nose or ears,[4] or both; and he may even take the life of his unfaithful wife with impunity. The squaw who has been mutilated for such a cause, is *ipso facto* divorced, and, it is said, for ever precluded from marrying again. The consequence is, that she becomes a confirmed harlot in the tribe. Owing in part, no doubt, to such severity in their customs, the Comanche squaws have ever been noted for their chastity. This may result also, in some degree, from the circumstance, that the Comanche husbands, fathers, and brothers, seldom or never subject their wives, daughters and sisters, to that debasing traffic practised among so many of the northern nations.

Like the other wild tribes, the Comanches tolerate polygamy, the chiefs and braves sometimes taking as many as eight or ten wives

[4] This custom was perhaps often quite extensive. It prevails among the Creeks to the present day, and was anciently practised by other southern nations; and "Among the Miamis," says Father Charlevoix, "the Husband has a right to cut off his wife's nose if she runs away from him."—GREGG.

433

at a time. Three is considered the usual number, however, for 'subjects' or common warriors, and nine for the chiefs. Their marriage ceremonies vary in different bands; but the following has been represented as the most usual. Unlike most other tribes, the consent of the maiden has to be obtained. This done, the lover, from apparent delicacy, goes not to the father of his intended, but, in accordance with a custom which prevails among some other tribes, communicates his desire to an uncle or other aged relative, who enters into the marriage contract. The parties, however, are not yet fully betrothed; but, as a test of the submission of the bride to the service of her proposed lord, the latter ties his riding-horse at her lodge door. If she turns him loose, she has resolved finally to reject him; but if she lead him to the *caballada*, it is an unequivocal agreement to take charge of his horses and other property; and the marriage is soon concluded. The 'uncle' now communicates the engagement to the chief, who causes the 'bans' to be published, that no other wooer may interfere. As the horse is with them the type of every important interest, the bridegroom next proceeds to kill the least valuable one that he is possessed of; and, taking out the heart, hangs it at the door of his betrothed, who takes and roasts it, and then dividing it into two parts, each eats a half, which perfects the bond of wedlock. The heart of the buffalo or other animal may perhaps be substituted, if the bridegroom has not a superabundance of horses. Should the circumstances of the parties admit of it, the marriage is usually celebrated with feasting and dances; though, in general, the Comanches are less fond of dancing than most other Indians.

The Comanche dress consists of the usual leggins, moccasins, flap and blanket or robe. Many wear in addition a kind of leathern jerkin, or tight jacket closed before. Their moccasins differ from those of other tribes, by having a lengthy tassel of leathern fringes attached to the heels, which trail the ground as they walk. Instead of this fringe, the tassel sometimes consists of the tail of a polecat or some other animal. When he can procure it, the young warrior is wont to wear a mantle and leggins of strouding. Both of these articles, according to the 'latest fashions,' should be one-half red, the other blue. The bi-colored mantle, as well as the blanket or buffalo rug, is carelessly thrown over the shoulders, and must be long enough to drag the ground; for they seem to have an instinct for the 'regal grandeur of a sweeping gown.'

Though all the far-western Indians wear their hair long, the Comanche seems to take most pride in the voluminousness of his 'tresses,' and the length of his *queue*, which is sometimes eked out with buffalo or other hair, till its tip reaches the ground, and is bedaubed with gum, grease and paint, and decorated with beads and other gewgaws. We are not to think that foppery and coxcombry are generated exclusively in civilized life. I am sure I never saw a vainer creature than a Comanche brave in full costume, of dress, trinkets and paint. He steps as if he disdained the very ground upon which he walks.

The dress of the Comanche squaw is usually a kind of loose gown or tunic of leather, or cotton if it can be procured, which hangs from the shoulders and is bound around the waist with a girdle; thus presenting a resemblance in its appearance to our ordinary female costume. They wear moccasins, to which short leggins are attached, and which constitute a sort of leathern hose. They are not permitted to wear long hair: that 'manly' prerogative would be degraded by such an association. It is therefore kept docked so scarcely to reach the shoulders.

A style of dress similar to that of the Comanche females, is worn by those of most of the erratic tribes. The squaws of the north usually embroider their leathern frocks in a fanciful manner with colored porcupine quills and beads, and bedeck the borders with rattling shells, tags, hawk-bells, and the like. Such as have the fortune to marry Canadian or American trappers, are those who usually dress most gaily.

The prairie Indians generally are an equestrian race; yet in horsemanship the Comanches stand decidedly pre-eminent; and can only be equalled by the Northern Mexicans, and perhaps the Arabs. Like the latter, they dote upon their steeds: one had as well undertake to purchase a Comanche's child as his favorite riding-horse. They have a peculiar mark for their animals: every one which has pertained to them may always be recognized by a slit in the tip of each ear; a practice apparently universal among all their tribe.

In their warlike expeditions they avail themselves of their equestrian skill with wonderful success. As they always fight on horseback, they depend chiefly upon the charge, at which they use their arrows and javelins[5] with wonderful efficacy. On such occasions a Comanche will often throw himself upon the opposite side of his charger, so as to be protected from the darts of the enemy; and, while clinging there, he will discharge his arrows with extraordinary dexterity from underneath his horse's neck. Different from the 'prowling' tribes, they seldom attack at night, or in timbered or rough regions; for they would then be unable to manoeuvre their courses to advantage.

Although not meriting the title of brave Indians, they are held by the Mexicans as the most valiant of their border: but when they come in contact with Americans or any of our frontier tribes, they generally appear timid and cowardly. Their predatory forays are therefore directed mostly westward. They make continual inroads upon the whole eastern frontier of Mexico, from Chihuahua to the coast; driving off immense numbers of horses and mules, and killing the citizens they may encounter, or making them prisoners—particularly the females and boys. Of the latter they make slaves, to perform such menial service as usually pertains to the squaws, particularly the herding of the stock. It is perhaps this alleviation of their labor by slaves, that has contributed to elevate the Comanche women above those of many of the northern tribes. Of their female captives they often make wives; a fate which has befallen some of those taken from Texas.

Strange as it may appear, their captives frequently become attached to their masters and to the savage life, and with difficulty are induced to leave them after a few years' captivity. In fact, these prisoners, it is said, in time often turn out to be the most formidable savages. Combining the subtlety of the Mexican with the barbarity of the Indian, they sometimes pilot into their native frontier and instigate horrid outrages. The department of Chihuahua has been the greatest sufferer from their inroads.

But, though at continual war with the south of the republic, for many years the Comanches have cultivated peace with the New Mex-

[5] The Comanches employ usually short-handled javelins or lances, declaring like the Spartan mother, that cowards only need long weapons.—GREGG.

icans—not only because the poverty of the country offers fewer inducements for their inroads, but because it is desirable, as with the interior Mexican tribes, to retain some friendly point with which to keep an amicable intercourse and traffic. Parties of them have therefore sometimes entered the settlements of New Mexico for trading purposes; while every season numerous bands of New Mexicans, known as *Comancheros*, supplied with arms, ammunitions, trinkets, provisions and other necessaries, launch upon the Prairies to barter for mules, and the different fruits of their ravages upon the South.

This powerful nation, combined with the petty southern tribes, has also waged an almost unceasing warfare upon Texas, ever since her independence. War-parties have frequently penetrated to the very heart of the settlements, perpetrating murderous outrages, and bearing away into captivity numerous women and children. They have entered the city of Austin, then the seat of government, in open day; and, at other times, have been known to descend to the very sea-coast, committing many frightful depredations. "On the 8th of August, 1840," writes a friend who resided at Linnville, on Matagorda Bay, "several hundred Comanches came down from the mountains, and charged upon us without the least notice. They burned and made a perfect destruction of the village and everything pertaining to it."[6]

Besides continual hostilities with Mexico and Texas, the Comanches are at war with most of the Indians of the Mexican interior, as also with the tribes of the most northern prairies—and particularly the Arrapahoes and Chayennes, with whom they have many bloody rencounters. But they generally remain on friendly terms with the petty tribes of the south, whom, indeed, they seem to hold as their vassals.

As these Indians always go to war on horseback, several days are often spent previous to a campaign in equestrian exercises and

[6] Open warfare between the Comanches and Texans broke out in 1837, and when truce talks at San Antonio collapsed in February, 1840, and a number of Comanche delegates were killed, the tribe descended upon Victoria and Linnville. At the latter, a village of only five houses, the inhabitants fled to a ship in the bay, and the Comanches destroyed their homes. A punitive expedition under General Felix Houston overtook the raiders, defeated them, and recovered the white captives.

ceremonies, which seem partly to supply the place of the war-dance of other tribes; though they sometimes join in preparatory dances also. It is not an unusual custom, when a campaign is in agitation, for a band of about twenty Comanche maidens to chant, for three nights in succession, the victories of their ancestors, the valor of their brothers and contemporaries, and the individual prowess of all such young warriors as they consider should engage in the contemplated enterprise: and all those designated by the serenading band are held as drafted for the campaign. Fired by the encomiums and excitations of the 'fair *cantatrices,*' they fly at once to the standard of their favorite chief: and the ceremony is concluded by a war-dance.

Upon their return from a successful expedition, the 'war-worn corps' halts on some elevation at a distance from the village, and a herald is sent forward to announce their arrival. Thereupon, one of their most respectable and aged matrons issues forth to receive them, carrying with her a very long-handled lance kept for the purpose. On the top of this the victorious Indians fasten all the scalps they may have taken, so arranged that each shall be conspicuous. The matron squaw then approaches the wigwams, holding her scalp-garnished lance high in the air, and chanting some favorite war-legend. She is soon joined by other squaws and Indian lasses, who dance around as the procession moves through the entire circuit of the village. If the victory has been brilliant, the dancing and feasting are apt to be kept up for several days, all parties joining in the general jubilee.

If the conquerors bring any prisoners with them, these have to encounter the scourgings and insults of the squaws and children. Each seems entitled to a blow, a kick, a pinch, a bite, or whatever simple punishment they may choose to inflict upon the unfortunate captives. This done, they are delivered over to the captors as slaves, and put to the service and drudgery of the camp.

After their first entrance it seems rare for them to treat their captives with much cruelty: though an instance was related to me by some Mexican prisoners, of a very barbarous massacre which they witnessed during their captivity. Two white men, supposed to be Texans, were tied to a stake, and a number of their marksmen, retiring to a distance and using the naked bodies of their victims as targets, began wantonly to fire at them, and continued their horrid sport, until some fatal balls put an end to their sufferings! The capture of these had probably been attended with some aggravating circumstances, which induced the savages to resort to this cruel method of satiating their revenge.

If a campaign has been unsuccessful, the warriors separate upon their return, and drop into the village one by one. Nothing is now heard for several days, but the wailings and howlings of the bereft relatives and friends. They will also scarify their arms and legs, and subject themselves to other carnal mortifications of the most powerful character. On these occasions their previous captives, and particularly such as may belong to the nation of their victorious enemy, are sure to be roughly treated, and sometimes massacred by the enraged relatives of the slain.

When a Comanche dies, a similar course of mourning is practised; and he is usually wrapped in his best blankets or robes, and interred with most of his 'jewelry' and other articles of esteem; accompanying which, it is said, an awl and some moccasin leather is generally added, as a provision, it would appear, for his use during his long journey to the 'happy hunting ground' beyond the grave. They also kill the favorite horses of the deceased, which are often buried by his side, doubtless with the same object.

The religious notions of the Comanches resemble, in most particulars, those of the other prairie tribes; yet they appear to have an occasional peculiarity. Some say the dry buffalo head or cranium is their idol. True it is that they show it great reverence, and use it in many of their mystic ceremonies. The Pawnees also hold these buffalo heads, with which the plains are strewed, in great reverence; and usually for many leagues around, these sculls are set up facing towards their villages, in the belief that the herds of buffalo will thus be conducted by them into their neighborhood. Of the Comanches the sun is no doubt the principal deity. When preparing for a campaign, it is said they do not fail to place their arms betimes every morning on the east side of their lodges, that they may receive the blessing of the fountain of light at his first appearance. This indeed seems the usual time for offering their devotions to the sun, of many tribes of the American aborigines.

GLOSSARY

[From 2nd edition, end of volume one]

Containing such Spanish or Hispano-Mexican words as occur undefined in this work, or recur without definition after having been once translated

A, al, to, to the
Abajo, down, under, below
Acequia, ditch, canal
Adelantado, [explorer, conqueror, or]governor of a [frontier] province
A dios, [adiós], adieu, farewell
Administrador de Rentas, a custom-house officer
Adobe, a sort of unburnt brick
Afuera, without, abroad
Aguador, water-carrier
Aguardiente, brandy
Alacran [alacrán], scorpion
Alameda, public walk with rows of trees, usually the *álamo*
Alamo (in Mexico), cotton-wood
Alcalde, justice of the peace
Alegria [alegría], mirth, a plant
Allí, there
Amigo, friend
Ancheta, adventure of goods
Angelito, little angel
Angostura, narrowness
Aparejo, sort of pack-saddle
Aqui, here

Arancel, tariff
Armas, arms
Arriba, up, above
Arriero, muleteer
Asambléa [asamblea], assembly
Astucia, cunning, artifice
Atajo, drove of pack mules, etc.
Atole, sort of thick gruel
Auto, act, edict
Ayotéa [azotea], flat roof, terrace

Baile, ball, dance
Bandolin [bandolín], species of small guitar
Bárbaro, barbarous; a savage
Barra, ingot, bar of silver, etc.
Baston [bastón], staff, cane
Blanco, white
Bolsa, pocket, purse
Bonanza, prosperity
Bonito, pretty
Bota, boot, leggin
Bravo, brave, bold [or savage]
Bueno, good
Burro, ass

Caballada, drove of horses, etc.

Caballero, gentleman, knight

Caballo, horse

Cacique, Indian chief or prince

Café, coffee; coffee-house

Calabozo, dungeon, jail

Caliente, warm, hot

Camino, road

Campo, field, camp

Campo santo, cemetery without a church

Cancion [canción], song, poem

Cañada, valley

Cañon [cañón], deep gorge or ravine; cannon

Capilla, chapel

Capitan [capitán], captain

Carajo, an oath; scoundrel

Caravana, caravan

Cárcel, prison, jail

Carga, load

Cargador, carrier

Cargamento, cargo

Carnero, male sheep

Carreta, cart

Carro, wagon, etc.

Casa, house

Cautivo, captive

Ceja, brow

Centralismo, central[ized] government

Cerro, mound

Chacal, jackal

Chico, small; small person

Chile, red pepper

Cibolero, buffalo-hunter

Cibolo, the American buffalo

Cigarrito, little cigar [cigarette]

Cigarro, cigar [paper-wrapped]

Cimarron [cimarrón], wild

Claco, small copper coin

Coche, coach

Cocina, kitchen

Cocinera, female cook

Cola, tail; glue

Colorado, red

Comanchero, Comanche trader

Comiso, confiscation

Consumo, consumption

Contra-revolución, counter-revolution

Cordillera, chain of mountains

Corral, yard, pen

Correr, to run

Coyote, prairie-wolf

Crepúsculo, dawn, twilight

Cristo, Christ

Cruz, cross

Cuñado, brother-in-law

De, del, of, of the, etc.

Decreto, decree

Derecho, tax; right

Descubrimiento, discovery

Dia [día], day

Diablo, devil

Dictador, dictator

Diligencia, diligence; stage-coach

Dios, God

Doblon [doblón], doubloon

Domingo, Sunday; Dominic

Don, Sir, Mr.; gift

Doña, Madam, Mrs., Miss

Dorado, gilt

Dos, two

Dulce, sweet

Eclesiástico, ecclesiastical

El, the; he, him

Enáguas, sort of petticoat

En junta, in council
Enmendadura, enmendation
Entrada, entrance
Entrerenglonadura, interlineation
Escritor, writer
Escuadron [escuadrón], squadron
Español, Spanish; Spaniard
Está, is, he is, it is, etc.

Estacado, staked
Estrangero, [extranjero], stranger, foreigner
Estufa, cell; stove

Factura, invoice
Fandango, dance; ball
Fiera, wild beast
Fe, faith
Feria, fair
Fierro, iron; branding-iron, etc.
Fiesta, feast
Fonda, eating-house, inn
Fraile, Fray, friar
Frijol, bean
Fueros, chartered privileges

Gachupin [gachupín], Spaniard in America
Gallina, hen
Gallo, cock
Ganado, cattle
Geje [jefe], chief
Gobernador, governor
Gobernadorcillo, petty governor, or chief
Gobierno, government
Grama, species of grass
Gran, grande, great, large
Grandeza, greatness, grandeur
Grano, grain
Gauge [Guaje], gourd, flask

Guardia, guard, watch; watch-house
Guerra, war
Guia [guía], sort of passport for goods
Guisado, cooked, stewed
Guitarra, guitar

Hacienda, estate; lands; treasure
Haciendero [hacendado], proprietor of an hacienda
Herradura, horse-shoe
Herrero, blacksmith
Hidalgo, nobleman
Hoja, leaf, husk, etc.
Hombre, man
Hombre bueno, arbitrator

Ilustrísimo, most illustrious
Imprenta, printing-office
Inocente, innocent

Jacal, hut, wigwam
Jola, copper coin, penny
Jornada, day's travel; journey
Juez, judge
Junta, council; union

La, las, the; her, it, them
Labor, labor; field; mining-pit
Labrador, laborer, farmer
Ladron [ladrón], thief, robber
Laguna, lake [lagoon]
Lanzada, thrust with a lance
Layador [lazador?], nooser
Lazito, little lazo
Lazo, noosing rope
Legua, league
Lépero, vagabond, *sans-culotte*
Ley, law

442

Limosnero, beggar
Llano, plain; prairie; smooth
Lo, los, the; it, them, etc.
Lobo, wolf

Madre, mother
Manifiesto, manifest; bill of goods presented to the custom-house
Manta, covering; cotton-cloth.
Marco, weight of eight ounces; mark
Mayor, great, superior
Mayordomo, overseer
Médano, sand-hill
Medio, half; picayune
Menor, less, inferior
Mesa, table; table-plain
Meson [*mesón*], inn, hotel
Mestizo, mongrel [of Indian and white parentage]
Mezquite, a tree, acacia
Mi, mis, my
Militar, military
Monte, a game; grove; mount
Mora, mulberry
Muerto, dead; dead man
Mula, mule; unsalable item.

Negro, black; a black person
Noria, machine for drawing water; well
Norte, north.
Noticioso, giving information
Número, number.

Oficial, official; officer
Ojo, eye; spring of water
Oro, gold

Padre, father; priest
Padrino, godfather, sponsor

Paisano, countryman
Palacio, palace
Panza, paunch
Papa, pope; potato
Parage [*paraje*], place; camping-site
Pariente, relative, kin
Parroquia, parish; parish church
Pasa, raisin
Paséo [*paseo*], pleasure walk or ride
Paso, pass, passage; step
Pastor, pastor; shepherd
Patio, court, enclosed yard
Pato, duck
Patriótico, patriotic
Pauta, rule, model
Pelo, hair
Penitencia, penance, penitence
Perro, dog
Peso, dollar; weight
Piedra, stone
Pinole, food of parched Indian meal stirred in water
Placer, pleasure; gold region
Plata, silver
Plaza, square; place; village
Poquito, very little
Portal, porch, corridor
Perfecto, perfect
Presidio, garrison, fort
Presto, quick, soon
Profano, profane
Pronunciamento [*pronunciamiento*], act of making a public declaration
Proyecto, project, plan
Público, public
Pueblo, people: Catholic Indians, etc.

Puerta, door
Puro, pure; pure tobacco cigar

Ranchera, country woman
Ranchería, village of wild Indians
Ranchero, inhabitant of a rancho
Rancho, stock-farm
Raspadura, erasure; rasping
Real, a coin, royal, real, grand
Rebozo, muffler, species of scarf
Remedio, remedy, medicine
Rey, king
Rico, rich; rich man.
Rio [*río*], river

Sala, hall, parlor
Salina, salt pond or pit
San, santo, santa, saint, holy
Sandía, watermelon
Sangre, blood
Santísimo, most holy
Saquéo [*saqueo*], sack, pillage
Sarape, sort of blanket
Semana, week
Señor, sir, Mr.; lord
Señora, Madam, Mrs.; lady
Señoría, lordship
Señoría ilustrísima, title of a bishop, etc.
Señorita, madam, miss, Mrs., etc.
Sierra, ridge of mountains; saw
Siesta, afternoon's sleep
Silla, chair; saddle
Sistema, system
Sol, sun
Soldado, soldier
Sombrero, hat

Sonoreño, citizen of Sonora
Su, sus, his, her, its, their

Tarde, evening
Tierra, country, land
Tierra Afuera (in Mexico), the exterior, or country near the coast, etc.
Tilma, Indian mantle
Tio [*tío*], uncle
Todo, all, every, whole
Tornillo, screw
Tortilla, thin cake, diminutive of *torta,* cake, loaf

Vado, ford
Valiente, valiant, brave
Valle, valley, dale
Vaquero, cowherd
Vaquita, diminutive of *vaca,* cow
Vara, Spanish yard of 33 inches
Venta, sale; sale-brand; inn
Verdadero, true.
Verde, green
Vicio, vice
Viernes, Friday

Un, uno, a, one

Y, é, and
Yeso, gypsum

Zambo, offspring of the Indian and negro
Zaguan [*zaguán*], entry, porch
Zarco, light blue
Zorra, fox

GREGG'S BIBLIOGRAPHY

(Reconstructed from his references by the editor[1])

Acosta, Juan de. *Historia natural y moral de las Indias.* Sevilla, Iuan de León, 1590. 1st. English ed., London, 1604.

Adair, James. *The History of the American Indians.* London, E. & C. Dilly, 1775.

Anghiera, Pierto Martire de. *De rubus oceanicis et novo orbe decades.* Compluti, Michaela d' Egina, 1530. 1st English ed., London, 1555.

Bacon, Francis, *Essayes. Religious Meditations. Places of Perswasion and Disswasion.* London, H. Hooper, 1597.

Brackenridge, Henry Marie. *Journal of a Voyage up the River Missouri in 1811.* Baltimore, Coale & Maxwell, 1815.

Burns, Robert. *Tam o' Shanter, a Tale.* Glasgow, R. Inglis & Co. [n.d.].

Calderón de la Barca, Frances Erskine. *Life in Mexico.* London, Chapman & Hall, 1843.

Cervantes Saavedra, Miguel de. *El ingenioso hidalgo Don Quixote de la Mancha.* Iuan de la Puesta, 1605, 1615. 1st English eds., London, 1612, 1620.

Charlevoix, Pierre François Xavier de. *Histoire et description générale de la Nouvelle France.* 6 vols. Paris, Chez la veuve Ganeau, 1774. 1st English ed., London, 1769.

Choctaw Almanac, 1843. Chahta Almanak. Hvpin Chitokaka yvt vtta tok a afvmmi holhtina. Park Hill, Cherokee Nation, Mission Press, 1843.

Clavijero, Francisco Javier. *Storia Antica del Messico.* 4 vols. Cessena, G. Biasina, 1780–81. 1st Mexican ed., Mégico, 1826.

Commissioner of Indian Affairs. *Annual Reports,* 1842, 1843. Washington, Government Printing Office, 1843, 1844.

---

[1]Citations are all to the first editions except where those used by Gregg are known.

Cowper, William. "The Entertaining and Facetious History of John Gilpin," *Public Advertizer* (London), November 14, 1792.

Espy, James Pollard. *Philosophy of Storms*. Boston, Little & Brown, 1841.

Farnham, Thomas Jefferson. *Travels in the Great Western Prairies, the Anahuac and Rocky Mountains, and in the Oregon Territory*. New York, Greeley & McElrath, 1843.

Forbes, Alexander. *California: A History of Upper and Lower California from Their First Discovery to the Present Time*. London, Smith & Elder, 1839.

Gass, Patrick. *Journal of the Voyage and Travels of a Corps of Discovery under the Command of Capt. Lewis and Capt. Clark*. Pittsburgh, Z. Cramer, 1807.

Hennepin, Louis. *A New Discovery of a Vast Country in America*. London, M. Bentley *et al.*, 1698.

Herrera y Tordesillas, Antonio de. *Historia general de los hechos de los Castellanos en las Islas y Tierra Firma de el Mar Occeano*. 4 vols. Madrid, Emprenta Real, 1601. 1st English ed., London, 1740.

Hoffman, Charles Fenno. *A Winter in the West*. 2 vols. New York, Harper, 1835.

————. *Wild Scenes in Forest and Prairie*. 2 vols. London, R. Bentley, 1839.

Humboldt, Frederich Heinrich Alexander von. *Essai politique sur le Royaume de la Nouvelle-Espagne*. 5 vols. Paris, F. Schoell, 1811. 1st English ed: 4 vols. London, 1811-22.

Irving, Washington. *Tour on the Prairies*. Philadelphia, Carey, Lea & Blanchard, 1835.

————. *Rocky Mountains, or Scenes, Incidents and Adventures in the Far West*. 2 vols. Philadelphia, Carey, Lea & Blanchard, 1837.

James, Edwin. *An Account of an Expedition from Pittsburgh to the Rocky Mountains*. 3 vols. Philadelphia, Carey & Lea, 1823.

Kendall, George Wilkins. *Narrative of the Texan Santa Fé Expedition*. 2 vols. New York, Harper, 1844.

Mariana, Juan de. *Historia de rebus Hispaniae*. Toledo, P. Roderici, 1592. 1st Spanish ed.: Toledo, 1601; 1st English ed.; London, 1699.

Marquette, Jacques. *Voyage et découverte de quelques pays et nations de l'Amérique*. In Melchisédech Thévenot (ed.), *Recueil de voyages*. Paris, E. Michallet, 1681.

Marryat, Frederick. *Travels and Adventures of Monsieur Violet among*

the Snake Indians and Wild Tribes of the Great Western Prairies.
3 vols. London, Longman, Brown & Green, 1843.

Mayer, Brantz. *Mexico as It Was and as It is.* New York, J. Winchester
et al., 1844.

Murray, Charles Augustus. *Travels in North America.* 2 vols. London,
R. Bentley, 1839.

Oñate, Juan de. "Petición al virrey don Luis de Velasco para la jornada
de descubrimiento . . . y capitulaciones del virrey con don Juan de
Oñate, México, 21 de septiembre de 1595." MS. Copy formerly
in Spanish Archives at Santa Fé. Original in Archivo General de la
Indias at Seville, Patronato Real, 1–1–3/22–12.

Otermín, Antonio de. "Salida para El Paso del Norte, 23 de agosto,
hasta 5 de octubre de 1680." MS. Now in Twitchell Collection,
Doc. No. 4, Historical Society of New Mexico at Santa Fé.

Pike, Zebulon Montgomery. *An Account of Expeditions to the Sources
of the Mississippi and Through the Western Parts of Louisiana.*
Philadelphia, C. & A. Conrad, 1810.

Poinsett, Joel R. *Notes on Mexico Made in 1822.* Philadelphia, Carey &
Lea, 1824.

Schoolcraft, Henry Rowe. *Travels in the Central Portion of the Mississippi Valley: Comprising Observations on its Mineral Geography,
Internal Resources, and Aboriginal Population.* New York, Collins, 1825.

Sibley, John. "Historical Sketch of several Indian tribes in Louisiana,
south of the Arkansas river, and between the Mississippi and river
Grande," [Report to General H. Dearborn, Natchitoches, April 5,
1805.] *American State Papers,* Vol. V, *Indian Affairs,* Pt. I (Washington, 1832), 721–25.

Storrs, Augustus. *Answers of Augustus Storrs, of Missouri, to Certain
Queries upon the Origin, present State, and future Prospects, of
Trade and Intercourse between Missouri and the Internal Provinces of Mexico, propounded by the Hon. Mr. Benton, Jan. 5, 1825.*
18 Cong., 1 sess., *Senate Document No. 7.* Washington, Government Printing Office, 1825.

EDITOR'S SOURCES

MANUSCRIPTS

Archivo de la Secretaría de Relaciones Exteriores, Mexico City.
Territorio de Nuevo México. Estado que manifiesta los estrangeros. Año de 1825. L–E–1075. Tomo XXI.
Territorio de Nuevo México. Estado que manifiesta los estrangeros. Año de 1828. L-E-1076, Tomo XXII.

Archivo General y Pública de la Nación, Mexico City.
Correspondence of George East, *et al.* with state government of Chihuahua, 1838. Fomento-Caminos, Tomo XI, Expediente 255.
Letter of Governor José Mariano Monterde to the Minister of Interior, Chihuahua, May 19, 1843. Fomento-Caminos, Tomo XIII, Expediente 283.

Archivo Histórico de Hacienda, Mexico City.
Aduana de Nuevo México. Libro de Carga y Data, 1834–35. Legajo 176–1.
Manifiesto de José Sutton y Josias Gregg, Santa Fé, 29 de Julio de 1834. Carpeta de Manifiestos, Nuevo México, 1834–35. Legajo 176–3.

National Archives, Washington.
Manuel Alvarez, Memorial to the Secretary of State, Washington City, February 2, 1842. Consular Dispatches, Santa Fé, Vol. I.
Manuel Alvarez, Memorial to the Secretary of State, Independence, Missouri, July 1, 1843. Consular Dispatches, Santa Fé, Vol. I.
Josiah Gregg, *et al.*, Memorial to Governor of New Mexico, Santa Fé, December 2, 1839. (Translation) Consular Dispatches, Santa Fé, Vol. I.

Miscellaneous Record Books, Vol. III (1845). American Consulate General, Mexico City.

Bancroft Library, Berkeley, California.
Tamarón, Pedro. "Visita del Obispo de Durango, 1759–1763." (Transcript).
Wilson, Benjamin Davis. "Observations on Early Days in California and New Mexico." (1877).

Historical Society of New Mexico, Santa Fé.
Josiah Gregg to Manuel Alvarez, Independence, Missouri, May 7, 1846. B. M. Read Collection, Folder G, No. 158.
J. H. Lyman to Manuel Alvarez, Santa Fé, December 7, 1840. B. M. Read Collection, Folder L, No. 174.
J. H. Lyman to Manuel Alvarez, Rancho de Taos, August 8, 1841. B. M. Read Collection, Folder L, No. 175.

OFFICIAL DOCUMENTS

American State Papers. 38 vols. Washington, Gales & Seaton, 1832–61.
Cherokee Nation. *Constitution and Laws of the Cherokee Nation.* St. Louis, R. & T. A. Ennis, 1875.
Department of War. *Report of the Secretary of War, March 1st, 1849.* 31 Cong., 1 sess., *Senate Executive Document No. 32.* Washington, Government Printing Office, 1850.
Dublán, Manuel and Lozano, José María (compilers). *Legislación mexicana ó colección completa de las disposiciones legislativas expedidas desde la independencia de la República.* 42 vols. in 54. Mexico City, Mexican government, 1876–1912.
Emory, Lieutenant William Hemsley. *Notes on a Military Reconnoissance.* 30 Cong., 1 sess., *House Executive Document 41.* Washington, Government Printing Office, 1848.
Ministerio de Hacienda. *Memoria de la Hacienda General de la República.* [Annual report; title varies.] Mexico City, Mexican government, 1837–46.
Pacheco, Joaquín F., Francisco de Cárdenas, and Luis Torres de Mendoza (compilers). *Colección de documentos inéditos relativos al descubrimiento, conquista y colonización de las posesiones españolas en América.* 42 vols. Madrid, Bernaldo de Quirós, *et al.*, 1864–84.
Wislizenus, Frederick Adolph. *Memoir of a Tour of Northern Mexico.* 30 Cong., 1 sess., *Senate Miscellaneous Document No. 26,* Washington, Government Printing Office, 1846.

BOOKS

Alessio Robles, Carmen. *La región arqueológica de Casas Grandes de Chihuahua.* Mexico City, Imprenta Núñez, 1929.

Bancroft, Hubert Howe. *History of New Mexico and Arizona.* San Francisco, The History Company, 1889.

——. *Native Races of the Pacific States.* 5 vols. San Francisco, The History Company, 1882.

Bandelier, Adolph F. *Final Report of Investigations Among the Indians of Southwestern United States.* 2 vols. [*Papers of the Archeological Institute of America,* Vols. III, IV.] Cambridge, Mass., J. Wilson, 1890–92.

Bartlett, John Russell. *Personal Narrative of Explorations and Incidents in Texas, New Mexico, California, Sonora and Chihuahua.* 2 vols. New York, D. Appleton, 1854.

Bigelow, John. *Retrospections of an Active Life.* 5 vols. New York, Baker & Taylor, 1909–13.

Bledsoe, Anthony Jennings. *Indian Wars in the Northwest.* San Francisco, Bacon, 1885.

Bolton, Herbert Eugene. *Coronado: Knight of Pueblo and Plains.* New York, Whittlesey House, 1949.

Bork, Albert William. *Nuevos aspectos del comercio entre Nuevo México y Misuri, 1822–1846.* Mexico City, The author, 1944.

Calderón de la Barca, Frances Erskine. *Life in Mexico.* London, Chapman & Hall, 1843.

Carroll, H. Bailey. *The Texan Santa Fe Trail.* Canyon, Texas, Panhandle-Plains Historical Society, 1951.

——, and J. Villasana Haggard, (eds.). *Three New Mexican Chronicles.* Albuquerque, Quivira Society, 1942.

The Catholic Encyclopedia. 15 vols. New York, Robert Appleton, 1907–12.

Chittenden, Hiram Martin. *The American Fur-Trade of the Far West.* 3 vols. New York, F. P. Harper, 1902.

Clapp, Margaret. *Forgotten First Citizen: John Bigelow.* Boston, Little & Brown, 1947.

Cleland, Robert Glass. *This Reckless Breed of Men: The Trappers and Fur Traders of the Southwest.* New York, Knopf, 1950.

Cooke, Philip St. George. *Scenes and Adventures in the Army.* Philadelphia, Lindsey & Blakiston, 1857.

Coues, Elliott (ed.). *The Expeditions of Zebulon Montgomery Pike.* 3 vols. New York, F. P. Harper, 1895.

———— (ed.). *The Journal of Jacob Fowler.* New York, F. P. Harper, 1898.

Daly, H. W. *Manual of Pack Transportation.* Washington, Government Printing Office, 1917.

Drumm, Stella M. (ed.). *Down the Santa Fe Trail and into Mexico; the Diary of Susan Shelby Magoffin, 1846–1847.* New Haven, Yale University Press, 1926.

Farnham, Thomas Jefferson. *Travels in the Great Western Prairies, the Anahuac and Rocky Mountains, and in Oregon Territory.* New York, Greeley & McElrath, 1843.

Escudero, José Antonio. *Noticias Estadísticas de Chihuahua.* Mexico City, J. Ojeda, 1834.

Foreman, Grant. *Indian Removal.* Norman, University of Oklahoma Press, 1932.

Fulton, Maurice G. (ed.). *The Diary and Letters of Josiah Gregg.* 2 vols. Norman, University of Oklahoma Press, 1941–1944.

Gregg, Josiah. *Commerce of the Prairies.* Ed. by Reuben Gold Thwaites. 2 vols. [Vols. XIX and XX of *Early Western Travels*]. Cleveland, Arthur H. Clark Co., 1905.

Gregg, Kate L. (ed.). *The Road to Santa Fe.* Albuquerque, University of New Mexico Press, 1952.

Hackett, Charles W. (ed.). *Historical Documents Relating to New Mexico, Nueva Vizcaya and Approaches Thereto, to 1773.* 3 vols. Washington, The Carnegie Institution, 1923.

———— (ed.). *The Revolt of the Pueblo Indians of New Mexico and Otermin's Attempted Reconquest, 1680–1682.* 2 vols. Albuquerque, University of New Mexico Press, 1942.

Hammond, George P. *Don Juan de Oñate and the Founding of New Mexico.* Santa Fe, Historical Society of New Mexico, 1927.

————, and Agapito Rey (eds.). *Expeditions into New Mexico Made by Antonio de Espejo, 1582–1583.* Los Angeles, Quivira Society, 1929.

Haring, Clarence H. *The Spanish Empire in America.* New York, Oxford University Press, 1947.

Hodge, Frederick Webb (ed.). *Handbook of American Indians North of Mexico.* Bureau of American Ethnology *Bulletin No. 30.* 2 vols. Washington, Government Printing Office, 1907–10.

Houck, Louis. *The Spanish Regime in Missouri.* 2 vols. Chicago, R. R. Donnelley, 1909.

Hughes, John T. *Doniphan's Expedition and the Conquest of New Mexico and California.* Ed. by William E. Connelley. Topeka, The editor, 1907.

Humboldt, Frederich Heinrich Alexander von. *Essai Politique sur le Royaume de la Nouvelle-Espagne.* 5 vols. Paris, F. Schoell, 1811.

James, Thomas. *Three Years among the Indians and Mexicans.* Ed. by Walter B. Douglas. St. Louis, Missouri Historical Society, 1916.

Kendall, George Wilkins. *Narrative of the Texan Santa Fé Expedition.* 2 vols. New York, Harper, 1844.

Leonard, Irving A. *Books of the Brave.* Cambridge, Mass., Harvard University Press, 1949.

Morse, Sydney Edwards, and S. Breese (eds.). *North American Atlas.* New York, Harper & Bros., 1842–45.

Norman, Benjamin Moore. *Rambles in Yucatan.* New York, J. & H. G. Langley, 1843.

Omwake, John. *The Conestoga Six-Horse Bell Teams of Eastern Pennsylvannia.* Cincinnati, Ebbert & Richardson, 1930.

Riddle, Kenyon. *Records and Maps of the Old Santa Fe Trail.* Raton, New Mexico, The author, 1949.

Ruxton, George Frederick Augustus. *Life in the Far West.* New York, Harper & Bros., 1849.

Sullivan, Maurice S. *The Life of Jedediah Smith, Trader and Trail Breaker.* New York, Pioneer Press, 1937.

Thwaites, Reuben Gold (ed.). *Early Western Travels, 1784–1846.* 32 vols. Cleveland, Arthur H. Clark Co., 1904–1907.

———— (ed.). *Hennepin's New Discovery.* 2 vols. Chicago, A. C. McClurg, 1903.

————(ed.). *The Jesuit Relations and Allied Documents.* 73 vols. Cleveland, The Burrows Brothers Co., 1896–1903.

———— (ed.). *Original Journals of the Lewis and Clark Expedition, 1804–1806.* 7 vols. and atlas. New York, Dodd & Mead, 1904–1905.

Twitchell, Ralph Emerson. *Dr. Josiah Gregg, Historian of the Santa Fe Trail.* Santa Fé, Historical Society of New Mexico, 1924.

————. *Leading Facts of New Mexican History.* 5 vols. Cedar Rapids, Iowa, The Torch Press, 1911–17.

Wagner, Henry Raup. *The Plains and the Rockies: A Bibliography of Original Narratives of Travel and Adventure, 1800–1865.* San Francisco, J. Howell, 1921.

Webb, James Josiah. *Adventures in the Santa Fe Trade, 1844–1847.* Ed. by Ralph P. Bieber. Glendale, California, Arthur H. Clark Co., 1931.

Wright, Muriel H. *A Guide to the Indians of Oklahoma.* Norman, University of Oklahoma Press, 1951.

Yoakum, Henderson K. *History of Texas.* 2 vols. New York, Redfield, 1855.

Young, Otis E. *The First Military Escort on the Santa Fe Trail, 1829.* Glendale, California, Arthur H. Clark Co., 1952.

ARTICLES

Atherton, Lewis E. "Business Techniques in the Santa Fe Trade," *Missouri Historical Review,* Vol. XXXIV, No. 3 (April, 1940), 335–41.

Bieber, Ralph P. (ed.). "Letters of James and Robert Aull," *Missouri Historical Society Collection,* Vol. V (St. Louis, 1928), 286–87.

Connelley, William E. "Dr. Josiah Gregg, Historian of the Old Santa Fe Trail," *Proceedings of the Mississippi Valley Historical Association,* Vol. X, Part 2 (1919–20), 334–48.

Falconer, Thomas. "Notes on a Journey Through Texas and New Mexico Made in the Years 1841 and 1842," *Journal of the Royal Geographical Society of London,* Vol. III (1843).

García Conde, Pedro. "Ensayo estadístico sobre el Estado de Chihuahua," *Boletín de la Sociedad Mexicana de Geografía y Estadística,* Vol. V (Mexico City, 1857).

Hammond, George P., and Agapito Rey. "The Rodríguez Expedition into New Mexico, 1581–82," *New Mexico Historical Review,* Vol. II, Nos. 3, 4 (July, October, 1927), 239–68, 334–64.

Horgan, Paul. "Josiah Gregg Himself: An Introduction," Maurice G. Fulton (ed.), *The Diary and Letters of Josiah Gregg,* Vol. I, 3–40; Vol. II, 3–30.

Hughes, Anne E. "The Beginnings of Spanish Settlement in the El Paso District," *University of California Publications in History,* Vol. I (Berkeley, 1914), 293–333.

"The Journals of Capt. Thomas Becknell, from Boone's Lick to Santa Fe, and from Santa Cruz to Green River," *Missouri Historical Review,* Vol. IV, No. 2 (January, 1910), 65–84.

Lee, John Thomas. "The Authorship of Gregg's *Commerce of the Prairies,*" *Mississippi Valley Historical Review,* Vol. XVI, No. 4 (March, 1930), 451–66.

————. "Josiah Gregg and George Engelmann," *ibid.*, Vol. XLI, No. 4 (October, 1931), 355–404.

————. "New Found Letters of Josiah Gregg," *Proceedings of the American Antiquarian Society*, Vol. XL, No. 2 (April, 1930), 47–68.

Mooney, James. "Calendar History of the Kiowas," Bureau of American Ethnology *Seventeenth Annual Report*, Part I. Washington, 1898.

Perrine, Fred S. "Military Escorts on the Santa Fe Trail," *New Mexico Historical Review*; Part 1, Vol. II, Nos. 2, 3 (April, July, 1927), 175–93, 269–304; Part 2, Vol. III, No. 3 (July, 1928), 265–300.

Sampson, F. A. (ed.). "Santa Fe Trail: M. M. Marmaduke Journal (1824)," *Missouri Historical Review*, Vol. VI, No. 1 (October, 1911), 1–10.

[Sargent, Charles S.] "Josiah Gregg," *Garden and Forest*, Vol. VII, No. 2 (January 10, 1894), 12.

Stephens, F. F. (ed.). "Major Alphonso Wetmore's Diary of a Journey to Santa Fe, 1828," *Missouri Historical Review*, Vol. VIII, No. 4 (July, 1914), 177–97.

————. "Missouri and the Santa Fé Trade," *ibid.*; Part 1, Vol. X, No. 4 (July, 1916), 233–62; Part 2, Vol. XI, Nos. 3, 4 (April, July, 1917), 289–312.

Viles, Jonas. "Old Franklin: A Frontier Town of the Twenties," *Mississippi Valley Historical Review*, Vol. IX, No. 4 (March, 1923), 269–82.

NEWSPAPERS

Daily Missouri Republican (St. Louis), March 5, 1833.
Missouri Intelligencer (Franklin), April 10, 1824.
Niles' Weekly Register (Baltimore), December 5, 1829; March 23, 1833; May 22, 1843.

INDEX

Abert, Lt. J. W.: 73 n.
Abiquiú pueblo (New Mexico): 118 n.
Abó pueblo (New Mexico): 117 n.
Abreu, Ramón: 92
Abreu, Santiago: 93
Acequias: 107, 108, 275, 285
Acoma pueblo (New Mexico): 193, 198
Acosta, Father José de: quoted, 386; work of cited, 386 n.
Adair, James: work of cited, 390 n.; quoted, 410 n.
Adobe: 144, 277, 299
Aguardiente: 273, 313
Aguascalientes, Mexico: 279, 285, 288
Alarid, Jesús María: 93
Albuquerque, New Mexico: 79 n., 95, 99 n., 100 n., 181 n.
Alcaldes: 92, 94, 108, 133, 161, 162, 164, 167, 221
Alemán camp (New Mexico): 269
Alessio Robles, Carmen: 197 n.
Alfalfa County (Oklahoma): 352 n.
Algodones, New Mexico: 161
Algonquin language: 395 n., 430.
Allen, Alfred: 12 n.
Allende, Mexico: 183
Alvarez, Manuel; *xxiii* n., 161 n., 162, 163 & n.
American Botanical Society: *xxvi*
Anáhuac: 196
Antelope: 37–38, 68, 138, 241, 355, 377–78
Antelope Hills (Oklahoma): 326 n.
Antón Chico, New Mexico: 341 n.
Apache Indians: 12 n., 88, 132 n., 198, 208, 228, 272, 274, 275, 277, 313, 339 n.; Jicarilla band, 198, 200, 210–

11; Mescalero band, 201; Coyotero band, 201; description, 201–208; population, 432 n.
Appleton and Company, D.: *xxx, xxi*
Arapaho Indians: 17–18, 30, 57, 437; language, 395 n.; population, 432 n.
Arbuckle, Gen. Matthew: 230, 231 n.
Arbuckle Mountains (Oklahoma): 230 n.
Arcata, Calfornia: *xxviii*
Archuleta, Col. Diego: 317 n.
Archuleta, Juan Andrés: 317.
Arikara Indians: 57 n.; language, 395 n.; population, 432 n.
Arkansas Indians: 395 n.
Arkansas River: 11 n., 12, 13, 14 n., 15, 19–21, 30, 39 n, 40–47, 49, 51 n., 55, 64, 65, 67, 74 n., 83 n., 209, 216, 217 n., 226–27, 228, 230 n., 231 n., 232, 255, 258, 327, 339, 343, 351–52, 354, 357–58, 366, 377, 381 n., 391, 432
Arkansas River fords: 45–46, 49 n., 216, 217 n.
Armijo, Antonio: 333 n.
Armijo, Gov. Manuel: *xxii*, 339–42; biography, 79 n., 94–97; administration, 79, 158–63, 201 n., 262–63
Armstrong County (Texas): 322 n.
Arrastre: 295
Artalejo, José: 309–11
Ash Creek (Kansas): 42, 43 n., 45, 217 n.
Ashley, Gen. William H.: 51 n., 64 n.
Assinaboin Indians: 372, 395 n.
Athapascan language: 199 n.
Atherton, Lewis E.: 20 n.

455

UNIVERSITY OF OKLAHOMA PRESS : NORMAN